What makes *SOC* special?

Scholarship + Pedagogy = M-Series

SOC offers instructors unmatched scholarship, content, and currency in a succinct, magazine format that engages students.

What's Inside

Engaging pedagogy designed to be eye-catching and visually appealing can be found throughout the text. *SOC* shows students how they can apply sociological concepts to their everyday lives.

POPSOC

PopSOC teaches sociological concepts through popular culture familiar to students.

Personal Sociology

Personal Sociology gives down-to-earth explanations of sociological concepts using the author's experiences as examples.

SOCVIEWS on . . .

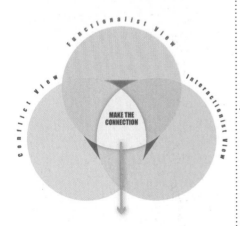

SOCViews provides students with a summary diagram of how each major perspective views key topics in sociology. **MAKE THE CONNECTION** prompt students to look at their own lives through the lens of sociological perspectives.

SOCTHINK

SOCThink questions throughout each chapter prompt students to think more deeply about a topic discussed in the text.

Get Involved advises students on how to actively participate in sociological issues that are relevant to them.

As You READ

As You Read begins the chapter with important questions discussed in the chapter.

At the Movies lists movies that relate to the sociological topics in each chapter.

For REVIEW

For Review summarizes the key points of each chapter in an easy-to-read format.

Pop Quiz

Pop Quiz allows students to review chapter material.

SOC 2013, THIRD EDITION

Published by McGraw-Hill, a business unit of The McGraw-Hill Companies, Inc., 1221 Avenue of the Americas, New York, NY 10020. Copyright © 2013 by The McGraw-Hill Companies, Inc. All rights reserved. Printed in the United States of America. editions © 2011 and 2009. No part of this publication may be reproduced or distributed in any form or by any means, or stored in a database or retrieval system, without the prior written consent of The McGraw-Hill Companies, Inc., including, but not limited to, in any network or other electronic storage or transmission, or broadcast for distance learning.

Some ancillaries, including electronic and print components, may not be available to customers outside the United States.

This book is printed on acid-free paper.

2 3 4 5 6 7 8 9 0 QVR/QVR 1 0 9 8 7 6 5 4 3

ISBN 978-0-07-802674-4
MHID 0-07-802674-1

Senior Vice President, Products & Markets: *Kurt L. Strand*
Vice President, General Manager, Products & Markets: *Michael Ryan*
Vice President, Content Production & Technology Services: *Kimberly Meriwether David*
Managing Director: *Gina Boedeker*
Brand Manager: *Gina Boedeker*
Director of Development: *Dawn Groundwater*
Marketing Manager: *Josh Zlatkus*
Development Editor: *Nicole Bridge*
Content Project Manager: *April R. Southwood*
Buyer: *Nicole Baumgartner*
Designer: *Jana Singer*
Interior Designer: *Laurie Entringer*
Cover Image: *Sam Edwards / Getty*
Content Licensing Specialist: *Shawntel Schmitt*
Compositor: *Laserwords Private Limited*
Typeface: *10/12 Minion Pro*
Printer: *Quad/Graphics*

All credits appearing on page or at the end of the book are considered to be an extension of the copyright page.

ISSN: 2164-0696

Name: Jon Witt (though my mom calls me Jonathan)

Education: I got my BA from Trinity College in Deerfield, IL, and earned my PhD from Loyola University in Chicago.

Occupations: Sociologist, father, and dog-walker

Hobbies: I like reading, writing, and riding a bike—and I'm addicted to my iPhone and iPad.

Childhood ambition: To be a printer like my dad until I decided to be a teacher like my mom.

Family: Lori and I have been married for 28 years, and we have two daughters, Emily, 18, and Eleanor, 16.

Last book read: Herman Melville's Moby Dick. It was on my book bucket list.

Favorite film: My most recent favorite is Departures—a Japanese film about a young undertaker.

Favorite soundtrack: Cowboy You by The Milkweeds

Latest accomplishment: This book!

Quote: There may be fields of sociological science quite beyond the average mind, and rightly left to the learned specialist; but that is no reason why we should not learn enough of the nature and habits of society to insure a more profitable and pleasant life.
—Charlotte Perkins Gilman, Human Work, 1904

My Blog: www.soc101.com or follow SOC on Twitter @soc101

WHAT'S NEW IN SOC

The Politics and Economy chapter has been completely revised to encompass the global economic crisis and its social consequences, like the Occupy Wall Street movement. There is new analysis of the representative democracy model and how that structure influences outcomes in the United States. A new "Movies in Sociology" feature gives students a chance to think about political and economic topics through cinema.

> A new PopSoc examines the story behind *Moneyball* and the idea that going against conventional wisdom can sometimes result in success.

> A new opening vignette in Chapter 4 examines "baby talk" as a cultural universal, despite the fact that the distinct sounds and relationships between them vary among cultures.

> A deeper discussion of Social Control examines our tendency to respect basic social norms and the circumstances under which power within a society can become oppressive. A new PopSoc "Zombie Apocalypse" considers how quickly social order would break down in the event of a zombie takeover.

> New discussion on social stratification considers the origins of class and the impact individuals can have in determining their own social position in the United States.

> There is a deeper discussion on social change resulting from the Arab Spring protests.

> Statistics and data have been updated throughout the book to reflect 2012 research.

> Key definitions have been reworded to be more accessible and easier to remember.

SOC 2013 Edition

BRIEF CONTENTS

* letters to the editor *

"I have taught this class for almost 10 years without a standard textbook, as I did not find one that worked for me. Too many were "highschooly," while others were dense with too many terms and not enough contemporary examples to keep the students' interest. . . . Quite frankly, I like *SOC* so much that I organized my course format/chronology around it."

—ANDREA M. BRENNER, *American University*

Thanks for your feedback. SOC was designed with students in mind. And one thing students appreciate is engaging content that can travel with them wherever they go.
—*The Editors*

"The tone and energy of the text are wonderful. I really like the graphics and the range of different ways the students have to interact with the material—At the Movies, SocThink, PopSoc, etc. The text has a lot of breadth and almost none of the boring textbook tone and heavy framing."

—LAUREN SMITH, *University of Wisconsin, Whitewater*

That's great news! Jon Witt developed the narrative and features to reach students where they are, so that instructors can take them where they need them to be. SOC asks students to think critically about issues close to their lives. We're glad you think this will work well for your students.
—*The Editors*

"The design of SOC is most appealing. What is good is that substance is not sacrificed for style. The students get good information in an engaging design that still adheres to the traditional framework of sociology classes."

—JOHN TENUTO, *College of Lake County*

"I like how the Witt text looks like a magazine. It also has lots of graphs, interesting facts, and cool pictures to hold my attention."

—SKYE PETERS, *student at Parkland College*

From the cover to the interior design, images, graphs, charts, and pedagogy, SOC was designed to make sociology accessible and thought-provoking for students. The visuals reinforce the solid scholarship throughout.
—*The Editors*

Table of Contents

8 > Education & Religion   178

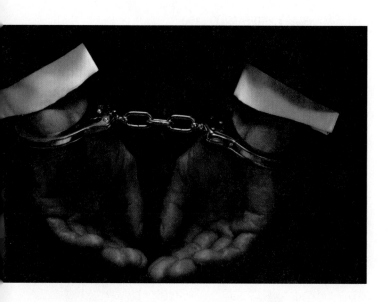

10 >   Social Class   236

11 >   Global Inequality   264

12 > Gender & Sexuality   290

13 > Race and Ethnicity   316

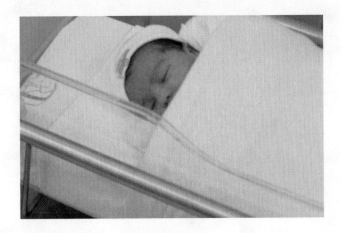

1

THE SOCIOLOG

THE INDIVIDUAL AND SOCIETY

On May 1, 2011, Osama bin Laden was shot and killed by U.S. forces in Abbottabad, Pakistan. In announcing this news to the world, President Barack Obama asserted that "Justice has been done." Even as he spoke, jubilant crowds began gathering outside the White House, at Ground Zero in New York City, and in many other locations around the country. People celebrated by singing the Star-Spangled Banner, reciting the Pledge of Allegiance, and chanting "USA! USA!"

For many people, bin Laden's death provided a sense of closure to a chapter that started with the September 11, 2001 attacks, which killed nearly 3,000 people. Bin Laden had eluded authorities for nearly 10 years. Now he was gone, and people expressed hope that his death might represent a new beginning. The day after, for example, CNN correspondent Carol Costello commented, "Americans are united again. . . . Osama bin Laden's death brought us together in a way we haven't experienced since the days of 9/11." That same day, at a Congressional bipartisan dinner, President Obama expressed a "fervent hope" that we could "harness some of that unity and some of that pride." For many, then, the effect of bin Laden's death was to draw people together, even in the face of differences.

Others looked to the same incident and came to different conclusions. The Pakistani government criticized the attack as "an unauthorized unilateral action" that violated Pakistan's national sovereignty. Followers of bin Laden viewed his killing as part of a larger war against their own deeply held beliefs and viewed him as a martyr who fought for his principles to the end. On the other end of the spectrum were those who weren't quite sure how to respond. One of the most common Internet search phrases in the hours after the attack was "Who was Osama bin Laden?" According to officials at Yahoo, 66 percent of those who entered this phrase were 13–17 years old and thus were likely too young to remember much, if anything, about 9/11.

How could this single event elicit so many different responses? Such variation points to a basic sociological premise about the significance of our place in society: how we think, what we do, and even how we feel, are shaped by the positions we occupy in society. In this chapter, and throughout this book, we will seek to more fully understand the implications of this claim.

ICAL
IMAGINATION

As You READ

>>
- What is sociology?
- How do sociologists look at the world?
- How might someone practice sociology?

>>What Is Sociology?

We need one another. We may like to think that we can make it on our own, but our individualism is made possible by our interdependence. We praise the Olympic gold medalist for her impressive skill, dedicated training, and single-minded determination. Yet, if it hadn't been for her mom driving her to the pool every day, for the building manager waking up at 4:00 A.M. to make sure the pool is open, for the women working overnight to make sure the locker room is clean and safe, and so many others who fade into the background in such moments of glory, she would never have had that chance to shine.

The people we depend upon are often unknown and invisible to us. Even though we may never meet them, we rely on farmers, truck drivers, secretaries, store clerks, custodians, software engineers, scientists, assembly-line workers, teachers, police officers, inventors, politicians, CEOs, and a whole host of others. Yet we mostly take their contributions for granted without fully appreciating the degree to which they make our lives possible. Sociologists seek to reveal the full extent of our interdependence. **Sociology** is defined as the systematic study of the relationship between the individual and society and of the consequences of difference. We will examine the various components of that definition in detail below, but at its heart is the intimate connection between self and society.

Through sociology we can ask and answer questions about our interdependence. With whom do we connect? How do we organize those connections? What gets in the way? Who benefits? Whether sitting in a classroom,

> **sociology** The systematic study of the relationship between the individual and society and of the consequences of difference.
>
> **sociological imagination** An awareness of the relationship between who we are as individuals and the social forces that shape our lives.

working in an office or a factory, or exercising in a health club, our options are shaped by the positions we occupy. As individuals, we do choose, but we cannot divorce our individual preferences from the influence of parents, coworkers, friends, enemies, the media, and more, or from our access to resources such as money, social networks, and knowledge. We influence and are influenced by the world around us. Sociology studies those influences.

THE SOCIOLOGICAL IMAGINATION

Sociology helps us to see our place in the world in new ways. In an effort to describe how we might do that, American sociologist C. Wright Mills (1959) created a concept called the **sociological imagination,** an awareness of the relationship between who we are as individuals and the social forces that shape our lives. Mills described the sociological imagination as our ability to see the interaction between history and biography. By "history" he meant not just the times in which we live but also our positions in society and the resources to which we have access. "Biography" encompasses our personal experience, our actions and thoughts, and the choices we make. As Mills put it, "neither the life of an individual nor the history of society can be understood without understanding both" (p. 3). As individuals, we act, but we do so within the context and confines of society.

The sociological imagination involves our recognition of the significance of our social location. In other words, it enables us to see how factors such as age, gender, race, ethnicity, class, and level of education shape our preferences, perceptions, and opportunities. One way to gain insight about ourselves and our social worlds is to imagine how our practices might look to an outsider. Consider sporting events, for example. In the United States, thousands of fans pack stadiums to cheer for well-trained football players. In Bali, Indonesia, dozens of spectators gather around a ring to cheer on well-trained roosters engaged in cockfights. In both instances, the spectators root for their favorites and might bet on the outcome. Yet what is considered a normal sporting event in one part of the world is considered unusual in another.

One way to develop our sociological imagination, according to Mills (1959), involves distinguishing between private troubles and public issues. **Private troubles** are problems we face in our immediate relationships with particular individuals in our personal lives. In such cases we

SOCTHINK

When someone says that something "sounds like a personal problem," what do they usually mean? How might we respond differently to people who lost a job, got divorced, or dropped out of high school if we viewed such events as public issues? What more might we learn by doing so?

5 Movies on THE SOCIOLOGICAL IMAGINATION

Idiocracy
A man travels forward a thousand years to an overpopulated, dumbed down America.

Children of Men
A dystopian vision of society where humans can no longer reproduce.

Harry Potter and the Sorcerer's Stone
An 11-year-old orphan is introduced to a new society of wizards.

Fish Tank
A volatile teenage girl tries to escape her chaotic life in a British housing project.

One Flew over the Cuckoo's Nest
A scheming convict sent to a mental institution takes on Nurse Ratched.

in February 2008 to 10.1 percent in October 2010 and then slowly declined to 8.3 percent in February 2012. Rising rates were shaped by factors such as the banking crisis, the stock market plunge, and the decline in new home construction. Taking into account social forces—in other words, treating unemployment as a public issue—enables individuals, companies, and governments to more effectively diagnose the problem and develop appropriate solutions. Used in this way, the sociological imagination is an empowering tool.

> **Private troubles** Problems we face in our immediate relationships with particular individuals in our personal lives.
>
> **Public issues** Problems we face as a consequence of the positions we occupy within the larger social structure.

THE HAMBURGER AS MIRACLE

Using the sociological imagination helps us better understand our interdependence. For example, many people take for granted that it would be easy to provide for their needs if they had to, and they are eager to strike out on their own and prove themselves. But suppose you had to do something as seemingly simple as making a hamburger and had to do so without relying on any knowledge, skills, tools, or resources obtained from anyone else.

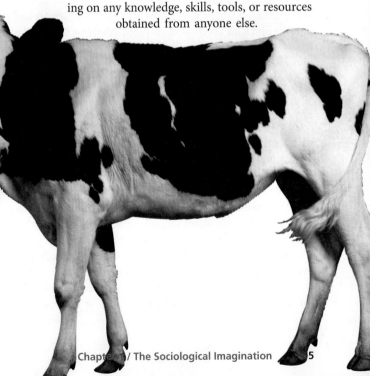

blame ourselves, or those close to us, for our struggles. Often, however, people in similar situations face the same troubles. In such cases, the real cause of our distress may well exist beyond our particular circumstances. **Public issues** are problems we face as a consequence of the positions we occupy within the larger social structure. Private troubles are personal problems, and public issues are social problems.

Unemployment provides a classic example of the relationship between private troubles and public issues. Losing a job is experienced as a private trouble for the individuals and families involved. It affects psychological well-being and is even associated with increased likelihood of divorce and suicide. But unemployment levels rise and fall depending upon what is happening in the larger economy. For example, the unemployment rate rose from 4.8 percent

Without an interdependent network of people performing myriad small tasks that we take for granted, we would be hard-pressed to provide for our most basic needs. A hamburger can serve as a symbol of our society's shared knowledge and skills.

How hard can it be to make a hamburger from scratch? Considering the ingredients, which seem fairly simple, there are any number of ways to proceed. Let's begin with the burger itself. First, you need to find a cow.

How hard can that be? Well, you can't buy one from a farmer, because doing so means relying on resources from others. For the same reason, you can't go out to the country (getting there itself might present something of a challenge) and steal one from a farm (which implies a farmer, which means dependence on another person). So you need to find a wild cow.

Assuming you do find a wild cow, you then have to kill it. Perhaps you might bash it with a large rock or stampede it off a cliff. Next, you need to butcher it, but cow hide is tough. Imagine what it takes to produce a metal knife (finding ore, smelting, forging, tempering, and so on). Perhaps a sharp rock will do. Assuming you came up with a cutting tool, you now have a chunk of raw cow meat. Given that it's hamburger we're after (though you might be ready to settle for steak at this point), next you need to grind the meat. You might use a couple of those rocks to pulverize the meat into something of a meat mash, although a meat grinder would work better if only it weren't so hard to make one. In any event, at last you have a raw hamburger patty.

Now you need to cook it. How will you do that? Where will you get the fire? Perhaps you could strike two rocks together in hopes of creating a spark, or maybe rub two sticks together. If you were allowed to get help from an outside source, you might check how Tom Hanks' character did it in the film *Cast Away*—but you aren't. Perhaps it would be easiest to wait around for lightning to strike a nearby tree. However you might accomplish it, after you get fire, you still have to cook the meat. No frying pans are available, so either you make one or perhaps cook it on that handy rock you used to kill the cow. Or you could just put the meat on a stick that you cut down and whittled with the knife you made (or was that a "sharp" stone?) and roast it over the fire.

Assuming you are successful, you now have a cooked hamburger patty. But, of course, you aren't done yet. There are still many steps that need to be completed. You need to bake a bun, which involves figuring out how to come up with flour, water, salt, oil, sugar, yeast, and an oven. What about condiments such as ketchup, mustard, pickles, and onions? What if at the end of all that you decide to make it a cheeseburger? We hope you milked the cow first.

Making something that seems so simple, that we take for granted, that we can get for a dollar at McDonald's,

turns out to be quite complicated. The knowledge and skill to acquire and prepare all the ingredients in a hamburger are beyond the capacity of most individuals. Yet if we eat a burger, we think nothing of it. When you think about it—when you apply the sociological imagination— a hamburger is a miracle. It's miraculous, not in a supernatural sense but as a symbol pointing to the astonishing complexity and taken-for-grantedness of our human interdependence and to the knowledge we share collectively without even realizing it. Of course, this is true not just for hamburgers but for virtually any product we use. It could be a veggieburger, a book, a desk, a shirt, a car, a house, or a computer. Look around you and try to imagine making, by yourself, all the things that we as humans have produced. The knowledge and skill that such products represent is astounding. Thankfully, our interdependence means that we do not have to rely on our own knowledge and skill alone for our survival.

> The function of sociology, as of every science, is to reveal that which is hidden.
>
> Pierre Bourdieu

DEFINING SOCIOLOGY

A more detailed breakdown of the four key components of the definition of sociology will help us to better understand the foundation upon which the sociological imagination is built.

Systematic Study Sociologists are engaged with the world, collecting empirical data through systematic research. Relying on such data means that sociologists draw their conclusions about society based on experiences or observations rather than beliefs or the authority of others. If they want to understand the impact of television on community or the phenomenon of binge drinking on college campuses, they must gather data from those involved in these activities and base their conclusions upon that information.

Sociological research historically has involved both quantitative and qualitative approaches to data collection. Quantitative approaches emphasize counting things and analyzing them mathematically or statistically. The most common way to collect this type of data is through surveys. In contrast, qualitative approaches focus on listening to and observing people and allowing them to interpret what is happening in their own lives. The most common way to collect this type of data is through participant observation, in which the researcher interacts with those she or he studies. In practice, sociologists often draw on both techniques in conducting their research. We will investigate these research techniques, along with others, in more detail in Chapter 2.

The Individual Although sociology is most commonly associated with the study of groups, there is no such thing as a group apart from the individuals who compose it.

As individuals we are constantly choosing what to do next. Most of the time, we follow guidelines for behavior we have learned from others, but we have the ability to reject those guidelines at any time. A term sociologists sometimes use to describe this capacity is **agency**, meaning the freedom individuals have to choose and to act. In professional sports, for example, we use the term "free agent" to describe a player who has the power to negotiate with whatever team he or she wishes. We, too, have such freedom. We could choose not to go to class, not to go to work, not to get out of bed in the morning, not to obey traffic signals, not to respond when spoken to, not to read the next sentence in this book, and on and on.

Because our self exists in an interactive relationship with its environment, we act within the context of our relationships. The same is true for that sports free agent. Although he or she can choose any team, in order to get a big payday, he or she is limited to choosing within the confines of

"*Actually, Lou, I think it was more than just my being in the right place at the right time. I think it was my being the right race, the right religion, the right sex, the right socioeconomic group, having the right accent, the right clothes, going to the right schools . . .*"

the league. Our choices, too, are constrained by our positions. Having access to varieties of resources, we choose among an array of options with knowledge of various possible outcomes. We usually follow "paths of least resistance"—the accepted and expected actions and beliefs—but the choice of whether to continue to follow them is ours each and every second of our lives (Johnson 1997).

Society The study of society is at the core of sociology. Although we will spend most of this book describing various aspects of society, we can begin by thinking of it as our social environment. Society consists of persistent patterns of relationships and social networks within which we operate. The social structure it provides

> **agency** The freedom individuals have to choose and to act.

is analogous to a building: The layout of a building both encourages and discourages different activities in different rooms (such as kitchens, bedrooms, and bathrooms), and

many of the most essential operations of a building (such as heating and air conditioning) are mostly invisible to us. In the same way, the structure of our *institutions*—a term sociologists use to describe some of the major components of social structure, including economy, family, education, government, and religion—shapes what is expected of us. For example, the choices that are available to us in the context of the modern family, such as to go off and pursue our own education and career, are much different from the obligations we would face in more traditional family contexts. Nested within institutions are the groups, subgroups, and statuses that we occupy. We will look at the details of these institutions in coming chapters, but it is helpful to remember that we construct culture and engage in social interaction within the context of society.

The Consequences of Difference The final part of the definition of sociology involves the consequences of difference. Sociology does more than just describe our structure, culture, and interaction; it also looks at how economic, social, and cultural resources are distributed and at the implications of these patterns in terms of the opportunities and obstacles they create for individuals and groups. Since the founding of sociology, sociologists have been concerned with the impact our social location has on our opportunities or lack thereof.

Sociologists have noted, for example, that the 2004 Indian Ocean tsunami affected Indonesian men and women differently. When the waves hit, following traditional cultural patterns, mothers and grandmothers were at home with the children; men were outside working, where they were more likely to become aware of the impending disaster. Moreover, most of the men knew how to swim, a survival skill that women in these traditional societies usually do not learn. As a result, many more men than women survived the catastrophe—about 10 men for every 1 woman. In one typical Indonesian village, 97 of 1,300 people survived; only 4 were women. The impact of this gender imbalance will be felt for some time, given women's primary role as caregivers for children and the elderly (BBC 2005).

The analysis of social power deserves particular attention because it shapes how and why we think and act as we do. The

U.S. Employment Trends

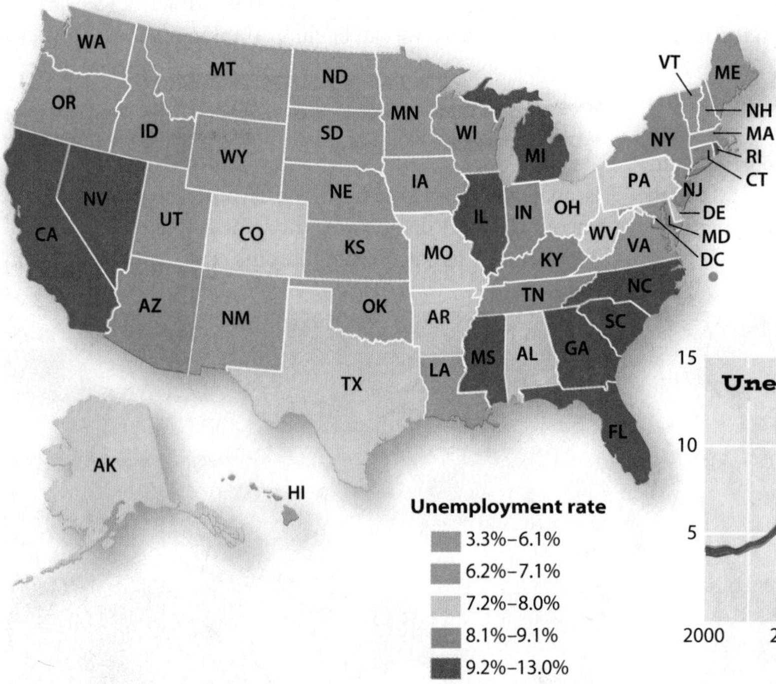

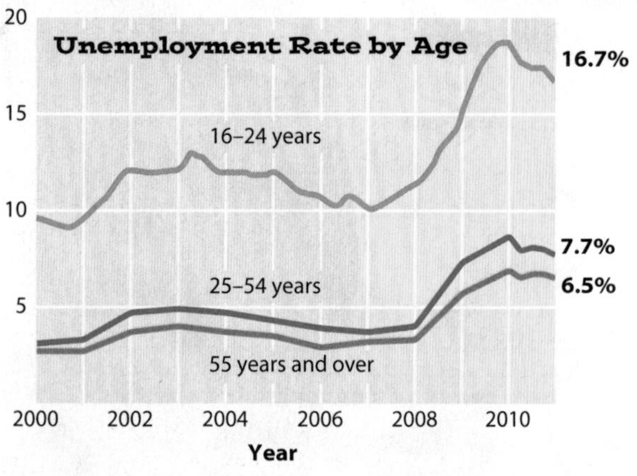

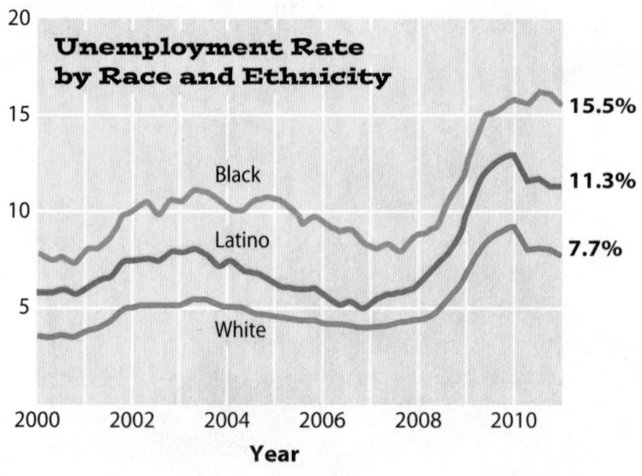

WA
OR
CA
NV
ID
MT
WY
UT
CO
AZ
NM
ND
SD
NE
KS
OK
TX
MN
IA
MO
AR
LA
WI
IL
MI
IN
OH
KY
TN
MS
AL
GA
FL
SC
NC
VA
WV
PA
NY
VT
ME
NH
MA
RI
CT
NJ
DE
MD
DC
AK
HI
Unemployment rate
3.3%–6.1%
6.2%–7.1%
7.2%–8.0%
8.1%–9.1%
9.2%–13.0%

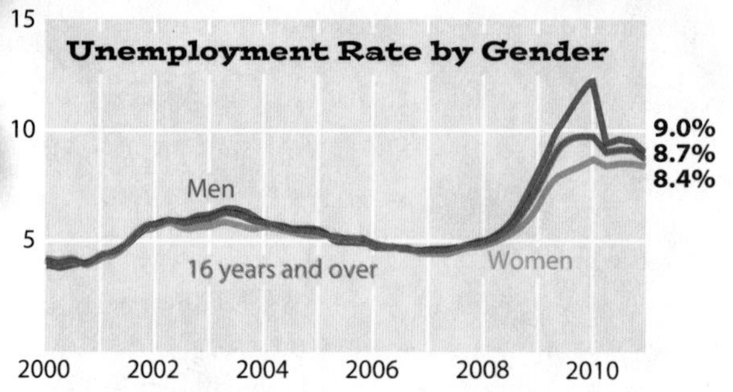

Unemployment Rate by Gender
Men
Women
16 years and over
9.0%
8.7%
8.4%
15
10
5
2000
2002
2004
2006
2008
2010

Unemployment Rate by Age
16–24 years
25–54 years
55 years and over
16.7%
7.7%
6.5%
20
15
10
5
2000
2002
2004
2006
2008
2010
Year

Unemployment Rate by Race and Ethnicity
Black
Latino
White
15.5%
11.3%
7.7%
20
15
10
5
2000
2002
2004
2006
2008
2010
Year

Source: Bureau of Labor Statistics 2012a.

Note: The unemployment rate includes people 16 years and older who are available for work but do not have a job and who have actively looked for work within the previous four weeks.

simple fact is that those who have access to and control over valued material, social, and cultural resources have different options available to them than do those without such access and control. One of the main tasks of sociology is to investigate and reveal levels of **social inequality**—a condition in which members of society have differing amounts of wealth, prestige, or power. That is why the definition of sociology draws particular attention to the consequences of difference.

In combination, these four aspects of sociology help us to understand the things that influence our beliefs and actions. Coming to terms with the reality that our choices are constrained by the positions we occupy can seem depressing, but sociology actually empowers us by providing a more complete picture of the worlds within which we live. French sociologist Pierre Bourdieu (1998a) put it this way: "Sociology teaches how groups function and how to make use of the laws governing the way they function so as to try to circumvent them" (p. 57). Only by appreciating the degree to which our thoughts and actions are shaped by our social location are we free to make more effective choices to change ourselves and our worlds.

SOCIOLOGY AND THE SOCIAL SCIENCES

Is sociology a science? The term **science** refers to the body of knowledge obtained by methods based on systematic observation. Just like other scientific disciplines, sociology involves the organized, systematic study of phenomena (in this case, human behavior) in order to enhance understanding. All scientists, whether studying mushrooms or murderers, attempt to collect precise information through methods of study that are as objective as possible. They rely on the careful recording of observations and the accumulation of data.

Of course, there is a great difference between sociology and physics, and between psychology and astronomy. For this reason, the sciences are commonly divided into natural and social sciences. **Natural science** is the study of the physical features of nature and the ways in which they interact and change. Astronomy, biology, chemistry, geology, and physics are all natural sciences. **Social science** is the study of the social features of humans and the ways in which they interact and change. The social sciences include sociology, anthropology, economics, history, psychology, and political science.

These social science disciplines have a common focus on the social behavior of people, yet each has a particular orientation. Anthropologists usually study past cultures and preindustrial societies that continue today, as well as the origins of humans. Economists explore the ways in which people produce and exchange goods and services, along with money and other resources. Historians are concerned with the peoples and events of the past and their significance for us today. Psychologists investigate personality and individual behavior. Political scientists study international relations, the workings of government, and

the exercise of power and authority. Sociologists, as we have already seen, study the influence that society has on people's attitudes and behavior and the ways in which people interact and shape society.

Let's consider how different social sciences might study the impact of the global economic crisis that began in late 2008. Historians would compare recent events to those that occurred in previous crises, such as the Great Depression of the 1930s. Economists would conduct research on the financial impact of the current crisis for individuals, nations, and the world as a whole. Psychologists would study the behavior and reactions of individuals to assess the emotional trauma such crises cause. And political scientists would study the stances taken by political leaders and their governments' responses to the crisis.

> **social inequality** A condition in which members of society have differing amounts of wealth, prestige, or power.
>
> **science** The body of knowledge obtained by methods based on systematic observation.
>
> **natural science** The study of the physical features of nature and the ways in which they interact and change.
>
> **social science** The study of the social features of humans and the ways in which they interact and change.

What approach would sociologists take? Following Mills' lead, they would analyze the economic downturn as a public issue. This necessitates gathering data about how this crisis affected people differently depending upon the social positions they occupied. As the map and graphs on page 8 demonstrate, a person's geographical location, age, gender, race, and ethnicity all influenced his or her likelihood of experiencing unemployment. Unemployment was more likely in the Southeast and West than in the Midwest. The level for young people was, and continues to be, substantially higher than for those who are older. Men experienced a more significant jump in joblessness than did women. Rates for African Americans and Latinos were, and are, significantly higher than those for Whites. Sociology teaches us that our social location matters. Understanding how different groups are affected helps policy makers decide which actions to take to address the crisis. A singular or universal solution to such a problem is unlikely to be effective in addressing the different needs of the various groups.

Sociological research shows that the choice of a marriage partner is heavily influenced by societal expectations.

Sociologists would take a similar approach in studying episodes of extreme violence. In January 2010, Congresswoman Gabrielle Giffords was meeting constituents at a supermarket near Tucson, Arizona, when a gunman walked up and started shooting. Eighteen people were hit. Six were killed, including a 9-year-old girl. Giffords was shot point-blank in the head but survived. Observers struggled to describe the events and place them in some social context. For sociologists in particular, events such as these raise numerous questions, including the role of the media in reporting breaking news events, the politics of gun control, concerns about gender, the adequacy of the nation's mental health care system, and the stereotyping and stigmatizing of people who suffer from mental illness (Force 2011; Glassner 2010; Sharp 2011).

SOCIOLOGY AND COMMON SENSE

At times all of us practice some form of the sociological imagination, weighing the balance between individual and society. So what's the difference between sociology and common sense—the knowledge we get from our experiences and conversations, from what we read, from what we see on television, and so forth? Commonsense knowledge, although sometimes accurate, is not always reliable, because it rests on commonly held beliefs rather than on systematic analysis of facts.

Contrary to the common notion that women tend to be chatty compared to men, for instance, researchers have found little difference between the sexes in terms of their

theory In sociology a set of statements that seeks to explain problems, actions, or behavior.

talkativeness. Over a five-year period, they placed unobtrusive microphones on 396 college students in various settings, on campuses in Mexico as well as the United States. They found that both men and women spoke about 16,000 words per day (Mehl et al. 2007).

Similarly, "common sense" tells us that in the United States today, military marriages are more likely to end in separation or divorce than in the past owing to the strain of long deployments in Iraq and Afghanistan. Yet a study released in 2007 shows no significant increase in the divorce rate among U.S. soldiers over the past decade. In fact, the rate of marital dissolution among members of the military is comparable to that of nonmilitary families. Interestingly, this is not the first study to disprove the widely held notion that military service strains the marital bond. Two generations earlier, during the Vietnam War era, researchers came to the same conclusion (Call and Teachman 1991; Karney and Crown 2007).

Like other social scientists, sociologists do not accept something as fact just because "everyone knows it." At times, the findings of sociologists may seem like common sense because they deal with familiar facets of everyday life. The difference is that such findings have been tested by researchers, analyzed in relation to other data, and evaluated in light of what is known by sociologists in the form of sociological theory.

>>What Is Sociological Theory?

Sociology, like all sciences, involves a conversation between theory and research. We gather data through systematic research, and we seek to describe and explain what we find using theories. Theories represent our attempts to tell the stories of our lives, but they do so in a particular way. Initially, theories might be general and vague. However, over time, as they become more fully informed by research, they are modified and refined into fuller, more accurate accounts of why we think and act as we do. We look here first at theories before turning to methods in Chapter 2.

FORMULATING SOCIOLOGICAL THEORIES

Why do people commit suicide? Émile Durkheim's answer to this question more than a hundred years ago helped to establish sociology as a discipline. Among the traditional commonsense answers that Durkheim rejected were the notions that people inherit the desire to kill themselves or that sunspots drive people to take their own lives. He suspected that existing psychological or biological theories that pointed toward depression or chemical imbalance as causal factors were insufficient. He believed that social forces existed that influenced an individual's likelihood of committing suicide and set out to test his theory.

Durkheim developed a theory that offered a general explanation of suicidal behavior. We can think of theories as attempts to explain events, forces, materials, ideas, or behavior in a comprehensive manner. In sociology a **theory** is a set of statements that seeks to explain problems, actions, or behavior. An effective theory may have both explanatory and predictive power. That is, it can help us to see the relationships among seemingly isolated

phenomena, as well as to understand how one type of change in an environment leads to other changes.

Durkheim theorized that people commit suicide because they lack the social connections and obligations to prevent them from taking this most final and individualistic of all acts. His hypothesis was this: "Suicide varies inversely with the degree of integration of the social groups of which the individual forms a part" ([1897] 1951:209). He initially chose religious affiliation as an indicator of social integration, arguing that Protestants are less socially integrated than are Roman Catholics. He claimed that Catholicism is a traditional faith with a hierarchical system of authority in which variation in belief (on such topics as birth control, abortion, married priests, and women priests) is not up to the individual. Protestantism, in contrast, puts the Bible into the believers' hands to interpret. The many schisms found among Protestants occurred as a consequence of individuals choosing to interpret matters of faith based on their own understanding of God's word. Whereas there is only one Roman Catholic Church, Protestantism includes Baptist, Methodist, Reformed, Episcopalian, Presbyterian, and many other denominational and nondenominational churches. These contrasting contexts shaped the degree to which individuals were integrated into the religious community, leading Durkheim to predict that Protestants would be more likely to commit suicide than Catholics.

TESTING SOCIOLOGICAL THEORIES

To test his theory, Durkheim gathered data from different countries to see if suicide rates varied. Looking at France, England, and Denmark, he found that England had 67 reported suicides per million inhabitants, France had 135

SOCTHINK

If Durkheim is correct and the level of social integration influences the likelihood of suicide, why do rates vary for the groups listed in the Suicide Rates figure? Why is the rate for men almost four times higher than that for women? Why is the rate for non-Hispanic Whites higher than that for any other racial/ethnic groups? Why are the rates for White, non-Hispanic males so high (22.9) and for Black, non-Hispanic females so low (1.7)? Why is there a midlife suicide peak? What might the top-five or bottom-five states have in common? What might these patterns suggest about the social integration of people in these categories?

Suicide Rates

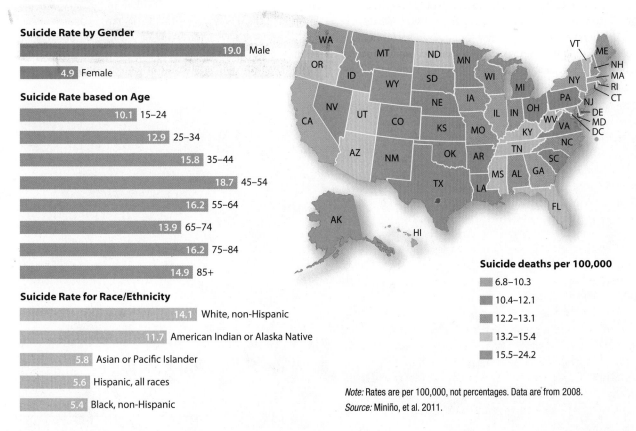

Suicide Rate by Gender

- 19.0 Male
- 4.9 Female

Suicide Rate based on Age

- 10.1 15–24
- 12.9 25–34
- 15.8 35–44
- 18.7 45–54
- 16.2 55–64
- 13.9 65–74
- 16.2 75–84
- 14.9 85+

Suicide Rate for Race/Ethnicity

- 14.1 White, non-Hispanic
- 11.7 American Indian or Alaska Native
- 5.8 Asian or Pacific Islander
- 5.6 Hispanic, all races
- 5.4 Black, non-Hispanic

Suicide deaths per 100,000

- 6.8–10.3
- 10.4–12.1
- 12.2–13.1
- 13.2–15.4
- 15.5–24.2

Note: Rates are per 100,000, not percentages. Data are from 2008.

Source: Miniño, et al. 2011.

per million, and Denmark had 277 per million. Durkheim concluded that Denmark's comparatively high suicide rate was due to the fact that Denmark was a more Protestant nation than either France or England. In other words, it was the social makeup of these nations that shaped their suicide rates. More recent research focusing on individual rather than national rates continues to find this same relationship.

In extending his analysis to look at other indicators of social integration, Durkheim continued to obtain results that confirmed his underlying theory: the unmarried had much higher rates of suicide than married people; and people without children were more likely to take their lives than people with children. In addition, there were higher rates in times of economic instability and recession than in times of prosperity. Durkheim concluded that his theory was correct: the suicide rate of a society reflects the extent to which people are or are not integrated into the group life of the society. Durkheim presented his results in his landmark work *Suicide,* published in 1897.

APPLYING SOCIOLOGICAL THEORIES

Built into Durkheim's theory is the presupposition that we find meaning in life through our interconnections with others. The more interconnected and interdependent we feel, the less likely we are to kill ourselves. Attempting to summarize the significance of our attachment to society, Durkheim put it this way: "The individual alone is not a sufficient end for his activity. He is too little. . . . When, therefore, we have no other object than ourselves we cannot avoid the thought that our efforts will finally end in nothingness. . . . Under these conditions one would lose the courage to live, that is, to act and struggle" ([1897] 1951:210). Human beings are, at their very foundation, social beings. According to Durkheim, we cannot consider what it means to be an individual apart from our position in society. This

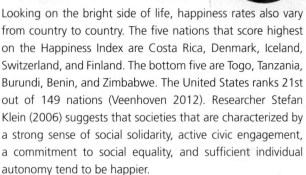

Going GLOBAL

What Makes a Country Happy?

Looking on the bright side of life, happiness rates also vary from country to country. The five nations that score highest on the Happiness Index are Costa Rica, Denmark, Iceland, Switzerland, and Finland. The bottom five are Togo, Tanzania, Burundi, Benin, and Zimbabwe. The United States ranks 21st out of 149 nations (Veenhoven 2012). Researcher Stefan Klein (2006) suggests that societies that are characterized by a strong sense of social solidarity, active civic engagement, a commitment to social equality, and sufficient individual autonomy tend to be happier.

social dimension of individual behavior is what Durkheim wants sociology to explore, elaborate, and explain.

Durkheim's work on suicide provides a classic case of sociological theory at work. He theorized that social forces shape individual actions. He tested this theory by investigating suicide as one such individual choice—perhaps the most individual of all choices—and demonstrated that the likelihood of committing suicide varied based on group membership. Analysis of more recent data (see figure on page 11) shows that suicide rates continue to vary based on social position. Durkheim concluded that if social forces are at work in this most extreme example of individual choice, they similarly shape all other individual choices. He argued that if social forces have such power in our lives, there should be a discipline dedicated to their study. As a result, Durkheim established Europe's first department of sociology at the University of Bordeaux in 1895.

>>The Development of Sociology

Given the complexity of human life, sociologists have developed a wide range of theories in which they describe and explain the diversity of social behavior. Sometimes their theories can be grand in scope, seeking to encompass the "big picture"; other times they can be more personal, intimate, and immediate. Although we spend most of the rest of this book investigating the insights sociological theories provide, here we will briefly address just five questions sociologists have frequently asked. These questions represent significant doors sociologists have opened to provide additional tools for the sociological imagination. The questions are these: How is social order maintained? How do power and inequality shape outcomes? How does interaction shape our world? How does group membership (especially class, race, and gender) shape opportunity? How should sociologists respond?

HOW IS SOCIAL ORDER MAINTAINED?

The discipline of sociology grew up in the midst of significant social upheaval. The advent of the Industrial Revolution and urbanization in the early 19th century led to changes in patterns of government, thought, work, and everyday life. Aristocracy was on the decline while democracy was spreading; people were moving from a primary reliance

POPSOC

Harriet Martineau ([1838] 1989) argued that we could learn a lot about a culture by analyzing the ideas, images, and themes reflected in their popular songs. She wrote, "The Songs of every nation must always be the most familiar and truly popular part of its poetry. . . . They present also the most prevalent feelings on subjects of the highest popular interest. If it were not so, they would not have been popular songs." What might we learn about American culture based on analysis of the lyrics of the current top-10 songs? What themes, ideas, images, and expectations are prevalent? (Lists are available at "The Billboard Hot 100" or www.top10songs.com.)

on religious explanations to more scientific ones; and the world of the village and farm was rapidly giving way to life in the city and factory. It was in this context that French sociologist and philosopher Auguste Comte (1798–1857), in hopes of emulating what natural scientists did for nature, sought to establish a science of society that would reveal the basic "laws of society." Comte believed that knowing these laws would help us to understand two key principles that he referred to as "social statics"—the principles by which societies hold together and order is maintained—and "social dynamics"—the factors that bring about change and that shape the nature and direction of that change. Sociologists would then use their knowledge of these laws to help lead us toward the good society, balancing the needs for social order with positive social change. To give this new discipline a name, Comte coined the term *sociology*—which literally means "the study of the processes of companionship" (Abercrombie, Hill, and Turner 2006:367).

English-speaking scholars learned of Comte's works largely through translations by the English sociologist Harriet Martineau (1802–1876). Seeking to systematize the research essential to conducting a science of society, Martineau ([1838] 1989) wrote the first book on sociological methods. She was also a pathbreaking theorist in her own right, introducing the significance of inequality and power into the discipline. Martineau's book *Society in America* ([1837] 1962) examined religion, politics, child rearing, and immigration in the young nation. It gave special attention to social class distinctions and to such factors as gender and race. In Martineau's ([1837] 1962) view, intellectuals and scholars should not simply offer observations of social conditions; they should act on their convictions in a manner that will benefit society. Martineau spoke out in favor of the rights of women, the emancipation of slaves, and religious tolerance.

These two themes—social order and social inequality—have shaped the theoretical and research paths sociologists have pursued since this beginning. In early sociological theory, they find their fullest development in the works of Émile Durkheim and Karl Marx, respectively. As we will see throughout this book, they continue to be primary concerns for sociologists.

Émile Durkheim (1858–1917) emphasized the significance of social order. As we saw in his analysis of suicide, he saw society as a real, external force existing above the level of the individual and exerting its influence on individual behavior. Durkheim was particularly concerned about what happens when the influence of society declines, resulting in weakened social integration. He theorized that an increase in the division of labor, a defining characteristic of modern societies, meant that individuals shared fewer common experiences, ideas, and values. As workers became much more specialized in their tasks, they were at greater risk of what Durkheim called **anomie**—the loss of direction felt in a society when social control of individual behavior has become ineffective. Anomie increases the likelihood of loneliness, isolation, and despair. Inspired by Comte's

> **anomie** The loss of direction felt in a society when social control of individual behavior has become ineffective.

vision, Durkheim sought to establish sociology as a science to study these processes.

HOW DO POWER AND INEQUALITY SHAPE OUTCOMES?

Karl Marx (1818–1883) took a different approach. He emphasized the role that power and control over resources played in how social order is established and maintained. Marx viewed our creative capacity to transform raw materials into products—for example, to take clay and make a pot, or cut down a tree and make a desk—as the key factor distinguishing humans from other animals (whose behavior is ruled by their instincts). For Marx, human history is the progressive unfolding of human creativity in the form of new technology through which we establish our relationship to the natural world and with each other. Unfortunately, for most of human history, we lacked sufficient technology to provide enough material goods (such as food, clothes, and shelter) to meet everyone's needs, so not all people had enough.

Social inequality for Marx, then, is determined by ownership, or lack thereof, of key material resources. The ruling class is defined by its ownership and control of the means of production—the tools and resources necessary for that transformation to happen. Members of the working class, in contrast, own only their capacity to transform raw materials into products, which requires access to the means of production controlled by the ruling class. Whereas Durkheim was concerned with anomie, Marx was concerned with alienation, by which he meant loss of control over our creative human capacity to produce, separation from the products we make, and isolation from our fellow workers. We will consider Marx's

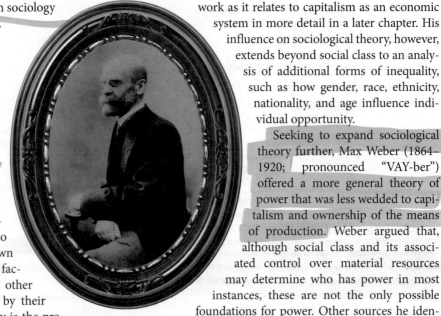

Émile Durkheim

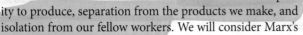

Karl Marx

work as it relates to capitalism as an economic system in more detail in a later chapter. His influence on sociological theory, however, extends beyond social class to an analysis of additional forms of inequality, such as how gender, race, ethnicity, nationality, and age influence individual opportunity.

Seeking to expand sociological theory further, Max Weber (1864–1920; pronounced "VAY-ber") offered a more general theory of power that was less wedded to capitalism and ownership of the means of production. Weber argued that, although social class and its associated control over material resources may determine who has power in most instances, these are not the only possible foundations for power. Other sources he identified include social status, in which people defer to others out of respect for their social position or prestige, and organizational resources, in which members of a group gain power through their ability to organize to accomplish some specific goal by maximizing their available resources. Weber argued that these social resources draw their power from people's willingness to obey the authority of another person, which in turn is based on their perception of the legitimacy of that person's right to rule.

HOW DOES INTERACTION SHAPE OUR WORLDS?

Much of the work of Durkheim, Marx, and Weber involves **macrosociology**, which concentrates on large-scale phenomena or entire civilizations. This top-down approach focuses on society as a whole and how broad social forces shape our lives. A later school of sociologists turned away from this approach in favor of **microsociology**, which stresses the study of small groups and the analysis of our everyday experiences and interactions. This bottom-up approach emphasizes the significance of perception, of how we see others and

Max Weber

how they see us. Sociologist Erving Goffman (1922–1982) popularized a method known as the *dramaturgical approach* (see Chapter 4), which compares everyday life to the setting of the theater and stage and sees people as theatrical performers. Just as actors project certain images to an audience, all of us seek to present particular features of our personalities to others even as we hide certain qualities. Thus, in a class, we may feel the need to project a serious image; at a party, we want to look relaxed and friendly. In this approach, sociologists must analyze our lived experience at the everyday level where our actions create, sustain, and modify our understanding of reality itself.

... According to the Thomas theorem, established by sociologists W. I. Thomas and Dorothy Swaine Thomas, "If men define situations as real, they are real in their consequences" (Thomas and Thomas 1928:571–572). In other words, our perceptions of what is real determine how we act more so than does reality itself.

Did You Know?

HOW DOES GROUP MEMBERSHIP INFLUENCE OPPORTUNITY?

Over time, sociologists came to more fully understand and appreciate the consequences that group membership, especially class, race, and gender, has for opportunity. Black sociologist W. E. B. Du Bois (1868–1963; pronounced "dew BOYS") combined an emphasis on the analysis of the everyday lived experience with a commitment to investigating power and inequality based on race. He was critical of those who relied on common sense or on all-too-brief investigations, arguing that a researcher has to be more than just a "car-window sociologist" because true understanding demands more than "the few leisure hours of a holiday trip to unravel the snarl of centuries" (Du Bois [1903] 1994:94). Through engaged and sustained research on the lives of African Americans, he documented their relatively low status in Philadelphia and Atlanta. His research revealed the social processes that contributed to the maintenance of racial separation, which extended beyond material differences to include social separation, which he referred to as the "color line."

Similarly, feminist scholarship has broadened our understanding of social behavior by extending the analysis beyond the male point of view that dominated classic sociology. An early example of this perspective can be seen in the life and writings of Ida Wells-Barnett (1862–1931). Carrying on a tradition begun with Martineau, Wells-Barnett argued that societies can be

judged based on whether the principles they claim to believe in match their actions. Wells-Barnett found that when it came to the principles of equality and opportunity for women and African Americans, America came up short. Part of the task for the sociologist, then, is to bring to light such inconsistencies that may otherwise go largely unnoticed. This is something Wells-Barnett sought to do in her groundbreaking publications in the 1890s on the practice of lynching African Americans, as well as with her advocacy of women's rights, especially the struggle to win the vote for women. Like feminist theorists who succeeded her, Wells-Barnett used her analysis of society as a means of resisting oppression. In her case, she researched what it meant to be African American, a woman in the United States, and a Black woman in the United States (Wells-Barnett [1928] 1970).

HOW SHOULD SOCIOLOGISTS RESPOND?

Throughout sociology's history, a recurring theme has been the idea that sociological theory and research should contribute to positive social change. In the early 1900s many leading sociologists in the United States saw themselves as social reformers dedicated to systematically studying and then improving a corrupt society. They were genuinely concerned about the lives of immigrants in the nation's growing cities, whether those immigrants came from Europe or from the rural American South. Early female sociologists,

> **macrosociology** Sociological investigation that concentrates on large-scale phenomena or entire civilizations.
>
> **microsociology** Sociological investigation that stresses the study of small groups and the analysis of our everyday experiences and interactions.

Did You Know?
... First Lady Michelle Obama received a bachelor of arts degree in sociology from Princeton University in 1985. She used that degree as a stepping-stone to law school at Harvard.

Jane Addams

in particular, often took active roles in poor urban areas as leaders of community centers known as settlement houses. For example, Jane Addams (1860–1935), an early member of the American Sociological Society, cofounded the famous Chicago settlement, Hull House, which provided social, education, and cultural programs for recent immigrants. Addams and other pioneering female sociologists commonly combined intellectual inquiry, social service work, and political activism—all with the goal of assisting the underprivileged and creating a more egalitarian society. Working with Ida Wells-Barnett, Addams successfully prevented racial segregation in the Chicago public schools, and her efforts to establish a juvenile court system and a women's trade union reflect the practical focus of her work (Addams 1910, 1930; Lengermann and Niebrugge-Brantley 1998).

This commitment to positive social change was not unique to Addams and her colleagues. From the very beginning and on down to the present, sociologists have recognized an obligation to go beyond explaining how the world works and become actively engaged in making the world a better place. In the words of French sociologist Pierre Bourdieu, "I have come to believe that those who have the good fortune to be able to devote their lives to the study of the social world cannot stand aside, neutral and indifferent, from the struggles in which the future of that world is at stake" (1998a:11). For some this has meant releasing the results of their research to the public so that we might make more informed decisions; for others it has meant active engagement in establishing social policy or assisting in the lives of others. For example, Durkheim, who considered an educated citizenry essential to democratic success, used his appointment to the Department of Science of Education and Sociology at the Sorbonne in Paris, along with his political connections and appointments, to shape French educational policy and practice. Du Bois cofounded the National Association for the Advancement of Colored People, better known as the NAACP. In fact, one of the dominant reasons students choose to major in sociology is that they want to make a difference, and sociology provides a pathway to do just that.

functionalist perspective
A sociological approach that emphasizes the way in which the parts of a society are structured to maintain its stability.

When I took "Soc101" in college, it took me a long time to understand the sociological imagination. I still remember feeling overwhelmed by all the concepts, facts, and figures. Eventually, as we studied the impact of the media and the power of inheritance, things began to fall into place; I took another course and was hooked. As you begin your study of sociology, my advice is to stay focused on how our individual choices are shaped by our social positions and access to resources. How do our circumstances influence how we understand ourselves and others? I hope that after encountering sociology, you will come away with a new way of seeing, equipped to act in new and more informed ways.

>>Three Sociological Perspectives

The answers to the five questions that sociologists ask provide us with a glimpse of the mosaic of sociological theories that have developed over time as sociologists consider the complexity of human behavior. Some theorists focus on society as a whole; others concentrate on individual interactions. Some are particularly concerned with inequality; others focus on maintaining social cohesion. Some approaches seem to overlap; others seem at odds with one another. But, regardless of their stance, all theorists share a common commitment to provide us with greater understanding of why we think and act the way we do. Each theory, whether broad or narrow, offers a way of seeing that allows us to perceive things we might have otherwise missed.

To simplify the rich array of sociological theories (especially for someone new to sociology) sociologists have classified various theories into three major theoreticial perspectives or approaches: functionalist, conflict, and interactionist. Each perspective offers a different set of lenses, focusing our attention in slightly different ways. Or, to put it another way, it is like three different people standing on the edge of a circle looking in at the same thing but each seeing it from a different point of view, able to recognize things that others might not even see.

According to the **functionalist perspective**, society is like a living organism with its various parts working together (or functioning) for the good of the whole. Functionalists posit that society and its parts are structured to provide social order and maintain stability. Aspects of

Three Sociological Perspectives

	Functionalist	Conflict	Interactionist
View of society	Stable, well integrated	Characterized by tension and struggle between groups	Active in influencing and affecting everyday social interaction
Level of analysis emphasized	Macro	Macro	Micro, as a way of understanding the larger macro phenomena
Key concepts	Social integration Institutions Anomie	Inequality Capitalism Stratification	Symbols Nonverbal communication Face-to-face interaction
View of the individual	People are socialized to perform societal functions	People are shaped by power, coercion, and authority	People manipulate symbols and create their social worlds through interaction
View of the social order	Maintained through cooperation and consensus	Maintained through force and coercion	Maintained by shared understanding of everyday behavior
View of social change	Predictable, reinforcing	Change takes place all the time and may have positive consequences	Reflected in people's social positions and their communications with others
Example	Public punishments reinforce the social order	Laws enforce the positions of those in power	People respect laws or disobey them based on their own past experience
Proponents	Émile Durkheim Talcott Parsons Robert Merton	Karl Marx W. E. B. Du Bois Ida Wells-Barnett	George Herbert Mead Charles Horton Cooley Erving Goffman

society that appear dysfunctional, seemingly contributing to a decrease in social order or integration, will either wither away over time or actually contribute some hidden benefits that researchers seek to reveal. Durkheim's research into social order and its challenges, especially within modern societies, is a classic example of the functionalist perspective. Durkheim assumed that, over time, society would progress toward greater order as it came to terms with apparent threats or challenges.

Whereas the functionalist perspective emphasizes consensus and cooperation, the **conflict perspective** focuses on power and the allocation of valued resources in society. According to conflict theorists, social order cannot be fully understood apart from an analysis of how the status quo is established and maintained by those who control key resources. Such resources include material resources (such as money, land, and property), social resources (such as family connections, social networks, and prestige), and

cultural resources (such as education, beliefs, knowledge, and taste). The existing social structure helps maintain the privileges of some groups and keep others in inferior positions. Marx's work on inequality, social class, and alienation provides a classic example of the conflict perspective.

Finally, whereas functionalist and conflict theorists both analyze large-scale, society-wide patterns of behavior, theorists who take the **interactionist perspective** generalize about everyday forms of social interaction in order to explain society as a whole. For interactionists, society is the product of our everyday interactions (with parents, friends, teachers, or strangers) through which we establish shared meanings and thus construct order. Because society is dependent on this ongoing construction, society is fluid and subject to change. Goffman's dramaturgical approach is an example of the interactionist perspective.

> **conflict perspective**
> A sociological approach that assumes social behavior is best understood in terms of tension between groups over power or the allocation of resources, including housing, money, access to services, and political representation.

> **interactionist perspective**
> A sociological approach that generalizes about everyday forms of social interaction in order to explain society as a whole.

The three-perspectives model has the advantage of providing us with conceptual hooks that allow us to recall some of the key concerns and issues sociologists have raised. A disadvantage, however, is that it gives the illusion that these three are discrete categories with fundamentally different and incompatible ways of looking at

SOCTHINK

To what extent was your decision to go to college driven by a desire to fit in and contribute to society? How might access to resources have shaped your decisions about going to college? What specific individuals influenced your decision and how did they do so?

the world. In practice, research rooted in one perspective almost inevitably draws on or addresses insights from the other two.

>>Practicing Sociology

One of the questions that students frequently ask about sociology is "What can I do with it?" This query often comes from students who really like sociology, and might want to pursue it further, but are uncertain about where it leads. The good news is that there are many ways people can practice sociology.

PERSONAL SOCIOLOGY

We don't have to become professional sociologists to practice what we have learned. The sociological imagination can help all of us to better understand our beliefs and actions and to make more informed choices. We can all practice **personal sociology** by recognizing the impact our individual position has on who we are, and how we think and act. Doing so also calls us to take responsibility for the effects our actions have on others. For example, by drawing on insights gained from

personal sociology The process of recognizing the impact our individual position has on who we are and how we think and act, and of taking responsibility for the impacts our actions have on others.

sociological theory and research, we might watch the news and ask whose interests are being represented. When we walk through the mall, we might observe how people display their social status and how they are treated accordingly. When we go in for a job interview, we might abide by the largely unspoken norms of conduct that shape interaction and influence our likelihood for success. Personal sociology empowers us by allowing us to see things that were previously invisible and to act on those insights.

ACADEMIC SOCIOLOGY

Many students opt to take their sociology education further, and the number of U.S. college students who have graduated with a degree in sociology has risen steadily (see figure below). The American Sociological Association (ASA) conducted research on recent sociology graduates and discovered that the top reasons for choosing sociology as a major are that students found the sociological concepts interesting, they particularly enjoyed the first course, sociology helped them to understand the relationship between social forces and individual relationships, they wanted to make a difference in the world, and it helped them to understand themselves better (American Sociological Association 2006a, 2006b). As part of their sociology education, sociology majors, cultivate a variety of skills, such as developing evidence-based arguments, evaluating research methods, writing a research

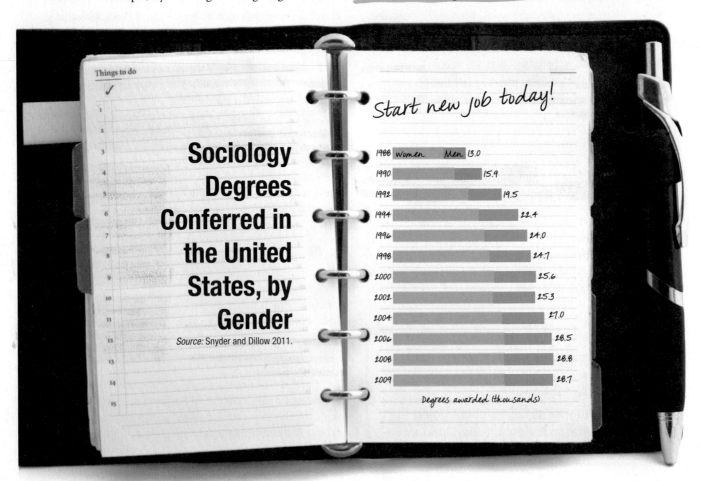

Things to do

Sociology Degrees Conferred in the United States, by Gender

Source: Snyder and Dillow 2011.

Start new job today!

	Women	Men	
1988			13.0
1990			15.9
1992			19.5
1994			22.4
1996			24.0
1998			24.7
2000			25.6
2002			25.3
2004			27.0
2006			28.5
2008			28.8
2009			28.7

Degrees awarded (thousands)

report understandable to nonsociologists, using computer resources including statistical software to organize and analyze data, and identifying ethical issues in research. Sociology graduates who later use these skills in their jobs express the highest levels of job satisfaction (Spalter-Roth and Van Vooren 2008a, 2008b).

The jobs that sociology majors find shortly after graduation, according to the ASA study, are in a range of fields. The most common occupational category is social services. Examples of jobs include caseworker for abused and neglected children, funds coordinator for Hurricane Katrina victims, manager for a not-for-profit organization, case manager for HIV-positive individuals, and child advocate. Researchers also found that graduates were employed in a variety of other positions, including teacher, librarian, paralegal, immigration specialist, office manager, quality assurance manager, crime scene investigator, police officer, probation officer, marketing consultant, research assistant, program evaluator, statistician, and editor (Spalter-Roth and Van Vooren 2008a).

According to the ASA study, of sociology majors who pursued graduate school degrees, only about one-quarter did so in sociology. Instead, most used their sociology major as a stepping-stone into graduate study in social work, education, law, psychology, engineering, and business management (Spalter-Roth and Van Vooren 2009:9). Overall, 51.9 percent of the majors completed a graduate degree within four years of college graduation. Of those who pursued advanced degrees in sociology, the majority enrolled in some form of an applied sociology program (Spalter-Roth and Van Vooren 2010).

SOCTHINK

How much responsibility do individuals have to make things better for society?

APPLIED SOCIOLOGY

Applied sociology is the use of the discipline of sociology with the specific intent of yielding practical applications for human behavior and organizations. Often, the goal of such work is to assist in resolving a social problem. For example, in the past 40 years, eight presidents of the United States have established commissions to delve into major societal concerns facing our nation. Sociologists are often asked to apply their expertise to studying such issues as violence, pornography, crime, immigration, and population.

> **applied sociology** The use of the discipline of sociology with the specific intent of yielding practical applications for human behavior and organizations.

One example of applied sociology involves the growing interest in the ways in which nationally recognized social problems manifest themselves locally. Sociologist Greg Scott and his colleagues sought to better understand the connection between illicit drug use and the spread of HIV/AIDS. The study employed 14 researchers from colleges and public health agencies, assisted by 15 graduate and 16 undergraduate students. By combining a variety of methods, including interviews and observation, with photo and video documentation, these researchers found that across all drug users, HIV/AIDS transmission is highest among users of crystal methamphetamine. Meth users are also most likely

Where Are They Now?

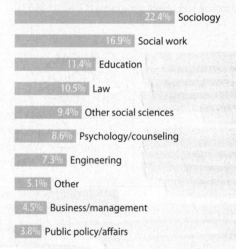

Occupational categories of recent sociology majors

Category	%
Social services	26.5%
Administrative, clerical support	15.8%
Management	14.4%
Other (includes PR and IT)	10.2%
Sales, marketing	10.1%
Services	8.3%
Education	8.1%
Research	5.7%

Graduate school programs of recent sociology majors

%	Program
22.4%	Sociology
16.9%	Social work
11.4%	Education
10.5%	Law
9.4%	Other social sciences
8.6%	Psychology/counseling
7.3%	Engineering
5.1%	Other
4.5%	Business/management
3.8%	Public policy/affairs

Note: Percentage based on sociology majors attending graduate school 18 months after graduation.

Source: Spalter-Roth and Van Vooren 2009.

in interventions for individual and social change. This professional group has developed a procedure for certifying clinical sociologists—much as physical therapists or psychologists are certified.

Applied sociologists generally leave it to others to act on their evaluations, but clinical sociologists take direct responsibility for implementation and view those with whom they work as their clients. This specialty has become increasingly attractive to graduate students in sociology because it offers an opportunity to apply intellectual learning in practical ways. A competitive job market in the academic world has made such alternative career routes appealing.

Regardless of the level at which it is done, practicing sociology is about so much more than a career; it is a way of looking at the world around us and understanding its complexity and interconnections in a new way. It is about understanding others from their perspective and even understanding ourselves through their eyes. It is a way of assessing the accuracy of claims and refining our knowledge about why we think the way we think and act the way we act. Sociology is something you do; it's a way of life.

>>Developing a Sociological Imagination

Though the expression has become something of a cliché, it truly is a small world after all. Social, cultural, political, and economic events around the world—including such things as the global financial meltdown and the death of Osama bin Laden—have a profound effect on how we think and what we do. The process of **globalization**—the worldwide integration of government policies, cultures, social movements, and financial markets through trade and the exchange of ideas—shows no signs of stopping. The sociological imagination presents us with the tools necessary to respond to these challenges.

College and university campuses often provide a microcosm of this trend. Students, faculty, staff, and administrators with radically different values, political views, customs, experiences, and expectations are drawn together from around the world into a relatively confined space. If the resulting interactions are to be meaningful, positive, and respectful, we must seek out ways to better understand factors that shape them. Conflicts with roommates,

to engage in risky sexual behavior and to have partners who do so. Fortunately, of all drug users, meth users are the ones most closely connected to treatment programs, which allows them to receive substance abuse education and treatment from their health care providers. Their cases, brought to the forefront by Scott and his team, highlight the need for public health officials to identify other individuals who engage in high-risk sexual behavior and to get them into appropriate treatment programs (G. Scott 2005).

clinical sociology The use of the discipline of sociology with the specific intent of altering organizations or restructuring social institutions.

globalization The worldwide integration of government policies, cultures, social movements, and financial markets through trade and the exchange of ideas.

CLINICAL SOCIOLOGY

The growing popularity of applied sociology has led to the rise of the specialty of clinical sociology. Whereas applied sociology may involve simply evaluating social issues, **clinical sociology** is dedicated to facilitating change by altering organizations (as in family therapy) or restructuring social institutions (as in the reorganization of a medical center). Louis Wirth (1931) wrote about clinical sociology more than 75 years ago, but the term itself has become popular only in recent years. The Association for Applied Clinical Sociology was founded in 1978 to promote the application of sociological knowledge

classmates, and professors are often chalked up to personality clashes and other individual attributes, but they cannot be fully understood or dealt with apart from coming to terms with the ways our social backgrounds have shaped how we think, act, and feel. For each of us, the social positions we occupy shape the opportunities and obstacles we face. We must learn to see the implications of this reality both for ourselves and for others. This self-knowledge necessitates a more complete appreciation of the intersection of history and biography in all of our lives.

Developing the sociological imagination enables us to make more informed choices about which pathways to follow. By opening our eyes to patterns and practices that are often invisible to us, sociology empowers us to act in more effective ways. It also facilitates our taking responsibility for the consequences of our actions. Practicing the sociological imagination enables us to ask ourselves what kind of world we want to live in and begin to take the steps necessary to make that world a reality.

SOCTHINK

Consider the obstacles to cross-cultural interaction on college campuses. Why might people be unwilling to interact with others who have different cultural practices? How might it perpetuate inequality?

get involved!

Investigate! The American Sociological Association (ASA) is an organization "dedicated to advancing sociology as a scientific discipline and profession serving the public good." Visit their website at asanet.org for more information on majoring in sociology and on career options for sociology majors.

For REVIEW

I. **What is sociology?**
   - Sociology is a way of seeing that joins theory and research to investigate the relationship between the individual and society and the impact unequal distribution of resources has on opportunity.

II. **How do sociologists look at the world?**
   - Sociologists developed theories to provide windows into our lives, including three primary perspectives: functionalist (emphasizing social order), conflict (focusing on inequality), and interactionist (highlighting the significance of our everyday relationships and exchanges).

III. **How might someone practice sociology?**
   - Sociology can provide a pathway to a career in a related applied, clinical, or academic context. But more than that, we can practice sociology in our everyday lives by utilizing the sociological imagination to better understand ourselves and others.

Functionalist View

Society is like a **living organism** with its various parts **working together** for the good of the whole.

The parts of society are structured to maintain **stability and social order.**

Society influences individual behavior and thus helps maintain **social integration through shared experiences.**

INTEGRATION
KEY CONCEPT

Conflict View

Society represents a **struggle over resources.** Those who control valued resources have **greater power** to get their way.

Valued resources include **material** (money, land, property), **social** (status, prestige, authority), and **cultural resources** (knowledge, beliefs, taste).

The existing social structure helps maintain the **privileges** of some groups while keeping others in subservient positions.

KEY CONCEPT
POWER

MAKE THE CONNECTION

After reviewing the chapter, answer the following questions:

KEY CONCEPT
CONSTRUCTING SOCIAL REALITY

Interactionist View

Society is the product of our everyday interactions by which we establish **shared meanings** and construct **social order.**

By generalizing from our everyday forms of social interaction (on the **micro level**), we can explain society as a whole.

The **self** exists in **relationship** with others and we come to **perceive** who we are and what our reality is through our interactions.

1

Why might having multiple theoretical perspectives help us when we practice the sociological imagination (p. 17)?

2

How might each perspective differ in how it looks at what it takes to produce something (such as a hamburger, a house, a book, and so on) (p. 17)?

3

How might each perspective approach the study of unemployment? Of suicide? (p. 17)

4

How does each perspective enable you to see the way you participate in sports, either as a fan or as an athlete, in a different light?

Pop Quiz

1. **Sociology is**
   a. the analysis of individual motivations and internal struggles.
   b. concerned with predicting what particular individuals do or do not do.
   c. the systematic study of the relationship between the individual and society and of the consequences of difference.
   d. the integration of government policies, cultures, social movements, and financial markets through trade and the exchange of ideas.

2. **According to C. Wright Mills, the sociological imagination focuses on the intersection between**
   a. natural science and social science.
   b. power and access to resources.
   c. theory and research.
   d. history and biography.

3. **What is the primary sociological lesson we learn from the hamburger as a miracle example?**
   a. We take our interdependence and the knowledge we collectively share for granted.
   b. An individual could easily survive on his or her own without assistance from others.
   c. Modern technology makes it difficult for us to provide for our individual needs.
   d. Interdependence is no longer necessary because we can provide for our needs through modern technology.

4. **In their attempts to describe the relationship between sociology and common sense, sociologists argue that**
   a. common sense provides time-tested answers that are reliable most of the time, whereas sociological facts change all the time.
   b. sociology depends on systematic analysis through research, whereas common sense does not.
   c. sociology cannot assess or test the truthfulness of commonsense claims.
   d. there is no significant difference between the two.

5. **Émile Durkheim's research on suicide found that**
   a. Catholics had much higher suicide rates than Protestants.
   b. the more socially integrated someone is the less likely he or she is to commit suicide.
   c. married people are more likely to take their lives than single people.
   d. suicide is a solitary act, unrelated to group life.

6. **Karl Marx argued that in order to understand social order we must include analysis of**
   a. anomie.
   b. ownership of the means of production.
   c. the sociological imagination.
   d. microsociology.

7. **Which sociologist made a major contribution to society through his in-depth studies of urban life, including both Blacks and Whites?**
   a. W. E. B. Du Bois
   b. Émile Durkheim
   c. Auguste Comte
   d. Erving Goffman

8. **What is the sociological term for the loss of direction felt in a society when social control of individual behavior has become ineffective?**
   a. suicide
   b. alienation
   c. anomie
   d. agency

9. **Thinking of society as a living organism in which each part of the organism contributes to its survival is a reflection of which theoretical perspective?**
   a. the functionalist perspective
   b. the conflict perspective
   c. the Marxist perspective
   d. the interactionist perspective

10. **The career path with the specific intent of altering social relationships or restructuring organizations is known as**
    a. dramaturgical sociology.
    b. applied sociology.
    c. academic sociology.
    d. clinical sociology.

1. (c); 2 (d); 3 (a); 4 (b); 5 (b); 6 (b); 7 (a); 8 (c); 9 (a); 10 (d)

2

SOCIOLOG

ASKING QUESTIONS AND FINDING ANSWERS

Part of the fun of sociology is asking questions and finding answers, and sociologists Patricia and Peter Adler seem to have had more fun than most. Their search to understand our social lives has led them to spend extended periods of time with college athletes, drug dealers, school kids, Hawaiian resort workers, graduate students, self-injurers, and others. In each such study their underlying sociological commitment has remained the same: to answer the questions "Why do we think the way we think?" and "Why do we act the way we act?"

To better understand the tourism industry, for example, the Adlers spent eight years gathering information at five Hawaiian hotels, studying the staff and operations in minute detail (Adler and Adler 2004). This allowed them to better understand how tourist experiences are scripted (including the ceremonial lei provided upon arrival) and the significance of race, ethnicity, and social class when it comes to access to resources (including the kinds of jobs available to new immigrants such as Filipinos, Samoans, and Vietnamese).

Similarly, in their effort to better understand self-injury—including self-cutting, burning, branding, biting, and bone-breaking—the Adlers (2011) analyzed more than 30,000 Internet sites, posts, chats, and exchanges and conducted lengthy, emotionally intense interviews with more than 100 self-injurers over a ten-year period, becoming friends with many. "Rather than remaining strictly detached from our subjects," they write, "we became involved in their lives, helping them and giving voice to their experiences and beliefs" (2007:542). They found that, for many, self-injury was a coping strategy, a form of self-therapy, and a means of empowerment.

In other studies they found that college athletes go to big-time college sports schools with the best of intentions to be good students but get worn down by the obligations of being an athlete, and resign themselves to inferior academic performance (Adler and Adler 1985).

As is the case with all good sociological research, such studies seek to tell our stories and help us to understand ourselves in light of our interdependence. Sociologists such as the Adlers systematically gather our stories through research and make sense of them with theory.

ICAL
RESEARCH

As You READ

>>

- What steps do sociologists take when seeking to answer why people think and act the way they do?
- What techniques do sociologists use to collect data?
- What ethical concerns must sociologists consider while conducting research?

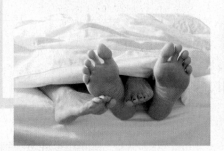

>>Steps in the Research Process

Sociology at its core represents a conversation between theory and research. Sociologists seek to describe and explain the patterns and practices of our lives through systematic investigation of what we do and why we do it. If we want to know why people think and act the way they do, we need to know more about what they actually think and do. We need to observe them, ask them questions, participate in their lives, or in other ways come to understand their experiences from their perspective. We cannot sit back and guess.

Sociology inherits this commitment in part from early attempts by some sociologists to emulate the scientific method, used in investigations of the natural world. The **scientific method** is a systematic, organized series of steps that ensures maximum objectivity and consistency in researching a problem. Although not all sociologists today would tie the task of sociology as strongly to the natural science model, the commitment to making sense of the world through engagement with the world remains.

scientific method A systematic, organized series of steps that ensures maximum objectivity and consistency in researching a problem.

Conducting sociological research in the spirit of the scientific method requires adherence to a series of steps designed to ensure the accuracy of the results. Sociologists and other researchers follow five basic steps in the scientific method: (1) defining the problem, (2) reviewing the literature, (3) formulating the hypothesis, (4) selecting the research design and then collecting and analyzing data, and (5) developing the conclusion (see the figure at right). To better understand the process, we will follow an example about the relationship between education and income from start to finish.

The Scientific Method

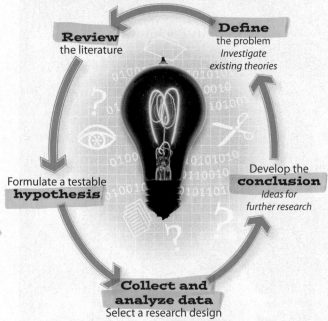

Review the literature

Define the problem *Investigate existing theories*

Formulate a testable **hypothesis**

Develop the **conclusion** *Ideas for further research*

Collect and analyze data Select a research design
Survey · Observation · Experiment · Existing sources

DEFINING THE PROBLEM

Does it "pay" to go to college? Many people make great sacrifices and work hard to get a college degree. Parents borrow money for their children's tuition. Students take part-time jobs or even work full-time while attending evening or weekend classes. Does it pay off? Are there sufficient monetary returns for getting that degree?

The first step in any research project is to state as clearly as possible what you hope to investigate—that is, to define the problem. Typically, this means explicitly identifying both the concepts we are interested in learning more about and the nature of the relationship we suspect might exist between those concepts. Doing so is necessary for the conversation between theory and research to occur.

Theory plays a central role in our definition of the problem. Theories represent our most informed explanations of what happens and why. When we come up against something we do not yet understand, theories can guide our investigation by suggesting possible research paths. For example, as we saw in Chapter 1, Émile Durkheim theorized that social integration shapes individual action. He set out to test this theory by conducting research on suicide as an example of the most extreme individual choice of all. Through research we assess and refine our theories so that our sociological explanations and descriptions of the world are fuller and richer, more accurately reflecting both the simplicity and the complexity of human behavior.

In our current example, we are interested in knowing how education affects a person's economic position. Several competing sociological theories exist concerning this relationship. One approach, growing out of the functionalist paradigm, presumes that, in order to realize its full potential, society needs people to take sufficient time to develop their skills. This leads to the supposition that people who make the sacrifices necessary to develop those skills will be rewarded for doing so (Davis and Moore 1945). Another theory, from conflict tradition, suggests that, instead of rewarding those with skills, education reinforces the existing system of inequality by providing the illusion of opportunity. In this theory, people more or less end up in the same economic position in which they began their educational journey (Bowles and Gintis 1976). Which theory we start with will shape the kind of data we collect. We look into both theories in a later chapter, but for the purpose of our example, we will focus on the first.

Often the concepts in our theories are too abstract to observe. To assess those theories, social science researchers develop an operational definition of each concept being studied. An **operational definition** transforms an abstract concept into indicators that are observable and measurable. For example, a sociologist interested in studying status might use membership in exclusive social clubs as an operational definition of status. Someone studying religiosity might consider the frequency of a person's participation in religious services or the amount of time in prayer or meditation as an operational definition of how religious the person is. In our example, we need operational definitions for both education and earnings. Although a person's level of education might mean more than just their years of schooling completed, it is conventional to operationalize it that way. Similarly, we will also use the common approach of operationalizing earnings as a person's total income received in the previous year.

REVIEWING THE LITERATURE

The next phase of research involves a review of the literature: investigating previous research conducted by sociologists and others regarding the concepts we wish to study. Analyzing how others have studied these concepts allows researchers to refine the problem under study, clarify possible techniques for collecting data, and eliminate or reduce avoidable mistakes. An excellent place to start such research is the many sociological journals that regularly publish articles in which sociologists carefully document their findings. (See the "Finding Information" table on page 28 for more useful tips.)

> **operational definition** Transformation of an abstract concept into indicators that are observable and measurable.
>
> **variable** A measurable trait or characteristic that is subject to change under different conditions.
>
> **hypothesis** A testable statement about the relationship between two or more variables.

In our example, we would need to seek out existing research about the relationship between education and income. In that literature we would find significant evidence that the two are linked. We would also learn that other factors besides years of schooling influence earning potential. For example, a person's occupational category (such as plumber, tool-and-die worker, secretary, or professor) might shape her or his income in a way different from educational level alone. We also find that additional background factors such as class, gender, and race affect income. For example, the children of rich parents are more likely to go to college than those from modest backgrounds, so we might consider the possibility that the same parents may later help their children secure better-paying jobs (Walpole 2007). This might lead us to consider adding additional concepts to our definition of the problem.

> *Without theory we are blind—we cannot see the world.*
>
> **Michael Burawoy**

FORMULATING THE HYPOTHESIS

After defining the problem in conversation with existing theories and refining the problem by reviewing previous research, we can identify the variables we want to study and indicate our expectations about the relationships between them. A **variable** is a measurable trait or characteristic that is subject to change under different conditions. Income, religion, occupation, and gender can all serve as variables in a study. A **hypothesis** is a testable statement about the relationship between two or more variables.

Finding Information

Begin with material you already have, including this text and others.

Beware of using online sources such as Wikipedia; they can be a helpful place to start, but always double-check claims with a reputable source or organization.

Use newspapers.

Search using computerized periodical indexes to find related academic journal articles.

Use the library catalog.

Examine government documents (including the U.S. Census).

Contact people, organizations, and agencies related to your topic.

Consult with your instructor, teaching assistant, or reference librarian.

causal logic A relationship exists between variables in which change in one brings about change in the other.

independent variable The variable in a causal relationship that causes or influences a change in a second variable.

dependent variable The variable in a causal relationship that is subject to the influence of another variable.

A hypothesis is more than just an educated guess. It represents an explicit attempt to indicate what we think is happening and why. It presupposes that **causal logic** is at work, meaning that a relationship exists between variables in which change in one brings about change in the other. Durkheim, for example, hypothesized that a cause and effect relationship existed between religious affiliation and suicide rates. In our example, we are hypothesizing that increased education leads to higher income.

In hypotheses, the causal variable that brings about change is called the **independent variable.** The variable that is affected is known as the **dependent variable,** because change in it depends on the influence of the independent variable. In other words, the researcher believes that the independent variable predicts or causes change in the dependent variable. For example, a researcher in sociology might anticipate that the availability of affordable housing (the independent variable; often referred to in equations as *x*) affects the level of homelessness in a community (the dependent variable; typically represented in equations as *y*).

We can put these pieces together to generate a generic hypothesis statement: knowledge of the independent variable (*x*) allows us to better explain or predict the value or position of the dependent variable (*y*). We could then place variables we are interested in studying, such as those in the "Causal Logic" figure to the right, into

Did You Know?

. . . U.S. government agencies regularly release reports on income, education, poverty, and health care. According to the Department of Education, 87.1 percent of people age 25 and older have received their high school diploma or equivalent, and 29.9 percent earned at least a bachelor's degree. According to the Census Bureau, the median income for full-time, year-round workers aged 25–64 was $43,990.

Source: Snyder and Dillow 2011: Table 8; U.S. Census Bureau 2011f: Table 28

Causal Logic

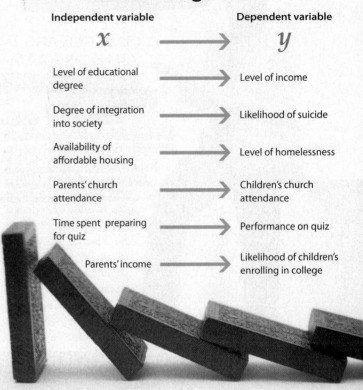

Independent variable	Dependent variable
x ⟶	y
Level of educational degree	Level of income
Degree of integration into society	Likelihood of suicide
Availability of affordable housing	Level of homelessness
Parents' church attendance	Children's church attendance
Time spent preparing for quiz	Performance on quiz
Parents' income	Likelihood of children's enrolling in college

this statement to clearly present the nature of the relationships we expect to find between variables we wish to study.

In our example, our hypothesis suggests that knowing how many years of schooling a person has completed will allow us to better predict how much money he or she will earn. Our independent variable is the level of education, and the dependent variable is income. Further, we expect the relationship to be positive, meaning the higher a person's educational attainment, the more money she or he will make. In a negative relationship, as the independent variable goes up, the dependent variable goes down, and vice versa.

We should note that just because two variables seem to co-vary does not mean that change in one causes change in the other. Such covariance is known as a **correlation,** which is a relationship between two variables in which change in one coincides with change in the other. It may well be that the apparent relationship is due to chance or to the influence of some other factors. It is the task of the researcher to demonstrate—drawing on the data, logical reasoning, and theory—that the correlation is also causal. Statistics alone are not enough.

Take, for example, the effect that divorce has on the well-being of children. Studies have shown that the two variables are correlated—children of divorce exhibit long-term adverse effects—but is that relationship causal? Before reaching a conclusion, we should consider other factors. Perhaps negative outcomes for children are due to levels of parental conflict rather than divorce itself, or to the nature

of the relationship between the parents and the children, or to contextual factors such as unemployment or geographic mobility (Bhrolcháin 2001; Sun and Li 2008). In the words of sociologist Pierre Bourdieu, "One has explained nothing by establishing the existence of a correlation between an 'independent' variable and a

correlation A relationship between two variables in which a change in one coincides with a change in the other.

Correlation

I USED TO THINK CORRELATION IMPLIED CAUSATION.

THEN I TOOK A STATISTICS CLASS. NOW I DON'T.

SOUNDS LIKE THE CLASS HELPED. WELL, MAYBE.

Source: http://xkcd.com/552/.

'dependent' variable" (1984:18). Correlation does not equal causation.

COLLECTING AND ANALYZING DATA

To assess their hypotheses, sociologists, like all scientists, collect data. There are a variety of ways, known as research designs, that sociologists go about doing this, including surveys, observation, experiments, and use of existing data. Because the design selected is so critical to the research process, we will go into greater depth about each of those research designs later in this chapter. For now we will focus on some key issues that researchers must address regardless of which research design they select.

Selecting the Sample

Often, especially in the case of large-scale research projects, sociologists cannot conduct a census, meaning they cannot gather information from everyone in the population they are interested in studying. In such instances, they conduct a **sample**—a selection from a larger population that is statistically representative of that population. To ensure that a sample is representative, sociologists frequently use a **random sample,** in which every member of the entire population being studied has an equal chance of being selected. Thus, if researchers want to examine the opinions of people listed in a city directory (a book that, unlike the telephone directory, lists all households in a community), they might use a computer to randomly select names from the directory. Doing so eliminates the possibility of bias or convenience negatively affecting who gets included.

When conducted properly, such sampling allows researchers to statistically estimate how

sample A selection from a larger population that is statistically representative of that population.

random sample A sample for which every member of an entire population has an equal chance of being selected.

validity The degree to which a measure or scale truly reflects the phenomenon under study.

representative their results are likely to be. The same cannot be said of most online polls, such as on Facebook, Yahoo, or news sites, because they usually do not control for who responds, relying instead on whoever logs in and chooses to participate. Though such surveys can be interesting, fun, or provocative, there is no way to tell if they are representative.

To better understand the relationship between education and income, we can draw on research collected by the National Opinion Research Center (NORC) or the U.S. Census Bureau. These two organizations provide invaluable sources of data for sociologists. NORC has administered the General Social Survey 28 times since 1972. In this national survey, administered in both English and Spanish, a representative sample of the adult population is interviewed in depth on a variety of topics, including both income and education. They frequently ask the same questions over multiple years, allowing for analysis of how responses change over time.

Although the Census Bureau is best known for the census it conducts every ten years of the entire U.S. population (most recently in 2010), researchers there also regularly collect data using representative samples of the U.S. population. Doing so provides them with more frequent updates and allows them to gather more detailed information about more variables than is possible in the decennial census. For example, with regard to our variables of interest, each fall they release an annual report on income, poverty, and health care coverage in the United States (DeNavas-Walt, Proctor, and Smith 2011).

Ensuring Validity and Reliability To have confidence in their findings, and in keeping with the scientific method, sociologists pursue research results that are both valid and reliable. **Validity** refers to the degree to which

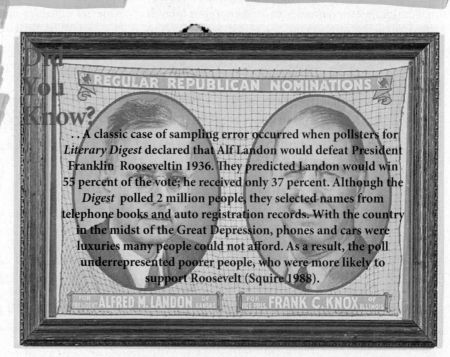

Did You Know?

REGULAR REPUBLICAN NOMINATIONS

. . A classic case of sampling error occurred when pollsters for *Literary Digest* declared that Alf Landon would defeat President Franklin Roosevelt in 1936. They predicted Landon would win 55 percent of the vote; he received only 37 percent. Although the *Digest* polled 2 million people, they selected names from telephone books and auto registration records. With the country in the midst of the Great Depression, phones and cars were luxuries many people could not afford. As a result, the poll underrepresented poorer people, who were more likely to support Roosevelt (Squire 1988).

FOR PRESIDENT ALFRED M. LANDON OF KANSAS   FOR VICE PRES. FRANK C. KNOX OF ILLINOIS

a measure or scale truly reflects the phenomenon under study. In our example, a valid measure of income would accurately represent how much money a person earned in a given year. If the question is not written clearly, some respondents might interpret it as asking for earnings from a job, others might add income from other sources, such as investments, and others might report household income, including earnings from children or a spouse. Studies show that, even though income can be a touchy subject, people respond accurately when asked a clear and unambiguous question about how much they have earned.

Reliability refers to the extent to which a measure produces consistent results. Using the same instrument to collect data from the same people in similar circumstances should provide the same results. For example, if you give people the same questionnaire about income and education at two different times, unless something significant has changed between times, the responses should be approximately the same.

DEVELOPING THE CONCLUSION

After having collected the data and analyzed the results, sociologists draw conclusions about what they have learned. They use the information they gathered so as to better explain why we act and think as we do. The research results inform our theories, which helps to generate new questions, and the whole cycle begins again with a new definition of the problem.

Supporting Hypotheses As we can see in the graph below, data from the U.S. Census support our hypothesis regarding education and income: people with more formal

schooling do earn more money than those with less schooling. Looking first at the top two income categories, we see that 47 percent for those with a college degree, compared to 16 percent of those without a college degree, earn $60,000 or more. Turning to the bottom two income categories, we notice that 26 percent for those with higher educational degrees versus 59 percent of those with no more than a high school diploma earn less than $40,000. When it comes to income, educational attainment matters.

> **reliability** The extent to which a measure produces consistent results.

> **control variable** A factor that is held constant to test the relative impact of an independent variable.

Of course, this is not true for all individuals. As we see in the graph, having a college degree does not guarantee a high income—15 percent of those with a college degree earn less than $20,000. Exceptions to the rule might include successful entrepreneurs lacking formal schooling or those with a doctorate who choose to work for a low-paying, not-for-profit institution. Sociologically, both of these findings—that education shapes income and that the relationship is not perfect—are interesting. To understand why such variation exists, we would need to consider the possible effects that additional variables have on income.

Sociological studies do not always generate data that support the original hypothesis. In many instances, the results refute the hypothesis, and researchers must reformulate their conclusions. This often leads to additional research in which sociologists reexamine their theory and methods, making appropriate changes in their research design.

Controlling for Other Factors Given the complexity of human behavior, it is seldom sufficient to study only one independent and dependent variable. Although such analyses can provide us with insight, we also need to consider other causal factors that might influence the dependent variable. One way to do this is to introduce a **control variable,** which is a factor that the researcher holds constant to test the relative impact of an independent variable. For example, if researchers wanted to explain neighborhood crime rates as a dependent variable, they might look at the

Impact of a College Degree on Income

High school diploma or less

7%	$80,000 and over
9%	$60,000–79,999
25%	
44%	$40,000–59,999
	$20,000–39,999
15%	under $20,000

Associate's degree or more

29%
18%
27%
22%
4%

Note: Data includes those age 25–64 working full-time, year-round. High school category includes those with some college but no degree.

Source: U.S. Census Bureau 2011f: Table PINC-03, part 28.

Sticking with education as our independent variable, what other dependent variables might we study to see the impact of education on society? What do we hope to get out of education both individually and collectively?

neighborhood's poverty rate as an independent variable. It is likely, however, that additional factors influence crime rates, so they might introduce familiarity—the degree to which neighbors know and regularly interact with each other—as a control variable. They would find that neighborhoods with a high level of familiarity do have lower crime rates than those with low familiarity rates. The introduction of the control variable allows us to see that some of the variation in neighborhood crime rates that was initially assumed to be due to poverty is actually due to the influence of the control variable.

research design A detailed plan or method for obtaining data scientifically.

survey A study, generally in the form of an interview or questionnaire, that provides researchers with information about how people think and act.

Looking at our variables, we cannot consider only the effect education has on income; we should also investigate the role that other variables might play. One possibility is that "who you know" matters as much as "what you know." To study this relationship, we could look at how a person's family background or social network connections influence income. In later chapters we consider such additional background factors that help to explain income differences, including gender, race, ethnicity, and social class.

IN SUMMARY: THE RESEARCH PROCESS

We began with a general question about the relationship between education and income. By following the steps in the research process—defining the problem, reviewing the literature, formulating a hypothesis, collecting and analyzing data, and developing a conclusion—we were able to show that education does pay. One of the ways we can check the validity of our findings is to share them with sociologists, policy makers, and others in a public forum in the form of a paper at a professional conference or an article in a refereed academic journal. By exposing what we did, how we did it, and what we found, others can serve as a useful check to make sure we did not miss anything and that we proceeded in an appropriate manner.

Research is cyclical in nature. At the end of the process, researchers almost always find that they have more questions they would like to pursue and ideas for further research, and most research papers include a specific section addressing how they might define the problem and carry out the research next time. Along the way, researchers

may have discovered new concepts they should consider, better ways to ask questions to get the information they need, individuals or groups they should include in the study, or a whole host of other possibilities. In the end, the studies researchers produce become part of the literature review for the next project, whether theirs or someone else's.

>>Major Research Designs

As we have seen, sociologists go about gathering and making sense of the stories of our lives in a variety of ways. Sometimes sociologists want to tell our larger collective story; other times they want to tell the stories of individuals and groups who are often left out of such large-scale accounts. Different research designs are available to tell these different types of stories. For example, large national surveys allow us to get a sense of the national mood about issues such as politics or religion, and statistics can give insight into where we stand in relation to each other on such issues. To explore the smaller-scale stories of individuals and groups, researchers may employ methods, such as observation, that emphasize more direct and personal interaction with their subjects.

Sociologists draw on four major types of research designs when considering how to collect their data. A **research design** is a detailed plan or method for obtaining data scientifically. Often a selection of research designs is based on the theories and hypotheses the researcher starts with (Denzin 2009; Merton 1948). The choice requires creativity and ingenuity, because it directly influences both the cost of the project and the time needed to collect the data (Vogt, Gardner, and Haeffele 2012). As noted previously, research designs that sociologists regularly use to generate data include surveys, observation, experiments, and existing sources.

SURVEYS

Almost all of us have responded to surveys of one kind or another. We may have been asked what kind of detergent we use, which presidential candidate we intend to vote for, or what our favorite television program is. A **survey** is a study, generally in the form of an interview or questionnaire, that provides researchers with information about how people think and act. Surveys become particularly commonplace during election seasons in the form of political polls. Major polling organizations include Gallup, SurveyUSA, ABC/Washington Post, and Rasmussen. All these firms seek to use careful techniques to ensure the accuracy of their results.

President Obama's Approval Ratings

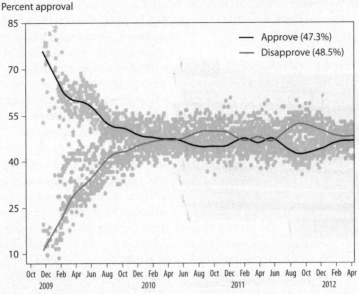

Percent approval

Legend:
— Approve (47.3%)
— Disapprove (48.5%)

Each point represents a single poll conducted by a major polling organization.

Source: www.pollkatz.homestead.com.

Issues in Designing Surveys As indicated earlier, a survey must be based on precise, representative sampling if it is to genuinely reflect a broad range of the population. We might be skeptical that feedback from just a few hundred people can provide an accurate picture of how more than 300 million people think, but properly run surveys can do just that. When it comes to presidential polling, for example, we can compare the results of such polls against actual election results. In a study of the historical accuracy of presidential polls, political scientist Michael W. Traugott (2005) reports that the polls from 1956 to 2004 were, on average, within 2 percent of accurately predicting the final result, as was also the case in 2008 (Panagopoulos 2009). We can also get a sense of the accuracy of polls by looking at "polls of polls" that combine various results into a single report or graph to better see the pattern that the polls collectively demonstrate (see the figure above). Examples of current polls for presidential and congressional approval ratings are available at sites such as pollster.com and pollingreport .com. Although the pollsters sometimes fail to "get it right" (for example, predicting that Dewey would defeat Truman in the 1948 presidential election), most often they do, and with amazing precision.

Going GLOBAL

Research Abroad

Researchers can gather information even under difficult circumstances. Even as the Obama administration was escalating the war in Afghanistan against the Taliban in 2009, researchers conducted surveys about people's attitudes in the region. In late 2009 they found that 79 percent of Afghans felt the Taliban had a negative influence, though residents in the south, a Taliban stronghold, were somewhat less negative. At the same time, 45 percent approved of U.S. leadership in Afghanistan, down from 50 percent earlier in the year (Ray and Srinivasan 2010a, 2010b).

In addition to developing representative samples, sociologists must exercise great care in the wording of questions. An effective survey question must be simple and clear enough for people to understand. It must also be specific enough that researchers have no problems interpreting the results. Open-ended questions ("What do you think of the programming on educational television?") must be carefully phrased to solicit the type of information desired. Surveys can be indispensable sources of information, but only if the sampling is done properly and the questions are worded accurately and without bias.

Studies have also shown that the characteristics of the interviewer influence survey data. For example, female interviewers tend to receive more feminist responses from female subjects than do male researchers, and African American interviewers tend to receive more detailed responses about race-related issues from Black subjects than do White interviewers. The possible impact of gender and race indicates again how much care social research requires (Chun et al. 2011 Davis and Silver 2003).

interview A face-to-face or telephone questioning of a respondent to obtain desired information.

questionnaire A printed, written, or computerized form used to obtain information from a respondent.

mean A number calculated by adding a series of values and then dividing by the number of values.

median The midpoint, or number that divides a series of values into two groups of equal numbers of values.

quantitative research Research that collects and reports data primarily in numerical form.

Types of Surveys There are two main forms of the survey: the **interview,** in which a researcher obtains information through face-to-face or telephone questioning, and the **questionnaire,** in which a researcher uses a printed, written, or computerized form to obtain information from a respondent. Each of these has its advantages. An interviewer can obtain a higher response rate because people find it more difficult to turn down a personal request for an interview than to throw away a written questionnaire. In addition, a skillful interviewer can go beyond written questions and probe for a subject's underlying feelings and reasons. For their part, questionnaires have the advantage of being cheaper, especially in large samples. Either way, what we can learn from surveys can be amazing.

Why, for example, do people have sex? That is a straightforward question, but until recently one that rarely

Top Reasons Why Men and Women Had Sex

Men	Reason	Women
1	I was attracted to the person	1
2	It feels good	3
3	I wanted to experience the physical pleasure	2
4	It's fun	8
5	I wanted to show my affection to the person	4
6	I was sexually aroused and wanted the release	6
7	I was "horny"	7
8	I wanted to express my love for the person	5
9	I wanted to achieve an orgasm	14
10	I wanted to please my partner	11
17	I realized I was in love	9
13	I was "in the heat of the moment"	10

Source: Meston and Buss 2007:506.

was investigated scientifically, despite its significance to public health, marital counseling, and criminology. In an exploratory study published in 2007, researchers surveyed nearly 2,000 undergraduates at the University of Texas at Austin. They began phase 1 of the research by asking approximately 400 students in a variety of psychology courses to answer this question: "Please list all the reasons you can think of why you, or someone you have known, has engaged in sexual intercourse in the past." The explanations were highly diverse, ranging from "I was drunk" to "I wanted to feel closer to God."

In phase 2 of the research, the team asked another sample of 1,500 students to rate the importance of each of the 287 reasons given by the first group. Nearly every one of the reasons was rated most important by at least some respondents. Although there were some gender differences in the replies, there was significant consensus between men and women on the top reasons (see the table below). Based on their overall results, the researchers identified four major categories of reasons why people have sex: Physical (pleasure, stress reduction), Goal Attainment (social status, revenge), Emotional (love, commitment), and Insecurity (self-esteem boost, duty/pressure) (Meston and Buss 2007, 2009). After reviewing the study results, critics argued that the researchers' sample was not sufficiently representative to permit generalizing their findings to the population as a whole. The researchers acknowledged as much from the beginning, having undertaken the project as exploratory research. They have since conducted research using a more representative sample, and their findings were largely the same (Melby 2007).

Quantitative and Qualitative Research Surveys most often represent an example of **quantitative research,** which collects and reports data primarily in numerical form. Analysis of these data depends on statistics, from the simple to the complex, which provide basic summaries describing what variables look like and how they are related. Basic descriptive statistics, such as percentages, are likely familiar. The **mean,** or average, is a number calculated by adding a series of values and then dividing by the number of values. The **median,** or midpoint, is the number that divides a series of values into two groups of equal numbers of values. The median is most often used when there are extreme scores that would distort the mean. The **mode** is the single most common value in a series of scores and is seldom used in sociological research. The mean, median, and mode all seek to provide a single score that is representative of or provides a summary for the whole distribution of scores. When it comes to analyzing relationships between variables, researchers usually rely on computer programs to deal with more complex analysis of quantitative data.

Although quantitative research can make use of large samples, it can't offer great depth on a topic. That is why researchers also make use of **qualitative research,** which relies on what they see in field and naturalistic settings, often focusing on small groups and communities rather than on large groups or whole nations. Here, too,

Research is formalized curiosity. It is poking and prying with a purpose.

Zora Neale Hurston

sociologists rely on computers to assist their analysis. Numerous software programs allow researchers not only to record observations but to identify common themes, concepts, or concerns expressed in interviews. The most common form of qualitative research is observation.

OBSERVATION

Investigators who collect information by participating directly and/or by closely watching a group or community are engaged in **observation.** This method allows sociologists to examine behaviors and communities in greater depth than is possible using other methods. Though observation may seem a relatively informal method compared to surveys, researchers are careful to take detailed notes while observing their subjects.

An increasingly popular form of qualitative research in sociology today is **ethnography**—the study of an entire social setting through extended systematic observation. Typically, the emphasis is on how the subjects themselves view their social life in some setting. In some cases, the sociologist actually joins the group for a period to get an accurate sense of how it operates. This approach is called *participant observation.*

During the late 1930s, in a classic example of participant observation research, sociologist William F. Whyte moved into a low-income Italian neighborhood in Boston. For nearly four years, he was a member of the social circle of "corner boys" whom he described in his classic book *Street Corner Society.* Whyte revealed his identity to these men and joined in their conversations, bowling, and other leisure-time activities. His goal was to gain greater insight into the community that these men had established. As Whyte ([1943] 1981:303) listened to Doc, the leader of the group, he "learned the answers to questions that I would not even have had the sense to ask if I had been getting my information solely on an interviewing basis." Whyte's work was especially valuable since, at the time, the academic world had little direct knowledge of the poor and tended to rely for information on the records of social service agencies, hospitals, and courts (P. Adler, Adler, and Johnson 1992).

The initial challenge that Whyte faced—and that every participant observer encounters—was to gain acceptance into an unfamiliar group. It is no simple matter for a college-trained sociologist to win the trust of a religious cult, a youth

mode The single most common value in a series of scores.

qualitative research Research that relies on what is seen in field or naturalistic settings more than on statistical data.

observation A research technique in which an investigator collects information through direct participation and/or by closely watching a group or community.

ethnography The study of an entire social setting through extended systematic observation.

gang, a poor Appalachian community, or a circle of skid row residents. It requires a great deal of patience and an accepting, nonthreatening type of personality on the part of the observer.

Observation research poses other complex challenges for investigators. Sociologists must be able to fully understand what they are observing. In a sense, then, researchers must learn to see the world as the group sees it in order to fully comprehend the events taking place around them.

SOC THINK

What social group or setting (such as a religious group, political organization, sorority/fraternity, laboratory, or office) might you want to learn more about through in-depth participant observation? How would you go about making contact? How would you gain members' trust?

This raises a delicate issue. If the research is to be successful, the observer cannot allow the close associations or even friendships that inevitably develop to influence the subjects' behavior or the conclusions of the study. Anson Shupe and David Bromley (1980), two sociologists who have used participant observation, have likened this challenge to that of walking a tightrope. Even while working hard to gain acceptance from the group being studied, the participant observer *must* maintain some degree of detachment.

In 2006 the issue of detachment became a controversial one for social scientists embedded with the U.S. military in Afghanistan and Iraq. Among other studies, researchers participated in the creation of the Army's Human Terrain System, a $4-million effort to identify the customs, kinship structures, and internal social conflicts in the two countries. The intention was to provide military leaders with information that would help them make better decisions. Although the idea of scholars cooperating in any way with soldiers struck many social science researchers as inappropriate, others countered that the information they developed would help the military to avoid needless violence and might even facilitate the withdrawal of troops from the region (Forte 2011; Glenn 2007; Gonzalez 2008).

experiment An artificially created situation that allows a researcher to manipulate variables.

experimental group The subjects in an experiment who are exposed to an independent variable introduced by a researcher.

control group The subjects in an experiment who are not introduced to the independent variable by the researcher.

Hawthorne effect The unintended influence that observers of experiments can have on their subjects.

EXPERIMENTS

When scientists want to study a possible cause-and-effect relationship, they conduct an **experiment**—an artificially created situation that allows a researcher to manipulate variables. Researchers carefully control the experimental

Have you ever asked yourself, "What were they thinking?" Maybe it's the music people like, the clothes they wear, the major they choose, the job they get, the person they date, the religion they practice, or the candidate they support. Although sociology cannot provide specific answers for why particular individuals think and act like they do, it does offer insight into the social factors that influence our choices. Imagine that you had the chance to answer some specific question such as those above. Which would you choose? What independent and dependent variables might you identify? What would your hypothesis be? What research design might you select? What makes sociology fun is that we get to ask questions and find answers.

context in order to measure the degree to which the independent variable causes change in the dependent variable under study. Although experiments can prove insightful, sociologists tend not to use them as frequently as the other research designs, because they are typically more interested in understanding people's natural responses, and there are ethical questions about manipulating people's responses.

In a classic experiment, researchers begin by dividing subjects with similar characteristics into two groups in order to see the impact of one independent variable. The **experimental group** is then exposed to an independent variable; the **control group** is not. Thus, if scientists were testing a new type of antibiotic, they would administer the drug to an experimental group but not to a control group.

One of the disadvantages of experiments, just as in observation research, is that the presence of a social scientist or other observer may affect the behavior of the people being studied. The recognition of this phenomenon grew out of an experiment conducted during the 1920s and 1930s at the Hawthorne plant of the Western Electric Company near Chicago. A group of researchers set out to determine how to improve the productivity of workers at the plant. The investigators manipulated such variables as lighting and working hours to see what impact the changes would

SOC THINK

Imagine you are a researcher interested in the effect playing computer or console games has on a college student's grades. How might you go about setting up an experiment to measure this effect?

have on how much workers produce. To their surprise, they found that every step they took seemed to increase output. Even measures that seemed likely to have the opposite effect, such as reducing the amount of lighting in the plant down to moonlight levels, led to higher productivity (Mayo 1933).

Why did the plant's employees work harder even under less favorable conditions? The researchers initially concluded that the workers modified their behavior because they knew they were being studied. They responded positively to the novelty of being subjects in an experiment and to the fact that researchers were interested in them. Since that time, sociologists have used the term **Hawthorne effect** to describe the unintended influence that observers of experiments can have on their subjects, even though later studies show the situation there was more complex (Brannigan and Zwerman 2001). It highlights the difficulties experiments present in seeking to understand how people behave in their real-world environments.

Sociologists do sometimes try to approximate experimental conditions in the field. Sociologist Devah Pager (2003) devised an experiment to assess the impact of a criminal background on individuals' employment opportunities. She sent four polite, well-dressed young men out to look for an entry-level job in Milwaukee, Wisconsin. All four were 23-year-old college students, but they presented themselves as high school graduates with similar job histories. Two of the men were Black and two were White. One Black applicant and one White applicant claimed to have served 18 months in jail for a felony conviction—possession of cocaine with intent to distribute.

The experiences of the four men with 350 potential employers were vastly different. The White applicant with a purported prison record received only half as many callbacks as the other White applicant—17 percent compared to 34 percent (see the graphic above). But as dramatic as the effect of his criminal record was, the effect of his race was more significant. Despite his prison record, he received slightly more callbacks than the Black applicant with no criminal record (17 percent compared to 14 percent).

White Privilege in Job Seeking

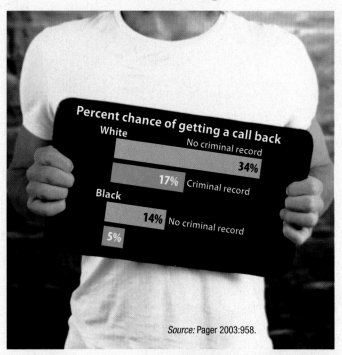

Percent chance of getting a call back

White
No criminal record — 34%
Criminal record — 17%

Black
No criminal record — 14%
5%

Source: Pager 2003:958.

To assess the validity of her findings, Pager and colleagues later conducted a similar experiment in New York City, and the results were the same (Pager, Western, and Bonikowski 2009; Pager, Western, and Sugie 2009). When it comes to getting a job, race matters.

secondary analysis A variety of research techniques that make use of previously collected and publicly accessible information and data.

USE OF EXISTING SOURCES

Sociologists do not necessarily need to collect new data to conduct research. The term **secondary analysis** refers to a variety of research techniques that make use of previously

What's in a Name?

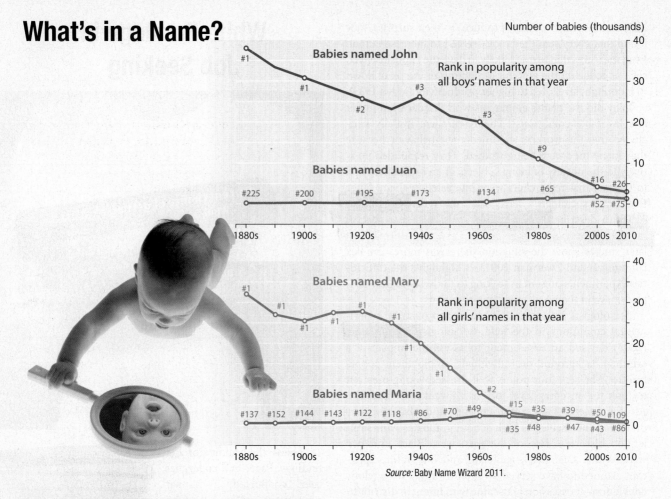

Number of babies (thousands)

Babies named John — Rank in popularity among all boys' names in that year
#1, #1, #2, #3, #3, #9, #16, #26

Babies named Juan
#225, #200, #195, #173, #134, #65, #52, #75

1880s 1900s 1920s 1940s 1960s 1980s 2000s 2010

Babies named Mary — Rank in popularity among all girls' names in that year
#1, #1, #1, #1, #1, #1, #1, #1, #2, #15, #35, #39, #50, #109

Babies named Maria
#137, #152, #144, #143, #122, #118, #86, #70, #49, #35, #48, #47, #43, #86

1880s 1900s 1920s 1940s 1960s 1980s 2000s 2010

Source: Baby Name Wizard 2011.

collected and publicly accessible information and data. As indicated above, the U.S. Census Bureau provides a treasure trove of such data.

Every 10 years, as required by the U.S. Constitution, the Bureau attempts to gather information from every household in the United States. In 2010 the initial response rate they received from the Census form they mailed out was 72 percent. After door-to-door contacts were completed, they were ultimately able to gather information from 99.62% of the nation's housing units. Gathering data on that scale is very expensive and time-consuming, so the

information the Census provides is extremely valuable to researchers. One difficulty, as is the case with all secondary analysis, is that researchers do not have control over the questions that get asked. As such, conclusions they can draw are limited by the available data.

Even though it was not explicitly conducted with the research questions sociologists have in mind, such data analysis can be extremely fruitful. For example, every year the Social Security Administration receives thousands of registrations for newborn babies. Using these data, we can recognize shifts in cultural trends in the population.

Major Research Designs

Method	Examples	Advantages	Limitations
Survey	Questionnaires Interviews	Yields information about specific issues	Can be expensive and time-consuming
Observation	Ethnography	Yields detailed information about specific groups or organizations	Involves months if not years of labor-intensive data collection
Experiment	Deliberate manipulation of people's social behavior	Yields direct measures of people's behavior	Has ethical limitations on the degree to which subjects' behavior can be manipulated
Existing sources/ Secondary analysis	Analysis of census or health data Analysis of films or TV commercials	Cost-efficiency; nonreactive	Limited to data collected for some other purpose

SOCTHINK

"NameVoyager" at www.babynamewizard.
com is an application that allows you to type
in any name to trace its popularity over time.
Go there and enter several names to see how
they have changed over time. Considering
some of the specific names you tried, what
factors might have contributed to their rise
and fall? How popular is your first name? How
and why has its popularity changed over time?

As the figure "What's in a Name?" on the previous page
shows, the popularity of the names John and Mary has
declined significantly—both were once number one—while
the names Juan and Maria have become more popular
(Baby Name Wizard 2011). These shifts reflect the growing
influence of the Latino population in the United States.

Existing data from another source confirms this shift.
Analysis of data released by the U.S. Census Bureau tracking people's family names in 2007 revealed that although
Smith remained the most common surname in the United
States, Garcia and Rodriguez had risen into the top 10. The
announcement marked the first time in the nation's history
that a non-Anglo name had been counted among the most
common names. Such name changes reflect an overall shift
in the U.S. population from a nation composed primarily of
European descendants to one that is more globally diverse,
a trend sociologists expect will continue (Baby Name
Wizard 2010; Levitt and Dubner 2005; Word et al. 2007).

Part of the appeal of secondary analysis to sociologists is
that it is nonreactive—that is, doing this type of study does
not influence what you find. For example, Émile Durkheim's
statistical analysis of existing suicide data neither increased
nor decreased human self-destruction. Researchers, then,
can avoid the Hawthorne effect by using secondary analysis.
However, there is one inherent problem: The researcher
who relies on data collected by someone else may not find
exactly what he or she needs. Social scientists who are studying family violence can use statistics from police and social
service agencies on reported cases of spouse abuse and child
abuse, but because not all incidents get reported, government bodies have no precise data on all cases of abuse.

Secondary analysis also allows us to study social contexts, both present and past, through careful analysis of
cultural, economic, and political documents, including
newspapers, periodicals, radio and television tapes, the
Internet, scripts, diaries, songs, folklore, and legal papers.
In examining these sources, researchers employ a technique known as **content analysis**—the systematic coding
and objective recording of data, guided by a given rationale.

Using content analysis, Erving Goffman (1979) conducted a pioneering exploration of how advertisements portray women. The ads he studied
typically showed women as
subordinate to or dependent
on others, or as taking instruc-
tion from men. Women engaged in caressing and touching
gestures more than men. Even when presented in leadership roles, women were likely to be shown striking seductive
poses or gazing out into space. Jeanne Kilbourne's content
analysis of ads demonstrates that women continue to be
portrayed as objects. She found that advertisers' primary
message is that women should spend their time, energy, and
money trying to attain the idealized, airbrushed image of
female beauty only achievable with the assistance of Photoshop. She quotes supermodel Cindy Crawford as saying, "I
wish I looked like Cindy Crawford" (Kilbourne 2010).

> **content analysis** The systematic
> coding and objective recording of
> data, guided by some rationale.

Researchers have also used content analysis to investigate
media portrayals of other public health issues. For example,
Sargent and Heatherton (2009) analyzed the top 25 films
for each year from 1990 to 2007 and found that the average number of smoking occurrences fell from 3.5 to 0.23 per
film. They compare this with the declining smoking levels of
U.S. eighth-graders, an average of 1.3 percent per year after
1996. Given the complexity of possible factors, they cannot
assert a direct causal link between the two, although they
point to other research that demonstrates that exposure to
smoking in films does affect youth smoking rates (National
Cancer Institute 2008).

Concerns about childhood obesity led researchers to
analyze commercials aired during Saturday children's

Primary Themes in Children's Television Food Commercials

47%	Fun/happiness
18%	Taste/flavor/smell
12%	Product's uniqueness
10%	Other
8%	Physical strength
5%	Popularity of product
0%	Healthy product

Source: Stitt and Kunkel 2008.

television programming on broadcast and cable channels. For example, in an analysis of more than 1,200 ads, Stitt and Kunkel (2008) found that food ads made up almost half of the commercial time, an average of 11 food ads per hour. Of these ads, 9 out of 10 were for high-calorie, low-nutrient food products such as sugared snacks, sugared cereals, and fast food. The researchers also found that the most common strategy used to persuade viewers to try the products was to associate the product with having fun or happiness.

> **code of ethics** The standards of acceptable behavior developed by and for members of a profession.

Other researchers have found a growing difference in the way men and women use sexually explicit language. For example, an analysis of the lyrics of *Billboard* magazine's top 100 hits indicates that, since 1958, male artists have increased their use of such language, whereas female artists have decreased theirs (Dukes et al. 2003). In all such cases, content analysis allows us a better understanding of our cultural practices.

>>Research Ethics

A biochemist cannot inject a drug into a human being unless the drug has been thoroughly tested and the subject agrees to the shot. To do otherwise would be both unethical and illegal. Sociologists, too, must abide by certain specific standards in conducting research, called a **code of ethics.** The professional society of the discipline, the American Sociological Association (ASA), first published its *Code of*

Ethics in 1971 and revised it most recently in 1997. It puts forth the following basic principles:

- Maintain objectivity and integrity in research.
- Respect the subject's right to privacy and dignity.
- Protect subjects from personal harm.
- Preserve confidentiality.
- Seek informed consent when data are collected from research participants or when behavior occurs in a private context.
- Acknowledge research collaboration and assistance.
- Disclose all sources of financial support.

Because most sociological research uses people as sources of information—as respondents to survey questions, subjects of observation, or participants in experiments—these principles are important.

CONFIDENTIALITY

In all cases, sociologists need to be certain they are not invading their subjects' privacy. Generally, they do so by assuring subjects of anonymity or by guaranteeing the confidentiality of personal information. In addition, research proposals that involve human subjects are now subject to oversight by a review board, whose members seek to ensure that the research does not place subjects at an unreasonable level of risk. If necessary, the board may ask researchers to revise their research designs to conform to the *Code of Ethics.*

These basic principles and procedures may seem clear-cut in the abstract but can be difficult to adhere to in practice. For example, should a sociologist who is engaged in participant observation research always protect the confidentiality of subjects? What if the subjects are members of a group involved in unethical or illegal activities? What if

Content analysis of popular song lyrics shows that over the past 50 years, top female artists such as Beyoncé Knowles have used fewer sexually explicit words, whereas male artists like Jay-Z have used more.

We often make decisions based on common sense, but doing so can result in errors. Analyzing data reveals underlying patterns that we might otherwise miss, enabling us to make more effective decisions. In the film *Moneyball*, and in the book it's based on, Michael Lewis (2003) tells the story of general manager Billy Beane, whose Oakland A's team lacked the money to afford big-money free agents. Beane goes against baseball's conventional wisdom and uses statistical analyses to make decisions about how best to produce runs; by bringing the nonobvious patterns to the surface, he turns the team into a winner.

the sociologist is interviewing political activists and is questioned by government authorities about the research?

Like journalists, sociologists occasionally find themselves facing the ethical dilemma of whether to reveal their sources to law enforcement authorities. In May 1993 sociologist Rik Scarce was jailed for contempt of court because he declined to tell a federal grand jury what he knew—or even whether he knew anything—about a 1991 raid on a university research laboratory by animal rights activists. At the time, Scarce was doing research for a book about environmental protestors and knew at least one suspect in the break-in. Although he was chastised by a federal judge, Scarce won respect from fellow prison inmates, who regarded him as a man who "won't snitch" (Monaghan 2012; Scarce 2005).

The ASA, in defense of the principle of confidentiality, supported Scarce's position when he appealed his sentence. Scarce maintained his silence. Ultimately, the judge ruled that nothing would be gained by further incarceration, and Scarce was released after spending 159 days in jail. The U.S. Supreme Court ultimately declined to hear Scarce's case on appeal. The Court's failure to consider his case led Scarce (1994, 1995, 2005) to argue that federal legislation is needed to clarify the right of scholars and members of the press to preserve the confidentiality of those they interview.

SOCTHINK

Should researchers sometimes deceive subjects, even if it might result in their emotional harm, in order to get genuine responses?

RESEARCH FUNDING

An additional concern of the ASA's *Code of Ethics* is the possibility that funding sources could influence research

findings. Accepting funds from a private organization or even a government agency that stands to benefit from a study's results can clash with the ASA's first principle of maintaining objectivity and integrity in research. As such, all sources of funding should be disclosed. The previously mentioned controversy surrounding the involvement of social scientists in the U.S. Army's Human Terrain System is one example of this conflict of interest.

Another example is the Exxon Corporation's support for research on jury verdicts. On March 24, 1989, the Exxon oil tanker *Valdez* hit a reef off the coast of Alaska, spilling over 11 million gallons of oil into Prince William Sound. Until the Deepwater Horizon spill in the Gulf of Mexico in 2010, the *Valdez* disaster was regarded as the world's worst oil spill in terms of its environmental impact. In 1994 a federal court ordered Exxon to pay $5.3 billion in damages for the accident. Exxon appealed the verdict and began approaching legal scholars, sociologists, and psychologists who might be willing to study jury deliberations. The corporation's objective was to develop academic support for its lawyers' contention that the punitive judgments in such cases result from faulty deliberations and do not deter future incidents.

Some scholars have questioned the propriety of accepting funds under these circumstances, even if the source is disclosed. The scholars who accepted Exxon's support deny that it influenced their work or changed their conclusions. To date, Exxon has spent more than $1 million on the research, and at least one compilation of studies congenial to the corporation's point of view has been published. As ethical considerations require, the academics who conducted the studies disclosed Exxon's role in funding the research. In 2006, drawing on these studies, Exxon's lawyers succeeded in persuading an appeals court to reduce the corporation's legal damages from $5.3 to $2.5 billion (Freudenburg 2005; Liptak 2008a, 2008b). In 2008, the amount was further reduced to $508 million, though in 2009 the Ninth U.S. Circuit Court of Appeals ordered Exxon to pay on additional $500 million in punitive damages, court costs, and interest payments.

VALUE NEUTRALITY

The ethical considerations of sociologists lie not only in the methods they use and the funding they accept but also in the way they interpret their results. Max Weber ([1904] 1949) recognized that personal values would influence the topics that sociologists select for research. In his view, that was perfectly acceptable, but he argued that researchers should not allow their personal feelings to influence the interpretation of data. In Weber's phrase, sociologists must practice **value neutrality** in their research.

-SOCTHINK-

To what extent is it possible to maintain value neutrality when studying a social group with which you might disagree (such as White supremacists or convicted child molesters)? Why might sociologists choose to study such groups?

As part of this neutrality, investigators have an ethical obligation to accept research findings even when the data run counter to their own personal views, to theoretically based explanations, or to widely accepted beliefs. For example, Émile Durkheim challenged popular conceptions when he reported that social (rather than supernatural) forces were an important factor in suicide.

Some sociologists believe that such neutrality is impossible. They worry that Weber's insistence on value-free sociology may lead the public to accept sociological conclusions without exploring researchers' biases. Others have suggested that sociologists may use objectivity as a justification for remaining uncritical of existing institutions and centers of power (Gouldner 1970). Despite the early work of W. E. B. Du Bois and Jane Addams, for example, sociologists still need to be reminded that the discipline often fails to adequately consider all people's social behavior. Sociologists should not focus only on those in the majority but must also seek out the stories of those who are often invisible due to their relative lack of power and resources. In fact, sociologists have learned much about society by listening to the voices of those who are excluded from mainstream sources of power and denied access to

value neutrality Max Weber's term for objectivity of sociologists in the interpretation of data.

> The greatest obstacle to discovery is not ignorance—it is the illusion of knowledge.
>
> Daniel Boorstin

valuable resources. In her book *The Death of White Sociology* (1973), Joyce Ladner called attention to the tendency of mainstream sociologists to investigate the lives of African Americans only in the context of social problems. Similarly, feminist sociologist Shulamit Reinharz (1992) has argued that sociological research should not only include the research of sociologists who are outside the mainstream but should also be open to drawing on relevant research by nonsociologists who might provide additional depth and understanding of social life. The issue of value neutrality does not mean that sociologists can't have opinions, but it does mean that they must work to overcome any biases, however unintentional, that they may bring to their analysis of research.

FEMINIST METHODOLOGY

Although researchers must be objective, their theoretical orientation necessarily influences the questions they ask—or, just as important, the questions they fail to ask. Because their contributions have opened up so many new lines of inquiry, sociologists using the feminist perspective have had perhaps the greatest impact on the current generation of social researchers. Until the 1960s, for example, researchers frequently studied work and family separately, as if they were two discrete institutions. Feminist theorists, however, reject the notion that

Movies on SOCIOLOGICAL RESEARCH

Kinsey
The father of modern sexual research employs individual case studies.

Thank You for Smoking
A satire about the tobacco industry, showing how statistics can lie.

Supersize Me
A reporter investigates the American fast-food industry by eating at McDonald's for one month.

49 Up
Documentary following 14 children as their lives progress from age 7 to 49.

Zeitgeist: Moving Forward
Documentary making the case for a transition from the current economy to a new resource-based economy.

5

these are separate spheres. They were the first sociologists to look at housework as real work and to investigate the struggles people face in balancing the demands of work and family (Hochschild 1989; Lopata 1971).

Feminist theorists have also drawn attention to researchers' tendency to overlook women in sociological studies. For most of the history of sociology, researchers conducted studies of male subjects or male-led groups and organizations, then generalized their findings to all people. For many decades, for example, ethnographic studies of urban life focused on street corners, neighborhood taverns, and bowling alleys—places where men typically congregated. Although researchers gained valuable insights in this way, they did not form a true impression of city life, because they overlooked the areas where women were likely to gather, such as playgrounds, grocery stores, and front stoops. These are the arenas that the feminist perspective focuses on.

Feminist scholars have also contributed to a greater global awareness within sociology. To feminist theorists, the traditional distinction between industrial nations and developing countries overlooks the close relationship between these two supposedly separate worlds. Feminist theorists have called for more research on the special role that immigrant women play in maintaining their households, on the use of domestic workers from less developed nations by households in industrial countries, and on the global trafficking of sex workers (Cheng 2003; K. Cooper et al. 2007).

Finally, feminist researchers tend to involve and consult their subjects more than other researchers, contributing to a significant increase in more qualitative and participatory research. They are also more oriented toward seeking change, raising the public consciousness, and influencing policy, which represents a return to sociology's roots (Harding 2003; Naples 2003; Sprague 2005).

Sociologists must be engaged with the world. Although there are numerous ways in which they accomplish this, first and foremost this involvement comes through research. As we have seen throughout this chapter, it is not enough for sociologists to stand back and theorize or even hypothesize about why we think and act the way we do. We must go out, collect data, and use it to inform our interpretations and explanations of human behavior. Having done so, we bear a responsibility for that knowledge, whether that means simply sharing it with other sociologists through conference presentations and journal articles or actively working for positive social change.

Investigate! Learn more about what sociologists are discovering. *Contexts* magazine provides a "thought-provoking take on modern life in our communities," including feature articles, accessible summaries of the latest findings from social science research, op-ed pieces from sociologists, and more. It is produced by the American Sociological Association and is available at contexts.org.

get involved!

For REVIEW

I. **What steps do sociologists take when seeking to answer why people think and act the way they do?**
   - They need to define the problem, review existing literature, formulate a hypothesis, collect and analyze data, and develop a conclusion.

II. **What techniques do they use to collect data?**
   - Research designs used to collect data include surveys, observation, experiments, and use of existing sources.

III. **What ethical concerns must they consider while conducting research?**
   - They have a responsibility to follow the ASA *Code of Ethics*, particularly respecting confidentiality, revealing research funding, maintaining value neutrality, and overall, treating their subjects with respect.

Functionalist View

Sociological research seeks to better understand how the various parts of society **fit together** to create social order and stability.

Researchers focus on **consensus and cooperation** and on the large-scale (or **macro**) level, looking at society from the top down.

Research can also help determine whether the facets of our society are **functioning** as intended. For example, does more education "pay off" in higher income?

STABILITY, CONSENSUS, COOPERATION
KEY CONCEPTS

Conflict View

Sociological research seeks to better understand how **power** operates and how **resources** are distributed and controlled.

Focus of research tends to be on the large-scale (or **macro**) level, looking at society from the top down.

Key questions behind research include: Who benefits? How does the status quo maintain **privileges** for some and denial of opportunity for others? How does **access** to resources shape outcomes?

KEY CONCEPTS
INEQUALITY, STRATIFICATION, INTERESTS

MAKE THE CONNECTION

After reviewing the chapter, answer the following questions:

Interactionist View

Sociological research seeks to better understand how we construct meaning and establish order through **everyday interactions** with others.

Focus of research is on the small-scale (or **micro**) level, looking at the construction of society from the bottom up.

Researchers are most likely to use **participant observation** because it provides a window into people's everyday lived experiences.

KEY CONCEPTS
ROLES, SYMBOLS, LABELING

1
Which perspective do Patricia Adler and Peter Adler (p. 25) seem to favor in their research? Why?

2
How might a researcher's perspective influence the research design he or she picks? Give an example for each perspective.

3
How might each perspective interpret Devah Pager's findings in her experiment about race and job seeking (p. 37)?

4
How might each perspective study the relationship between education and income in a slightly different way?

Pop Quiz

1. **The first step in any sociological research project is to**
   a. collect data.
   b. define the problem.
   c. review previous research.
   d. formulate a hypothesis.

2. **An explanation of an abstract concept that is specific enough to allow a researcher to measure the concept is a(n)**
   a. hypothesis.
   b. correlation.
   c. operational definition.
   d. variable.

3. **In sociological and scientific research, a hypothesis**
   a. is an educated guess.
   b. is a testable statement about the relationship between two or more variables.
   c. insists that science can deal only with observable entities known directly to experience.
   d. ensures that the people being studied are representative of the population as a whole.

4. **The variable hypothesized to cause or influence another is called the**
   a. dependent variable.
   b. hypothetical variable.
   c. correlation variable.
   d. independent variable.

5. **The degree to which a measure or scale truly reflects the phenomenon under study is known as**
   a. reliability.
   b. sampling.
   c. validity.
   d. control.

6. **Which research technique do sociologists use to ensure that data are statistically representative of the population being studied?**
   a. sampling
   b. experiments
   c. correlation
   d. control variables

7. **Ethnography is an example of which type of research design?**
   a. surveys
   b. observation
   c. experiments
   d. use of existing resources

8. **In the 1930s William F. Whyte moved into a low-income Italian neighborhood in Boston. For nearly four years he was a member of the social circle of "corner boys," whom he describes in *Street Corner Society*. His goal was to gain greater insight into the community established by these men. What type of research technique did Whyte use?**
   a. experiment
   b. survey
   c. secondary analysis
   d. participant observation

9. **The unintended influence that observers of experiments can have on their subjects is known as**
   a. the correlation effect.
   b. confidentiality.
   c. validity.
   d. the Hawthorne effect.

10. **According to Max Weber, researchers should not allow their personal feelings to influence the interpretation of data. He referred to this as**
    a. the code of ethics.
    b. content analysis.
    c. value neutrality.
    d. secondary analysis.

1. (b); 2. (c); 3. (b); 4. (d); 5. (c); 6. (a); 7. (b); 8. (d); 9. (d); 10. (c)

3

CULTURE

BREAKING RULES AND LOWERING BARRIERS

On January 8th, 2012, Charlie Todd took a train ride on the New York City subway. He wasn't wearing any pants. Charlie was not alone. In fact, he was joined by nearly 4,000 other pantsless riders in New York City that day. They gathered in six locations around the city, boarded various trains, and headed toward a rendezvous at Union Station. They spaced themselves out across many subway cars, had minimal interaction with one another, and acted as normally as possible. The event was all part of the now annual No Pants Subway Ride coordinated by Improv Everywhere, a self-described "prank collective that causes scenes of chaos and joy in public places," which Charlie Todd founded in 2001.

Improv Everywhere has sponsored over 100 missions, some of which may be familiar because their videos have often gone viral. The No Pants event started in 2002 with just seven participants and grew larger each year, celebrating its eleventh anniversary in 2012 with over 5,000 partici- pants in 59 cities across 27 countries, for the first time including Istanbul, Turkey, and Bangalore, India. In 2008, over 200 participants ("agents") con- verged on Grand Central Station and simultaneously froze in place for five minutes, after which they resumed what they were doing as if nothing had happened. In 2009, they randomly picked a just-married couple depart- ing the City Clerk's Office and threw them a wedding reception complete with a formally attired wedding party, cake, a toast, gifts, and dancing. In 2010 several hundred agents, formally dressed in tuxedos and ball gowns, headed to the Coney Island beach, where they laid out in the sun, played games, and swam in the ocean. In 2011, they performed a spontaneous musical by interrupting a technology conference and breaking into song celebrating the joys of ubiquitous online connectivity. (Videos for these and many other missions are available at ImprovEverywhere.com.)

The scenes that Improv Everywhere creates help to reveal our taken- for-granted rules for behavior. In our daily lives we follow routines that are largely invisible to us, and we expect others to do likewise. When people do things differently, we tend to get uncomfortable. It disrupts our sense of order. One of the best parts of their videos is watching how people respond. Initial confusion and nervousness are often followed by smiles as people realize they are seeing a performance. We want and need the actions of others to be predictable, so we create both formal and informal rules to guide our behaviors. Such rules are an important component of culture.

As You READ

>>

- Why do humans create culture?
- What does culture consist of?
- How does culture both enable and constrain?

>>Culture and Society

We need culture. As humans, we lack the complex instincts other species are born with that enable them to survive. Unlike birds, for example, our genes do not provide us with the knowledge to build nests (or homes) for ourselves, and we can choose whether to seek out warmer climates for the winter or cooler ones in the summer. Because our actions are not narrowly determined by such instincts, we must construct their equivalent in order to provide food, clothes, shelter, and a host of other human needs. **Culture** consists of everything humans create in establishing our relationships to nature and with each other. It includes language, knowledge, material creations, and rules for behavior. In other words, it encompasses all that we say, know, make, and do in our efforts to survive and thrive.

culture Everything humans create in establishing our relationships to nature and with each other.

Culture mediates between individuals and the external world. While we experience the natural world through our senses—hearing, sight, touch, smell, and taste—we depend on culture to interpret those sensations. Our retinas may send visual images to our brains, but recognition of patterns is made possible through culture. For example, we might fail to see an image in an optical illusion until someone nudges us to "look at it this way." Nothing about the physical image changed, but our perspective on it, with the help of others, has. We do not perceive nature directly; we perceive the world around us through the lens of culture.

Shared culture also enables us to work together. It provides us with a tool kit of similar habits, skills, and styles (Swidler 1986). It simplifies day-to-day interactions by allowing us to take for granted that others will understand what we mean, making it possible for us to accomplish our

Do you see the old woman or the young one?

SOC THINK

Sometimes we can see something over and over and still not recognize patterns until someone points them out (such as the arrow in the FedEx logo). What might this tell us about the importance of authorities for recognition?

Cultural preferences vary across societies. Educational methods, marriage ceremonies, religious doctrines, and other aspects of culture are learned and transmitted through human interaction within specific societies. Parents in India are accustomed to arranging marriages for their children; in the United States, parents typically leave marital decisions up to their children. Lifelong residents of Cairo consider it natural to speak Arabic; lifelong residents of Buenos Aires feel the same way about Spanish.

goals. For example, when we say hello, we expect a similar response in return. If we buy a flat screen TV or an airline ticket, we expect that the clerk will accept a credit card rather than demand huge sums of cash. When we show up for the first day of class, we assume that students will sit at their desks and the professor will take his or her place up front. Culture facilitates social interaction.

Because we need culture in order to interact and survive, we both preserve it and pass it along to others. We preserve it in the form of books, art, video recordings, and other means of expression. We pass it along in families, through mass media, among peers, and, more formally, at school, investing substantial amounts of resources to do so. If we didn't socially transmit culture in these ways, each generation would have to start from scratch, reinventing not just the wheel but all other elements of culture as well.

Although we establish a relationship to the external world through culture, society provides the context within which those relationships develop. **Society** consists of the structure of relationships within which culture is created and shared through regularized patterns of social interaction. How we structure society constrains the kind of culture we construct. Some ways of thinking, acting, and making are more acceptable, whereas other ways may not even be recognized as possible. People often confront this reality when they travel abroad and find their taken-for-granted ideas and actions to be out of place and inappropriate.

SOCTHINK

How does social context influence how we relate to others? If you were talking about how school is going, how might you respond differently at home with your parents compared to in a dorm with friends or at work with colleagues?

>>Creating Culture

Because we are not narrowly determined by our genes, human beings throughout history have demonstrated the innovative capacity to create amazing cultural artifacts. Examples include the cave paintings at Lascaux, France, poems by Langston Hughes, novels by Toni Morrison, and films such as *Schindler's List*. We now take for granted what once seemed impossible, from air travel, to the cloning of cells, to organ transplants, to always-on wireless Internet access. We can peer into the outermost reaches of the universe or analyze our innermost feelings. In all these ways, our cultural creativity sets us apart as remarkably different from other species of the animal kingdom.

society The structure of relationships within which culture is created and shared through regularized patterns of social interaction.

CULTURAL UNIVERSALS

Given that we have a certain amount of freedom to construct culture in a multitude of ways, one of the early sociological questions was whether there are any aspects of culture

...Marc Platt, producer of the Broadway play *Wicked* and numerous movies, including *Legally Blonde*, *Rachel Getting Married*, and *Drive*, was a sociology major.

The foods people eat, and the customs around eating and preparation of food, reflect their culture as well as their economic circumstances.

shared by all people. Some sociologists, such as Comte, sought to discover whether there are fundamental laws of society equivalent to the laws of nature. Such patterns were referred to as **cultural universals**—common practices and beliefs shared by all societies. Anthropologist George Murdock (1945) compared results from studies of hundreds of cultures and concluded that, although there are common denominators shared by all cultures, how cultures go about addressing each varies significantly. Included among his list of seventy categories were athletic sports, community organization, dancing, division of labor, folklore, funeral rites, housing, incest taboos, marriage, personal names, property rights, religious ritual, sexual restrictions, and trade.

cultural universal A common practice or belief shared by all societies.

The debate about the existence of general cultural universals raises an important question: Are our actions shaped by biology, or are we free to construct culture as we might choose? Historically, this nature versus nurture debate has been put in either/or terms in which "nature" means that the genes we inherit determine our outcomes, as if our fates were programmed by computer code over which we have limited control. On the other side, "nurture" means that our destiny is shaped primarily by the social and psychological influences of others around us (especially parents); human nature is malleable, and we become who we are in the contexts of the societies we create. Over time most researchers have realized that this either-or argument is inadequate or misleading, because the relationship between the two forces is more fluid, better represented by shades of gray.

sociobiology The systematic study of how biology affects human social behavior.

Although researchers are increasingly coming to the conclusion that this nature-nurture dichotomy is too simplistic, significant differences remain. **Sociobiology** is a discipline that places primary emphasis on studying how biology affects human social behavior. For example, sociobiologists

look at the development of cultural universals as a product of our biological evolution. They argue that explanations of our thoughts and actions as a species must ultimately take into account our genetic makeup. On the other hand, although most sociologists would agree that our biology influences our social behavior, the degree of variation within and between societies suggests that sociobiological theories are limited as a means to explain complex human behavior. For example, one society may not allow marriage between first cousins, whereas another encourages it.

Not only does the expression of cultural universals vary from one society to another, but it can also change dramatically over time. For example, in the nineteenth century, it was thought that, biologically speaking, women were not capable of success in college because their brains were too small and their reproductive organs made them too emotional. Over time we learned that such presuppositions are false—women now make up almost 60 percent of college graduates—but at one time these assertions were accepted as "natural" and therefore resistant to change. Similar biologically based claims have been used in the past to justify inequality (claims that were later revealed to be scientifically untrue), leading many sociologists to question biological explanations for human behavior (Lucal 2010). One of the lessons we learn about culture throughout human history is that variety and change are the norm.

More recently, researchers in both the natural sciences and sociology have sought a nuanced understanding of the relationship between biology and culture. In the scientific community there has been growing support for gene-culture coevolution, in which each shapes the other through the course of human development. From this perspective, how

at predetermined times (Rutter 2010; Rutter, Moffitt, and Caspi 2006; Shenk 2010). In pursuit of a more informed understanding of this interplay, the American Sociological Association established a new section called "Evolution, Biology, and Society" in 2005 (Machalek and Martin 2010).

innovation The process of introducing a new idea or object to a culture through discovery or invention.

INNOVATION

Humans have the freedom and ability to create new things. Whereas a robin's nest in the year 2013 looks very much like one in 2003 or 1013 because robins act on a nest-building instinct, human abodes vary widely. We can live in a cave, a castle, a sod house, a pueblo, a high-rise apartment, a McMansion, or a dorm room. Such variation is possible because we are free to innovate. **Innovation**—the process of introducing a new idea or object to a culture—interests sociologists because it can have ripple effects across a society.

Going GLOBAL

Success in life is determined by forces outside our control

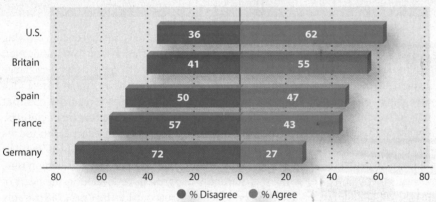

	% Disagree	% Agree
U.S.	36	62
Britain	41	55
Spain	50	47
France	57	43
Germany	72	27

Source: Pew research Center 2011d.

As the graph above demonstrates, the perceptions of people in the United States differ from those of people in Western Europe. As part of their Global Attitude Project, researchers at Pew Research Center (2011d) found significant differences in cultural values in a number of areas, including belief in God, the role of the state, the use of military force, and presumption of cultural superiority.

individuals turn out isn't simply a matter of whether they inherited a set of "bad genes" or "good genes." Instead, researchers argue that an interdependent relationship exists between genes and environment. How genes are expressed (whether or not they are triggered, in other words) can depend on our natural, social, and cultural contexts. From this perspective, genes are responsive to environmental factors and do not inevitably trigger predetermined responses

SOCTHINK

Increasingly, mass communication, corporations, and consumerism combine to spread particular cultural preferences around the globe. What are the consequences of such diffusion for local cultures?

There are two main forms of innovation: discovery and invention. **Discovery** involves making known or sharing the existence of an aspect of reality. The identification of the DNA molecule and the sighting of a new moon of Saturn are both acts of discovery. A significant factor in the process of discovery is the sharing of newfound knowledge with others. By contrast, an **invention** results when existing cultural items are combined into a form that did not exist before. The bow and arrow, the automobile, and the television are all examples of inventions, as are abstract concepts such as Protestantism and democracy.

discovery The process of making known or sharing the existence of an aspect of reality.

invention The combination of existing cultural items into a form that did not exist before.

DIFFUSION AND GLOBALIZATION

More and more cultural expressions and practices are crossing national borders and influencing the traditions and customs of the societies exposed to them. Sociologists use the term **diffusion** to refer to the process by which some aspect of culture spreads from group to group or society to society. Historically, diffusion typically occurred through a variety of means, including exploration, war, military conquest, and missionary work. Today,

diffusion The process by which a cultural item spreads from group to group or society to society.

societal boundaries that were once relatively closed owing to the constraints of transportation and communication have become more permeable, with cross-cultural exchange occurring more quickly. Through the mass media, the Internet, immigration, and tourism, we regularly confront the people, beliefs, practices, and artifacts of other cultures.

Cultural innovation has global consequences in today's world. Imagine walking into Starbucks, with its familiar green logo, and ordering a decaf latte and a cinnamon ring. Only this Starbucks happens to be located in the heart of Beijing's Forbidden City, just outside the Palace of Heavenly Purity, the former residence of Chinese emperors. The first Starbucks in mainland China opened in 1999. As of spring 2012, there were 550 with plans for more than 1,500 by 2015. The success of Starbucks in a country in which coffee drinking is still a novelty (most Chinese are tea drinkers) has been striking. In fact, for many, drinking coffee has now become a status symbol of middle-class success (Burkitt 2011, Christian 2009; Rein 2012).

The emergence of Starbucks in China demonstrates the cultural impact of globalization. Starbuck's expansion affects not only coffee consumption patterns but also the international trade in coffee beans, which are harvested mainly in developing countries. Our consumption-oriented culture supports a retail price of three to five dollars for a single cup of premium coffee. Even though coffee prices have reached all-time highs, millions of farmers around the world can barely eke out a living. Worldwide, the growing

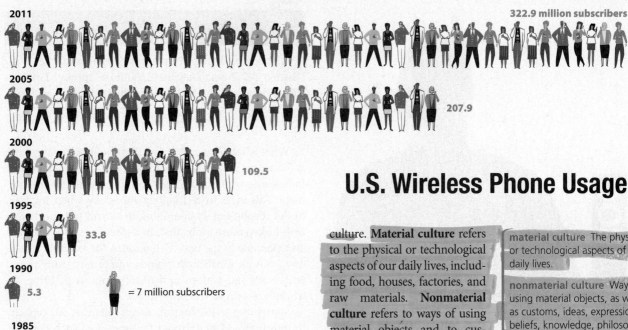

2011   322.9 million subscribers

2005   207.9

2000   109.5

1995   33.8

1990   5.3   = 7 million subscribers

1985   0.3

Technology makes it possible for us to keep in touch with almost anyone anywhere, as these numbers showing the explosion in the number of wireless phone subscribers since 1985 demonstrates.
Source: CTIA 2011.

demand for coffee, tea, chocolate, fruit, and other natural resources is straining the environment, as poor farmers in developing countries clear more and more forestland to enlarge their fields (Herman 2010). Even as people in Asia have begun to drink coffee, people in North America have discovered the Japanese cuisine known as sushi.

Diffusion often comes at a cost. In practice, globalization has led to the cultural domination of developing nations by more affluent nations. In these encounters, people in developed nations often pick and choose the cultural practices they find intriguing or exotic, whereas people in developing nations often lose their traditional values and begin to identify with the culture of the dominant nations. They may discard or neglect their native language and dress, attempting to imitate the icons of mass-market entertainment and fashion. In this way, Western popular culture represents a threat to native cultures. Similarly, Walt Disney's critics have called his work "perhaps the primary example of America's cultural imperialism, supplanting the myths of native cultures with his own" (Gabler 2006). So something is gained and something is lost through diffusion, and often it is the poorer societies that sacrifice more of their culture.

>>Elements of Culture

To better understand how culture operates, it is helpful to distinguish among its different forms. A classic twofold model of culture was proposed by sociologist William F. Ogburn (1922). He drew a line between material and nonmaterial

U.S. Wireless Phone Usage

culture. **Material culture** refers to the physical or technological aspects of our daily lives, including food, houses, factories, and raw materials. **Nonmaterial culture** refers to ways of using material objects and to customs, ideas, expressions, beliefs, knowledge, philosophies, governments, and patterns of communication. Although this simple division is helpful, the concept of nonmaterial culture is so inclusive that we break it down here into four key components: language, values, norms, and sanctions.

> **material culture** The physical or technological aspects of our daily lives.
>
> **nonmaterial culture** Ways of using material objects, as well as customs, ideas, expressions, beliefs, knowledge, philosophies, governments, and patterns of communication.

MATERIAL CULTURE AND TECHNOLOGY

It is easy to underestimate the degree to which we live in a humanly constructed world. Even for those of us who live close to nature, material culture is everywhere. It includes the clothes we wear, the books we read, the chairs we sit in, the carpets we walk on, the lights we use, the buildings we live in, the cars we drive, the roads we drive on, and so much more. Even those things that seem natural, like yards or parks, are human constructs.

SOCTHINK

People in the United States sent an average of 6.0 billion text messages per day in 2011— the equivalent of 19.5 messages per day per person. How might frequent "texting" and less talking affect the nature of our relationships, both positively and negatively?

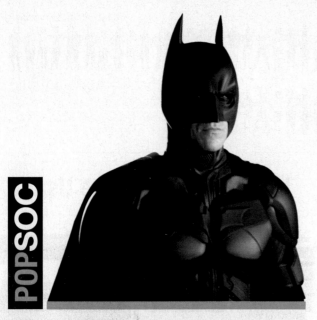

POPSOC

Culture, Technology, and Superheroes

Some superheroes (Superman and the X-Men) are born that way, but others gain their powers the old-fashioned way: they invent them. Characters such as Ironman and Batman appeal to us in part because they rely on human innovation for their strength and stamina. Technology makes them faster than a speeding bullet or more powerful than a locomotive. To what extent does technology provide us with superhuman powers?

What is sociologically important about material culture is the role it plays, like all forms of culture, in connecting individuals with one another and to the external environment. Advances in technology, especially when it comes to the revolutions in communication and transportation, have linked more individuals in a global network than was ever possible in the past. Cell phones, for example, enable us to stay in touch with friends and family from almost anywhere, and laptops and iPads allow us to bring the workplace with us wherever we go.

Sometimes technological change outstrips our capacity to interpret and understand the impact of such changes. Because it goes to the core of our perception of reality, nonmaterial culture is often more resistant to change than is the material culture. Ogburn (1922) introduced the term **cultural lag** to refer to the period of adjustment when the nonmaterial culture is struggling to adapt to new conditions of the material culture. For example, the ethics of the Internet—particularly issues concerning privacy and censorship—have not yet caught up with the explosion in Internet use and technology.

The most common term we use to refer to material culture is technology. **Technology** is a form of culture in which humans modify the natural environment to meet our wants and needs. It is the means by which we establish our relationship to the natural world, enabling us to provide the food, clothes, and shelter necessary for our survival. It includes not only high-tech items such as computers, cars, and cell phones, but low-tech items including spoons, paper, and chalk.

Technology enhances our human abilities, giving us power, speed, and even flight. The steam engine, for example, represented a critical turning point during the Industrial Revolution. It provided us with historically unprecedented strength and stamina—the ability to lift and move extremely heavy objects and to do so over sustained periods of time. It made modern coal mining practical, provided manufacturing machinery with the power needed for early factories, and powered early tractors and locomotives, setting the stage for modern global mobility (Rosen 2010).

technology A form of culture in which humans modify the natural environment to meet our wants and needs.

cultural lag A period of adjustment when the nonmaterial culture is still struggling to adapt to new material conditions.

language A system of shared symbols; it includes speech, written characters, numerals, symbols, and nonverbal gestures and expressions.

LANGUAGE

Turning to nonmaterial culture, we begin with language, its most basic building block. **Language** is a system of shared symbols; it includes speech, written characters, numerals, symbols, and nonverbal gestures and expressions. It provides the foundation of a common culture because it facilitates day-to-day exchanges with others, making collective action possible. There are approximately 7,000 languages spoken in the world today. Of these, approximately 43 percent are considered endangered. There are 324 languages with fewer than 50 speakers, and 230 languages have become extinct since 1950 (UNESCO 2010).

Language is fundamentally social in nature. There are no inherent meanings in the sounds we make when talking or in the written alphabet we use. Instead,

Inventing New Words

I was reminded of our ability to create new words while on a family hiking trip in Oregon. Eleanor, who was four at the time, was riding on my shoulders along the trail while her sister, Emily, and my wife, Lori, were falling behind. Eleanor turned and yelled as loud as she could, "Stop chickenjagging!" We knew immediately what she meant and have used this word ever since. Anyone can create words, but they become meaningful only when they are shared with others. For Eleanor's new word to become part of the common language, the chickenjagging network must extend beyond our immediate family into the wider world. Have you ever done something similar with friends or family?

words get their meaning from us. We come together to agree that certain sounds or shapes mean certain things, and then we act based on those shared meanings. What matters most is our shared perception rather than the actual sound or image we use. We could, for example, teach a dog the wrong meanings of commands (*fetch* means stay, *roll over* means shake, and so on). The dog would never know the difference, but we would laugh because its responses would clash with our expectations. In fact, when we start to learn a new language, we are at the mercy of those who teach us. We rely on their authority, and the only way to test our fluency is through interactions with other speakers. Because language is socially constructed, it allows change. We create new words and modify existing ones—especially in our modern global culture where innovation is never-ending. Dictionaries are regularly modified in an effort to try to keep up. In 2011, the *Merriam-Webster Collegiate Dictionary* added over 150 new words, including *tweet, social media, bromance, cougar, walk-off, fist bump, hypermiling, helicopter parents,* and *boomerang child.*

Some linguists, including amateurs, have seized on the socially constructed nature of language in hopes of creating whole new languages from scratch, with varying motivations (Okrent 2009). Some, inspired by the scientific revolution, were appalled by the inefficiencies and irregularities of existing languages. They invented new languages in the 17th and 18th centuries (such as Francis Lodwick's *Common Writing* or John Wilkins' *Philosophical Language*) in hopes of providing us with a logical system of communication in which the relationships between concepts were rational and everything fit together into a coherent whole. They didn't want words to be arbitrary sounds we attach to things, hoping instead to map the essence of things through language. Even though they succeeded in creating coherent

systems, the languages they created were difficult to use and failed to attract widespread acceptance.

During the 20th century, other language inventors, driven in part by a desire to come to terms with globalization and increased contact across cultures, combined various aspects of existing languages. Their goal was to create a universally accepted language that would transcend national and ethnic differences. Rather than focus on purity of representation, such inventors emphasized pragmatic communication. The most successful language of this type was Esperanto, which continues to be used today. It was originally created by Ludwik Zamenhof in 1887 and literally means "one who hopes." It was Zamenhof's hope that his hybrid language would not only facilitate international commerce and communication but also contribute to world peace by reducing the cultural differences that separate us.

In spite of the relative success of Esperanto, none of these invented languages has achieved widespread adoption. Part of what such attempts seem to miss is that language is a community endeavor built up over generations of shared experiences that lead to common understandings of how the world works. Though it is technically possible to create a language from scratch, doing so undercuts the importance that such experiences have in shaping who we are. As linguist Arika Okrent put it in her history of invented languages, "[Languages] are the repositories of our very identities. . . . [Esperanto, along with other invented languages,] asks us to turn away from what makes our languages personal and unique and choose one that is generic and universal. It asks us to give up what distinguishes us from the rest of the world for something that makes everyone in the world the same" (Okrent 2009:112). To the extent that Esperanto has succeeded, it has done so by creating a community of shared participants who are committed to keeping the language alive.

Because different groups share different languages, the ability to speak other languages is crucial to intercultural relations. Throughout the Cold War era, beginning in the 1950s and continuing well into the 1970s, the U.S. government encouraged the study of Russian by developing special language schools for diplomats, intelligence agents, and military advisors. And following the terrorist attacks of September 11, 2001, the nation recognized how few skilled translators it had for Arabic and other languages spoken in Muslim countries. Language quickly became a key not only to tracking potential terrorists but also to building diplomatic bridges with Muslim countries willing to help in the war against terrorism (Furman, Goldberg, and Lusin 2007; Taha 2007).

Sapir-Whorf Hypothesis Language does more than simply describe reality; it also shapes what we see. For example, the Slave Indians of northern Canada, who live in a frigid climate, have 14 terms to describe ice, including eight kinds of "solid ice" and other terms for "seamed ice," "cracked ice," and "floating ice" (Basso 1972). Most people in the United States lack such verbal distinctions and thus are less likely to notice different types of ice.

Linguists Edward Sapir and Benjamin Whorf studied the relationship between language and perception. In what

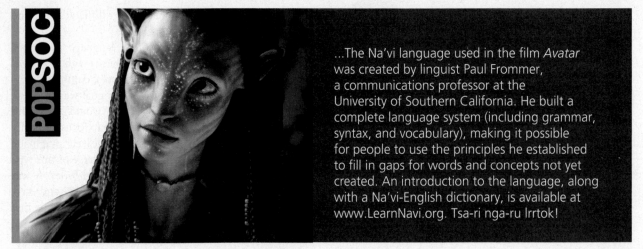

...The Na'vi language used in the film *Avatar* was created by linguist Paul Frommer, a communications professor at the University of Southern California. He built a complete language system (including grammar, syntax, and vocabulary), making it possible for people to use the principles he established to fill in gaps for words and concepts not yet created. An introduction to the language, along with a Na'vi-English dictionary, is available at www.LearnNavi.org. Tsa-ri nga-ru lrrtok!

Source: Okrent 2010.

has come to be known as the **Sapir-Whorf hypothesis,** they concluded that the language a person uses shapes his or her perception of reality and therefore his or her thoughts and actions. Based on their research, they argued that because people can conceptualize the world only through language, language *precedes* thought. Thus, the word symbols and grammar of our language organize the world for us. The Sapir-Whorf hypothesis also holds that language is not a given. Rather, it is culturally determined and encourages a distinctive interpretation of reality by focusing our attention on certain phenomena (Sedivy 2012; Skerrett 2010).

Sapir-Whorf hypothesis The idea that the language a person uses shapes his or her perception of reality and therefore his or her thoughts and actions.

In a literal sense, language may color how we see the world. Berlin and Kay (1991) noted that humans possess the physical ability to make millions of color distinctions, yet languages differ in the number of colors they recognize. For example, the English language distinguishes between yellow and orange, but some other languages do not. In the Dugum Dani language of New Guinea's West Highlands, there are only two basic color terms—*modla* for "white" and *mili* for "black." By contrast, there are 11 basic terms in English. Russian and Hungarian, though, have 12 color terms. Russians have terms for light blue and dark blue, while Hungarians have terms for two different shades of red (Roberson, Davies, and Davidoff 2000; Wierzbicka 2008).

Feminists have noted that gender-related language can reflect—although in itself it does not determine—the traditional acceptance of men and women in certain occupations. Each time we use a term such as *mailman, policeman,* or *fireman,* we are implying (especially to young children) that these occupations can be filled only by males. Yet many women work as *letter carriers, police officers,* and *firefighters*—a fact that is being increasingly recognized and legitimized through the use of such nonsexist language (Eckert and McConnell-Ginet 2003; McConnell-Ginet 2011).

Linguist Suzette Haden Elgin went so far as to invent a new language that gives voice to women's experience (Elgin 1984). She argued that "existing human languages are inadequate to express the perceptions of women," which leads to inadequate perception of critical issues in the lives of women (Elgin 1988). Drawing on her expertise in the Navajo language (*Diné bizaad*), she created Láadan as a test of the Sapir-Whorf hypothesis. She argued that using Láadan would open up new dimensions of reality that are not easily accessible using such languages as English. Láadan lessons for beginners are available at www.LáadanLanguage.org.

Language can also transmit stereotypes related to race. Look up the meanings of the adjective *black* in dictionaries published in the United States, and you will find "dismal, gloomy or forbidding, destitute of moral light or goodness, atrocious, evil, threatening, clouded with anger." By contrast, dictionaries list "pure" and "innocent" among the meanings of the adjective *white*. Through such patterns of language, our culture reinforces positive associations with the term (and skin color) *white* and negative associations with *black*. Is it surprising, then, that a list meant to prevent people from working in a profession is called a "blacklist," and a fib that we think of as somewhat acceptable is called a "white lie"? Such examples demonstrate that language can shape how we see, taste, smell, feel, and hear (Henderson 2003; Moore 1976; Reitman 2006).

SOCTHINK

What are some slang terms we use to refer to men and to women? What images do such terms convey for what it means to be male or female?

Nonverbal Communication Of course, we communicate using more than just words. If you do not like the way a meeting is going, you might suddenly sit back, fold your arms, and turn down the corners of your mouth. When you see a friend in tears, you may give her a quick hug. After winning a big game, you may high-five your teammates. These are all examples of **nonverbal communication**—the use of gestures, facial expressions, and other visual images to communicate. We are not born with these expressions. We learn them, just as we learn other forms of language, from people who share our culture. We learn how to show—and to recognize—happiness, sadness, pleasure, shame, distress, and other emotional states (Burgoon, Guerrero, and Floyd 2010).

Like other forms of language, nonverbal communication is not the same in all cultures. For example, people from various cultures differ in the degree to which they touch others during the course of normal social interactions. Even experienced travelers are sometimes caught off guard by these differences. In Saudi Arabia a middle-aged man may want to hold hands with a male partner after closing a business deal. The gesture, which would surprise most Americans, is considered a compliment in that culture. The meaning of hand signals is another form of nonverbal communication that can differ from one culture to the next. For instance, in both Australia and Iraq the thumbs-up sign is considered rude (Koerner 2003; Lefevre 2011).

VALUES

Although each of us has our own personal set of standards—which may include caring or fitness or entrepreneurship—we also share a general set of beliefs as members of a society. **Values** are these collective conceptions of what is considered good, desirable, and proper—or bad, undesirable, and improper—in a culture. Values may be specific, such as honoring one's parents and owning a home, or they may be more general, such as health, love, and democracy. Even individualism represents a collective value. As American essayist Richard Rodriguez points out, "American individualism is a communally derived value, not truly an expression of individuality. The teenager persists in rebelling against her parents, against tradition or custom, because she is shielded . . . by American culture from the knowledge that she inherited her rebellion from dead ancestors and living parents" (2002:130). Of course, all members of a society do not uniformly agree on its values. Angry political debates and billboards promoting conflicting causes tell us that much.

The values of a culture may change, but most remain relatively stable during any one person's lifetime. Socially shared, intensely felt values are a fundamental part of our lives in the United States. Sociologist Robin Williams (1970) has offered a list of U.S. basic values. These include freedom, equality, democracy, morality, conformity, progress, humanitarianism, and material comfort. Obviously, not all 313 million people in the United States agree on all these values, but such a list serves as a starting point in defining America's national character.

In recent decades, scholars have made extensive efforts to compare values in different nations, even while recognizing the challenges in interpreting value concepts in a

> **nonverbal communication** The use of gestures, facial expressions, and other visual images to communicate.
>
> **value** A collective conception of what is considered good, desirable, and proper—or bad, undesirable, and improper—in a culture.

SOCTHINK

Consider Williams's list of basic values. Do you think most people value these things? How might some values, such as freedom and conformity, conflict? How do we resolve such conflicts?

In Arab cultures, men sometimes hold hands as a sign of affection and friendship.

Life Goals of First-Year College Students in the United States

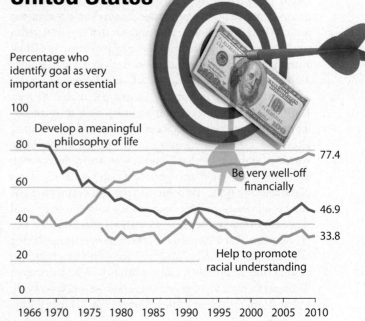

Percentage who identify goal as very important or essential

- Develop a meaningful philosophy of life
- Be very well-off financially — 77.4
- 46.9
- Help to promote racial understanding — 33.8

1966 1970 1975 1980 1985 1990 1995 2000 2005 2010

Source: Pryor et al. 2007, 2011.

similar manner across cultures. Social psychologist Shalom Schwartz has measured values in more than 60 countries. Around the world, certain values are widely shared, including benevolence, which is defined as "forgiveness and loyalty." In contrast, power, defined as "control or dominance over people and resources," is a value that is endorsed much less often (Davidov, Schmidt, and Schwartz 2008; Pew Research Center 2011d).

Each year more than 200,000 first-year college students at approximately 270 of the nation's four-year colleges fill out a questionnaire asking them which values are most important to them. Because of its coverage, content, and scope, this survey provides a kind of barometer of the nation's values. The top value of the freshman class of 1966, the year the survey was first conducted, was "developing a meaningful

philosophy of life," with 80 percent of the new students identifying it as either essential or very important. By contrast, only 44 percent choose "being well off financially." Since that time, the relative position of these two values has flipped (see graph above). Among the freshman class of 2011, for example, 79.6 percent identified being well-off as a significant value compared to 46.8 percent who selected developing a meaningful philosophy (Pryor et al. 2011).

Researchers have also studied other family and community values among first-year students. The second-highest rated value identified by the 2011 class was "raising a family," at 73 percent. This value has remained at approximately the same level for the past forty years (Pryor et al. 2007). Students in 2011 were also committed to "helping others who were in difficulty" (70 percent), although only 30 percent selected "participating in a community action program" as either essential or very important. The proportion that identified "helping to promote racial understanding," fell slightly over the previous year to 33.5 percent. As these numbers demonstrate, a nation's values are not necessarily set in stone.

Because it challenges honesty as a shared value, cheating is a significant concern on college campuses. Professors who take advantage of computerized services that can identify plagiarism, such as the search engine Google or TurnItIn.com, have found that many of the papers their students hand in are plagiarized, in whole or in part. When high school students were asked about academic honesty, 34 percent admitted to copying an

Internet document for a classroom assignment, 59 percent said they'd cheated during a test at school, and 81 percent had copied someone's homework, all within the past year. When asked whether it's not worth it to lie or cheat because it hurts your character, 84 percent agreed or strongly agreed (Josephson Institute of Ethics 2011). Perhaps cheating has become a normal part of student culture even if it is at odds with dominant school values.

Sometimes values shift in response to historic events. Americans have always valued their right to privacy and resented government intrusions into their personal lives. In the aftermath of the terrorist attacks of September 11, 2001, however, many citizens called for greater protection against the threat of terrorism. In response, the federal government broadened its surveillance powers and increased its ability to monitor people's behavior without court approval. In 2001, shortly after the attacks, Congress passed the USA PATRIOT Act, which empowers the FBI to access individuals' medical, library, student, and phone records without informing them or obtaining a search warrant.

NORMS

While values express our core beliefs, norms provide guidance for how to act: "Wash your hands before dinner." "Thou shalt not kill." "Respect your elders." All societies have ways of encouraging and enforcing what they view as appropriate behavior while discouraging and sanctioning what they consider to be improper behavior. **Norms** are the established standards of behavior maintained by a society. However, they are more than just the rules we think about and know—we come to embody them as part of our everyday actions.

For a norm to become significant, it must be widely shared and understood. For example, in movie theaters in the United States, we typically expect that people will be quiet while the film is shown. Of course, context matters, and the application of this norm can vary, depending on the particular film and type of audience. People who are viewing a serious artistic film will be more likely to insist on the norm of silence than those who are watching a slapstick comedy or a horror movie.

Types of Norms Sociologists distinguish between norms in two ways. First, norms are classified by their relative importance to society. When presented this way, they are known as *folkways* and *mores*. **Folkways** are norms governing everyday behavior. They play an important role in providing general guidelines for how to act within a culture. Such norms are less rigid in their application, and their violation raises comparatively little concern. **Mores** (pronounced "MOR-ays") are norms deemed highly necessary to the welfare of a society, often because they embody the most cherished principles. Each society demands obedience to its mores; violation can lead to severe penalties. Thus, the United States has strong mores against murder, treason, and child abuse, which have been institutionalized into formal norms.

Clothing provides an example of the difference between the two. For example, fashion is a folkway, and there is wide latitude in what we might wear. But what about not wearing any clothes in public? For most of us, most of the time (except perhaps on No Pants Subway Ride days) that would be crossing the line into the territory of mores, and we might expect a strong and swift response if we did so. However, even this may be undergoing a change: in recent years, the nude vacation business has been booming (Higgins 2008).

Norms are also classified as either formal or informal. **Formal norms** generally have been written down and specify strict punishments for violators. In the United States we often formalize norms into laws, which are very precise in defining proper and improper behavior. Sociologist Donald Black (1995) defined *law* as "governmental social control"; that is, **laws** are formal norms enforced by the state. But laws are just one example of formal norms. The requirements for a college major and the rules of a card game are also considered formal norms.

By contrast, **informal norms** are generally understood but not precisely recorded. We follow

norm An established standard of behavior maintained by a society.

folkways Norms governing everyday behavior, whose violation raises comparatively little concern.

mores Norms deemed highly necessary to the welfare of a society.

formal norm A norm that generally has been written down and that specifies strict punishments for violators.

laws Formal norms enforced by the state.

informal norm A norm that is generally understood but not precisely recorded.

5 Movies on U.S. CULTURE

Revolutionary Road
A look at the social isolation and gender roles of 1950s America.

The Invention of Lying
What would society be like if we never told a lie?

Whip It
A misfit finds her place on a Texas Roller Derby team.

The Greatest Movie Ever Sold
Morgan Spurlock attempts to finance a movie completely with product placement.

Good Hair
Chris Rock's documentary about the culture of hair in the Black community.

largely unspoken rules for all kinds of everyday interactions, such as how to ride on an elevator, how to pass someone on a sidewalk, and how to behave in a college classroom. Knowledge of such norms is often taken for granted.

In many societies around the world, norms reinforce patterns of male dominance. For example, various folkways reveal men's hierarchical position above women within the traditional Buddhist areas of Southeast Asia. In the sleeping cars of trains, women do not sleep in upper berths, above men. Hospitals that house men on the first floor do not place female patients on the second floor. Even on clotheslines, folkways in Southeast Asia dictate male dominance: women's attire is hung lower than that of men (Bulle 1987).

Acceptance of Norms People do not follow norms, whether mores or folkways, in all situations. In some cases they can evade a norm because they know it is weakly enforced. For instance, it is illegal for American teenagers to drink alcoholic beverages, yet drinking by minors is common throughout the nation. In fact, teenage alcoholism is a serious social problem.

In some instances behavior that appears to violate society's collective norms may actually represent adherence to the norms of a particular group. Teenage drinkers are often conforming to the standards of their peer group when they violate norms that condemn underage drinking. Similarly, business executives who use shady accounting techniques may be responding to a corporate culture that demands the maximization of profits at any cost, including the deception of investors and government regulatory agencies.

Norms are violated in some instances because one norm conflicts with another. For example, suppose you live in an apartment building and one night hear the screams of the woman next door, who is being beaten by her husband. If you decide to intervene by knocking on their door or

Break-a-Norm Day

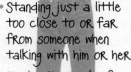

- Wearing formal clothes in an informal setting
- Eating with the wrong utensil or none at all
- Responding to friends or family the same as to a boss or teacher
- Having long gaps in speech when talking with someone
- Standing just a little too close to or far from someone when talking with him or her
- Facing the back of an elevator instead of getting in and turning around

Norms provide us with rules that guide our everyday behavior. All we need to do is step outside the lines even a little bit to see the influence they have over our lives. These are some examples of how people violate norms. How would you feel about violating any of these norms? How might others respond to you?

calling the police, you are violating the norm of minding your own business while at the same time following the norm of assisting a victim of domestic violence.

Even if norms do not conflict, there are exceptions to any norm. The same action, under different circumstances, can cause one to be viewed as either a hero or a villain. For instance, secretly taping telephone conversations is normally considered not just intrusive but illegal. However, it can be done with a court order to obtain valid evidence for a criminal trial. We would heap praise on a government agent who used such methods to convict an organized crime figure. In our culture we tolerate killing another human being in self-defense, and we actually reward killing in warfare, as was evident in the celebrations that followed the death of Osama bin Laden.

Acceptance of norms is subject to change as the political, economic, and social conditions of a culture are transformed. Until the 1960s, for example, formal norms throughout much of the United States prohibited the marriage of people from different racial groups. Over the past

"Strangers in a new culture see only what they know."

Anomymous

A female U.S. soldier searches Iraqi women.

half century, however, such legal prohibitions have been cast aside. The process of change can be seen today in the increasing acceptance of single parents and the growing support for the legalization of marriage for same-sex couples.

When circumstances require the sudden violation of longstanding cultural norms, the change can upset an entire population. In Iraq, where Muslim custom strictly forbids touching by strangers for men and especially for women, the war that began in 2003 has brought numerous daily violations of the norm. Outside mosques, government offices, and other facilities likely to be targeted by terrorists, visitors must now be patted down and have their bags searched by Iraqi security forces. To reduce the discomfort caused by the procedure, women are searched by female guards and men by male guards. Despite that concession, and the fact that many Iraqis admit to or even insist on the need for such measures, people still wince at the invasion of their personal privacy. In reaction to the searches, Iraqi women have begun to limit the contents of the bags they carry or simply to leave them at home (Rubin 2003).

A Guide to Raising Your Hand in Class

Start

Is there something you would like to say? — Yes. → Is class almost over? — No. → Do you just like to hear yourself talk? — No. → Would others benefit from what you have to say? — No. → Is class almost over yet? — Yes. → How about now? — Yes.

No. ↓ Great!

Yes. ↓ Keep your hand down.

Yes. ↓ I hate you.

Yes. ↓ Congratulations. you may speak without annoying your classmates.

No. ↓

Informal norms are often unspoken and taken for granted, yet we rely on learned principles to decide how we (and we hope others) should proceed, as this cartoon humorously demonstrates

SANCTIONS

When norms are violated, we can usually expect a response designed to bring our behavior back into line. If a basketball coach sends a sixth player into the game, we count on the referee to call a foul. If a candidate shows up for a formal job interview in shorts and a T-shirt, we predict that no job offer will follow. If we park without putting money into the meter, we should expect a ticket. In each of these cases, some form of negative repercussion results from our failure to abide by expected norms.

Sanctions are penalties and rewards for conduct concerning a social norm. They include both negative and positive responses to behavior; their purpose is to influence future behavior. Adhering to norms can lead to positive sanctions such as a pay raise, a medal, a word of gratitude, or a pat on the back. Negative sanctions might include fines, threats, imprisonment, and stares of contempt. In this way sanctions work to enforce the order that the norms represent. Most of the time we do not even need others to sanction our acts. Having internalized society's

sanction A penalty or reward for conduct concerning a social norm.

norms, we police ourselves, using such internal motivations as guilt or self-satisfaction to regulate our own behavior.

As we saw with the No Pants Subway Ride, norms provide order, but norms change, and change can result in confusion. As social scientist Gustave Le Bon said in 1895, "Civilization is impossible without traditions, and progress impossible without the destruction of those traditions. The difficulty, and it is an immense difficulty, is to find a proper equilibrium between stability and variability." In a world of norms, we constantly face this tension: to obey or not to obey.

>>Cultural Variation

Together the elements of culture provide us with social coherence and order. Culture clarifies for us what we think is good and bad, and right and wrong, giving us a sense of direction. That is not to say, however, that there is universal agreement on values and norms or that culture works on behalf of all for the greater good. Culture helps to unify and provide meaning, but it also serves the interests of some individuals and groups to the detriment of others. Some people benefit from existing norms and values, while others are denied opportunities or access to resources simply due to the positions they occupy—positions we have culturally defined as inferior.

dominant ideology A set of cultural beliefs and practices that legitimates existing powerful social, economic, and political interests.

Agricultural strikes and boycotts in the 1960s and 1970s alerted the nation to the harsh economic plight of migrant workers.

DOMINANT IDEOLOGY

One of the ways culture can function to maintain the privileges of certain groups is through the establishment of a **dominant ideology**—the set of cultural beliefs and practices that legitimate existing powerful social, economic, and political interests. The dominant ideology helps to explain and justify who gets what and why in a way that supports and maintains the status quo. Dominant ideas can even squelch alternative expressions of what might be, casting such alternatives as threats to the existing order. This concept was first proposed by Hungarian Marxist Georg Lukács (1923) and Italian Marxist Antonio Gramsci (1929), but it did not gain an audience in the United States until the early 1970s. In Karl Marx's view, a capitalist society has a dominant ideology that serves the interests of the ruling class.

A society's most powerful groups and institutions control wealth and property. Armed with a dominant ideology, they can also shape beliefs about reality through religion, education, and the media. In so doing, they can influence what we come to accept as true. For example, feminists would argue that if all of society's most important institutions send the message that women should be subservient to men, this dominant ideology will help to control and subordinate women.

One of the limitations of the dominant ideology thesis is that, in the United States, it is not easy to identify a singular, all-inclusive "core culture." Studies report a lack of consensus on national values and a wide range of cultural traits from a variety of cultural traditions. In addition, as we saw in the surveys of young people's values, significant shifts in cultural values can occur. Yet there is no denying that certain expressions of values have greater influence than others, even in so complex a society as the United States. For example, the value of competition in the marketplace—a cornerstone of any capitalist economy—remains powerful, and we often look down on those who we suspect might be lazy.

ASPECTS OF CULTURAL VARIATION

Although societies can be defined in part by the culture their inhabitants share, culture varies both between and within societies. Inuit tribes in northern Canada, clad in furs and dieting on whale blubber, have little in common with farmers in Southeast Asia, who dress for the heat and subsist mainly on the rice they grow in their paddies. Cultures adapt to meet specific sets of circumstances, such as climate, level of technology, population, and geography. This adaptation to different conditions shows up in differences in all elements of culture, including language, values, norms, and sanctions. Thus, despite the presence of cultural universals such as courtship and religion, great diversity exists among the world's many cultures. Moreover, even within a single nation, certain segments of the populace develop cultural patterns that differ from the patterns of the dominant society. Cultural variation, as described by sociologists, takes a number of forms.

Subcultures Rodeo riders, residents of a retirement community, workers on an offshore oil rig—all are examples of what sociologists refer to as *subcultures*. A **subculture** is a segment of society that shares a distinctive pattern of mores, folkways, and values that differs from the pattern of the larger society. In a sense, a subculture can be thought of as a culture existing within a larger, dominant culture. The existence of many subcultures is characteristic of complex societies such as the United States.

SOCTHINK

What subcultures are common on college and university campuses? What indicators make them recognizable? Why might such subcultures be more likely to form there?

Members of a subculture participate in the dominant culture while engaging in unique and distinctive forms of behavior. Frequently, a subculture will develop its own slang, known as **argot**—specialized language that distinguishes it from the wider society. For example, back in the 1940s and 1950s, New York City's sanitation workers developed a humorous argot used to this day to describe the dirty and smelly aspects of their job. They call themselves *g-men* (a term more typically applied to government agents); a garbage scow or barge is known as a *honey boat*; and trash thrown from an upper-story window is called *airmail.* More recent coinages include *disco rice* (maggots)

and *urban whitefish* (used condoms). Administrators at the Sanitation Department practice a more reserved humor than those who work on the trucks. When they send a *honey boat* to New Jersey, they are not dumping the city's garbage; they're *exporting* it. Policy makers at the department have also invented some novel acronyms to describe New Yorkers' attitude toward the construction of new sanitation facilities: *banana* (build absolutely nothing anywhere near anyone) and *nope* (not on planet earth) (Urbina 2004).

Such argot allows insiders—the members of the subculture—to understand words with special meanings and establishes patterns of communication that outsiders cannot understand. In so doing, it clarifies the boundary between "us" and "them" and reinforces a shared identity. We see something like this in the taken-for-granted words and acronyms in the instant-messaging and text-messaging world. There, abbreviations come fast and furious, from the well-known, such as *lol* (laughing out loud), *brb* (be right back), and *g2g* (got to go), to the more obscure, such as *1337* (meaning "elite" and referring to symbolic language or "leet-speak") or *pwned* (leet term meaning "defeated").

In India a new subculture has developed among employees at the international call centers established by multinational corporations. To serve customers in the United States and Europe, the young men and women who work there must be fluent speakers of English. But the corporations

> **subculture** A segment of society that shares a distinctive pattern of mores, folkways, and values that differs from the pattern of the larger society.
>
> **argot** Specialized language used by members of a group or subculture.

Subculture Slang

Anime and Manga Fans

chibi eyes: the characteristic, big childlike eyes used in anime

majoko: a girl anime character with magical powers who must save the world

Con Artists & Scammers

grifter: a person who steals through deception

phishing: seeking personal information by sending out emails that appear to be from legitimate companies

Graffiti Writers

bite: to copy another graffiti writer's work

burner: a stylistically impressive, brilliantly colored piece of graffiti, usually written in a complex pattern of interlocking letters and other visual elements

toy: an inexperienced or unskilled graffiti writer

kill: to saturate an area with one's graffiti

Bikers (Motorcyclists)

brain bucket: a helmet

ink slinger: a tattoo artist

pucker factor: the degree of panic felt during a near-accident

yard shark: a dog that races out to attack passing motorcyclists

Skateboarders

deck: a skateboard platform

face plant: a face-first crash

sketchy: in reference to a trick, poorly done

Subcultures often produce their own unique jargon. The words may be appropriate in those subcultures, but they have the effect of drawing a line between insiders and the rest of us.
Source: Reid 2006.

that employ them demand more than proficiency in a foreign language; they expect their Indian employees to adopt Western values and work habits, including the grueling pace that U.S. workers take for granted. In return, the corporations offer perks such as Western-style dinners and dances and coveted consumer goods. Ironically, they allow employees to take the day off only on such American holidays as Labor Day and Thanksgiving—not on Indian holidays such as Diwali, the Hindu festival of lights. While most Indian families are home celebrating, call center employees see mostly one another. When they have the day off, no one

counterculture A subculture that deliberately opposes certain aspects of the larger culture.

else is free to socialize with them. As a result, these employees have formed a tight-knit subculture based on hard work and a taste for Western luxury goods and leisure-time pursuits. Increasingly, they are the object of criticism from Indians who live a more conventional Indian lifestyle centered on family and holiday traditions (Kalita 2006).

Countercultures Sometimes a subculture can develop that seeks to set itself up as an alternative to the dominant culture. When a subculture conspicuously and deliberately opposes certain aspects of the larger culture, it is known as a **counterculture.** Countercultures typically thrive among the young, who have the least investment in the existing culture.

The 1960s, now often characterized by the phrase "sex and drugs and rock 'n' roll," provide a classic case of an extensive counterculture. Largely composed of young people, members of this counterculture were turned off by a society they believed was too materialistic and technological. It included many political radicals and "hippies" who had "dropped out" of mainstream social institutions, but its membership was extensive and diverse. The young people expressed in their writings, speeches, and songs their visions, hopes, and dreams for a new society. As was reflected in the 1966 survey of first-year college students, these young women and men rejected the pressure to accumulate more expensive cars, larger homes, and an endless array of material goods. Instead, they expressed a desire to live in a culture based on more humanistic values, such as sharing, love, and coexistence with the environment. As a political force, they worked for peace—opposing U.S. involvement in the war in Vietnam and encouraging draft resistance—as well as racial and gender equality (Anderson 2007; Gitlin 1993).

In the wake of the attacks of September 11, 2001, people around the United States learned of the existence of terrorist groups operating as a counterculture within their own country. Many nations have had to deal with internal counterculture groups—often rooted in long-standing national, ethnic, or political differences—whose members strongly disagree with the values and norms of the dominant culture. In most cases this does not result in violence, but in some cases, as in Northern Ireland and Israel, groups have used attacks, including suicide bombings, to make a statement, both symbolic and real, seeking to bring attention to their situation and an end to their repression (Juergensmeyer 2003). In Northern Ireland, Israel, the Palestinian territory, and other parts of the world, many generations have lived in such circumstances. But terrorist cells are not necessarily fueled only by outsiders. Frequently, people become disenchanted with the policies of their own country, and a few take very violent steps (Juergensmeyer 2003).

Culture Shock Today we are more and more likely to come into contact with and even immerse ourselves in cultures unlike our own. For example, it has become increasingly common for students to study abroad. Though they may well have predeparture orientation sessions, when they get in-country, they often have a difficult time adjusting because so many of the little things that they took for granted, things they barely noticed before, no longer apply. Anyone who feels disoriented, uncertain, out of place, or even fearful

when they encounter unfamiliar cultural practices may be experiencing **culture shock.** For example, a resident of the United States who visits certain areas in Cambodia and wants meat for dinner may be stunned to learn that a local specialty is rat meat. Similarly, someone from a strict Islamic culture may be shocked upon first seeing

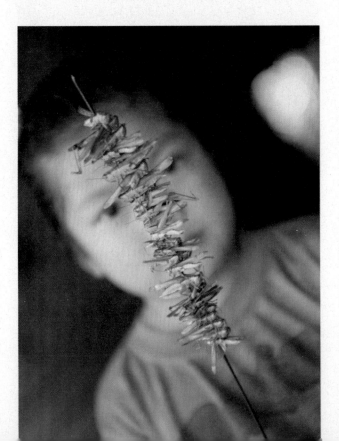

the comparatively provocative dress styles and open displays of affection that are common in the United States and other Western cultures.

Interestingly, after students who study abroad return home, they may experience a kind of reverse culture shock. Their time away has changed them, often in ways they were unaware of, and they find that they cannot so easily slip back into the old routines that those who remained at home expect of them. Culture shock reveals to us both the power and the taken-for-granted nature of culture. The rules we follow are so ingrained that we barely notice that we were following them until they are no longer there to provide the structure and order we assume as a given.

All of us, to some extent, take for granted the cultural practices of our society. As a result, it can be surprising and even disturbing to realize that other cultures do not follow our way of life. The fact is, customs that seem strange to us are considered normal and proper in other cultures, which may view our own mores and folkways as odd.

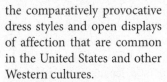

> **culture shock** The feelings of disorientation, uncertainty, and even fear that people experience when they encounter unfamiliar cultural practices.
>
> **ethnocentrism** The tendency to assume that one's own culture and way of life represent what's normal or are superior to all others.

ATTITUDES TOWARD CULTURAL VARIATION

Ethnocentrism Because we are now more likely to encounter people from a whole range of cultural backgrounds than we were in the past, we are also more likely to struggle with what we think about the beliefs, values, and practices of others. When we hear people talking about "our" culture versus "their" culture, we are often confronted with statements that reflect the attitude that "our" culture is best. Terms such as *underdeveloped, backward,* and *primitive* may be used to refer to other societies. What "we" believe is a religion; what "they" believe is superstition and mythology.

It is tempting to evaluate the practices of other cultures on the basis of our own perspectives. Sociologist William Graham Sumner (1906) coined the term **ethnocentrism** to refer to the tendency to assume that one's own culture and way of life represent what's normal or are superior to all others. The ethnocentric person sees his or her own group as the center or defining point of culture and views all other cultures as deviations from what is "normal." Thus, Westerners who see cattle as a food source might look down on the Hindu religion and culture, which view the cow as sacred. People in one culture may dismiss as unthinkable the mate selection or child-rearing practices of another culture.

Ethnocentric value judgments have complicated U.S. efforts at democratic reform of the Iraqi government. Before the 2003 war in Iraq, U.S. planners had assumed that Iraqis would adapt to a new form of government in the same way the Germans and Japanese did following World War II. But in the Iraqi culture, unlike the German and Japanese cultures, loyalty to the family and the extended clan comes before patriotism and the common good. In a country in which almost half of all people, even those in the cities, marry a first or second cousin, citizens are predisposed to favor their own kin in government and business dealings. Why trust a stranger from outside the family? What Westerners would criticize as nepotism, then, is actually an acceptable, even admirable, practice to Iraqis (J. Tierney 2003).

One of the reasons ethnocentrism develops is that it contributes to a sense of solidarity by promoting group pride. Denigrating other nations and cultures can enhance our own patriotic feelings and belief in our way of life. Yet this type of social stability is established at the expense of other peoples. One of the negative consequences of ethnocentric value judgments is that they serve to devalue groups and to deny equal opportunities.

Of course, ethnocentrism is hardly limited to citizens of the United States. Visitors from many African cultures are surprised at the disrespect that children in the United States show their parents. People from India may be repelled by our practice of living in the same household with dogs and cats. Many Islamic fundamentalists in the Arab world and Asia view the United States as corrupt, decadent, and doomed to destruction. All these people may feel comforted by membership in cultures that in their view are superior to ours (Juergensmeyer 2003).

Cultural Relativism Whereas ethnocentrism means evaluating foreign cultures using the familiar culture of the observer as a standard of correct behavior, **cultural relativism** means viewing people's behavior from the perspective of their own culture. It places a priority on understanding other cultures, rather than dismissing them as "strange" or "exotic." Unlike ethnocentrists, cultural relativists seek to employ the kind of value neutrality that Max Weber saw as so important.

cultural relativism The viewing of people's behavior from the perspective of their own culture.

> You never really understand a person until you consider things from his point of view . . . until you climb into his skin and walk around in it.
>
> Harper Lee, *To Kill a Mockingbird*

Cultural relativism stresses that different social contexts give rise to different norms and values. Thus, we must examine practices such as polygamy, bullfighting, and monarchy within the particular contexts of the cultures in which they are found. Cultural relativism is not the same as moral relativism, which implies that no ultimate normative standards exist, and thus does not suggest that we must unquestionably accept every cultural variation. But it does require a serious and unbiased effort to evaluate norms, values, and customs in light of their distinctive culture.

Practicing the sociological imagination calls for us to be more fully aware of the culture we as humans have created for ourselves and to be better attuned to the varieties of culture other people have established for themselves. Culture shapes our everyday behaviors all the time, and we select from the tools it provides. For the most part, we are not aware of the degree to which we are immersed in a world of our own making. Whether that includes the capacity to read a book, make a meal, or hug a stranger on the street, it is through culture that we establish our relationship to the external world and with one another.

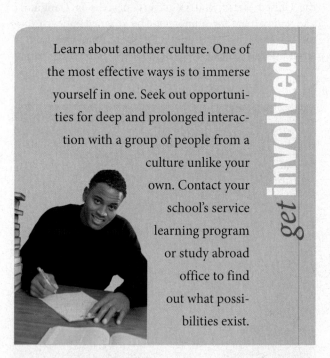

Learn about another culture. One of the most effective ways is to immerse yourself in one. Seek out opportunities for deep and prolonged interaction with a group of people from a culture unlike your own. Contact your school's service learning program or study abroad office to find out what possibilities exist.

get involved!

For REVIEW

I. **Why do humans create culture?**
- Humans lack the complex instincts present in other animals, and as such they must construct a relationship to nature and with each other. We do this through the construction of shared culture.

II. **What does culture consist of?**
- Culture can be broken down into two categories. The first is material culture, which consists of our modification of the physical environment and includes technology. The second is nonmaterial culture, which consists of a number of components including language, values, norms, and sanctions.

III. **How does culture both enable and constrain?**
- While culture provides us with the knowledge, rules, and artifacts we need to survive, it also limits our options. Words enable us to see, and tools enable us to make things, but both are designed for particular purposes and shield us from alternative possibilities. Further, with ethnocentrism, we cut ourselves off from new possibilities from different cultures.

Functionalist View

Sharing a culture helps to define the society to which one belongs, establishing **social order**.

Society **preserves** its culture by transmitting shared language, norms, and values from one generation to the next, thus providing social **stability**.

The interests of **subgroups** within a culture are served by formation of **subcultures**.

PRESERVATION, FACILITATION, COMMUNICATION
KEY CONCEPTS

Conflict View

While a common culture helps to unify a society, it also **privileges** some to the detriment of others.

The **dominant ideology** reinforces the power of the ruling class.

The existence of subcultures reflects **unequal social arrangements**, as brought to light by the civil rights and feminist movements.

Language in a culture can be a source of conflict, as in the case of **sexist** language or language that transmits **racial stereotypes**.

KEY CONCEPTS
PRIVILEGE, DOMINANCE, INEQUALITY

MAKE THE CONNECTION

After reviewing the chapter, answer the following questions:

Interactionist View

Without social interaction, people would not be able to **construct their culture** or transmit it to others. In turn, having a common culture simplifies everyday transactions.

Cultural diffusion is enhanced by interactions involved in immigration, tourism, the Internet, and the mass media.

Both a culture's **language** and **nonverbal communication** facilitate day-to-day exchanges between people.

KEY CONCEPTS
SOCIAL CONSTRUCTION, NONVERBAL COMMUNICATION

1
How would each of the three perspectives make the case that "we need culture"?

2
How would each perspective explain the existence of ethnocentrism (p. 65)?

3
How would each perspective approach the role that dominant ideology (p. 62) performs in a culture?

4
How would you use the perspectives to describe one of the subcultures at your school?

Pop Quiz

1. What do sociologists refer to as the structure of relationships within which a culture is created and shared through regularized patterns of social interaction?

   a. norms

   b. diffusion

   c. globalization

   d. society

2. People's need for food, shelter, and clothing is an example of what George Murdock referred to as

   a. norms.

   b. folkways.

   c. cultural universals.

   d. cultural practices.

3. What is an invention?

   a. introducing a new idea or object to a culture

   b. combining existing cultural items into a form that did not exist before

   c. making known or sharing the existence of an aspect of reality

   d. the physical or technological aspects of our daily lives

4. What term do sociologists use to refer to the process by which a cultural item spreads from group to group or society to society?

   a. diffusion

   b. globalization

   c. innovation

   d. cultural relativism

5. Which of the following statements is true according to the Sapir-Whorf hypothesis?

   a. Language simply describes reality.

   b. Language legitimates existing social, economic, and political interests.

   c. Language shapes our perception of reality.

   d. Language formation is constrained by cultural universals.

6. Values represent shared _____, whereas norms provide guidelines for shared _____.

   a. rules; ideas

   b. beliefs; behaviors

   c. language; technologies

   d. actions; knowledge

7. What type of norms is deemed highly necessary to the welfare of a society, often because these norms embody the most cherished principles of a people?

   a. formal norms

   b. informal norms

   c. mores

   d. folkways

8. Which of the following terms describes the set of cultural beliefs and practices that help to maintain powerful social, economic, and political interests?

   a. mores

   b. dominant ideology

   c. consensus

   d. values

9. Terrorist groups are examples of

   a. cultural universals.

   b. subcultures.

   c. countercultures.

   d. dominant ideologies.

10. What is the term used when one seeks to understand another culture from its perspective, rather than dismissing it as "strange" or "exotic"?

    a. ethnocentrism

    b. culture shock

    c. cultural relativism

    d. cultural value

1. (d); 2. (c); 3. (b); 4. (a); 5. (c); 6. (b); 7. (c); 8. (b); 9. (c); 10. (c)

4

SOCIALIZATION

LEARNING LANGUAGE

Babies are culture magnets. At birth, we as humans are extremely vulnerable, but soon elements of culture begin to stick to us. Imagine what the world must look like through a newborn's eyes. Without language to give names to things, without beliefs to give things meaning, without norms to know what to do, without skills to use tools or utensils, how could we possibly survive? Slowly, as we interact with others, we internalize what we need to know.

One of the most basic elements of culture is language, and we begin teaching it to infants right away. We start doing so using baby talk. Researchers often refer to this singsong style of speaking as "Motherese" or Infant Directed speech. It is characterized by a higher and more varied pitch, longer vowel sounds, and slower speech. Infants prefer baby talk until they are about 8 months old. Such speech provides important building blocks for what will later become a child's native language. In fact, missing out on such exposure due to social deprivation can have a devastating impact on language acquisition (Soderstrom 2007).

Even though baby talk is a near cultural universal, the frequency of sounds, including both vowels and consonants, and the relationships between them, vary from culture to culture. An infant in an English speaking environment hears different combinations than one in a Swedish- or Japanese-speaking context. Such variation provides the foundation for children learning the particulars of their native tongue. For example, English has 10 vowel sounds, whereas Swedish has 16 and Japanese has 5. Baby talk in these different contexts varies accordingly, opening some linguistic pathways while closing others. As linguist Patricia Kuhl (2004) puts it, "early learning promotes future learning that conforms to and builds on the patterns already learned, but limits future learning of patterns that do not conform to those already learned" (p. 832).

Babies can appear especially cute when they themselves begin experimenting with sounds, mimicking what they hear even before they know any words. This was evident when a video of bantering twins went viral. In the video, available at TwinMamaRama.com, the two 17-month-olds "talked" back and forth, saying little more than "da da da." But they did so with expression, hand gestures, turn taking, and laughter in what seemed like all the right places. They knew what language sounded like—they'd learned that through interactions with family, friends, and others—and it was only a matter of time until they also learned the words that go with it.

As You READ

>>

- How do we become ourselves?
- Who shapes our socialization?
- How does our development change over time?

>>The Role of Socialization

As a species, humans aren't fully formed at birth. We depend on others in the earliest years of our lives to survive. They care for the physical needs we are not yet able to provide for on our own, but, as we saw with language, they also set us up for the future by teaching us how to talk, think, behave, and create. We must internalize the culture that has been created by those who have come before us, and parents, teachers, friends, and others enable us to

socialization The lifelong process through which people learn the attitudes, values, and behaviors appropriate for members of a particular culture.

do so. Sociologists refer to this formation as **socialization**, the lifelong process through which people learn the attitudes, values, and behaviors appropriate for members of a particular culture. Although biology plays a role in shaping who we become, sociologists argue that the language we speak, the values we believe in, and the rules we follow have less to do with our DNA than with the cultural context into hich we emerge.

SOCTHINK

What skills that you learned before age two do you now take for granted? From whom did you learn them? In what contexts?

SOCIAL ENVIRONMENT: THE IMPACT OF ISOLATION

Socialization at a young age plays a major role in shaping who we become. We see its power when considering cases in which such interaction is limited or denied. For example, studies of children who have experienced extreme childhood isolation, and research on primates who are denied care suggest how much we need such interaction.

Extreme Childhood Isolation Children who have been isolated or severely neglected (sometimes called *feral children* to suggest that they have reverted to a wild or untamed state) typically have a difficult time recovering from the loss of early childhood socialization. One famous case was Isabelle, who was discovered and rescued in Ohio in 1938. Isabelle had been hidden away from the world at birth and received only minimal human contact from that time on. When she was rescued at the age of six, she could not speak. She was extremely fearful of strangers, reacting almost like a wild animal when confronted with an unfamiliar person. On tests of her educational development, she scored at the level of an infant (Davis 1940, 1947).

Another such case was Genie, a 14-year-old girl discovered by California authorities in 1970. Genie had been kept in isolation since she was 20 months old. During that time no family member had spoken to her, nor could she hear anything other than swearing. Because there was no television or radio in her home, she had never heard the sounds of normal human speech. One year after beginning extensive therapy, Genie's grammar resembled that of a typical 18-month-old. Though she made further advances with continued therapy, she never achieved full language ability.

Today Genie, now in her mid 50s, lives in a home for developmentally disabled adults in California (Curtiss 1977; James 2008; Rymer 1993).

Though such individual cases of near total isolation are relatively rare, children raised in extremely neglectful circumstances also face difficult developmental challenges. For example, earlier in many Romanian orphanages, babies lay in their cribs 18–20 hours a day, curled

Ten Modern Cases of Feral Children

Shamdeo, the Sultanpur Wolf Boy	He was about 4 years old when discovered playing with wolves in 1974.
Memmie LeBlanc, the Wild Girl of Champagne	About 18 to 20 years old when found, she had learned language before having been abandoned.
John Ssebunya, the Ugandan Monkey Boy	Found living with a pack of monkeys in 1991 at age 6, he now gives talks about his experience.
The Syrian Gazelle Boy	An agile runner, he was found among gazelles at about the age of 10 in 1946.
Oxana Malaya, the Ukrainian Dog Girl	She was found living in the dog pen in her family's back yard in 1991 at the age of 8.
The Russian Bird Boy	Found in February 2008, he was cared for by his mother but never spoken to and chirps like a bird.
The Leopard Boy of Dihungi	He was found among leopards at age 5 in 1915 after having been in the wild three years.
Kamala and Amala, the Wolf Girls of Midnapore	These two girls were found living among wolves at about the ages of 8 and 2 in 1920.
The Turkish Bear Girl	This 9-year-old girl was found living with bears in 1937.
Natasha, the Siberian Dog Girl	A 5-year-old Russian girl, discovered in 2009, who was raised like a pet in a room full of dogs and cats.

Source: www.feralchildren.com.

A cloth-covered "artificial mother" of the type used by Harry Harlow.

adopting families concluded that they were ill-suited to be adoptive parents. Many of them have asked for assistance in dealing with the children. After these conditions were brought to light by international aid workers, the Romanian government made efforts to introduce the deprived youngsters to social interaction and its consequent feelings of attachment, which they had never experienced before (Groza, Ryan, and Thomas 2008; Ionescu 2005; Craig Smith 2006a).

Cases of extreme isolation demonstrate the importance of the earliest socialization experiences for children. We now know that it is not enough to attend only to an infant's physical needs; parents must also concern themselves with children's social development. If parents discourage their children from having friends—even as toddlers—those children miss out on social interactions with peers that are critical for emotional growth.

Primate Studies Our need for early socialization is reinforced by studies of animals raised in isolation. Although we would never conduct such experiments on human babies, psychologist Harry Harlow (1971) conducted tests with rhesus monkeys that had been raised away from their mothers and away from contact with other monkeys. As was the case with Isabelle and Genie, the rhesus monkeys raised in isolation were fearful and easily frightened. They did not mate, and the females, who were artificially inseminated, became abusive mothers. Early isolation had long-term damaging effects on the monkeys.

A creative aspect of Harlow's experimentation was his use of "artificial mothers." In one such experiment, Harlow presented monkeys raised in isolation with two substitute mothers—one a cloth-covered replica and one a wire-covered model that had the capacity to offer milk. Monkey after monkey went to the wire mother for the life-giving milk, yet spent much more time clinging to the more motherlike cloth model. Apparently, the infant monkeys developed greater social attachments based on their need for warmth, comfort, and intimacy than their need for food.

against their feeding bottles and receiving little adult care. Such minimal attention continued for the first five years of their lives. Many of them were fearful of human contact and prone to unpredictable antisocial behavior.

This situation came to light only when families in North America and Europe began adopting thousands of these children in the 1990s. The adjustment problems were often so dramatic that about 20 percent of the

THE INFLUENCE OF HEREDITY

Researchers who argue for a stronger role for biological explanations of our behavior point to different research to support their position—studies of twins, especially identical twins raised apart from each other. Oskar Stohr and Jack Yufe, identical twins separated soon after their birth, were raised on different continents and in very different cultural settings. Oskar was reared as a strict Catholic by his maternal grandmother in the Sudetenland of Czechoslovakia. As a member of the Hitler Youth movement in Nazi Germany, he learned to hate Jews. By contrast, his brother, Jack, was reared in Trinidad by the twins' Jewish father. Jack joined an Israeli kibbutz (a collective settlement) at age 17 and later served in the Israeli army. When the twins were reunited in middle age, however, some startling similarities emerged. They both wore wire-rimmed glasses and had mustaches. They both liked spicy foods and sweet liqueurs, were absentminded, flushed the toilet before using it, stored rubber bands on their wrists, and dipped buttered toast in their coffee (Holden 1980).

It is tempting in such cases to focus almost exclusively on such quirky similarities, but the twins also differed in many important respects. For example, Jack was a workaholic, and Oskar enjoyed leisure-time activities. Whereas Oskar was a traditionalist who was domineering toward women, Jack was a political liberal much more accepting of feminism. Finally, Jack was extremely proud of being Jewish, but Oskar never mentioned his Jewish heritage. Oskar and Jack are prime examples of the interplay of heredity and environment (Holden 1987).

To better understand the nature–nurture interplay, since 1983 the Minnesota Twin Family Study has been following pairs of identical twins reared apart to determine what similarities, if any, they show in personality traits, behavior, and intelligence. Results from the available twin studies indicate that both genetic factors and socialization experiences are influential in human development. Certain characteristics—such as temperament, voice patterns, nervous habits, and leadership or dominance tendencies—appear to be strikingly similar even in twins reared apart, suggesting that these qualities may be linked to heredity. However, identical twins reared apart differ far more in their attitudes; values; chosen mates; need for intimacy, comfort, and assistance; and even drinking habits. These qualities, it would seem, are influenced by environmental factors.

Researchers have also been impressed with the similar scores on intelligence tests of twins reared apart in *roughly similar* social settings. Most of the identical twins register scores even closer than those that would be expected if the same person took a test twice. However, identical twins brought up in *dramatically different* social environments score quite differently on intelligence tests—a finding that supports the importance of socialization in human development (Joseph 2004; McGue and Bouchard 1998; Minnesota Center for Twin and Family Research 2012).

> It matters not what someone is born, but what they grow to be.
>
> J. K. Rowling

Did You Know?

. . . The birthrate for twins has risen 70 percent since 1980, and the birthrate for triplets-plus rose 400 percent from 1980 to 1998 (although it has declined in the years since then). Technological advances in both in vitro fertilization and embryo transfer are the primary cause for these increases, providing more cases for researchers to investigate to better understand the interplay between nature and nurture.

Results from twin studies suggest that the nature–nurture debate is likely to continue. As sociologists we cannot dismiss the significance of biology in shaping human behavior. It does appear, however, that although some general behavioral propensities may be shaped by our genes, their manifestation is dependent upon socialization and cultural context. For example, we may inherit tendencies toward temperament, but the ways we express anger (or other emotions) depend on our environment (Shenk 2010).

>>The Self and Socialization

At the heart of this debate about nature versus nurture is the question "Who am I?" In both approaches the implicit assumption is that we are shaped by factors beyond our control. Sociologically speaking, however, we are not simply passive recipients of external forces. As individuals we are engaged in an ongoing dance with the world.

We choose what to think and how to act, but we do so within the confines of the cultural resources to which we have access.

SOCIOLOGICAL APPROACHES TO THE SELF

We come to be who we are in the context of our relationships with others. The **self** is our sense of who we are, distinct from others and shaped by the unique combination of our social interactions. It is not a static entity; instead, it develops and changes as we seek to make sense of our life experiences. Sociologists and psychologists alike have expressed interest in how the individual develops and modifies his or her sense of self as a result of social interaction.

self Our sense of who we are, distinct from others, and shaped by the unique combination of our social interactions.

Cooley: The Looking-Glass Self

According to American sociologist Charles Horton Cooley (1864–1929), we become our self through our interactions with others. We use their responses to what we say and do as a mirror that shapes our understanding of our self. Cooley used the expression the **looking-glass self** to describe his theory that we become who we are based on how we think others see us.

looking-glass self A theory that we become who we are based on how we think others see us.

I The acting self that exists in relation to the Me.

Me The socialized self that plans actions and judges performances based on the standards we have learned from others.

Our understanding of our self, according to Cooley, involves a complex calculation in which we constantly read and react. This process of self-development has three phases. First, we imagine how others see us—relatives, friends, even strangers on the street. Second, we imagine how others evaluate what we think they see—as intelligent, attractive, shy, or strange. Finally, we define our self as a result of these assumptions—"I am smart" or "I am beautiful" (Cooley 1902). This process is ongoing; it happens during each and every one of our interactions. According to Cooley, we become who we are based not on how others actually see us, and not on how they judge us, but on how we think they will judge us based on what we think they perceive.

In Cooley's model, our sense of self results from our "imagination" of how others view us. Because we never truly know what others think, we can develop self-identities based on often *incorrect* perceptions of how others see us. Imagine you are on a first date or a job interview. All the cues you receive throughout the interaction are positive—your date or interviewer smiles, laughs and nods at all the right times. You go home feeling happy, confident that things went really well. But your date never returns your call, or the expected job offer never comes. You go from a feeling of elation and confidence to a sense of disappointment, doubt, and recrimination, asking yourself, "What's wrong with me?" without ever really knowing what they truly thought about you. In Cooley's world, who we are is very much dependent on our interpretations of the interactions we have with others.

Mead: Stages of the Self

George Herbert Mead (1863–1931), another American sociologist, sought to expand on Cooley's theory that we become our self through interaction with others. Mead especially sought to clarify the relationship between our self and our environment. He argued that there are two core components of the self: "I" and "Me." The **I** is our acting self. It is the part of us that walks, reads, sings, smiles, speaks, and performs any other action we might undertake. The **Me** is our socialized self. It draws on all our previous training and experience to plan our actions and then uses these standards to judge our performance afterward.

SOC THINK

What cues do you rely on to know if things are going well on a first date? How about on a job interview? To what extent do you think it is possible to fake such cues?

For Mead the self represents an ongoing interaction between our socialized self and our acting self. The Me plans. The I acts. The Me judges. For example, in a

classroom discussion, our Me may have something to say but fears that the words won't come out quite right, which could lead to embarrassment. So our I stays silent. Our Me then kicks our self afterward when someone else says exactly what we planned to say and receives praise from the professor for having said it.

In all our interactions, we rely on a feedback loop in which we gather information, process it, and use it to guide our reaction. In some respects, this relationship is not unlike the technique math teachers turn to when using the "guess and check" problem solving strategy for certain types of story problems. In this approach, you try a solution to see if it works out, and if it doesn't, you try again. With each successive attempt, you use the information you've gained to make more informed guesses and in so doing find the appropriate pathway to the correct solution. Similarly, in our interactions with others, pathways of appropriate action emerge over time. We become more confident that certain responses are appropriate, making our decisions about how to act in the future easier and providing us with greater self-confidence.

In developing our sense of who we are and what is appropriate, we rely on the interactions we have with our parents, friends, co-workers, coaches, and teachers. Mead used the expression **significant others** to describe the particular individuals we interact with who are most important in the development of our self. Over time, however, we begin to see that the positions these significant others occupy are part of a larger social network. Mead (1934, 1964a, 1964b) described that realization as a three-stage process of self-development: preparatory stage, play stage, and game stage.

Preparatory Stage

During the *preparatory stage,* which lasts until about age three, children merely imitate the people around them, especially family members with whom they continually interact. Thus, a small child will bang on a piece of wood while a parent is engaged in carpentry work or will try to throw a ball if an older sibling is doing so nearby. This imitation is largely mindless—simple parroting of the actions of others.

As they grow older, children begin to realize that we attach meanings to our actions, and they become more adept at using symbols to communicate with others. **Symbols** are the gestures, objects, and words that form the basis of human

Self and others do not exist as mutually exclusive facts

Charles Horton Cooley

communication. By interacting with family and friends, as well as by watching cartoons on television and looking at picture books, children in the preparatory stage begin to develop interaction skills they will use throughout their lives. They learn that they can use symbols to get their way, such as saying please and thank you, or perhaps throwing a tantrum in the candy aisle of the local supermarket.

Play Stage

As children develop skill in communicating through symbols, they gradually become more aware of social relationships out of which those symbols grow. During the *play stage,* from about ages three through five, they begin to pretend to be other people: a doctor, parent, superhero, or teacher. Such play need not make a lot of sense or be particularly coherent to adults, and children, especially when they are young, are able to move in and out of various characters with ease. For Mead, playing make-believe is more than just fun; it is a critical part of our self-development.

> **significant other** An individual who is most important in the development of the self, such as a parent, friend, or teacher.
>
> **symbol** A gesture, object, or word that forms the basis of human communication.
>
> **role taking** The process of mentally assuming the perspective of another and responding from that imagined viewpoint.

Mead, in fact, noted that an important aspect of the play stage is role playing. **Role taking** is the process of mentally assuming the perspective of another and responding from that imagined viewpoint. Through this process a young child internalizes the performances of other people and gradually learns, for example, when it is best to ask a parent for favors. If the parent usually comes home from work in a bad mood, the child might wait until after dinner, when the parent is more relaxed and approachable.

Game Stage

In Mead's third stage, the *game stage,* the child of about six to nine years of age no longer merely plays roles but now begins to consider several tasks and relationships simultaneously. At this point in development, children grasp not only their own social positions but also those of others around them. The transition from play to game is evident when teaching kids to play team sports such as T-ball or soccer. When they are little, you will often see a clump of kids chasing after a ball or moving up the field together. They have yet to learn that different people

play different positions and that they will be more successful as a team if everyone plays the position to which they are assigned. When they do, they can take for granted that someone will be covering a base so they can throw a runner out or that a goalie will be there to make a save if the ball gets behind them. This map of who should be where and who should do what serves as a kind of blueprint for society, and internalizing it represents the final stage of development in Mead's model.

Mead uses the term **generalized other** to refer to the attitudes, viewpoints, and expectations of society as a whole that a child takes into account in his or her behav-

> **generalized other** The attitudes, viewpoints, and expectations of society as a whole that a child takes into account in his or her behavior.
>
> **dramaturgical approach** A view of social interaction in which people are seen as actors on a stage attempting to put on a successful performance.

ior. Simply put, this concept suggests that when an individual acts, he or she takes into account the relative positions, contributions, and expectations for an entire group of people. For example, a child will not act courteously merely to please a particular parent. Rather, the child comes to understand that courtesy is a widespread social value endorsed by parents, teachers, and religious leaders.

At this stage, children begin to see that there really is something like a game going on with an underlying logic and shared rules and expectations for its various players. They may know their principal, Ms. Sanchez, as a significant other, but also see that the position of principal exists independent of Ms. Sanchez and that it carries with it certain expectations that make sense in the context of a school in which other positions include teacher, custodian, aide, and student. And if the individuals who come to occupy the various positions in the game fail to do their part, the whole thing falls apart.

Goffman: Presentation of the Self This idea that we must all play our parts as part of something larger led Erving Goffman, a Canadian sociologist, to study our everyday social interactions using the **dramaturgical approach**, which studies interaction as if we were all actors on a stage seeking to put on a successful performance. He was inspired, in part, by the William Shakespeare quote, "All the world's a stage, And all the men and women merely players: They have their exits and their entrances; And one man in his time plays many parts." As we perform our parts, according to Goffman, each of us seeks to convey impressions of who we are to others, even as those others are doing the same with us.

Building on this analogy, Goffman draws our attention to various aspects of performance, analysis of which allow us to better understand what makes a show a success. Performances take place on a stage. Front stage is where we perform for our audience and includes appropriate sets and props and may involve other cast members with whom we work as a team. We largely follow scripts and, although some improvisation is permissible, too much may threaten the credibility of the character we are trying to portray. Backstage is where we prepare, including getting into costumes and gathering together appropriate props so as to

SOCTHINK

Imagine that going to class is like performing in a play. Who are the key players? What are some of their most-used lines? What props do people use to be convincing? How might the performance break down, and what steps might be taken to save the show?

make our performance believable. Ultimately, the audience judges how well we did. Whether in our role as students, restaurant servers, or even lovers, we all know that we have a part to play and that if we don't say the right lines or use the correct props, the show will collapse, undermining our sense of self.

Early in life, we learn to slant our presentation of our self to create distinctive appearances and satisfy particular audiences. Goffman (1959) referred to this altering of the presentation of the self as **impression management**. To maintain a proper image and avoid public embarrassment, we engage in **face-work**. We often initiate some kind of face-saving behavior when we are feeling flustered or rejected. In response to a rejection at a singles bar, a person may engage in face-work by saying, "There really isn't an interesting person in this entire crowd." Or, if we do poorly on an exam, we may say to a friend who did likewise, "This professor is incompetent." We feel the need to maintain a proper image of the self if we are to continue social interaction.

In some cultures, people engage in elaborate deceptions to avoid losing face. In Japan, for example, where lifetime employment has until recently been the norm, "company men" thrown out of work during a severe economic recession may feign employment, rising as usual in the morning, donning suit and tie, and heading for the business district. But instead of going to the office, they congregate at places such as Tokyo's Hibiya Library, where they pass the time by reading before returning home at the usual hour. Many of these men are trying to protect family members, who would be shamed if neighbors discovered that the family

breadwinner was unemployed. Others are deceiving their wives and families as well (French 2000).

For Goffman, Mead, and Cooley, our self is fundamentally social. Each encounter we have provides opportunities for self-assessment. Even though our sense of self may seem relatively fixed over time, it is always subject to revision as we move into and out of relationships with others. A novel interaction or experience is often all it takes to get us to question things we have taken for granted, leading to new understandings of who we really are.

PSYCHOLOGICAL APPROACHES TO THE SELF

Psychologists have shared the interest of Cooley, Mead, and other sociologists in the development of the self. Early work in psychology, such as that of Sigmund Freud (1856–1939), stressed the role of inborn drives—among them the drive for sexual gratification—in channeling human behavior. Later psychologists such as Jean Piaget emphasized the stages through which human beings progress as the self develops.

impression management The altering of the presentation of the self in order to create distinctive appearances and satisfy particular audiences.

face-work The efforts people make to maintain a proper image and avoid public embarrassment.

cognitive theory of development The theory that children's thought progresses through four stages of development.

Like Cooley and Mead, Freud believed that the self is a social product and that aspects of one's personality are influenced by other people (especially one's parents). However, unlike Cooley and Mead, Freud suggested that the self has components that work in opposition. According to Freud, we have a natural instinct that seeks limitless pleasure, but this is at odds with our societal needs for order and constraint. By interacting with others, we learn the expectations of society and then select behavior most appropriate to our own culture.

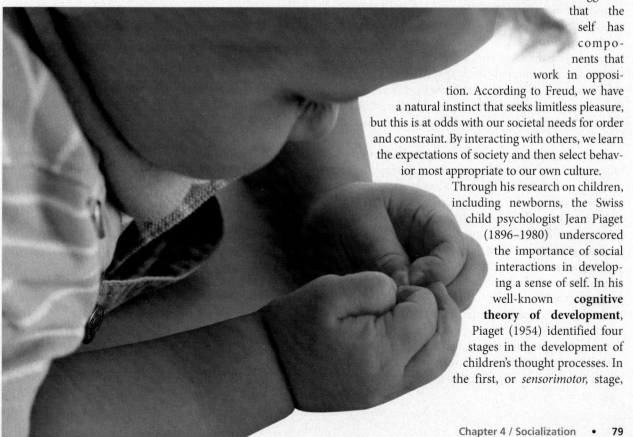

Through his research on children, including newborns, the Swiss child psychologist Jean Piaget (1896–1980) underscored the importance of social interactions in developing a sense of self. In his well-known **cognitive theory of development**, Piaget (1954) identified four stages in the development of children's thought processes. In the first, or *sensorimotor,* stage,

young children use their senses to make discoveries. For example, through touching they discover that their hands are actually a part of themselves. During the second, or *preoperational,* stage, children begin to use words and symbols to distinguish objects and ideas. The milestone in the third, or *concrete operational,* stage is that children engage in more logical thinking. For example, they learn that even when a formless lump of clay is shaped into a snake, it is still the same clay. Finally, in the fourth, or *formal operational,* stage, adolescents become capable of sophisticated abstract thought and can deal with ideas and values in a logical manner.

Piaget suggested that moral development becomes an important part of socialization as children develop the ability to think more abstractly. When children learn the rules of a game such as hopscotch or Candy Land, they are learning to obey societal norms. Those under eight years of age display a rather basic level of morality: rules are rules, and there is no concept of "extenuating circumstances." As they mature, children become capable of greater autonomy, and they begin to experience moral dilemmas and doubts as to what constitutes proper behavior.

According to Piaget, social interaction is the key to development. As children grow older, they pay increasing attention to how other people think and why they act in particular ways. In order to develop a distinct personality, each of us needs opportunities to interact with others.

As we saw earlier, Isabelle and Genie were deprived of the chance for normal social interactions, and the consequences were severe (Kitchener 1991).

>>Agents of Socialization

The people with whom we interact influence how we think about ourselves and how we represent ourselves to others, and the positions they occupy determine the kind of influence they have. Family, friends, schools, peers, the mass media, the workplace, religion, and the state are among the agents of socialization that play the most powerful roles in shaping the self.

FAMILY

The family is the most important agent of socialization, especially for children. We can see the power of family socialization among the Amish. Children in Amish communities are raised in a highly structured and disciplined manner, but they are not immune to the temptations posed by their peers in the non-Amish world. During a period of discovery called *rumspringa,* a term that means "running around," Amish young people attend barn dances where taboos like drinking, smoking, and driving cars are commonly violated. Parents often react by looking the other way, sometimes literally, pretending not to notice. They remain secure in the knowledge that, after a lifetime of Amish socialization, their children almost always return to the traditional Amish lifestyle. Research shows that only about 20 percent of Amish youths leave the fold, and most of them join one of the only somewhat more modern Mennonite groups. Rarely does a baptized adult leave (Schachtman 2006; Zellner and Schaefer 2006).

Although the Amish provide what seems like an extreme case, the truth is that all families play a powerful role in shaping their children. Although peer groups and the media do influence us, research shows that the role of the family in socializing a child cannot be overestimated (McDowell and Parke 2009). As we saw with baby talk and language, the lifelong process of learning begins shortly after birth. Because newborns can hear, see, smell, and taste, and can feel heat, cold, and pain, they are constantly orienting themselves to the surrounding world. Human beings, especially family members, constitute an important part of their social environment. People minister to the baby's needs by feeding, cleaning, carrying, and comforting her or him. In the context of families, we learn to talk, walk, feed ourselves, go to the bathroom, and so on—basic skills that we take for granted as natural but that we learned thanks to our families.

Cross-Cultural Variation As both Cooley and Mead noted, the development of the self is a critical aspect of the early years of one's life. How children develop this sense of self, however, can vary from one society to another. For example, most parents in the United States do not send six-year-olds to school unsupervised. However, that is the norm in Japan, where parents push their children to commute to school on their own from an early age. In cities like Tokyo, first-graders must learn to negotiate buses, subways, and long walks. To ensure their safety, parents carefully lay out rules: never talk to strangers; check

with a station attendant if you get off at the wrong stop; stay on to the end of the line, then call, if you miss your stop; take stairs, not escalators; don't fall asleep. Some parents equip the children with cell phones or pagers. One parent acknowledges that she worries, "but after they are 6, children are supposed to start being independent from the mother. If you're still taking your child to school after the first month, everyone looks at you funny" (Tolbert 2000:17).

Family structures also reproduce themselves through socialization. In the contexts of families, children learn expectations regarding marriage and parenthood. Children observe their parents expressing affection, dealing

with finances, quarreling, complaining about in-laws, and so forth. Their learning represents an informal process of anticipatory socialization in which they develop a tentative model of what being married and being a parent are like.

The Influence of Race and Gender In the United States, social development includes exposure to cultural assumptions regarding gender and race. African American parents, for example, have learned that children as young as two years old can absorb negative messages about Blacks in children's books, toys, and television shows—the vast majority of which are designed primarily for White consumers. At the same time, African American children are exposed more often than others to the inner-city youth gang culture. Because most Blacks, even those who are middle class, live near very poor neighborhoods, their children are susceptible to these influences, despite their parents' strong family values (Benhorin and McMahon 2008; Kliewar and Sullivan 2009; Pattillo 2005).

The term **gender roles** refers to expectations regarding the proper behavior, attitudes, and activities of males and females. For example, we traditionally think of "toughness" as masculine—and desirable only in men—while we view "tenderness" as feminine. As we will see in Chapter 12, other cultures do not necessarily assign these qualities to each gender in the way that our culture does. As the primary agents of childhood socialization, parents play a critical role in guiding children into those gender roles deemed appropriate in a society.

gender role Expectations regarding the proper behavior, attitudes, and activities of males and females.

Other adults, older siblings, the mass media, and religious and educational institutions also have a noticeable influence on a child's socialization into feminine and masculine norms. A culture or subculture may require that one sex or the other take primary responsibility for the socialization of children, economic support of the family, or religious or intellectual leadership. In some societies girls are socialized mainly by their mothers and boys by their fathers—an arrangement that may prevent girls from learning critical survival skills. In South Asia, for example, fathers teach their sons to swim to prepare them for a life as fishermen; girls typically do not learn to swim. When the deadly tsunami hit the coast of South Asia in 2004, many more men than women survived.

While we consider the family's role in socialization, we need to remember, however, that children are not simply robots who lack agency. They do not play a passive role in their socialization. As Mead's "I" implies, they choose, sometimes to the disappointment of their parents, and in so doing are active participants in their self-creation. Through the choices they make, they influence and alter the families, schools, and communities of which they are a part.

SCHOOL

In school we typically move beyond the more sheltered confines of our family and learn to become members of the larger social groups to which we belong. Schools teach us the taken-for-granted knowledge of the broader society—not only basic skills such as reading, writing, and 'rithmatic but also shared cultural knowledge, such as the national anthem, the heroes of the American Revolution, and the pillars of good character. Like the family, schools have an explicit mandate to socialize people in the United States—and especially children—into the norms and values of U.S. culture.

Schools teach children the values and customs of the larger society because that shared culture provides the glue that holds us together as a society. If we did not transmit our knowledge and skills from one generation to the next, society would collapse. The knowledge we gain there, however, goes beyond the official curriculum to include the more informal lessons we learn on the playground. We do learn the facts and figures of history, science, reading, math, and more, but we also learn how to stand up for ourselves when our parents or teachers are not there to hover over us or to bail us out.

In addition to providing social order, schools open doors for us as individuals. We are exposed to new ways of thinking and acting that allow us to make new choices about our future. Although this can include training for careers that allow us to "get ahead," it also involves exposure to new cultures, ideas, practices, and possibilities. It might even lead us to an unexpected future such as a career in sociology!

Although schools provide both social order and individual opportunity, they can also reinforce existing inequality through the ways students are socialized. As economists Samuel Bowles and Herbert Gintis (1976) have observed, schools produce teachable students who become

manageable workers. They argue that schools have less to do with transmitting academic content than with socializing students into the proper attitudes and behaviors of the workplace. Schools teach students how to work for rewards, how to work in teams, how to meet deadlines, how to take responsibility for a task or work product, how to comply with instructions, and so on. The students who internalize these skills best are rewarded with opportunities in the workplace while others are left behind.

These differential outcomes are compounded by the fact that the positions we occupy when we enter school shape where we end up. For example, higher education in the United States is costly despite the existence of public colleges and universities and financial aid programs. Students from affluent backgrounds, therefore, have an advantage in gaining access to universities and professional training. At the same time, less affluent young people may never receive the preparation that would qualify them for the best-paying and most prestigious jobs.

PEER GROUPS

Families and schools do shape us, but if you ask any 13-year-old who matters most in his or her life, the likely answer is "friends." As children grow older, the family becomes somewhat less important in social development. Instead, peer group members increasingly assume the role of Mead's significant other. Within the peer group, young people associate with others who are approximately their own age and who often enjoy a similar social status (Giordano 2003).

In the context of peer groups, a hierarchy often develops. Sociologists Patricia and Peter Adler conducted

In the TV series *Glee*, the most popular couple in the high school loses face when Quinn, the head cheerleader, is revealed to be pregnant and joins the glee club with her boyfriend, Finn, the star quarterback. The respect from others that they took for granted quickly vanishes. In a meeting with the school counselor, Quinn gives voice to the power that people's perceptions of us can have in our lives: "Status is like currency. When your bank account is full, you can get away with doing just about anything. But right now, we're like toxic assets."

participant observation at elementary schools to investigate how popularity works among fourth- through sixth-grade students. They found that, even this early, a pecking order is established ranging from the "popular clique" at the top that includes the "cool kids" on down to what they call the "social isolates" at the bottom, whom other kids sometimes call "dweebs" or "nerds" (Adler and Adler 1996). Children get the message about where they fit and how they should behave.

High School Popularity

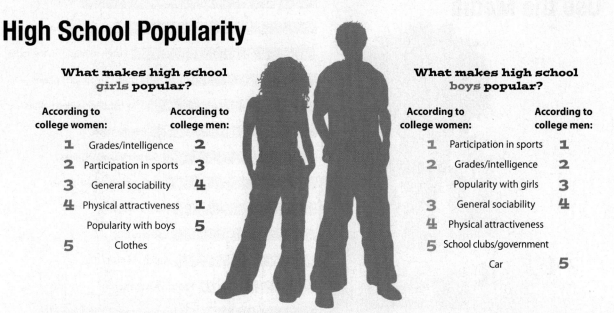

What makes high school girls popular?

According to college women:		According to college men:
1	Grades/intelligence	2
2	Participation in sports	3
3	General sociability	4
4	Physical attractiveness	1
	Popularity with boys	5
5	Clothes	

What makes high school boys popular?

According to college women:		According to college men:
1	Participation in sports	1
2	Grades/intelligence	2
	Popularity with girls	3
3	General sociability	4
4	Physical attractiveness	
5	School clubs/government	
	Car	5

Note: Students at the following universities were asked in which ways adolescents in their high schools had gained prestige with their peers: Cornell University, Louisiana State University, Southeastern Louisiana University, State University of New York at Albany, State University of New York at Stony Brook, the University of Georgia, and the University of New Hampshire.

Source: Suitor et al. 2001:445.

In other research the Adlers also found that popularity reinforces gender stereotypes. To be popular as a boy is to be athletic, tough, and not too academic. To be popular as a girl is to be attractive, to be able to manipulate others using social skills, and to come from a family wealthy enough to permit shopping for the latest cool stuff (Adler, Kless, and Adler 1992). In similar research, college students were asked to reflect on what made people popular in high school. Researchers found that male and female students named many of the same paths to popularity—such as physical attractiveness, participation in sports, and grades/intelligence—but gave them different orders of importance. Neither men nor women named sexual activity, drug use, or alcohol use as one of the top five paths, but college men were much more likely than women to mention those behaviors as a means to becoming popular when they were boys and girls (Suitor et al. 2001). Other researchers have found that being considered popular early in high school increases the likelihood of using tobacco and engaging in sexual activity later in high school (Mayeux, Sandstrom, and Cillessen 2008).

Though we value the importance of kids establishing themselves as individuals, the irony is that peer culture is not individualistic. Children, especially adolescents, run in packs and look, talk, and act alike (often in the name of individualism). Of course, although parents often lecture their kids about not giving in to peer pressure, they don't really mean it. What they mean is to not give in to the *wrong kinds* of peer

pressure. They love peer pressure if it makes their children more like the "good kids" or, even better, if the form of social pressure they give in to is parental pressure.

Did You Know?

Source: Nielsen 2012a.

. . . The average person in the United States watches 32 hours and 33 minutes of television per week and spends 4 hours and 7 minutes per week using the Internet on a computer.

How Young People Use the Media

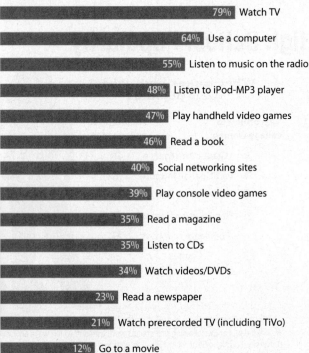

Percentage of 8- to 18-year-olds in a typical day

79%	Watch TV
64%	Use a computer
55%	Listen to music on the radio
48%	Listen to iPod-MP3 player
47%	Play handheld video games
46%	Read a book
40%	Social networking sites
39%	Play console video games
35%	Read a magazine
35%	Listen to CDs
34%	Watch videos/DVDs
23%	Read a newspaper
21%	Watch prerecorded TV (including TiVo)
12%	Go to a movie

Source: Rideout et al. 2010:44–45.

MASS MEDIA AND TECHNOLOGY

In the past 80 or so years, media innovations—radio, motion pictures, recorded music, television, and the Internet—have become important agents of socialization. One national survey indicates that 71 percent of U.S. children have a television in their bedroom, and 70 percent of all youths ages 8–18 use the Internet every day (Rideout, Foehr, and Roberts 2010; Wartella et al. 2009). We are spending more and more of our time interacting with technology, which has an inevitable impact on our interactions with each other. Adding up totals from television, radio, print media, phones, computers, movies, and music—and taking multitasking (doing more than one task at a time) into account—Americans consume the equivalent of 11.8 hours of information per day outside of work (Bohn and Short 2010).

Television programs and even commercials can introduce young people to unfamiliar lifestyles and cultures. On PBS alone, children are exposed to life in the city, on the farm, and across the world. The same thing happens in other countries and regions. In the Palestinian-held Gaza Strip, for example, Hamas—a group better known for its suicide bombing campaigns—has launched a television program meant to familiarize children with the Palestinian position on the disputed territories. In between lectures on revered sites such as Nablus and Al Aksa Mosque, the show's host, known as Uncle Hazim, takes on-air phone calls from viewers and talks with animal characters reminiscent of those on *Sesame Street*. Designed with a child-age audience in mind, the show omits all mention of violence and armed conflict in pursuit of Hamas' goals

(Craig Smith 2006b). On a different Palestinian network, an alternative called *Shara's Simsim* is affiliated with the official *Sesame Street* franchise and promotes its core values of optimism and tolerance (Shapiro 2009).

New technologies are changing how we interact with family, friends, and even strangers. Through email, cell phones, texting, and instant messaging, we can maintain close, almost constant, connections with family and friends both near and far. Services such as Facebook and Twitter can expand our worlds, enabling us to establish and extend networks with "friends" both known and unknown (Hampton, Sessions, Her, and Rainie 2009). But new technologies can also lead to narrowcasting, in which we interact mainly with people who are most like ourselves. Social scientist Sherry Turkle (2011) argues that such technologies detract from even our more intimate relationships, which require concentrated time together to flourish.

SOCTHINK

Among tablet and smartphone owners, 57 percent check email while watching TV and 44 percent visit social network sites. They also download applications, check sports scores, look up information related to the program they are watching, and more (Nielsen 2012b). What are possible effects, both positive and negative, of such multitasking?

Telephones and Cell Phones by Country (rates per 100 people)

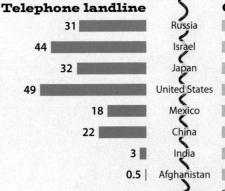
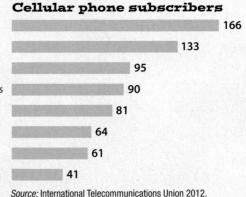

Telephone landline

31	Russia
44	Israel
32	Japan
49	United States
18	Mexico
22	China
3	India
0.5	Afghanistan

Cellular phone subscribers

Russia	166
Israel	133
Japan	95
United States	90
Mexico	81
China	64
India	61
Afghanistan	41

Source: International Telecommunications Union 2012.

In a similar vein, Nicholas Carr (2010) suggests that the Internet is making us shallow, arguing that even though we have access to more information, we are not sufficiently attentive to ideas or to one another.

Around the world, including Africa and other developing areas, people have been socialized into relying on new communications technologies. For instance, not long ago, if Zadhe Iyombe wanted to talk to his mother, he had to make an eight-day trip from the capital city of Kinshasa (in the Democratic Republic of the Congo) up the Congo River by boat to the rural town where he was born. Now both he and his mother have access to a cell phone, and they send text messages to each other daily. And Iyombe and his mother are not atypical. Although cell phones aren't cheap, 3.2 billion owners in developing countries have come to consider them a necessity. Today, there are more than twice as many cell phones in developing countries as there are in industrial nations—the first time in history that developing countries have outpaced the developed world in the adoption of a telecommunications technology (International Telecommunications Union 2010; K. Sullivan 2006).

Access to media can also increase social cohesion by presenting a common, more or less standardized view of culture through mass communication. Sociologist Robert Park (1922) studied how newspapers helped immigrants to the United States adjust to their environment by changing their customary habits and teaching them the values and views of people in their new home country. Unquestionably, the mass media play a significant role in providing a collective experience for members of society. Think about how the mass media bring together members of a community or even a nation by broadcasting important events and ceremonies (such as inaugurations, press conferences, parades, state funerals, and the Olympics) and by covering disasters.

Which media outlets did people turn to in the aftermath of

Did You Know?

The National Day of Unplugging is an annual event encouraging people to take a 24-hour break from the "relentless deluge of technology and information" by shutting down their computers and turning off their cell phones. Participants are urged to use the time they gain to connect with loved ones, get outside, nurture their health, find silence, and give back.

Child Care Arrangements for Preschoolers

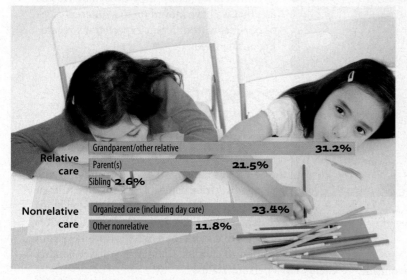

Relative care		
Grandparent/other relative		31.2%
Parent(s)		21.5%
Sibling	2.6%	

Nonrelative care		
Organized care (including day care)		23.4%
Other nonrelative	11.8%	

Note: Organized care includes day care, Head Start, preschool, and school.

Source: U.S. Census Bureau 2011g:Table 1B.

the September 11, 2001, terrorist attacks? Television and telephone were the primary means by which people in the United States bonded. But the Internet also played a prominent role. About half of all Internet users—more than 53 million people—received some kind of news about the attacks online. Nearly three-fourths of Internet users communicated via email to show their patriotism, discuss events with their families, or reconnect with old friends. More than a third of Internet users read or posted material in online forums. In the first 30 days alone, the Library of Congress collected from one Internet site more than half a million pages having to do with the terrorist attacks. As a library director noted, "The Internet has become for many the public commons, a place where they can come together and talk" (D. L. Miller and Darlington 2002; Mirapaul 2001:E2; Rainie 2001).

THE WORKPLACE

Learning to behave appropriately in an occupation is a fundamental aspect of human socialization. In the United States, working full-time confirms adult status; it indicates that one has passed out of adolescence. In a sense, socialization into an occupation can represent both a harsh reality ("I have to work in order to buy food and pay the rent") and the realization of an ambition ("I've always wanted to be an airline pilot") (W. Moore 1968:862; Simmons 2009).

It used to be that our work life began with the end of our formal schooling, but that is no longer necessarily the case, at least not in the United States. More and more young people work today, and not just for a parent or relative. Adolescents generally seek jobs to earn spending money; 80 percent of high school seniors say that little or none of

what they earn goes to family expenses. These teens rarely look on their employment as a means of exploring vocational interests or getting on-the-job training (Hirschman and Voloshin 2007).

Some observers believe that the increasing number of teenagers who are working earlier in life and for longer hours are finding the workplace to be almost as important an agent of socialization as school. In fact, a number of educators complain that time spent at work is adversely affecting students' schoolwork. The level of teenage employment in the United States is the highest among industrial countries, which may provide one explanation for why U.S. high school students lag behind those in other countries on international achievement tests.

Socialization in the workplace changes when it involves a more permanent shift from an after-school job to full-time employment. Occupational socialization can be most intense during the transition from school to job, but it continues throughout one's work history. Technological advances and corporate reorganization may alter the requirements of the position and necessitate new training. According to the Bureau of Labor Statistics (2008b), between the ages of 18 and 42 alone, the typical person holds 11 different jobs. We can no longer assume that we will have a job-for-life, so whether by choice or by necessity, we must be open to ongoing occupational socialization.

RELIGION AND THE STATE

Increasingly, social scientists are recognizing the growing importance of government ("the state") and the continued significance of religion as agents of socialization. Traditionally, family members served as the primary caregivers in U.S. culture, but in the 20th century, the family's

Leh Village, India schoolchildren.

Although many 18-year-olds choose not to vote, voter turnout in the 2008 presidential election was the highest it had been in decades, causing long lines at some polling stations.

strict rites of passage—most 18-year-olds choose not to vote, and most people choose their age of retirement without reference to government dictates—they do symbolize the fact that we have moved on to a different stage of our life, with different expectations regarding our behavior.

>> Socialization Throughout the Life Course

Adolescents among the Kota people of the Congo in Africa paint themselves blue. Cuban American girls go on a day-long religious retreat before dancing the night away. These are both **rites of passage**—rituals that mark the symbolic transition from one social position to another, dramatizing and validating changes in a person's status.

In the Kota rite the color blue—the color of death—symbolizes the death of childhood and the passage to adulthood. For adolescent girls in Miami's Cuban American

Body painting is a ritual marking the passage to puberty in some cultures.

protective function was steadily transferred to outside agencies such as public schools, hospitals, mental health clinics, and child care centers, many of which are run by the state. Historically, religious groups also provided such care and protection. Despite early sociological predictions that religion would cease to play a substantial role in modern society, these groups continue to play a significant role in identity formation and collective life (Warner 2005).

rite of passage A ritual marking the symbolic transition from one social position to another.

Preschool children in particular are often cared for by someone other than a parent. Ninety-one percent of employed mothers depend on others to care for their children, and 37 percent of mothers who aren't employed have regular care arrangements. More than a third of children under age five are cared for by nonrelatives in nursery schools, Head Start programs, day care centers, family day care, and other providers. Children this age are also more likely to be cared for on a daily basis by grandparents than by their parents (U.S. Census Bureau 2011g:Table 1B).

Both government and organized religion act to provide markers representing significant life course transitions. For example, religious organizations continue to celebrate meaningful ritual events—such as baptism, bismillah, or bar/bat mitzvah—that often bring together all the members of an extended family, even if they never meet for any other reason. Government regulations stipulate the ages at which a person may drive a car, drink alcohol, vote in elections, marry without parental permission, work overtime, and retire. Although these regulations do not constitute

—SOCTHINK—
Should government play a larger role in socializing children by funding public education for all children starting at the age of two?

Milestones in the Transition to Adulthood

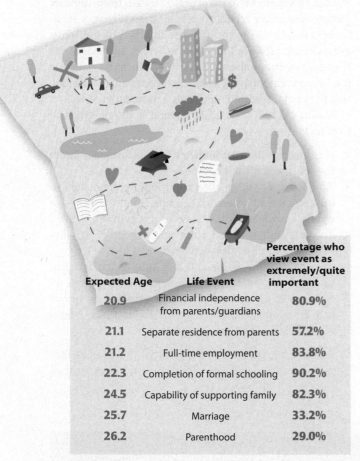

Expected Age	Life Event	Percentage who view event as extremely/quite important
20.9	Financial independence from parents/guardians	80.9%
21.1	Separate residence from parents	57.2%
21.2	Full-time employment	83.8%
22.3	Completion of formal schooling	90.2%
24.5	Capability of supporting family	82.3%
25.7	Marriage	33.2%
26.2	Parenthood	29.0%

Source: T. Smith 2004.

community, the *quinceañera* ceremony celebrating the attainment of womanhood at age 15 supports a network of party planners, caterers, dress designers, and the Miss Quinceañera Latina pageant. For thousands of years, Egyptian mothers have welcomed their newborns to the world in the Soboa ceremony by stepping over the seven-day-old infant seven times. And Naval Academy seniors celebrate their graduation from college by hurling their hats skyward.

THE LIFE COURSE

Such specific ceremonies mark stages of development in the life course. They indicate that the process of socialization continues through all stages of the life cycle. In fact, some researchers have chosen to concentrate on socialization as a lifelong process. Sociologists and other social scientists who take such a **life course approach** look closely at the social factors, including gender and income, that influence people throughout their lives, from birth to death. They recognize that biological changes help mold but do not dictate human behavior.

In the transition from childhood to adulthood, we can identify certain markers that signify the passage from one life stage to the next. These milestones vary from one society and even one generation to the next. In the United States, according to one national survey, completion of formal schooling has risen to the top, with 90 percent of people identifying it as an important rite of passage. On average, Americans expect this milestone to be attained by a person's 23rd birthday. Other major events in the life course, such as getting married or becoming a parent, are expected to follow three or four years later. Interestingly, the significance of these markers has declined, with only about one-third of survey respondents identifying marriage and less than one-third identifying parenthood as important milestones representing adulthood (Furstenberg 2010; T. Smith 2004).

One result of these staggered steps to independence is that in the United States, unlike some other societies, no clear dividing line exists between adolescence and adulthood. Nowadays, the number of years between childhood and adulthood has grown, and few young people finish school, get married, and leave home at about the same age, clearly establishing their transition to adulthood. The term *youthhood* has been coined to describe the prolonged ambiguous status that young people in their 20s experience (Côté 2000).

> **life course approach** A research orientation in which sociologists and other social scientists look closely at the social factors that influence people throughout their lives, from birth to death.
>
> **anticipatory socialization** Processes of socialization in which a person "rehearses" for future positions, occupations, and social relationships.

SOC THINK

What are some of the markers of youthhood? When does it begin? When does it end? To what extent do you feel like an adult (regardless of your age)? What characteristics of our society contribute to ambiguity in our passage into adulthood?

ANTICIPATORY SOCIALIZATION AND RESOCIALIZATION

In our journey through our lives, we seek to prepare ourselves for what is coming and to adapt to change as necessary. To prepare, we undergo **anticipatory socialization**, which refers to processes of socialization in which a person "rehearses" for future positions, occupations, and social relationships. A culture can function more efficiently and smoothly if members become acquainted with the norms, values, and behavior associated with a social position before actually assuming that status. Preparation for many aspects of adult life begins with anticipatory socialization during childhood and adolescence and continues throughout our lives as we prepare for new responsibilities (Levine and Hoffner 2006).

High school students experience a bit of anticipatory socialization when they prepare for college. They begin to imagine what college life will be like and what kind of person they will be when they get there. They may seek out information from friends and family to get a better sense of what to expect, but increasingly, they also rely on campus websites and Facebook entries. To assist in this process and to attract more students, colleges are investing more time and money in websites through which students can take "virtual" campus tours, listen to podcasts, and stream videos of everything from the school song to a sample zoology lecture.

Occasionally, assuming a new social or occupational position requires that we *unlearn* an established orientation. **Resocialization** refers to the process of discarding old behavior patterns and accepting new ones as part of a life transition. Often resocialization results from explicit efforts to transform an individual, as happens in reform schools, therapy groups, prisons, religious conversion settings, and political indoctrination camps. The process of resocialization typically involves considerable stress for the individual—much more so than socialization in general, or even anticipatory socialization (Hart, Miller, and Johnson 2003).

resocialization The process of discarding former behavior patterns and accepting new ones as part of a transition in one's life.

total institution An institution that regulates all aspects of a person's life under a single authority, such as a prison, the military, a mental hospital, or a convent.

Resocialization is particularly effective when it occurs within a total institution. Erving Goffman (1961) coined the term **total institution** to refer to an institution that regulates all aspects of a person's life under a single authority. Examples can be more or less extreme, from summer camp or boarding school to prison, the military, a mental hospital, or a convent. Because the total institution is generally cut off from the rest of society, it provides for all the needs of its members. In its extreme form, so elaborate are its requirements, and so all-encompassing its activities, that the total institution represents a miniature society.

Goffman (1961) identified several common traits of total institutions:

- All aspects of life are conducted in the same place under the control of a single authority.
- Any activities within the institution are conducted in the company of others in the same circumstances—for example, army recruits or novices in a convent.
- The authorities devise rules and schedule activities without consulting the participants.
- All aspects of life within a total institution are designed to fulfill the purpose of the organization. Thus, all activities in a monastery might be centered on prayer and communion with God (Malacrida 2005; Mapel 2007; Williams and Warren 2009).

People often lose their individuality within total institutions. For example, a person entering prison may experience

Life in prison is highly regulated—even recreation time.

SOCTHINK

To what extent is summer camp, a cruise, or even life at a residential college similar to a total institution? In what ways is it different?

the humiliation of a **degradation ceremony** as he or she is stripped of clothing, jewelry, and other personal possessions. From that point on, scheduled daily routines allow for little or no personal initiative. The individual becomes secondary and rather invisible in the overbearing social environment (Garfinkel 1956).

ROLE TRANSITIONS DURING THE LIFE COURSE

As we have seen, one of the key transitional stages we pass through occurs as we enter the adult world, perhaps by moving out of the parental home, beginning a career, or entering a marriage. As we age we move into the midlife transition, which typically begins at about age 40. Men and women often experience a stressful period of self-evaluation, commonly known as the **midlife crisis**, in which they realize that they have not achieved basic goals and ambitions and may feel they have little time left to do so. This conflict between their hopes and their outcomes causes strain. Compounding such stresses that are often associated with one's career or partner is the growing responsibility for caring for two generations at once (Mortimer and Shanahan 2006; Wethington 2000).

During the late 1990s, social scientists began focusing on the **sandwich generation**—adults who simultaneously try to meet the competing needs of their parents and their children. Their caregiving goes in two directions:

to children, who even as young adults may still require significant support and direction; and to aging parents, whose health and economic problems may demand intervention by their adult children.

Like the role of caring for children, that of caring for aging parents falls disproportionately on women. Overall, women provide 60 percent of the care their parents receive, and even more as the demands of the role grow more intense and time consuming. Increasingly, middle-aged women and younger are finding themselves on the "daughter track," as their time and attention are diverted by the needs of their aging mothers and fathers (Gross 2005; Taylor et al. 2009).

degradation ceremony An aspect of the socialization process within some total institutions, in which people are subjected to humiliating rituals.

midlife crisis A stressful period of self-evaluation that begins at about age 40.

sandwich generation The generation of adults who simultaneously try to meet the competing needs of their parents and their children.

>>Aging and Society

Due to advances in areas such as health care, nutrition, and working conditions, life expectancy has risen significantly both in the United States and around the world. Someone born in 1900 in the United States had an average life expectancy of 47 years, but babies born in the U.S. in 2007 can anticipate living to 75 if they're boys and 80 if they're girls (National Center for Health Statistics 2011: Table 22). Globally, life expectancy in more developed nations is 78 years compared to 59 years in least developed nations (Population Reference Bureau 2011:10).

How societies deal with their elderly population varies significantly across cultures. One society may treat older people with reverence, whereas another sees them as unproductive and "difficult." The Sherpas—a Tibetan-speaking Buddhist people in Nepal—live in a culture that idealizes old age. Almost all elderly members of the Sherpa culture (picture above) own their homes, and most are in relatively good physical condition. Typically, older Sherpas value their independence and prefer not to live with their children. Among the Fulani of Africa, however, older men and women move to the edge of

5 Movies

SOCIALIZATION on

An Education
A middle-class British schoolgirl and her family are seduced by a slick older man.

Bully
The true story of the tragic costs of peer group intimidation.

Children Underground
Documentary about children surviving in the subway systems of Romania.

Half Nelson
A young teacher in Brooklyn struggles in and out of the classroom.

Training Day
A day in the life of a rookie narcotics officer in the LAPD.

Aging Around the world

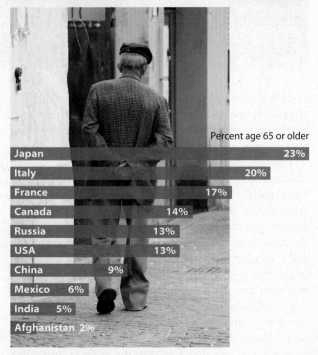

	Percent age 65 or older
Japan	23%
Italy	20%
France	17%
Canada	14%
Russia	13%
USA	13%
China	9%
Mexico	6%
India	5%
Afghanistan	2%

Source: Population Reference Bureau 2011.

the family homestead. Since that is where people are buried, the elderly sleep over their own graves, for they are viewed socially as already dead (Goldstein and Beall 1981; Stenning 1958; Tonkinson 1978).

Understandably, all societies have some system of age stratification that associates certain social roles with distinct periods in life. Some of this age differentiation seems inevitable; it would make little sense to send young children off to war or to expect older citizens to handle physically demanding tasks, such as loading freight at shipyards.

In the United States, the proportion of the population that was 65 and older grew from 4.1 percent in 1900 to 13.0 percent in 2010; it is expected to rise to approximately 20 percent by 2050 (Howden and Meyer 2011). These rates vary by race and ethnicity. In 2010, 16.1 percent of non-Hispanic Whites were older than 65, compared to 8.6 percent of African Americans, 9.2 percent of Asian Americans, and 5.7 percent of Hispanics. In part, these differences reflect the shorter life spans of the latter groups. They also stem from immigration patterns among Asians and Hispanics, who tend to be young when they enter the country (U.S. Census Bureau 2011h: Table 12).

The aging pattern in the United States also varies by state. Whereas Florida leads the country with 17.3 percent of its population over 65, Alaska comes in with the lowest U.S. rate

at 7.7 percent. As of 2010, the top five states with the highest proportion of older people included Florida, West Virginia, Maine, Pennsylvania, and Iowa (Howden and Meyer 2011). As a result of these trends, the development of retirement communities, along with various other amenities geared toward senior citizens, is particularly common in these states.

ADJUSTING TO RETIREMENT

Making the role transition into retirement can be a difficult process. Retirement is a rite of passage that typically marks a transition out of active participation in the full-time labor market. Symbolic events are associated with this rite of passage, such as retirement gifts, a retirement party, and special moments on the last day on the job. The pre-retirement period itself can be emotionally charged, especially if the retiree is expected to train his or her successor (Reitzes and Mutran 2004).

Gerontologist Robert Atchley (1976) has identified several phases of the retirement experience:

- *Preretirement,* a period of anticipatory socialization as the person prepares for retirement.

Actual and Projected Growth of the Elderly Population of the United States

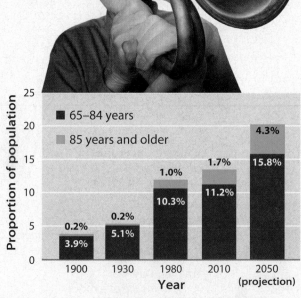

	65–84 years	85 years and older
1900	3.9%	0.2%
1930	5.1%	0.2%
1980	10.3%	1.0%
2010	11.2%	1.7%
2050 (projection)	15.8%	4.3%

Source: He et al. 2005:9; U.S. Census Bureau 2008g:Table 1 Werner 2011.

"Good news, honey—seventy is the new fifty."

- *The near phase,* when the person establishes a specific departure date from his or her job.
- *The honeymoon phase,* an often euphoric period in which the person pursues activities that he or she never had time for before.
- *The disenchantment phase,* in which retirees feel a sense of letdown or even depression as they cope with their new lives, which may include illness or poverty.
- *The reorientation phase,* which involves the development of a more realistic view of retirement alternatives.
- *The stability phase,* in which the person has learned to deal with life after retirement in a reasonable and comfortable fashion.
- *The termination phase,* which begins when the person can no longer engage in basic, day-to-day activities such as self-care and housework.

Retirement is not a single transition, then, but a series of adjustments that varies from one person to another. The length and timing of each phase will differ for each individual, depending on such factors as financial and health status. In fact, a person will not necessarily go through all the phases identified by Atchley. For example, people who are forced to retire or who face financial difficulties may never experience a honeymoon phase. And many retirees continue to be part of the paid labor force of the United States, often taking part-time jobs to supplement their pensions, either because they want to or because they need to.

>>Perspectives on Aging

Aging is an important aspect of socialization throughout the life course. The particular problems of the elderly have become the focus of a specialized field of research and inquiry known as **gerontology**—the study of the sociological and psychological aspects of aging and the problems of the aged. It originated in the 1930s, as an increasing number of social scientists became aware of the plight of the elderly.

Gerontologists rely heavily on sociological principles and theories to explain the effects of aging on the individual and society. They also draw on psychology, anthropology, physical education, counseling, and medicine in their study of the aging process. Three perspectives on aging—disengagement theory, activity theory, and age discrimination—arise out of these studies.

SOCTHINK

What age do you think counts as getting "old"? What factors influence our conception of what counts as old?

DISENGAGEMENT THEORY

After studying elderly people in good health and relatively comfortable economic circumstances, Elaine Cumming and William Henry (1961) introduced their **disengagement theory**, which implicitly suggests that society and the aging individual mutually sever many of their relationships. Highlighting the significance of social order in society, disengagement theory emphasizes that passing social roles on from one generation to another ensures social stability.

According to this theory, the approach of death forces people to drop most of their social roles—including those of worker, volunteer, spouse, hobby enthusiast, and even reader. Younger members of society then take on these functions. The aging person, it is held, withdraws into an increasing state of inactivity while preparing for death. At the same time, society withdraws from the elderly by segregating them residentially (in retirement homes and communities), educationally (in programs

> **gerontology** The study of the sociological and psychological aspects of aging and the problems of the aged.
>
> **disengagement theory** A theory of aging that suggests that society and the aging individual mutually sever many of their relationships.

designed solely for senior citizens), and recreationally (in senior citizens' centers). Implicit in disengagement theory is the view that society should help older people to withdraw from their accustomed social roles.

Since it was first outlined more than five decades ago, disengagement theory has generated considerable controversy. Some gerontologists have objected to the implication that older people want to be ignored and put away—and even more to the idea that they should be encouraged to withdraw from meaningful social roles. Critics of disengagement theory insist that society forces the elderly into an involuntary and painful withdrawal from the paid labor force and from meaningful social relationships. Rather than voluntarily seeking to disengage, older employees find themselves pushed out of their jobs—in many instances, even before they are entitled to maximum retirement benefits (Boaz 1987).

ACTIVITY THEORY

How important is it for older people to stay actively involved, whether at a job or in other pursuits? A tragic disaster in Chicago in 1995 showed that it can be a matter of life and death. An intense heat wave lasting more than a week—with a heat index exceeding 115 degrees on two consecutive days—resulted in 733 heat-related deaths. About three-fourths of the deceased were 65 or older. Subsequent analysis showed that older people who lived alone had the highest risk of dying, suggesting that support networks for the elderly literally help to save lives. Older Hispanics and Asian Americans had lower death rates from the heat wave than other racial and ethnic groups. Their stronger social networks probably resulted in more regular contact with family members and friends (Klinenberg 2002; Schaefer 1998a).

5 Movies on AGING

Gran Torino
A widowed veteran confronts gang violence in his neighborhood.

Up
A cranky old man and a young boy embark on an unusual adventure.

Harold and Maude
Not your average couple.

Crazy Heart
Life takes a country music singer down paths he never saw coming.

The Bucket List
Two men confront death by ticking off items on their to-do list.

Rising Labor Force Participation Rates Among the Elderly

Often seen as the opposite of disengagement theory, **activity theory** suggests that those elderly people who remain active and socially involved will have an improved quality of life. Proponents of this perspective acknowledge that a 70-year-old person may not have the ability or desire to perform various social roles that he or she had at age 40. Yet they contend that old people have essentially the same need for social interaction as any other group.

The improved health of older people—sometimes overlooked by social scientists—has strengthened the arguments of activity theorists. Illness and chronic disease are no longer quite the scourge of the elderly that they once were. The recent emphasis on fitness, the availability of better medical care, greater control of infectious diseases, and the reduction in the number of fatal strokes and heart attacks have combined to reduce the traumas of growing old.

Accumulating medical research also points to the importance of remaining socially involved. Among those who decline in their mental capacities later in life, deterioration is most rapid in those who withdraw from social relationships and activities. Fortunately, the aged are finding new ways to remain socially

Percentage change in labor force participation rates since 1994

65–69 years		70–74 years		75 years and older	
Men 28%	Women 43.6%	34.2%	60.9%	11.6%	37.1%

Source: Gendell 2008:47.

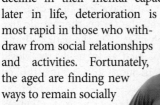

In 2002, the Senate Special Committee on Aging convened a panel on the media's portrayal of older people and sharply criticized media and marketing executives for bombarding audiences with negative images of the aged. How many characters on top TV shows today can you think of who are over 65? How does that compare to the number of characters you can think of who are under 30?

engaged, as evidenced by their increasing use of the Internet, especially to keep in touch with family and friends (Taylor et al. 2009; Williams et al. 2010).

> **activity theory** A theory of aging that suggests that those elderly people who remain active and socially involved will have an improved quality of life.

Admittedly, many activities open to the elderly involve unpaid labor, for which younger adults may receive salaries. Unpaid elderly workers include hospital volunteers (versus aides and orderlies), drivers for charities such as the Red Cross (versus chauffeurs), tutors (in contrast to teachers), and craftspeople for charity bazaars (in contrast to carpenters and dressmakers). However, some companies have recently begun programs to hire retirees for full- or part-time work.

Continued engagement in the workforce has been a growing trend. In 2009, 26 percent of those aged 65–74 worked full- or part-time. Of those who consider themselves retired but who continue to work, almost 70 percent say they do so primarily because they want to, not because they need to for financial reasons. In fact, the percentage of those who choose to work after what we conventionally think of as retirement age continues to rise, even among the oldest in the population (Gendell 2008; Taylor et al. 2009:91). Though many continue to work into old age for social engagement, those who must do so for financial reasons often find their workforce experience to be a challenge.

AGEISM AND DISCRIMINATION

Physician Robert Butler (1990) became concerned 30 years ago when he learned that a housing development near his home in metropolitan Washington, D.C., barred the elderly.

Butler coined the term **ageism** to refer to prejudice and discrimination based on a person's age. For example, we may choose to assume that someone cannot handle a rigorous job because he is "too old," or we may refuse to give someone a job with authority because she is "too young."

To more fully understand issues regarding aging, we must also consider the impact of social structure on patterns of aging. Critics argue that neither disengagement nor activity theory answers the question of *why* social interaction must change or decrease in old age. The low status of older people is seen in prejudice and discrimination against them, in age segregation, and in unfair job practices—none of which are directly addressed by either disengagement or activity theory.

Although firing people simply because they are old violates federal law, courts have upheld the right to lay off older workers for economic reasons. Critics contend that, later, the same firms hire young, cheaper workers to replace experienced older workers. When economic growth slows and companies cut back on their workforces, the number of complaints of age bias rises sharply as older workers begin to suspect they were bearing a disproportionate share of the layoffs. According to the Equal Employment Opportunity Commission, between 2000 and 2010, complaints of age discrimination rose more than 45 percent. However, evidence of a countertrend has emerged. To hang on to experienced workers, some firms have been giving larger raises to older workers, to encourage their retirement at the higher salary—a tactic that prompts younger workers to complain of age discrimination (EEOC 2011; Roscigno 2010).

ageism Prejudice and discrimination based on a person's age.

A controlled experiment conducted by the AARP (formerly known as the American Association of Retired Persons) confirmed that older people often face discrimination when applying for jobs. Comparable résumés for two applicants—one 57 years old and the other 32 years old—were sent to 775 large firms and employment agencies around the United States. In situations for which positions were actually available, the younger applicant received a favorable response 43 percent of the time. By contrast, the older applicant received favorable responses only 17 percent of the time. One Fortune 500 corporation asked the younger applicant for more information while informing the older applicant that no appropriate positions were open (Bendick, Jackson, and Romero 1993; Neumark 2008).

As a group, elderly people in the United States enjoy a standard of living that is much higher now than at any point in the nation's past. Class differences among the elderly remain evident but tend to narrow somewhat.

> First you are young; then you are middle-aged; then you are old; then you are wonderful.
>
> Lady Diana Cooper

Those older people who enjoyed middle-class incomes while younger tend to remain better off after retirement, but less so than before (Smith 2003).

To some extent, older people owe their overall improved standard of living to a greater accumulation of wealth—in the form of home ownership, private pensions, and other financial assets. But much of the improvement is due to more generous Social Security benefits. Although modest when compared with other countries' pension programs, Social Security nevertheless provides 37 percent of all income received by older people in the United States. Still, in 2010, 9 percent of people age 65 or older lived below the poverty line (DeNavas-Walt et al. 2011; Proctor and Smith 2009b; Social Security Administration 2008).

Members of groups who face a greater likelihood of income inequality earlier in their lives, including women and members of racial and ethnic minorities, continue to do so when they are older. For women aged 65 or older, the poverty rate is 10.7 percent compared to the rate for elderly men of 6.7 percent. Considering race and ethnicity, in 2010, the 18 percent poverty rates for both African Americans and Hispanics aged 65 or older was more than twice the 6.8 percent rate for non-Hispanic Whites of the same age (U.S. Census Bureau 2011i: Table Pov01).

DEATH AND DYING

In the film *The Bucket List,* Morgan Freeman and Jack Nicholson play the two main characters who are diagnosed with terminal cancer and have less than one year to live. They make a list of all the things they would like to do before they "kick the bucket." On the list are things they had never dared to do, such as traveling the world and skydiving, but it also includes reconciling broken relationships.

Until recently, death was a taboo topic in the United States. Death represents a fundamental disruption that cannot be undone, so we often find it easier to live with a sense of denial about our mortality. In the words of sociologist Peter Berger, "Death presents society with a formidable problem . . . because it threatens the basic assumptions of order on which society rests" (1969:23). However, psychologist Elisabeth Kübler-Ross (1969), through her pioneering book *On Death and Dying,* greatly encouraged open discussion of the process of dying. Drawing on her work with 200 cancer patients, Kübler-Ross identified five stages of the experience: denial, anger, bargaining, depression, and finally acceptance.

Although we may still be uncomfortable with the topic, *The Bucket List*'s portrayal of a "good death" represents one of the ways we have become more open about it. Gerontologist Richard Kalish (1985) laid out some of the issues people must face to prepare for a "good death." These included completing unfinished business, such as settling insurance and inheritance matters; restoring harmony to social relationships and saying farewell to friends and family; dealing with medical needs; and making funeral plans and other arrangements for survivors. In accomplishing these tasks, the dying person actively contributes to smooth intergenerational transitions, role continuity, compliance with medical procedures, and minimal disruption of the social system, despite the loss of a loved one.

We have also begun to create institutions to facilitate our wishes for a good death. The practice of **hospice care**, introduced in England in the 1960s, is devoted to easing this final transition. Hospice workers seek to improve the quality of a dying person's last days by offering comfort and by helping the person to remain at home, or in a homelike setting at a hospital or other special facility, until the end. Currently, more than 5,100 hospice programs serve almost 1.6 million people a year (NHPCO 2012).

Recent studies in the United States suggest additional ways in which people have broken through the historical taboos about death. For example, bereavement practices—once highly structured—are becoming increasingly varied and therapeutic. More and more people are actively addressing the inevitability of death by making wills, establishing "living wills" (health care proxies that explain their feelings about the use of life support equipment), donating organs, and providing instructions for family members about funerals, cremations, and burials. Given medical and technological advances and increasingly open discussion and negotiation regarding death and dying, it is possible that good deaths may become a social norm in the United States (Pew Research Center 2006).

We encounter some of the most difficult socialization challenges (and rites of passage) in these later years of life.

Retirement undermines the sense of self we had that was based in our occupation, a particularly significant source of identity in the United States. Similarly, taking stock of our accomplishments and disappointments, coping with declining physical abilities, and recognizing the inevitability of death may lead to painful adjustments. Part of the difficulty is that potential answers to the "Now what?" question that we might have asked in previous life stages are dwindling, and we begin to face the end of our days.

> **hospice care** Treatment of the terminally ill in their own homes, or in special hospital units or other facilities, with the goal of helping them to die comfortably, without pain.

And yet, as we reflect on the story of our lives, we can look back to see all the people who shaped us into becoming who we are. Such relationships play a crucial role in our overall self-concept and self-satisfaction. As we have already seen, we are interdependent. And, though the influences of others on our life can be both a blessing and a curse, we wouldn't be who we are without them.

Stop! Go on a "technology fast," and give up email, blogs, Facebook, Twitter, texting, computers, and even your cell phone for a day. Keep a journal of how you respond.

get involved!

For REVIEW

I. **How do we become our self?**
- We are born with innate tendencies, but we depend on the socializing influences of others with whom we interact to provide us with the cultural tools necessary for our survival.

II. **Who shapes our socialization?**
- Although almost anyone with whom we interact can have a significant influence on us, particularly important to our development are the family, school, peer group, mass media, religion, and the state.

III. **How does our development change over time?**
- We learn new things at various stages of our life course, experiencing significant transitions as we pass from childhood to adulthood and again from adulthood into retirement. At each stage, the kinds of things expected of us by others shift significantly.

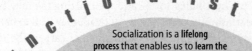

Functionalist View

Socialization is a **lifelong process** that enables us to **learn the attitudes, values, and behaviors** appropriate for our culture.

Socialization promotes **integration** and **intimacy** with others and keeps us from being isolated.

The institutions of the family, school, mass media, workplace, government, and religion act as **agents of socialization** from childhood through adulthood.

INTEGRATION, AGENTS OF SOCIALIZATION
KEY CONCEPTS

Conflict View

We learn to accept a culture's dominant ideology as natural, which **reinforces existing inequalities.**

Alternative perspectives and experiences are often underrepresented and devalued.

Schools help reproduce the status quo in the way they socialize students into the proper attitudes and behaviors of the workplace.

KEY CONCEPTS
GENDER AND RACE, INEQUALITY

MAKE THE CONNECTION

After reviewing the chapter, answer the following questions:

Interactionist View

Our **concept of the self,** who we are, emerges from our interactions with others.

Parents, friends, co-workers, coaches, teachers are among the **significant others** who play a major role in socialization and shaping a person's self.

Role taking, impression management, and face-work are concepts that convey the idea of social interactions as **performances.**

KEY CONCEPTS
CONCEPT OF SELF, PERFORMANCE

1

How would each perspective describe the impact that extreme isolation has on people (p. 73)?

2

How would each perspective explain the role socialization performs among children (pp. 75-78)?

3

How would a functionalist look at anticipatory socialization (p. 81)? How might this view differ from a conflict approach (p. 90)?

4

Which agents of socialization have been most influential in your life? How does each perspective help shed light on those influences?

Pop Quiz

1. **The nurture side of the nature–nurture debate argues that**
   a. socialization plays a critical role in shaping our attitudes, values, and behaviors.
   b. our attitudes, values, and behaviors are largely inherited biologically through our DNA.
   c. sociology has a limited role in explaining our behaviors before age two.
   d. we cannot determine the degree to which our behaviors are shaped by heredity or environment.

2. **According to Charles Horton Cooley, the process of developing a self-identity by imagining how others see us is known as**
   a. socialization.
   b. the looking-glass self.
   c. the Me.
   d. the generalized other.

3. **In George Herbert Mead's *play stage* of socialization, people mentally assume the perspectives of others, thereby enabling them to respond from that imagined viewpoint. This process is referred to as**
   a. symbolization.
   b. the significant other.
   c. impression management.
   d. role taking.

4. **Suppose a clerk tries to appear busier than he or she actually is when a supervisor happens to be watching. Erving Goffman would say this is a form of what?**
   a. degradation ceremony
   b. impression management
   c. resocialization
   d. looking-glass self

5. **Which social institution is considered to be the most important agent of socialization in the United States, especially for children?**
   a. family
   b. school
   c. peer group
   d. mass media

6. **The term *gender role* refers to**
   a. the biological fact that we are male or female.
   b. a role that is given to us by a teacher.
   c. a role that is given to us in a play.
   d. expectations regarding the proper behavior, attitudes, and activities of males and females.

7. **On the first day of basic training in the army, a male recruit has his civilian clothes replaced with army "greens," has his hair shaved off, loses his privacy, and finds that he must use a communal bathroom. All these humiliating activities are part of**
   a. becoming a significant other.
   b. impression management.
   c. a degradation ceremony.
   d. face-work.

8. **What do sociologists call the symbolic representations of major change in a person's status throughout their life course?**
   a. rites of passage
   b. anticipatory socialization
   c. impression management
   d. role taking

9. **The process of discarding former behavior patterns and taking on new ones is known as what?**
   a. resocialization
   b. impression management
   c. anticipatory socialization
   d. the I

10. **Which theory argues that elderly people have essentially the same need for social interaction as any other group and that those who remain active and socially involved will be best adjusted?**
    a. disengagement theory
    b. institutional discrimination theory
    c. activity theory
    d. ageism theory

1. (a); 2. (b); 3. (d); 4. (b); 5. (a); 6. (d); 7. (c); 8. (a); 9. (a); 10. (c)

5

SOCIAL

WINNING AND LOSING

Life is a like a game. Saying so has become something of a cliché, the kind of thing that appears on greeting cards and motivational posters, usually followed by some inspirational comments about how one should play. And yet, sociologically speaking, paying attention to how games operate can help us to better understand what happens in our lives and why.

In the United States, players in most games start with the same basic chances—equal numbers of cards, identical amounts of cash, or the same space on the board. Card shuffling or dice throwing introduce randomness that could tilt the odds, but the presupposition is that winners and losers are determined more by skill than by anything else. In some games, however, the structure of the game shapes likely outcomes. One example is the traditional Chinese card game Zheng Shangyou (争上游), meaning "struggling upstream." Many variations of this game exist, including Dai Hin Min (大貧民) in Japan and Tiên Lên in Vietnam. In the United States, adaptations include Kings and Servants, the Great Dalmuti, President, and Scum.

What makes such games distinctive is that the position each player occupies conveys advantages or disadvantages. In one version, positions include king, queen, jack, merchant, peasant, and servant. After all the cards have been dealt, the servant gives the king his or her best three cards, receiving the king's three worst cards in return. The peasant and queen similarly exchange two cards and the merchant and jack exchange one. Play then commences with people seeking to get rid of their cards by laying higher cards than those played by the person with the lead. At the end of each hand, after all the cards have been played, players change seats: the first person to go out, having played all his or her cards, becomes the new king, continuing until the last one out becomes the new servant. Because of the card exchanges, people at the top tend to stay at the top and vice versa.

As a player at the top, you can easily feel good about yourself and chalk your success up to skill. As a player at the bottom, you can get discouraged, doubt your skill, and resent the unfair advantages of those at the top. There's nothing like having to give up two aces and a king only to receive worthless cards in return to make transparent the consequences of the game's unequal structure.

The choices we make do not occur in a vacuum. What these games suggest for those at the bottom is that, even if you play your cards right, you can still lose. In these games, as in life, our structural positions shape the options and opportunities available to us.

& STRUCTURE INTERACTION

As You READ

>>

- What makes up society?
- How does social structure shape individual action?
- How do sociologists describe traditional versus modern societies?

>>Social Interaction

Whether we are working together to construct culture or learning from each other through socialization, we do so via **social interaction,** a reciprocal exchange in which two or more people read, react, and respond to each other. Through this process we come to know what is expected of us. When parents discipline us or teachers praise us, we use those punishments and rewards to better inform how we might act in the future. The choices we make create patterns of behavior over time; thus our everyday interactions form the building blocks of society.

social interaction A reciprocal exchange in which two or more people read, react, and respond to each other.

SELF AND SOCIETY

We come to be who we are through the daily interactions we have with others—whether going to class, working on the job, or driving in traffic. We seek to make sense of our interactions as they occur and then respond accordingly. Our self, as we saw in Chapter 4, must be understood as an ongoing project constantly created through our interactions with others rather than as an isolated, singular unchanging object. Society provides the context within which that dynamic process of self-creation occurs. In the words of George Herbert Mead, "Selves can only exist in definite relationships to other selves. No hard-and-fast line can be drawn between our own selves and the selves of others" (1934: 164). This social or relational conception of the self runs counter to the dominant sense of the self in the United States expressed in phrases such as "rugged individualism" or "I did it my way." But even these phrases are collective sentiments learned in the context of U.S. culture.

Over time we develop routine patterns of behavior that we take for granted—sitting at the same desk, having lunch with the same co-workers, traveling the same route. We do the same things and think many of the same thoughts, day after day. And so do others. Eventually such repeated practices can solidify into formal and informal norms, or become institutionalized in the form of laws. The resulting predictability allows us to know what to do most of the time.

In time, the positions we occupy relative to others (such as student, boss, or traffic cop) also solidify, and we develop mutual expectations of how people in such positions should act. As these perceptions are shared with others beyond our immediate sphere of experience, it becomes possible to talk about the positions themselves—and the various relationships between them—apart from the individuals who occupy them. The end result is society—the structure of relationships within which culture is created and shared through regularized patterns of social interaction.

SOCIAL CONSTRUCTION OF REALITY

In working out the relationship between our self and society, we are engaged in the "social construction of reality." Sociologists Peter Berger and Thomas Luckmann (1966) use this phrase to describe the interdependent relationship in which we as individuals create society through our actions and, at the same time, become products of the society we construct. They present their argument in their three-part model of world construction. The three parts include

- *Constructing culture.* Our actions are not strictly determined by biological instincts. To survive, we must establish a relationship to nature and with one another. We do so by creating tools, language, ideas, beliefs, rules for behavior, and so on to establish order and meaning. Culture enables us to make sense of our experiences and to pattern our actions. (See Chapter 3 on culture.)

- *Constructing the self.* We become products of the worlds we create. Anytime we enter into a new social world (for example, at birth, going away to college, the first day at a new job, marriage), we do not begin from scratch. We are shaped by the tools, ideas, and rules for action that have been constructed by others who have gone before us. We learn how we should think and act through our interactions with others, sharing ideas and experiences. Through socialization, we are constrained by the very culture we construct. (See Chapter 4 on socialization.)
- *Constructing society.* Between these first two steps is an intervening stage in which we share the culture we create with others. After it is shared, we lose control over it as individuals. It is no longer something "I" control; it is now in "our" hands. As a result of our shared acceptance, it comes to feel solid, real, or natural, even though we created it in the first place. One way to think of it is as an environment, a social world, or a structure within which we live. We come to take for granted that it simply "is."

In short, the social construction of reality is an ongoing process of constructing the objects, knowledge, and rules for behavior that we come to share collectively. These creations then shape or limit the ideas and actions that are available to us. We then use them to create new culture. The result is predictability and order that are necessary for social interaction and collective action. Through social interaction, we are always creating and being created, producers and products.

The more we share culture with others, the more resistant it becomes to change. The ability to define social reality often reflects a group's power within a society. In fact, one of the crucial aspects of the relationship between dominant and subordinate groups is the ability of the former to set values and norms. Those who wield power and influence in a society are often reluctant to relinquish their positions of control. As a result, it is a struggle to change the meanings attached to the positions people occupy. Since the mid-1900s—starting with the civil rights movement of the 1950s and 1960s and continuing among women, the elderly, gays and lesbians, and people with disabilities—an important aspect of the process of social change has involved redefining or reconstructing social reality.

When members of subordinate groups challenge traditional social assumptions, they can raise our collective awareness about the consequences of group membership or social position and help us to perceive and experience reality in a new way. For example, when Olympic gold medalist Muhammad Ali began his professional boxing career in the early 1960s, he was much like any other young Black fighter. He was managed and sponsored by a White boxing syndicate and went by his given name, Cassius Clay. Soon, however, the young boxer rebelled against the stereotypes of the self-effacing Black athlete and began to define his own social role. He converted to Islam, becoming a member of the U.S.-based Nation of Islam, and abandoned his "slave name" to take the name Muhammad Ali. He insisted on expressing his own political views, including refusing to fight in the Vietnam War. Ali changed the terms of social interaction for Black athletes by rebelling against racist thinking and terminology. In redefining social reality, he helped open up greater opportunities for himself and for other African Americans in the world of sports and beyond.

>>Elements of Social Structure

Although not all sociologists accept the idea that society is a real, external, objective thing, the concepts of society and social structure provide tools useful when trying to make sense of why we act and think the way we do. **Social structure** represents the underlying framework of society consisting of the positions people occupy and the relationships between them. Structure provides order. Its existence appears to transcend the particular individuals who populate it. We take its reality as a given and learn to move into social positions that already exist. Thinking of structure as something like a skeleton that holds us together—or as analogous to the framework of a building—helps us better understand ourselves and others. We can identify the following elements that make up social structure: statuses, social roles, groups, social networks, virtual worlds, and social institutions.

social structure The underlying framework of society consisting of the positions people occupy and the relationships between them.

status The social positions we occupy relative to others.

STATUSES

Status is perhaps the most basic component of social structure. It refers to the social positions we occupy relative to others. Such positions exist independent of the individuals who occupy them. Within our society, a person can occupy the status of student, fruit picker, son or daughter,

Did You Know?

... Muhammad Ali was found guilty of draft evasion and sentenced to five years in prison. In 1967, he refused induction into the Army because of his pacifist religious convictions as a Muslim. Ultimately, the U.S. Supreme Court reversed his draft evasion conviction, and he avoided serving jail time.

Social Statuses

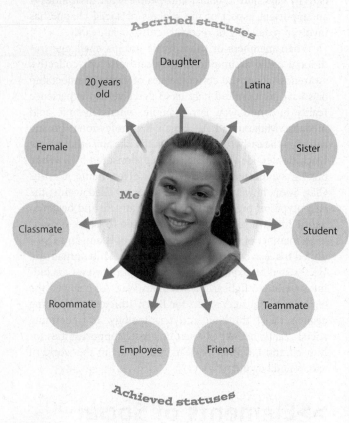

Ascribed statuses

- Daughter
- 20 years old
- Latina
- Female
- Sister
- Me
- Classmate
- Student
- Roommate
- Teammate
- Employee
- Friend

Achieved statuses

violinist, teenager, resident of St. Louis, dental technician, or neighbor. A person can also occupy a number of different statuses at the same time.

Ascribed and Achieved Status

Sociologists categorize statuses as either ascribed or achieved. An **ascribed status** is assigned to a person by society without regard for the person's unique talents or characteristics. Generally, the assignment takes place at birth; thus a person's age, race/ethnicity, and sex are all considered ascribed statuses. Though such characteristics are biological in origin, the key is the social meaning we attach to such categories. Ascribed statuses are often used to justify privileges or reflect a person's membership in a subordinate group, and we will analyze the impacts of race, ethnicity, and gender as ascribed statuses in Chapters 12 and 13.

In most cases, we can do little to change an ascribed status. We can, however, attempt to change the traditional constraints associated with it. For

> **ascribed status** A social position assigned to a person by society without regard for the person's unique talents or characteristics.
>
> **achieved status** A social position that is within our power to change.

example, since its founding in 1971, the activist political group Gray Panthers has worked for the rights of older people and tried to modify society's negative and confining stereotypes of the elderly. As a result of their work and that of other groups supporting older citizens, the ascribed status of "senior citizen" is no longer as difficult for millions of older people.

An ascribed status does not necessarily have the same social meaning in every society. In China, for example, respect for the elderly, known as filial piety, is an important norm. There, in many cases, the prefix "old" is used respectfully: calling someone "old teacher" or "old person" is like calling a judge in the United States "your honor." In countries such as the United States or Britain, which put a premium on youth, the term "old man" is often more of an insult than a celebration of seniority and wisdom (Huang 1988; Kline and Zhang 2009; Laidlaw et al. 2010).

Unlike ascribed statuses, an **achieved status** is a social position we have earned as a consequence of something we have done. Those accomplishments can be either positive or negative. For example, pianist, college student, sorority member, and lawyer are all achieved statuses. Each is attained by taking actions necessary for their accomplishment—practicing, going to school, pledging, and getting a law degree. But becoming a prisoner is also an achieved status, a consequence of committing a crime. The line between attained and achieved statuses can, however, become fuzzy as happens when someone is given the benefit of the doubt, or denied it, because of inheritance rather than effort.

Master Status Each of us holds many different and sometimes conflicting statuses; some may signify a higher social position, and others a lower position. How, then, do others view our overall social position? According to sociologist Everett Hughes (1945), societies deal with inconsistencies by agreeing that certain statuses are

more important than others. A **master status** is a status that dominates others and thereby determines a person's general position in society. For example, in 1998, Michael J. Fox revealed that he was diagnosed with Parkinson's disease. He had a remarkable career in films and television, but now his status as a well-known personality with Parkinson's may outweigh his statuses as actor, author, and political activist.

SOCTHINK

Why do factors such as race, gender, and disability become master statuses? What might master status tell us about how powerful our definition of "normal" is?

People with disabilities frequently observe that the nondisabled see them only as blind, or only as wheelchair users, and so on, rather than as complex human beings with individual strengths and weaknesses whose disability is merely one aspect of their lives. Often people with disabilities find that their status as "disabled" receives undue weight, overshadowing their actual ability to hold meaningful employment and contributing to widespread prejudice, discrimination, and segregation (Banks and Lawrence 2006). For example, most voting places are inaccessible to wheelchair users and fail to provide ballots that can be used by the blind. Activists argue that such unnecessary and discriminatory barriers restrict people with disabilities more than do any biological limitations.

Ascribed statuses frequently influence our achieved status. The African American activist Malcolm X (1925–1965), an eloquent and controversial advocate of Black power and Black pride in the 1960s, recalled that his feelings and perspectives changed dramatically while in eighth grade. When his English teacher, a White man, advised him that his goal of becoming a lawyer was ridiculous and suggested he become a carpenter instead, Malcolm X (1964:37) found that his position as a Black man (ascribed status) was an obstacle to his dream of becoming a lawyer (achieved status). In the United States, the ascribed statuses of race and gender can function as master statuses that play an important part in one's efforts to achieve a desired professional and social status (Brownfield, Sorenson, and Thompson 2001).

SOCIAL ROLES

The statuses we occupy imply both rights and responsibilities. A **social role** is a set of expected behaviors for people who occupy a given social status. While we occupy a status, we play a role. Thus, in the United States, we expect that cab drivers will know how to get around a city, that receptionists will handle phone messages, and that police officers will take action if they see a citizen being threatened.

With each distinctive social status—whether ascribed or achieved—come particular role expectations. However, actual performance varies from individual to individual. One executive assistant may assume extensive administrative responsibilities, whereas another may focus on clerical duties.

Roles are a significant component of social structure. Roles contribute to a society's stability by enabling members to anticipate the behavior of others and to pattern their own actions accordingly. Yet social roles also restrict people's interactions and relationships. If we view a person *only* as a police officer or a supervisor, it will be difficult to relate to him or her as a friend or neighbor.

master status A status that dominates others and thereby determines a person's general position in society.

social role A set of expected behaviors for people who occupy a given social status.

role conflict The situation that occurs when incompatible expectations arise from two or more social statuses held by the same person.

Role Conflict Sometimes the statuses we occupy can clash. **Role conflict** occurs when incompatible expectations arise from two or more social statuses held by the same person. Fulfillment of the roles associated with one position may directly violate the roles linked to a second status.

SOCTHINK

List the social statuses you occupy. Which ones are ascribed, and which are achieved? What roles are you expected to play as a consequence of the positions you occupy? How do you resolve possible role conflicts?

Imagine the delicate situation of a woman who has worked for a decade on an assembly line in an electrical plant and has recently been named supervisor of her unit. She now must balance her status as a friend with her status as the boss. How should she treat her longtime friends and co-workers? Should she still have lunch with them? Should she recommend the firing of an old friend who cannot keep up with the demands of the assembly line? She will most likely experience a sharp conflict between her friendship and supervisory roles. Such role conflicts involve difficult ethical choices. The new supervisor will have to make a difficult decision about how much allegiance she owes her friend and how much she owes her employers, who have given her supervisory responsibilities.

Another type of role conflict occurs when individuals move into occupations that are not common among people with their ascribed status. Male preschool teachers and female police officers experience this type of role conflict. In the latter case, the women must strive to reconcile their workplace status in law enforcement with the societal view of the status of women, which historically has not embraced many skills associated with police work. And even as female police officers encounter sexual harassment, as women do throughout the labor force, they must also deal with the "code of silence," an informal norm that precludes their implicating fellow officers in wrongdoing (Maher 2008; Pershing 2003).

—SOCTHINK—

Is there no such thing as our true self? Are we only actors performing roles based on the positions we occupy?

Role Strain Role conflict describes the situation of a person dealing with the challenge of occupying two social statuses simultaneously. However, even a single status can cause problems. Sociologists use the term **role strain** to describe the difficulty that arises when the same social status imposes conflicting demands and expectations.

People who belong to minority cultures may experience role strain while working in the mainstream culture. Criminologist Larry Gould (2002) interviewed officers of the Navajo Nation Police Department and found that they faced role strain when responding to the majority and minority communities. They were expected to follow the official policies and procedures defined by conventional law enforcement officials (sheriffs and FBI agents). At the same time, Navajo Nation officers practice an alternative form of justice known as Peacemaking, in which they seek reconciliation between the parties to a crime or grievance. The officers expressed great confidence in Peacemaking but worried that if they did not make arrests, other law enforcement officials would think they were too soft or were "just taking care of their own." All felt the strain of being considered "too Navajo" or "not Navajo enough."

role strain The difficulty that arises when the same social status imposes conflicting demands and expectations.

role exit The process of disengagement from a role that is central to one's self-identity in order to establish a new role and identity.

Role Exit Often, when we think of assuming a social role, we focus on the preparation and anticipatory socialization a person undergoes for that role. Such is true if a person is about to become an attorney, a chef, a spouse, or a parent. Yet, sociologists also pay attention to the adjustments involved in leaving social roles.

Sociologist Helen Rose Fuchs Ebaugh (1988) used the term **role exit** to describe the process of disengagement from a role that is central to one's self-identity in order to establish a new role and identity. Drawing on interviews—with, among others, ex-convicts, divorced men and women,

Sociologist Helen Rose Fuchs Ebaugh interviewed transsexuals (as pictured here) and others exiting from significant social roles in order to develop her four-stage model of role exit.

Although I love teaching, I hate grading. When I mention that to students they say I have no one to blame but myself; if I didn't assign things I wouldn't have to grade them. But I don't teach in a vacuum. If I didn't assign papers and tests, students would focus their time and energy on their looming chemistry test or their literature paper instead of reading for, participating in, or even attending my course. It is not that students aren't interested or sincere; it's that they are forced to budget their time for which professors compete using assignments. Because we exist in social systems, the expectations of those systems limit the amount of innovation we might desire.

may take a leave of absence; an unhappily married couple may begin what they see as a trial separation.

The third stage of role exit is the action stage, or departure. Ebaugh found that the vast majority of her respondents could identify a clear turning point when it became essential to take final action and leave their jobs, end their marriages, or engage in some other type of role exit. Only 20 percent of respondents saw their role exit as a gradual, evolutionary process that had no single turning point.

The last stage of role exit involves the creation of a new identity. Traditionally, students experience a form of role exit when they make the transition from high school to college. They may leave behind the role of a child living at home and take on the role of a somewhat independent college student living with peers in a dorm. Sociologist Ira Silver (1996) has studied the central role that material objects play in this transition. The objects students choose to leave at home (like stuffed animals and dolls) are associated with their prior identities. They may remain deeply attached to those objects but not want them to be seen as part of their new identities at college. The objects they bring with them symbolize how they now see themselves and how they wish to be perceived. iPads and wall posters, for example, are calculated to say, "This is who I am."

> **group** Any number of people with shared norms, values, and goals who interact with one another on a regular basis.

recovering alcoholics, ex-nuns, former doctors, retirees, and transsexuals—Ebaugh (herself a former nun) studied the process of voluntarily exiting from significant social roles.

Ebaugh has offered a four-stage model of role exit. The first stage begins with doubt. The person experiences frustration, burnout, or simply unhappiness with an accustomed status and the roles associated with that social position. The second stage involves a search for alternatives. An individual who is unhappy with his or her career

GROUPS

Statuses combine in various ways to form social groups. In sociological terms, a **group** is any number of people

SOCTHINK

Whether from a sports team, a religious group, the military, or some other close-knit group, what experience, if any, have you had with role exiting? To what extent does your experience match the four stages Ebaugh describes?

Comparison of Primary and Secondary Groups

Primary group	Secondary group
Generally small	Usually large
Relatively long period of interaction	Relatively short duration, often temporary
Intimate, face-to-face association	Little social intimacy or mutual understanding
Some emotional depth to relationships	Relationships generally superficial
Cooperative, friendly	More formal and impersonal

with shared norms, values, and goals who interact with one another on a regular basis. The members of a women's basketball team, a hospital's business office, a synagogue, or a symphony orchestra constitute a group. However, the residents of a suburb would not be considered a group, because they rarely interact with one another at one time.

We spend much of our time interacting in group settings. The type of group we are in influences our level of commitment and participation. Some groups demand our almost undivided attention and shape our core identity; others allow us to more easily accomplish specific goals.

Primary and Secondary Groups

Charles Horton Cooley (1902) coined the term **primary group** to refer to a small group characterized by intimate, face-to-face association and cooperation. Such groups often entail long-term commitment and involve more of what we think of as our whole self. Families constitute primary groups for many, although people also build close-knit, in-depth relationships with teammates, like-minded religious believers, coworkers, and fellow street gang members. In sports, for example, commitment to the

primary group A small group characterized by intimate, face-to-face association and cooperation.

secondary group A formal, impersonal group in which there is little social intimacy or mutual understanding.

cliché that there is "no 'I' in 'team'" often leads to a sense that teammates are "like family." Their level of trust and interdependence grows. Teammates come to know that the pitcher, outfielder, or catcher on the team will be there for them not only on the field, she will also have their backs when they need it in other circumstances.

We also participate in many groups that are not characterized by close bonds of friendship, such as large college classes and business associations. The term **secondary group** refers to a formal, impersonal group in which there is little social intimacy or mutual understanding. Participation in such groups is typically more instrumental or goal-directed, often involving only what we think of as one part of our self. Given these characteristics, we are more likely to move into and out of such groups as suits our needs.

The distinction between primary and secondary groups is not always clear-cut, however. Some social clubs may become so large and impersonal that they no longer function as primary groups; similarly, some work groups can become so close-knit that they are experienced as primary groups (Hochschild 1989). The accompanying table demonstrates some significant differences between primary and secondary groups.

In-Groups and Out-Groups

The shared norms, values, and goals of group members, along with their common experiences,

create a boundary distinguishing insiders and outsiders. The resulting us/them divide can lead to a strong sense of group identity, but it can also serve as a basis for exclusion, especially if "they" are perceived as different either culturally or racially. Sociologists use the terms in-group and out-group to identify these two classifications.

An **in-group** consists of a category of people who share a common identity and sense of belonging. Members differentiate between themselves and everybody else (Sumner 1906). The in-group may be as narrow as a teenage clique or as broad as an entire nation. An **out-group** is defined, relative to the in-group, as a category of people who do not belong or do not fit in. Among an in-group of high school "jocks," for example, a science "geek" might be considered an out-group member, and vice versa.

In-group members typically feel distinct and superior, seeing themselves as better than people in the out-group. Proper behavior for the in-group can be simultaneously viewed as unacceptable behavior for the out-group. This double standard enhances the sense of superiority. Sociologist Robert Merton (1968) described this process as the conversion of "in-group virtues" into "out-group vices." We can see this differential standard operating in the context of terrorism. When a group or a nation takes aggressive actions, it usually justifies them as necessary

> Every society honors its live conformists, and its dead troublemakers.
>
> Mignon McLaughlin

in-group A category of people who share a common identity and sense of belonging.

out-group A category of people who do not belong or do not fit in.

SOCTHINK

How do in-groups and out-groups function in a typical U.S. high school? What groups are common? How are boundaries separating insiders and outsiders maintained?

even if civilians are hurt or killed. Opponents are quick to assign the emotion-laden label of *terrorist* to such actions and to appeal to the world community for condemnation. Yet these same people may themselves retaliate with actions that hurt civilians, which the first group will then condemn as terrorist acts (Juergensmeyer 2003).

Reference Groups Both in-groups and primary groups can dramatically influence the way an individual thinks and behaves. Sociologists call any group that individuals use as a standard for evaluating themselves and their own behavior a **reference group.** For example, a high school student who aspires to join a social circle of hip-hop music devotees will pattern his or her behavior after that of the group. The student will begin dressing like these peers, listening to the same downloads and DVDs, and hanging out at the same stores and clubs.

> **reference group** Any group that individuals use as a standard for evaluating themselves and their own behavior.
>
> **coalition** A temporary or permanent alliance geared toward a common goal.
>
> **social network** A series of social relationships that links individuals directly to others and, through them, indirectly to still more people.

Reference groups have two basic purposes. They serve a normative function by setting and enforcing standards of conduct and belief. The high school student who wants the approval of the hip-hop crowd will have to follow the group's dictates, at least to some extent. Reference groups also perform a comparison function by serving as a standard against which people can measure themselves and others. An actor will evaluate him- or herself against a reference group composed of others in the acting profession (Merton and Kitt 1950).

Often, two or more reference groups influence us at the same time. Our family members, neighbors, and co-workers all shape different aspects of our self-evaluation. In addition, reference group attachments change during the life cycle. A corporate executive who quits the rat race at age 45 to become a social worker will find new reference groups to use as standards for evaluation. We shift reference groups as we take on different statuses during our lives.

Coalitions As groups grow larger, coalitions begin to develop. A **coalition** is an alliance, whether temporary or permanent, geared toward a common goal. Coalitions can be broad-based or narrow and can take on many different objectives. Sociologist William Julius Wilson (1999) has reported on community-based organizations in Texas that include Whites and Latinos, working-class and affluent, who banded together to work for improved sidewalks, better drainage systems, and comprehensive street paving. Out of this type of coalition building, Wilson hopes, will emerge better interracial understanding.

Some coalitions are intentionally short-lived. Short-term coalition building is a key to success in popular TV programs like *Survivor* and *Big Brother* in which players gain a strategic advantage by banding together to vote others off the island or out of the house. The political world is also the scene of many temporary coalitions. For example, in 2003 President George W. Bush established a "Coalition of the Willing": 45 nations dedicated to removing Saddam Hussein from power in Iraq and willing to provide troops to accomplish that goal. The Iraq invasion began in March 2003 and Hussein was captured in December 2003.

SOCIAL NETWORKS

Groups do not merely serve to define other elements of the social structure, such as roles and statuses; they also link the individual with the larger society. We all belong to a number of groups, and through our acquaintances, we connect with people in different social circles. Such connections comprise a **social network**—a series of social relationships that link individuals directly to others, and through them indirectly to still more people. Social networks can center on virtually any activity, from sharing job information to exchanging news and gossip. Some networks may constrain people by limiting the range of their interactions, yet networks can also empower people by making vast resources available to them (Watts 2004).

Sometimes the connections are intentional and public; other times networks can develop that link us together in ways that are not intentional or apparent. Sociologists Peter Bearman, James Moody, and Katherine Stovel (2004) investigated one such network, asking themselves this question: If you drew a chart of the romantic relationship network at a typical American high school, what would

Adolescent Sexual Networks

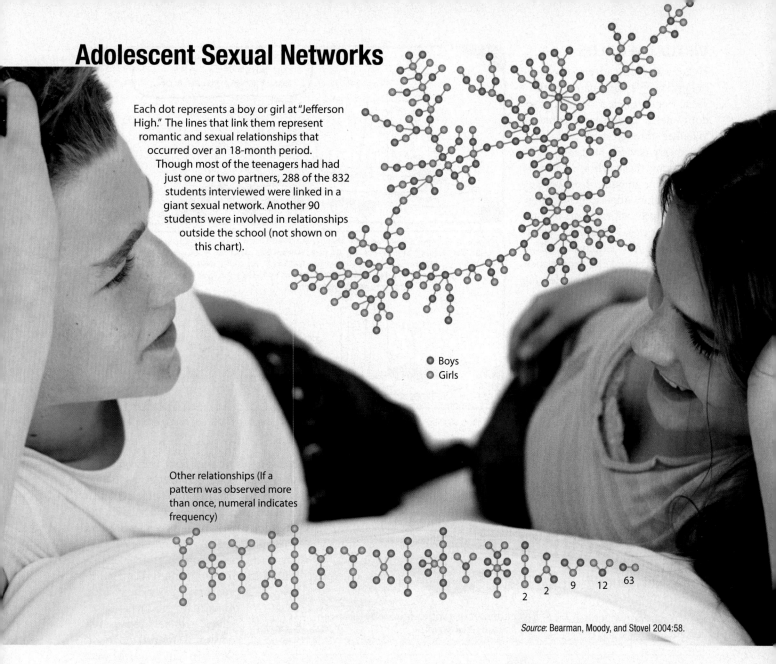

Each dot represents a boy or girl at "Jefferson High." The lines that link them represent romantic and sexual relationships that occurred over an 18-month period. Though most of the teenagers had had just one or two partners, 288 of the 832 students interviewed were linked in a giant sexual network. Another 90 students were involved in relationships outside the school (not shown on this chart).

● Boys
● Girls

Other relationships (If a pattern was observed more than once, numeral indicates frequency)

2   2   9   12   63

Source: Bearman, Moody, and Stovel 2004:58.

it look like? Using careful data collection techniques to enhance the validity of their findings, they found that 573 of the 832 students they surveyed had been either romantically or sexually involved in the previous 18 months. Of these, 63 couples connected only with each other as pairs with no other partners. Other students connected directly or indirectly with a handful of partners. One larger group, however, connected 288 students directly or indirectly into a single extended network (see the figure "Adolescent Sexual Networks"). Such an example points to the fact that the choices we make often link us with others both known and unknown.

Networks can also serve as a social resource that is every bit as valuable to us as economic resources when it comes to shaping our opportunities. Involvement in social networks—commonly known as "networking"—can be especially valuable in finding employment. For example, a 2011 survey found that 92% of executive jobs with salaries over $200,000 per year were not posted publicly online. Instead, networking accounted for 46 percent of hires and an additional 23 percent came from the firm's database, which is built using network connections (ExecuNet 2011).

In the workplace, networking often pays off more for men than for women because of the traditional presence of men in leadership positions. One survey of executives found that 63 percent of the men used networking to find new jobs, compared to 41 percent of the women. Thirty-one percent of the women used classified ads to find jobs, compared to only 13 percent of the men. Still, women at all levels of the paid labor force are beginning to make effective use of social networks. A study of women who were leaving the welfare rolls to enter the paid workforce found that networking was an effective tool in their search for employment. Informal networking also helped them to locate child care and better housing—keys to successful employment (Benschop 2009; Carey and McLean 1997).

VIRTUAL WORLDS

Today, with recent advances in technology, people can maintain their social networks electronically; they don't need face-to-face contacts. Whether through text messaging, Blackberry devices, Skype, or social networking sites such as Facebook, a significant amount of networking occurs online. Adolescents can now interact freely with distant friends, even under close scrutiny by parents or teachers. And employees with a taste for adventure can escape their work environments without leaving their cubicles.

The future of virtual networking and the effects it will have are difficult to predict. Consider Second Life (SL), a virtual world that included more than 15 million networked residents with approximately 20,000 / new registrations per day and over 1 million regular users per month as of October 2011. Participants in such virtual worlds typically create an **avatar** that is their online representation as a character, whether in the form of

THE BEST THING ABOUT THE INTERNET IS THEY DON'T KNOW YOU'RE A DOG.

You're a four-year-old German Shepherd - Schnauser mix, likes to shop for rawhide chews, 213 visits to Lassie website, chatroom conversation 8-29-99 said third Lassie was the hottest, downloaded photos of third Lassie 10-12-99, e-mailed them to five other dogs whose identities are...

DID YOU MARK ALL THAT?

a 2-D or 3-D image or simply through text. The avatar that a player assumes may represent a very different looking-glass self from his or her actual identity. Once equipped with an avatar, the player goes about his or her life in the virtual world, establishing a business and even buying and decorating a home (Bainbridge 2007; Second Life 2011).

In fact, virtual products have become a profitable business enterprise. Within the SL world, enterprising entrepreneurs sell a whole array of virtual products (land, houses, clothes, and even rainstorms) for real money. In 2009, $567 million USD were spent in user-to-user transactions within the SL world, and the top 25 SL avatars made a combined total of more than $12 million. Similarly, estimates are that Zynga, the company that produced the games Farmville and Mafia Wars, accounted for $445 million, or 12 percent, of Facebook's revenue in 2011 by selling virtual products, including seeds, chickens, and crates (Linden 2011; Rosenwald 2010; Takahashi 2012).

Second Life is being used for more than just entertainment and business. A team from Indiana University of Pennsylvania used SL to simulate key events in the Civil

Going GLOBAL

Social Networking

■ Social networking users   ■ Internet use without social networking   ■ No Internet use

Percentage

100 · 80 · 60 · 40 · 20 · 0

Israel   U.S.   Britain   Russia   Poland   Germany   France   China   Turkey   Egypt   Japan   Mexico   Lebanon   Kenya   India   Pakistan

Note: Don't know/Refused responses are not shown. Samples in China, India, and Pakistan are disproportionately urban.

Source: Pew Research Center 2010.

Shirky's Four Steps Toward Increased Internet Interaction

Step	Site
Sharing	Flikr; Bit Torrent; Del.icio.us
Conversation	Forums; MAKE; How To
Collaboration	Linux; Aegisub
Collective action	Flash Mob activism; NetRoots activism

Source: Based on Shirky 2008.

Rights Movement to give students a sense of being there (McCoy 2011). The U.S. Army uses it as a place for troops and their families to go to address their physical and emotional well-being (Lim 2011). Filmmaker Ariella Furman uses SL to create short animated films, known as Machinima, for clients including IBM and Eli Lilly (Spencer 2011). And Amaretto Breedables, a SL horse breeding group, sold limited edition virtual horses to raise $82,264.30 for victims of the earthquake and tsunami that hit Japan in March, 2011 (Cooperstone 2011).

Sociologist Manuel Castells (1997, 1998, 2000) views these emerging electronic social networks as fundamental to new organizations and to the growth of existing businesses and associations; analysts such as Clay Shirky (2008) are trying to understand them. Shirky suggests that the Internet has radically transformed the possibilities for collective action. He argues that previous technologies either allowed two-way communication that was small-scale because it was limited to individuals (for example, the telephone), or facilitated large-scale group formation through broadcasting but was limited to one-way communication (for example, talk radio listeners or fans of *Glee*). With the Internet, he suggests, "group action just got easier" because it supports interactive, large-scale group formation as occurred during the "Arab Spring" protests in countries including Egypt, Tunisia, and Libya in 2011. He identifies a series of steps toward that end (see the accompanying table).

Finally, virtual networks can help to preserve real-world networks interrupted by war and other dislocations. In 2003 the deployment of U.S. troops in the Middle East increased many people's reliance on email. Today, digital photos and sound files accompany email messages between soldiers and their families and friends. GIs can even view siblings' graduations or children's birthday parties live, via webcams. And U.S. soldiers and Iraqi citizens have begun to post their opinions of the war in Iraq in online journals or blogs. Though critics are skeptical of the identity of some of the authors, these postings have become yet another source of news about the war (Faith 2005; O'Connor 2004; Sisson 2007).

> **avatar** A person's online representation as a character, whether in the form of a 2-D or 3-D image or simply through text.
>
> **social institution** An organized pattern of beliefs and behavior centered on basic social needs.

SOCIAL INSTITUTIONS

Combinations of statuses, groups, and networks can coalesce to address the needs of a particular sector of society, forming what sociologists refer to as institutions. A **social institution** is an organized pattern of beliefs and behavior centered on basic social needs. Sociologists have tended to focus on five major institutions that serve as key elements of the larger social structure: family, education, religion, economy, and government. Though these institutions frequently overlap and interact, considering each institution individually provides us with a perspective within which we can analyze the larger social system. We

In February 2010, an Austin man flew his plane into the city's IRS building.

look in depth at all five in future chapters, but we begin here by considering the contributions each makes to the social structure.

How we organize social interaction within each of these institutions helps contribute to social order. If a society is to survive, certain functions must be performed, and focusing on these institutions allows us to see how different societies fulfill these needs (Aberle et al. 1950). It is within the context of *families,* for example, that we ensure the society's continued existence by producing the next generation. Families carry out both biological reproduction (having children) and social reproduction (teaching them the culture they need for survival). Families also provide care and protection for members. Through *education* we teach the more formal and public culture necessary to be members of the larger society. This includes the formal curriculum (history, math, science, and so on) but also includes learning to interact with others outside our immediate families. We rely on *religion* to be the glue that holds society together by establishing a clear identity with shared beliefs and practices, answering basic questions about meaning, and enforcing both individual and collective discipline. *Government* helps to maintain internal order through laws, policing, and punishment and seeks to establish stable relations with other societies through diplomacy. Finally, the *economy* regulates the production, distribution, and consumption of goods and services.

How societies choose to fulfill these functions can vary significantly, as can the degree to which these institutions overlap. For example, one society may protect itself from external attack by amassing a large arsenal of weaponry; another may make determined efforts to remain neutral in world politics and to promote cooperative relationships with its neighbors. No matter what its particular strategy, any society or relatively permanent group must address all these functional prerequisites for survival.

Focusing on the functions institutions fulfill can help us to better understand social order, but it often implies that the way things are is the way things should be. Sociologists

SOCTHINK

How is it possible for education to represent both a path for opportunity and an instrument for maintaining inequality? Where in your experience have you seen both at work?

using the conflict paradigm focus more on power, the consequences of difference, and resource distribution. They suggest that we must also look at the ways our construction of these institutions reinforces inequality. We can meet these functional needs in a variety of ways, so we should consider why some groups might seek to maintain the status quo.

Major institutions, such as education, help to perpetuate the privileges of the most powerful individuals and groups within a society while contributing to the powerlessness of others. To give one example, public schools in the United States are financed largely through property taxes. This arrangement allows more affluent areas to provide their children with better-equipped schools and better-paid teachers than low-income areas can afford. As a result, children from prosperous communities are better prepared to compete academically than children from impoverished communities. The structure of the nation's educational system permits and even promotes such unequal treatment of schoolchildren (Kozol 2005).

"Frankly, at this point in the flow chart, we don't know what happens to these people..."

Cartoon by Chris Wildt, www.CartoonStock.com.

Using the interactionist paradigm to study what goes on within these institutions provides additional insight into why we think and act the way we do. Focusing on the economy, sociologist Mitchell Duneier (1994a, 1994b) studied the social behavior of the word processors, all women, who worked in the service center of a large Chicago law firm. Duneier was interested in the informal social norms that emerged in this work environment and the rich social network these female employees created.

Duneier learned that, despite working in a large office, these women found private moments to talk (often in the halls or outside the washroom) and shared a critical view of the firm's attorneys and day-shift secretaries. Expressing their frustration about their relative lack of power and

respect, the word processors routinely suggested that their assignments represented work that the "lazy" secretaries should have completed during the normal workday. One word processor, seeking to reclaim a sense of personal power, reacted to the lawyers' superior attitude and pointedly refused to recognize or speak with any attorney who would not address her by name (Duneier 1994b).

Such approaches to viewing life in the contexts of social institutions allow us to better understand what it means to live in the world as it is structured today. Looking at society through the lens of social structure gives us a sense of what is going on with regard to both the "big picture" and the intimate details of our daily interactions. One of the ways that sociologists have characterized the structure of our modern world is in terms of bureaucracy.

>>Bureaucracy

A **bureaucracy** is a component of a formal organization that uses rules and hierarchical ranking to achieve efficiency. The impressions we have of bureaucracies—rows of cubicles staffed with seemingly faceless people, endless waiting, complex language, and frustrating encounters with red tape—are often negative. But bureaucracy was established to provide fair and efficient means of organizing social life.

> **bureaucracy** A component of formal organization that uses rules and hierarchical ranking to achieve efficiency.

CHARACTERISTICS OF A BUREAUCRACY

Max Weber ([1913–1922] 1947) provided the first detailed sociological analysis of bureaucracy. He recognized that

Characteristics of a Bureaucracy

	Positive consequences	Negative consequences	
		For the individual	For the organization
Division of labor	Produces efficiency in a large-scale corporation	Produces trained incapacity	Produces a narrow perspective
Hierarchy of authority	Clarifies who is in command	Deprives employees of a voice in decision making	Permits concealment of mistakes
Written rules and regulations	Let workers know what is expected of them	Stifles initiative and imagination	Leads to goal displacement
Impersonality	Reduces bias	Contributes to feelings of alienation	Discourages loyalty to company
Employment based on technical qualifications	Discourages favoritism and reduces petty rivalries	Discourages ambition to improve oneself elsewhere	Inhibits innovative thinking

its underlying structure remained the same regardless of location, whether in religion, government, education, or business. Weber argued that bureaucracy was quite different from traditional forms of organization, such as those used to run a family business, and he set out to identify its core components. He did so by constructing what he called an **ideal type,** an abstract model of the essential characteristics of a phenomenon. In actuality, perfect bureaucracies do not exist; no real-world organization corresponds exactly to Weber's ideal type.

ideal type An abstract model of the essential characteristics of a phenomenon.

alienation Loss of control over our creative human capacity to produce, separation from the products we make, and isolation from our fellow producers.

trained incapacity The tendency of workers in a bureaucracy to become so specialized that they develop blind spots and fail to notice potential problems.

Weber proposed that whether the purpose is to run a church, a corporation, or an army, the ideal bureaucracy displays five basic characteristics: division of labor, hierarchy of authority, written rules and regulations, impersonality, and employment based on technical qualifications. Let's look at each in turn; the accompanying table provides a summary.

Division of Labor
In bureaucracies, specialized experts perform specific tasks. In a college bureaucracy, for example, the admissions officer does not do the job of registrar; the academic advisor doesn't see to the maintenance of buildings. By working at a specific task, people are more likely to become highly skilled and carry out a job with maximum efficiency. This emphasis on specialization is

A Chief Executive Officer typically rests atop the pyramid structure of bureaucratic hierarchy. Don Thompson, pictured above, became the CEO for McDonald's in 2012.

Another potential downside of the division of labor is that, even though it makes us more interdependent, our relative isolation can result in our failing to recognize our links with others. As we saw with the "hamburger as miracle" example in Chapter 1, we take other people's skills for granted and assume they will do their jobs, even though we are unaware of what most of those jobs are. In some cases this can lead to **trained incapacity**—a situation in which workers become so specialized that they develop blind spots and fail to notice potential problems. Even worse, workers can become so isolated that they may not care about what is happening in the next department. Some observers believe that such developments have caused workers in the United States to become less productive on the job (Wais 2005).

such a basic a part of our lives that we may not realize it is a fairly recent development in Western culture.

Division of labor has freed up people to specialize, enhancing their knowledge and skill and leading to significant advances and innovation. However, fragmenting work into smaller and smaller tasks can isolate workers from one another and weaken any connection they might feel to the overall objective of the bureaucracy. In *The Communist Manifesto* ([1847] 1955), Karl Marx and Friedrich Engels charged that capitalism's inherent drive toward increased efficiency and productivity reduces workers to a mere "appendage of the machine." Such a work arrangement, they wrote, produces extreme **alienation**—loss of control over our creative human capacity to produce, separation from the products we make, and isolation from our fellow producers. Restricting workers to very small tasks also can lessen their job security because new employees can easily be trained to replace them.

In some cases, the bureaucratic division of labor can have tragic results. In the wake of the terrorist attacks on the World Trade Center and the Pentagon on September 11, 2001, many Americans wondered how the FBI and CIA could have failed to detect the terrorists' elaborately planned operation. The problem, in part, turned out to be the division of labor between the FBI, which focuses on domestic matters, and the CIA, which operates overseas. Officials at these intelligence-gathering organizations, both of which are huge bureaucracies, are well known for jealously guarding information from one another. Subsequent investigation revealed that they knew about Osama bin Laden and his al Qaeda terrorist network in the early 1990s. Unfortunately, five federal agencies—the CIA, FBI, National Security Agency, Defense Intelligence Agency, and National Reconnaissance Office—failed to share their information on the network. Although the hijacking of the four commercial airliners used in the massive attacks may not have been preventable, the bureaucratic division of labor definitely hindered efforts to defend against terrorism, undermining U.S. national security.

Hierarchy of Authority Bureaucracies follow the principle of hierarchy; that is, each position is under the supervision of a higher authority. A president heads a college bureaucracy; he or she selects members of the administration, who in turn hire their own staff. In the Roman Catholic Church, the pope is the supreme authority; under him are cardinals, bishops, and so forth. In businesses, the most basic relation is between boss and worker, but in large corporations there are various levels of authority. To track relationships, such companies map those connections using organizational charts that identify all the links of who answers to whom, ultimately leading up to the president or CEO at the top.

Written Rules and Regulations Through written rules and regulations, bureaucracies generally offer employees clear standards for an adequate (or exceptional) performance. If situations arise that are not covered by the

> ## Bureaucracy is . . . the most rational known means of exercising authority over human beings.
>
> Max Weber

rules, bureaucracies are self-correcting. They have rules in place to ensure that new rules are established that make work expectations as clear and comprehensive as possible. Because bureaucracies are hierarchical systems of interrelated positions, such procedures provide a valuable sense of continuity for the organization. Individual workers may come and go, but the structure and past records of the organization give it a life of its own that outlives the services of any one particular person.

SOCTHINK

Why do we tend to associate bureaucracies with red tape and inefficiency when they are explicitly organized to be the opposite? To what extent is our desire to be treated as an individual at odds with the principles of bureaucracies?

Of course, rules and regulations can overshadow the larger goals of an organization to the point that they become dysfunctional. What if a hospital emergency room physician failed to treat a seriously injured person because he or she had no valid proof of U.S. citizenship? If blindly applied, rules no longer serve as a means to achieving an objective but instead become important (perhaps too important) in their own right. Robert Merton (1968) used the term **goal displacement** to refer to overzealous conformity to official regulations in which we lose sight of the larger principle from which the rule was created.

> **goal displacement** Overzealous conformity to official regulations of a bureaucracy.

Impersonality Max Weber wrote that, in a bureaucracy, work is carried out "without hatred or passion." Bureaucratic norms dictate that officials judge people based on performance rather than personality. The intent is to ensure equal treatment for each person. But it can also contribute to the cold, uncaring feeling often associated with modern organizations.

We typically think of big government and big business when we think of impersonal bureaucracies, and bureaucratic impersonality often produces frustration and disaffection. Whether it involves registering for college classes or getting tech support for a malfunctioning computer, most people have had some experience of feeling like a number and longing for some personal attention. The larger the organization or society, however, the less possible such personal care becomes because attending to individual wants and needs is inefficient.

Did You Know?

In the 2010 Census, the U.S. Census Bureau identified 539 distinct occupational categories including Chief Executive, Aerospace Engineer, Phlebotomist, Crossing Guard, and Sociologist. They organized these occupations into six major categories.

Employment Based on Technical Qualifications Within the ideal bureaucracy, hiring is based on technical qualifications rather than on favoritism, and performance is measured against specific standards. Written personnel policies dictate who gets promoted, and people often have a right to appeal if they believe that particular rules have been violated. In combination with the principle of impersonality, the driving personnel principle is supposed to be that it is "what you know, not who you know" that counts. Such procedures protect workers against arbitrary dismissal, provide a measure of security, and encourage loyalty to the organization.

Weber developed his five indicators of bureaucracy almost 100 years ago, and they continue to describe the ideal type. Not every formal organization will fully realize all of Weber's characteristics. The underlying logic they represent, however, points toward a way of doing things that is typical of life in modern societies.

BUREAUCRATIZATION AS A WAY OF LIFE

Bureaucracy for Weber was an indicator of a larger trend in modern society toward rational calculation of all decision making using efficiency and productivity as the primary standards of success. We recognize this pattern first at the level of businesses and organizations. More companies seek greater efficiency through **bureaucratization**—the process by which a group, organization, or social movement increasingly relies on technical-rational decision making in the pursuit of efficiency. Over time, however, the technical-rational approach pervades more and more areas of our lives.

The Spread of Bureaucratization One example of the expansion of bureaucratization is found in the spread of what sociologist George Ritzer (2008) calls **McDonaldization**—the process by which the principles of efficiency, calculability, predictability, and control shape organization and decision making, in the United States and around the world. Ritzer argues that these principles, which are at the heart of the McDonald's fast-food chain's success, have been emulated

> ## "The chains of tormented mankind are made out of red tape."
>
> Franz Kafka

by many organizations, ranging from medical care to wedding planning to education. Even sporting events reflect the influence of McDonaldization. Around the world, stadiums are becoming increasingly similar, both physically and in the way they present the sport to spectators. Swipe cards, "sports city" garages and parking lots, and automated ticket sales maximize efficiency. All seats offer spectators an unrestricted view, and a big screen guarantees them access to instant replays. Scores, player statistics, and attendance figures are updated by computer and displayed on an automated scoreboard. Spectator enthusiasm is manufactured through video displays urging applause or rhythmic chanting. At food counters, refreshments include well-known brands whose customer loyalty has been nourished by advertisers for decades. And, of course, the merchandising of teams' and even players' names and images is highly controlled.

Normally, we think of bureaucratization in terms of large organizations, but bureaucratization also takes place within small-group settings. Sociologist Jennifer Bickman Mendez (1998) studied domestic houseworkers employed in central California by a nationwide franchise. She found that housekeeping tasks were minutely defined, to the point that employees had to follow 22 written steps for cleaning a bathroom. Complaints and special requests went not to the workers but to an office-based manager.

Weber predicted that eventually even the private sphere would become rationalized. That is, we would turn to rational techniques in an effort to manage our self in order to handle the many challenges of modern life. A trip to any bookstore would seem to prove his point: we find countless self-help books, each with its own system of steps to help us solve life's problems and reach our goals.

Weber was concerned about the depersonalizing consequences of such rationalization, but he saw no way out. Because it is guided by the principle of maximum efficiency, the only way to beat bureaucratization, he thought, was to be more bureaucratic. He argued that, unfortunately, something human gets lost in the process. Culture critic Mike

www.buttersafe.com © 2011 Alex Culang and Raynato Castro Buttersafe.

Daisey describes something like this through his experience working at Amazon.com. His job performance was measured based on five factors: time spent on each call, number of phone contacts per hour, time spent on each customer email, number of email contacts per hour, and the sum total of phone and email contacts per hour. Of these calculations, he writes, "Those five numbers are who you are. They are, in fact, all you are. . . . Metrics will do exactly what it claims to do: It will track everything your employees do, say, and breathe, and consequently create a measurable increase in their productivity" (Daisey 2002:114). Metrics do work, but they do so by

dehumanizing the worker. "The sad thing," Daisey continues, "is that metrics work so well precisely because it strips away dignity—it's that absence that makes it possible to see precisely who is pulling his weight and who is not" (p. 114). When workers' performance is measured only in numbers, the only part of the self that counts is that part that produces those numbers. Weber predicted that those parts of the self deemed not necessary to the job, such as emotional needs and family responsibilities, would be dismissed as irrelevant.

From Bureaucracy to Oligarchy

One of the dangers, then, is that bureaucratization overwhelms other values and principles, that how we organize to accomplish our goals overwhelms and alters the goals themselves. Sociologist Robert Michels ([1915] 1949) studied socialist parties and labor unions in Europe prior to World War I and found that such organizations were becoming increasingly bureaucratic. The emerging leaders of the organizations—even some of the most egalitarian—had a vested interest in clinging to power. If they lost their leadership posts, they would have to return to full-time work as manual laborers.

Through his research, Michels originated the idea of the **iron law of oligarchy,** the principle that all organizations, even democratic ones, tend to develop into a bureaucracy ruled by an elite few (called an oligarchy). Why do oligarchies emerge? People who achieve leadership roles usually have the skills, knowledge, or charisma to direct, if not control, others. Michels argued that the rank and file of a movement or organization look to leaders for direction and thereby reinforce the process of rule by a few. In addition, members of an oligarchy are strongly motivated to maintain their leadership roles, privileges, and power.

Concerns about oligarchy are often raised when ideologically driven social and political movements become institutionalized. In U.S. politics, ideologically committed followers, who often represent their party's base, frequently complain that elected leaders become "Washington insiders" who look out only for their self-interests. For example, during debates about the federal budget deficit in the summer of 2011, Tea Party conservatives, who are ideologically committed to small government and fiscal restraint, challenged Republican leaders to be true to their ideals and not raise taxes regardless of the electoral consequences. Similarly, progressive Democrats, ideologically committed to equality and opportunity, argued that Democratic leaders should not agree to cuts in funding for education, Social Security, Medicare, Medicaid, and other social support programs. In both cases, questions were raised about whether the craving to stay in office trumped the desire to do the right thing (Clemons 2011; Jones 2011).

bureaucratization The process by which a group, organization, or social movement increasingly relies on technical-rational decision making in the pursuit of efficiency.

McDonaldization The process by which the principles of efficiency, calculability, predictability, and control shape organization and decision making, in the United States and around the world.

iron law of oligarchy The principle that all organizations, even democratic ones, tend to develop into a bureaucracy ruled by an elite few.

BUREAUCRACY AND ORGANIZATIONAL CULTURE

Weber's model also predicted that bureaucratic organizations were self-correcting and would take steps to remedy worker concerns. Faced with sabotage and decreasingly productive workers, for example, early bureaucratic managers realized that they could not totally dismiss workers' emotional needs as irrelevant. As a result, new management philosophies arose to counter the negative effects of depersonalization.

According to the **classical theory** of formal organizations, also known as the **scientific management approach,** workers are motivated almost entirely by economic rewards. This theory stresses that only the physical constraints on workers limit their productivity. Therefore, workers may be treated as a resource, much like the machines that began to replace them in the 20th century. Under the scientific management approach, management attempts to achieve maximum work efficiency through scientific planning, established performance standards, and careful supervision of workers and production. Planning involves efficiency studies but not studies of workers' attitudes or job satisfaction (Taylor 1911).

classical theory An approach to the study of formal organizations that views workers as being motivated almost entirely by economic rewards.

scientific management approach Another name for the classical theory of formal organizations.

human relations approach An approach to the study of formal organizations that emphasizes the role of people, communication, and participation in a bureaucracy and tends to focus on the informal structure of the organization.

Not until workers organized unions—and forced management to recognize that they were not objects—did theorists of formal organizations begin to revise the classical approach. Along with management and administrators, social scientists became aware that informal groups of workers have an important impact on organizations (Perrow 1986). An alternative management philosophy, the **human relations approach,** emphasizes the role of people, communication, and participation in a bureaucracy. This type of analysis reflects the significance of interaction and small-group behavior. Unlike planning under the scientific management approach, planning based on the human relations perspective focuses on workers' feelings, frustrations, and emotional need for job satisfaction (Mayo 1933). Today, many workplaces—primarily for those in higher-status occupations—have been transformed to family-friendly environments (Hochshchild 1997). To the extent that managers are convinced that helping workers meet all their needs increases productivity, care and concern are instituted as a result of rational calculation.

>>Social Structure in Global Perspective

Principles of bureaucratization may influence more and more spheres of our lives today, but it has not always been thus. In fact, sociology arose as a discipline in order to better understand and direct the transition from traditional to modern society. Early sociologists sought to develop models that described the basic differences between the two. They hoped that by better understanding how traditional societies operate, we might more effectively identify the underlying factors that shape core concerns in modern society, such as social order, inequality, and interaction.

GEMEINSCHAFT AND GESELLSCHAFT

Ferdinand Tönnies (1855–1936) was appalled by the rise of industrial cities in his native Germany during the late 1800s. In his view, the city marked a dramatic change from the ideal of a close-knit community, which Tönnies termed a *Gemeinschaft,* to that of an impersonal mass society, or *Gesellschaft* (Tönnies [1887] 1988).

The **Gemeinschaft** (pronounced "guh-MINE-shahft") is typical of rural life. It is a small community in which people have similar backgrounds and life experiences. Virtually everyone knows one another, and social interactions are intimate and familiar, almost like an extended family. In this community there is a sense of commitment to the larger social group and a sense of togetherness among members. People relate to others in a personal way, not just as, say, clerk or manager. However, with such personal interaction comes little privacy and high expectations of individual sacrifice.

Social control in the *Gemeinschaft* is maintained through informal means, such as moral persuasion, gossip, and even gestures. These techniques work effectively because people genuinely care how others feel about them. Social change is relatively limited in the *Gemeinschaft;* the lives of members of one generation may be quite similar to those of their parents, grandparents, and so on.

In contrast, the **Gesellschaft** (pronounced "guh-ZELL-shahft") is characteristic of modern urban life. In modern societies, most people are strangers who feel little in common with other residents. Relationships are governed by social roles that grow out of immediate tasks, such as purchasing a product or arranging a business meeting. Self-interest dominates, and there is little consensus concerning values or commitment to the group. As a result, social control must rest on formal techniques, such as laws and legally defined sanctions. Social change is a normal part of life in the *Gesellschaft,* with substantial shifts evident even within a single generation.

Sociologists have used these two terms to compare social structures that stress close relationships with those that feature less personal ties. It is easy to view the *Gemeinschaft* with nostalgia, as a far better way of life than the rat race of contemporary existence. However, the more intimate relationships of the *Gemeinschaft* come at a price. The prejudice and discrimination found there can be quite confining; ascribed statuses such as family background often outweigh a person's unique talents and achievements. In addition, the *Gemeinschaft* tends to distrust individuals who are creative or simply different (Garrett 2003).

SOC THINK

What might be appealing about living in a community characterized by *Gemeinschaft?* What are possible drawbacks?

MECHANICAL AND ORGANIC SOLIDARITY

While Tönnies looked nostalgically back on the *Gemeinschaft*, Émile Durkheim was more interested in the transition to modern society, which he felt represented the birth of a new form of social order. Durkheim hoped to use sociology as a science to better understand this transition. In his book *The Division of Labor in Society* ([1893] 1933), Durkheim highlighted the seemingly inverse relationship between the division of labor and the collective conscience. As jobs became more specialized, the shared sentiments that united communities grew weaker.

In societies in which there is minimal division of labor, a sense of group solidarity develops because people do the same things together over time. Such societies are characterized by what Durkheim calls **mechanical solidarity,** a type of social cohesion based on shared experiences, knowledge, and skill in which social relations function more or less the way they always have. Societies with strong mechanical solidarity operate like a machine with limited change over time. Most individuals perform the same basic tasks—as did their parents and grandparents before them—and they do so together. These shared experiences—whether hunting, farming, preparing meals, making clothes, or building homes—result in shared perspectives and common values. Each individual acts, thinks, and believes very much like the next. Among the Amish, for example, what you will be when you grow up is virtually set at birth. There is limited opportunity for individual variation, because deviation from expected pathways represents a threat to social solidarity (Kraybill 2001).

As societies become more advanced technologically, their division of labor expands, and jobs become increasingly specialized. The person who cuts down timber is no longer the same person who builds your house. In most cases, it now takes many people with diverse sets of skills to produce even a single item, such as a chair or a cellphone. As a result, the solidarity that arose through common experience breaks down as differences emerge in how the members of the society view the world and their place in it. While Tönnies saw this and despaired, Durkheim suggested that a new form of solidarity would develop in its place.

As we saw in the "hamburger is a miracle" example in Chapter 1, specialization breeds interdependence. The irony of modern society is that we combine extreme interdependence with a strong sense of individualism.

We couldn't be self-sufficient because of our extreme division of labor, but we have a strong desire to be independent. We need one another more than ever, but we realize it less. Durkheim argued that society would evolve to address this tension and ensure social order. He maintained that mechanical solidarity would give way to **organic solidarity**—a type of social cohesion based on our mutual interdependence in the context of extreme division of labor. The various components of society would recognize how much they need one another and work together in the same way as do organs of the human body, each performing a vital function, but none capable of surviving alone.

Gemeinschaft A close-knit community, often found in rural areas, in which strong personal bonds unite members.

Gesellschaft A community, often urban, that is large and impersonal, with little commitment to the group or consensus on values.

mechanical solidarity Social cohesion based on shared experiences, knowledge, and skills in which things function more or less the way they always have.

organic solidarity Social cohesion based on mutual interdependence in the context of extreme division of labor.

TECHNOLOGY AND SOCIETY

Some sociologists focus more explicitly on technology than on social organization, expressed as division of labor, to understand distinctions between traditional and modern societies. In sociologist Gerhard Lenski's view, a society's level of technology is critical to the way it is organized. Lenski defines technology as "cultural information about how to use the material resources of the environment to satisfy human needs and desires" (Nolan and Lenski 2006:361). As technology changes, new social forms arise, from preindustrial, to industrial, to postindustrial.

The available technology does not completely define the form that a particular society and its social structure will take. Nevertheless, a low level of technology may limit the degree to which a society can depend on such things as irrigation or complex machinery.

Preindustrial Societies Perhaps the earliest form of preindustrial society to emerge in human history was the **hunting-and-gathering society,** in which people simply rely on whatever foods and fibers are readily available. Such groups are typically small and widely dispersed, and technology in such societies is minimal. Organized into groups, people move constantly in search of food. There is little division of labor into specialized tasks because everyone is engaged in the same basic activities. Because resources are scarce, there is relatively little inequality in terms of material goods.

In **horticultural societies,** people plant seeds and crops rather than merely subsist on available foods. Members of horticultural societies are much less nomadic than hunter-gatherers. They place greater emphasis on the production of tools and household objects. Yet technology remains rather limited in these societies, whose members cultivate crops with the aid of digging sticks or hoes (Wilford 1997).

The third type of preindustrial development is the **agrarian society.** As in horticultural societies, members of agrarian societies are engaged primarily in the production of food, but technological innovations such as the plow allow farmers to dramatically increase their crop yields and cultivate the same fields over generations. As a result it becomes possible for larger, more permanent settlements to develop.

Agrarian societies continue to rely on the physical power of humans and animals (in contrast to mechanical power). Division of labor increases because technological advances free up some people from food production to focus on specialized tasks, such as the repair of fishing nets or blacksmithing. As human settlements become stabler and more established, social institutions become more elaborate and property rights more important. The comparative permanence and greater surpluses of an agrarian society allow members to specialize in creating artifacts such as statues, public monuments, and art objects and to pass them on from one generation to the next.

Industrial Societies The Industrial Revolution transformed social life in England during the late 1700s, and within a century its impact on society had extended around the world. An **industrial society** is one that depends on mechanization to produce its goods and services. The strength and stamina humans gained from new inventions such as the steam engine opened up a new world of possibilities by applying nonanimal (mechanical) sources of power to most labor tasks. As such, industrialization significantly altered the way people lived and worked, and it undercut taken-for-granted norms and values.

During the Industrial Revolution, many societies underwent an irrevocable shift from an agrarian-oriented economy to an industrial base. Specialization of tasks and manufacture of goods increasingly replaced the practice of individuals or families making an entire product in a home workshop. Workers, generally men but also women and even children, left their family homesteads to work in central locations such as urban factories.

The process of industrialization had distinctive social consequences. Families and communities could not continue to function as self-sufficient units. Individuals, villages, and regions began to exchange goods and services and to become interdependent. As people came to rely on the labor of members of other communities, the family lost its unique position as the main source of power and authority. The need for specialized knowledge led to formalized schooling, and education emerged as a social institution distinct from the family.

Postindustrial Societies Mechanized production continues to play a substantial role in shaping social order, relationships, and opportunities, but technological

hunting-and-gathering society A preindustrial society in which people rely on whatever foods and fibers are readily available in order to survive.

horticultural society A preindustrial society in which people plant seeds and crops rather than merely subsist on available foods.

agrarian society The most technologically advanced form of preindustrial society. Members are engaged primarily in the production of food, but they increase their crop yields through technological innovations such as the plow.

Did You Know?

... TV talk-show host Regis Philbin was a sociology major. He graduated from the University of Notre Dame with a B.A. in sociology in 1953. Sociology, he says, "gave me a great insight into human nature."

innovation once again has reshaped social structure by freeing up some people from the demands of material production. This has led to the rise of the service sector of the economy in many technologically advanced countries. In the 1970s sociologist Daniel Bell wrote about the technologically advanced **postindustrial society,** whose economic system is engaged primarily in the processing and control of information. The main output of a postindustrial society is services rather than manufactured goods. Large numbers of people become involved in occupations devoted to the teaching, generation, or dissemination of ideas. Jobs in fields such as advertising, public relations, human resources, and computer information systems are typical of a postindustrial society (Bell 1999).

Some sociologists, including Bell, view this transition from industrial to postindustrial society as largely a positive development. Others, however, point to the often hidden consequences that result from differential access to resources in postindustrial society. For example, Michael Harrington (1980), who alerted the nation to the problems of the poor in his book *The Other America,* questions the significance that Bell attaches to the growing class of white-collar workers. Harrington concedes that scientists, engineers, and economists are involved in important political and economic decisions, but he disagrees with Bell's claim that they have a free hand in decision making, independent of the interests of the rich. Harrington follows in the tradition of Marx by arguing that conflict between social classes will continue in the postindustrial society.

POSTMODERN LIFE

Sociologists recently have gone beyond discussion of the postindustrial society to contemplate the emergence of postmodern society. A **postmodern society** is a technologically sophisticated, pluralistic, interconnected, globalized society. Although it is difficult to summarize what a whole range of thinkers have said about postmodern life, four elements provide a sense of the key characteristics of such societies today: stories, images, choices, and networks.

industrial society A society that depends on mechanization to produce its goods and services.

postindustrial society A society whose economic system is engaged primarily in the processing and control of information.

postmodern society A technologically sophisticated, pluralistic, interconnected, globalized society.

Stories Because postmodern societies are pluralistic and individualistic, people hold many different, often competing, sets of norms and values. Fewer people assume that a single, all-inclusive story—whether a particular religious tradition, or an all-encompassing scientific theory of everything, or even the faith many early sociologists had in the inevitability of modern progress—can unite us all under a common umbrella. Instead, we embrace the various individual and group stories that help us to make sense of the world and our place in it. We do so in the full knowledge that others out there are doing exactly the same thing and often coming to dramatically different conclusions. This multiplicity of stories undercuts the authority that singular accounts of reality have had in the past.

Going **GLOBAL**

International U.S. Favorability Ratings

Bottom seven nations | Top seven nations

China	44%	Japan 85%
India	41%	Kenya 83%
Egypt	20%	France 75%
Palestinian territories 18%		Lithuania 73%
Jordan	13%	Israel 72%
Pakistan	12%	Poland 70%
Turkey	10%	Spain 64%

Note: Data are for 2011.
Source: Pew Research Center 2012a.

Because we exist in an interdependent global network, the consequences of our actions, both large and small, reverberate throughout the world. In a global survey of 23 nations conducted in 2011, the Pew Research Center looked at international favorability ratings for the United States. How favorably do other nations view the United States? The average national score was 53 percent, a decrease of 4 points over 2010.

Images Postmodern society is also characterized by the explosion of the mass media, which emphasizes the importance of images. As we saw in Chapter 4, the average person in the United States watches almost 4.9 hours of television per day (Bureau of the Census 2008a). This works out to the equivalent of more than 71 full days per year. We are bombarded by images everywhere we turn, but in postmodern theory, the significance of the image goes much deeper than television and advertisements; it impacts our taken-for-granted notion of material reality itself. Theorists argue that we do not confront or interact with the material world directly. Just as language shapes our perception of reality according to the Sapir-Whorf hypothesis, our experience of "reality" is always mediated through representations of reality in the form of signs, symbols, and words. According to postmodernists, our images or models of reality come before reality itself. Postmodern theorists use a geography metaphor to illuminate this concept: "The map precedes the territory" (Baudrillard [1981] 1994). In other words, the images we construct draw our attention to certain features that we might not otherwise single out. A road map, for example, highlights different features, and for different purposes, than does a topographical map or political map. In so doing, it shapes what we see. We cannot step around or look through such cultural constructs to approach the thing itself, and so our knowledge of what is real is always constrained by the images we construct.

Choices In a postmodern world, reality is not simply given; it is negotiated. We pick and choose our reality from the buffet of images and experiences presented to us. In fact, we *must* choose. In contrast to societies characterized by mechanical solidarity, where one's life path is virtually set at birth, members of postmodern societies must make life choices all the time. Assuming we have access to sufficient resources, we choose what to eat, what to wear, and what to drive. Shopping, which in the past would have been viewed primarily as an instrumental necessity to provide for our basic needs, becomes an act of self-creation. As advertising professor James B. Twitchell (2000) put it, "We don't buy things, we buy meanings" (p. 47). An iPhone, a Coach purse, and a MINI Cooper are more than just a phone, a handbag, and a car. They are statements about the kind of person we are or want to be. The significance of choice goes much deeper than just consumer products. We also choose our partners, our schools, our jobs, our faith, and even our identities. As individuals, we may choose to affirm traditions, language, diet, and values we inherited from our family through socialization, but we can also choose to pursue our own path.

Networks Members of postmodern societies live in a globally interconnected world. The food we eat, the clothes we wear, the books we read, and the products we choose often come to us from the other side of the world. The computer technician we talk to for assistance in the United States may be located in India. McDonald's has even experimented with centralized drive-through attendants—who might even be located in another state—who take your order and transmit it to the restaurant you are

ordering from (Richtel 2006). Increasingly, all corners of the globe are linked into a vast, interrelated social, cultural, political, and economic system. A rural Iowa farmer, for example, must be concerned with more than just the local weather and community concerns; he or she must know about international innovations in farming technology, including biotech, as well as the current and future state of international markets.

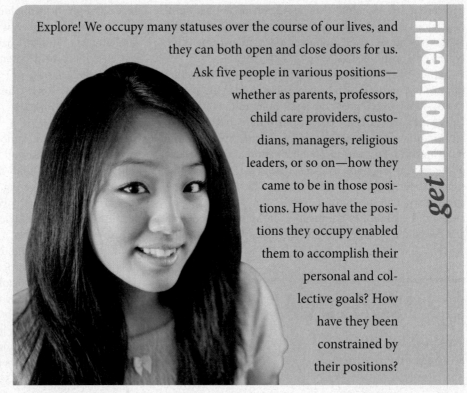

Explore! We occupy many statuses over the course of our lives, and they can both open and close doors for us. Ask five people in various positions— whether as parents, professors, child care providers, custodians, managers, religious leaders, or so on—how they came to be in those positions. How have the positions they occupy enabled them to accomplish their personal and collective goals? How have they been constrained by their positions?

get involved!

Whether in the form of traditional, modern, or postmodern society, social structure provides order, shaping the options that are available to us. It provides the context within which we interact with others. The statuses we occupy shape the roles we perform. What we think and do is influenced by the relationships we have with others in the contexts of groups, networks, and institutions. Sociology as a discipline is committed to making sense of our structural context and the impact it has on our lives.

Still, society and social structure are not singular things. Though we are, in many respects, products of society, socialized to think and act in appropriate ways, we always have the option to think and act in new ways and to construct new culture. The possibility for such change may be more apparent in our pluralistic world. Ours is a world not of "the" structure, "the" family, and "the" religion, but of structures, families, and religions. We have the possibility for more contact with more people who have more ways of thinking and acting than at any time in the past. As such, we can become aware of more alternatives for how we might think and act that might lead us to change our worlds.

For REVIEW

I. **What makes up society?**

- Society provides a structure that is built from the statuses we occupy; the roles we perform; and the groups, networks, and institutions that connect us.

II. **How does social structure shape individual action?**

- The positions we occupy shape our perceptions, the resources to which we have access, and the options that are available. For example, in the context of bureaucracies, our social position, connections, and performance expectations are clearly defined.

III. **How do sociologists describe traditional versus modern societies?**

- Sociologists highlight the impact that division of labor and technological development have on the organization of community, work, and social interaction in traditional and modern societies.

Functionalist View

The **elements of social structure**—statuses, groups, social networks, and social institutions—provide order, shape our options, and give context to our lives.

Social roles create a **stable society** by allowing people to anticipate the behavior of others and to act accordingly.

Institutions contribute to **social order** by performing **vital functions**, whether it is producing children (family), teaching them (schools), establishing order (government), or distributing goods and services (economy).

STRUCTURE, ORDER
KEY CONCEPTS

Conflict View

The elements of the social structure justify and reinforce existing systems of inequality and unequal distributions of resources.

Ascribed statuses, often conferred at birth, can be used to justify **privileges** for some while limiting opportunities for others by consigning them to a **subordinate group.**

In-groups and out-groups serve to highlight **differences** between people and can foster antagonism.

SUBORDINATION, INEQUALITY, PRIVILEGE
KEY CONCEPTS

MAKE THE CONNECTION

After reviewing the chapter, answer the following questions:

Interactionist View

It is through social interaction—the **shared experiences** through which we relate to others—that the elements of social structure are constructed.

Our social roles are governed by a set of expectations, but how we actually **perform** those roles can vary from individual to individual.

A **micro, bottom-up perspective** of social structure reinforces the significance of our actions, and helping us to appreciate how we can think and act in new ways to bring about social change.

SHARED EXPERIENCES, MICRO PERSPECTIVE
KEY CONCEPTS

1

How does Berger and Luckmann's social construction of reality model integrate elements of functionalist, conflict, and interactionist perspectives?

2

Briefly describe how a functionalist, a conflict theorist, and an interactionist would view institutions (pp. 113–114).

3

Sociologists Daniel Bell and Michael Harrington have differing views of postindustrial society. Which perspectives do you think their views reflect (p. 122)?

4

Have you ever been part of an in- or out-group (p. 108)? If so, how might each perspective shed light on your experience?

Pop Quiz

1. The three stages of Berger and Luckmann's model describing the interdependent relationship between the individual and society are
   a. statuses, groups, and institutions.
   b. telling stories, making choices, and establishing networks.
   c. constructing culture, constructing the self, and constructing society.
   d. role conflict, role strain, and role exit.

2. In the United States, we expect that cab drivers know how to get around a city. This expectation is an example of which of the following?
   a. role conflict
   b. role strain
   c. social role
   d. master status

3. What occurs when incompatible expectations arise from two or more social positions held by the same person?
   a. role conflict
   b. role strain
   c. role exit
   d. role playing

4. In sociological terms, what do we call any number of people with similar norms, values, and expectations who interact with one another on a regular basis?
   a. a category
   b. a group
   c. an aggregate
   d. a society

5. Primary groups are characterized by
   a. a series of relationships that link individuals directly to others and, through them, indirectly to still more people.
   b. formal, impersonal relationships with minimal social intimacy or mutual understanding.
   c. social positions that are within our power to change.
   d. intimate, face-to-face association and cooperation.

6. What is the definition of a social institution?
   a. A series of social relationships that link individuals directly to others, and through them indirectly to still more people.
   b. An alliance, whether temporary or permanent, geared toward a common goal.
   c. An organized pattern of beliefs and behavior centered on basic social needs.
   d. A component of a formal organization that uses rules and hierarchical ranking to achieve efficiency.

7. The principle of bureaucracy that establishes that work should be carried out "without hatred or passion" is known as
   a. impersonality.
   b. hierarchy of authority.
   c. written rules and regulations.
   d. division of labor.

8. What type of society did Ferdinand Tönnies describe as a close-knit community in which members have strong personal bonds?
   a. *Gesellschaft*
   b. mechanical
   c. *Gemeinschaft*
   d. organic

9. Sociologist Daniel Bell uses which of the following terms to refer to a society whose economic system is engaged primarily in the processing and control of information?
   a. postmodern
   b. horticultural
   c. industrial
   d. postindustrial

10. What characteristic of postmodern life emphasizes the importance of consumption on identity creation?
    a. stories
    b. images
    c. choices
    d. networks

1. (c); 2. (c); 3. (a); 4. (b); 5. (d); 6. (c); 7. (a); 8. (c); 9. (d); 10. (c)

6

DEVIANCE

LIVING THE GANG LIFE

Sociology student Sudhir Venkatesh (2008), wanting to better understand the lives of poor African Americans, ventured into the housing projects in inner-city Chicago. After a rocky beginning, his naïveté and genuine curiosity helped to open the door to what became a seven-year, in-depth participation research project about gangs, drugs, crime, public housing, and more.

Venkatesh's commitment to going beyond what W. E. B. Du Bois dismissed as "car-window sociology" ultimately provided him access to information about crime and deviance that he could never have found through a survey. Through his research he learned that gangs have a highly organized structure, with those at the top of the gang hierarchy doing well financially, and the foot soldiers at the bottom, who make up 95 percent of the membership, averaging only $3.30 per hour (Levitt and Dubner 2005). They also have an astonishingly high death rate. These two facts led one of Venkatesh's collaborators to say that selling drugs for a gang is perhaps "the worst job in all of America."

Although it may not yield much money for most members, dealing drugs does allow gang members to help support their families. Venkatesh argued that their willingness to work these jobs, even in the face of minimal return and high risk, demonstrated their desire to work, but they found so few viable options that some actually worked at McDonald's to supplement their drug-dealing income.

Venkatesh also found that gangs seek to contribute to the local community, giving money to women who work in the buildings looking after children and the elderly. They require their young members to stay in school and prohibit members from using hard drugs—in part because they cannot be good at business if they are high and in part because it is bad for the image of the gang.

Through research like Venkatesh's, sociologists can better understand crime and deviance. The gang Venkatesh studied tried to create a level of stability in their neighborhood, but they relied on crime and violence as tools of their trade. What social factors lead to such outcomes, and can those factors or outcomes be changed? In this chapter we look at these questions and more.

As You READ

>>

- How do groups maintain social control?
- What is the difference between deviance and crime?
- How do sociologists explain deviance and crime?

>>Social Control

At some point in our lives all of us have likely asked our-selves, "Should I do what *they* want or should I do what *I* want?" Perhaps it happened when we were little and our parents asked us to clean up our toys or maybe at college when a professor assigned a lot of reading or at a job when the boss requested that we work an extra shift. We may not want to give in to the demands of others, yet we know that there are conse-

> **Social control** The techniques and strategies for preventing deviant human behavior in any society.

quences for not doing so. To better understand the power that others wield over us, and how we respond to it, soci-ologists study social control, deviance, and crime.

As a species, we need the social order that norms pro-vide. Knowing that others will follow shared rules for behavior makes coordinated action possible, thus enabling us to meet our individual and collective needs. To ensure sufficient obe-dience regarding norms, we use **social control**—the techniques and strategies for preventing deviant human behav-ior in any society. Social control occurs throughout society. Parents have taken-for-granted authority to discipline their children. Peer groups introduce informal norms, such as dress codes, that govern the behav-ior of their members. Colleges establish requirements that must be met for graduation. Govern-ments pass laws and enforce pun-ishments for violators.

Most of us accept and respect basic social norms most of the time. We

have internalized the notion that it is appropriate to obey the instructions of police officers, follow the day-to-day rules at our jobs, and move to the rear of elevators when people enter. Such acquiescence reflects effective socialization to the dominant standards of a culture. We also know that fail-ure to do so can result in negative sanctions (see Chapter 3).

Sanctions point to the power that societies, institutions, and groups have over our lives. People in positions of author-ity have the capacity to reward and punish, thus encourag-ing and discouraging particular outcomes. For example, a parent might heap praise upon a child, a police officer might write a speeding ticket, a boss might grant a promotion, or a teacher might give a student an F on an exam.

Although social control contributes to social order, such power can be oppressive, limiting individual free-dom and advancing the interests of some at the expense of others. Entrenched interests often seek to maintain the status quo and use their power over sanctions to do so. In fact, positive social change often comes through active resistance to the status quo, with individuals and groups rejecting existing norms and following new paths. Such attempts may meet with significant opposition, as was evident in the struggle to end slavery, the fight for women's right to vote, the civil rights movement, and the protests to end the war in Vietnam.

CONFORMITY AND OBEDIENCE

Techniques for social control operate on both the group and the societal level. People we think of as peers or equals influence us to act in particular ways; the same is true of people who hold authority over us or whose positions we respect. Social psychologist Stanley Milgram (1975) made a useful distinction between these two levels of social control.

According to Milgram, **conformity** means going along with peers—individuals of our own status who have no special right to direct our behavior. **Obedience,** in contrast, is compliance with higher authorities in a hierarchical structure. A recruit entering military service will typically conform to the habits and language of other recruits and obey the orders of superiors. Students will conform to the drinking behavior of their peers and obey the requests of campus security officers.

In a classic experiment, Milgram (1963, 1975) sought to test how far people would go when obeying authority. Would they administer increasingly painful electric shocks to another person if asked to do so by a scientific researcher? Contrary to what we might believe about ourselves, Milgram found that most of us would obey the researcher. In his words, "Behavior that is unthinkable in an individual . . . acting on his own may be executed without hesitation when carried out under orders" (1975:xi).

To set up his experiment, Milgram placed ads in local newspapers to recruit subjects for an experiment at Yale University. His participants included postal clerks, engineers, high school teachers, and laborers. They were told that the purpose of the research was to investigate the effects of punishment on learning. The scientist, dressed in a gray technician's coat, explained that in each test, one subject would be randomly selected as the "learner" and another would function as the "teacher." However, the experiment was rigged so that the "real" subject would always be the teacher while an associate of Milgram's served as the learner.

To begin, each teacher was given a sample shock of 45 volts to convince him or her of the authenticity of the experiment. A learner was then strapped to an electric apparatus, and the teacher was taken to an electronic "shock generator" with 30 switches labeled from 15 to 450 volts. The experimenter then instructed the teacher to apply shocks of increasing voltage each time the learner gave an incorrect answer on a memory test. Teachers were told that "although the shocks can be extremely painful, they cause no permanent tissue damage." In reality, the learner did not receive any shocks.

conformity The act of going along with peers—individuals of our own status who have no special right to direct our behavior.

obedience Compliance with higher authorities in a hierarchical structure.

In a prearranged script, the learner deliberately gave incorrect answers and pretended to be in pain when "shocked." For example, at 150 volts the learner would cry out, "Get me out of here!" At 270 volts the learner would scream in agony. When the shock reached 350 volts, the learner would fall silent. If the teacher wanted to stop the experiment, the experimenter would insist that the teacher continue, using such statements as "The experiment requires that you continue" and "You have no other choice; you *must* go on" (Milgram 1975: 19–23).

The results of this unusual experiment stunned and dismayed Milgram and other social scientists. A sample of

POPSOC

The zombie apocalypse has become a pop culture staple. Examples include George Romero's *Living Dead* films, Max Brooks's *World War Z* book and film, and *The Walking Dead* graphic novel and TV series. Such accounts often say more about humans and the breakdown of social order than they do about zombies. In the event of a zombie apocalypse, how quickly do you think social order would break down? What factors might minimize social chaos? What steps should people take?

SOCTHINK

According to the American Sociological Association *Code of Ethics,* researchers must "protect subjects from personal harm." To what extent might Milgram's subjects have experienced emotional harm? How and why might a researcher seek to justify such a risk?

psychiatrists had predicted that virtually all subjects would refuse to shock innocent victims. In their view, only a "pathological fringe" of fewer than 2 percent would continue administering shocks up to the maximum level. Yet almost two-thirds of participants fell into the category of "obedient subjects."

Why did these subjects obey? Why were they willing to inflict seemingly painful shocks on innocent victims who had never done them any harm? There is no evidence that these subjects were unusually sadistic; few seemed to enjoy administering the shocks. Instead, in Milgram's view, the key to obedience was the experimenter's social role as "scientist" and "seeker of knowledge."

Milgram pointed out that in the modern industrial world, we are accustomed to submitting to impersonal authority figures whose status is indicated by a title (professor, lieutenant, doctor) or by a uniform (the technician's coat). Because we view the authority as more important than the individual, we shift responsibility for our behavior to the authority figure. Afterward, Milgram's subjects frequently stated, "If it were up to me, I would not have administered shocks." They saw themselves as merely doing their duty (Milgram 1975).

Milgram launched his experimental study of obedience in part to better understand the involvement of Germans in the murder of 6 million Jews and millions of other people during World War II. In an interview conducted long after the publication of his study, he suggested that

"if a system of death camps were set up in the United States of the sort we had seen in Nazi Germany, one would be able to find sufficient personnel for those camps in any medium-sized American town" (CBS News 1979:7–8). Though many people questioned this statement, the revealing photos taken at Iraq's Abu Ghraib prison in 2004, showing U.S. military guards humiliating if not torturing Iraqi prisoners, recalled the experiment Milgram had done two generations earlier. Under conducive circumstances, otherwise normal people can and often do treat one another inhumanely (Hayden 2004; Zimbardo 2007).

SOCTHINK

Do you think a person's background factors would influence how far he or she would go in Milgram's experiment? How might age, gender, religion, or education make a difference?

INFORMAL AND FORMAL SOCIAL CONTROL

The sanctions that society uses to encourage conformity and obedience—and to discourage violation of social norms—are carried out through both informal and formal social control. As the term implies, people use **informal social control** casually to enforce norms. Examples include smiles, laughter, a raised eyebrow, and ridicule. We seek to read such cues in new situations such as a first date or a job interview so that we might adjust our behavior accordingly.

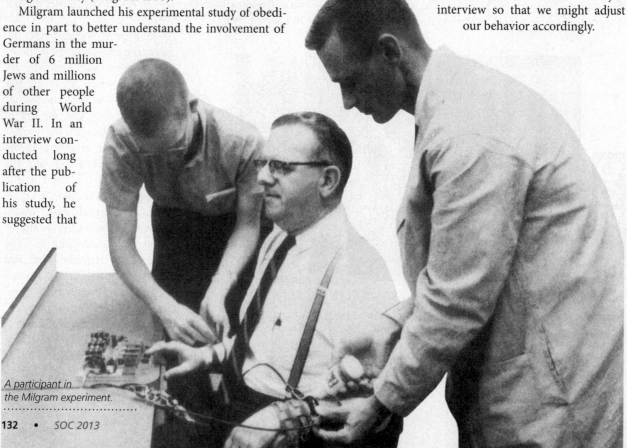

A participant in the Milgram experiment.

All groups must use some form of social control if they are to maintain any sense of order. What mechanisms of formal and informal social control are evident in your college classes and in day-to-day life and social interactions at your school?

Formal social control is carried out by authorized agents, such as police officers, judges, school administrators, employers, military officers, and managers. It can serve as a last resort when socialization and informal sanctions do not bring about desired behavior. An increasingly significant means of formal social control in the United States is imprisonment. In 2010 more than 7.1 million adults underwent some form of correctional supervision—jail, prison, probation, or parole. Put another way, 3.0 percent, or 1 out of every 33 adult Americans, was subject to this very formal type of social control (Glaze 2011).

In the wake of mass campus shootings, such as those at Virginia Tech in 2007 and Oikos University in Oakland in 2012, many college officials reviewed security measures on their campuses. Administrators were reluctant to end or even limit the relative freedom of movement students on their campuses enjoyed. Instead, they concentrated on improving emergency communications between campus police and students, faculty, and staff. Reflecting a reliance on technology to maintain social control, college leaders called for replacement of the "old" technology of email with instant alerts that could be sent to people's cell phones via instant messaging.

Similarly, in the aftermath of the terrorist attacks of September 11, 2001, new measures of social control became the norm in the United States. Some of them, such as stepped-up security at airports and high-rise buildings, were highly visible to the public. The federal government also publicly urged citizens to engage in informal social control by watching for and reporting people whose actions seem suspicious. But many other measures taken by the government have increased the covert surveillance of private records and communications.

Only a month and a half after September 11, and with virtually no debate, Congress passed the USA PATRIOT Act of 2001. It was reauthorized in 2005 and 2006, and extended by the Obama administration in 2011. Sections of this sweeping legislation revoked legal checks on the power of law enforcement agencies. Without a warrant or probable cause, the FBI can now secretly access most private records, including medical histories, library accounts, and student registrations. In 2002, for example, the FBI searched the records of hundreds of dive shops and scuba organizations. Agents had been directed to identify every person who had taken diving lessons in the past three years because of speculation that terrorists might try to approach their targets underwater (Moss and Fessenden 2002).

Many people think that this kind of social control goes too far. Civil rights advocates also worry that the government's request for information on suspicious activities may encourage negative stereotyping of Muslims and Arab Americans. Clearly, there is a trade-off between the benefits of surveillance and violation of the right to privacy.

The interplay between formal and informal social control can be complicated, because we sometimes have to balance one source of control against another. College students, for example, receive conflicting messages about the acceptability of binge drinking. On the one hand, it represents deviance from the standards of conduct expected of those in an academic context. On the other hand, binge drinking shows conformity to the peer culture, especially in the context of sororities and fraternities (see the figure "Binge Drinking on Campus"). Increasingly, colleges and

informal social control Social control that is carried out casually by ordinary people through such means as laughter, smiles, and ridicule.

formal social control Social control that is carried out by authorized agents, such as police officers, judges, school administrators, and employers.

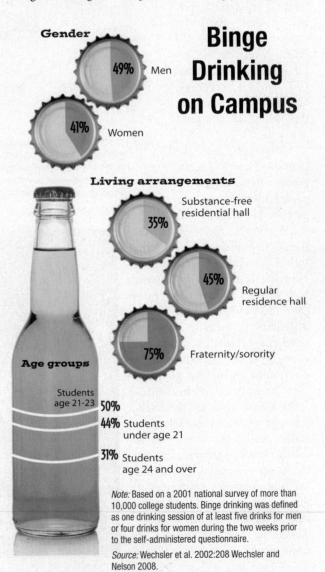

Binge Drinking on Campus

Gender

49% Men

41% Women

Living arrangements

35% Substance-free residential hall

45% Regular residence hall

75% Fraternity/sorority

Age groups

Students age 21-23 50%

44% Students under age 21

31% Students age 24 and over

Note: Based on a 2001 national survey of more than 10,000 college students. Binge drinking was defined as one drinking session of at least five drinks for men or four drinks for women during the two weeks prior to the self-administered questionnaire.

Source: Wechsler et al. 2002:208 Wechsler and Nelson 2008.

universities are taking steps to exert greater social control by instituting rules banning kegs, closing fraternities and sororities that violate standards of conduct, expelling students after multiple alcohol-related violations, and working with local liquor retailers to discourage high-volume sales to students (Wechsler and Nelson 2008).

LAW AND SOCIETY

Some norms are so important to a society that they are formalized into laws limiting people's behavior. Laws—formal norms enforced by the state—are a form of governmental social control. Some laws, such as the prohibition against murder, are directed at all members of society. Others, such as fishing and hunting regulations, primarily affect particular categories of people. Still others govern the behavior of social institutions (for instance, corporate law and laws regarding the taxing of nonprofit enterprises).

Sociologists see the creation of laws as a social process. Because laws are passed in response to a perceived need for formal social control, sociologists have sought to explain how and why such a perception arises. In their view law is not merely a static body of rules handed down from generation to generation. Rather, it reflects continually changing standards of what is right and wrong, of how violations are to be determined, and of what sanctions are to be applied (Deflem 2008).

In diverse societies the establishment of laws inevitably generates conflicts over whose values should prevail, and so the creation of civil and criminal laws can be controversial. For example, should it be against the law to employ illegal immigrants? To have an abortion? To allow prayer in public schools?

To smoke on an airplane? Such issues have been bitterly debated because they require a choice among competing values. Not surprisingly, unpopular laws—such as the 18th Amendment, which prohibited the manufacture and sale of alcohol (ratified in 1919), or the nationwide 55-mile-per-hour speed limit that was imposed in 1974—become difficult to enforce when there is no consensus supporting the norms. In both cases the public commonly violated the stated government policy, and the laws proved

Medical Marijuana Laws

■ Washington, DC

16 states and the District of Columbia have legalized the possession and use of marijuana for medical purposes. The amount a person can possess and the legality of growing your own varies by state.

Source: Marijuana Policy Project 2011.

unenforceable; the states repealed Prohibition in 1933, and Congress overturned the national speed-limit policy in 1987.

The current debate over the legalization of marijuana illustrates the difficulty in crafting public laws governing private behavior. For example, even though federal law prohibits all uses of marijuana, 73 percent of U.S. adults support legalization for medical purposes (Pew Research Center 2010b). As the map below shows, 16 states and the District of Columbia have responded by legalizing the possession and use of medical marijuana. In 2009 the U.S. Supreme Court upheld the right of states to pass such statutes, despite existing federal laws. Overall, support for the outright legalization of

marijuana has risen from 12 percent in 1969 to 50 percent in 2011 (Gallup 2011c).

Socialization is the primary vehicle for instilling conforming and obedient behavior, including obedience to law. Generally, it is not external pressure from a peer group or authority figure that makes us go along with social norms. Rather, we have internalized such norms as valid and desirable and are self-policing. In a profound sense, we want to see ourselves (and to be seen) as loyal, cooperative, responsible, and respectful of others. In the United States and other societies around the world, people are socialized both to want to belong and to fear being viewed as different or deviant.

Control theory suggests that our connection to other members of society leads us to conform systematically to society's norms. According to sociologist Travis Hirschi and other control theorists, our bonds to family members, friends, and peers induce us to follow the mores and folkways of our society. We give little conscious thought to whether we will be sanctioned if we fail to conform. Socialization develops our self-control so well that we don't need further pressure to obey social norms. Although control theory does not explain the rationale for every conforming act, it nevertheless reminds us that although the media may focus on crime and disorder, most members of most societies conform to and obey basic norms most of the time (Gottfredson and Hirschi 1990; Hirschi 1969).

>>Deviance

The flip side of social control is deviance. **Deviance** is behavior that violates the standards of conduct or expectations of a group or society (Wickman 1991:85). In the United States, most people classify those who are alcoholics, compulsive gamblers, or mentally ill as deviant. Being late for class is categorized as a deviant act, as is wearing jeans to a formal wedding. On the basis of the sociological definition, we are all deviant from time to time. Each of us violates common social norms in certain situations.

> **control theory** A view of conformity and deviance that suggests our connection to members of society leads us to systematically conform to society's norms.
>
> **deviance** Behavior that violates the standards of conduct or expectations of a group or society.

WHAT BEHAVIOR IS DEVIANT?

Because deviance involves violation of some group's norms, defining an act as deviant depends on the context. File sharing on the Internet—including MP3s, movies, computer games, books, and almost anything else that can be digitized—provides an example of how deviance can be in the eye of the beholder. Sharing files, whether through BitTorrent or eMule, has become widespread. New movies are sometimes available online even before they have been released in the theater. Because the "property" these files represent is not physical, it can be reproduced for virtually no cost. Anyone with a computer and an Internet connection can grab them from people who are willing to share, then pass them along to others. Just how deviant is this? Record and movie companies take it very seriously; they have actively pursued lawsuits against those who share files in part

Present-day fans of bullfighting, which has a long and rich history in Spain and elsewhere, are now often stigmatized for their admiration of a sport that can result in pain and death for the bulls.

... In 2006 the Spanish Association of Fashion Designers banned overly thin models—those with a *body mass index* score under 18—from the runway during Madrid Fashion Week. Similarly, in 2009, Germany's most popular women's magazine, *Brigitte*, banned professional models from its pages, replacing them with "real life" women. Both groups established these policies to encourage healthier practices for the models and in response to protests that such ultrathin images of women contribute to eating disorders.

examples of this, such as when nonviolent protesters at sit-ins and marches were met with attack dogs, fire hoses, beatings, and jail time. In the end, however, these protests led to greater political, legal, and economic opportunity for African Americans and others. Part of what makes such change difficult is that those with the greatest status have the capacity to define what is acceptable and what is deviant. It often takes a concerted effort, and the mobilization of substantial resources, to counteract such power.

DEVIANCE AND SOCIAL STIGMA

Some people are unwillingly cast in negative social roles because of physical or behavioral characteristics. Whole groups of people—for instance, "short people" or "blondes"—may be labeled in this way. Once individuals have been assigned a deviant role, they can have trouble presenting a positive image to others and may even experience lowered self-esteem. Sociologist Erving Goffman coined the term **stigma** to describe the labels society uses to devalue members of certain social groups (Goffman 1963).

We face pressure not to deviate too far from expected norms. To avoid stigma, for example, women can feel pressured to approximate what Naomi Wolf (1992) refers to as the "beauty myth"—an exaggerated ideal of beauty, beyond the reach of all but a few females. As a result, many of the 12.1 million cosmetic procedures performed by physicians on women in 2011 were performed on women who would be defined objectively as having a normal appearance. Although feminist sociologists have accurately noted that the beauty myth makes many women feel uncomfortable with themselves, men, too, seek to improve their appearance. In 2011, 1.2 million men underwent cosmetic surgery, making up 9 percent of total patients. Overall, the total number of cosmetic procedures for both men and women rose 87 percent from 2000 to 2011 (American Society of Plastic Surgeons 2011).

Often people are stigmatized for deviant behaviors that they may no longer practice. The labels "former gambler," "ex-convict," and "ex–mental patient" can stick to a person for life. Goffman draws a useful distinction between a prestige symbol that calls attention to a positive aspect of one's identity, such as a wedding band or a badge, and a stigma symbol that discredits or debases

to scare those who might think of doing it. However, the widespread availability of these files suggests that many people do not view this practice as particularly deviant. Some even view it as an act of protest against what they consider unfair prices charged by big corporations.

stigma A label used to devalue members of certain social groups.

Although we tend to think of deviance as something negative, deviance is also the source for positive social change. Because we usually conform to expected social norms, it can be difficult to see how our existing practices may violate our core principles. At times such as these, people who stand up for what they believe is right are often punished. The civil rights movement provided numerous

one's identity, such as a conviction for child molestation. Although stigma symbols may not always be obvious, they can become a matter of public knowledge. Starting in 1994 many states required convicted sex offenders to register with local police departments. Some communities publish the names and addresses, and in some instances even the pictures, of convicted sex offenders on the Web.

Being stigmatized can limit a person's opportunities. For example, people who are homeless often have trouble getting a job because employers are wary of applicants who cannot provide a home address. Though many hiring agencies use a telephone for contacts, cell phones are expensive, and owning one while homeless is often looked at with suspicion by others. If a homeless person has access to a telephone at a shelter, the staff generally answers by announcing the name of the institution, which discourages prospective employers from hiring the applicant. And, even if the person is hired, the stigma attached to homelessness, should the employee's past or present situation become known, can negatively impact opportunities, even in the face of positive work performance.

>>Crime

If deviance means breaking group norms, **crime** is a violation of law for which some governmental authority applies formal penalties. It is a type of deviance representing a violation of social norms administered by the state. Laws divide crimes into various categories, depending on the severity of the offense, the age of the offender, the potential punishment, and the court that holds jurisdiction over the case.

OFFICIAL CRIME REPORTS

When we think of crime, the categories most likely to come to mind involve what we might think of as street crimes. The FBI breaks such crimes into two major categories: violent crimes and property crimes. They do not include all types of crime in these reports, focusing only on four major types within each category. Violent crimes include murder, forcible rape, robbery, and aggravated assault; property crimes include burglary, larceny-theft, motor vehicle theft, and arson. The FBI provides an annual account of the number of these crimes in their *Uniform Crime Reports* (UCR), which is available online. Because they are tracked so closely by the FBI and have been for a long time, these crimes have come to be known as **index crimes**.

crime A violation of criminal law for which some governmental authority applies formal penalties.

index crimes The eight types of crime reported annually by the FBI in the *Uniform Crime Reports:* murder, forcible rape, robbery, aggravated assault, burglary, larceny-theft, motor vehicle theft, and arson.

As we can see in the accompanying table, property crimes occur at a much higher rate than do violent crimes. In fact, according to the "crime clock" that the FBI provides as part of its report, a property crime occurs on average every 3.5 seconds. The most frequent property crime is larceny-theft, which includes incidents such as shoplifting and stealing items from cars. By contrast, a violent crime occurs every 25.3 seconds. Robbery, which involves the

National Crime Rates and Percentage Change

Offenses in 2010	Number reported	Rate per 100,000 inhabitants	Percent change in rate Since 2001 Since 2006
Violent crimes Murder	14,748	4.8	-17.4 / -15.0
Forcible rape	84,767	27.5	-13.0 / -13.8
Robbery	367,832	119.1	-20.6 / -19.7
Aggravated assault	778,901	252.3	-13.6 / -20.8
Total	1,246,248	403.6	-15.8 / -20.0
Property crimes Burglary	2,159,878	699.6	-4.6 / -5.7
Larceny-theft	6,185,867	2,003.5	-9.5 / -19.4
Motor vehicle theft	737,142	238.8	-40.3 / -44.5
Total	9,082,887	2,941.9	-12.1 / -19.6

= 10,000 Offenses

Note: Insufficient data are available on arson to estimate accurate totals. Because of rounding, the offenses may not add to totals.

Source: U.S. Department of Justice 2011a: Tables 1, 1A.

Crimes Reported to Police

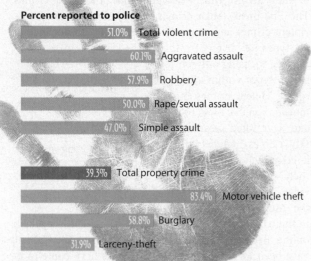

Percent reported to police

- 51.0% Total violent crime
- 60.1% Aggravated assault
- 57.9% Robbery
- 50.0% Rape/sexual assault
- 47.0% Simple assault

- 39.3% Total property crime
- 83.4% Motor vehicle theft
- 58.8% Burglary
- 31.9% Larceny-theft

Note: Percentages based on the National Crime Victimization Survey for 2010.

Source: Truman 2011: Table 7

use or threat of force, is the most frequent violent crime, with one occurring every 1.4 minutes. Murder is the least frequent of the index crimes, with one occurring every 35.6 minutes (U.S. Department of Justice 2011b).

Trends in Crime Crime rates vary over time, and sociologists seek to explain factors that contribute to these changes. In the past ten years, as indicated in the accompanying table, crime rates have fallen in every major category. Murder rates, for example, declined 15 percent since 2001 (U.S. Department of Justice 2011a: Table 1a). To explain these trends, sociologists would seek to identify possible causal factors, including the potential effects of

> **victimization survey** A questionnaire or interview given to a sample of the population to determine whether people have been victims of crime.

- The overall aging of the population, because people are more likely to commit crimes when they are young;

- Changes in the economy, including the economic downturn in the early 2000s and again starting in 2008;
- The expansion of community-oriented policing and crime prevention programs;
- Increased incarceration rates, removing potential offenders from the streets;
- New prison education programs designed to reduce the number of repeat offenders.

Knowledge of the impact of these and other possible factors would help us to establish more effective policies designed to further reduce the crime rate in the future.

Victimization Surveys Official crime reports, such as the UCR, underreport the actual number of crimes that occur. This is primarily because not everyone reports crimes to the police. In the case of larceny-theft, for example, people may conclude that, because there is little chance of getting stolen items back, it simply isn't worth the hassle. More significantly, members of racial and ethnic minority

—SOCTHINK—

The Clery Act, passed in 1990, requires schools to provide students with timely reports of campus crimes. How much do you trust official campus crime reports? Why might reports of crime on college campuses underestimate the actual number of incidents?

groups often distrust law enforcement agencies and may not contact the police when they are victimized. Further, many women do not report rape or spousal abuse out of fear they will be blamed for the crime.

To address such deficiencies in official statistics, the U.S. Department of Justice conducts its annual National Crime Victimization Survey. **Victimization surveys** are questionnaires or interviews given to a sample of the population to determine whether people have been victims of crime. In their yearly report, Department of Justice officials draw on interviews with more than 70,000 people in over 40,000 households in the United States. They interview each household in their sample twice during the

"I swear I wasn't looking at smut—I was just stealing music."

given year. Over 90 percent of selected households agree to participate (Truman 2011).

Results from the National Crime Victimization Survey demonstrate significant variability in which types of crimes are reported to police. As shown in the graph on the previous page, motor vehicle theft is the most likely to be reported, with 83.4 percent of victims contacting the authorities. Larceny-theft is the least likely at 31.9 percent. When it comes to violent crimes, only about one-half of victims contact the police (Truman 2011). What these numbers suggest is that a substantial amount of crime goes unreported and, as such, many offenses never see justice served within the U.S. legal system.

Movies 5 on CRIME

Drive
A man moonlights as a getaway car driver.

Enron: The Smartest Guys in the Room
A huge company's white-collar crime practices.

The Town
Bank robbery as a way of life in South Boston.

No Country for Old Men
A violent cat-and-mouse game between a witness, a hit man, and a sheriff.

Girl with the Dragon Tattoo
A journalist and a young computer hacker search for a woman who has been missing for 40 years.

Another limitation of the UCR official statistics is that they exclude many offenses that we would count as criminal. In so doing, they minimize the degree to which we see perpetrators of other types of crime as criminal in the same way as violators of the index crimes. We turn next to several such categories, including white-collar crime, victimless crimes, and organized crime.

WHITE-COLLAR CRIME

Income tax evasion, stock manipulation, consumer fraud, bribery and extraction of kickbacks, embezzlement, and misrepresentation in advertising—these are all examples of **white-collar crime,** or illegal acts committed in the

course of business activities, often by affluent, "respectable" people. Historically, we have viewed such crimes differently because they are often perpetrated through respected occupational roles (Sutherland 1949, 1983).

Sociologist Edwin Sutherland (1940) coined the term *white-collar crime* to refer to acts by individuals, but the term is now used more broadly to include offenses by businesses and corporations as well. Corporate crime, or any act by a corporation that is punishable by the government, takes many forms and includes individuals, organizations, and institutions among its victims. Corporations may engage in anticompetitive behavior, environmental pollution, medical fraud, tax fraud, stock fraud and manipulation, accounting fraud, the production of unsafe goods, bribery and corruption, and health and safety violations (J. Coleman 2006).

The downfall of Bernie Madoff represents the largest case of white-collar crime of its type in history. Madoff, an American businessman who managed people's financial investments, promised investors annual returns of 15 to 20 percent and delivered on that promise for years. This enabled him to attract extremely wealthy clients from around the world, even charitable organizations. In the end, he was just running a scam. Madoff had provided investors with false statements showing nonexistent trades and profits. Estimates are that he defrauded his clients out of $65 billion in purported assets. Life savings and family fortunes were gone in an instant (Gaviria and Smith 2009).

The scheme collapsed in December 2008, after Madoff confessed to his sons that his investment company was a "giant Ponzi scheme." After consulting an attorney, they reported their father to the FBI. Madoff was arrested the next day. In a Ponzi scheme, the fraudulent investor uses money from new investors to pay off old ones rather than investing the money. The payoff is at higher-than-average rates of return, which encourages new investors who are attracted by the profits. The whole system topples if current investors want to pull their money out, or if there aren't enough new investors to cover profits and payouts to existing investors. Both happened with the economic collapse in late 2008. On March 12, 2009, Madoff pled guilty to 11 felony counts, including securities fraud, mail fraud, money laundering, and perjury. He was sent directly to jail and was sentenced to the maximum of 150 years in prison (Henriques and Healy 2009).

white-collar crime Illegal acts committed by affluent, "respectable" individuals in the course of business activities.

What is particularly interesting about the Madoff case is that officials at the Securities and Exchange Commission (SEC) were tipped off numerous times to the possibility that Madoff's investments were a scam. Finally, after receiving documented accusations that he was running a Ponzi scheme, the SEC launched an official investigation

SOCTHINK
Should gambling, prostitution, and recreational drugs be legalized? What are the potential consequences, both positive and negative, of doing so?

victimless crime Acts involving the willing exchange among adults of widely desired, but illegal, goods and services.

organized crime The work of a group that regulates relations among criminal enterprises involved in illegal activities, including prostitution, gambling, and the smuggling and sale of illegal drugs.

in 2006. Two years later they concluded that there was "no evidence of fraud." The SEC failed to see what analysts now say should have been obvious. Red flags were ignored, but why? Sociologists suggest that white-collar criminals are often given the benefit of the doubt. In fact, during each previous investigation, Madoff deliberately and successfully used his status as a respected businessman as evidence of his innocence. He might have avoided detection had it not been for his own confession (Berenson and Henriques 2008).

VICTIMLESS CRIMES

Another category of crimes that raises questions about how we define deviance consists of so-called victimless crimes. **Victimless crime** refers to the willing exchange among adults of widely desired, but illegal, goods and services, such as drugs or prostitution (Schur 1965, 1985). The fact that the parties involved are willing participants has led some people to suggest that such transactions should not constitute crimes.

> Where there are rules there will always be violations of those rules.

Joel M. Charon

The HBO series *The Wire* has been widely praised for its realistic portrayal of urban life in Baltimore including its coverage of drugs, gangs, and law enforcement. A growing number of sociologists teach courses based on the show to demonstrate lessons about community, crime, poverty, and corruption. Sociologist William Julius Wilson, who teaches such a course at Harvard, maintains, "Although *The Wire* is fiction, not a documentary, its depiction of [the] systemic urban inequality that constrains the lives of the urban poor is more poignant and compelling [than] that of any published study, including my own" (Bennett 2010).

Some activists are working to decriminalize many of these illegal practices. Supporters of decriminalization are troubled by the attempt to legislate a moral code for adults. In their view, prostitution, drug use, gambling, and other victimless crimes are expensive to enforce and impossible to prevent. The already overburdened criminal justice system should instead devote its resources to "street crimes" and other offenses with obvious victims.

Despite widespread use of the term *victimless crime*, however, many people object to the notion that there is no victim other than the offender in such crimes. Excessive drinking, compulsive gambling, and illegal drug use contribute to an enormous amount of personal and property damage. A person with a drinking problem can become abusive to a spouse or children; a compulsive gambler or drug user may steal to pursue his or her obsession. Feminist sociologists contend that prostitution, as well as the more disturbing aspects of pornography, reinforce the misconception that women are "toys" who can be treated as objects rather than people. According to critics of decriminalization, society must not give tacit approval to conduct that has such harmful consequences (Farley and Malarek 2008; Meier and Geis 1997).

ORGANIZED CRIME

When it comes to organized crime, the name Tony Soprano is the first that comes to mind for many people. He was the fictional boss of the DiMeo crime family on HBO's hit series *The Sopranos*. In real life, examples of organized crime groups go beyond the Mafia to include the Japanese Yakuza, the Russian Organization, Colombian drug cartels, and many other international crime syndicates. **Organized crime** is the work of a group that regulates relations among criminal enterprises involved in illegal activities, including prostitution, gambling, and the smuggling and sale of illegal drugs (National Institute of Justice 2007).

Organized crime dominates the world of illegal business, just as large corporations dominate the conventional business world. It allocates territory, sets prices for goods and services, and acts as an arbiter in internal disputes. A secret, conspiratorial activity, organized crime generally evades law enforcement. It takes over legitimate businesses, gains influence over labor unions, corrupts public officials, intimidates witnesses in criminal trials, and even "taxes" merchants in exchange for "protection" (Federal Bureau of Investigation 2012).

Historically, organized crime has provided a means of upward mobility for groups of people struggling to escape poverty. Sociologist Daniel Bell (1953) used the term *ethnic succession* to describe the sequential passage of leadership from Irish Americans in the early 1900s to Jewish Americans in the 1920s and then to Italian Americans in the early 1930s. Recently, ethnic succession has become more complex, reflecting the diversity of the nation's latest immigrants. Colombian, Mexican, Russian, Chinese,

Going GLOBAL

International Incarceration Rates

Rank
out of 219 nations

International incarceration rates
(prison population rates per 100,000 of the national population)

Rank	Nation	Rate
1	United States of America	730
5	Russian Federation	522
33	South Africa	310
54	Israel	236
64	Mexico	201
90	England and Wales	90
117	Kenya	126
121	China	122
130	Canada	117
174	Sweden	70
193	Japan	55
211	India	30

Source: International Centre for Prison Studies 2012.

Pakistani, and Nigerian immigrants are among those who have begun to play a significant role in organized crime activities (Friman 2004; Kleinknecht 1996).

There has always been a global element in organized crime. However, law enforcement officials and policy makers now acknowledge the emergence of a new form of organized crime that takes advantage of advances in electronic communications. International organized crime includes drug and arms smuggling, money laundering, and trafficking in illegal immigrants and stolen goods (Lumpe 2003; National Institute of Justice 2007).

INTERNATIONAL CRIME

In the past, international crime was often limited to the clandestine shipment of goods across the border between two countries. Increasingly, however, crime is no more restricted by such borders than is legal commerce. Rather than concentrating on specific countries, international crime now spans the globe.

Transnational Crime More and more, scholars and law enforcement officials are turning their attention to **transnational crime**, or crime that occurs across multiple national borders. Historically, probably the most dreaded example of transnational crime has been slavery. At first, governments did not regard slavery as a crime but merely regulated it as they would trade in any other good. In the 20th century, transnational crime grew to include trafficking in endangered species, drugs, and stolen art and antiquities.

Transnational crime is not exclusive of some of the other types of crime we have discussed. For example, organized criminal networks are increasingly global. Technology definitely facilitates their illegal activities, such as trafficking in child pornography. The United Nations tracks a variety of transnational crimes, such as trafficking in persons, smuggling migrants, drug trafficking, counterfeiting, and cybercrime (UNODC 2010).

One way to fight such crime has been through multilateral cooperation in which countries cooperate to pursue border-crossing crime. The first global effort to control international crime was the International Criminal Police Organization (Interpol), a cooperative network of European police forces founded to stem the movement of political revolutionaries across borders. Although such efforts to fight transnational crime may seem lofty—an activity with which any government would want to cooperate—they are complicated by sensitive legal and security issues. Most nations that have signed protocols issued by the United Nations, including the United States, have expressed concern over potential encroachments on their national judicial systems, as well as concern over their national security. Thus, they have been reluctant to share certain types of intelligence data. The terrorist attacks of September 11, 2001, increased both the interest in combating transnational crime and sensitivity to the risks of sharing intelligence data (Deflem 2005; Felson and Kalaitzidis 2005).

> **transnational crime** Crime that occurs across multiple national borders.

International Crime Rates Taking an international perspective on crime reinforces one of the key sociological lessons about crime and deviance: place matters. Although cross-national data comparison can be difficult, we can offer insight about how crime rates differ around the world.

During the 1980s and 1990s, violent crimes were much more common in the United States than in the nations of western Europe. Murders, rapes, and robberies were reported to the police at much higher rates in the United States. Yet the incidence of certain other types of crime appears to be higher elsewhere. For example, England, Italy, Australia, and New Zealand all have higher rates of car theft than the United States. Developing nations have significant rates of reported homicide due to civil unrest and political conflict among civilians (van Dijk, van Kesteren, and Schmit 2007; World Bank 2003a). But when it comes to putting offenders in jail, the United States tops them all. On a typical day, the United States imprisons 730 of every 100,000 adults, compared to 522 in Russia, fewer than 200 in Mexico, and 117 in Canada (International Centre for Prison Studies 2012).

Why are rates of violent crime so much higher in the United States than in western Europe? Sociologist Elliot Currie (1985, 1998) has suggested that our society places greater emphasis on individual economic achievement than other societies. At the same time, many observers have noted that the culture of the United States has long tolerated, if not condoned, many forms of violence. Coupled with sharp disparities between poor and affluent citizens, significant unemployment, and substantial alcohol and drug abuse, these factors combine to produce a climate conducive to crime.

Violent crime remains a serious problem in nations around the world. In Mexico, for example, drug-related homicides rose from 2,826 in 2007 to 15,273 in 2010 (Archibold 2011). Attacks have been especially concentrated in the area around Ciudad Juárez, a major transportation gateway to the U.S. drug market owing to its location near El Paso, Texas. The violence is a consequence, in part, of governmental attempts to crack down on the illegal drug trade. After his election in 2006, President Felipe Calderón sent in tens of thousands of troops to enforce the law. As a result, drug cartels fought both the authorities and one another in a struggle to maintain their local power (Camp 2010a, 2010b).

>>Sociological Perspectives on Deviance and Crime

Why do people violate social norms? We have seen that deviant acts are subject to both informal and formal social control. The nonconforming or disobedient person may face disapproval, loss of friends, fines, or even imprisonment. Why, then, does deviance occur?

Sociologists have been interested in crime and deviance from the very beginning and have generated numerous theories of deviance and crime. Though we might wish otherwise, there is no one, simple, universal theory that explains all such acts. Here we look to just a few of the theories that sociologists have offered in order to identify significant factors that we must consider in our attempt to understand deviance and crime more fully.

SOCIAL ORDER, DEVIANCE, AND CRIME

Émile Durkheim's ([1895] 1964) emphasis on the importance of social order led him to investigate the nature and causes of deviance and crime. He wondered why deviance, which would seem to undermine order, is found in all societies. For Durkheim the answer rested with how such actions were perceived by others.

Durkheim's Theory of Deviance Durkheim argued that there is nothing inherently deviant or criminal in any act; the key is how society responds to the act. He put it this way: "We must not say that an action shocks the common consciousness because it is criminal, but rather that it is criminal because it shocks that consciousness"

([1895] 1964:123–24). In other words, nothing is criminal or worthy of condemnation unless we decide it is. For example, we do not regard killing in self-defense or in combat in the same way we view killing in cold blood. At least, that is the case until we change our minds about how we view wartime killing, as has happened at various times in our past. When it comes to war, for example, our attitudes about what is appropriate can shift. In both Vietnam and Iraq, strong public support gave way to serious misgivings about U.S. involvement in these nations. In both cases, this was driven in part by images from the conflict, including, for example, the killing of civilians at My Lai

and the treatment of prisoners at Abu Ghraib. In this way, our understanding of what constitutes deviance and crime are tied to issues of social solidarity.

In fact, Durkheim concluded that deviance and crime actually can have a positive impact on society in a variety of ways. For example, identifying acts as deviant clarifies our shared beliefs and values and thus brings us closer together. We say, in effect, "This is who we are, and if you want to be one of us you cannot cross this line. Some things we might let go, but if you push the limits too far you will face sanctions." Punishment, too, can draw a group together, uniting members in their opposition to the offender. Sanctions also discourage others from similar violations, thus increasing conformity. When we see a driver receiving a speeding ticket, a department store cashier being fired for yelling at a customer, or a college student getting a failing grade for plagiarizing a term paper, we are reminded of our collective norms and values and of the consequences of their violation. Finally, Durkheim did recognize that deviant acts might also force us to recognize the limits of our existing beliefs and practices, opening up new doors and leading to cultural innovation.

Based on Durkheim's analysis, it is possible to conclude that all societies identify criminals for the sake of social order. No matter how much unity a society might appear to have, there will always be some who push the limits. Regardless of how "good" such people may appear to be to outsiders, they may face sanction within the group for the good of the whole.

Durkheim did, however, also recognize that some social circumstances increase the likelihood of turning toward deviance and crime. As we have already seen, Durkheim ([1897] 1951) introduced the term *anomie* into the sociological literature to describe the loss

> ## Law and justice are not always the same.
>
> Gloria Steinem

─SOC THINK─

Durkheim argues that increased division of labor results in fewer shared experiences and thus a weakened sense of community. What impact might a strong commitment to individualism have on our likelihood of committing crime?

of direction felt in a society when social control of individual behavior has become ineffective. Anomie is a state of normlessness that typically occurs during a period of profound social change and disorder, such as a time of economic collapse, political or social revolution, or even sudden prosperity. The power of society to constrain deviant action at such times is limited because there is no clear consensus on shared norms and values. Just as we saw with Durkheim's analysis of suicide, at times when social integration is weak, people are freer to pursue their own deviant paths.

Merton's Theory of Deviance Sociologist Robert Merton (1968) took Durkheim's theory a step farther. He suggested that a disconnect can exist between a society's goals and the means people have to attain them. By *goals* he meant the dominant values that most members of a society share, and by *means* he meant the material, social, and cultural resources necessary for success. He did not assume that all people in a society would be equally committed to those values. He also did not assume that everyone would have the same opportunity to attain those goals. Putting these together, he developed the **strain theory of deviance** which views deviance as an adaptation of socially prescribed goals or of the means governing their attainment, or both.

Every office has its ritualist.

We can better understand Merton's model by looking at economic success as an important goal in the United States. Socially agreed upon pathways exist in order to attain that goal—go to school, work hard, do not quit, take advantage of opportunities, and so forth. Merton wondered what happened when someone who shared the goal of economic success lacked the means to attain that end. For example, a mugger and a merchant may share a common goal of making money, but their means of attaining it are radically different. Merton put together various combinations of goals and means and developed a model with five possible adaptations.

> **strain theory of deviance** Merton's theory of deviance as an adaptation of socially prescribed goals or of the means governing their attainment, or both.

Conformity to social norms, the most common adaptation in Merton's typology, is the opposite of deviance. The "conformist" accepts both the overall societal goal (for example, to become wealthy) and the approved means

DWIGHT SCHRUTE

DETERMINED
WORKER
INTENSE
GOOD WORKER
HARD WORKER
TERRIFIC

(hard work). In Merton's view, there must be some consensus regarding accepted cultural goals and the legitimate means for attaining them. Without such a consensus, societies could exist only as collectives of people rather than as unified cultures, and they might experience continual chaos.

cultural transmission A school of criminology that argues criminal behavior is learned through social interactions.

differential association A theory of deviance that holds violation of rules results from exposure to attitudes favorable to criminal acts.

The other four types of behavior all involve some departure from conformity. The "innovator" accepts the goals of society but pursues them with means that are regarded as improper. For instance, a safecracker may steal money to buy consumer goods and take expensive vacations.

In Merton's typology, the "ritualist" has abandoned the goal of material success and become compulsively committed to the institutional means. Work becomes simply a way of life rather than a means to the goal of success. An example would be the bureaucratic official who blindly applies rules and regulations without remembering the larger goals of the organization. Certainly, that would be true of a welfare caseworker who refuses to assist a homeless family because their last apartment was in another district.

The "retreatist," as described by Merton, has basically withdrawn (or retreated) from both the goals and the means of society. In the United States, drug addicts and vagrants are typically portrayed as retreatists. Concern has been growing that adolescents who are addicted to alcohol will become retreatists at an early age.

The final adaptation identified by Merton reflects people's attempts to create a *new* social structure. The "rebel" feels alienated from the dominant means and goals and may seek a dramatically different social order. Members of a revolutionary political organization, such as a militia group, can be categorized as rebels according to Merton's model.

Merton's theory, though popular, does not fully account for patterns of deviance and crime. Although it is useful in explaining certain types of behavior, such as illegal gambling by disadvantaged "innovators," it fails to explain key differences in crime rates. Why, for example, do some disadvantaged groups have lower rates of reported crime than others? Why do many people in adverse circumstances reject criminal activity as a viable alternative? Merton's theory does not easily answer such questions (Clinard and Miller 1998). To more fully appreciate such nuances, we must add to what we can learn from Merton by turning to additional theories that seek to better understand deviance and crime at an interpersonal level.

INTERPERSONAL INTERACTION AND LOCAL CONTEXT

Perhaps the likelihood of committing deviant acts is not solely shaped by social integration or the acceptance of society's larger goals and means to attain them. Maybe parents around the world were right all along that it really does depend on who your friends are. If we are to understand and explain such acts, we must also consider the importance of social interaction and the local context.

Cultural Transmission As humans, we learn how to behave in social situations, whether properly or improperly. Sociologist Edwin Sutherland (1883–1950) proposed that, just as individuals are socialized to conform to society's basic norms and values, so also are they socialized to learn deviant acts. It's not that we are born to be wild; we learn to be wild.

Sutherland drew on the **cultural transmission** school, which emphasizes that individuals learn criminal behavior by interacting with others. Such learning includes not only the techniques of lawbreaking (for example, how to break into a car quickly and quietly), but also the motives, drives, and rationalizations of the criminal. The cultural transmission approach can also be used to explain the behavior of those who habitually abuse alcohol or drugs.

Sutherland maintained that through interactions with a primary group and significant others, people acquire definitions of proper and improper behavior. He used the term **differential association** to describe the process through which exposure to attitudes favorable to criminal acts leads to the violation of rules. Research suggests that this view of differential association also applies to noncriminal deviant acts, such as smoking, binge drinking, and cheating (Higgins, Tewksbury, and Mustaine, 2007; Nofziger and Hye-Ryeon 2006; Vowell and Chen 2004).

To what extent will a given person engage in an activity that is regarded as

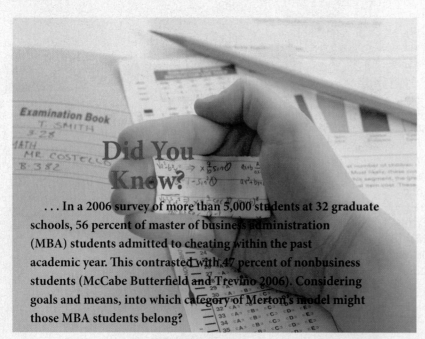

Did You Know?

... In a 2006 survey of more than 5,000 students at 32 graduate schools, 56 percent of master of business administration (MBA) students admitted to cheating within the past academic year. This contrasted with 47 percent of nonbusiness students (McCabe Butterfield and Trevino 2006). Considering goals and means, into which category of Merton's model might those MBA students belong?

proper or improper? For each individual, it will depend on the frequency, duration, and importance of two types of social interaction—those experiences that endorse deviant behavior and those that promote acceptance of social norms. People are more likely to engage in norm-defying behavior if they are part of a group or subculture that stresses deviant values, such as a street gang.

Sutherland offers the example of a boy who is sociable, outgoing, and athletic and who lives in an area with a high rate of delinquency. The youth is very likely to come into contact with peers who commit acts of vandalism, fail to attend school, and so forth, and he may come to adopt such behavior. However, an introverted boy who lives in the same neighborhood may stay away from his peers and avoid delinquency. In another community, an outgoing and athletic boy may join a Little League baseball team or a scout troop because of his interactions with peers. Thus, Sutherland views improper behavior as the result of the types of groups to which one belongs and the kinds of friendships one has (Sutherland, Cressey, and Luckenbill 1992).

Although the cultural transmission approach may not explain the conduct of the first-time, impulsive shoplifter or the impoverished person who steals out of necessity, it does help to explain the deviant behavior of juvenile delinquents or graffiti artists. It directs our attention to the paramount role of social interaction and context in increasing a person's motivation to engage in deviant behavior (Morselli, Tremblay, and McCarthy 2006; Sutherland et al. 1992).

Social Disorganization Theory The relative strength of social relationships in a community or neighborhood influences the behavior of its members. Social psychologist Philip Zimbardo (2007) studied the effect of these communal relationships by conducting the following experiment. He abandoned a car in each of two different neighborhoods, leaving its hood up and removing its hub caps. In one neighborhood, people started to strip the car for parts even before Zimbardo had finished setting up a remote video camera to record their behavior. In the other neighborhood, weeks passed without the car being touched, except for a pedestrian who stopped to close the hood during a rainstorm.

Social disorganization theory attributes increases in crime and deviance to the absence or breakdown of communal relationships and social institutions, such as the family, school, church, and local government.

The lack of such local community connections, with their associated cross-age relationships, makes it difficult to exert informal control within the community, especially of children. Without community supervision and controls, playing outside becomes an opportunity for deviance, and older violators to socialize children into inappropriate paths. Crime becomes a normal response to a local context.

This theory was developed at the University of Chicago in the early 1900s to describe the apparent disorganization that occurred as cities expanded with immigrants from abroad and migrants from rural areas. Using precise survey techniques, Clifford Shaw and Henry McKay (1969) literally mapped the distribution of social problems in Chicago. They found high rates of social problems in neighborhoods where buildings had deteriorated and the population had declined. Interestingly, the patterns persisted over time, despite changes in the neighborhoods' ethnic and racial composition.

> **social disorganization theory** The theory that attributes increases in crime and deviance to the absence or breakdown of communal relationships and social institutions, such as the family, school, church, and local government.

Labeling Theory Sometimes when it comes to deviance, what you see determines what you get. The Saints and Roughnecks were two groups of high school males who were continually engaged in excessive drinking, reckless driving, truancy, petty theft, and vandalism. There the similarity ended. None of the Saints was ever arrested, but every Roughneck was frequently in trouble with police and townspeople. Why the disparity in their treatment? On the basis of observation research in their high school, sociologist William Chambliss (1973) concluded that how they were seen, as rooted in their social class positions, played an important role in the varying fortunes of the two groups.

The Saints hid behind a facade of respectability. They came from "good families," were active in school organizations, planned on attending college, and received good grades. People generally viewed their delinquent acts as a few isolated cases of sowing wild oats. The Roughnecks had no such aura of respectability. They drove around town in beat-up cars, were generally unsuccessful in school, and aroused suspicion no matter what they did.

We can understand such discrepancies by using an approach to deviance known as **labeling theory,** which emphasizes how a person comes to be labeled as deviant or to accept that label. Unlike Sutherland's work, labeling theory does not focus on why some individuals come to commit deviant acts. Instead, it attempts to explain why society views certain people (such as the Roughnecks) as deviants, delinquents, bad kids, losers, and criminals, while it sees others whose behavior is similar (such as the Saints) in less harsh terms. Sociologist Howard Becker (1963:9; 1964), who popularized this approach, summed up labeling theory with this statement: "Deviant behavior is behavior that people so label."

Labeling theory is also called the **societal-reaction approach,** reminding us that it is the response to an act, not the act itself, that determines deviance. Traditionally, research on deviance has focused on people who violate social norms. In contrast, labeling theory focuses on police, probation officers, psychiatrists, judges, teachers, employers, school officials, and other regulators of social

labeling theory An approach to deviance that attempts to explain why certain people are viewed as deviants while others engaged in the same behavior are not.

societal-reaction approach Another name for *labeling theory.*

control. These agents, it is argued, play a significant role in creating the deviant identity by designating certain people (and not others) as deviant (Bernburg, Krohn, and Rivera 2006). An important aspect of labeling theory is the recognition that some individuals or groups have the power to define labels and apply them to others. This view

ties into the conflict perspective's emphasis on the social significance of power.

In recent years, the practice of racial profiling, in which people are identified as criminal suspects purely on the basis of their race, has come under public scrutiny. Studies confirm the public's suspicion that in some jurisdictions, police officers are much more likely to stop African American males than White males for routine traffic violations, in the expectation of finding drugs or guns in their cars. Civil rights activists refer to these cases sarcastically as DWB (Driving While Black) violations (Warren et al. 2006). The shooting death of 17-year-old Trayvon Martin in February 2012 raised substantial concerns about the life-and-death consequences of labeling young African American males as threats.

Although the labeling approach does not fully explain why certain people accept a label and others manage to reject it, labeling theorists do suggest that the power an individual has relative to others is important in determining his or her ability to resist an undesirable label. It opens the door to additional emphasis on the undeniably important actions of people with power who can shape what counts as deviance.

POWER AND INEQUALITY

In addition to its significance for labeling theory, the story of the Saints and Roughnecks points toward the role that power and control over valued resources can play in defining deviance. Sociologist Richard Quinney (1974, 1979, 1980) is a leading proponent of the view that the criminal justice system serves the interests of the powerful; people with power protect their own interests and define deviance to suit their own needs. Crime, according to Quinney (1970), is defined as such by legislators who may be influenced by the economic elites to advance their interests.

Race and Class Looking at crime from this perspective draws our attention to the effects that

Executions by State Since 1976

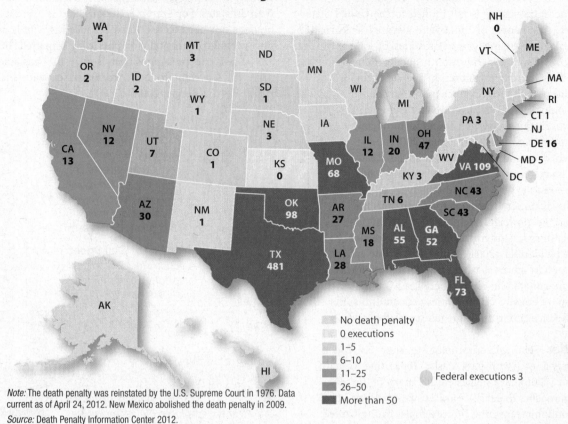

	Legend
	No death penalty
	0 executions
	1–5
	6–10
	11–25
	26–50
	More than 50

Federal executions 3

Note: The death penalty was reinstated by the U.S. Supreme Court in 1976. Data current as of April 24, 2012. New Mexico abolished the death penalty in 2009.

Source: Death Penalty Information Center 2012.

power and position might have throughout the criminal justice system in the United States. Researchers have found that the system treats suspects differently based on their racial, ethnic, or social class background. In many cases, officials using their own discretion make biased decisions about whether to press charges or drop them, whether to set bail and how much, and whether to offer parole or deny it. Researchers have found that this kind of **differential justice**—differences in the way social control is exercised over different groups—puts African Americans and Latinos at a disadvantage in the justice system, both as juveniles and as adults. On average, White offenders receive shorter sentences than comparable Latino and African American offenders, even when prior arrest records and the relative severity of the crime are taken into consideration (Brewer and Heitzeg 2008; Quinney 1974).

We see this pattern of differential justice at work with death penalty cases. Simply put, poor people cannot afford to hire the best lawyer and often must rely on court-appointed attorneys, who typically are overworked and underpaid. With capital punishment in place, these unequal resources may mean the difference between life

> Whenever you find yourself on the side of the majority, it is time to pause and reflect.
>
> Mark Twain

and death for poor defendants. Indeed, the American Bar Association (2009) has repeatedly expressed concern about the limited defense most defendants facing the death penalty receive. Through mid-2012, DNA analysis and other new technologies had exonerated 17 death row inmates and 289 inmates overall, 62 percent of whom were African American (Innocence Project 2012).

differential justice Differences in the way social control is exercised over different groups.

Various studies show that defendants are more likely to be sentenced to death if their victims were White rather than Black. Approximately 76 percent of the victims in death penalty cases are White, even though about half of *all* murder victims are White. There is some evidence that Black defendants, who constituted 42 percent of all death row inmates in 2012, are more likely to face execution than Whites in the same legal circumstances. Overall, 70 percent of those who have been exonerated by DNA testing were members of minority groups. Evidence exists, too, that capital defendants receive poor legal services because of the racist attitudes of their own defense counsel. Apparently, discrimination and racism do not end even when the stakes are life and death (Death Penalty Information Center 2012; Innocence Project 2012; D. Jacobs et al. 2007).

Differential justice is not limited to the United States. In 2007, the people of India were alarmed to learn that police had never investigated a series of killings in the slums of New Delhi. Only after residents found 17 bodies of recently murdered children in a sewer drain on the edge of a slum were police moved to act. For many onlookers, it was just the latest example of the two-tier justice system found in India and many other countries (Gentleman 2007).

Such dramatic differences in social treatment may lead to heightened violence and crime. People who view themselves as the victims of unfair treatment may lash out, not against the powerful so much as against fellow victims. In studying crime in rural Mexico, Andrés Villarreal (2004) found that crime rates were high in the areas where land distribution was most inequitable. In areas where land was distributed more equally, communities appeared to suffer less violence and to enjoy greater social cohesion.

Gender Feminist criminologists such as Meda Chesney-Lind (with Lisa Pasko 2004) and Gillian Balfour (2006) have suggested that many of the existing approaches to deviance and crime were developed with only men in mind. For example, in the United States, for many years any husband who forced his wife to have sexual intercourse—without her consent and against her will—was not legally considered to have committed rape. The law defined rape as pertaining only to sexual relations between people who were not married to each other, reflecting the overwhelmingly male composition of state legislatures at the time.

It took repeated protests by feminist organizations to get changes in the criminal law defining rape. It was not until 1993 that husbands in all 50 states could be prosecuted under most circumstances for the rape of their wives. However, significant exceptions remain in no fewer than 30 states. For example, the husband is exempt when he does not need to use force because his wife is asleep, unconscious, or mentally or physically impaired. In such cases, the presupposition is that the husband has a right to nonconsensual sex with his wife (Bergen 2006).

5 Movies on ORGANIZED CRIME/CORPORATE CRIME

Margin Call
A group of employees at an investment firm react to sensitive information in the immediate wake of the 2008 financial collapse.

Wall Street
A young stockbroker gets swept away with greed and insider trading on his ruthless climb to the top of the corporate ladder.

Inside Job
A documentary detailing the lax regulatory environment behind the 2008 recession.

The Informant!
An eccentric employee blows the whistle on his corporation's price-fixing scheme.

Eastern Promises
The inner workings of the Russian mafia.

When it comes to crime and to deviance in general, society tends to treat women in a stereotypical fashion. For example, consider how women who have many and frequent sexual partners are more likely to be viewed with scorn than men who are promiscuous. Cultural views and attitudes toward women influence how they are perceived and labeled. The feminist perspective also emphasizes that deviance, including crime, tends to flow from economic relationships. Traditionally, men have had greater earning power than their wives. As a result, wives may be reluctant to report acts of abuse to the authorities and thereby lose what may be their primary or even sole source of income. In the workplace, men have exercised greater power than women in pricing, accounting, and product control, giving them greater opportunity to engage in such crimes as embezzlement and fraud. But as women have taken more active and powerful roles both in the household and in business, these gender differences in deviance and crime have narrowed (Bisi 2002; Chesney-Lind 1989; Kruttschnitt and Carbone-Lopez 2010).

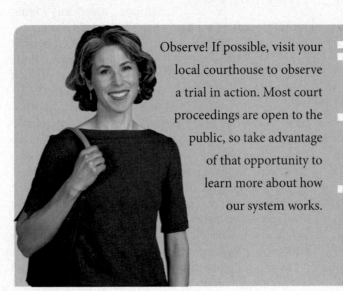

get involved! Observe! If possible, visit your local courthouse to observe a trial in action. Most court proceedings are open to the public, so take advantage of that opportunity to learn more about how our system works.

Together, sociological perspectives on crime and deviance help us to better understand and explain such acts. No single explanation is sufficient. We must consider multiple factors from a variety of perspectives, including the extent to which deviance exists for the sake of social order; the degree of opportunity to attain both means and ends; the role of socialization in deviance; the strength of local community networks; the power to administer labels and make them stick; and differential access to valuable resources based on class, race, and gender. As Sudhir Venkatesh found in his research on gangs, if we are to fully understand something, we need to dig deep enough and consider what is going on from enough angles and with sufficient care, concern, and curiosity.

For REVIEW

I. How do groups maintain social control?
- They use positive and negative sanctions in both formal and informal ways to bring about conformity and obedience.

II. What is the difference between deviance and crime?
- Deviance involves violating a group's expected norms, which may lead the offender to be stigmatized. Crime is a form of deviance that involves violating the formal norms administered by the state for which the offender may receive formal sanctions.

III. How do sociologists explain deviance and crime?
- Sociologists offer a number of theories of crime, each of which provides additional factors to be considered—such as the need for social order, the significance of interpersonal relationships and local context, and the importance of power and access to resources—that help us to better understand why deviance and crime occur.

Functionalist View

Agents of **social control** aim to limit deviant social behavior by enforcing norms and providing negative sanctions for disobedience. Government exerts formal social control through its **laws**.

Deviance can actually contribute to social stability by defining the limits of proper behavior and encouraging **conformity** to laws and rules.

Social **integration** constrains deviant acts because it provides a clear **consensus** on shared norms and values.

CONFORMITY, OBEDIENCE, LAW, ORDER
KEY CONCEPTS

Conflict View

In diverse societies, the process of making laws generates conflicts over whose values should prevail.

Individuals and groups with the greatest **status and power** generally define who or what is deviant in a society.

The criminal justice system **treats suspects differently** based on their racial, ethnic, or class background, which leads to distrust in the criminal system.

POWER, DIFFERENTIAL JUSTICE
KEY CONCEPTS

Interactionist View

People learn what is proper and improper behavior through their interactions with others—an idea known as **cultural transmission**.

Informal social control is achieved through casual interactions—a smile, a raised eyebrow, ridicule—that prompt us to adjust our behavior.

A breakdown in interpersonal social relationships in a local community can lead to increases in crime and deviance.

LABELING, CULTURAL TRANSMISSION
KEY CONCEPTS

MAKE THE CONNECTION

After reviewing the chapter, answer the following questions:

1

How would each perspective approach the conclusions of Venkatesh's study of gang life in Chicago (p. 129)?

2

What perspective do you think provides the best explanation for the results of Milgram's experiment on obedience (p. 132)? Why?

3

Describe victimless crime from the point of view of each of the three perspectives, using one of the following examples in your response: drug use, gambling, or prostitution (p. 139).

4

Which perspective best describes the way you learned proper social behavior? Were social norms socialized and internalized (functionalist), imposed by powerful authority figures (conflict), or learned from observing others (interactionist)? Provide examples.

Pop Quiz

1. **Society brings about acceptance of basic norms through techniques and strategies for preventing deviant human behavior. This process is termed**
   a. stigmatization.
   b. labeling.
   c. law.
   d. social control.

2. **The penalties and rewards we face for conduct concerning a social norm are known as**
   a. informal social controls.
   b. stigmas.
   c. sanctions.
   d. conformities.

3. **Stanley Milgram used the word *conformity* to mean**
   a. going along with peers.
   b. compliance with higher authorities in a hierarchical structure.
   c. techniques and strategies for preventing deviant behavior in any society.
   d. penalties and rewards for conduct concerning a social norm.

4. **According to Hirschi's control theory,**
   a. deviance involves acceptance and/or rejection of society's goals and means.
   b. our connection to members of society leads us to systematically conform to society's norms.
   c. we come to view ourselves as deviant based on how others view us.
   d. power and access to resources shape whose norms and values determine individual action.

5. **Which of the following statements is true of deviance?**
   a. Deviance is always criminal behavior.
   b. Deviance is behavior that violates the standards of conduct or expectations of a group or society.
   c. Deviance is perverse behavior.
   d. Deviance is inappropriate behavior that cuts across all cultures and social orders.

6. **The FBI reports which two major categories of crime in its annual Uniform Crime Reports?**
   a. violent crime and property crime
   b. organized crime and white-collar crime
   c. victimless crime and transnational crime
   d. transnational crime and victimization crime

7. **Which type of crime involves the willing exchange among adults of widely desired, but illegal, goods and services?**
   a. index crimes
   b. white-collar crime
   c. victimless crime
   d. organized crime

8. **Which of the following is *not* one of the basic forms of adaptation specified in Robert Merton's strain theory of deviance?**
   a. conformity
   b. innovation
   c. ritualism
   d. hostility

9. **Which of the following theories contends that criminal victimization increases when communal relationships and social institutions break down?**
   a. labeling theory
   b. conflict theory
   c. social disorganization theory
   d. differential association theory

10. **Even though they committed the same deviant acts, the Saints and the Roughnecks did not receive the same treatment from authorities. Sociologist William Chambliss suggests this was due to the fact that authorities viewed members of the groups differently. Which theory supports that conclusion?**
    a. Merton's strain theory
    b. culture transmission theory
    c. differential association theory
    d. labeling theory

1. (d); 2. (c); 3. (a); 4. (b); 5. (b); 6. (a); 7. (c); 8. (d); 9. (c); 10. (d)

FAMILIES

LOVE AND MARRIAGE

On April 29, 2011, Prince William married Catherine Middleton at Westminster Abbey in London. Though William's status as second-in-line to the British throne ensured much pomp and circumstance, as royal weddings go, it included both something old and even more of something new. Although William and Catherine respected traditions, including the kiss on the Buckingham Palace balcony after the ceremony, their marriage was in a variety of ways unconventional. Instead of a fancy sit-down wedding feast, they opted for a buffet-style lunch. In lieu of wedding presents, they requested that people contribute to the Royal Wedding Charity Fund. Prince William is the first king-to-be to have openly lived with his future bride before marriage. Kate is the first royal bride with a university education to marry an heir to the throne. At age 29 she is the oldest not-previously-married bride to marry a king-in-waiting. And, on top of all that, she is the first commoner to marry someone in the direct line of succession to the throne since the year 1660 (Chu 2011; Pearson 2011; Rayner 2011).

Although such innovations may have been shocking in the past, now they are in keeping with broader cultural shifts regarding the norms of partner selection and marriage. Even among other royals, traditional norms have become much less binding. Since 1945, a majority (71 percent) of European princes have married commoners. Often these relationships began, like William's and Kate's, at a university, where love trumped lineage (Badoo 2011).

In the United States people are, just as the royal couple did, waiting longer to get married. In 1960, 60 percent of 20- to 24-year-olds had already married, but now it is only 14 percent; this change is related to the rise of couples living together. Approximately 12 percent of U.S. couples now are unmarried, and 44 percent of all adults have cohabited at some point in their lives. Overall, the percentage of U.S. adults who are married fell from 72 percent in 1960 to 51 percent in 2010 (Cohn, Passel, Wang, and Livingston 2012; El Nasser and Overberg 2011; Pew Research Center 2010e).

In many ways, rather than breaking new ground, Prince William and Kate simply conformed to emerging norms influencing who, when, and whether to marry. Throughout this chapter we investigate these and other shifts in current marriage and family practices.

As You READ

>>

- What is the family?
- How do people pick partners?
- How do families vary?

>>Global View of the Family

Families around the world come in many shapes and sizes. Among Tibetans, a woman may be married simultaneously to more than one man, usually brothers. This system allows sons to share the limited amount of good land. Among the Betsileo of Madagascar, a man has multiple wives, each one living in a different village where he cultivates rice. Wherever he has the best rice field, that woman is considered his first or senior wife. Among the Yanomami of Brazil and Venezuela, it is considered proper to have sexual relations with one's opposite-sex cousins if they are the children of one's mother's brother or father's sister. But if one's opposite-sex cousins are the children of one's mother's

sister or father's brother, the same practice is considered to be incest (Haviland et al. 2005; Kottak 2004).

In the United States families of today often look different than they did a century or even a generation ago. New roles, new gender distinctions, and new child-rearing patterns have all combined to create new forms of family life. These days, for example, more and more women are taking the breadwinner's role, whether as a spouse or as a single parent. Blended families—the result of divorce and remarriage—are common. And many people are seeking intimate relationships outside

Did You Know?

More than 2 million couples get married in the United States every year. That works out to almost 6,000 per day. In 2009, Nevada had by far the highest marriage rate with 108,150 couples tying the knot, so perhaps not everything that happens in Vegas stays in Vegas.

Source: Tejada-Vera and Sutton 2010.

marriage, whether in gay or lesbian partnerships or in cohabiting arrangements (Fry and Cohn 2010; O'Connell and Feliz 2011; Patten and Parker 2012).

We see such changes reflected in popular culture representations of families. The 1950s U.S. family was epitomized on television by shows such as *Leave It to Beaver* and *Father Knows Best* with a stay-at-home mom, working dad, and assorted kids. Times have changed. *Modern Family* features three interrelated families; *Parenthood* depicts families across three generations; and then there's *Desperate Housewives*. Perhaps the closest you get these days to the 1950s family is *The Simpsons* with Homer, Marge, Bart, Lisa, and Maggie. This shift in how families are portrayed is consistent with changes we have seen both in practice and in our understanding of what constitutes a family.

Because families as we experience them are varied in structure and style, we need a sociological approach that is sufficiently broad to encompass all those relationships we experience as family. Two definitional approaches are helpful. The first is a substantive definition that focuses on what a family *is,* and the second is a functional definition that focuses on what families *do.*

SUBSTANCE: WHAT A FAMILY IS

Perhaps the most conventional approach to defining family is the **substantive definition,** which focuses on blood and law. Blood, in this case, means that people are related because they share a biological heritage passed on directly from parent to child, linking people indirectly to grandparents, aunts and uncles, and other biological relatives. Law means the formal social recognition and affirmation of a bond as family, particularly in the form of marriage and adoption.

The primary advantage of this definitional approach is that boundaries are clear; we can tell who is in and who is out. This makes it easier to count such families, so perhaps it is no surprise that the U.S. Census relies on a substantive approach: "A family is a group of two people or more (one of whom is the householder) related by birth,

marriage, or adoption and residing together" (U.S. Census Bureau 2012a). It also allows us to track who is related to whom over time.

Kinship Patterns Many of us can trace our roots by looking at a family tree or by listening to elderly family members talk about their lives—and about ancestors who lived and died long before we were born. Yet a person's lineage is more than simply a personal history; it also reflects societal traditions that govern descent. In every culture, children encounter relatives to whom they are expected to show an emotional attachment. The state of being related to others is called **kinship.** Kinship is culturally learned, however, and is not totally determined by biological or marital ties. For example, adoption creates a kinship tie that is legally acknowledged and socially accepted.

The family and the kin group are not necessarily one and the same. Whereas the family is a household unit, kin do not always live together or function as a collective body on a daily basis. Kin groups include aunts, uncles, cousins, in-laws, and so forth. In a society such as the United States, the kinship group may come together only rarely, for a wedding or funeral. However, kinship ties frequently involve obligations and responsibilities. We may feel compelled to assist our kin, and we feel free to call on them for many types of aid, including loans and babysitting (Pew Research Center 2010).

How do we identify kinship groups? The principle of descent assigns people to kinship groups according to their relationship to a mother or father. There are three primary ways of determining descent. The United States follows the system of **bilateral descent,** which means that both sides

substantive definition of the family A definition of the family based on blood, meaning shared genetic heritage, and law, meaning social recognition and affirmation of the bond including both marriage and adoption.

kinship The state of being related to others.

bilateral descent A kinship system in which both sides of a person's family are regarded as equally important.

SOCTHINK

How important are intergenerational kinship networks and extended family members in your family? How has this changed since your parents' and grandparents' generations?

of a person's family are regarded as equally important. For example, no higher value is given to the brothers of one's father than to the brothers of one's mother. However, most societies—according to anthropologist George Murdock, 64 percent of societies—give preference to one side of the family or the other in tracing descent. In **patrilineal** (from the Latin *pater*, "father") **descent,** only the father's relatives are significant in terms of property, inheritance, and emotional ties. Conversely, in societies that favor **matrilineal** (from the Latin *mater*, "mother") **descent,** only the mother's relatives are significant.

Family Types The substantive approach also shapes what we traditionally view as common family types. If we assume that we are connected through blood and law, we can analyze how we structure those relationships. Families might place greater emphasis on immediate family members or on extended family networks. They also are shaped by the number of partners deemed appropriate.

Historically, family connections served as a valuable resource, providing us with access to material, social, and cultural resources. We depended on relatives for food, shelter, opportunities, and knowledge. In fact, historian Stephanie Coontz (2005) argues that, historically, the primary reason to get married was to obtain not a partner but in-laws, thus extending one's network of cooperative relationships. This was the logic of the matchmaker tradition in which resource distribution mattered more than romantic love. The matchmaker, as a member of the community, sought to maximize social network connections for the good of the whole.

A family in which relatives—such as grandparents, aunts, or uncles—live in the same household as parents and their children is known as an **extended family.** Although not common, such living arrangements do exist in the United States. The structure of the extended family offers certain advantages over that of the nuclear family. Crises such as death, divorce, and illness put less strain on family members because more people can provide assistance and emotional support. In addition, the extended family constitutes a larger economic unit than the nuclear family. If the family is engaged in a common enterprise—a farm or a small business—the additional family members may represent the difference between prosperity and failure.

patrilineal descent A kinship system in which only the father's relatives are significant.

matrilineal descent A kinship system in which only the mother's relatives are significant.

extended family A family in which relatives—such as grandparents, aunts, or uncles—live in the same household as parents and their children.

nuclear family A married couple and their unmarried children living together.

monogamy A form of marriage in which one woman and one man are married only to each other.

serial monogamy A form of marriage in which a person may have several spouses in his or her lifetime but only one spouse at a time.

With the advent of the Industrial Revolution, the economy shifted away from agricultural production and its corresponding small-town life and toward industrial production in urban areas. Families became smaller and more mobile in response to these structural changes. The obligations of the extended family could hold individuals back, and so we saw a move toward a smaller family unit that came to be known as the nuclear family. The **nuclear family** includes a married couple and their unmarried children living together. The concept of nuclear family builds on the essence or nucleus of the substantive definition of blood and law, including as it does both the parent-to-child and the marriage relationship.

Most people in the United States assume that the nuclear family is by far the most common arrangement. In fact, married couples with children under 18 make up 29.8 percent of total families. The breadwinner father and stay-at-home mom model idealized in 1950s television makes up only 9.1 percent of total families and 30.4 percent of families with children under 18 (Bureau of Labor Statistics 2012b). In contrast, the percentage of single-parent and nonfamily households has risen steadily over the past 50 years.

Types of Marriage In considering these different family types, we have limited ourselves to the form of marriage that is characteristic of the United States—monogamy. The term **monogamy** describes a form of marriage in which one woman and one man are married only to each other. Individuals in the United States are more likely to move into and out of a number of serious romantic relationships, what sociologist Andrew Cherlin (2009) refers to as the "marriage-go-round." Termed **serial monogamy,**

U.S. Households by Family Type

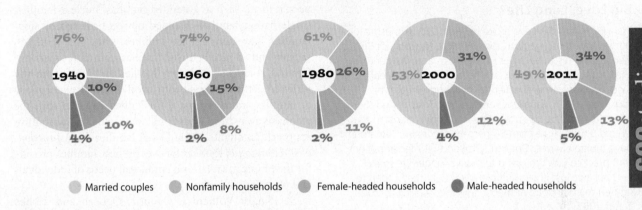

- Married couples
- Nonfamily households
- Female-headed households
- Male-headed households

Note: Nonfamily households include women and men living alone or exclusively with people to whom they are not related, as in a college dormitory, homeless shelter, or military base.

Source: U.S. Census Bureau 2011j:Table HH-1.

a person may have several spouses in his or her lifetime, but only one spouse at a time.

Some cultures allow an individual to have several husbands or wives simultaneously. This form of marriage is known as **polygamy.** In fact, most societies throughout the world, past and present, have preferred polygamy to monogamy. Anthropologist George Murdock (1949, 1957) sampled 565 societies and found that in more than 80 percent, some type of polygamy was the preferred form. While polygamy declined steadily through most of the 20th century, in 28 sub-Saharan African countries, at least 10 percent of men still have polygamous marriages (Tertilt 2005).

There are two basic types of polygamy. The more common is **polygyny,** which refers to the marriage of a man to more than one woman at the same time. Less common is **polyandry,** in which a woman may have more than one husband at the same time. Such is the case, for example, in the Nyinba culture of Nepal and Tibet, in which brothers share a common wife. This arrangement provides a sufficient number of physical laborers in the difficult farming environment yet minimizes the number of offspring.

Most people assumed that polygamy was a thing of the past in the United States. However, in 2008, law enforcement officials in Texas received an anonymous phone call purported to be from a 16-year-old girl who claimed that she had been forced into a polygamous marriage with an adult man. Shortly thereafter, Texas officials raided the Yearning for Zion ranch, where the girl claimed to be living, and took 462 children into temporary legal custody. The 1,700-acre ranch was run by members of the Fundamentalist Church of Jesus Christ of Latter Day Saints (FLDS), a group with more than 10,000 members that continues to practice polygamy even though it is illegal in the United States and was banned over 100 years ago by the mainstream LDS denomination (whose members are commonly referred to as Mormons). Officials found evidence of both polygamy and marriage between adult

polygamy A form of marriage in which an individual may have several husbands or wives simultaneously.

polygyny A form of polygamy in which a man may have more than one wife at the same time.

polyandry A form of polygamy in which a woman may have more than one husband at the same time.

SOCTHINK

Why do you think that polygamy was the most common form of marriage historically? Why has it given way to monogamy in modern societies?

Big Love, Long Life?

The HBO series *Big Love* broke new ground with its fictional portrayal of a polygamous family. It told the story of Bill Henrickson, his three wives (Barb, Nicki, and Margene), and their eight children. Its success helped inspire the reality TV series *Sister Wives,* which follows Kody Brown, his four wives (Meri, Janelle, Christine, and Robyn), and their 17 children. Although polygamy is unconventional in the United States, more than 50 percent of men in Cameroon have multiple wives. One study found that men in nations that practice polygyny tend to have a longer life span, perhaps because their multiple wives bear the burden to lighten the workload of men's daily lives (Callaway 2008; Tertilt 2005).

men and minor girls. Twelve FLDS men—including the group's leader, the 55-year-old Warren Jeffs who counted both a 12- and a 15-year-old girl among his numerous plural wives—were eventually convicted of crimes related to unlawful sexual relations with minors and bigamy. This case brought out into the open the continued existence of polygamy in the United States.

When we begin to look at the varieties of family types around the world, we see the main limitation of the substantive definition: There are people who seem to be family but who do not fit neatly into blood or law. For example, the biological parent-to-child tie was expanded by including adoption as part of law. We accept stepparents and stepsiblings as family members even when the children have not been formally adopted by the stepparent. We are currently debating whether to grant same-sex couples legal standing as families. But what about pushing the definition of family still further? Is dad's college friend "Uncle" Bob part of the family? New forms of reproductive technology, involving donated sperm and eggs and surrogate parents, also challenge conventional thinking. Any substantive definition we might come up with runs the risk of excluding those whom we think of as family members. In response, sociologists turn toward the more inclusive functionalist definition of families to address such limitations.

functionalist definition of families A definition of families that focuses on how families provide for the physical, social, and emotional needs of individuals and of society as a whole.

FUNCTIONS: WHAT FAMILIES DO

People in the United States seem to agree that traditional definitions of family are too restrictive. When they are asked how they would define family, their conception is much more inclusive than the substantive definition implies. In one survey, only 22 percent of the respondents defined family in the same way as the U.S. Census Bureau. Instead, 74 percent considered a family to be "any group whose members love and care for one another" (Coontz 1992:21).

We need a definition of family that is inclusive enough to encompass the broad range of intimate groups that people form, such as extended families, nuclear families, single-parent families, blended or reconstituted or step-families, gay and lesbian families, child-free families, racially and ethnically mixed families, commuter marriage families, surrogate or chosen families, and more. One way to avoid getting trapped into overly narrow conceptions of families and to embrace their diversity is to shift the emphasis away from what families *are*, which a substantive approach highlights, toward what families do. A *functionalist definition of families* focuses on how families provide for the physical, social, and emotional needs of individuals and of society as a whole.

Sociologist William F. Ogburn (Ogburn and Tibbits 1934) identified six primary functions that families perform for us:

- *Reproduction.* For a society to maintain itself, it must replace dying members. Families provide the context within which biological reproduction takes place.
- *Socialization.* Parents and other family members monitor a child's behavior and transmit the norms, values, and language of their culture to the child.
- *Protection.* Unlike the young of other animal species, human infants need constant care and economic security. In all cultures, the family assumes the ultimate responsibility for the protection and upbringing of children.
- *Regulation of sexual behavior.* Sexual norms are subject to change both over time (for instance, in the customs for dating) and across cultures (compare strict Saudi Arabia to the more permissive Denmark). However, whatever the time period or cultural values of a society,

158 • *SOC 2013*

Personal Sociology

Pets As Family

When we discuss families in terms of what they do instead of what they are, my students inevitably ask, "Do pets count as family?" Some strongly agree, while others think it is the most ridiculous thing they have ever heard. Over time, more and more students have begun coming down on the side of pets as family. When Lori and I "adopted" Jessie, our Pembroke Welsh corgi, I better understood why. People develop strong emotional bonds with their pets and some refer to them as their "fur kids." Pets provide a source of comfort and companionship. They give us someone to care about, and they care for us in their own ways. Isn't that what family is all about?

standards of sexual behavior are most clearly defined within the family circle.

- *Affection and companionship.* Ideally, families provide members with warm and intimate relationships, helping them to feel satisfied and secure. Of course, a family member may find such rewards outside the family—from peers, in school, at work—and may even perceive the home as an unpleasant or abusive setting. Nevertheless, we expect our relatives to understand us, to care for us, and to be there for us when we need them.

- *Provision of social status.* We inherit a social position because of the family background and reputation of our parents and siblings. For example, the race, ethnicity, social class, education level, occupation, and religion of our parents all shape the material, social, and cultural resources to which we have access and therefore the options we might have.

No matter how it is composed, any group that fulfills these functions is family to us. We might count teammates, close college dorm mates, or a long-term circle of friends as family. We look to such groups in moments of need for all kinds of support, including care and affection, guidance in how to think and act, dating advice, and sometimes even material support, whether borrowing a car or just some money for pizza. We may use the expression that they are "like family" to convey that sense, or we may even refer to such significant people in our lives as our sister, brother, mom, or dad. In fact, given the survey results above, people may already be defining as family any group that provides sufficient love and care for group members. According to this functionalist definition, a family *is* what a family *does.*

AUTHORITY PATTERNS: WHO RULES?

Regardless of what a family looks like, within the context of any group we define as family, we will inevitably have to address issues of power. Imagine, for example, that you have recently married and must begin to make decisions about the future of your new family. You and your partner face many questions: Where will you live? How will you furnish your home? Who will do the cooking, shopping, and cleaning? Whose friends will be invited to dinner? Each time a decision must be made, an issue is raised: who has the power to make the decision? In simple terms, who rules the family?

Societies vary in the way that power is distributed with-in the family; historically, however, the answer to that question has largely been shaped by gender. A society that expects males to dominate in all family decision making is termed a **patriarchy.** In patriarchal societies, such as Iran, the eldest male often wields the greatest power, although wives are expected to be treated with respect and kindness. An Iranian woman's status is typically defined by her relationship to a male relative, usually as a wife or daughter. In many patriarchal societies, women find it more difficult to obtain a divorce than a man does (Farr 1999). In contrast, in a **matriarchy,** women have greater authority than men. Formal matriarchies, which are uncommon, emerged among Native American tribal societies and in nations in which men were absent for long periods because of warfare or food-gathering expeditions.

patriarchy A society in which men dominate in family decision making.

matriarchy A society in which women dominate in family decision making.

More than a century ago, Friedrich Engels ([1884] 1959), a colleague of Karl Marx, went so far as to say that the family is the ultimate source of social inequality because of its role in the transfer of power, property, and privilege. Historically, he argues, the family has legitimized and perpetuated male dominance. It has contributed to societal injustice, denied women opportunities that are extended to men, and limited freedom in sexual expression and mate selection. In the United States, it was not until the first wave of contemporary feminism, in the mid-1800s, that there was a substantial challenge to the historical status of wives and children as the legal property of husbands and fathers.

Partly because of the efforts of women and men in similar movements over the years, we have seen the rise of a third type of authority pattern. In the **egalitarian family,** spouses are regarded as equals. This shift has been driven at least in part by occupational and financial opportunities for women that previously had been denied them (Wills and Risman 2006). That does not mean, however, that all decisions are shared in such families. Wives may hold authority in some spheres, and husbands in others. For example, sociologists have found that, in terms of paid and unpaid labor in two-parent families, the total hours worked by mothers and fathers is roughly equal at about 65 hours per week, though the distribution of tasks varies (Bianchi, Robinson, and Milkie 2006).

egalitarian family An authority pattern in which spouses are regarded as equals.

Historian Stephanie Coontz (2008) suggests that, when it works, marriage today is better than ever. She writes that it "delivers more benefits to its members—adults and children—than ever before. A good marriage is fairer and more fulfilling for both men and women than couples of the past could ever have imagined." She points to shared decision making and housework, increases in time spent with children, and declines in violence and sexual coercion and in the likelihood of adultery.

Although the egalitarian family has become a more common pattern in the United States in recent decades, male dominance over the family has hardly disappeared. Sociologists have found that although married men are increasing their involvement in child care, their wives still perform a disproportionate amount of it. Furthermore, with 5 million stay-at-home moms versus 176,000 stay-at-home dads, a ratio of 28 to 1, the dominant practice reinforces normative expectations (U.S. Census Bureau 2011k:Table SHP-1). And unfortunately, many husbands reinforce their power and control over wives and children through acts of domestic violence.

In addition to such internal power struggles, families also continue to provide a foundation for power within the larger society. Family serves as the basis for transferring power, property, and privilege from one generation to the next. Although the United States is widely viewed as a land of opportunity, social mobility is restricted in important ways. Children inherit the privileged or less-than-privileged social and economic status of their parents (and in some cases, of earlier generations as well). The social class of parents significantly influences children's socialization experiences and the degree of protection they receive. Thus, the socioeconomic status of a child's family will have a marked influence on his or her nutrition, health care, housing, educational opportunities, and in many respects, life chances as an adult. In many ways the family helps to maintain inequality.

>>Marriage and Family

Despite concerns about power and inequality in the family sphere, people's faith in marriage persists. Currently, more than 95 percent of all men and women in the United States marry at least once during their lifetimes. Though people

SOC THINK

Why might people turn to matchmaking services today? What are the disadvantages of relying on our own contacts and judgment when it comes to finding a romantic partner?

Ten Questions Couples Should Ask (or Wish They Had) Before Marrying

Do you want to have children?

Who will do what when it comes to housework?

What are your expectations regarding sex?

What do you think about having a television in the bedroom?

What do you expect regarding religious training for our children?

How much money do you owe?

Do you like and respect my friends?

What do you really think about my parents?

What does my family do that annoys you?

Are there some things you are not willing to give up in the marriage?

Source: New York Times 2006.

wait a bit longer to marry now than in the past, the most historically consistent aspect of family life in this country has been the high rate of marriage. In the United States the median age at first marriage is 26.5 years for women and 28.9 years for men. In 1960, the median age was 20.3 for women and 22.8 for men (Cherlin 2009; U.S. Census Bureau 2011:Table MS-2).

Going GLOBAL

Percentage of People Aged 20–24 Ever Married, Selected Countries

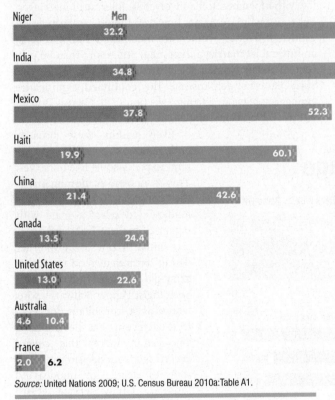

	Men	Women
Niger	32.2	89.7
India	34.8	77.0
Mexico	37.8	52.3
Haiti	19.9	60.1
China	21.4	42.6
Canada	13.5	24.4
United States	13.0	22.6
Australia	4.6	10.4
France	2.0	6.2

Source: United Nations 2009; U.S. Census Bureau 2010a:Table A1.

COURTSHIP AND MATE SELECTION

There are many ways that we might go about finding someone to marry. Historically, it was not uncommon for marriages to be arranged by families or matchmakers. This is a practice that continues in many cultures today. In the Asian nation of Uzbekistan, for example, courtship is largely orchestrated by the couple's parents. A young Uzbekistani woman is socialized to eagerly anticipate her marriage to a man whom she has met only once, at the final inspection of her dowry (Kamp 2008; Rand 2006).

> **endogamy** The restriction of mate selection to people within the same group.

When it comes to marriage in the United States, most of us assume that true love will guide the way. We can't imagine allowing others, including parents and matchmakers, to select partners for us through arranged marriages. Many are surprised to hear that this practice continues today in some subcultures in the United States. We often take for granted that we are best suited to make this personal and intimate selection. We may look to advice from family and friends, but the deciding factor is how we feel about the other person. We assume that the pool of potential partners is wide open so long as they get our heart racing.

In practice, however, our pool of potential partners is substantially reduced by our social location. We are sometimes blind to the basic social rules that inevitably narrow our choices (Kalmijn 1998):

- We are limited to those who are available and with whom we have contact.
- We are heavily influenced by opinions of family, friends, and the organizations to which we belong (including religious groups and the workplace).
- We are most attracted to people like ourselves.

In the first case, our position in the social structure influences the degree to which we have the opportunity to establish a relationship with someone. Second, partner selection involves more than just the happy couple; those close to us play a significant role in shaping which characteristics we perceive as acceptable. Finally, as the saying goes, like attracts like (or at least it tends to).

When sociologists analyze social factors that shape our selection of partners, they pay particular attention to the balance between endogamy and exogamy. **Endogamy** (from the Greek *endon,* "within") specifies the groups within which a spouse must be found and prohibits marriage with outsiders. For example, in the United States, many people are expected to marry within their own racial, ethnic, or religious group and are strongly discouraged or even prohibited from marrying outside the group. Endogamy is intended to reinforce the cohesiveness of the group by suggesting to young people that they should marry someone "of their own kind."

In contrast, **exogamy** (from the Greek *exo,* "outside") requires mate selection outside certain groups, usually one's own family or certain kinfolk. The **incest taboo,** a social norm common to virtually all societies, prohibits sexual relationships between certain culturally specified relatives. In the United States, this taboo means that we must marry outside the nuclear family. We cannot marry our siblings, and in most states, we cannot marry our first cousins.

exogamy The requirement that people select a mate outside certain groups.

incest taboo The prohibition of sexual relationships between certain culturally specified relatives.

homogamy The conscious or unconscious tendency to select a mate with personal characteristics and interests similar to one's own.

Endogamy influences a number of social location variables. We tend to pick partners who are the same age, race, ethnicity, education, and religion. Though the degree of influence of these variables has shifted over time, each continues to play a significant role.

For example, in one study researchers found that the average age difference between spouses was 3.8 years, though the significance of the age gap decreases as we get older. A five-year age difference is more significant when someone is 18 than when the person is 38 or 58. Age is one of the factors for which third-party pressure can exert significant influence; people tend to look suspiciously at relationships in which the age difference is perceived to be too large (Blossfeld 2009; Rosenfeld 2008; Sherkat 2004; Thomas and Sawhill 2002).

The role of race in selecting partners demonstrates how social norms can both change and remain the same. For a long time, interracial marriage was illegal in the United States. This was still the case in some states until a 1967 Supreme Court ruling overturned these laws. In the past 50 years, the number of marriages between African Americans and Whites in the United States has increased more than tenfold, jumping from 157,000 in 1960 to 2.5 million in 2011. Including all racial groups, the percentage of interracial marriages rose from 0.4 percent in 1960 to 4.1 percent in 2011 (U.S. Census Bureau 1998:Table 1; 2011m:Table FG4).

Despite the overall increase in the acceptance and practice of interracial marriage, most married people continue to select a partner of the same race. As we can see from the accompanying table, however, there is some variation both by race and by gender. Those who are White are the most likely to practice racial endogamy; more than 98 percent of both men and women select a marital partner of the same race. Among African Americans, men are more likely than women to be involved in interracial marriages. For those who are Asian, however, there is an even larger gender difference; women are much more likely to be in an interracial marriage than men. Still, more than 80 percent of Asian women select a partner of the same race. Such patterns demonstrate the continued significance endogamy plays in partner selection (U.S. Census Bureau 2011m:Table FG4; Wang 2012).

Even within these broader endogamous social categories, we tend to pick people like ourselves. This is known as **homogamy**—the conscious or unconscious tendency to select a mate with personal characteristics and interests similar to one's own. Internet dating services depend upon this principle to help find matches. Sociologist Pepper Schwartz, who works as a consultant for PerfectMatch.com, has developed a 48-question survey that covers everything from decision-making style to degree of impulsivity. Internet dating service eHarmony claims that its technique of matching people on the basis of similar characteristics, interests, and abilities—that is, relying on the principles of endogamy and homogamy—results in 542 marriages per day (Gottlieb 2006; Logue 2009; Peel 2008).

Patterns of Interracial Marriage

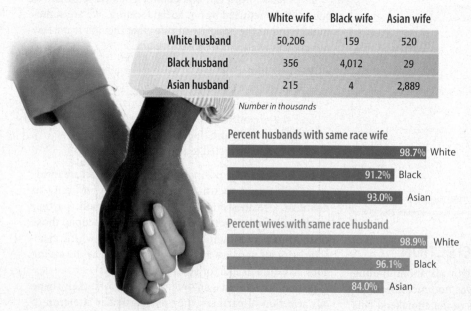

	White wife	Black wife	Asian wife
White husband	50,206	159	520
Black husband	356	4,012	29
Asian husband	215	4	2,889

Number in thousands

Percent husbands with same race wife

98.7% White
91.2% Black
93.0% Asian

Percent wives with same race husband

98.9% White
96.1% Black
84.0% Asian

Note: Numbers in thousands. Table does not show data for Other Race husbands and wives.
Source: Based on U.S. Census Bureau 2011m:Table FG4.

In theory, Cupid's arrow could strike anyone on our behalf. But love is not blind. Love is a product of the social and cultural forces that shape the choices we make. Of course, knowledge of the ways our choices are patterned can free us up to follow different paths.

5 Movies on MARRIAGE AND FAMILIES

The Loving Story
A couple's true love conquers all, even the Supreme Court.

Monsoon Wedding
An Indian wedding celebration.

The Squid and the Whale
How divorce affects children.

It's Complicated
A divorced couple with adult children reunite with mixed results.

A Home at the End of the World
An alternative marriage and family.

VARIATIONS IN FAMILY LIFE AND INTIMATE RELATIONSHIPS

Within the United States, social class, race, and ethnicity create variations in family life. Studying these variations will give us a more sophisticated understanding of contemporary family styles in our country. The desire to avoid having to negotiate such differences also helps to explain why people often practice homogamy.

Social Class Differences Social class differences matter when it comes to parenting. Historically, poor and working-class families were more authoritarian, and middle-class families were more permissive and less likely to use physical punishment. Starting in the 1950s, exposure to common child-rearing advice in books, magazines, and on television reduced the extremes by creating a shared understanding of appropriate parenting techniques, but recent research shows that parenting practices still differ. For example, middle-class parents provide more structure through participation in organized activities, and working-class parents allow their children greater freedom so long as they don't overstep disciplinary bounds. The material, social, and cultural resources children inherit from their parents (whether in the form of money, connections, language, tastes, attitudes, or experience) help to reproduce social class across generations (Kronstadt and Favreault 2008; Lareau 2003).

Among people who are poor, women often play a significant role in the economic support of the family. Men may earn low wages, may be unemployed, or may be entirely absent from the family. In 2010, 31.6 percent of all families headed by women with no husband present were below the official poverty line. The rate for married couples was only 6.2 percent (DeNavas-Walt, Proctor, and Smith 2011:16). Racial and class factors are often closely related. In examining family life among racial and ethnic minorities, keep in mind that certain patterns may result from class as well as cultural factors.

Racial and Ethnic Differences The subordinate status of racial and ethnic minorities in the United States profoundly affects their family lives. For example, the lower incomes of African Americans, Native Americans, most Hispanic groups, and selected Asian American groups make creating and maintaining successful marital unions a difficult task. The economic restructuring of the past 50 years, described by sociologist William Julius Wilson (1996) and others, in which blue-collar jobs disappeared from urban areas as companies moved production facilities abroad, has especially affected people living in inner cities and desolate rural areas. Furthermore, the immigration policy of the United States has complicated the successful relocation of intact families from Asia and Latin America.

The African American family suffers from many negative and inaccurate stereotypes. It is true that in a significantly higher proportion of Black than White families, no husband is present in the home. Yet Black single mothers often belong to stable, functioning kin networks, which mitigate the pressures of sexism and racism. Members of these networks—predominantly female kin such as mothers, grandmothers, and aunts—ease financial strains by sharing goods and services. In addition to these strong kinship bonds, Black family life has emphasized deep religious commitment and high aspirations for achievement (F. Furstenberg 2007; Stack 1974).

> The goal in marriage is not to think alike, but to think together.
>
> Robert C. Dodds

Like African Americans, Native Americans draw on family ties to cushion many of the hardships they face. On the Navajo reservation, for example, teenage parenthood is not regarded as the crisis that it is elsewhere in the United States. The Navajo trace their descent matrilineally. Traditionally, couples reside with the wife's family after marriage, allowing the grandparents to help with the child rearing. While the Navajo do not approve of teenage parenthood, the deep emotional commitment of their extended families provides a warm home environment for fatherless children (Dalla and Gamble 2001).

Sociologists also have taken note of differences in family patterns among other racial and ethnic groups. For example, although Mexican American men have been described as exhibiting a sense of virility, personal worth, and pride in their maleness that is called **machismo,** Mexican Americans are also described as being more familistic than many other subcultures. **Familism** refers to pride in the extended family, expressed through the maintenance of close ties and strong obligations to kinfolk outside the immediate family.

machismo A sense of virility, personal worth, and pride in one's maleness.

familism Pride in the extended family, expressed through the maintenance of close ties and strong obligations to kinfolk outside the immediate family.

Traditionally, Mexican Americans have placed proximity to their extended families above other needs and desires.

These family patterns are changing, however, in response to changes in Latinos' social class standing, educational achievements, and occupations. Like other Americans, career-oriented Latinos in search of a mate but short on spare time are turning to the Internet. As Latinos and other groups assimilate into the dominant culture of the United States, their family lives take on both the positive and the negative characteristics associated with non-Hispanic White households (Landale and Orapesa 2007).

CHILD-REARING PATTERNS

Caring for children is a universal function of the family, yet the ways in which different societies assign this function to family members can vary significantly. The Nayars of southern India acknowledge the biological role of fathers, but the mother's eldest brother is responsible for her children. In contrast, uncles play only a peripheral role in child care in the United States. Even within the United States, child-rearing patterns are varied. Just as our conception of families has changed, so also has our practice of child rearing.

Parenthood and Grandparenthood The socialization of children is essential to the maintenance of any culture. Consequently, parenthood is one of the most important (and most demanding) social roles in the United States. Sociologist Alice Rossi (1968, 1984) has identified four factors that complicate the transition to parenthood and the role of socialization. First, there is little anticipatory socialization for the social role of caregiver. The normal school curriculum gives scant attention to the subjects

POPSOC

Parenthood has been a frequent source of entertainment in the movies. Examples of such films include *Mr. Mom, Parenthood, Finding Nemo, Freaky Friday, Cheaper by the Dozen, Mars Needs Moms, Juno, Baby Mama, The Blind Side,* and even *Alvin and the Chipmunks.* They all convey messages of what it means to be a parent. What lessons might we learn from an analysis of how mothers and fathers are portrayed in such films? What recurring images and themes occur? How common is the bungling dad or the career mom who wonders if she is making the right choices? What are the consequences of such films for how we practice parenting?

most relevant to successful family life, such as child care and home maintenance. Second, only limited learning occurs during the period of pregnancy itself. Third, the transition to parenthood is quite abrupt. Unlike adolescence, it is not prolonged; unlike the transition to work, the duties of caregiving cannot be taken on gradually. Finally, in Rossi's view, our society lacks clear and helpful guidelines for successful parenthood. There is little agreement on how parents can produce happy and well-adjusted offspring—or even on what it means to be well adjusted. For these reasons, socialization for parenthood involves difficult challenges for most men and women in the United States.

One recent development in family life in the United States has been the extension of parenthood, as adult children continue to live at home or return home after college. In 2011, 59 percent of men and 50 percent of women aged 18–24 lived with their parents, compared to 52 and 35 percent, respectively, in 1960 (U.S. Census Bureau 2011n:Table AD-1). Some of these adult children were still pursuing an education, but in many instances, financial difficulties underlay these living arrangements. While rents and real estate prices have skyrocketed, salaries for younger workers have not kept pace, and many find themselves unable to afford to buy a house. Moreover, with many marriages now ending in divorce, divorced sons and daughters often return to live with their parents, sometimes with their own children.

In some homes, child-rearing responsibilities fall to grandparents. In 2011, 7.6 million children in the United States, 10.1 percent overall, lived in a household with a grandparent. Of these, 1.3 million (1.7 percent) had no parent present to assist in child rearing (U.S. Census Bureau 2011m: Table C4). Special difficulties are inherent in such relationships, including legal custodial concerns, financial issues, and emotional problems for adults and youths alike. Perhaps not surprisingly, support groups such as Grandparents as Parents have emerged to provide assistance.

Adoption

In a legal sense, **adoption** is a "process that allows for the transfer of the legal rights, responsibilities, and privileges of parenthood" to a new legal parent or parents (E. Cole 1985:638). In many cases, these rights are transferred from a biological parent or parents (often called birth parents) to an adoptive parent or parents.

Approximately 1.2 percent of U.S. children live with at least one adoptive parent (U.S. Census Bureau 2011m:Table

Hollywood stars Angelina Jolie and Brad Pitt and several of their children, many from overseas adoptions.

C9). There are two legal methods of adopting an unrelated person: (1) the adoption may be arranged through a licensed agency, or (2) in some states it may be arranged through a private agreement sanctioned by the courts. Adopted children may come from the United States or from abroad. In 2011, more than 9,320 children entered the United States as the adopted children of U.S. citizens. The top three nations of origin for U.S. adoptions in 2011 were China with 2,589, Ethiopia with 1,727, and Russia with 970. The median fee for adopting a child from China was $15,930 (Carr 2007; U.S. Department of State 2011). Although the number of international adoptions remains substantial, it has declined in recent years, down from 23,000 in 2004.

In the United States, one of the limitations historically was that only married couples could adopt. In 1995 an important court decision in New York held that a couple does not have to be married to adopt a child. Under this ruling, unmarried heterosexual couples, lesbian couples, and gay couples can all legally adopt children in New York. Writing for the majority, Chief Justice Judith Kaye argued that by expanding the boundaries of who can be legally recognized as parents, the state may be able to assist more children in securing "the best possible home." With this ruling, New York became the third state (after Vermont and Massachusetts) to recognize the right of unmarried couples to adopt children (Dao 1995; Human Rights Campaign 2009).

> **adoption** In a legal sense, a process that allows for the transfer of the legal rights, responsibilities, and privileges of parenthood to a new legal parent or parents.

For every child who is adopted, many more remain the wards of state-sponsored child protective services. In 2010, 408,425 children in the United States were living in foster care. Of these children 107,011 were waiting for adoption (U.S. Department of Human Services 2011).

Dual-Income Families

The idea of a family consisting of a wage-earning husband and a stay-at-home wife has largely given way to the dual-income household. Among married couples with children under 6, 53 percent have both husband and wife in the labor force (Bureau of Labor Statistics 2012b:Table 4).

SOCTHINK

What are the advantages and disadvantages of the dual-income model for women, for men, for children, and for society as a whole?

Both opportunity and need have driven the rise in the number of dual-income couples. Women now have the chance to pursue opportunities in a way that previously had been closed due to cultural expectations regarding gender. This has resulted in increased education levels for women and increased participation in

Did You Know?

... Until 1978 it was legal in the United States to fire a woman for being pregnant. The Supreme Court upheld that principle in key cases in 1974 and 1976. Two years later, in response to these rulings, Congress passed the Pregnancy Discrimination Act, which prohibited denying benefits to, firing, or refusing to hire someone for being pregnant.

occupational fields that had been largely closed. At the same time, however, couples find it harder to make it on a single income. Evidence of this trend can be found in the rise of married couples living apart for reasons other than marital discord. The 3.6 million couples who now live apart represent 1 out of every 33 marriages. More than half live farther than 100 miles apart, and half of those live 1,000 or more miles apart. Of course, couples living apart are nothing new; men have worked at transient jobs for generations as soldiers, truck drivers, or traveling salesmen. The existence of such household arrangements reflects an acceptance of the egalitarian family type (L. Cullen 2007; Holmes 2006; Stafford 2010).

single-parent family A family in which only one parent is present to care for the children.

Single-Parent Families

The 2004 *American Idol* winner Fantasia Barrino's song "Baby Mama" offers a tribute to young single mothers—a subject she knows about. Barrino was 17 when she became pregnant with her daughter. Though critics charged that the song sends the wrong message to teenage girls, Barrino says it is not about encouraging teens to have sex. Rather, she sees the song as an anthem for young mothers courageously trying to raise their children alone (Cherlin 2006).

In recent decades, the stigma attached to unwed mothers and other single parents has significantly diminished. **Single-parent families,** in which only one parent is present to care for the children, can hardly be viewed as a rarity in the United States. In 2011, 27.2 percent of all children lived with only one parent. This varied by race and ethnicity with 19.9 percent of White, non-Hispanic children, 54.7 percent of African American children, 10.3 percent of Asian children, and 29.2 percent of Hispanic children living with one parent (U.S. Census Bureau 2011m:Table C9).

The life of single parents and their children is not inevitably more difficult than that of a traditional nuclear family. It is as inaccurate to assume that a single-parent family is necessarily deprived as it is to assume that a two-parent family is always secure and happy. Nevertheless, to the extent that such families have to rely on a single income or a sole caregiver, life in the single-parent family can be extremely stressful. A family headed by a single mother faces especially difficult problems when the mother is a teenager, especially when she lacks access to significant social and economic resources (Sawhill 2006).

Why might low-income teenage women wish to have children and face the obvious financial difficulties of motherhood? Some theorists argue that these women tend to have low self-esteem and limited options; a child may provide a sense of motivation and purpose for the teenager whose economic worth in our society is limited at best. Given the barriers that many young women face because of their gender, race, ethnicity, and class, many teenagers may believe they have little to lose and much to gain by having a child (Edin and Kefalas 2005).

Although 87 percent of single parents in the United States are mothers, the number of households headed by single fathers more than tripled (3.5) between 1970 and 2011. Single mothers often develop social networks, but single fathers are typically more isolated. In addition, they must deal with schools and social service agencies that are more accustomed to women as custodial parents (U.S. Census Bureau 2011o:Table CH1).

Stepfamilies

As a result of single parents who marry or divorced parents who remarry, approximately 5.8 percent of children under 18 live with at least one stepparent (U.S. Census Bureau 2011m:Table C9). But stepfamilies can involve more than just young children in these relationships. Sociologist Susan Stewart (2007) recommends expanding our definition of stepfamilies to include cohabitating couples with children from previous relationships, families whose stepchildren do not live with them full-time, gay or lesbian couples with children from former heterosexual relationships, and stepfamilies with adult children. The expanded definition highlights the

What greater thing is there for human souls than to feel that they are joined for life— to be with each other in silent unspeakable memories.

George Eliot

Comedians Tina Fey and Amy Poehler starred, along with Sigourney Weaver, in the 2008 film *Baby Mama*, in which Fey played a would-be single mother.

fact that stepfamily membership extends throughout the life course. The exact nature of blended families has social significance for adults and children alike.

Family members in stepfamilies must deal with resocialization issues when an adult becomes a stepparent or a child becomes a stepchild and stepsibling. In evaluating these stepfamilies, some observers have assumed that children would benefit from remarriage, because they would be gaining a second custodial parent and would potentially enjoy greater economic security. However, after reviewing many studies of stepfamilies, sociologist Andrew J. Cherlin (2008b:800) concluded that "the well-being of children in stepfamilies is no better, on average, than the well-being of children in divorced, single-parent households."

Stepparents can and do play valuable and unique roles in their stepchildren's lives, but their involvement does not guarantee an improvement in family life. In fact, standards may decline. Studies suggest that children raised in families with stepmothers are likely to have less health care, education, and money spent on their food than children raised by biological mothers. The measures are also negative for children raised by stepfathers, but only half as

negative as in the case of stepmothers. This may be due to the stepmother holding back out of concern for seeming too intrusive or relying on the biological father to carry out parental duties (Schmeeckle 2007; Schmeeckle et al. 2006).

>>Diverse Lifestyles

Marriage is no longer the presumed route from adolescence to adulthood. In fact, it has lost much of its social significance as a rite of passage. Now, establishing oneself through education and a career has taken precedence (Cherlin 2004, 2009). The nation's marriage rate has declined since 1970 because people are postponing marriage until later in life and because more couples, including same-sex couples, are deciding to form partnerships without marriage (Mather and Lavery 2010).

COHABITATION

In the United States, testing the relationship waters by living together without being married is an increasingly

Living Arrangements of Children with Parents

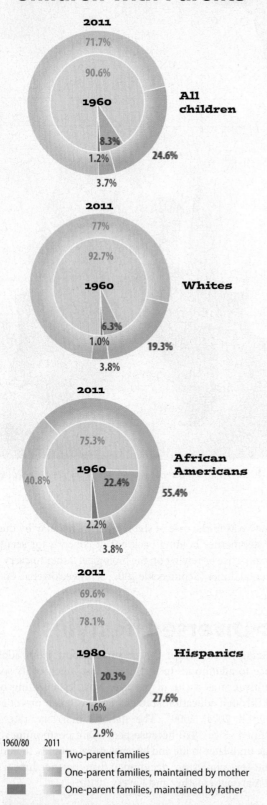

2011

71.7%

90.6%

1960

All children

8.3%

1.2%

24.6%

3.7%

2011

77%

92.7%

1960

Whites

6.3%

1.0%

19.3%

3.8%

2011

75.3%

1960

40.8%

22.4%

African Americans

55.4%

2.2%

3.8%

2011

69.6%

78.1%

1980

20.3%

Hispanics

27.6%

1.6%

2.9%

1960/80	2011	
		Two-parent families
		One-parent families, maintained by mother
		One-parent families, maintained by father

Note: Graphs show the percentage of children under 18 who live with at least one parent. Persons of Hispanic origin can be of any race. Data for Hispanics are from 1980 and 2011.

Source: Based on U.S. Census Bureau 2011o: Tables Ch-1, Ch-2, Ch-3, Ch-4.

common practice. **Cohabitation** is conventionally defined as the practice of a man and a woman living together in a sexual relationship without being married. The percentage of currently cohabiting adults age 30- to 44-year-olds rose from 3 percent in 1995 to 7 percent in 2010 (Fry and Cohn 2011).

About half of all currently married couples in the United States say that they lived together before marriage. And this percentage is likely to increase. The number of unmarried-couple households in the United States rose sixfold in the 1960s and increased another 72 percent between 1990 and 2000. Adults aged 30-44 without a college education are more likely to cohabit than those with a college degree. Cohabitation is more common among African Americans and American Indians than among other racial and ethnic groups; it is least common among Asian Americans. The map on page 169 shows how cohabitation varies by region (Goodwin et al. 2010; Kreider 2010; T. Simmons and O'Connell 2003).

In much of Europe, cohabitation is so common that the general sentiment seems to be "Love, yes; marriage, maybe." In Iceland, 62 percent of all children are born to single mothers; in France, Great Britain, and Norway, the proportion is about 40 percent. Government policies in these countries make few legal distinctions between married and unmarried couples or households (Lyall 2002; M. Moore 2006; Thomson and Bernhardt 2010).

Unmarried-Couple Households by State

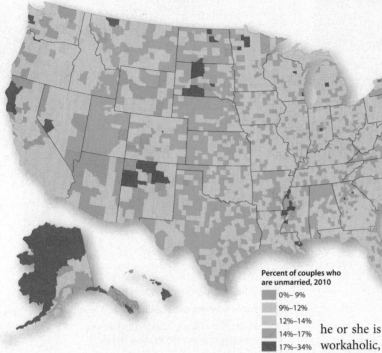

Percent of couples who are unmarried, 2010

- 0%– 9%
- 9%–12%
- 12%–14%
- 14%–17%
- 17%–34%

Source: El Nasser and Overberg 2011.

People commonly associate cohabitation only with younger couples, but according to a study done in Los Angeles, working couples are almost twice as likely to cohabit as college students. And census data show that in 2008, 9.6 percent of U.S. births were to women living with a cohabiting partner (Dye 2010). These cohabitants are more like spouses than dating partners. Moreover, in contrast to the common perception that people who cohabit have never been married, researchers report that about half of all people involved in cohabitation in the United States have been previously married. Cohabitation serves as a temporary or permanent alternative to matrimony for many men and women who have experienced their own or their parents' divorces (Fields 2004; Popenoe and Whitehead 1999).

REMAINING SINGLE

Increasingly, people are opting to remain single. The percentage of the U.S. adult population that has never married grew from 15 percent in 1960 to 28 percent in 2010. A variety of factors help to explain this trend, including rising cohabitation rates and, as we saw earlier, the fact that those who do marry are waiting longer to do so. Of those who have never married, 61 percent say they want to, 27 percent aren't sure, and 12 percent do not want to marry (Cohn et al. 2011).

There are many reasons a person may choose not to marry. Some singles do not want to limit their sexual intimacy to one lifetime partner. Some men and women do not want to become highly dependent on any one person—and do not want anyone depending heavily on them. In a society that values individuality and self-fulfillment, the single lifestyle can offer certain freedoms that marriage may not.

Remaining single represents a clear departure from societal expectations and can feel targeted in a society that presumes marriage. A single adult must confront the inaccurate view that he or she is always lonely, is a workaholic, or is immature. These stereotypes help to support the traditional assumption in the United States and most other societies that to be truly happy and fulfilled, a person must get married and raise a family. To counter these societal expectations, singles have formed numerous support groups (Hertz 2006; Lundquist 2006).

cohabitation The practice of a man and a woman living together in a sexual relationship without being married.

REMAINING CHILDLESS

There has also been a significant increase in childlessness in the United States. According to Census data, 19 percent of women age 40 to 44 have never had children. Those with at least a college degree are more likely to opt out of parenthood than those who have less education (U.S. Census Bureau 2010k: Table 1).

Childlessness within marriage has generally been viewed as a problem that can be solved through such means as adoption and artificial insemination. More and more couples today, however, choose not to have children and regard themselves as child-free rather than childless. They do not believe that having children automatically follows from marriage, nor do they feel that reproduction is the duty of all married couples. Childless couples have formed

> Call it a clan, call it a network, call it a tribe, call it a family. Whatever you call it, whoever you are, you need one.
>
> **Jane Howard**

support groups (with names like No Kidding and Child-less by Choice) and set up websites (K. Park 2005; Terry 2000).

Economic considerations have contributed to this shift in attitudes; having children has become quite expensive. Estimates are that middle-income parents of children born in 2010 can anticipate spending $286,860 to feed, clothe, and shelter a child from birth to age 18. If the child attends college, that amount could double, depending on the college chosen. Aware of the financial pressures, some couples are having fewer children than they otherwise might, and others are weighing the advantages of a child-free marriage (Lino 2011).

Same-Sex Marriage Laws

■ States that define marriage as a male-female union

■ States in which same-sex marriage is legal

■ States that officially recognize same-sex marriages conducted in other states

■ States with laws providing the equivalent of state-level spousal rights (including domestic partnerships and civil unions)

■ States with laws providing limited statewide spousal rights to same-sex couples

Note: Current as of May 2012.

Source: Human Rights Campaign 2012.

LESBIAN AND GAY RELATIONSHIPS

One of the more active political debates about families in recent years has involved marriage of same-sex couples. Such couples highlight the difficulty of defining families in too narrow terms. If we stick with a narrow, substantive definition, such relationships have not counted as families. When we define families in terms of what they do—what functions they perform—however, we find a growing acceptance that such relationships do constitute families.

The lifestyles of lesbians and gays are varied, just like those of heterosexuals. Some live in long-term, monogamous relationships; others live alone or with roommates. Some remain in "empty shell" heterosexual marriages and do not publicly acknowledge their homosexuality; others live with children from a former marriage or with adopted children. Based on 2008 election exit polls, researchers found that 4 percent of the adult voting population identify

themselves as either gay or lesbian. As of 2010, according to the Census Bureau, there were 646,464 unmarried same-sex couples in the United States. On average, these couples had more education, a greater likelihood of both members being employed, and higher incomes than married opposite-sex couples (CNN 2008; Lofquist, Lugaila, O'Connell, and Feliz 2012).

Starting with the 2010 Census, it became easier to get statistics on same-sex couples. Previously, if same-sex partners checked the "husband" or "wife" box to indicate the nature of their relationship, they were categorized as unmarried partners. With the legalization of same-sex marriage in some states, and to get a more accurate count, the Census is encouraging gay and lesbian couples who perceive themselves as married to check the "married" box, even if they do not live in a state where such marriages are legal.

Despite such symbolic progress, gay and lesbian couples continue to face discrimination on both a personal and a legal level. Their inability to marry in most states denies them many rights that married couples take for granted, from the ability to make decisions for an incapacitated

Couple getting married in San Francisco after a state Supreme Court ruling to allow same-sex marriage and before Proposition 8, a state constitutional amendment, banned the practice.

partner to the right to receive government benefits to dependents, such as Social Security payments. Though gay couples consider themselves families, legally they are usually treated as if they are not in most states. Precisely because of such inequities, many gay and lesbian couples continue to fight to expand the right to marry to more states.

Though the majority of states have laws that define marriage as between a man and a woman, recent changes in state laws have expanded legal rights for gay and lesbian couples. In 1999 Vermont provided legal rights through civil unions but stopped short of calling such relationships marriage. Then, in 2003, Massachusetts became the first state to legalize same-sex marriage when its Supreme Court ruled 4–3 that under the state's constitution, gay couples have the right to marry—a ruling the U.S. Supreme Court has refused to review. In 2008 Connecticut's Supreme Court reached the same conclusion, as did Iowa's in 2009. Vermont then became the first state to pass a law that legalized same-sex marriage; New Hampshire followed shortly thereafter, as did New York in July 2011. As a result, as of May 2012 six states provided gay and lesbian couples the same right to marry as guaranteed to heterosexual couples.

In the United States, state and local jurisdictions have proactively passed legislation allowing for the registration of domestic partnerships and have extended employee benefits to those relationships. Under such policies, a **domestic partnership** may be defined as two unrelated adults who share a mutually caring relationship, reside together, and agree to be jointly responsible for their dependents, basic living expenses, and other common necessities. Domestic partnership benefits can apply to couples' inheritance, parenting, pensions, taxation, housing, immigration, workplace fringe benefits, and health care. Even though the most passionate support for domestic partnership

Attitudes Toward Gay Rights Depend on Who You Know

	Doesn't know someone gay or lesbian	Knows someone gay or lesbian
Gay couples should be able to adopt	28%	50%
Gay partners should have Social Security benefits	43%	60%
Gay and lesbian people should serve openly in the military	48%	63%
Hate-crime laws should include violence committed against gay and lesbian people	54%	69%
Gay partners should have inheritance rights	50%	73%
Gay and lesbian people should have equal rights in employment	77%	90%

Doesn't know someone gay or lesbian

Knows someone gay or lesbian

Source: www.hrc.org. October 4, 2006.

legislation has come from lesbian and gay activists, the majority of those eligible for such benefits would be cohabiting heterosexual partners.

Recently, national surveys of attitudes toward gay marriage in the United States have shown an even split among the public. In 2012, 47 percent of those surveyed felt that marriages between same-sex couples should be considered legal, while 43 percent felt that they should not be recognized. These results reflect the gradual shift in the level of acceptance of gay marriage since 2004, when 31 percent of respondents felt that it should be legal (Pew Research Center 2012a).

>> Divorce

"Do you promise to love, honor, and cherish . . . until death do you part?" Every year, people of all social classes and racial and ethnic groups make this legally binding agreement. Yet a significant number of these promises shatter before divorce.

STATISTICAL TRENDS IN DIVORCE

Just how common is divorce? Surprisingly, this is not a simple question to answer; divorce statistics are difficult to interpret. The media frequently report that one out of every two marriages ends in divorce. But that figure is misleading in that many marriages last for decades. It is based on a comparison of all divorces that occur in a single year (regardless of when the couples were married) with the number of new marriages in that same year. We get a somewhat more complete picture by looking at marital milestones people reach based on the year they first married (as shown in the table on page 172). These data include marriages that end owing to the

> **domestic partnership** Two unrelated adults who share a mutually caring relationship, reside together, and agree to be jointly responsible for their dependents, basic living expenses, and other common necessities.

Percentage of Marriages to Reach Milestones*

Men, year of first marriage	Anniversary (percentage still married)*							
	5th	10th	15th	20th	25th	30th	35th	40th
1960–64	94.6	83.4	74.7	70.2	66.9	64.5	62.1	60.1
1965–69	91.7	88.0	69.9	65.8	62.7	60.5	57.9	
1970–74	88.0	75.0	65.7	60.2	56.8	53.8		
1975–79	88.2	73.4	63.7	58.7	54.4			
1980–84	90.6	74.3	65.2	60.0				
1985–89	87.7	75.4	66.6					
1990–94	89.7	77.3						
1995–99	89.6							

*Counts marriages ended by divorce, separation, and death

Women, year of first marriage	Anniversary (percentage still married)*							
	5th	10th	15th	20th	25th	30th	35th	40th
1960–64	93.0	82.8	73.5	67.0	60.8	57.2	53.6	49.7
1965–69	90.7	79.3	69.6	64.0	59.1	55.8	52.1	
1970–74	89.2	74.5	66.1	61.3	56.2	52.6		
1975–79	86.9	72.8	63.2	57.4	53.2			
1980–84	87.8	71.1	62.9	56.6				
1985–89	87.9	74.5	66.4					
1990–94	87.1	74.5						
1995–99	89.5							

Source: Kreider and Ellis 2011:Table 4.

death of the partner; given that life expectancy has increased, the data do provide a sense of shifting patterns. Following either the rows or the columns provides insight into both the generational effect and the effects of changing attitudes and practices over time.

Of first marriages that ended in divorce, the median duration is 8 years. Overall, in the United States 20.5 percent of men and 22.4 percent of women age 15 and older have been divorced. Among adults age 50 to 59, 35.7 percent of men and 37.3 percent of women divorced at some point in their lives (Kreider and Ellis 2011).

In the United States overall divorce rates increased significantly in the 1960s but then leveled off; since the late 1980s the divorce rate has declined by 30 percent. This trend is due partly to the aging of the baby boomer generation and the corresponding decline in the proportion of people of marriageable age. But it also indicates an increase in marital stability in recent years (Coontz 2006; Kreider and Ellis 2011).

Getting divorced does not necessarily sour people on marriage. About 63 percent of all divorced people in the United States have remarried. The median time between their divorce and second marriage is four years. Women are less likely than men to remarry, because many retain custody of their children after a divorce, which complicates

a new adult relationship (Kreider and Ellis 2011; Saad 2004).

FACTORS ASSOCIATED WITH DIVORCE

One of the major factors shaping the increase in divorce over the past 100 years has been the greater social acceptance of divorce. It is no longer considered necessary to endure an unhappy marriage. Even major religious groups have relaxed what were often negative attitudes toward divorce, commonly having treated it as a sin in the past.

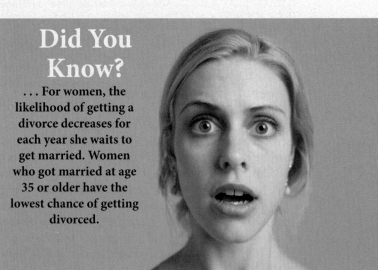

Did You Know?

. . . For women, the likelihood of getting a divorce decreases for each year she waits to get married. Women who got married at age 35 or older have the lowest chance of getting divorced.

The growing acceptance of divorce is a worldwide phenomenon. Only a decade ago, Sunoo, South Korea's foremost matchmaking service, had no divorced clients. Few Koreans divorced, and those who did felt social pressure to resign themselves to the single life. In one recent seven-year period, South Korea's divorce rate doubled. Now, 15 percent of Sunoo's membership is divorced (Onishi 2003).

Trends in Marriage and Divorce in the United States

Rate per 1,000 total population

Sources: Bureau of the Census 1975:64; Tejada-Vera and Sutton 2010.

In the United States, a variety of factors have contributed to the growing social acceptance of divorce. For instance, most states have adopted less restrictive divorce laws in the past three decades. No-fault divorce laws, which allow a couple to end their marriage without assigning blame (by specifying adultery, for instance), accounted for an initial surge in the divorce rate after they were introduced in the 1970s, though these laws appear to have had little effect beyond that. Additionally, a general increase in family incomes, coupled with the availability of free legal aid to some poor people, has meant that more couples can afford costly divorce proceedings. Also, as society provides greater opportunities for women, more and more wives are becoming less dependent on their husbands, both economically and emotionally. They may feel more able to leave a marriage if it seems hopeless (Coontz 2011).

IMPACT OF DIVORCE ON CHILDREN

Divorce is traumatic for all involved, but it has special meaning for the more than 1 million children whose parents divorce each year. There is significant sociological debate on the effects divorce has on children. One major study tracked 131 children of divorce

over a 25-year period. It concluded that the impacts of divorce are substantial and long-lasting, including higher rates of drug and alcohol abuse, limited resources for college, and fear of intimacy in adulthood (Wallerstein, Lewis, and Blakeslee 2000). These researchers recommended that parents should stay together in a "good enough" marriage for the sake of the children. One of the limitations of this research is the relatively small sample size, raising questions about the degree to which the results can be generalized.

Other sociologists have concluded that, for many children, divorce signals the welcome end to a highly dysfunctional relationship. A national study conducted by sociologists Paul R. Amato and Alan Booth (1997) showed that in about a third of divorces, the children actually benefited from parental separation because it lessened their exposure to conflict. Additional researchers, also using larger samples, have concluded that the long-term harmful effects of divorce affect only a minority of children (Booth and Amato 2001; Cherlin 2009; Hetherington and Kelly 2002; Sun and Li 2008).

The debates surrounding issues such as divorce, cohabitation, and same-sex families highlight many of the issues sociologists seek to address in their investigation of family life. What families are, what they do, how they do it, and what obstacles they face are issues relevant for all families. In our modern, pluralistic world, the singular traditions of the past can no longer be taken for granted. People come from many different cultures with multiple taken-for-granted assumptions. Sociology investigates such complexity, providing us with tools so that we might better understand how we think and act in the context of families.

SOCstudies

Volunteer! There are numerous organizations designed to assist children in situations of need, including Big Brothers and Big Sisters, CASA (Court Appointed Special Advocates), and school tutoring programs. Such programs can fulfill some of the functions of families. Seek out one of these organizations, and find out ways that you can help.

get involved!

For REVIEW

I. **What is the family?**

- Sociologists define the family in terms of both what a family is, with an emphasis on blood and law, and what families do or what functions they perform, including reproduction, socialization, protection, regulation of sexual behavior, affection and companionship, and provision of social status.

II. **How do people pick partners?**

- Social factors shape the pool of potential partners from which individuals select. People balance selection, favoring someone who is from within their group (endogamy) but not too close (exogamy). People tend to pick people with similar social characteristics (homogamy), including age, education, class, race, and ethnicity.

III. **How do families vary?**

- There is significant variation in terms of proximity (extended versus nuclear), authority (patriarchal, matriarchal, and egalitarian), duration (divorce), and structure (dual-income, single-parent, stepfamilies, cohabitation, singlehood, child-free, and same-sex).

SOCVIEWS on Families

Functionalist View

The family contributes to **social stability** by performing important functions: reproduction, protection, socialization, regulation of sexual behavior, affection and companionship, and providing social status.

Kinship ties involve both obligations and responsibilities, but also serve as a source of aid in time of trouble.

Parenthood is a crucial **social role** because one of its tasks is the **socialization** of children, which is essential to maintain any culture.

STABILITY, SOCIAL ROLES, SOCIALIZATION
KEY CONCEPTS

Conflict View

A family's social position helps determine a child's opportunities in life as a result of **power, property, and privilege** that is passed from generation to the next.

Endogamous restrictions on marriage perpetuates existing inequality and may raise **racial barriers**.

Discrimination against gay and lesbian partners is seen in bans on same-sex marriage, denial of legal rights that married couples enjoy, and restrictions on adoption of children.

KEY CONCEPTS
POWER, DISCRIMINATION

Interactionist View

Families provide the context within which we are born, **socialized**, and establish our basic identities.

We construct new family patterns—whether dual-career, single-parent, blended, or gay or lesbian—in response to social and historical changes we both experience and cause.

In egalitarian marriages, couples **interact as equals**, sharing decision making, housework, and child care.

KEY CONCEPTS
MICRO LEVEL, INTIMATE RELATIONSHIPS

MAKE THE CONNECTION

After reviewing the chapter, answer the following questions:

1

How would each perspective shed light on shifts represented by William and Kate's wedding? (p. 153)

2

Take a look at the pie charts family types (p. 157). What factors would each perspective focus on to explain the changes over the years?

3

Why does a functionalist definition of what the family *does* provide additional insight into families today than trying to define what it *is* (p. 158)?

4

Who rules in your family? Would a functionalist, conflict, or interactionist perspective best describe your family dynamics?

Pop Quiz

1. **Which definition of the family focuses on the importance of blood and law?**
   a. functionalist
   b. matrilineal
   c. substantive
   d. extended

2. **Which system of descent is followed in the United States?**
   a. matrilineal
   b. patrilineal
   c. bilateral
   d. unilateral

3. **Alice, age seven, lives at home with her parents, her grandmother, and her aunt. Alice's family is an example of a(n)**
   a. nuclear family.
   b. patrilineal family.
   c. extended family.
   d. polygynous family.

4. **In which form of marriage may a person have several spouses in his or her lifetime but only one spouse at a time?**
   a. serial monogamy
   b. monogamy
   c. polygamy
   d. polyandry

5. **The marriage of a woman to more than one man at the same time is referred to as**
   a. polygyny.
   b. monogamy.
   c. serial monogamy.
   d. polyandry.

6. **In what type of societies do women dominate in family decision making?**
   a. polygyny
   b. egalitarian
   c. patriarchy
   d. matriarchy

7. **Which norm requires mate selection outside certain groups, usually one's own family or certain kinfolk?**
   a. exogamy
   b. endogamy
   c. matriarchy
   d. patriarchy

8. **The principle that prohibits sexual relationships between certain culturally specified relatives is known as**
   a. monogamy.
   b. the incest taboo.
   c. polygamy.
   d. endogamy.

9. **What is the projected cost of raising a child born in 2010 until she or he is 18 years old?**
   a. $107,011
   b. $286,860
   c. $408,425
   d. $646,464

10. **Overall, the divorce rate in the United States in the past 30 years**
    a. has risen dramatically.
    b. has risen slowly but steadily.
    c. has declined after having risen significantly in the 1960s and 1970s.
    d. shows no clear pattern.

1. (c); 2. (c); 3. (c); 4. (a); 5. (d); 6. (d); 7. (a); 8. (b); 9. (b); 10. (c)

8

EDUCATION & RELIGION

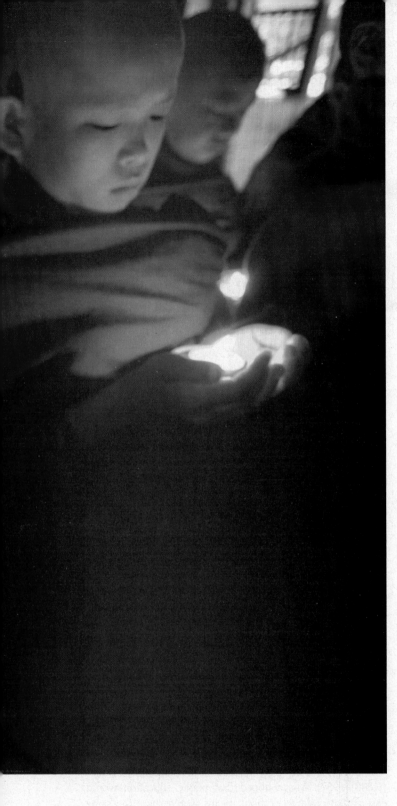

FAITH AND LEARNING

Patrick Henry College, located near Washington, D.C., was founded in 2000 with the explicit intention of competing with Ivy League schools. The elite students it pursues, however, come from a particular niche: approximately 80 percent of them were homeschooled, and they all share a strong commitment to evangelical Christian faith.

In keeping with the school's expectation of a high level of religious commitment, students must sign a "Statement of Faith" that sets out a series of Christian beliefs, including the virgin birth of Jesus Christ, the existence of Satan, and eternal punishment in hell for non-Christians. Students are required to abide by a strict dress code, attend daily chapel, and abstain from alcohol, smoking, and premarital sex.

The students by and large take these commitments quite seriously. As journalist Hannah Rosin (2007) recounts in her book on Patrick Henry College titled *God's Harvard,* "To them, a 'Christian' keeps a running conversation with God in his or her head . . . and believes that at any moment God might in some palpable way step in and show He either cares or disapproves" (p. 5).

Student Elisa Muench was something of a trailblazer at Patrick Henry College. She was the first woman to run for a leadership position in student government, in the face of disapproval by students who thought it inappropriate that a woman should serve in such an office. As a junior, she had an internship in the White House. Yet she found herself fearing that what counted as success in the eyes of the dominant society, including a professional career, might conflict with success in the eyes of God (Rosin 2007:85). Elisa struggled to be true to both her educational and her religious teachings.

It is within such educational and religious communities that we learn what to believe and how to act. All of us are, in some respects, like Elisa, seeking to balance the sometimes conflicting demands of the various spheres of our lives, including family, education, religion, work, and politics. In this chapter we focus on the roles education and religion play both for individuals and for society as a whole.

- How does education help to maintain social order?
- How does education support the existing system of inequality?
- How do sociologists define religion?

>>Education in Society

We need schools. They are so important, in fact, that we often take their existence and necessity for granted. Historically, families had the primary responsibility for teaching us the knowledge and skills we needed to survive and thrive in society. With the advent of the Industrial Revolution and the rise of globalization, however, schools became essential agents of socialization. As a society, we now invest a substantial amount of time and money in **education**. We do so because we believe the individual and collective benefits are worth it.

education A social institution dedicated to the formal process of transmitting culture from teachers to students.

Schools provide a place where we are exposed to the knowledge of those who have gone before us, enabling us to build on their wisdom as we carve out our pathways into the future. They expose us to beauty and help us to investigate the deeper meanings of life. As sociologist W. E. B. Du Bois ([1903] 1994) put it, "The true college will ever have one goal—not to earn meat, but to know the end and aim of that life which meat nourishes" (p. 51). But schools also provide us with the practical knowledge and skills we need as members of society, enabling us to get good jobs, become better parents, exercise our citizenship responsibilities, and more.

In the United States this commitment to education is built on a belief that our outcomes should not be determined

Did You Know?

. . . Among high school graduates from the class of 2011, 68.3 percent enrolled in college the following fall. Of these, 62 percent enrolled in 4-year programs, and 38 percent enrolled in 2-year schools.

Source: Bureau of Labor Statistics 2012c.

by birth but by ability and effort. According to this value, being born to wealthy parents should not ensure economic and social privilege any more than being born into meager circumstances should consign one to a life of poverty. Early American political leaders such as Benjamin Franklin and Thomas Jefferson advocated public education as an essential component of democratic societies because it provides individuals with opportunities and society with informed citizens. Horace Mann, often called the father of American public education, wrote in 1848, "Education, beyond all other devices of human origin, is the great equalizer of the conditions of men" ([1848] 1957). Mann hoped that public education would ensure that children without means would share the same classrooms, curriculum, and experiences with children of the well-off, thus providing everyone a chance for success.

Over time, education as an institution in the United States became more inclusive and expansive. Initially, public schools were open only to White males. In the 19th century, education was for the most part racially segregated, a practice that was affirmed by the 1896 Supreme Court decision in *Plessy v. Ferguson,* which reinforced the principle of "separate, but equal." Through education reform

SOC THINK

Who most influenced you to go to college? Considering people you know who did not go to college, what influenced them to make that choice? How powerful are socialization and social networks in making such decisions?

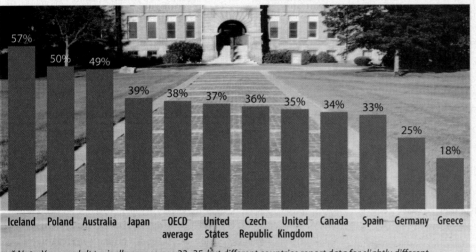

Percentage of Young Adults
with University Degrees*

57% Iceland
50% Poland
49% Australia
39% Japan
38% OECD average
37% United States
36% Czech Republic
35% United Kingdom
34% Canada
33% Spain
25% Germany
18% Greece

Note: Young adult typically means age 22–25, but different countries report data for slightly different ranges. University degree is the equivalent of a BA or BS. The Organization for Economic Cooperation and Development (OECD) is an international organization composed of 30 democratic nations.

Source: OECD 2010: Table A3.2.

efforts and legal decisions over two centuries, public education eventually opened up to include everyone regardless of race, ethnicity, sex, or national origin. Examples of education reformers include Emma Hart Willard, who opened the first college-level school for women in 1821, and sociologists such as Du Bois and Jane Addams, both of whom fought for racial and gender equality in the late 19th century. Legal decisions, such as Brown v. Board of Education in 1954, found that separate facilities are inherently unequal, and laws such as Title IX in 1972 required equal educational opportunities for both males and females as a requisite for receiving federal funding. Its expansion is reflected in higher levels of educational attainment. From 1940 to 2011 the proportion of people with a high school diploma increased from 24.5 to 87.6 percent, and the number with a college degree rose from 4.6 to 30.4 percent (U.S. Census Bureau 2012:Table A-2). In spite of these accomplishments, questions remain about the degree to which the principle of opportunity is fully achieved in practice.

>>Sociological Perspectives on Education

Sociologists have closely examined the degree to which education actually succeeds in providing social order and individual opportunity. They have found that although it does offer opportunity and helps to establish social order,

it also perpetuates inequality. Fulfilling the hopes of Jefferson, Franklin, Emma Hart Willard, and Mann, it has produced an educated citizenry equipped to take on the challenges of modern life. At the same time, however, it reinforces existing beliefs, values, and norms that justify the status quo and its inequalities. Sociologists seek to understand how education can do both at the same time.

EDUCATION AND SOCIAL ORDER

Society needs people with the knowledge and skills to perform the tasks necessary for its continued existence, and individuals need this know-how to survive and prosper. Schools teach students how to read, speak foreign languages, repair automobiles, and much more. Sociologists have identified five positive functions that education serves for both individuals and society.

Transmitting Culture Each society has a common stock of cultural knowledge deemed important for its members. As a social institution, education preserves and transmits society's norms, values, beliefs, ideas, and skills, thus reinforcing society's dominant culture. This endorsed knowledge is transmitted through the formal curriculum taught in schools including "the three 'Rs" (reading, 'riting, and 'rithmatic), as well as history, science, and much more. As a result, young people of each generation learn what they need to survive and succeed. In addition, ensuring that a critical mass of new members share common knowledge and beliefs secures society's survival into the future.

Education connects us with others beyond our immediate circumstances, enabling us to work together. For example, in addition to shared norms and values, if we could not take for granted that those we meet on a daily basis share common languages, collective action would be almost impossible. We would have to spend a significant amount of time working out how to communicate with each other in order to get anything accomplished. Shared language, including knowledge of multiple languages learned in schools, provides a shortcut facilitating such action.

In addition to the formal curriculum, schools create social space for children to transmit unofficial culture among their peers and to establish themselves as individuals separate from their families. Parents aren't hovering over their shoulders to ensure their children say the right things or keep their coats on at recess, and they can't protect children from getting hurt. School is the place where children learn to stand on their own and to establish relationships with their peer group (Adler and Adler 1996). As children get older, peer relationships grow stronger, and the distance from the parental world grows greater.

Promoting Social Integration Why do we need to know things such as, "in 1492 Columbus sailed the ocean blue" and $a^2 + b^2 = c^2$? The answer is simple: the culture we share binds us together. Even if no one individual possess all of it—and even if any single item seems necessary only for contestants on *Jeopardy!*—such knowledge represents who we are and what we believe is important. To put it in Durkheim's terms, it is part of our collective conscience, the social glue that holds us together; or, in Mead's terms, the shared culture we learn in schools contributes to our sense of the generalized other, the map of society we hold in our heads.

SOCTHINK

Why do students often feel like schools teach a lot of useless facts? What might this attitude suggest about social integration in modern society?

In an effort to promote social integration, many colleges and universities have established learning communities within which students share common experiences, or they may require first- and second-year students to live on campus. Such programs become more important when students come from diverse backgrounds with different cultural expectations. The goal is to provide experiences that will unify a population composed of diverse racial, ethnic, and religious groups into a community whose members share—to some extent—a common identity. The social integration fostered by education contributes to societal stability and consensus.

SOCTHINK

Does offering bilingual education to accommodate non-English-speaking students undermine social integration in the United States?

In the past the integrative function of education was most obvious in its emphasis on promoting a common language. Immigrant children were expected to learn English. In some instances, they were even forbidden to speak their native language on school grounds. More recently, bilingualism has been defended both for its educational value and as a means of encouraging cultural diversity. However, critics argue that bilingualism undermines the social and political integration that education traditionally has promoted.

Training and Social Control In schools, students learn general behaviors that are expected of them as members of society and specialized skills they will need in the workforce. In the early grades in particular, significant time and effort are spent getting students to do what the teacher wants them to do, when and how the teacher wants them to do it. Through the exercise of social control, schools teach students various skills essential to their future positions in society. Norms provide us with the order and stability we need to make our individual and collective lives predictable, and schools help us internalize normative expectations. Students learn manners, punctuality, creativity, discipline,

Education Pays

Education level	Median annual earnings
Some high school, no degree	$20,270
High school graduate (includes GED)	$30,888
Some college, no degree	$32,803
Associate's degree	$37,393
Bachelor's degree	$46,415
Master's degree	$52,547
Professional degree	$63,244
Doctorate degree	$67,470

Your efforts will pay.

* Includes full-time, full-year wage and salary for workers aged 25–34.
Source: U.S. Census Bureau 2011f:Part 46.

techniques, knowledge, and practices. Cultural innovation on campuses goes beyond such concrete results, however, because college provides a context within which we can challenge existing ideas and try out new practices. Such experimentation sometimes leads people to accuse professors, especially those with innovative or unpopular ideas, of being out of touch or out of line, but we need people to experiment with new ideas so that our culture does not stagnate.

Campuses also provide an environment in which students from around the world with widely divergent ideas and experiences can interact. In 2010–2011, U.S. campuses hosted 723,277 international students. Such exposure provides opportunities for cultural innovation as people from various cultures are exposed to and experiment with new and different cultural norms and values (Institute of International Education 2012).

Child Care Historically, family members had the primary responsibility to teach and care for their children until adulthood. Increasingly, we expect schools and teachers to do more of the job—and at younger and younger ages. The movement toward day care and preschool is driven in part by changes in the economy. Although this shift does provide children with a head start in learning the skills they will need in a globally competitive world, working parents have come to depend on schools to essentially babysit their kids, making sure they are cared for and protected. Because they take responsibility for the children during the school day, schools effectively free up parents to participate in the paid labor force.

EDUCATION AND INEQUALITY

What if, instead of leveling the playing field, schools reinforce existing systems of inequality? We rely on schools to provide a fair chance of success for all, but researchers have found that the social positions students occupy when they start school are often reproduced when they finish. Take, for example, the impact a parent's education

Government policies at the national, state, and local levels all influence what happens within the classroom.

and responsibility—skills and abilities we need well beyond the classroom. In effect, schools serve as a transitional agent of social control, bridging the gap between childhood and entry into the labor force and wider society.

In a society with a complex division of labor, we especially count on schools to select and train students so that they can become effective workers in specialized jobs. We expect schools to choose those with the most ability to pursue degrees in fields that demand the greatest skill. For example, we want students with aptitude in math and science to become engineers. We use grades as an indicator of such ability and provide degrees to certify that the graduate has sufficient training to perform the job well. We hold out the promise of higher pay to reward those who make the sacrifices that higher education calls for in terms of time and money. As we will see below, however, many people are concerned about the degree to which this ideal is achieved.

Stimulating Cultural Innovation

Although schools do preserve and transmit existing culture, education can also stimulate social change. In response to the soaring pregnancy rate among teenagers, for example, public schools began to offer sex education classes. As a means of countering discrimination based on sex or race, many schools turned to affirmative action in admissions—giving priority to females or minorities. Project Head Start, an early-childhood program that serves more than 904,000 children annually, has sought to compensate for the disadvantages in school readiness experienced by children from low-income families (Administration for Children and Families 2010). To ensure school readiness, it provides classes for preschool children from families below a certain income level, working with them on letter recognition, vocabulary, nutrition, and other basic skills.

Colleges and universities are particularly committed to cultural innovation. Faculty members, especially at large universities, must pursue research and publish articles and books. In so doing, they produce new technology,

Effect of Parents' Education on Students' Test Performance

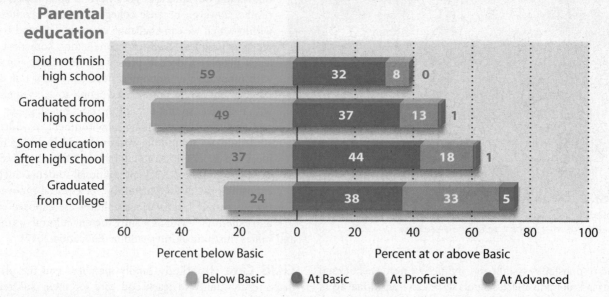

Parental education

Did not finish high school — 59 | 32 | 8 | 0

Graduated from high school — 49 | 37 | 13 | 1

Some education after high school — 37 | 44 | 18 | 1

Graduated from college — 24 | 38 | 33 | 5

Percent below Basic | Percent at or above Basic

60 40 20 0 20 40 60 80 100

● Below Basic   ● At Basic   ● At Proficient   ● At Advanced

Note: Percentage distribution of 12th-grade students across NAEP mathematics achievement levels, by highest level of parental education, 2009.
Source: NAEP 2011.

level can have on a child's success in school, as described by sociologist Annette Lareau (2003):

> Children of highly educated mothers continue to outperform children of less educated mothers throughout their school careers. By the time young people take the SAT examinations for admission to college, the gap is dramatic, averaging 150 points (relative to an average score of 500 points) between children of parents who are high school dropouts, and those with parents who have a graduate degree. (p. 29)

This example points to one of our basic sociological insights: social position matters, shaping both the resources available to us and our likely outcomes. More recent data continues to show that SAT performance varies by family income and parents' education, race, and

ethnicity, challenging our faith that schools provide a fair chance for mobility regardless of position (Snyder and Dillow 2011:Table 151, 153). We don't expect our education systems to perpetuate a system of inequality, serving the interests of those who already have economic, social, and cultural resources. But sociologists point to a number of ways in which this very thing can happen.

One of the ways we see education systems perpetuate inequality is through school funding. Jonathan Kozol (2005), who has studied educational inequality for decades, argues that wealthier districts have the money to offer programs and facilities that poor districts cannot hope to match, including AP (Advanced Placement) classes, high-tech labs, athletic facilities, and elective courses in art, music, and languages. As but one example among many, in 2009–2010 the Chicago public school district spent

In the classic comic strip *Calvin and Hobbes,* Calvin is a first-grader who often struggles with balancing what he wants to do versus doing what is expected of him. That is especially true when it comes to school. He gives voice to the experience many of us have had as we are socialized to accept the institutional expectations of the larger society at the cost of our individual freedom.

$13,078 per student while the wealthy northern suburban Highland Park and Deerfield school district spent $19,920 (Illinois State Board of Education 2012). As a former New York City principal, in an interview with Kozol, put it, "I'll believe money doesn't count the day the rich stop spending so much on their own children" (Kozol 2005:59). In this section we look at a number of such ways that the experience of and outcomes from education are not equal for everyone.

Personal Sociology

Unearned Advantages

My daughters Emily and Eleanor make me proud. They get good grades, and their scores on the standardized exams are sky high. But as a sociologist, I know that they benefit from the fact that their parents are college graduates. As parents, Lori and I provide Em and El with economic, social, and cultural resources in the form of books, activities, and even vacations to historic locations. Kids from such families tend to do better in school than children who lack such opportunities. It's almost as if they are cheating. They did nothing to deserve such advantages, and yet, as a society, we act as if educational outcomes—good or bad—are solely based on merit.

SOCTHINK

Funding for public schools comes mostly from local and state governments, each contributing approximately 45 percent. The federal government provides about 9 percent (Snyder and Dillow 2011:67). What are possible consequences of this model for equitable funding of education nationwide? Why might some local districts resist changing this model?

The Hidden Curriculum One of the ways that schools reinforce the existing system of inequality is through the teaching of what sociologists call the **hidden curriculum**—standards of behavior that society deems proper and that teachers subtly communicate to students (Langhout and Mitchell 2008; Thornberg 2008). It prepares students to submit to authority. For example, children learn not to speak until the teacher calls on them, and they learn to regulate their activities according to the clock or bells. A classroom environment that is overly focused on obedience rewards students for pleasing the teacher and remaining compliant rather than for creative thought and academic learning. In this way, schools socialize students to submit to authority figures, including bosses and political leaders.

Teacher Expectancy Student outcomes can also become a self-fulfilling prophecy based on how teachers perceive students. Psychologist Robert Rosenthal and school principal Lenore Jacobson (1968) documented what they referred to as a **teacher-expectancy effect**—the impact that a teacher's expectations about a student's performance may have on the student's actual achievements. They conducted experiments to document this effect.

Rosenthal and Jacobson informed teachers that they were administering a verbal and reasoning pretest to children in a San Francisco elementary school. After administering the tests, the researchers told the teachers that some of the students were "spurters"—children who showed particular academic potential. However, rather than using the actual

PRINCIPAL

hidden curriculum Standards of behavior that are deemed proper by society and are taught subtly in schools.

teacher-expectancy effect The impact that a teacher's expectations about a student's performance may have on the student's actual achievements.

test scores to make this determination, the researchers randomly selected the 20 percent of the students they identified as spurters. When the students were later retested, the spurters scored not only significantly higher than they had in previous tests but also significantly higher than their peers. Moreover, teachers evaluated the spurters as more interesting, more curious, and better adjusted than their classmates. This is a classic case of a self-fulfilling prophecy at work. Teachers expected some students to do well, and so they did. Such effects are of particular concern if factors such as race, ethnicity, class, or gender shape teachers' perceptions. Recent research continues to affirm the significant role that teacher expectations have on student performance and also finds that students' race and ethnicity can shape those expectations and, therefore, outcomes (McKown and Weinstein 2008; Rubie-Davies 2010; van den Bergh et al. 2010).

Did You Know?

SOCTHINK

What experiences have you had with tracking? To what extent do you believe it was effective for both high-track and low-track students? What are its limitations in terms of equal opportunity?

Bestowal of Status As we saw above, part of the public school ideal was that education would contribute to the creation of opportunity and the establishment of a more open society. In a classic sociology study, Kingsley Davis and Wilbert E. Moore (1945) argued that all societies have positions that are more important for the society's survival or that require greater skill or knowledge to perform. Ideally, the institution of education selects those with ability and trains them for such positions. We reward people in such positions with social prestige and high pay, Davis and Moore claim, because we value such skills and respect the fact that these individuals sacrificed the time and energy necessary to acquire those skills. For example, not everyone has the skill necessary to become a medical doctor, and in order to encourage people who do have the potential to pursue that path, we promise them sufficient social and economic compensation.

The problem with this model is that, in practice, factors other than potential and ability shape outcomes such as social class, race, ethnicity, and gender. Although the educational system helps certain poor children to move into middle-class professional positions, it denies most disadvantaged children the same educational opportunities afforded to children of the affluent. In this way, schools tend to preserve social class inequalities in each new generation (Giroux 1988; Pinkerton 2003).

One way schools reinforce class differences is by putting students in tracks. The term **tracking** refers to the practice of placing students in specific curriculum groups on the basis of their test scores and other criteria. In theory, tracking is beneficial because it allows students to be taught at a level and pace most consistent with their abilities. In practice, however, tracking often starts at a young age, and student selection for low-versus high-ability groups is often correlated with their social class, race, or ethnicity. In effect, the differences children bring with them on their first day of kindergarten shape their likely long-term educational outcomes (Oakes 2008).

Research on tracking raises questions about its effectiveness, especially for low-ability students. In one study of low-income schools in California, researchers discovered a staggering difference between students who were tracked and those who were not. At one school, all interested students were allowed to enroll in advanced placement (AP) courses, not just those who were selected by the administration. Half the open-enrollment students scored high enough to qualify for college credit—a much higher proportion than in selective programs, in which only 17 percent of students qualified for college credit. Tracking programs do not necessarily identify those students with the potential to succeed (B. Ellison 2008; Sacks 2007).

Sociologists Samuel Bowles and Herbert Gintis (1976) have argued that the educational inequalities produced by tracking are designed to meet the needs of modern capitalist societies. They claim that capitalism requires a skilled, disciplined labor force and that the educational system of the United States is structured with that objective in mind. Citing numerous studies, they offer support for what they call the **correspondence principle**. According to this approach, schools promote the values expected of individuals in each social class and perpetuate social class divisions from one generation to the next. Thus, working-class children, assumed to be destined for subordinate positions, are likely to be placed in high school vocational and general tracks, which emphasize close supervision and compliance with authority. In contrast, young people from more affluent families are likely to be directed to college preparatory tracks, which stress leadership and decision making—the skills they are expected to need as adults.

tracking The practice of placing students in specific curriculum groups on the basis of their test scores and other criteria.

correspondence principle The tendency of schools to promote the values expected of individuals in each social class and to prepare students for the types of jobs typically held by members of their class.

Did You Know?

Credentialism Students today also face elevated expectations. When it comes to educational attainment, they now have to go further just to stay in the same place. Fifty years ago, a high school diploma was enough to get a good job. Today, it often takes a college diploma to get that same job. This change reflects the process of **credentialism**—a term used to describe an increase in the lowest level of education needed to enter a field.

> Good schools, like good societies and good families, celebrate and cherish diversity.
>
> Deborah Meier

One of the driving factors in the rise of credentialism has been the expansion of occupations considered to be professions. Employers and occupational associations typically contend that reclassifying jobs is a logical response to the increasing complexity of many jobs. However, in many cases, employers raise the degree requirements for a position simply because all applicants have achieved the existing minimum credential (D. Brown 2001; G. Brown 2006).

One potential effect of credentialism is to reinforce social inequality. Applicants from poor and minority backgrounds are especially likely to suffer from the escalation of qualifications, because they may lack the financial resources needed to obtain degree after degree. In addition, upgrading of credentials serves the self-interest of the two groups most responsible for this trend. First, educational institutions profit because people must spend more time and money on schooling. Moreover, current jobholders have a stake in raising occupational requirements because credentialism can increase the status of an occupation and demands for higher pay. Max Weber anticipated this possibility as early as 1916, concluding that the "universal clamor for the creation of educational certificates in all fields makes for the formation of a privileged stratum in businesses and in offices" (Weber [1921] 1958c).

> **credentialism** An increase in the lowest level of education required to enter a field.

Women in Higher Education

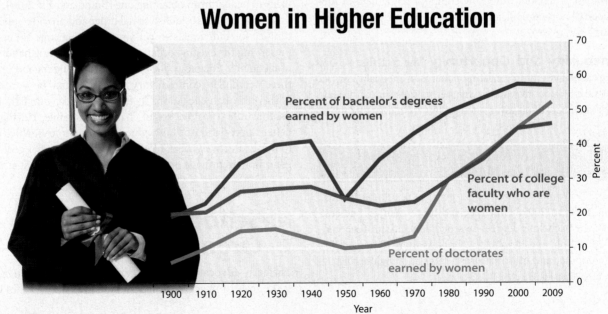

Percent of bachelor's degrees earned by women

Percent of college faculty who are women

Percent of doctorates earned by women

Year

Percent

Source: Snyder and Dillow 2011:Table 196.

Gender The educational system of the United States, like many other social institutions, has long been characterized by discriminatory treatment of women. It took until 1833 for Oberlin College to become the first institution of higher learning to admit female students—some 200 years after the founding of Harvard, the first men's college in the United States. Even so, Oberlin believed that women should aspire to become wives and mothers, not lawyers and intellectuals. In addition to attending classes, female students washed men's clothing, cared for their rooms, and served them meals.

In the 20th century, sexism in education showed up in many ways—in textbooks with negative stereotypes of women, in counselors' pressure on female students to prepare for "women's work," and in unequal funding for women's and men's athletic programs. In fact, throughout much of the century, only about one-third of college students were women. During that time they sat in classrooms staffed predominantly by male professors, because few college faculty members were female (Snyder and Dillow 2010:Table 188).

Today women have much greater educational opportunity, largely as a result of women's movements that worked for social change. Title IX of the Education Amendments of 1972 played a pivotal role in expanding access. It states, "No person in the United States shall, on the basis of sex, be excluded from participation in, be denied the benefits of, or be subjected to discrimination under any education program or activity receiving Federal financial assistance." While Title IX is most commonly associated with equal opportunity for women in athletics, among other things, it also eliminated sex-segregated classes and prohibited sex discrimination in admissions. And women have made the most of this opportunity. Starting in the late 1960s, the percentage of women earning college degrees began rising dramatically. In 1980 women earned 49 percent of degrees conferred, and the 2009 rate was 57.2 percent. Women students are also more likely to be taught by women professors, who now compose 45 percent of total faculty (Corbett, Hill, and St. Rose 2008;Snyder and Dillow 2011:Table 196).

Inequality and Opportunity The fact that schools can actually reinforce existing patterns of inequality has led some educators to wonder whether schools should discourage members of disadvantaged groups from even attempting

SOCTHINK

Women's participation in NCAA college athletics has increased more than 500 percent since 1972, from 31,852 then to 193,232 in 2010–2011. And high school rates rose from 294,015 in 1972 to nearly 3.2 million participants in 2011 (NFHS 2011). To what extent would we have seen such an increase had it not been for a law that mandated increased opportunity? How might increased opportunity for women in athletics have an impact on increased opportunity in other areas?

college. They fear that the long-term emotional toll of failure would be too great. Sociologists John R. Reynolds and Chardie L. Baird (2010) sought to answer the question "Do students who try but fail to achieve their educational dreams experience long-term frustration and anxiety?" Based on research from two national longitudinal studies, they concluded that the answer to this question is no. Those who fail to fulfill their aspirations develop "adaptive resilience," allowing them to cope with their lack of college success. Reynolds summarizes it this way: "Aiming high and failing is not consequential for mental health, while trying may lead to higher achievements and the mental and material benefits that go along with those achievements" (quoted in Elish 2010). As a result of their research, Reynolds and Baird recommend encouraging students to aim higher because it significantly increases students' chances of getting ahead, as the experience of women in higher education demonstrates. In fact, researchers have found that those with characteristics making them least likely to pursue a college degree—such as coming from low-income families, having parents with less education, or being African American or Latino—are most likely to benefit from obtaining one (Brand and Xie 2010).

Education does establish social order and provide opportunities for individuals to get ahead. At the same time, in preserving the existing order, it reproduces existing patterns of inequality. Sociology allows us to better understand how these seemingly contradictory outcomes can be accomplished through education. As the experience with Title IX demonstrates, positive social change is possible. Having a better appreciation of how education functions enables us to more effectively work toward realizing the initial goal of education: to provide opportunity and a more open society.

>>Schools as Formal Organizations

The early advocates of public education would be amazed at the scale of the education system in the United States in

Average Salaries for Teachers

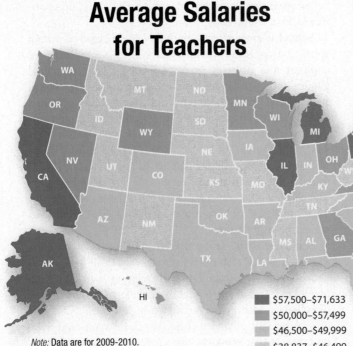

Note: Data are for 2009-2010.

Source: National Education Association 2010: Table C-11.

■	$57,500–$71,633
■	$50,000–$57,499
■	$46,500–$49,999
■	$38,837–$46,499

Teacher Turnover

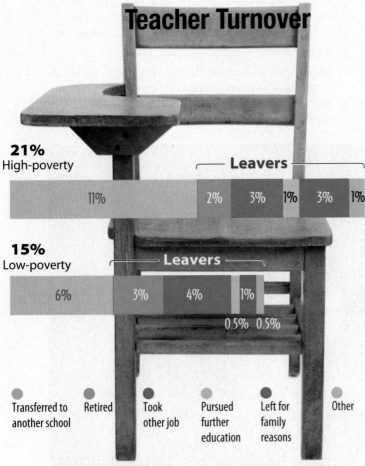

21%
High-poverty

11% | Leavers | 2% | 3% | 1% | 3% | 1%

15%
Low-poverty

6% | Leavers | 3% | 4% | 1% | 0.5% | 0.5%

● Transferred to another school   ● Retired   ● Took other job   ● Pursued further education   ● Left for family reasons   ● Other

Note: Percentage of public K–12 teachers who did not teach in the same school the following year, by poverty level of school and the reason teachers left.

Source: Planty et al. 2008:51.

---

the 21st century. In many respects, today's schools, when viewed as an example of a formal organization, are similar to factories, hospitals, and business firms. Instead of producing cars, patients, or profits, they pump out millions of students per year. In doing so, schools must be responsive to the various constituencies outside of the student body, including parents, employers, neighborhoods, and politicians. To handle their complex mission, schools have had to become increasingly institutionalized.

THE BUREAUCRATIZATION OF SCHOOLS

It simply is not possible for a single teacher to transmit all the necessary culture and skills to children who will enter many diverse occupations. The growing number of students being served by school systems and the greater degree of specialization required within a technologically complex society have combined to bureaucratize schools.

In many respects, schools put into practice all of Max Weber's principles of bureaucracy that we considered in Chapter 5. When it comes to the division of labor, teachers specialize in particular age levels and specific subjects. Schools are hierarchically organized, with teachers reporting to principals, who are themselves answerable to the superintendent of schools and the board of education. In terms of written rules and regulations, teachers must submit written lesson plans, and students, teachers, and administrators must all adhere to established policies and procedures or face sanctions for not doing so. As schools grow, they become increasingly impersonal, and teachers are expected to treat all students in the same way, regardless of their distinctive personalities and learning needs. Finally, hiring and promotion—and even grading—are based on technical qualifications alone, and standards are established and rubrics created in an effort to ensure this practice (Vanderstraeten 2007).

The trend toward more centralized education particularly affects disadvantaged people, for whom education promises to be a path to opportunity. The standardization of educational curricula, including textbooks, generally reflects the values, interests, and lifestyles of the most powerful groups in our society and may ignore those of racial and ethnic minorities. In addition, in comparison to the affluent, the resource poor often lack the time, financial resources, and knowledge necessary to sort through complex educational bureaucracies and to organize effective lobbying groups. As a result, low-income and minority parents will have even less influence over citywide and statewide educational administrators than they have over local school officials (Kozol 2005).

TEACHING AS A PROFESSION

As schools become more bureaucratic, teachers increasingly encounter the conflicts inherent in serving as a professional within the context of a bureaucracy. Teachers must work within the system, submitting to its hierarchical structure and abiding by its established rules. At the same time, teachers want to practice their profession with some degree of autonomy and respect for their judgment. Conflicts arise from having to serve simultaneously as instructor, disciplinarian, administrator, and employee of a school district.

As professionals, teachers feel pressure from a number of directions. First, the level of formal schooling required for teaching remains high, and the public has begun to call for new competency examinations. Second, teachers' salaries are significantly lower than those of many comparably educated professionals and skilled workers. Finally, respect for teachers as competent and responsible professionals has been challenged in the political arena. Many teachers, disappointed and frustrated, have left the educational world for careers in other professions. In fact, between a quarter and a third of new teachers quit within their first three years, and as many as half leave poor urban schools within their first five years (Wallis 2008). Even within a single year, teacher turnover is significant; in high-poverty areas, more than 20 percent of teachers did not teach in the same school the following year.

STUDENT SUBCULTURES

Schools also provide an arena for students' social and recreational needs. Education helps toddlers and young children develop interpersonal skills that are essential during adolescence and adulthood. In their high school and college years, students may meet future spouses and establish lifelong friendships.

School leaders often seek to develop a sense of school spirit and collective identity, but student subcultures are complex and diverse. As we saw in Chapter 4, school cliques and social groups may crop up according to race, social class, physical attractiveness, academic placement, athletic ability, and leadership roles in the school and community (Adler and Adler 1996; Milner 2006; Suitor, Minyard, and Carter 2001). In his classic community study of "Elmtown," sociologist August B. Hollingshead (1975) found some 259 distinct cliques in a single high school. The cliques, whose average size was five, were centered on the school itself, on recreational activities, and on religious and community groups.

Amid these close-knit and often rigidly segregated cliques, some students get left out. Historically, gay and lesbian students have been particularly vulnerable to such exclusion. Many have organized to establish their own stronger sense of collective identity, including through the establishment of gay–straight alliances (GSAs)—school-sponsored support groups that bring gay teens together with sympathetic straight peers. Begun in Los Angeles in 1984, these programs numbered more than 4,000 nationwide in 2011.

We can find a similar diversity of student groups at the college level. Sociologists have identified four distinctive subcultures among college students (Clark and Trow 1966; Horowitz 1987):

- The *collegiate* subculture focuses on having fun and socializing. These students define what constitutes a "reasonable" amount of academic work (and what amount of work is "excessive" and leads to being labeled as a "grind").

The High School Class of 2021

Asian/Pacific Islander
4.4%   7.9%

American Indian/Alaska Native
0.9%
1.1%

Note: Projected high school graduating class of 2021 by race and ethernity

Source: Projections of Education Statistics to 2020

Hispanic
19.3%
9.6%

2020-21

1995-96

Black
12.9%
14.3%

72.1%

White

57.3%

The typology used by the researchers reminds us that the school is a complex social organization—almost like a community with different neighborhoods. Of course, these four subcultures are not the only ones evident on college campuses in the United States. For example, one might find subcultures of Iraq or Afghanistan war veterans or former full-time homemakers, or students may gather together on the basis of race, ethnicity, or nationality.

COMMUNITY COLLEGES

Community colleges exist as a testament to the ideals put forth by Jefferson, Franklin, and Mann. The GI bill in the 1940s and Pell Grants in the 1960s provided significant college financial aid for those with limited means, opening wide the doors to college. However, availability of financial aid, especially in the form of grants, has declined significantly in recent years. Community colleges continue to give students a chance to prove themselves, however, and their relatively low cost and open enrollment lower the barriers to success. As a result, an increasing number of students have turned to community colleges, including a surge that started in the fall of 2009 because of a weak economy.

There are now more than 7.8 million community college students in the United States, making up 36 percent of all postsecondary students. This represents an almost 750 percent increase in students since 1963. These students are more likely to be older, female, Black, Hispanic, low-income, and part-time, compared to their peers at four-year schools. In fact, the more income and education a student's parents have, the less likely she or he is to attend a community college. This

Members of the collegiate subculture have little commitment to academic pursuits. Athletes often fit into this subculture.

- The *academic* subculture identifies with the intellectual concerns of the faculty and values knowledge for its own sake.
- The *vocational* subculture is interested primarily in career prospects and views college as a means of obtaining degrees that are essential for advancement.
- The *nonconformist* subculture is hostile to the college environment and seeks out ideas that may or may not relate to academic studies. This group may find outlets through campus publications or issue-oriented groups.

Each college student is eventually exposed to these competing subcultures and must determine which (if any) seems most in line with his or her feelings and interests.

SOCTHINK

To what extent do you fit into one of the four college subcultures? What background influences, including friends, teachers, or parents, might have contributed to your following that path instead of the others?

high-lights the role these schools play in providing opportunity for those with limited resources. Enrollment at community colleges raises the aspirations of students. Whether they initially expected to take only a few courses or to finish with a two-year degree, almost one-half of these students later aspired to more education, including a four-year degree or beyond (Knapp, Kelly-Reid, and Ginder 2012; Provasnik and Planty 2008).

One of the concerns raised about community colleges is persistence—the degree to which students pursue an education. The rate at which such students leave community college without completing a degree or certificate program (45 percent) is significantly higher than that for students at four-year schools (16 to 17 percent). Even those who had initially enrolled intending to pursue a four-year degree left school early at a rate of 39 percent. Such high rates led some theorists to suggest that community colleges serve a "cooling out" function. They argue that the limited number of good jobs in society is a given, so not everyone can succeed in obtaining one. Because community colleges appear to provide opportunities for anyone to succeed, failure to do so is perceived to be the individual's responsibility alone. Thus, students are more likely to blame themselves than to develop a critique of the social structure that shaped their likely outcomes. In other words, community colleges do provide opportunity for some, but they also help to justify the existing system of inequality (Bahr 2008; Clark 1960, 1980).

HOMESCHOOLING

Some parents view formal schooling as a path to opportunity; others have decided to opt out altogether. More than 1.5 million students are now being educated at home—about 2.9 percent of the K–12 school population. Homeschooled families are more likely to be White, have two parents in the household with only one in the labor force, have parents with a bachelor's degree, and have three or more children (Planty et al. 2009).

religion Is a social institution dedicated to establishing a shared sense of identity, encouraging social integration, and offering believers a sense of meaning and purpose.

In a sense this represents a return to the pre–public school days of American education, in which the primary responsibility for teaching rested with parents. When asked to identify the most important reason for choosing this path, 36 percent of parents said they were motivated by a desire to provide religious or moral instruction (the most common response), and 83 percent overall identified that as an important factor. A concern about the environment of schools—safety, drugs, and negative peer pressure—was most important to 21 percent, and 17 percent attributed their decision primarily to dissatisfaction with the school's academic instruction (Planty et al. 2009). In addition, some immigrants choose homeschooling as a way to ease their children's transition to a new society. For example, increasing numbers of the nation's growing Arab American population have joined the movement toward homeschooling (Cooper and Sureau 2007; MacFarquhar 2008). Other parents see it as a good alternative for children who suffer from attention deficit hyperactivity disorder (ADHD) and learning disorders (LDs). A study by the Home School Legal Defense Association (2005), a homeschool advocacy organization, found that homeschooled students score higher than others on standardized exams in every subject and in every grade.

The rise in homeschooling points toward a growing dissatisfaction with the institutionalized practice of education. Early public school advocates argued for the importance of a common curriculum rooted in a shared sense of values. Homeschooling, however, points toward pluralism and the desire to retain the unique subcultural values of a community. Although new forms of schooling may meet the individual needs of diverse groups in today's society, they also undermine the historical commitment to public education as a means of fostering unity within society.

─SOC THINK─

What do you think are the advantages and disadvantages of being homeschooled? How might it contribute to a stronger sense of identity? How might it threaten the social order?

>>Defining Religion

Education plays a major role in socializing members of society into shared values and norms, and religion helps to cement those beliefs and practices into people's hearts and minds. **Religion** is a social institution dedicated to establishing a shared sense of identity, encouraging social integration, and offering believers a sense of meaning and purpose. Though levels of religious participation vary from place to place, religion continues to be a major force both on the world stage and in the lives of individuals. To fully understand its various forms, sociologists take two basic approaches to defining religion. The first focuses on what religion is, and the second focuses on what it does.

SUBSTANCE: WHAT RELIGION IS

According to a substantive approach to studying religion, religion has a unique content or substance that separates it from other forms of knowledge and belief. Most commonly, this unique focus involves some conception of a supernatural realm, such as heaven, but it does not have to be outside the physical world. The key is that religion centers on something that goes above and beyond the mundane realities of our everyday existence, that points to something larger, and that calls for some response from us in terms of how we think and act. Sociologist Peter Berger (1969) provided a substantive definition of religion as "the human enterprise by which a sacred cosmos is established" (p. 25). The sacred here refers to that extraordinary realm that becomes the focus of religious faith and practice. It provides believers with meaning, order, and coherence. In describing that sacred realm, people might touch on concepts such as gods and goddess, angels and demons, heaven and hell, nirvana, or other beings or realms. A society with broad agreement about the nature and importance of this sacred realm is, by definition, more religious.

Sociologists that follow a substantive approach focus on the ways in which religious groups rally around what they define to be sacred. The **sacred** encompasses elements beyond everyday life that inspire respect, awe, and even fear. People interact with the sacred realm through ritual practices, such as prayer or sacrifice. Because believers have faith in the sacred, they accept what they cannot understand. The sacred realm exists in contrast to the **profane**, which includes the ordinary and commonplace.

Different religious groups define their understanding of the sacred or profane in different ways. For example, who or what constitutes "god" varies among Muslims, Christians, and Hindus. Even within a group, different believers may treat the same object as sacred or profane, depending on whether it connects them to the sacred realm. Ordinarily, a piece of bread is profane, but it becomes sacred for Christians during their practice of communion because through it believers enter into connection with God. Similarly, a candelabrum becomes sacred to Jews if it is a menorah. For Confucians and Taoists, incense sticks are not mere decorative items, but highly valued offerings to the gods in religious ceremonies that mark the new and full moons.

FUNCTION: WHAT RELIGIONS DO

A functionalist approach focuses less on what religion is than on what religions do, with a particular emphasis on how religions contribute to social order. According to a functionalist approach to studying religion, religion unifies believers into a community through shared practices and a common set of beliefs relative to sacred things. The emphasis is on the unifying dimension of religion rather than on the substance of that which unifies. For functionalists, the supernatural or something like it is not an essential part of religion. Religion need not have gods or goddesses, an afterlife, or other such conventional elements. In fact, any social practices that strongly unite us, such as being a sports fan, can function like religion for the individual and for society.

The functional approach to defining religion has roots in the work of Émile Durkheim. He defined religion as "a unified system of beliefs and practices relative to sacred things, that is to say things set apart and forbidden—beliefs and practices which unite into a single moral community, called a 'church,' all those who adhere to them" ([1887] 1972:224). This definition points to three aspects sociologists focus on when studying religion: a unified system of beliefs and practices, involving sacred things, in the context of community.

> **sacred** Elements beyond everyday life that inspire respect, awe, and even fear.
>
> **profane** The ordinary and commonplace elements of life, as distinguished from the sacred.

The first element of Durkheim's functional approach is the unified system of beliefs and practices. What those beliefs and practices are matters less than the fact that they are shared. Terms historically used to describe religious beliefs include *doctrine, dogma, creeds,* and *scripture,* all representing principles believers share through faith. Practices refer to shared rituals such as attendance at services, prayer, meditation, and fasting. Because beliefs and practices are central to religion, we look at them in more detail below.

Unlike the substantive approach, Durkheim's emphasis on sacred things focuses less on the objects themselves than on the believers' attitude toward those objects. Sacred objects and sacred places convey a sense of awe,

---

SOC THINK

Do you think it is appropriate for religious leaders, such as pastors, priests, rabbis, or imams, to discuss political issues during religious services? Why or why not?

Personal Sociology

Victory Dance

I confess to being a Green Bay Packers fan. I follow them religiously. Even though I know better, I practice superstitions in the hope that they will help, including wearing a lucky shirt, not talking on the phone during the game, and though I am embarrassed to admit it, doing a "touchdown dance" around the dining-room table after the Packers score, with high-fives for everyone including our dog. My wife Lori is an even bigger fan, and together we have made numerous pilgrimages to "the frozen tundra of Lambeau Field" to cheer them on. Each season I renew my faith that they can win it all. In 2011 all those efforts paid off when the Packers won the Super Bowl, their 13th NFL championship. And there was much rejoicing.

and religion calls upon believers to treat them with reverence and care. Roman Catholics, for example, treat the bread and wine of communion with respect because they believe that the sacrament transforms those elements into the body and blood of Christ. For Muslims, the Qur'an is a sacred object, and the Kaaba in Mecca is a sacred place. In the functional approach to religion, however, sacredness is in the eyes of the beholders. Any object can be sacred so long as people define it as such and treat it accordingly.

religious belief A statement to which members of a particular religion adhere.

The most important component of Durkheim's definition is this third part: community. It is not the church, mosque, or temple as a building that matters, but the unification of a body of believers into a shared community.

What they believe, what they practice, or what they view as sacred is less important than that they have these beliefs, practices, and shared sacred things in common.

As suggested above, according to this approach, religion need not look like what we conventionally think of as religion. Anything that does what Durkheim's three elements do can function as religion. Just as our understanding of what families are has expanded to include people who are "like family" to us, so also has the definition of religion expanded to include things that function like religion. Sports provides a classic example. When it comes to beliefs and practices, sports fans—short for *fanatics,* a term that historically had religious connotations—share beliefs about the superiority of their team and regularly practice rituals in hopes that it will help their team win. They may wear the same jersey to watch the game, sit in the same chair, or do a touchdown dance after their team scores, all out of superstitious fear that failure to do so will make their team lose. In terms of sacred things, there are autographs, jerseys, balls; and the stadium where the team plays, often referred to by fans as a shrine, represents a sacred space. Finally, fans are united into a community with other fans of the team. Being a fan of the team becomes part of their identity. It provides them with joy, satisfaction, and even a sense of purpose. In a personal essay recounting his obsession with soccer, journalist Michael Elliott (2005) put it this way: "What does being a fan mean? It means you will never walk alone" (p. 76).

>>Components of Religion

In studying religion, regardless of which definitional approach they take, sociologists investigate components of religion that are common to most groups. Their goal is to gain a more complete picture of the role religion plays for both individuals and groups. Sociologists using both approaches focus on how religious groups organize beliefs, rituals, experience, and community.

BELIEFS

Some people believe in life after death, in supreme beings with unlimited powers, or in supernatural forces. **Religious beliefs** are statements to which members of a particular religion adhere. The focus can vary dramatically from religion to religion.

In the late 1960s a significant shift occurred in the nature of religious belief in the United States. Denominations that held to relatively liberal interpretations of religious scripture (such as the Presbyterians, Methodists, and Lutherans) declined in membership, while those that held to more conservative interpretations and sought a return to the fundamentals of the faith grew in numbers. The term **fundamentalism** refers to a rigid adherence to core religious doctrines. Often, fundamentalism is accompanied by a literal application of scripture or historical beliefs to today's world. Fundamentalism grows out of a sense that the world is falling apart due to a decline in true religious belief and practice. Fundamentalists see themselves as presenting a positive vision for the future through a return to the purity of the original religious message.

The phrase "religious fundamentalism" was first applied to Protestants in the United States who took a literal interpretation of the Bible, but fundamentalism is found worldwide among most major religious groups, including Roman Catholicism, Islam, and Judaism. Fundamentalists vary immensely in their beliefs and behavior. Some stress the need to be strict in their own personal faith but take little interest in broad social issues. Others are watchful of societal actions, such as government policies, that they see as conflicting with fundamentalist doctrine (Emerson et al. 2006).

Christian fundamentalists in the United States have fought against the teaching of evolution in public schools because they believe not only that it represents a threat to their beliefs, but also that it is itself a type of religious faith in naturalism (as opposed to the supernaturalism of God). The first, and most famous, court case over the teaching of evolution in public schools occurred in 1925 and is often referred to as the "Scopes Monkey Trial." In that trial, high school biology teacher John T. Scopes was convicted of violating a Tennessee law that made it a crime to teach the scientific theory of evolution in public schools (Larson 2006). Since that time there have been numerous other court challenges, including *Kitzmiller v. Dover Area School District* in Pennsylvania in 2005. In this major case, those opposed to the teaching of evolution sought to force schools to teach the "science" of intelligent design—the idea that life is so complex that there had to be some form of intelligence behind its creation. The judge ruled that intelligent design was a variation on creationism, the teaching of which in a public school would violate the separation of church and state (Padian 2007).

> **fundamentalism** Rigid adherence to core religious doctrines, often accompanied by a literal application of scripture or historical beliefs to today's world.
>
> **religious ritual** A practice required or expected of members of a faith.

RITUALS

Religious rituals are practices required or expected of members of a faith. Rituals usually honor the divine power (or powers) worshiped by believers; they also remind adherents of their religious duties and responsibilities. Rituals and beliefs can be interdependent; rituals generally affirm beliefs, as in a public or private statement confessing a sin. Like any social institution, religion develops distinctive norms to structure people's behavior. Moreover, sanctions are attached to religious rituals, in the form of either rewards (such as bar mitzvah gifts) or penalties (such as expulsion from a religious institution for violation of norms).

Rituals may be very simple, such as saying grace at a meal or observing a moment of silence to commemorate someone's death. Other rituals, such as the process of canonizing a saint, are quite elaborate. Most religious rituals in the United States focus on services conducted at houses of worship. Attendance at a service, silent and spoken prayers,

Going GLOBAL

How Often Do You Attend Religious Services?

Percentage attending religious services once a week or more

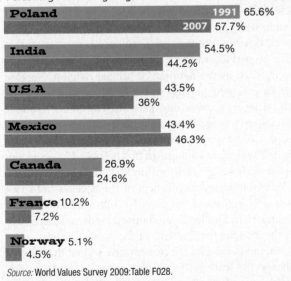

Country	Year	Percentage
Poland	1991	65.6%
	2007	57.7%
India		54.5%
		44.2%
U.S.A		43.5%
		36%
Mexico		43.4%
		46.3%
Canada		26.9%
		24.6%
France		10.2%
		7.2%
Norway		5.1%
		4.5%

Source: World Values Survey 2009:Table F028.

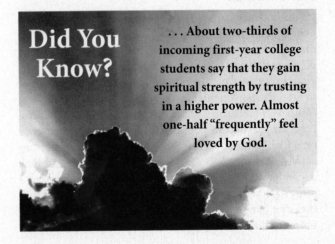

Did You Know? ... About two-thirds of incoming first-year college students say that they gain spiritual strength by trusting in a higher power. Almost one-half "frequently" feel loved by God.

Another profound religious experience for many Christians is being "born again," which involves making a personal commitment to Jesus Christ, marking a major turning point in one's life. According to a 2008 national survey, 34 percent of people in the United States claim they have had a born-again Christian experience at some time in their lives (Kosmin and Keysar 2009). Another survey found that 81 percent of Assembly of God attendees reported having had such experiences, with Baptists coming in at 67 percent. In contrast, only 25 percent of Catholics responded that they had been born again (Barna Group 2001).

The collective nature of religion, as emphasized by Durkheim, is evident in these statistics. The beliefs and rituals of a particular faith can create an atmosphere either friendly toward or less conducive to this type of religious experience. Thus, an Assembly member would be encouraged to "come forward" to make such a commitment and then to share her or his experience with others. A Roman Catholic who claimed to have been born again, on the other hand, would receive much less attention within his or her church (Gallup 2008c).

COMMUNITY

Religious communities organize themselves in varieties of ways. Specific structures such as churches and synagogues have been constructed for religious worship; individuals have been trained for occupational roles within various fields. These developments make it possible to distinguish clearly between the sacred and secular parts of one's life—a distinction that could not be made easily in earlier times, when religion was largely a family activity carried out in the home.

Sociologists find it useful to distinguish between four basic forms of organization: the ecclesia, the denomination, the sect, and the new religious movement, or cult. We can see differences among these four forms of organization in their size, power, degree of commitment expected from members, and historical ties to other faiths (Dawson 2009).

Ecclesiae When studying how groups organize their communities, sociologists have used the term **ecclesia** (plural, *ecclesiae*) to describe a religious organization that claims to include most or all members of a society and is recognized as the national or official religion. Because virtually everyone belongs to the faith, membership is by birth rather than conscious decision. The classic example in sociology was the Roman Catholic Church in medieval Europe. Contemporary examples of ecclesiae include Islam in Saudi Arabia and Buddhism in Thailand. However, significant differences exist within this category. In Saudi Arabia's Islamic regime, leaders of the ecclesia hold vast power over actions of the state. In contrast, the historical state church in Sweden, Lutheranism, holds no such power over the Riksdag (parliament) or the prime minister.

Generally, ecclesiae are conservative in that they do not challenge the leaders of a secular government. In a society with an ecclesia, the political and religious institutions

religious experience The feeling or perception of being in direct contact with the ultimate reality, such as a divine being, or of being overcome with religious emotion.

ecclesia A religious organization that claims to include most or all members of a society and is recognized as the national or official religion.

communion, and the singing of hymns and chants are common forms of ritual behavior that generally take place in group settings. These rituals serve as important face-to-face encounters in which people reinforce their religious beliefs and their commitment to their faith. Religious participation varies widely from country to country.

For Muslims, a very important ritual is the *hajj*—a pilgrimage to the Grand Mosque in Mecca, Saudi Arabia. Every Muslim who is physically and financially able is expected to make this trip at least once. Each year 2 million pilgrims go to Mecca during the one-week period indicated by the Islamic lunar calendar. Muslims from all over the world make the *hajj*, including those in the United States, where many tours are arranged to facilitate the trip.

EXPERIENCE

In the sociological study of religion, the term **religious experience** refers to the feeling or perception of being in direct contact with the ultimate reality, such as a divine being, or of being overcome with religious emotion. A religious experience may be rather slight, such as the feeling of exaltation a person might receive from hearing a choir sing Handel's "Hallelujah Chorus." Many religious experiences, however, are more profound, such as a Muslim's experience on a *hajj*. In his autobiography, the late African American activist Malcolm X (1964:338) wrote of his *hajj* and how deeply moved he was by the way that Muslims in Mecca came together across racial and color lines. For Malcolm X, the color blindness of the Muslim world "proved to me the power of the One God."

Major Religious Traditions in the United States

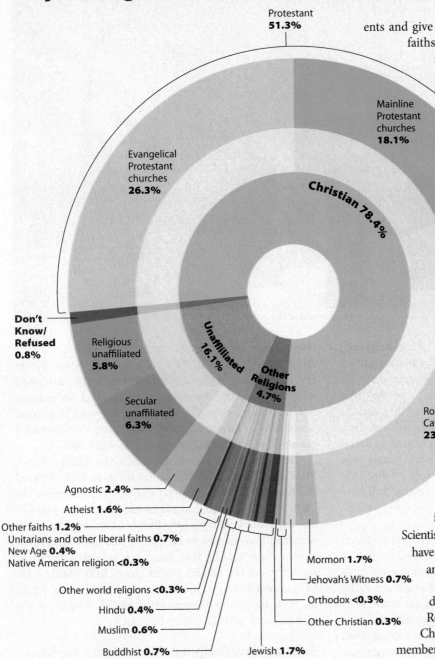

Protestant 51.3%

Mainline Protestant churches **18.1%**

Evangelical Protestant churches **26.3%**

Historically Black, Protestant churches **6.9%**

Christian 78.4%

Unaffiliated 16.1%

Other Religions **4.7%**

Don't Know/ Refused **0.8%**

Religious unaffiliated **5.8%**

Secular unaffiliated **6.3%**

Roman Catholic **23.9%**

Agnostic **2.4%**

Atheist **1.6%**

Other faiths **1.2%**
Unitarians and other liberal faiths **0.7%**
New Age **0.4%**
Native American religion **<0.3%**

Other world religions **<0.3%**

Hindu **0.4%**

Muslim **0.6%**

Buddhist **0.7%**

Jewish **1.7%**

Mormon **1.7%**

Jehovah's Witness **0.7%**

Orthodox **<0.3%**

Other Christian **0.3%**

Note: Due to rounding, figures may not add to 100 and nested figures may not add to the subtotal indicated.
Source: Pew Research Center 2008a.

often act in harmony and reinforce each other's power in their relative spheres of influence. In the modern world, ecclesiae are declining in power.

Denominations A **denomination** is a large, organized religion that is not officially linked to the state or government. Like an ecclesia, it tends to have an explicit set of beliefs, a defined system of authority, and a generally respected position in society. Denominations often claim large segments of a population as members. Generally,

children accept the denomination of their parents and give little thought to membership in other faiths. Although considered respectable and not viewed as a challenge to the secular government, unlike ecclesia, denominations lack the official recognition and power held by an ecclesia (Doress and Porter 1977).

The United States is home to a large number of denominations. This diversity is largely the result of the nation's immigrant heritage. Many settlers brought with them the religious commitments native to their homelands. Some Christian denominations in the United States, such as the Roman Catholics, Episcopalians, and Lutherans, are the outgrowth of ecclesiae established in Europe. New Christian denominations also emerged, including the Mormons and Christian Scientists. Within the last generation, immigrants have increased the number of Muslims, Hindus, and Buddhists living in the United States.

Although by far the largest single denomination in the United States is Roman Catholicism, at least 24 other Christian faiths have 1 million or more members. Protestants collectively account for about 51.3 percent of the nation's adult population, compared to 23.9 percent for Roman Catholics and 1.7 percent for Jews. Muslims account for approximately 0.6 percent, Buddhists about 0.7 percent, and Hindus about 0.4 percent. Self-described atheists and agnostics make up about 4 percent of the population (Pew Research Center 2008a).

Sects A **sect** can be defined as a relatively small religious group that has broken away from some other religious organization to renew what it considers the original vision

> **denomination** A large, organized religion that is not officially linked to the state or government.
>
> **sect** A relatively small religious group that has broken away from some other religious organization to renew what it considers the original vision of the faith.

of the faith. Many sects, such as that led by Martin Luther during the Reformation in the 1500s, claim to be the "true church" because they seek to cleanse the established faith of what they regard as extraneous beliefs and rituals. Max Weber ([1916] 1958b: 114) termed the sect a "believer's church" because affiliation is based on conscious acceptance of a specific religious dogma.

Sects are at odds with the dominant society and do not seek to become established national religions. Unlike ecclesiae and denominations, they require intensive commitments and demonstrations of belief by members. Partly owing to their outsider status, sects frequently exhibit a higher degree of religious fervor and loyalty than more established religious groups. They actively recruit adults as new members, and acceptance comes through conversion.

Sects are often short-lived. Those that are able to survive may become less antagonistic to society over time and begin to resemble denominations.

In a few instances, sects have been able to endure over several generations while remaining fairly separate from society. Sociologist J. Milton Yinger (1970:226–73) uses the term **established sect** to describe a religious group that is the outgrowth of a sect, yet remains isolated from society. The Hutterites, Jehovah's Witnesses, Seventh-Day Adventists, and Amish are contemporary examples of established sects in the United States.

Throughout the world, including the United States, Muslims are divided into a variety of sects, such as Sunni and Shia (or Shiite). The great majority of Muslims in the United States are Sunni Muslims—literally, those who follow the *Sunnah,* or way of the Prophet. Compared to other Muslims, Sunnis tend to be more moderate in their religious orthodoxy. The Shia, who come primarily from Iraq and Iran, are the second-largest group. Shia Muslims are more attentive to guidance from accepted Islamic scholars than are Sunnis. About two-thirds of Muslims in the United States are native-born citizens.

Cults or New Religious Movements Historically, sociologists have used the term *cult* to describe alternative religious groups with unconventional religious beliefs. Partly as a result of the notoriety generated by some of these more extreme groups—such as the Heaven's Gate cult members who committed mass suicide in 1997 so that their spirits might be freed to catch a ride on the spaceship hidden behind the Hale-Bopp comet—many sociologists have abandoned the use of the term. In its place they have adopted the expression "new religious movement."

A **new religious movement (NRM)** or **cult** is generally a small, alternative religious group that represents either a new faith community or a major innovation in an existing faith. NRMs are similar to sects in that they tend to be small and are often viewed as less respectable than more established faiths. Unlike sects, however, NRMs normally do not result from schisms or breaks with established ecclesiae or denominations. Some cults, such as those focused on UFO sightings, may be totally unrelated to existing faiths. Even when a cult does accept certain fundamental tenets of a dominant faith—such as a belief in Jesus as divine or in Mohammad as a messenger of God—it will offer new revelations or insights to justify its claim to being a more advanced religion (Stark and Bainbridge 1979, 1985).

Like sects, NRMs may be transformed over time into other types of religious organization. An example is the Christian Science Church, which began as a new religious movement under the leadership of Mary Baker Eddy. Today, this church exhibits the characteristics of a denomination. In fact, most major religions, including Christianity, began as cults. NRMs may be in the early stages of developing into a denomination or new religion, or they may just as easily fade away through the loss of members or weak leadership (Schaefer and Zellner 2007).

To summarize, ecclesiae are recognized as national churches. Denominations, although not officially approved by the state, are widely accepted as legitimate. On the other hand, sects are countercultures at odds with society's dominant norms and values. NRMs provide innovative, though not necessarily exclusive, types of faith. The boundaries between these four types are somewhat fluid, and it is helpful to view them as a continuum based on their level of acceptance in the larger society.

secularization Religion's diminishing influence in the public sphere, especially in politics and the economy.

>>World Religions

Early sociologists predicted that modern societies would experience widespread **secularization**, which involves religion's diminishing influence in the public sphere, especially in politics and the economy. In the United States today, those who are nonreligious account for about 10–14 percent of the population; in 1900, however, they constituted a mere 1.3 percent of all Americans. In 2011, 24.5 percent of incoming

Going GLOBAL

Religions of the World

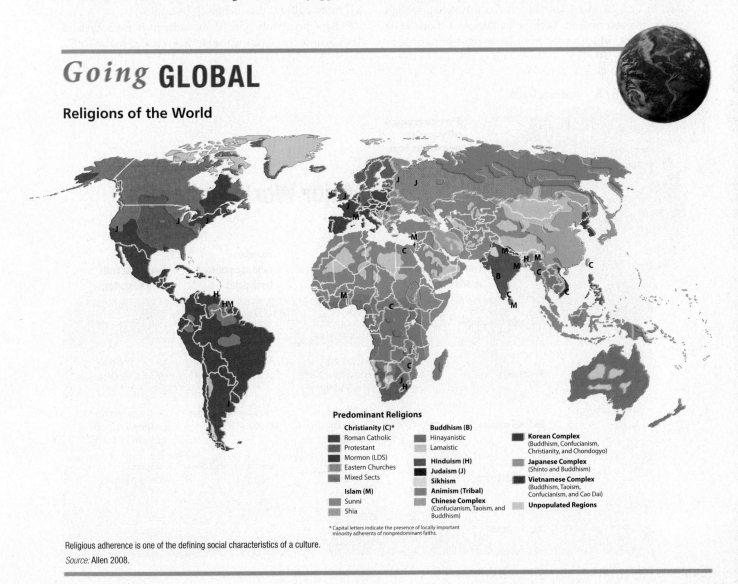

Predominant Religions

Christianity (C)*
Roman Catholic
Protestant
Mormon (LDS)
Eastern Churches
Mixed Sects

Islam (M)
Sunni
Shia

Buddhism (B)
Hinayanistic
Lamaistic

Hinduism (H)
Judaism (J)
Sikhism
Animism (Tribal)
Chinese Complex
(Confucianism, Taoism, and Buddhism)

Korean Complex
(Buddhism, Confucianism, Christianity, and Chondogyo)
Japanese Complex
(Shinto and Buddhism)
Vietnamese Complex
(Buddhism, Taoism, Confucianism, and Cao Dai)
Unpopulated Regions

* Capital letters indicate the presence of locally important minority adherents of nonpredominant faiths.

Religious adherence is one of the defining social characteristics of a culture.

Source: Allen 2008.

U.S. college students had no religious preference compared to 12.2 percent of their mothers (Hout and Fischer 2002; Pryor et al. 2011). Though the percentage of those who opt out of organized religion continues to rise, tremendous diversity exists worldwide in religious beliefs and practices. Overall, about 85 percent of the world's population adheres to some religion. Major religions continue to exert a significant influence both collectively and individually.

Christianity is the largest single faith in the world; the second largest is Islam (see the table below). Although global news events often suggest an inherent conflict between Christians and Muslims, the two faiths are similar in many ways. Both are monotheistic (that is, based on a single deity), and both include a belief in prophets, an afterlife, and a judgment day. In fact, Islam recognizes Jesus as a prophet, though not as the son of God. Both faiths impose a moral code on believers, which varies from fairly rigid proscriptions for fundamentalists to relatively relaxed guidelines for liberals.

The followers of Islam, called Muslims, believe that the prophet Muhammad received Islam's holy scriptures from Allah (God) nearly 1,400 years ago. They see Muhammad as the last in a long line of prophets, preceded by Adam, Abraham, Moses, and Jesus. Islam is more communal in its expression than Christianity, particularly the more individualistic Protestant denominations. Consequently, in countries that are predominantly Muslim, the separation of religion and the state is not considered necessary or even desirable. In fact, Muslim governments often reinforce Islamic practices through their laws. Muslims do vary sharply in their interpretation of several traditions, some of which—such as the wearing of veils by women—are more cultural than religious in origin.

Like Christianity and Islam, Judaism is monotheistic. Jews believe that God's true nature is revealed in the Torah,

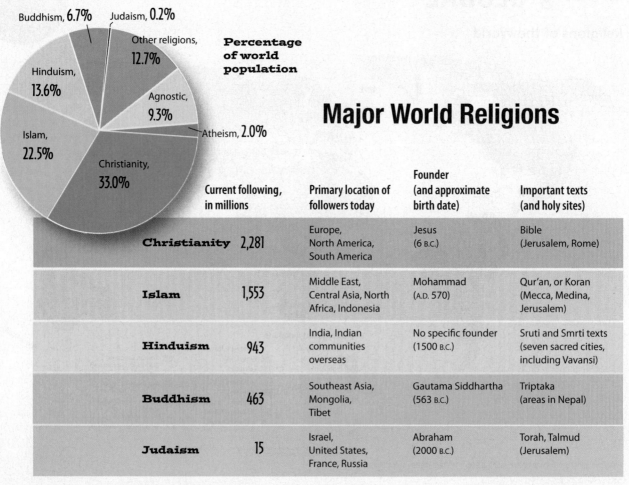

Major World Religions

	Current following, in millions	Primary location of followers today	Founder (and approximate birth date)	Important texts (and holy sites)
Christianity	2,281	Europe, North America, South America	Jesus (6 B.C.)	Bible (Jerusalem, Rome)
Islam	1,553	Middle East, Central Asia, North Africa, Indonesia	Mohammad (A.D. 570)	Qur'an, or Koran (Mecca, Medina, Jerusalem)
Hinduism	943	India, Indian communities overseas	No specific founder (1500 B.C.)	Sruti and Smrti texts (seven sacred cities, including Vavansi)
Buddhism	463	Southeast Asia, Mongolia, Tibet	Gautama Siddhartha (563 B.C.)	Triptaka (areas in Nepal)
Judaism	15	Israel, United States, France, Russia	Abraham (2000 B.C.)	Torah, Talmud (Jerusalem)

Percentage of world population

- Buddhism, 6.7%
- Judaism, 0.2%
- Other religions, 12.7%
- Hinduism, 13.6%
- Agnostic, 9.3%
- Islam, 22.5%
- Atheism, 2.0%
- Christianity, 33.0%

Sources: Based on Barrett, Johnson, and Crossing 2011; Swatos 2011.

which Christians know as the first five books of the Old Testament. According to these scriptures, God formed a covenant, or pact, with Abraham and Sarah, the ancestors of the twelve tribes of Israel. Even today, religious Jews believe this covenant holds them accountable to God's will. If they follow both the letter and the spirit of the Torah, a long-awaited Messiah will one day bring paradise to earth. Although Judaism has a relatively small following compared to other major faiths, it forms the historical foundation for both Christianity and Islam. That is why Jews revere many of the same sacred Middle Eastern sites as Christians and Muslims.

Two other major faiths developed in a different part of the world—India. The earliest, Hinduism, originated around 1500 B.C.E. Hinduism differs from Judaism, Christianity, and Islam in that it embraces a number of gods and minor gods, although most worshipers are devoted primarily to a single deity, such as Shiva or Vishnu. Hinduism is also distinguished by a belief in reincarnation, or the perpetual rebirth of the soul after death. Unlike Judaism, Christianity, and Islam, which are based largely on sacred texts, Hindu beliefs have been preserved mostly through oral tradition.

Buddhism developed in the sixth century B.C.E. as a reaction against Hinduism. This faith is founded on the teachings of Siddhartha (later called Buddha, or "The Enlightened One"). Through meditation, followers of Buddhism strive to overcome selfish cravings for physical or material pleasures, with the goal of reaching a state of enlightenment, or nirvana. Buddhists created the first monastic orders, which are thought to be the models for monastic orders in other religions, including Christianity. Though Buddhism emerged in India, its followers were eventually driven out of that country by the Hindus. It is now found primarily in other parts of Asia.

Although the differences among religions are striking, they are exceeded by variations within faiths. Consider the differences within Christianity, from relatively liberal denominations such as Presbyterians or Episcopalians to the more conservative Mormons and Greek Orthodox Catholics. Similar divisions exist within Hinduism, Islam, and other world religions (Barrett, Johnson, and Crossing 2006; Swatos 1998).

>>Sociological Perspectives on Religion

Sociology emerged as a discipline in the 19th century in the context of significant intellectual, political, and economic upheaval. Intellectuals at the time felt that the religious teachings that had guided society in times of crisis in the past were failing. Auguste Comte and other early sociologists sought to provide a science of society that would tap the ways of knowing built into the scientific method and apply them to the study of society. They recognized the significant role that religion had played in maintaining social order in the past and believed it essential to understand how it had accomplished this, so the study of religion became a significant topic in early sociology. Among classical theorists, for example, Émile Durkheim concluded that religion promoted social order; Max Weber maintained that it helped generate social change; and Karl Marx argued that it reinforced the interests of the powerful.

INTEGRATION

Durkheim viewed religion as an integrative force in human society. He sought to answer a perplexing question: "How can human societies be held together when they are generally composed of individuals and social groups with diverse interests and aspirations?" In his view, religious bonds often transcend these personal and divisive forces.

How does religion provide this "societal glue"? Religion, whether it be Buddhism, Islam, Christianity, or Judaism, gives meaning and purpose to people's lives. It offers ultimate values and ends to hold in common. Although they are subjective and not always fully accepted, these values and ends help society to function as an integrated social system. For example, funerals, weddings, bar and bat mitzvahs, and confirmations serve to integrate people into larger communities by reaffirming shared beliefs and values related to the ultimate questions of life.

Religion also serves to bind people together in times of crisis and confusion. Immediately after the terrorist attacks of September 11, 2001, on New York City and Washington, D.C., attendance at worship services in the United States increased dramatically. Muslim, Jewish, and Christian clerics made joint appearances to honor the dead and to urge citizens not to retaliate against those who looked, dressed, or sounded different from others. A year later, however, attendance levels had returned to normal (D. Moore 2002).

The integrative power of religion can be seen, too, in the role that churches, synagogues, and mosques have traditionally played and continue to play for immigrant groups in the United States. For example, Roman Catholic immigrants may settle near a parish church that offers services in their native language, such as Polish or Spanish. Similarly, Korean immigrants may join a Presbyterian church that has many Korean American

Income and Education Levels, Selected Denominations

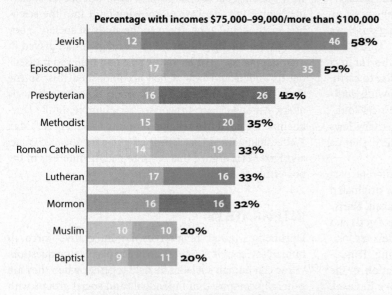

Percentage with incomes $75,000–99,000/more than $100,000

Denomination			Total
Jewish	12	46	**58%**
Episcopalian	17	35	**52%**
Presbyterian	16	26	**42%**
Methodist	15	20	**35%**
Roman Catholic	14	19	**33%**
Lutheran	17	16	**33%**
Mormon	16	16	**32%**
Muslim	10	10	**20%**
Baptist	9	11	**20%**

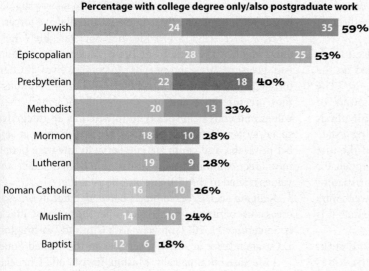

Percentage with college degree only/also postgraduate work

Denomination			Total
Jewish	24	35	**59%**
Episcopalian	28	25	**53%**
Presbyterian	22	18	**40%**
Methodist	20	13	**33%**
Mormon	18	10	**28%**
Lutheran	19	9	**28%**
Roman Catholic	16	10	**26%**
Muslim	14	10	**24%**
Baptist	12	6	**18%**

Source: Pew Research Center 2008a.

Protestant ethic Max Weber's term for the disciplined commitment to worldly labor driven by a desire to bring glory to God, shared by followers of Martin Luther and John Calvin.

members and follows religious practices similar to those of churches in Korea. Like other religious organizations, these Roman Catholic and Presbyterian churches help to integrate immigrants into their new homeland (Warner 2007).

Religion also strengthens feelings of social integration within specific faiths and denominations. In many faiths, members share certain characteristics that help to bind them together, including their race, ethnicity, and social class.

Such integration, while unifying believers, can come at the expense of outsiders. In this sense, religion can contribute to tension and even conflict between groups or nations. During the Second World War, Nazi Germany attempted to exterminate the Jewish people; approximately 6 million European Jews were killed. In modern times, nations such as Lebanon (Muslims versus Christians), Israel (Jews versus Muslims, as well as Orthodox versus secular Jews), Northern Ireland (Roman Catholics versus Protestants), and India (Hindus versus Muslims and, more recently, Sikhs) have been torn by clashes that are in large part based on religion. Such conflicts often do, however, have the effect of drawing the believers closer together.

SOCIAL CHANGE

Max Weber sought to understand how religion, which so often seems conservative in that it works to maintain order, might also contribute to social change. To do so, he focused on the relationship between religious faith and the rise of capitalism. Weber's findings appeared in his sociology classic, *The Protestant Ethic and the Spirit of Capitalism* ([1904] 2009).

The Weberian Thesis Weber noted that in European nations with both Protestant and Catholic citizens, an overwhelming number of business leaders, owners of capital, and skilled workers were Protestant. In his view, this was no mere coincidence. Weber explained it as a consequence of what he called the **Protestant ethic**—a disciplined commitment to worldly labor driven by a desire to bring glory to God that was shared by followers of Martin Luther and John Calvin. Weber argued that this emphasis on hard work and self-denial provided capitalism with an approach toward labor that was essential to capitalism's development.

To explain the impact of the Protestant ethic on the rise of capitalism, Weber highlights three keys: Luther's concept of a calling, Calvin's concept of predestination, and Protestant believers' resulting experience of "salvation panic." According to Protestant reformer Martin Luther (1483–1546), God called believers to their position in life, and they had to work hard in that calling so as to bring glory to God, regardless of whether they were rich or poor. Protestant Reformer John Calvin (1509–1564) added to this the concept of predestination, according to which God, before the beginning of time, picked who would go to heaven and who would go to hell, and there was nothing anyone could do to change their fate. It was impossible to earn salvation through good works; salvation was totally dependent on the grace of God. Complicating this was the fact that no individual could ever know for sure that he or she was saved because none could presume to know the mind of God. Weber concluded that this created a sense of salvation panic among believers who wanted assurance that they were going to heaven.

Weber theorized that believers would seek to resolve this uncertainty by leading the kinds of lives they thought God would expect godly people to lead. This meant hard work, humility, and self-denial, not for the sake of salvation or individual gain, but for the sake of God. Although doing so would not earn them salvation, to do otherwise would be an almost certain sign that they were not among the chosen. But they could never fully be sure, so they could never let up in their commitment to do God's will. Thus they worked hard not because they had to (either for subsistence or because they were forced) but because they wanted to in response to the salvation they hoped would come from God. It was precisely this

example of macrolevel analysis. Like Durkheim, Weber demonstrated that religion is not solely a matter of intimate personal beliefs. He stressed that the collective nature of religion has consequences for society as a whole.

SOC THINK

To what extent do you think religion can be a force for social change? What examples have you seen in your lifetime?

Liberation Theology A more contemporary example of religion serving as a force for social change came through liberation theology, in which the clergy were at the forefront. Many religious activists, especially in the Roman Catholic Church in Latin America, support **liberation theology**—the use of a church in a political effort to eliminate poverty, discrimination, and other forms of injustice from a secular society. Advocates of this religious movement sometimes sympathize with Marxism. Many believe that radical change, rather than economic development in itself, is the only acceptable solution to the desperation of the masses in impoverished developing countries. Activists associated with liberation theology believe that organized religion has a moral responsibility to take a strong public stand against the oppression of the poor, racial and ethnic minorities, and women (Bell 2001; Rowland 2007).

> **liberation theology** Use of a church, primarily Roman Catholicism, in a political effort to eliminate poverty, discrimination, and other forms of injustice from a secular society.

The term *liberation theology* dates back to the publication in 1973 of the English translation of *A Theology of Liberation*. The book was written by a Peruvian priest, Gustavo Gutiérrez, who lived in a slum area of Lima in the early 1960s. After years of exposure to the vast poverty around him, Gutiérrez concluded that "in order to serve the poor, one had to move into political action" (R. M. Brown 1980:23; Gutiérrez 1990). Eventually, politically committed Latin American theologians came under the influence of social scientists who viewed the domination of capitalist multinational corporations as central to the hemisphere's problems. One result was a new approach to theology that built on the cultural

5 Movies on RELIGION

Jonestown: The Life and Death of People's Temple
Documentary about American cult leader Jim Jones.

The Apostle
A Pentecostal preacher in the South.

Everything Is Illuminated
A young man explores his Jewish family's past.

The Tree of Life
An exploration on the meaning of life through the experiences of a 1950s Texas family.

Four Lions
A dark comedy about four Jihadists who bumble their way toward enacting a terrorist plot.

kind of worker, internally motivated to work hard and willing to show up every day even after getting paid, that capitalism needed if it was to engage in rationally planned production. This "spirit of capitalism," to use Weber's phrase, contrasted with the moderate work hours, leisurely work habits, and lack of ambition that Weber saw as typical of traditional labor.

In this way, religion contributed, through the Protestant Reformation, to one of the most significant examples of social change, in the form of the rise of capitalism and its effects, in human history. Weber's argument has been hailed as one of the most important theoretical works in the field and as an excellent

> But the poor person does not exist as an inescapable fact of destiny. . . . The poor are a by-product of the system in which we live and for which we are responsible.

Liberation Theologian Gustavo Gutiérrez

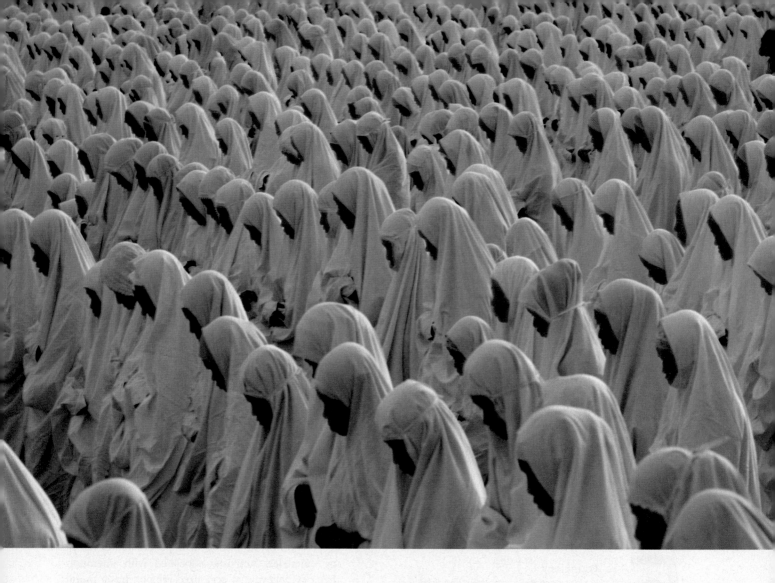

and religious traditions of Latin America rather than on models developed in Europe and the United States.

SOCIAL CONTROL

Liberation theology is a relatively recent phenomenon that marks a break with the traditional role of churches. It was this traditional role that Karl Marx opposed. In his view, religion inhibited social change by encouraging oppressed people to focus on other-worldly concerns rather than on their immediate poverty or exploitation.

Marx on Religion Marx described religion as an "opiate" that was particularly harmful to oppressed peoples. He felt that religion often, in essence, drugged the masses into submission by offering a consolation for their harsh lives on earth: the hope of salvation in an ideal afterlife. For example, during the period of slavery in the United States, White masters forbade Blacks to practice native African religions. Instead, they encouraged slaves to adopt Christianity, which taught that obedience would lead to salvation and eternal happiness in the hereafter. Viewed from this perspective, Christianity may have pacified certain slaves and blunted the rage that often fuels rebellion.

For Marx, religion plays an important role in propping up the existing social structure. The values of religion, as already noted, tend to reinforce other social institutions and the social order as a whole. From Marx's perspective, however, religion's promotion of social stability only helps to perpetuate patterns of social inequality. According to Marx, the dominant religion reinforces the interests of those in power.

From a Marxist perspective, religion keeps people from seeing their lives and societal conditions in political terms—for example, by obscuring the overriding significance of conflicting economic interests. Marxists suggest that by inducing a "false consciousness" among the disadvantaged, religion lessens the possibility of collective political action that could end capitalist oppression and transform society. Sociological analysis in this tradition seeks to reveal the ways in which religion serves the interests of the powerful at the expense of others.

Gender and Religion Drawing on the feminist approach, researchers and theorists point to the fundamental role women play in religious socialization. Women play a critical role in the functioning of religious organizations, yet when it comes to positions of leadership, women generally take a subordinate role in religious governance. Indeed, most faiths have a long tradition of exclusively male spiritual leadership. Furthermore, because most religions are patriarchal, religious beliefs tend to reinforce men's dominance in secular as well as spiritual matters. Women are more likely than men to say religion is important in their lives, more likely to pray daily, and more likely to attend weekly services. Women play a vital role as volunteers, staff, and religious educators, but even today, religious decision making and leadership typically falls to men. Exceptions to this rule, such as the Shakers and Christian Scientists, as well as Hinduism with its long goddess heritage, are rare (Pew Research Center 2009d; Schaefer and Zellner 2007).

In the United States, women compose 17.5 percent of the clergy, even though they account for 51 percent of students enrolled in theological institutions. Female clerics typically have shorter careers than men and are often relegated to fields that do not involve congregational leadership, such as counseling. In faiths that restrict leadership positions to men, women still serve unofficially. For example, about 4 percent of Roman Catholic congregations are led by women who hold nonordained pastoral positions—a necessity in a church that faces a shortage of male priests (Adams 2007; Banerjee 2006; Bureau of Labor Statistics 2012: Table 11).

In this chapter we have looked at both education and religion. In both cases we find institutions that play a powerful role in shaping how we think and act. Each provides opportunity and reinforces the status quo, including its system of inequality. Sociologists believe that by having a better appreciation for both the opportunities and constraints such institutions present, we can better act both individually and collectively to bring about positive social change.

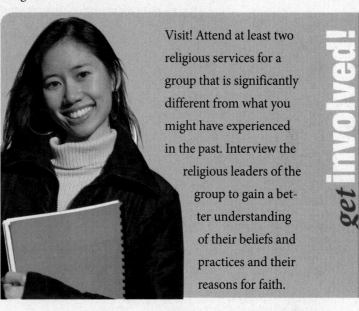

Visit! Attend at least two religious services for a group that is significantly different from what you might have experienced in the past. Interview the religious leaders of the group to gain a better understanding of their beliefs and practices and their reasons for faith.

get involved!

For REVIEW

I. **How does education help to maintain social order?**
- Education transmits culture, promotes social integration, provides training and social control, and contributes to cultural innovation.

II. **How does education support the existing system of inequality?**
- Education reinforces the status quo, and therefore its existing inequalities, through the hidden curriculum, teacher expectancy, bestowal of status, and credentialism.

III. **How do sociologists define religion?**
- One approach focuses on the substance of what religion is, defining religion as knowledge and beliefs relating to the sacred realm. The other approach looks at what religions do for society in terms of social order and integration. Both approaches analyze common components including belief, ritual, experience, and community.

Functionalist View

Education serves five positive functions: transmitting culture, promoting **social integration**, training and social control, stimulating cultural innovation, and child care.

As societies have become more diverse, education has taken on more of the task of formal **socialization.**

Religion provides **social order,** a sense of **shared identity,** and meaning and purpose in people's lives.

SOCIAL INTEGRATION, SOCIALIZATION, SOCIAL ORDER
KEY CONCEPTS

Conflict View

The education system helps reproduce the existing system of **inequality.**

Unequal funding, **tracking,** the **hidden curriculum** and **credentialism** serve to reinforce the status quo.

According to Marx, religion can function like a drug that blinds people to their true interests, prompting them instead to accept **submission to authority,** thereby reinforcing the interests of those in power.

INEQUALITY, SUBMISSION TO AUTHORITY
KEY CONCEPTS

MAKE THE CONNECTION

After reviewing the chapter, answer the following questions:

Interactionist View

Students from grade school through graduate school learn formal and informal norms, values, and interpersonal skills through classroom interactions.

A teacher's **expectations** about a student impact on student performance and achievement.

Religious rituals generally involve important **face-to-face interactions** with fellow at services.

EXPECTATIONS, INTERACTIONS
KEY CONCEPTS

1

The graph on p. 182 shows one way that "education pays." Using each perspective, how does education pay? Who benefits?

2

How do educational institutions bestow status from both the functionalist and conflict perspectives (p. 185)?

3

Using the conflict perspective, describe how women experience (or have experienced) discrimination in both the educational and religious spheres (pp. 187, 204).

4

Which perspective do you, think best describes the dynamics of a typical classroom setting? Explain, including examples.

Pop Quiz

1. Horace Mann, often called the "father of public education," refers to education as
   a. the great equalizer.
   b. the opiate of the masses.
   c. an instrument for social control.
   d. an opportunity engine.

2. One of the ways education contributes to social order is by providing an environment within which we can challenge existing ideas and experiment with new norms and values. This is known as
   a. transmitting culture.
   b. promoting social integration.
   c. training and social control.
   d. cultural innovation.

3. Samuel Bowles and Herbert Gintis have argued that capitalism requires a skilled, disciplined labor force and that the educational system of the United States is structured with that objective in mind. Citing numerous studies, they offer support for what they call
   a. tracking.
   b. credentialism.
   c. the correspondence principle.
   d. the teacher-expectancy effect.

4. Fifty years ago, a high school diploma was often enough to get a good job. Today it typically takes a college degree or more. This change reflects the process of
   a. tracking.
   b. credentialism.
   c. the hidden curriculum.
   d. the correspondence principle.

5. The college student subculture that focuses on having fun and socializing and doesn't take its studies too seriously is the
   a. collegiate subculture.
   b. academic subculture.
   c. vocational subculture.
   d. nonconformist subculture.

6. The approach to defining religion that emphasizes the significance of the sacred, most often super-natural, realm is known as the
   a. functionalist approach.
   b. conflict approach.
   c. substantive approach.
   d. ecclesiae approach.

7. Religious rituals are
   a. statements to which members of a particular religion adhere.
   b. the feelings or perceptions of being in direct contact with the ultimate reality, such as a divine being.
   c. the religious structures through which faith communities organize themselves.
   d. practices required or expected of members of a faith.

8. Of the world religions, the one with the most followers is
   a. Buddhism.
   b. Islam.
   c. Judaism.
   d. Christianity.

9. Sociologist Max Weber pointed out that the followers of John Calvin emphasized a disciplined work ethic, worldly concerns, and a rational orientation to life. Collectively, this point of view has been referred to as
   a. capitalism.
   b. the Protestant ethic.
   c. the sacred.
   d. the profane.

10. The use of a church, primarily Roman Catholic, in a political effort to eliminate poverty, discrimination, and other forms of injustice evident in a secular society is referred to as
    a. creationism.
    b. ritualism.
    c. religious experience.
    d. liberation theology.

1. (a); 2. (d); 3. (c); 4. (b); 5. (a); 6. (c); 7. (d); 8. (d); 9. (b); 10. (d)

GOVERNMENT AND ECONOMY

MONEY & POLITICS

On February 15, 2011, thousands of protesters streamed into Wisconsin's state capitol building to protest Governor Scott Walker's proposed legislation to cut the wages, benefits, and collective bargaining power of most public employees. Protestors came bearing signs, singing songs, and chanting slogans including "Kill the bill," and "This is what democracy looks like." They stayed for weeks. They failed (at least in terms of their immediate goals).

Scott Walker was elected governor of Wisconsin in November 2010 as part of a national wave of Republican victories. Dissatisfied with the apparent failure of Democratic leadership to fix the weak economy, voters turned to Republicans. Walker ran on a platform of economic growth via lower taxes and reduced government spending. At his inauguration he declared, "Wisconsin is open for business," and he immediately went into action.

The protests were triggered by Governor Walker's "Budget Repair Bill." He claimed that drastic measures were required to address a projected $3.6 billion budget shortfall. Union representatives for the affected employees agreed to his wage and benefit cuts, but they refused to budge on collective bargaining rights, negotiations between the government and union representatives that deal with wages, benefits, working conditions, and other workplace issues. Walker's bill denied negotiation rights over benefits, including health care, and capped salary increases at no more than the rate of inflation. Critics argued that his real goal was to bust the unions rather than balance the budget. Walker claimed that curtailing collective bargaining was economically necessary.

With Republican majorities in both the State Senate and Assembly, it was assumed that the bill would quickly become law. But, because it involved spending, the bill required a minimum of 20 voting senators. Senate Democrats left the state denying Republicans that quorum. The standoff, with a boost from the protestors, continued for over three weeks before Republicans stripped all spending provisions from the bill and passed it 18-1. Governor Walker signed the bill on March 11, but a judge struck down the bill, ruling Republican legislators did not provide enough public notice before passing the measure, a ruling that was appealed to the state's Supreme Court.

In the end, the Republicans wielded their power, yet the unintended consequence was to reenergize Democrats. The conflict is sociologically interesting, because it represents a struggle between institutions (economy vs. government), interests (business vs. labor), and ideologies (conservative vs. liberal). It raises important questions about who rules and why.

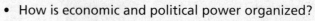

As You READ >>

- How is economic and political power organized?
- How does power operate?
- How has the economy changed over time?

>>Economic Change

The upheaval that overtook Wisconsin's capitol building was a manifestation of widespread frustration about the state of the economy and politics in the United States. The protests occurred in the context of a global recession that was triggered by a global financial crisis. That crisis started when a decline in the housing market revealed fault lines in the financial sector which led to the economic collapse of the nation's top investment banks, including Bear Stearns, Lehman Brothers, Merrill Lynch, Goldman Sachs, and Morgan Stanley. Banks around the world, including those in England, Germany, and the Netherlands, faced similar crises and the overall ripple effects resulted in global economic destabilization. Stocks crashed, businesses went bankrupt, unemployment skyrocketed, and governments around the world struggled to figure out how best to respond.

Economy A social institution dedicated to the production, distribution, and consumption of goods and services.

As these negative economic effects lingered, frustration grew. People looked for political solutions. Barack Obama's 2008 campaign for the presidency drew heavily upon the themes of hope and change, and his election turned control of the White House over to Democrats When the economy remained weak, beleaguered voters in the 2010 midterm elections handed control of the House of Representatives over to Republicans. In September, 2011, as the economy continued to stagnate, a group of protestors expressed their frustration by establishing a sit-in protest in a park in New York City's Wall Street financial district. Known as Occupy Wall Street, the group's primary intent was to call attention to extreme economic inequality in the United States. They argued that

the current economic and political system was stacked so that the interests of the top 1 percent of income earners were served at the expense of the bottom 99 percent. They called for systemic economic and political change. The Occupy movement spread to various cities throughout the United States and around the world, though most encampments, including the one in New York City, were ultimately shut down and evacuated by police.

Using the sociological imagination allows us to better understand such economic and political change. Doing so draws our attention to the fact that the economic and political systems we construct influence likely outcomes for individuals. In other words, structures have consequences. Adopting a capitalist economy or a democratic system of government leads us down different paths than we would likely have followed had we adopted alternatives. In this chapter we will look at economic and political systems and their consequences.

INDUSTRIALIZATION

The **economy** is a social institution dedicated to the production, distribution, and consumption of goods and services. We depend on it to coordinate and provide for our wants and needs. The structure of the economy reflects and reinforces our core values. For example, the degree of inequality societies accept when it comes to the distribution of valued economic resources varies widely.

The U.S. economy continues to be shaped by changes brought about during the Industrial Revolution.

Sociology developed as a discipline in part to come to terms with the economic transition from a preindustrial to an industrial society, one

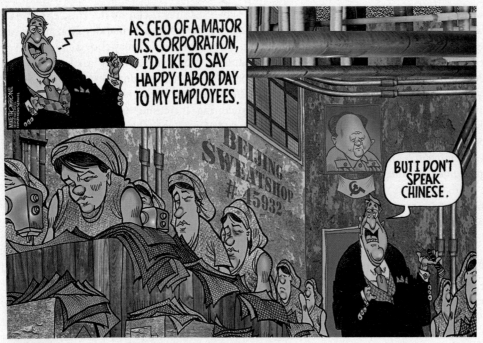

Reprinted with the permission of Mike Thompson and Creators Syndicate.

have land lines and 44 percent have cell phones, and there are 5 Internet users per 100 inhabitants (International Telecommunications Union 2011). Instead of improving these people's lives, the new business centers have siphoned water and electricity away from those who are most in need. Even the high-tech workers are experiencing negative consequences. Many suffer from stress disorders such as stomach problems and difficulty sleeping; more than half quit their jobs before the end of a year (International Telecommunications Union 2009; Waldman 2004a, 2004b, 2004c).

foreign workers as well. Although outsourcing is a significant source of employment for India's upper-middle class, hundreds of millions of other Indians have benefited little if at all from the trend. Most households in India do not possess any form of high technology: only about 3 percent

The effects of the economic downturn have been widespread. Recent college graduates have found a difficult job market. Many people have expressed frustration that large corporations have received billions while individual workers struggle.

THE GREAT RECESSION

The process of deindustrialization was part of a larger economic shift toward a global economy consisting of complex, worldwide networks of producers and consumers. The resulting interdependent connections increased the possibility that, if one part of the system collapsed, it

that depends on mechanization to produce its goods and services (as discussed in Chapter 5). At the heart of this shift, the Industrial Revolution changed where we live (from rural to urban settings) and the type of work we do (from agricultural to industrial jobs). The mechanization of production gave rise to factories (especially in the textile industries) and contributed to the decline of home-based or craft production. The steam engine provided the early power necessary to expand industrial production on a large scale. It did so by effectively enhancing workers' strength and stamina. Workers were then able to exert superhuman amounts of power for superhuman amounts of time. In pursuit of greater productivity, and guided by bureaucratic principles, work became increasingly specialized and routinized.

DEINDUSTRIALIZATION

The emphasis on industrial production continued through much of the twentieth century. But a significant shift occurred starting in the 1970s when the U.S. economy moved away from its industrial base through the process of **deindustrialization,** which refers to the systematic, widespread withdrawal of investment in basic aspects of productivity, such as factories and plants. Giant corporations that deindustrialize are not necessarily refusing to invest in new economic opportunities. Rather, the targets and locations of investment change, and the need for labor decreases as advances in technology continue to automate production. Historically, this transition began with companies moving their plants from the nation's central cities to the suburbs. The next step was to relocate from suburban areas of the Northeast and Midwest to the South, where labor laws place more restrictions on unions. Finally, corporations may simply relocate outside the United States to a country with a lower rate of prevailing wages. For example, from 2000 to 2009 U.S. multinational corporations cut 2.9 million U.S. workers from their total workforce while adding 2.4 million workers abroad (Wessel 2011).

Although deindustrialization often involves relocation, it can also take the form of corporate restructuring known as **downsizing,** which involves reducing the size of a company's workforce. The goal is to increase efficiency and reduce costs in the face of growing worldwide competition. When such restructuring occurs, the impact on the bureaucratic hierarchy of formal organizations can be significant. A large corporation may choose to sell off or entirely abandon less productive divisions and to eliminate layers of management it views as unnecessary. Wages and salaries may be frozen and fringe benefits cut—all in the name of restructuring. Increasing reliance on automation also spells the end of work as we have known it.

U.S. firms have been outsourcing certain types of work for generations. For example, moderate-sized businesses such as furniture stores and commercial laundries have long relied on outside trucking firms to make deliveries to their customers. The more recent trend toward **offshoring** carries this practice one step further by transferring other types of work to foreign contractors. Now, even large companies are turning to overseas firms, many of them located in developing countries. Offshoring has become the latest tactic in the timeworn business strategy of raising profits by reducing costs.

Offshoring began when U.S. companies started transferring manufacturing jobs to foreign factories, where wage rates were much lower. But the transfer of work from one country to another is no longer limited to manufacturing. Office and professional jobs are being exported, too, thanks to advanced telecommunications and the growth of skilled, English-speaking labor forces in developing nations with relatively low wage scales. The trend includes even those jobs that require considerable training, such as accounting and financial analysis, computer programming, claims adjustment, telemarketing, and hotel and airline reservations. Today, when you call a toll-free number to reach a customer service representative, chances are that the person who answers the phone will not be speaking from the United States.

deindustrialization The systematic, widespread withdrawal of investment in aspects of productivity, such factories and plants.

downsizing Reductions in company's workforce as pa of deindustrialization.

offshoring The transfer of to foreign contractors.

The social costs of deindustrialization and downsizing cannot be overemphasized. Plant closings lead to substantial unemployment in a community, which can have a devastating impact on both the micro and macro levels. On the micro level, the unemployed person and his or her family must adjust to a loss of spending power. Painting or re-siding the house, buying health insurance or saving for retirement, even thinking about having another child— all must be put aside. Both marital happiness and family cohesion may suffer as a result. Although many dismissed workers eventually reenter the paid labor force, they often must accept less desirable positions with lower salaries and fewer benefits. Unemployment and underemployment are tied to many of the social problems discussed throughout this textbook, among them the need for child care and the controversy over welfare.

While this shift has brought jobs and technology to nations such as India, there is a downside to offshoring for

SOCTHINK

If you were the CEO of an American manufacturing company that was facing declining profits because of international competition, what would you do? Would you move your production facilities overseas to reduce labor costs? What other options might exist? To what extent does the system within which companies operate shape the choices that are available to them?

could have global consequences. That is precisely what happened starting in 2007 when the global financial collapse, described above, occurred. The resulting economic crisis, often referred to as the Great Recession, had significant and long-term consequences. People's taken-for-granted assumptions about how their lives would and should proceed—get a good education, work hard in your job, and success will follow—were called into question.

Unemployment became a widespread problem. Rates more than doubled from February 2008 to October 2010 and remained high for an extended period of time. On top of that, increasing numbers of people experienced long-term unemployment. In the first quarter or 2012, for example, 29.5 percent of the 13.3 million people who were unemployed had been jobless for a year or more, many of whom had exhausted unemployment benefits (GAO 2012; Pew Charitable Trusts 2012).

Among those who were working, wages were flat for most and fell for many; young adults were particularly hard hit. The employment rate among 18-24 year-olds reached a record low of 54 percent and their wages declined more than those of any other age group since the economic downturn began (Levanon, Chen, and Chang 2012; Pew Research Center 2012b). A record percentage of young adults turned toward higher education which accounts for part of their decreased employment rate (Taylor 2011). The hope for many was that getting a degree would bolster their employability, yet the job prospects for recent college graduates have also dimmed.

Among recent college graduates, 43 percent report they are working in a job that does not require a college degree (Stone, Van Horn, and Zukin 2012). On top of that, most graduates faced the prospect of paying back the substantial student loan debt they incurred in order to get their degrees. For college graduates in the Class of 2010, among the two-thirds who graduated with student loan debt, the average owed was $25,250 (Project on Student Debt 2011). Among those who graduated with college debt, 27 percent of borrowers had balances that were past due and 27 percent moved in with parents or family members to save money (Brown, Haughwout, Lee, Mabutas, and van der Klaauw 2012; Stone, Van Horn, and Zukin 2012).

SOCTHINK

What impact did the global economic crisis have on you, your friends, and family? How did it figure in to your plans for the future?

For many people, bad news seemed everywhere, but not for all. There was an increase in the number of people who were working yet not earning enough to get out of poverty (Smiley and West 2012), and the age at which people could expect to retire was going up (Brandon 2012). And, yet, for some, things were looking up. In 2010, overall average income rose 2.3 percent, but the benefits of a slowly improving economy were not equally shared. Income for the top 1 percent grew 11.6 percent while bottom 99 percent saw only a 0.2% increase (Saez 2012). Corporations also did well, earning record profits in part because they reduced their costs by cutting their workforce and expecting more productivity from their remaining employees (Tully 2012).

THE CHANGING FACE OF THE WORKFORCE

The workforce in the United States constantly adapts to such economic changes. During World War II, when men were mobilized to fight abroad, women entered the workforce in large numbers. With the coming of the civil rights movement in the 1960s, minorities found numerous job opportunities opening to them. Sociologists and labor specialists foresee a workforce increasingly composed of women and racial and ethnic minorities. In 1960 there were twice as many men in the labor force as women. By March 2009 women made up 49.7 percent of the labour force, an increase in part because 80 percent of the layoffs were men (Boushey 2009). The dynamics for minority group workers are even more dramatic, as the number of Black, Latino, and Asian American workers continues to increase at a faster rate than the number of White workers owing to demograpic changes.

More and more, then, the workforce reflects the diversity of the population, as ethnic minorities enter the labor force and immigrants and their children move from marginal jobs or employment in the informal economy to positions of greater visibility and responsibility. A sociological study of workplace programs designed to increase managerial diversity found that 39 percent of employers had diversity training programs. Researchers discovered that relying solely on education programs designed to reduce managerial bias was not particularly effective. The most successful approach is to have a point person, task force, or affirmative action plan that holds people responsible for change (Kalev, Dobbin, and Kelly 2006).

To better understand all these changes, it is helpful to better understand the economic and political systems we construct because they provide the context within which actions occur. To do so we will analyze what sociologists have to say about power and authority, economic systems, types of government, political participation, and the power structure in the United States. Such analysis allows us to take a step back and gain better perspective on our own thoughts and actions.

Sociologists have always been interested in how power is achieved and maintained. In the midst of major political and economic shifts, early sociologists developed theories

Workforce Diversity: Past, Present, and Future

Percentage of the workforce

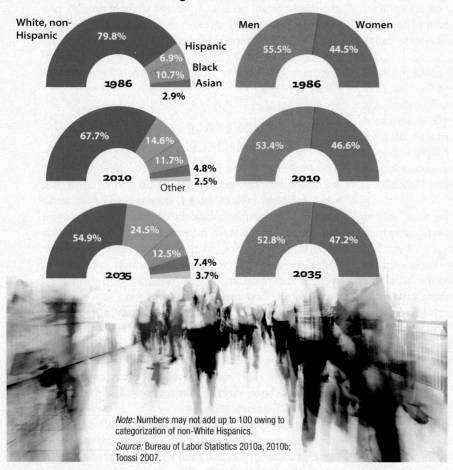

White, non-Hispanic **79.8%**

Hispanic **6.9%**
Black **10.7%**
Asian **2.9%**

1986

Men **55.5%** Women **44.5%**

1986

67.7% **14.6%**
11.7%
4.8%
2.5%
Other

2010

53.4% **46.6%**

2010

54.9% **24.5%**
12.5%
7.4%
3.7%

2035

52.8% **47.2%**

2035

Note: Numbers may not add up to 100 owing to categorization of non-White Hispanics.

Source: Bureau of Labor Statistics 2010a, 2010b; Toossi 2007.

of power intended to be sufficiently broad to explain the rise of democracy or the expansion of market-based capitalism yet sufficiently narrow to explain who gets their way within interpersonal relationships.

POWER

According to Max Weber, **power** is the ability to exercise one's will over others, even if they resist. To put it another way, if you can make people do what you want them to do— whether that is to go to war, coordinate a business meeting, clean their room, or even take an exam—you have power. Power relations can involve large organizations, small groups, or even people in intimate relationships.

Weber conceived of power as a continuum based on the extent to which it is accepted as legitimate by those over whom it is exercised. On one end is **force,** the actual or threatened use of coercion to impose one's will on others. When leaders imprison or execute political dissidents, they are applying force; so, too, are terrorists when they seize or bomb an embassy or assassinate a political leader. Slave-based economies typically rely on force. Such systems are not terribly efficient due to the policing costs necessary to make people do what they do not wish to do.

On the other end of the continuum is what Weber calls **authority,** power that is recognized as legitimate by the people over whom it is exercised. This type of power depends upon people's faith in their leader's right to rule. In a democracy, for example, people who continue to obey the laws even if the candidates they voted for do not win demonstrate an underlying faith in the legitimacy of the system. Weber views authority as more efficient than force because the motivation to obey comes from inside the follower rather than having to be externally imposed.

TYPES OF AUTHORITY

Weber identified three major types of authority: traditional, charismatic, and rational-legal. Oftentimes the legitimacy of leaders depends primarily upon only one, though elements of all three can be present at the same time.

Analyzing power using Weber's model focuses our attention in a way that allows us to better understand economic and political relationships. The degree to which we accept the legitimacy of the people that rule over us shapes the kind of power they are likely to use. For example, when police evacuated Occupy Wall Street protestors from their encampments, some degree of force was used. Protestors were made to do things that they did not otherwise wish to do, and failure to do so resulted in physical injury and jail time for some of those who questioned the legitimacy of the current system. Yet the presupposition that police and political leaders had the legitimate right to act in this way was widespread. As Weber suggested, when the legitimacy to rule is internalized in the form of authority, most people will simply comply with the wishes of the leader and will expect others to do likewise.

Personal Sociology

Because I Said So

I am astonished at how often my daughters, Emily and Eleanor, do what I ask. When they were little, if they disobeyed, they had to "sit in the green chair." It wasn't much of a punishment. The chair is located in our living room in full view of the television and not isolated from the rest of the family. In time, just the threat of having to sit there was enough. Eventually they simply accepted the traditional authority of "because I said so" as sufficient justification. Of course, as they grew, they began to question the legitimacy of my authority, seeking reasons for why they should obey. And yet, even now, they are usually willing to do as I say simply because I am their dad.

SOCTHINK

Which of these three forms of power do parents, bosses, or professors most rely on? Are there times when each of those groups use each of the three types of power?

Traditional Authority Until the middle of the 20th century, Japan was ruled for generations by a revered emperor whose absolute authority went largely unquestioned. In a political system based on **traditional authority,** legitimate power is conferred by custom and accepted practice. In other words, past practice justifies our present actions. As Weber put it, such authority rests in the belief that "everyday routine [provides] an inviolable norm of conduct" ([1922] 1978: 241). We do things the way the person in authority wishes, because we have always done them that way. The emperor, queen, or tribal leader may be loved or hated, competent or destructive; in terms

of legitimacy, that does not matter. For the traditional leader, authority depends on people's faith in custom, not in the leader's personal appeal, technical competence, or even written law.

Charismatic Authority Joan of Arc was a simple peasant girl in medieval France, yet she was able to rally the French people and lead them into major battles against English invaders despite having no formally recognized position of power. How was this possible? As Weber observed, power can be legitimized by the charisma of an individual. **Charismatic authority** refers to power made legitimate by a leader's exceptional personal or emotional appeal to his or her followers.

Charisma lets a person such as Joan of Arc lead or inspire without relying on set rules or traditions. In fact, charismatic authority is derived more from the beliefs of followers than from the actual qualities of leaders. So long as people perceive a charismatic leader such as Jesus, Joan of Arc, Gandhi, Malcolm X, or Martin Luther King Jr. as having qualities that set him or her apart from ordinary citizens, that leader's authority will remain secure and often unquestioned (Adair-Toteff 2005; Potts 2009). That unfortunately is also the case with malevolent figures such as Adolf Hitler, whose charismatic appeal turned people toward violent and destructive ends in Nazi Germany.

> **traditional authority** Legitimate power conferred by custom and accepted practice.
>
> **charismatic authority** Power made legitimate by a leader's exceptional personal or emotional appeal to his or her followers.

Political leaders increasingly depend on television, radio, and the Internet to establish and maintain charismatic authority. This practice took hold with President Franklin D. Roosevelt's use of fireside chats over the radio to calm a nation that faced the Great Depression and World War II. Barack Obama had high approval ratings early on in his presidency and news reports frequently mentioned his capacity to charm. Over time, however, these ratings declined as faith in his capacity to deliver waivered (Bligh and Kohles 2009). President George W. Bush learned a similar lesson. His approval ratings reached a high of 85 percent after the 9/11 terrorist attacks, but by the end of his second term they hovered around 25 percent, making it difficult for him to advance his legislative agenda (see graph on page 33).

Analyzing power using Weber's model focuses our attention in a way that allows us to better understand economic and political relationships. The degree to which we accept the legitimacy of the people that rule over us shapes the kind of power they are likely to use. For example, when police evacuated Occupy Wall Street protestors from their encampments, some degree of force was used. Protestors were made to do things that they did not otherwise wish to do, and failure to do so resulted in physical injury and jail time for some of those who questioned the legitimacy of the current system. Yet the presupposition that police and political leaders had the legitimate right to act in this way was widespread. As Weber suggested, when the legitimacy to rule is internalized in the form of authority, most people will simply comply with the wishes of the leader and will expect others to do likewise.

Rational-Legal Authority

The U.S. Constitution gives Congress and the president the authority to make and enforce laws and policies. Power made legitimate by law is a form of rational-legal authority. **Rational-legal authority** involves formally agreed-on and accepted rules, principles, and procedures of conduct that are established in order to accomplish goals in the most efficient manner possible. Such authority extends beyond governments to include any organization. Bureaucracies are the purest form of rational-legal authority. Generally, in societies based on rational-legal authority, leaders are thought to have specific areas of competence and authority, but are not thought to be endowed with divine inspiration, as in certain societies with traditional forms of authority.

rational-legal authority Authority based on formally agreed-upon and accepted rules, principles, and procedures of conduct that are established in order to accomplish goals in the most efficient manner possible.

capitalism An economic system based on private property, in which profit-seeking individuals, companies, and corporations compete in the marketplace.

>>Economic Systems

For the most part, we accept the legitimacy of the economic systems within which we operate. We may even find it difficult to accept the viability of alternatives. Yet people throughout history and around the world

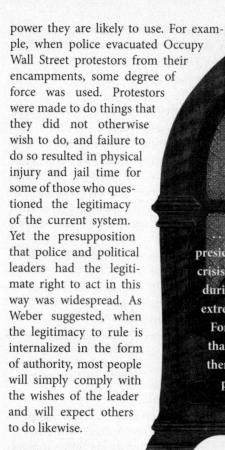

Did You Know?

… FDR gave 30 fireside chats during his presidency on topics ranging from the banking crisis of the Great Depression to the war effort during World War II. These broadcasts were extremely popular and drew large audiences. For the first time ever, people had a sense that the president was speaking directly to them, and the warm, simple manner of the presentation encouraged this feeling.

continue to provide for their needs using varieties of economic principles such as gift exchange, bartering, or shared ownership of goods. Analyzing the characteristics of the dominant economic systems of our time allows us to better understand how and why events happen as they do.

CAPITALISM

Capitalism is an economic system based on private property, in which profit-seeking individuals, companies, and corporations compete in the marketplace. Value under capitalism is determined based on what people are willing and able to pay for available goods and services. The basic principles of capitalism were laid out by Adam Smith in 1776 in his book *The Wealth of Nations*, including four key concepts: pursuit of profit, competition in the market, the law of supply and demand, and laissez-faire.

- *Pursuit of profit.* One of the basic presuppositions of capitalism is that, in our exchanges with others, human beings naturally seek to get the greatest return on their investments. This extends beyond economic exchanges (i.e., making a financial profit) to include social and cultural exchanges (in which even a conversation represents an exchange of symbolic resources such as status or attention). Pursuit of personal profit is not just morally acceptable; it is at the core of our identity as humans.
- *Competition in the market.* The marketplace is the context in which we exchange goods and services (such as shoes, cell phones, and college degrees); we do so in competition with other producers and consumers. Competition keeps prices in check. The marketplace must be open to whoever has the ability to compete so that no individual or firm controls a disproportionate share of the market.
- *Law of supply and demand.* In a competitive marketplace, a natural balance will be reached between production and consumption at the appropriate price. If the demand for a good or service is high and the supply is low, prices will go up, and vice versa. If a producer charges too much, another producer will step in to provide the good or service at a more reasonable price.

the one hand, capitalism tends toward the establishment of **monopolies,** in which a single business firm controls the market. Though the system needs competition, capitalists, in their pursuit of profits, seek to dominate the market to the point of monopolizing it. This violates the principle of competition. On the other hand, governments often respond by intervening in the marketplace—through policies such as antitrust legislation—to ensure sufficient competition, thus violating the principle of laissez-faire. In addition, some goods and services (such as police, fire protection, roads, national defense, and public education) are deemed important enough for the public good to be provided for all, even at the expense of government intervention.

> **laissez-faire** The principle that people should be able to compete freely, without government intervention, in the capitalist marketplace.
>
> **monopoly** Control of a market by a single business firm.
>
> **socialism** An economic system under which the means of production and distribution are collectively owned.

Adam Smith described this process as the "invisible hand" of the marketplace through which prices reach their natural level. Companies that don't respond to the prompting of the invisible hand—for example, by charging too much or too little—will ultimately fail.

- *Laissez-faire.* The expression **laissez-faire** means "let them do [as they please]," and in this context it means that outside entities, especially the government, should not intervene in the marketplace. Instead, the market should be allowed to function free from external influence. Ideally, markets self-correct using the invisible hand. Though governments may mean well, they cannot bring about a better result for society as a whole than can individuals who are allowed to compete on their own. In capitalism, the greatest social good is attained through the competition of profit-seeking individuals.

> Nowadays people know the price of everything and the value of nothing.
>
>
>
> Oscar Wilde

SOCIALISM

Socialism is an economic system in which the means of production and distribution in a society are collectively rather than privately owned. Value under socialism is determined by the amount of work it takes to produce products and the use we get out of those products. The basic principles of socialism were laid out by Karl Marx in the middle- to late 1800s in a variety of publications, including *The Communist Manifesto.* Marx believed socialism to be inevitable for the following reasons: humans must produce, production makes us uniquely human, we pour ourselves into our products, economy determines society, and scarcity and distribution are obstacles to the good of society.

- *Humans must produce.* Unlike animals, humans lack the complex instincts that direct how we provide for our basic human needs (food, shelter, and clothing) from nature. Therefore, we must fulfill those basic needs through technological innovation and culture creation.
- *Production makes us uniquely human.* Our capacity to produce distinguishes humans from the rest of the natural world. It is this free and creative productive ability, what Marx referred to as labor power, that must

SOCTHINK

Why is competition essential to capitalism? Why might capitalists seek to establish monopolies?

In practice, capitalism struggles to stick to these ideals because of contradictions that inevitably arise. On

contended that this shift brought about the transition from feudalism to capitalism—when the agricultural power base that gave rise to royalty gave way to the industrial power base of capitalists and corporations—and he predicted it will shift again from capitalism to communism.

- *Scarcity and distribution are obstacles to the good society.* For Marx, the ideal society is one in which we as humans have control over, and reap the full benefits of, our labor power. Until this point in history, however, no large-scale society has fully attained this ideal because we lacked the technological capacity to produce enough for everyone. This has resulted in social systems that divide the haves and have-nots: slavery's separation between masters and slaves, feudalism's separation between lords and peasants, capitalism's separation between owners and workers. Thanks to technological innovation—a consequence of our creative capacity to produce—we can eventually solve the problem of inadequate production. In fact, Marx praised capitalism, because it ultimately solves this problem by placing pressure on producers for constant innovation. Once we are technically capable of producing enough for all, any continued poverty, hunger, or extreme inequality is due to how we choose to distribute the products we make, rather than to our inability to produce enough. In other words, it's a social problem, solvable by the establishment of a new set of social relations that ensures equitable distribution. According to Marx, people will eventually decide that it doesn't make sense to maintain such economic extremes in the face of material abundance; thus a revolution in social relations toward socialism is inevitable.

In practice, the socialist ideal of collective ownership has been difficult to attain. The grand experiment in what was known as the Soviet Union—uniting Russia and neighboring countries as one large socialist bloc—ultimately collapsed in 1989. It did so under the weight of bureaucratic inefficiency, political corruption, and insufficient productivity—problems that seem endemic to socialist states. In addition, crackdowns on dissidents by the totalitarian socialist governments in both the Soviet Union and communist China have led to the murders of millions of their own people, purportedly for the good of the state. Recent surveys show that majorities in almost all of the former Soviet-bloc nations approve of the steady transition from socialism to democracy and free markets (Pew 2009e).

THE MIXED ECONOMY

In practice, national economic systems combine elements of both capitalism and socialism. A **mixed economy** features elements of more than one economic system. Starting from a socialist ideal and moving toward a mixed economy (as China has done in recent years) involves opening up some aspects of the state-controlled economy

be protected, nourished, and valued because it is at the core of our identity as humans.

- *We pour ourselves into our products.* For Marx, when we make something, we put part of who we are into each product; this is most apparent in craft labor. For example, a handmade bookshelf inspires pride because our labor power is the difference between the original stack of lumber and the finished shelf. To put it in an equation: *Raw materials + Labor power = Products.* According to Marx we naturally find joy in labor and take pleasure in sharing both the process and products with others.
- *Economy determines society.* Marx argued that, because our capacity and need to produce is at the core of who we are, it serves as the foundation for society. In essence, how we organize the economy determines all other forms of social relations, such as government, family, education, and religion. In most agrarian societies production is rooted in the land, so ownership and control of land becomes the foundation of power. Social institutions may reinforce the privileged position of landowners, for example, by rooting a king's "divine right" to rule in religious authority. Over time, this foundation shifts as our capacity to produce evolves through technological innovation. Eventually, the systems of social relations that grew out of that particular set of economic relations no longer match the new economic base, and a revolution to a new set of social relations occurs. Marx

mixed economy An economic system that combines elements of both capitalism and socialism.

Fifty Years of Growth, 1970–2020

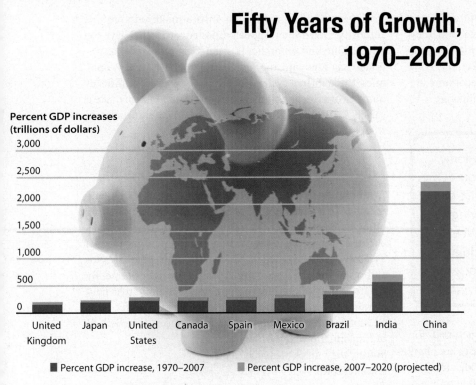

Percent GDP increases (trillions of dollars)

- ■ Percent GDP increase, 1970–2007
- ■ Percent GDP increase, 2007–2020 (projected)

Source: U.S. Department of Agriculture 2007.

years was the world's largest company, went bankrupt. The U.S. government became its majority stockholder, owning 60 percent of its shares. These funds helped many firms survive that otherwise would have failed. Now that they are back on their feet, some companies have paid back the loans they received from the government. For example, General Motors has paid back its $8.4 billion of government loans in full, with interest, and five years early. The U.S. government remains its single largest shareholder.

Though critics charged that Presidents Bush and Obama were moving the nation toward socialism, most people hoped that their efforts would minimize the negative effects the economic downturn had on their lives. The majority of citizens ultimately accepted these huge government expenditures as a means to save capitalism from its own excesses. Billionaire investor Warren Buffett later reflected on the government intervention and concluded, "Only one counterforce was available, and that was you, Uncle Sam. . . . Well, Uncle Sam, you delivered" (Buffett 2010).

to competition and the free market. Conversely, moving from a capitalist ideal toward a mixed economy removes some goods and services from the competitive free market and provides them for all or subsidizes them to assure broader access. In the United States, we are provided with goods and services such as police and fire protection, roads, and public schools. Most agree that we should all have access to such public goods without regard for our ability to pay. There is currently a debate under way about whether health care should be considered a similar public good.

There has long been a debate in the United States about the degree to which the government should be involved in the economy, but the economic upheaval of the Great Recession challenged people's commitment to *laissez-faire* principles. Government officials decided that some companies were "too big to fail," meaning that the domino effect of their failure would be greater than the cost of violating the non-intervention ideal. The Bush administration, itself a strong proponent of free market principles, took the first steps toward government intervention in the economy during this crisis. In September 2008 it pushed the Troubled Assets Relief Program (TARP) through Congress to provide up to $700 billion to buy mortgage-backed securities and to prop up the financial sector. The Obama administration continued along the same lines. For example, in an effort to kick-start the U.S. economy, Congress passed the American Recovery and Reinvestment Act in February 2009, providing almost $800 billion for infrastructure projects, education and health care funding, and tax cuts. And in June 2009 General Motors, which for

—SOCTHINK—

Should the U.S. government let companies fail regardless of apparent economic consequences?

THE INFORMAL ECONOMY

An informal economy operates within the confines of the dominant macroeconomic system in many countries, whether capitalist or socialist. In this **informal economy,** transfers of money, goods, or services take place but are not reported to the government. Examples of the informal economy include bartering, in which people trade goods and services with someone (say, exchanging a haircut for a computer lesson), selling goods on the street, and engaging in illegal transactions, such as gambling or drug deals. Participants in this type of economy avoid taxes and government regulations.

> **informal economy** Transfers of money, goods, or services that are not reported to the government.

In the developing world, governments often create burdensome business regulations that overworked bureaucrats must administer. When requests for licenses and permits pile up, delaying business projects, legitimate entrepreneurs find that they need to "go underground" to get anything done. Despite its apparent efficiency, this type of informal economy is dysfunctional for a country's overall political and economic well-being. Because informal firms typically operate in remote locales to avoid detection, they cannot easily expand when they become profitable. And given the limited protection for their property and contractual rights, participants in the informal economy are less likely than others to save and invest their income.

Informal economies can also be dysfunctional for workers. Working conditions in these businesses are often unsafe or dangerous, and the jobs rarely provide any benefits to those who become ill or cannot continue to work. Perhaps more significant, the longer a worker remains in the informal economy, the less likely he or she is to make the transition to the regular economy. No matter how efficient or productive a worker may be, employers expect to see experience in the formal economy on a job application. Experience as a successful street vendor or self-employed cleaning person does not carry much weight with interviewers (Venkatesh 2006).

>>Political Systems

Just as new economic systems developed in response to broader historical changes, political systems also adapted. In all societies, someone or some group—whether it be a tribal chief, a dictator, a council, or a parliament—makes important decisions about how to use resources and allocate goods. Inevitably, the struggle for power and authority involves **politics**, the competition between individuals or groups over the allocation of valued resources. Politics takes place within the context of a **political system**, which is the social institution that is founded on a recognized set of procedures for implementing and achieving society's goals.

politics The competition between individuals or groups over the allocation of valued resources.

political system The social institution that is founded on a recognized set of procedures for implementing and achieving society's goals.

monarchy A form of government headed by a single member of a royal family, usually a king, queen, or some other hereditary ruler.

oligarchy A form of government in which a few individuals rule.

Government represents an institutionalized form of authority. Given the responsibilities governments have for establishing and enforcing laws and the scope of international relations and the globalization of national economies, these formal systems of authority make a significant number of critical political decisions. Such systems take a variety of forms, including monarchy, oligarchy, dictatorship, totalitarianism, and democracy.

MONARCHY

A **monarchy** is a form of government headed by a single member of a royal family, usually a king, queen, or some other hereditary ruler. In earlier times, many monarchs claimed that God had granted them a divine right to rule. Typically, they governed on the basis of traditional forms of authority, sometimes accompanied by the use of force. By the beginning of the 21st century, however, monarchs held genuine governmental power in only a few nations, such as Monaco. Most monarchs, such as Queen Elizabeth II in England, now have little practical power; they serve primarily ceremonial roles.

OLIGARCHY

An **oligarchy** is a form of government in which a few individuals rule. A venerable method of governing that flourished in ancient Greece and Egypt, oligarchy now often takes the

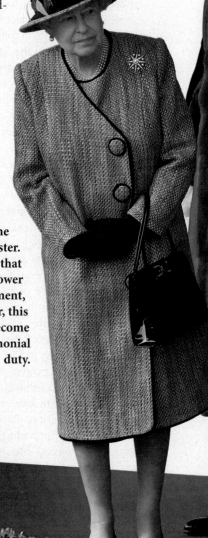

Did You Know?

. . . One of Queen Elizabeth's official duties is to appoint the prime minister. Given that political power rests with Parliament, however, this too has become largely a ceremonial duty.

form of military rule. In developing nations in Africa, Asia, and Latin America, small factions of military officers may forcibly seize power, either from legally elected regimes or from other military cliques (Michels [1915] 1949).

Strictly speaking, the term *oligarchy* is reserved for governments that are run by a few selected individuals. However, the People's Republic of China can be classified as an oligarchy if we stretch the meaning of the term. In China, power rests in the hands of a large but exclusive ruling *group,* the Communist Party. In a similar vein, we might argue that many industrialized nations of the West should be considered oligarchies (rather than democracies), because only a powerful few—leaders of big business, government, and the military—actually rule. Later in this chapter, we will examine the "elite model" of the U.S. political system in greater detail.

DICTATORSHIP AND TOTALITARIANISM

A **dictatorship** is a government in which one person has nearly total power to make and enforce laws. Dictators rule primarily through the use of force, which often includes imprisonment, torture, and executions. Typically, they seize power rather than being freely elected (as in a democracy) or inheriting power (as in a monarchy). Some dictators are quite charismatic and manage to achieve a certain popularity, although their supporters' enthusiasm is almost certainly tinged with fear. Other dictators rely on coercion and are often bitterly hated by their people.

Frequently, dictators develop such overwhelming control over people's lives that their governments are called totalitarian. (Monarchies and oligarchies may also achieve this type of dominance.) **Totalitarianism** involves virtually complete government control and surveillance over all aspects of a society's social and political life. Germany during Hitler's reign, the Soviet Union under Stalin in the 1930s, and North Korea today are classified as totalitarian states.

> **dictatorship** A government in which one person has nearly total power to make and enforce laws.
>
> **totalitarianism** Virtually complete government control and surveillance over all aspects of a society's social and political life.
>
> **democracy** In a literal sense, government by the people.
>
> **representative democracy** A system of government in which citizens elect political leaders to make decisions on behalf of the people.

DEMOCRACY

In a literal sense, **democracy** means government by the people. The word comes from two Greek roots—*demos,* meaning "the populace" or "the common people," and *kratia,* meaning "rule." In a democracy, power is not vested in a particular person or position. Individual citizens provide the foundation for political authority, and the underlying principle of power is "one person, one vote." This principle implies that, in theory at least, everyone has equal power when it comes to decision-making. Direct democracy, in which all citizens vote on all major decisions and the most votes win, provides perhaps the purest example. In large, populous nations such as the United States, direct democracy is impractical at the national level. All Americans cannot vote on every important issue. Consequently, popular rule occurs in the form of **representative democracy,** a system of government in which citizens elect political leaders to make decisions on behalf of the people.

The way representatives are chosen can vary, and the system used to select them influences the kind of politics we get. For example, the two-party system that dominates in the United States is a consequence, in part, of

-**SOC**THINK-

In 2001, expressing a sentiment shared by many past presidents, George W. Bush joked that, when it came to working with Congress, "a dictatorship would be a heck of a lot easier." In what ways is the U.S. system of government intentionally inefficient? Why might that be on purpose?

how legislators are selected. To select members to the House of Representatives, the country is divided into 435 geographically distinct congressional districts. Each district has a single seat. Elections are held within each, and the winner becomes the representative for that district. As a result of this winner-take-all system, candidates have an incentive to appeal to a majority of voters which tends to result in the creation of two parties, each vying to gain that majority. Even though there are plenty of "third parties" in the United States—in the 2012 election, for example, there were candidates on the ballot for the Constitution Party, Green Party, Libertarian Party, Party of Socialism and Liberation, and many others—the winner-take-all system makes it difficult for a minority party to break through to win a majority of votes, especially against the entrenched power and influence of the two major parties.

An alternative system for selecting legislators involves proportional representation, some form of which exists in Brazil, Israel, the Netherlands, and South Africa. In such cases, a single district can be represented by multiple seats, and winners are determined based on the percentage of votes received in that district. For example, if a party receives 15 percent of the vote, that party would receive approximately 15 percent of the legislative seats. In such a system, parties that might never be able to win a majority of votes can still win seats in the legislature. In addition, the likelihood that a single party secures a majority of seats declines. As a result, parties often need to work together

to create a ruling coalition which has the effect of giving those minority parties more power than they might otherwise have.

If citizens in a democracy are unhappy with the current direction of things, they can vote to establish new policies or elect new leaders. Over time, significant changes in policy can occur in response to the changing will of the people. For example, early on in U.S. history, the "self-evident" truth that everyone was created equal and endowed with unalienable rights only applied to White, property-holding men. Over time the definition of who counts as a citizen expanded to include others. Debates about citizenship rights in the United States continue to this day as evidenced, for example, in arguments regarding the rights of children or immigrants.

Citizenship rights involve more than just the right to vote. Sociologist T. H. Marshall (1950) identified three categories of such rights including civil rights, political rights, and social rights:

- *Civil rights.* These citizenship rights protect individual freedoms. We find some of them articulated in the Bill of Rights, the first ten amendments to the U.S. Constitution. Included are protections such as freedom of speech, freedom of assembly, the right to bear arms, and freedom of religion.
- *Political rights.* These ensure the right to full participation in the political process. In principle, any citizen can be involved in politics, by voting or running for office. But universal political participation wasn't always guaranteed. The 15th Amendment to the U.S. Constitution extended political rights to African Americans in 1870 and the 19th Amendment secured those rights for women in 1920.
- *Social rights.* These rights provide for our welfare and security. They are based on the presupposition that a minimum standard of living is necessary in order to ensure the ability of all to exercise their civil and political rights. To secure these rights, some goods and services—such as public education or police and fire protection—are taken out of the marketplace, ensuring that everyone has at least a minimum amount of access regardless of their ability to pay. Substantial debates exist over the role government should play in ensuring access to basic material, social, and cultural resources.

Making this distinction between categories of rights allows us to better understand the evolution of rights in the United States. We often take for granted that basic civil and political rights are secured for all, yet ongoing debates about the rights of immigrants or same-sex couples often fall within these two categories. Arguments regarding the extension of social rights to cover more items, for example the ongoing debate about securing health-care coverage for all, are particularly contentious.

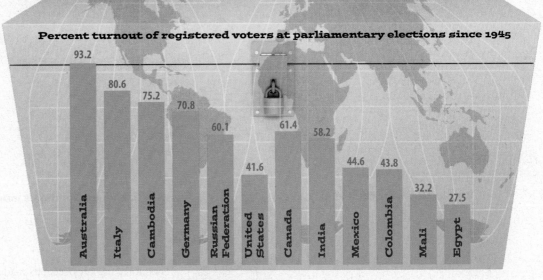

Percent turnout of registered voters at parliamentary elections since 1945

Country	Percent
Australia	93.2
Italy	80.6
Cambodia	75.2
Germany	70.8
Russian Federation	60.1
United States	41.6
Canada	61.4
India	58.2
Mexico	44.6
Colombia	43.8
Mali	32.2
Egypt	27.5

Note: Includes national elections to the legislative body. U.S. results are for the 2008 mid-term elections.

Source: International Institute for Democracy and Electoral Assistance 2011.

Debates over social rights are due, in part, to a basic tension between core values in the United States. On the one hand is the principle of equality, a basic presupposition at the heart of democracy. On the other, is the principle of competition, which is an essential premise of capitalism. A capitalist economy assumes that an economic hierarchy exists and that there will be winners and losers, but in a democracy all are created equal. Economist Arthur Okun (1975) described this tension as "the double standard of a capitalist democracy, professing and pursuing an egalitarian political and social system and simultaneously generating gaping disparities in economic well-being" (p. 1). The simultaneous adherence to these two principles helps to explain why social policies regarding the extension of social rights go back and forth over time with one or the other becoming dominant in public discourse. Leading up to the 2008 mid-term Congressional elections, for example, Tea

SOCTHINK

To what extent do you think that the principles of political equality and economic competition are at odds with each other in the United States?

Party conservatives advocated strongly in favor of lower taxes and substantial cuts in federal funding for social welfare programs. Not long thereafter, as we saw above, Occupy Wall Street protestors advocated in favor of higher taxes on the wealthy and a stronger social support safety net.

>>The Power Structure in the United States

The issue of power extends beyond just politics and the people who occupy formally recognized offices. Over the years, sociologists repeatedly have sought to discover who really holds power in the United States. Do "we the people" genuinely run the country through our elected representatives? Or does a small elite behind the scenes control both the government and the economic system? In exploring these questions, social scientists have developed two basic models of our nation's power structure: political pluralism versus the power elite.

POWER ELITE MODELS

Such criticisms lend support for an alternative model of how power functions. This model traces its roots back to

Power Elite Models

THE POWER ELITE

Corporate rich
Executive branch
Military leaders

Interest group leaders
Legislators
Local opinion leaders

Unorganized, exploited masses

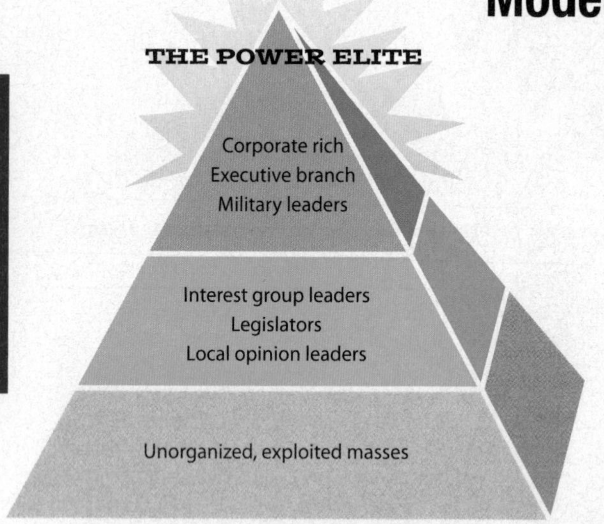

C. Wright Mills's model, 1956

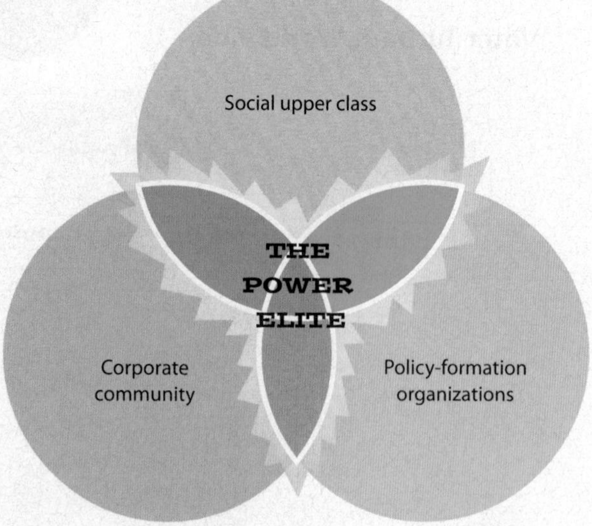

Source: Left, based on C. W. Mills (1956) 2000; right, Domhoff 2006:105.

Social upper class

THE POWER ELITE

Corporate community

Policy-formation organizations

G. William Domhoff's model, 2006

5 Movies on ECONOMY AND POLITICS

Inside Job
A global financial crisis whodunit.

The Artist
With technological innovation, something's gained and something's lost.

Capitalism: A Love Story
Capitalism on trial.

The Messenger
On being the bearer of bad news in times of war.

All the President's Men
A president's fall from grace.

Karl Marx, who believed that 19th-century representative democracy was essentially a sham. He argued that industrial societies were dominated by relatively small numbers of people who owned the factories and controlled natural resources. In Marx's view, government officials and military leaders were essentially servants of this capitalist class and followed their wishes.

elite model A view of society as being ruled by a small group of individuals who share a common set of political and economic interests.

power elite A small group of military, industrial, and government leaders who control the fate of the United States.

Therefore, any key decisions made by politicians inevitably reflected the interests of the dominant business owners. Like others who hold an **elite model** of power relations, Marx believed that society is ruled by a small group of individuals who share political and economic interests.

Mills's Model Sociologist C. Wright Mills, who developed the concept of the sociological imagination that we looked at in Chapter 1, put forth a model similar to Marx's in his pioneering work *The Power Elite* ([1956] 2000). Mills described a small group of military, industrial, and government leaders who controlled the fate of the United States—the **power elite.** Power rested in the hands of a few, both inside and outside government.

A pyramid illustrates the power structure of the United States in Mills's model. The power elite rests at the top and includes the corporate rich, leaders of the executive branch of government, and heads of the military (whom Mills called the "warlords"). Directly below are local opinion leaders, members of the legislative branch of government, and leaders of special-interest groups. Mills contended that these individuals and groups basically follow the wishes of the dominant power elite. At the bottom of the pyramid are the unorganized, exploited masses.

A fundamental element in Mills's thesis is that the power elite not only includes relatively few members but also operates as a self-conscious, cohesive unit. Although not necessarily diabolical or ruthless, the elite comprises

Public Trust in Government

Source: Pew Research Center 2010c; 2011f.

Note: The percentage represents those who say they "can trust the government in Washington to do what is right" either "just about always" or "most of the time."

similar types of people who interact regularly with one another and have essentially the same political and economic interests. Mills's power elite represents not a conspiracy but rather a community of interest and sentiment among a small number of influential people (Jenness, Smith, and Stepan-Norris 2006).

Critics claim that Mills failed to clarify when the elite opposes protests and when it tolerates them, making it difficult to test his model. Furthermore, they say, he failed to provide detailed case studies that would substantiate the interrelationships among members of the power elite.

> Majority rule only works if you're also considering individual rights. Because you can't have five wolves and one sheep voting on what to have for supper.

Larry Flynt

Nevertheless, his challenging theories forced scholars to look more critically at the democratic political system of the United States.

In analyzing the scandals that have rocked major corporations such as Enron and Lehman Brothers over the past decade, observers have noted that members of the business elite are closely interrelated. In a study of the members of the boards of directors of Fortune 1000 corporations, researchers found that each director can reach *every* other board of directors in just 3.7 steps. That is, by consulting acquaintances of acquaintances, each director can quickly reach someone who sits on each of the other 999 boards. Furthermore, the face-to-face contact directors regularly have in their board meetings makes them a highly cohesive elite. Finally, the corporate elite not only is wealthy, powerful, and cohesive but also is overwhelmingly White and male (G. Davis 2003, 2004; Kentor and Jang 2004; Mizruchi 1996; Strauss 2002).

Domhoff's Model Sociologist G. William Domhoff (2006, 2009) agrees with Mills that a powerful elite runs the United States. Domhoff stresses the role played by elites from within networks of organizations, including the corporate community; policy formation organizations such as think tanks, chambers of commerce, and labor unions; and the social upper class. Membership in these groups overlaps, and members with connections in more than one of these spheres have more power and influence. Domhoff finds that those in this latter group are still largely White, male, and upper class, but he notes the presence of a small number of women and minority men in key positions—groups that were excluded from Mills's top echelon and are still underrepresented today (Zweigenhaft and Domhoff 2006).

─**SOC**THINK─

Is it possible for a small and unified group of powerful people in the United States to use their power and influence to, in effect, rule the country?

Although the three groups in Domhoff's power elite model do overlap, they do not necessarily agree on specific policies. Domhoff notes that in politics, two different coalitions have exercised influence. A corporate-conservative coalition has played a large role in both political parties, generating support for particular candidates through direct-mail appeals. A liberal-labor coalition is based in unions, local environmental organizations, a segment of the minority group community, liberal churches, and the university and arts communities (Zweigenhaft and Domhoff 2006). The power this coalition wields suggests that the interests of members of the power elite are not always singular or uniform but that overall they do work together to advance their larger interests.

pluralist model A view of society in which many competing groups within the community have access to government, so that no single group is dominant.

THE PLURALIST MODEL

According to the pluralist approach, power is widely dispersed throughout society. Though some groups may have more power in certain areas at particular times, there is no core group at the top that is able to consistently advance its interests at the expense of others. According to this **pluralist model,** many competing groups have access to government so that no single group is dominant.

To support their claims, advocates of the pluralist model point to data gathered from intensive case studies of communities gathered using observation research. One of the most famous—an investigation of decision making in New Haven, Connecticut—was reported by Robert Dahl (1961). Dahl found that, although the number of people involved in any important decision was rather small, community power was nonetheless diffuse. Few political actors exercised decision-making power on all issues, and no one group got its way all the time. One individual or group might be influential in a battle over urban renewal but have little effect on educational policy.

Historically, pluralists have stressed ways in which large numbers of people can participate in or influence governmental decision making. New communications technologies like the Internet are increasing the opportunity to be heard, not just in countries like the United States but in developing countries the world over. The ability to communicate with political leaders via email, for example, increases the opportunity for the average citizen to have a voice in politics.

The pluralist model, has its critics. Sociologist G. William Domhoff (1978, 2006) reexamined Dahl's study of decision making in New Haven and argued that Dahl and other pluralists had failed to trace how local elites who were prominent in decision making belonged to a larger national ruling class. In addition, studies of community power, such as Dahl's work in New Haven, can examine decision making only on issues that become part of the political agenda. They fail to address the potential power of elites to keep certain matters entirely out of the realm of political debate.

Dianne Pinderhughes (1987) has criticized the pluralist model for failing to account for the exclusion of African Americans from the political process. Drawing on her studies of Chicago politics, Pinderhughes points out that the residential and occupational segregation of Blacks and their long political disenfranchisement violate the logic of pluralism—which would hold that such a substantial minority should always have been influential in community decision making. This critique applies to many cities across the United States, where other large racial and ethnic minorities, among them Asian Americans, Puerto Ricans, and Mexican Americans, are relatively powerless.

>>Political Participation in the United States

Citizens of the United States take for granted many aspects of their political system. They are accustomed to living in a nation with a Bill of Rights, two major political parties, voting by secret ballot, an elected president, state and local governments distinct from the national government,

Did You Know?

. . . Young voters were much more likely to vote for Obama in 2008 than any other age group. Of voters aged 18–29, 66 percent voted for Obama. This compares to 52 percent among 30–44 year-olds and 50 percent for those aged 45–64. People 65 and older preferred McCain; only 45 percent of that age group chose Obama.

and so forth. Because political representatives still must be elected to serve, citizens have substantial potential power to shape the nature and direction of pubic policy. Yet, if not all participate, either because they choose not to or they are discouraged or even prevented from doing so, some interests might be better served than others. In practice, two particular concerns—voter participation and race and gender representation—raise questions about the degree to which this is happening.

VOTER PARTICIPATION

In a democratic system, voters have the right to select their political leaders. They are free to vote for whom they choose, and political parties seek to persuade voters to support their positions. In May

2012, 39.6 percent of registered voters in the United States saw themselves as Democrats, 35.6 percent as Republicans, and 25.4 percent as independents (Pollster.com 2012).

Historically, voter participation rates in the United States were highest from 1848 to 1896, during which an average of about 80 percent of eligible voters participated in presidential elections. (Of course, that does not count women or African Americans, who were not legally permitted to vote.) The rate declined steadily until it reached 48.9 percent in 1928. It fluctuated throughout the rest of the 20th century, rising to more than 60 percent in 1940 and 1960 and falling to around 50 percent in 1948, 1988, and 1996. Concerns about voter apathy were expressed going into the 21st century, so the increases in the new millennium were greeted as a welcomed trend (McDonald 2009).

In the 2008 presidential election, voter turnout hit a 40-year high, representing the third straight presidential election with an increase in voter participation. In the battle between Barack Obama and John McCain, 61.7 percent of eligible voters participated. Compare this to 60.1 percent in the race between George W. Bush and John Kerry in 2004 and 54.2 percent in the 2000 election, which pitted George W. Bush against Al Gore (McDonald 2009).

Although a few nations still command high voter turnout, it is increasingly common to hear national leaders of other countries complain of voter apathy. Still, among the 194 countries that have held parliamentary elections since 1992, the United States ranked only 126th in voter turnout in 2011 (International Institute for Democracy and Electoral Assistance 2011).

Political participation makes government accountable to the voters. If participation declines, government operates with less of a sense of accountability to society. This issue is most serious for the least powerful individuals and groups in the United States. Historically, voter turnout has been particularly low among members of racial and ethnic minorities, although in the 2008 presidential election participation rates increased 9 percent among African Americans and 5 percent among Hispanics (Lopez and Taylor 2009). Those in poverty—whose focus understandably is on survival—are also traditionally underrepresented among voters. The low turnout found among these groups is due at least in part to their common feeling of powerlessness. By the same token, by declining to vote, they encourage political power brokers to continue to ignore the interests of the less affluent and the nation's minorities. The segment of the voting population that has consistently shown the most voter apathy is the 18- to 24-year-olds (Holder 2006). In the 2010 Congressional elections, for example, only 24 percent of this age group voted, compared to 61 percent of those aged 65 and older (Circle 2011).

Reasons for Not Voting, among Young adults

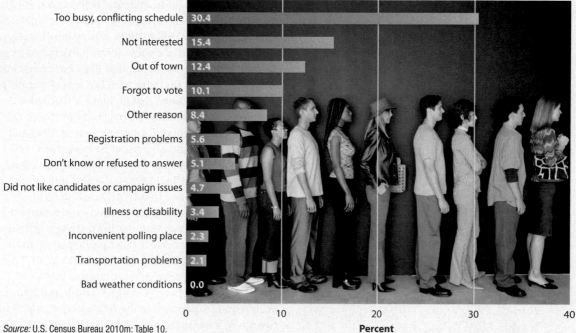

Reason	Percent
Too busy, conflicting schedule	30.4
Not interested	15.4
Out of town	12.4
Forgot to vote	10.1
Other reason	8.4
Registration problems	5.6
Don't know or refused to answer	5.1
Did not like candidates or campaign issues	4.7
Illness or disability	3.4
Inconvenient polling place	2.3
Transportation problems	2.1
Bad weather conditions	0.0

Source: U.S. Census Bureau 2010m: Table 10.

Note: Young adults include 18- to 24-year olds. Results are for the 2010 mid-term elections.

RACE AND GENDER IN POLITICS

Because politics is synonymous with power and authority, we should not be surprised that marginalized groups lack political strength. Nationally, women did not get the vote until 1920. Most Chinese Americans were turned away from the polls until 1926. American Indians did not win the right to vote until 1954. And African Americans were, in practice, largely disenfranchised until 1965, when national voting rights legislation was passed. It has taken these groups some time to develop their political power and begin to exercise it fully.

Progress toward the inclusion of minority groups in government has been slow as well. As of 2011, only 17 of 100 U.S. senators were women. No senator was African American, although 2 were Latino, and 2 were Asian American

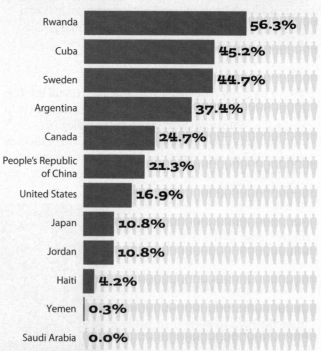

Going **GLOBAL**

Women in National Legislatures, Selected Countries

Country	Percent
Rwanda	56.3%
Cuba	45.2%
Sweden	44.7%
Argentina	37.4%
Canada	24.7%
People's Republic of China	21.3%
United States	16.9%
Japan	10.8%
Jordan	10.8%
Haiti	4.2%
Yemen	0.3%
Saudi Arabia	0.0%

Note: Data are for lower legislative houses only, as of March 31, 2012; data on upper houses, such as the U.S. Senate or the U.K. House of Lords, are not included.

Source: Inter-Parliamentary Union 2012.

(Under) Representation in Congress Compared to Overall Population

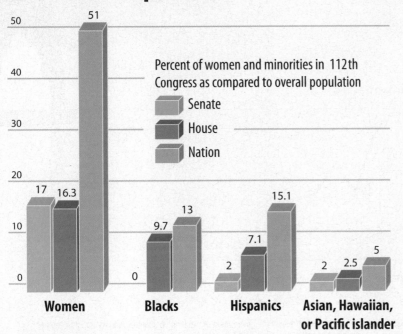

Percent of women and minorities in 112th Congress as compared to overall population

- Senate
- House
- Nation

Women: Senate 17, House 16.3, Nation 51
Blacks: Senate 0, House 9.7, Nation 13
Hispanics: Senate 2, House 7.1, Nation 15.1
Asian, Hawaiian, or Pacific islander: Senate 2, House 2.5, Nation 5

Source: Manning 2011.

record. Furthermore, when political issues were raised in newspaper articles, reporters were more likely to illustrate them with statements made by male candidates than by female candidates (Devitt 1999; Jost 2008; Paxton Kunovich, and Hughes 2007).

Whereas the proportion of women in national legislatures has increased in the United States and many other nations, women account for at least half the members of the national legislature in only two countries. The African Republic of Rwanda ranks the highest, with 56.3 percent, and the European nation Andorra has 50.0. Overall, the United States ranked 96th among 189 nations in the proportion of women serving as national legislators in 2012 (Inter-Parliamentary Union 2012).

To remedy this situation, many countries have adopted quotas for female representatives. In some, the government sets aside a certain percentage of seats for women, usually 10–30 percent. In others, political parties have decided that 20–40 percent of their candidates should be women. Fifty-seven countries now have some kind of quota system (Inter-Parliamentary Union 2011; Quota Project 2012).

or Native Hawaiian/Pacific Islander, leaving 79 White non-Hispanic men. Among the 435 members of the U.S. House of Representatives, 310 were White non-Hispanic men. Seventy-one were women, 42 were African Americans (including 13 women), 25 were Latinos (including 6 Latinas), 9 were Asian Americans or Native Hawaiian/Pacific Islanders (including four women), and 1 was an American Indian. These numbers, though low, represent a high-water mark for these groups.

Many critics within minority communities decry what they term "fiesta politics." This refers to the tendency of White power brokers to visit racial and ethnic minority communities only when they need electoral support, making a quick appearance on a national or ethnic holiday to get their picture taken and then vanishing. When the election is over, they too often forget to consult the residents who supported them about community needs and concerns.

Female politicians may be enjoying more electoral success now than in the past, but there is evidence that the media cover them differently from male politicians. A content analysis of newspaper coverage of gubernatorial races showed that reporters wrote more often about a female candidate's personal life, appearance, or personality than a male candidate's, and less often about her political viewpoints and voting

>>War and Peace

When it comes to political power, perhaps no decision is as weighty as the decision to go to war. Conflict is a central aspect of social relations. Sociologists Theodore Caplow and Louis Hicks (2002:3) have defined **war** as conflict between organizations that possess trained combat forces equipped with deadly weapons. This meaning is broader than the legal definition, which typically requires a formal declaration of hostilities.

> **war** Conflict between organizations that possess trained combat forces equipped with deadly weapons.

WAR

Sociologists approach war in three different ways. Those who take a global view study how and why two or more nations become engaged in military conflict. Those who take a nation-state view stress the interaction of internal political, socioeconomic, and cultural forces. And those who take a micro view focus on the social impact of war on individuals and the groups to which they belong.

Analysis at the global level focuses on macro issues such as the distribution

U.S. Public Opinion on Defense Spending

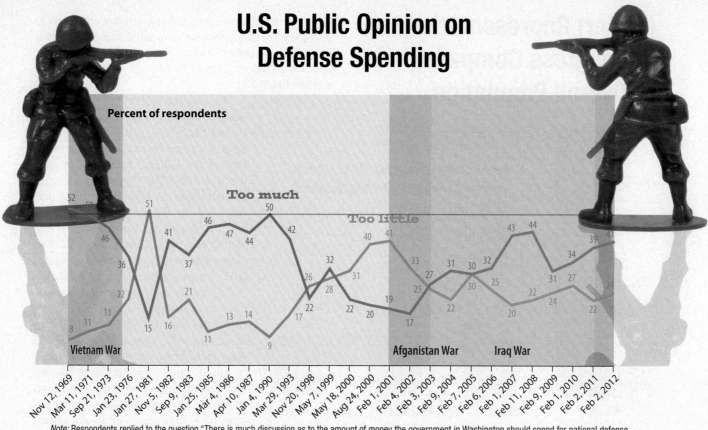

Percent of respondents

Too much

Too little

Vietnam War

Afganistan War

Iraq War

Nov 12, 1969 — Mar 11, 1971 — Sep 21, 1973 — Jan 23, 1976 — Jan 27, 1981 — Nov 5, 1982 — Sep 9, 1983 — Jan 25, 1985 — Mar 4, 1986 — Apr 10, 1987 — Jan 4, 1990 — Mar 29, 1993 — Nov 20, 1998 — May 7, 1999 — May 18, 2000 — Aug 24, 2000 — Feb 1, 2001 — Feb 4, 2002 — Feb 3, 2003 — Feb 9, 2004 — Feb 7, 2005 — Feb 6, 2006 — Feb 1, 2007 — Feb 11, 2008 — Feb 9, 2009 — Feb 1, 2010 — Feb 2, 2011 — Feb 2, 2012

Note: Respondents replied to the question "There is much discussion as to the amount of money the government in Washington should spend for national defense and military purposes. How do you feel about this? Do you think we are spending too little, about the right amount, or too much?"

Source: Gallup 2012a.

of resources, struggles over political philosophies, and debates about boundaries. Often it involves nations with competing political and economic systems, as was the case in World War I, World War II, and the Cold War. Some have argued that the conflict in Iraq is about bringing freedom and democracy to the Middle East, and others argue it is motivated by oil and profits.

Sociologists have devoted much effort to studying the internal decision-making process that leads to war. During the Vietnam War, Presidents Johnson and Nixon both misled Congress, painting a falsely optimistic picture of the likely outcome. Based on their intentional distortions, Congress appropriated the military funds the two administrations requested. However, in 1971, *The New York Times* published a set of classified documents now known as "The Pentagon Papers," which revealed that many members of both administrations had knowingly distorted the real prospects for the war. Two years later—over Nixon's veto—Congress passed the War Powers Act, which requires the president to notify Congress of the reasons for committing combat troops to a hostile situation (Patterson 2003).

Even though government leaders make the decision to go to war, public opinion plays a significant role in its execution. By 1971 the number of U.S. soldiers killed in Vietnam had surpassed 50,000, and antiwar sentiment was strong. Wars conducted by the United States since that time have tended to follow a similar pattern. Initial

support both for the importance of going to war and for military spending to support it tend to give way the longer it takes to finish the job. This proved true for the conflicts in both Iraq and Afghanistan.

A major change relating to the conduct of war involves the composition of the U.S. military. Women represent a growing presence among the troops. As of September, 2011, there were 207,308 women serving on active duty and women made up 14.5 percent of active military personnel (Department of Defense 2011). Increasingly, women are serving not just as support personnel but also as an integral part of combat units. The first casualty of the war in Iraq, in fact, was Private First Class Lori Piestewa, a member of the Hopi tribe and a descendant of Mexican settlers in the Southwest.

At the level of interpersonal interaction, war can bring out the worst as well as the best in people. In 2004, graphic images of the abuse of Iraqi prisoners by U.S. soldiers at Iraq's Abu Ghraib prison shocked the world. For social scientists, the deterioration of the guards' behavior brought to mind psychology professor Philip Zimbardo's mock prison experiment at Stanford University, in which volunteer guards in a simulated prison acted sadistically toward volunteer prisoners. Zimbardo concluded it was the positions of power the guards occupied relative to the inmates that led to their behavior rather than the characteristics of the individuals themselves. In July 2004 the U.S. military began using a documentary film about the experiment to train military interrogators to avoid mistreatment of prisoners (Zarembo 2004).

During World War II, the U.S. government sponsored films to garner support for the war effort, boost people's morale, and even demonize the enemy. From cartoons featuring Mickey Mouse and Donald Duck to films including *This Is the Army* (which starred Ronald Reagan), Hollywood cooperated in getting the message out in the 1940s. In more recent years, antiwar films have also raised difficult questions that governments would sometimes rather not be aired. During the Cold War, *Dr. Strangelove* called into question the insanity of the nuclear standoff; in 1970, the film version of *M*A*S*H*, though set in Korea, raised questions about the conflict in Vietnam. More recently, there have been numerous films about the war in Iraq, including *The Hurt Locker, The Messenger, In the Valley of Elah,* and *No End in Sight*.

TERRORISM

As people in the United States learned on September 11, 2001, the ability to instill fear through large-scale violent acts is not limited to recognized political states, and it can involve political groups that operate outside the bounds of legitimate authority. Acts of terror, whether perpetrated by a few or by many people, can be a powerful force. Formally defined, **terrorism** is the use or threat of violence against random or symbolic targets in pursuit of political aims. For terrorists, the end justifies the means. They believe that the status quo is oppressive and that desperate measures are essential to end the suffering of the deprived.

An essential aspect of contemporary terrorism involves use of the media. Terrorists may wish to keep secret their individual identities, but they want their political messages and goals to receive as much publicity as possible. The purpose of many acts of terrorist violence is more symbolic than strategic or tactical. These attacks represent a statement made by people who feel that the world has gone awry, that accepted political paths to problem resolution are ineffective or blocked, and that there is a larger or cosmic struggle going on, raising the stakes and so justifying the means (Juergensmeyer 2003). Whether through calls to the media, anonymous manifestos, or other means, terrorists typically admit responsibility for and defend their violent acts.

> **terrorism** The use or threat of violence against random or symbolic targets in pursuit of political aims.

Terrorism is a global concern. In 2010, there were 11,595 terrorist attacks worldwide resulting in 13,183 deaths (National Counterterrorism Center 2011). Since September 11, 2001, governments around the world have renewed their efforts to fight terrorism. Even though the public generally regards increased surveillance and social control as a necessary evil, these measures have nonetheless raised governance issues. For example, some citizens in the United States and elsewhere have expressed concern that measures such as the USA PATRIOT Act of 2001 threaten civil liberties. Citizens also complain about the heightened anxiety created by the vague "terror alerts" the federal government issues from time to time. Worldwide, immigration and the processing of refugees have slowed to a crawl, separating families and preventing employers from filling job openings. As these efforts to combat political violence illustrate, the term *terrorism* is an apt one (R. Howard and Sawyer 2003).

Aftermath of a 2009 suicide blast attack of a five-star hotel in Pakistan.

peace The absence of war or, more broadly, a proactive effort to develop cooperative relations among nations.

PEACE

Sociologists have considered **peace** both as the absence of war and as a proactive effort to develop cooperative relations among nations. It is important to note, however, that armed conflict involves more than just warring nations. From 1945 to the end of the 20th century, the 25 major wars that occurred between countries killed a total of 3.3 million people. Although this is significant, the 127 civil wars that occurred in the same time period resulted in 16 million deaths. In other words, five times as many people died as a result of conflicts *within* nations as died in wars *between* nations (Fearon and Laitin 2003).

Sociologists and other social scientists who draw on sociological theory and research have tried to identify conditions that deter war. One of their findings is that international trade may act as a deterrent to armed conflict. As countries exchange goods, people, and then cultures, they become more integrated and less likely to threaten each other's security. Viewed from this perspective, not just trade but also immigration and foreign exchange programs have a beneficial effect on international relations.

Another means of fostering peace is the activity of international charities and activist groups, or nongovernmental organizations (NGOs). The Red Cross and Red Crescent, Doctors Without Borders, and Amnesty International

Going GLOBAL

Terrorist Attacks, 2010

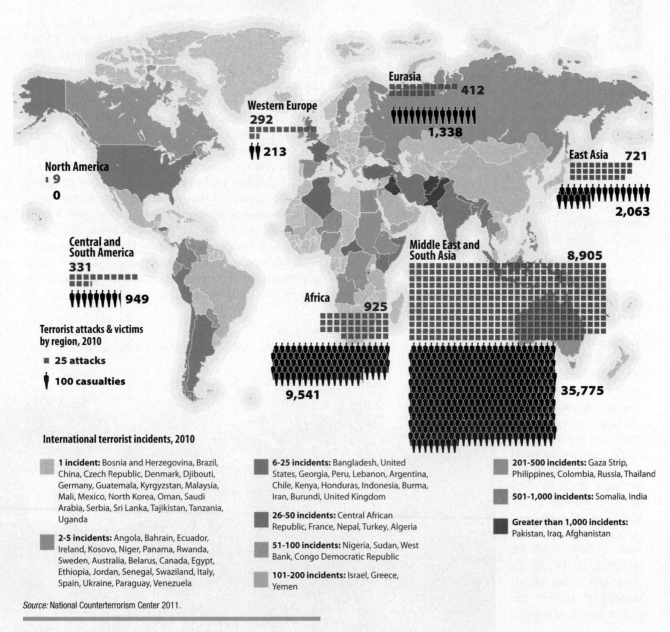

Terrorist attacks & victims by region, 2010

■ **25 attacks**

♦ **100 casualties**

North America
9
0

Western Europe
292
213

Eurasia
412
1,338

East Asia 721
2,063

Central and South America
331
949

Africa
925
9,541

Middle East and South Asia
8,905
35,775

International terrorist incidents, 2010

1 incident: Bosnia and Herzegovina, Brazil, China, Czech Republic, Denmark, Djibouti, Germany, Guatemala, Kyrgyzstan, Malaysia, Mali, Mexico, North Korea, Oman, Saudi Arabia, Serbia, Sri Lanka, Tajikistan, Tanzania, Uganda

2-5 incidents: Angola, Bahrain, Ecuador, Ireland, Kosovo, Niger, Panama, Rwanda, Sweden, Australia, Belarus, Canada, Egypt, Ethiopia, Jordan, Senegal, Swaziland, Italy, Spain, Ukraine, Paraguay, Venezuela

6-25 incidents: Bangladesh, United States, Georgia, Peru, Lebanon, Argentina, Chile, Kenya, Honduras, Indonesia, Burma, Iran, Burundi, United Kingdom

26-50 incidents: Central African Republic, France, Nepal, Turkey, Algeria

51-100 incidents: Nigeria, Sudan, West Bank, Congo Democratic Republic

101-200 incidents: Israel, Greece, Yemen

201-500 incidents: Gaza Strip, Philippines, Colombia, Russia, Thailand

501-1,000 incidents: Somalia, India

Greater than 1,000 incidents: Pakistan, Iraq, Afghanistan

Source: National Counterterrorism Center 2011.

donate their services wherever they are needed, without regard to nationality. In the past decade or so, these NGOs have been expanding in number, size, and scope. By sharing news of local conditions and clarifying local issues, they often prevent conflicts from escalating into violence and war. Some NGOs have initiated cease-fires, reached settlements, and even ended warfare between former adversaries.

Finally, many analysts stress that nations cannot maintain their security by threatening violence. Peace, they contend, can best be maintained by developing strong mutual security agreements among potential adversaries (Etzioni 1965; Shostak 2002). Following this path involves active diplomacy and, to the extent that it involves negotiations with countries viewed as enemies, can be controversial.

From election protests to peace movements, stories such as these provide hope that people can make a difference. Even though large-scale economic trends can have negative impacts on companies, communities, and individuals, as well as shaping political outcomes, positive social change is possible. Sociological analysis helps us to see the underlying processes at work in the economy and politics, and in so doing can assist us in recognizing places in those systems where opportunities for bringing about such change exist.

get Involved!

Investigate! Who contributed and how much to the senators and representatives in your state? What interests do those contributors represent? OpenSecrets.org provides an easily searchable database to track down who gives what to whom.

For REVIEW

I. How is economic and political power organized?

- The two major economic systems are capitalism and socialism, though in practice most economies are some mix of the two. Political systems of government include monarchy, oligarchy, dictatorship, totalitarianism, and democracy. A debate exists when looking at formal power in the United States about the degree to which there is a small, cohesive group of power elites who effectively rule or if leadership is more diverse and pluralistic, operating through democratic processes.

II. How does power operate?

- Power involves the capacity to get others to do what you want, ranging from use of force to acceptance of authority. In the case of authority, followers accept your power as legitimate, whether based on a traditional, rational-legal, or charismatic foundation.

III. How has the economy changed over time?

- From the Industrial Revolution through deindustrialization to the more recent global economic crisis, the modern economy is more dynamic and the consequences of change more far reaching both for nations and for individuals. Through political engagement people have the potential to influence the direction of that change.

Functionalist View

Power and authority are exercised in society to maintain social order for the good of the whole.

The economic system is a social institution that organizes the production, distribution, and consumption of goods and services.

The political system maintains **order** in society through internal policing and diplomatic relations with outsiders.

ORDER, SYSTEMS, ALLOCATION OF RESOURCES
KEY CONCEPTS

Conflict View

Power and authority are exercised to preserve and extend the integrity of the elites in society.

Capitalism primarily benefits the owners of the means of production; **socialism** allows workers to benefit from their own **labor power.**

The **power elite**, a small group of military, industrial, and government leaders, shape the direction of society.

KEY CONCEPTS
COERCION, POWER ELITE, LABOR POWER

Interactionist View

Power and authority are **socially constructed** through interactions with others.

Authority depends upon followers accepting the legitimacy of their leader's right to rule.

In the U.S. political system, leaders are selected by those who **vote**; the political parties try to **persuade** the voters to support their positions.

KEY CONCEPTS
AUTHORITY, PERSUASION

MAKE THE CONNECTION

After reviewing the chapter, answer the following questions:

1
How would each perspective explain the political battles in Wisconsin over rights and responsibilities? (p. 209)

2
How might each perspective seek to explain charismatic authority (p. 211)?

3
How might theorists from each perspective explain war (p. 227)?

4
Are you an active or an apathetic voter? What factors influence your approach? Which perspective best describes the way you participate in the political world?

Pop Quiz

1. **The systematic, widespread withdrawal of investment in basic aspects of productivity such as factories and plants is called**
   a. deindustrialization.
   b. downsizing.
   c. postindustrialization.
   d. gentrification.

2. **What is the term used to describe transfer of work to foreign contractors?**
   a. Exploitation
   b. Offshoring
   c. Alienation
   d. Downsizing

3. **According to Max Weber, what is the definition of power?**
   a. The recognized set of procedures for implementing and achieving societies goals.
   b. The combination of strength and stamina.
   c. The mechanical and electrical energy that provided the foundation for the Industrial Revolution.
   d. The ability to exercise one's will over others, even if they resist.

4. **Which of the following is *not* part of the classification system of authority developed by Max Weber?**
   a. traditional authority
   b. pluralist authority
   c. legal-rational authority
   d. charismatic authority

5. **Within a capitalist economy, what does laissez-faire mean?**
   a. The means of production and distribution in a society are collectively held.
   b. People should compete freely, with minimal government intervention in the economy.
   c. A single business firm controls the market.
   d. Society depends on mechanization to produce its goods and services.

6. **Which of the following are primarily characterized by the transfers of moneys, goods, and services which are not reported to the government?**
   a. globalization
   b. the mixed economy
   c. laissez-faire capitalism
   d. the informal economy

7. **In which type of government do only a few individuals rule?**
   a. a monarchy
   b. a democracy
   c. a dictatorship
   d. an oligarchy

8. **According to the model proposed by C. Wright Mills, in whose hands does power rest?**
   a. the people
   b. the power elite
   c. the aristocracy
   d. representative democracy

9. **When it comes to voter turnout, where does the United States rank compared to other nations?**
   a. the first, with the highest level of turnout
   b. in the top 10 internationally
   c. in about the top third of all nations
   d. in the bottom half of all nations

10. **Which of the following terms best describes the threat of violence against random or symbolic targets in pursuit of political aims?**
   a. politics
   b. power
   c. terrorism
   d. authority

Answers: 1. (a); 2. (b); 3. (d); 4. (b); 5. (b); 6. (d); 7. (d); 8. (b); 9. (d); 10. (c)

SOCIAL CLASS

LIFE CHANGES

Grayer is four years old. He takes lessons in French, Latin, music, swimming, ice skating, karate, and physical education—in addition to attending preschool. When he failed to get into the elite kindergarten of his mother's choice, she hired a grief counselor for him. He lives on Park Avenue in Manhattan with his mother and father, but the person with whom he spends most of his time is his nanny.

Grayer's fictional character was drawn from the real-life experiences of Emma McLaughlin and Nicola Kraus (2002), who worked as nannies to help pay their way through college. They told their stories in the book *The Nanny Diaries,* which later became a film (2007). They depict a world in which, like ours, social class matters.

Sima, one of the nannies in the novel, was an engineer in her home country of El Salvador. She came to the United States with her husband and children, but when he was unable to obtain a green card her husband went back to El Salvador with the kids. Nan, the main nanny character in the book, refers to Sima as "a woman who has a higher degree than I will ever receive, in a subject I couldn't get a passing grade in, and who has been home [to see her husband and children] less than one month in the last twenty-four" (p. 173).

In her book *Just Like Family,* Tasha Blaine (2009) interviewed more than 100 nannies and found that stories of immigrant women leaving their own families for months or years at a time to raise the children of others were not uncommon. They often felt guilty about leaving their children behind only to, in essence, mother someone else's, but they did so to give their own kids a better life financially. The nannies Blaine interviewed frequently found themselves caught in between being an employee and being "like family." This ambiguous relationship often led to their being taken advantage of economically and emotionally. In this chapter we see how the social class positions we occupy, from corporate executive to nanny, shape our hopes, dreams, and likely life outcomes.

>>
- What is social class?
- How does social class operate?
- What are the consequences of social class?

>>Understanding Stratification

Since sociology's inception, sociologists have studied the consequences of difference. In other words, they sought to understand how the social positions we occupy impact our access to resources and opportunities for success. Such analysis seemed particularly urgent in light of the changes wrought by the Industrial Revolution and the resulting transition from traditional to modern society. Emile Durkheim, for example, studied how increased division of labor threatened social integration, and Karl Marx claimed that the expansion of capitalism would result in the concentration of resources in the hands of the few and the impoverishment of the many.

> **stratification** A structured ranking of entire groups of people that perpetuates unequal economic rewards and power in a society.

One of the most significant ways difference is manifested in modern, capitalistic societies is in terms of social class. In the United States, however, class is a touchy subject. When the topic comes up, people often deny that it exists or claim that individual effort alone determines outcomes. Yet, we know that having money opens doors and that some people come from "the wrong side of the tracks." To better understand the consequences of class, we begin by contrasting stratification systems.

SYSTEMS OF STRATIFICATION

Ever since people first began to speculate about the nature of human society, they have focused on the differences between individuals and groups within society. The term *social inequality* (p. 9) describes a condition in which members of society have different amounts of wealth, prestige, or power. Some degree of social inequality characterizes every society. Sociologists refer to social inequality that is built into the structure of society as **stratification**—the structured ranking of entire groups of people that perpetuates unequal economic rewards and power in a society.

Stratification shapes individual opportunity based on the layer or stratum that one occupies in the system. Certain groups of people stand higher in social rankings, control scarce resources, wield power, and receive special treatment. Unequal rewards include income and wealth, but they are also related to the power conveyed by social networks (who you know) and knowledge (what you know). Control over such resources enables one generation to pass on social advantages to the next, producing groups of people arranged in rank order, from low to high.

Sociologists focus on four major systems of stratification: slavery, caste, estate, and class. To understand how each system functions, we should recall the distinction between achieved status and ascribed status from Chapter 5, p. 104. *Ascribed status* is a social position assigned to a person by society without regard for his or her unique talents or characteristics. In contrast, *achieved status* is a social position that a person attains largely through his or her own efforts. The nation's most affluent families generally inherit wealth and status, whereas many members of racial and ethnic

Did You Know?

... Slavery continues to be practiced around the world. Approximately 12.3 million people worldwide—80 percent of whom are female and about half of whom are children—are in bondage to forced labor in areas such as agriculture, mining, textiles, and sex trafficking.

Source: Andrees and Belser 2009.

prisoners of war or individuals captured and sold by pirates. Although succeeding generations could inherit slave status, it was not necessarily permanent. A person's status might change, depending on which city-state happened to triumph in a military conflict. In effect, all citizens had the potential to become slaves or gain freedom, depending on the historical circumstances. By contrast, slavery in the United States and Latin America was an ascribed status, and slaves faced racial and legal barriers to freedom.

> **slavery** A system of enforced servitude in which some people are owned by others as property.
>
> **caste** A hereditary rank, usually religiously dictated, that tends to be fixed and immobile.

Today, the Universal Declaration of Human Rights, which is binding on all members of the United Nations, prohibits slavery in all its forms. According to the United Nations (2010), contemporary forms of slavery include debt bondage, forced labor, child labor and child servitude, sexual slavery, sale of children, forced marriage, and the sale of wives. In many developing countries, bonded laborers are imprisoned in lifetime employment. Though slavery is outlawed in the United States and Europe, guest workers and illegal immigrants have been forced to labor for years under terrible conditions, either to pay off debts or to avoid being turned over to immigration authorities. According to a U.S. Department of Justice report, 82 percent of the trafficking incidents they investigated involved sex trafficking, with 40 percent involving the sexual exploitation of a child (Banks and Kyckelhahn 2011).

minorities inherit disadvantaged status. Age and gender are additional ascribed statuses that influence a person's wealth and social position.

Slavery The most extreme form of legalized social inequality for individuals and groups is **slavery.** Enslaved individuals are the property of other people, who have the right to treat them as they please, as if they were tools or draft animals.

The practice of slavery has varied over different times and places. Most of the slaves in ancient Greece were

Castes Castes are hereditary ranks, usually dictated by religion, that tend to be fixed and immobile. The caste system is generally associated with Hinduism in India and other countries. In India there are four major castes, or *varnas:* priests (*Brahman*), warriors (*Kshatriya*), merchants (*Vaishya*), and artisans/farmers (*Shudra*). A fifth category of outcastes, referred to as the *dalit,* or untouchables, is considered to be so lowly and unclean

military protection against bandits and rival nobles. The basis for the system was the nobles' ownership of land, which was critical to their superior and privileged status. As in systems based on slavery and caste, inheritance of one's position largely defined the estate system. The nobles inherited their titles and property; the peasants were born into a subservient position within an agrarian society.

As the estate system developed, it became more differentiated. Nobles began to achieve varying degrees of authority. By the 12th century a priesthood had emerged in most of Europe, along with classes of merchants and artisans. For the first time, there were groups of people whose wealth did not depend on land ownership or agriculture. This economic change had profound social consequences as the estate system ended and a class system of stratification came into existence.

Social Classes A **class system** is a social ranking based primarily on economic position in which achieved characteristics can influence social mobility. In contrast to slavery and caste systems, in a class system the boundaries between classes are imprecisely defined, and one can move from one stratum, or level, of society to another. Even so, the various layers of social classes are fairly stable over time; a person's position within them shapes her or his access to material, social, and cultural resources. Class standing, though it can be improved, is heavily dependent on ascribed characteristics including family background, race, and ethnicity.

Sociologists commonly use a five-class model to describe the class system in the United States: upper, upper-middle, middle, working, and under class (Beeghley 2007; Rossides 1997). Although the lines separating social classes are not as sharp as the divisions between castes, there are differences between the five classes in terms of key resources. Among these are income, occupation, bureaucratic authority, educational attainment, social networks, and political connections.

The *upper class* is the smallest and most exclusive class, including 1–2 percent of the U.S. population. Members are wealthy, well respected, and politically powerful. Just beneath them are members of the *upper-middle class,* which is composed of business executives and upper-level management, doctors, lawyers, architects, and other professionals. Making up about 15 percent of the population, they have high salaries, participate extensively in politics, and take leadership roles in voluntary associations.

The *middle class* includes less affluent professionals (such as elementary school teachers and nurses), owners of small businesses, and a sizable number of clerical workers. Although not all members of this varied class hold a college degree, they typically hope to send their children

as to have no place within this system of stratification. There are also many minor castes. Caste membership is an ascribed status (at birth, children automatically assume the same position as their parents). Each caste is sharply defined, and members are expected to marry within that caste.

In 1950, after gaining independence from Great Britain, India adopted a new constitution that formally outlawed the caste system. Over the past decade or two, however, urbanization and technological advances have brought more change to India's caste system than the government has in more than half a century. The anonymity of city life tends to blur caste boundaries, allowing the *dalit* to pass unrecognized in temples, schools, and workplaces. The globalization of high technology also has opened up India's social order, bringing new opportunities to those who

possess the skills and ability to capitalize on them, regardless of caste.

Estates A third type of stratification system developed within the feudal societies of medieval Europe. Under the **estate system,** or feudalism, nobles owned the land, which they leased to peasants who worked it and lived on it. The peasants turned over a portion of what they produced to the landowner, who in return offered the peasants

estate system A system of stratification under which peasants were required to work land leased to them by nobles in exchange for military protection and other services. Also known as feudalism.

class system A social ranking based primarily on economic position in which achieved characteristics can influence social mobility.

to college. They make up 30–35 percent of the population. Members of the *working class,* who make up an additional 30–35 percent of population, usually hold jobs that involve manual labor. Some blue-collar members of this class, such as electricians, may have higher incomes than people in the middle class. Yet, even if they have achieved some degree of economic security, they tend to identify with manual workers and have a long history of involvement in the labor movement. Members of the working class are particularly vulnerable, because jobs that once required physical labor are disappearing because of deindustrialization and offshoring of jobs to countries where labor is cheaper.

At the bottom end of the spectrum is the *under class,* known more commonly as "the poor." This class, constituting 15–20 percent of the population, has limited access to the paid labor force, lacks wealth, and is too weak politically to exert significant power. It consists of a disproportionate number of Blacks, Hispanics, immigrants, and single mothers with dependent children.

SOCIAL MOBILITY

A key component of each of these systems of stratification is **social mobility**—the degree to which one can change the social stratum into which one is born. The ascent of a person from a poor background to a position of prestige, power, or financial reward—such as in the film *Maid in Manhattan*—is an example of social mobility. In the film, Jennifer Lopez plays a chambermaid in a big-city hotel who rises to become a company supervisor and the girlfriend of a well-to-do politician. While stories in which the commoner marries the prince truly were fairy tales in the era of the estate system, today they are metaphors for the potential permeability of modern class boundaries.

> **social mobility** Movement of individuals or groups from one position in a society's stratification system to another.
>
> **open system** A social system in which the position of each individual is influenced by his or her achieved status.
>
> **closed system** A social system in which there is little or no possibility of individual social mobility.

Open versus Closed Stratification Systems

Sociologists distinguish between stratification systems that are open versus closed to indicate the degree of social mobility in a society. An **open system** implies that a person's achieved status influences his or her social position. Such a system encourages competition among members of society. The United States has sought to move toward this ideal by removing once-legal barriers faced by women, racial and ethnic minorities, and people born in lower social classes.

At the other extreme is the **closed system,** which allows little or no possibility of individual social mobility. Caste systems are examples of closed systems. In such societies, social placement is based on ascribed statuses, such as race or family background, which cannot be changed.

Types of Social Mobility Sociologists also distinguish between mobility *within* a stratum versus movement *between* levels. For example, a bus driver who becomes a hotel clerk moves from one social position to another of approximately the same rank. Sociologists call this kind of movement **horizontal mobility.** However, if the bus driver were to become a lawyer, he or she would experience **vertical mobility**—the movement of an individual from one social position to another of a different rank (Sorokin [1927] 1959). Vertical mobility can involve moving upward or downward in a society's stratification system.

> **horizontal mobility** The movement of an individual from one social position to another of the same rank.
>
> **vertical mobility** The movement of an individual from one social position to another of a different rank.
>
> **intergenerational mobility** Changes in the social position of children relative to their parents.
>
> **intragenerational mobility** Changes in social position within a person's adult life.

Sociologists also contrast the significance of mobility across an individual's career or lifetime versus movement that spans generations. **Intergenerational mobility** involves changes in the social position of children relative to their parents. Thus, a plumber whose father was a physician provides an example of downward intergenerational mobility. A film star whose parents were both factory workers illustrates upward intergenerational mobility. Because education contributes significantly to upward mobility, any barrier to the pursuit of advanced degrees limits intergenerational mobility (Isaacs, Sawhill, and Haskins 2008).

Intragenerational mobility, in contrast, involves changes in social position within a person's adult life. Thus, a woman who enters the paid labor force as a teacher's aide and eventually becomes superintendent of the school district experiences upward intragenerational mobility. A man who becomes a cab driver after his accounting firm goes bankrupt undergoes downward intragenerational mobility.

SOC THINK

What is the story of social mobility in your family? To what extent have there been shifts both across and within generations? What factors, such as family connections or historical events, contributed to the social mobility that occurred?

In the United States one way to define the "American Dream" is as upward vertical mobility that is intragenerational. In other words, a person could experience a significant shift in social class position over the course of her or his career, from a relatively low-level position to one of significant wealth and power. Though this does happen, as we will see below, the "American reality" is that we tend to end up in positions relatively close to where we began.

5 Movies on SOCIAL CLASS

The Help
In the 1960s South, three women from different classes build an unlikely friendship.

Winter's Bone
A teen living in the Ozarks investigates her father's criminal dealings.

Water
An Indian widow attempts to escape the social restrictions of her position.

Trouble the Water
Two street hustlers become heroes in the aftermath of Hurricane Katrina.

Pride and Prejudice
Social class dictates young women's lives in 19th-century English society.

>>Sociological Perspectives on Stratification

From early on in the discipline, sociologists have examined the role that control over valued resources plays in social stratification. As we saw in Chapter 9, Karl Marx was critical of capitalism because the social class system prevented workers from receiving the full benefits of their labor power. Max Weber, who sought to extend Marx's model and make it more broadly applicable, argued that three primary resources shape social position: class, status, and party. More recently, Pierre Bourdieu has highlighted the significance of culture as an additional resource. We will look at each of their models in turn.

MARX ON CLASS

In Karl Marx's view, social relations during any period of history depend on who owns the means of production, such as land, factories, machines, and tools. Control over production was important to Marx because people cannot produce—the very ability that he placed at the

Did You Know?

In 2011, CEOs at the top 500 U.S. companies received an average of $10.5 million in total compensation, including salary, bonuses, and stock options. McKesson's John Hammergren topped the list at $131 million.

Source: DeCarlo 2012.

center of what makes us unique—without access to such resources (see Chapter 9). For Marx, the group that owns the material means of production possesses the most significant source of power in a society. Under the feudal estate system, for example, most production was agricultural, and the nobility owned the land. Peasants had little choice but to work according to terms dictated by the landowners.

As we saw in Chapter 9, Marx argued that so long as scarcity exists, there will always be a divide between the haves and the have-nots. Under capitalism, the two main classes are the bourgeoisie and the proletariat. The **bourgeoisie,** or capitalist class, owns the means of production, such as factories and machinery; the **proletariat,** or working class, lacks such ownership.

The competition that is at the heart of capitalism initially pits capitalists against each other in their pursuit of profit in the marketplace. Their success, however, also depends on competition between the bourgeoisie and the proletariat. In order to succeed against their competitors, individual capitalists seek to reduce production costs so that they can lower prices, increase sales, and maintain profits. One of their major expenses is the cost of labor. They reduce these costs through mechanization (inventing new machines capable of taking over more of the labor), de-skilling (simplifying the work process by breaking it down into its most basic steps so that minimal knowledge is required), and offshoring (finding labor in other parts of the world capable of doing the work for less money). It's not that capitalists are personally greedier than others or have a particular desire to exploit their workers; they act based on the principles inherent in the system. If they don't match the steps taken by their competitors, they run the risk of losing market share and going out of business.

Marx argued that this downward pressure on workers' wages and working conditions is unrelenting. It ultimately leads to the development of a massive global working class of largely poor, unskilled workers competing against each

other for low-wage jobs, resulting in racial, ethnic, and nationalistic conflict among the proletariat. Ironically, it is the technological innovation of capitalism that makes a better future possible. Marx praised this aspect of capitalism because it solves the problem of production like no other previous economic system. Capitalism, he writes, was "the first to show what man's activity can bring about. It has accomplished wonders far surpassing Egyptian pyramids, Roman aqueducts, and Gothic cathedrals" (Marx and Engels [1848] 1998:38). As a result, we no longer face inevitable scarcity. We can now produce enough so that no one in the world needs to go hungry.

Once this technological obstacle to providing for all our needs was solved, Marx felt that the only obstacle to an equitable society would be the capitalist system of social relations. Its emphasis on private property enabled the few at the top, the bourgeoisie, to own and control much more than they could ever hope to need or want while the majority at the bottom, the proletariat, struggled. Eventually, Marx argued, the proletariat would see that they had no real interest in the existing set of social relations. They would develop **class consciousness**—a subjective awareness of common vested interests and the need for collective political action to bring about social change. This would lead to the overthrow of capitalism in favor of a system of more equitable distribution in the form of socialism and then communism.

A question that often arises in response to Marx's work is this: why hasn't that revolution happened? One answer is that Marx thought capitalists would work against the development of such class consciousness by shaping society's accepted values and norms. The term *dominant ideology* describes a set of cultural beliefs and practices that helps to maintain powerful social, economic, and political interests. Private property is a core principle of this ideology, but our failure to recognize the collective efforts that go into the production of any products and services contributes as well. For Marx, the bourgeoisie controlled not only material resources but also the means of producing beliefs about reality through religion, education, and the media (Abercrombie, Hill, and Turner 1980, 1990; Marx [1845] 2000). As a result, workers had to overcome what Marx termed **false consciousness**—an attitude held by members of a class that does not accurately reflect their objective position. A worker with false consciousness may adopt an individualistic viewpoint toward capitalist exploitation ("*I* am being exploited by *my* boss").

bourgeoisie Karl Marx's term for the capitalist class, comprising the owners of the means of production.

proletariat Karl Marx's term for the working class in a capitalist society who lack ownership of the means of production.

class consciousness In Karl Marx's view, a subjective awareness held by members of a class regarding their common vested interests and need for collective political action to bring about social change.

false consciousness A term used by Karl Marx to describe an attitude held by members of a class that does not accurately reflect their objective position.

In contrast, the class-conscious worker realizes that all workers are being exploited by the bourgeoisie and have a common stake in revolution.

WEBER ON POWER

Max Weber accepted Marx's premise that social class plays a substantial role in shaping outcomes, but he argued that Marx's conception of power was too narrow, because it focused almost exclusively on ownership of the means of production. Weber argued that power was multidimensional, and he identified class, status, and party as its three critical components.

Weber used the term **class** to refer to a group of people who have a similar level of economic resources. He identified two core elements of class: material resources and skill knowledge in the marketplace. In the first instance, class is about how much you own. Like Marx, this included ownership of the means of production, but Weber argued that ownership of other economic resources, including land, savings, and stocks, also defined a person's class position. And, while Marx maintained that mechanization and extreme division of labor would make skilled labor less valuable under capitalism, Weber argued that, given the complexity of modern society, knowledge would continue to be a valuable commodity in the labor market,

class A group of people who have a similar level of economic resources.

status group People who share the same perceived level of prestige.

something that employers would reward. By developing our skill knowledge—for example, by going to college—we enhance our class position.

Whereas class represents an economic resource, status is a social resource. Weber used the term **status group** to refer to people who share the same perceived level of prestige. The power that your status provides depends upon how others view you, including both positive and negative estimations of honor. Membership in a highly regarded group "has its privileges," whether as a medical doctor or a Supreme Court justice. Similarly, being part of a group defined as low status by members of the dominant society, such as ex-cons or "illegal immigrants," limits opportunity (even if the skill knowledge members of such groups possess would be of particular value to possible employers). Membership in status groups is often associated with a particular lifestyle, including the kind of car you drive or the vacations you take. Class and status are not necessarily linked. It is possible to have a high status and low class standing, as is the case for many clergy members who are highly regarded within their communities of faith, but who often earn a relatively modest income.

The third major element in Weber's multidimensional model of stratification focuses on organizational resources. **Party** refers to the capacity to organize to accomplish some particular goal. This is what we mean when we talk of a political party, but such organization extends beyond politics to all spheres of life. As we have seen previously with Weber, bureaucracies represent the

Personal Sociology

Cultural Capital

As a professor, I have seen that grades are shaped by more than just effort and inherent intellectual ability. Students with more cultural capital, including significant background educational resources, simply do not have to work as hard. Seniors in my introductory course, for example, know the rules of the game. In comparison, first-year students often have a hard time distinguishing what is essential versus what is secondary. Over time, however, most learn how to study effectively. This same principle is at work before students even arrive on campus. Students who come to college with the kinds of cultural capital that professors reward have advantages over those who lack such resources.

ideal form of this resource because they are organized explicitly to maximize available resources and to accomplish their goals in the most efficient manner possible. For Weber, party was a potential resource, available to any individuals or groups who would seize it. The civil rights movement in the United States provides a classic example. With minimal class or status resources as defined by the larger society, organization was critical to the success of this movement.

SOCTHINK

How might a group coordinate its class, status, and party resources to accomplish its goals? Pick a group on campus or in your community that is seeking to bring about social change, and imagine how you might advise group members using Weber's principles.

Weber maintained that, in practice, these three resources work together to shape individual and group power. Each factor influences the other two, and in fact the rankings on these three dimensions often tend to coincide. For example, George W. Bush came from an extremely wealthy family, attended exclusive preparatory schools, received a B.A from Yale and an M.B.A. from Harvard, and went on to become president of the United States. Like Bush, many people from affluent backgrounds achieve high status and demonstrate impressive political organization.

BOURDIEU ON CULTURE

Marx emphasized material resources, and Weber highlighted the significance of social resources in the form of both status and party. Sociologist Pierre Bourdieu added to these the significance of cultural resources. Bourdieu introduced the concept of **cultural capital,** by which he meant our tastes, knowledge, attitudes, language, and ways of thinking that we exchange in interaction with others. Often associated with artistic or literary preferences, cultural capital goes much deeper than this because it is rooted in our perception of reality itself. For Bourdieu, because some culture is more highly valued than other culture, it is a form of power.

> **party** The capacity to organize to accomplish some particular goal.
>
> **cultural capital** Our tastes, knowledge, attitudes, language, and ways of thinking that we exchange in interaction with others.

Bourdieu argued that people in different social class positions possess different types of cultural capital. From NASCAR to Mozart, for example, the tastes of the working class typically differ from those of the upper class. Symphonic concerts, operas, and foreign films, for instance, are considered "high culture," whereas "pop culture," including popular movies, TV shows, and most music CDs, is considered "middle-brow" or below. People draw distinctions, for example, between watching *Masterpiece* on PBS versus *Wipeout* and listening to Placido Domingo versus

Whether it is the rags-to-riches dreams of *American Idol,* the glitz of *Dancing with the Stars,* the upper-middle-class aspirations of *The Apprentice,* or the voyeuristic appeal of *Jersey Shore,* TV shows have found social class lifestyle differences a tempting topic. In the show *Undercover Boss,* a corporate executive puts on a disguise to work at an entry-level job in his or her firm. They almost inevitably discover that their class-based, taken-for-granted assumptions about these workers are wrong. They find that the jobs these workers do are much more complex and demanding than they assumed and that the people who do them are committed and hardworking.

Lady Gaga. Such judgments are based on a certain level of cultural elitism in which those at the top are able to define their preferences as apparently superior to those of the masses (Wilson 2007). The cultural capital of people who are working class, often disparaged as redneck or ghetto, is valued least of all—until it is claimed by others as their own, as was the case with jazz, blues, rock and roll, and rap (Gans 1971).

When we interact with others, we draw on the cultural capital resources we possess. Such interaction is fairly easy with others who share the same basic set of resources. When interaction occurs with others who possess a different stock of cultural capital, however, it becomes more complex. We see these kinds of difficulties when executives try to interact casually with workers on the factory floor or when we find ourselves dining in a place where we aren't quite sure what the rules are. If this were only a matter of social difference between various subcultures, it might not be a big deal. But the cultural capital of the elite is also tied to their control over economic and social resources. As a result, cultural capital can be used as a form of exclusion from jobs, organizations, and opportunities. For example, a qualified applicant may not be hired because, during the interview, he or she used inappropriate syntax or was not adequately familiar with cultural references, such as current news events or the latest in the world of golf. Employers tend to hire people they feel comfortable with, and cultural capital plays a significant role in that process (Kanter 1993).

Compounding this problem of cultural inequality is the fact that our preferences and perceptions often pass down from parent to child in the same way that material capital is inherited. Parents teach their children linguistic patterns and cultural tastes, from the use of double negatives to the appreciation of literature (Rothstein 2009). Cultural capital is also reproduced in the next generation in the context of schools, where class distinctions within the community shape the curriculum and patterns of discipline. Sociologist Jessi Streib (2011) found that, already by age four, children had adopted cultural conventions based on their social class positions. For eight months she conducted research at a diverse preschool and found that children from upper-middle-class families were more talkative and demanding of the teacher's time and attention than were working-class kids. The linguistic style of the higher-class children was more consistent with the classroom culture, and, as a result, they were more likely to get their needs met.

Social mobility from this perspective involves more than just acquiring more money and better social connections. Winning the lottery, for example, does not transform a person at the bottom of the hierarchy into one at the top, or, as Bourdieu put it, "Having a million does not in itself make one able to live like a millionaire" (1984:374). Such movement requires a social and cultural transformation as well. For mobility to happen, individuals must earn and learn a different set of knowledge and skills, as well as a whole new lifestyle: new tastes, attitudes, language, and thoughts.

MATERIAL, SOCIAL, AND CULTURAL RESOURCES

Combining insights from these perspectives, we can point to three critical categories of resources that shape the positions we occupy and influence our likelihood for social mobility. Material resources refer to economic resources that we own or control, including money, property, and land. Social resources include prestige based on the position we occupy and connections based on the social networks we are a part of. It turns out that the old saying "It's not what you know; it's who you know" has some truth to it. Position and connections make it possible for us to increase the likelihood of accomplishing

> Anyone who has ever struggled with poverty knows how extremely expensive it is to be poor.
>
> James A. Baldwin

Did You Know?

. . . Six members of the Walton family, heirs of Wal-Mart founder Sam Walton, own more wealth than the bottom 40 percent of U.S. families combined.

our goals. Finally, cultural resources include our tastes, language, and way of looking at the world. They represent our knowledge of cognitive, normative, and material elements of culture that we can draw on when acting to accomplish our goals. A simple but classic example involves knowing which fork to use for the various courses of a formal dinner. But it also includes knowing how to respond when we are put on the spot, whether in a business meeting, at a rock concert, or in class. Viewing social class in terms of material, social, and cultural resources makes social class a much more useful concept when trying to map our social lives or figure out why we think and act as we do.

All societies are characterized by some degree of stratification. Tracking how material, social, and cultural resources are defined, distributed, and exchanged provides a more complete picture of how stratification works in any given context. Some amount of inequality may be inevitable, but the extent of inequality practiced is variable. We turn next to an analysis of the distribution of such resources in the United States, a society committed to the potentially conflicting values of equality, which is built on the principle of sameness, and competition, which presumes difference.

>>Social Class in the United States

Social class dividing lines in the United States are not as clear-cut or firm as they were historically in, say, England. When we take a step back, however, we see that social class differences do affect our everyday lives. We may not label them as such, and we might want to dismiss their significance. Nevertheless, looking through the lens of class as highlighted by these three resources brings to the surface differences that we already recognize as important.

CULTURAL CAPITAL

In some ways it is helpful to look first at cultural resources because, although we recognize that such differences exist, we may not recognize how significant they can be. If one person likes Chopin and another likes Taylor Swift, what difference does that make? As indicated above, however, such tastes do not exist in isolation; rather, they are tied to social and material resources and can serve as a means of exclusion (Halle 1993; Wilson 2007). Looking at just a few examples, we can appreciate the degree to which we already see class, even if we don't usually identify it as such.

We can recognize class in the clothes we wear, and even in the terms we use to describe them, such as "business casual" or "blue collar." Some people would not be caught dead wearing a suit and tie (or maybe that's the only way they will wear them), whereas others are incapable of being comfortable at work in blue jeans and a T-shirt. And brands can matter, whether it's Lilly Pulitzer, Sean Jean, J. McLaughlin, Gap, Rocawear, H&M, Christian Louboutin, Baby Phat, Juicy Couture, Wrangler, Calypso, Abercrombie & Fitch, Coach, or Gucci. Even the fabrics clothes are made of suggest class differences, with higher classes more likely to wear clothes made out of organic materials (such as wool, silk, or cotton) and lower classes more likely to wear synthetic fabrics (including nylon, rayon, and orlon). This is likely driven not only by the initial cost differences for such materials, but also by the long-term care costs for dry-cleaning.

─SOCTHINK─

Paul Fussell (1992), in his book *Class: A Guide through the American Status System,* argued that the writing on our clothes says a lot about our social class. What story do the logos, brands, and writing on your clothes tell about you? How might your clothing choices have differed had you been in a different class position?

We also see class differences when it comes to houses. Just driving through neighborhoods, we recognize class indicators of houses: the distance they are located from the street; the composition of a driveway, if there is one; the fastidiousness of lawn care; the existence of flamingoes, gnomes, or gazing balls; and the presence of pillars or fountains. When it comes to where we live, expressions such as "the wrong side of the tracks," "snob hill," and "McMansion" point to our recognition that class matters.

Similarly, class makes a difference when it comes to vacations. Elites might head to Martha's Vineyard or the Hamptons, or they might "summer" in Nepal or Istanbul. Middle-class people are more likely to head to Disney World or perhaps go on a cruise, though either dream vacation may be possible only after having saved for years or by going into debt.

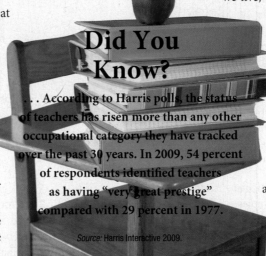

Did You Know?

. . . According to Harris polls, the status of teachers has risen more than any other occupational category they have tracked over the past 30 years. In 2009, 54 percent of respondents identified teachers as having "very great prestige" compared with 29 percent in 1977.

Source: Harris Interactive 2009.

Because money and vacation time are often limited, working-class families are more likely to go on a one-week trip, probably not too far from home, to which they are more likely to drive, and it might involve camping.

We could look at other areas, too, including what we eat (fast food versus haute cuisine), what we drink (Bud Light versus fine wine), and what sports we watch (NASCAR and professional wrestling versus tennis and America's Cup yachting). In all kinds of ways, our preferences are shaped by our social class positions. Yet we seldom take seriously the source of such preferences or their effect on the choices we make and the doors that these choices may open or close to us.

STATUS AND PRESTIGE

We have a sense of where people fit relative to one another. Some we see as higher, whereas others we see as lower. We have seen as much already with regard to cultural preferences, but when it comes to status, it is not just what people like that we rank, but also who they are. Sociologists seek to describe those systems of ranking and the advantages and disadvantages they convey.

Occupational Prestige One way sociologists describe the relative social class positions people occupy is by focusing on their occupational prestige. The term **prestige** refers to the respect and admiration that an occupation holds in a society. Fairly or not, "my daughter, the physicist" connotes something very different from "my daughter, the waitress." Prestige is independent of the

Prestige Rankings of Occupations

Occupation	Score
Physician	86
Lawyer	75
College professor	74
Architect	73
Dentist	72
Psychologist	69
Clergy	69
Pharmacist	68
Registered nurse	66
High school teacher	66
Accountant	65
Athlete	65
Elementary school teacher	64
Banker	63
Veterinarian	62
Legislator	61
Airline pilot	61
Police officer or detective	60
Actors and directors	58
Librarian	54
Firefighter	53
Social worker	52
Dental hygienist	52
Electrician	51
Funeral director	49
Farm manager	48
Mail carrier	47
Secretary	46
Insurance agent	45
Bank teller	43
Nurse's aide	42

Occupation	Score
Farmer	40
Correctional officer	40
Receptionist	39
Carpenter	39
Barber	36
Child care worker	36
Hotel clerk	32
Bus driver	32
Auto body repairer	31
Truck driver	30
Salesworker (shoes)	28
Garbage collector	28
Waiter and waitress	28
Bartender	25
Bill collector	24
Farm worker	23
Janitor	22
Maid	20
Newspaper vendor	19
Car washer	19

Note: 100 is the highest and 0 the lowest possible prestige score.

Source: J. Davis, Smith, and Marsden 2007.

prestige The respect and admiration that an occupation holds in a society.

esteem The reputation that a specific person has earned within an occupation.

particular individual who occupies a job, a characteristic that distinguishes it from esteem. **Esteem** refers to the reputation that a specific person has earned within an occupation. Therefore, we can say that the position of president of the United States has high prestige even though it has been occupied by people with varying degrees of esteem. A hairdresser may have the esteem of his clients, but he lacks the prestige of a corporate executive.

Socioeconomic Status As a single variable, occupation provides us with a sense of where people stand, but status involves more than just occupational prestige. In their research, sociologists add variables to the mix to gain a more complete picture of social class standing. These include such things as the value of homes, sources of income, assets, years in present occupations, neighborhoods, and considerations regarding dual careers. Adding these variables will not necessarily paint an alternative picture of class differentiation in the United States, but it does allow sociologists to measure class in a more complex and multidimensional way. When researchers use multiple measures, they typically speak of **socioeconomic status (SES),** a measure of social class that is based on income, education, occupation, and related variables.

> **socioeconomic status (SES)** A measure of class that is based on income, education, occupation, and related variables.
>
> **income** Wages and salaries measured over some period, such as per hour or year.
>
> **wealth** The total of all a person's material assets, including savings, land, stocks, and other types of property, minus his or her debt at a single point in time.

One of the lessons we learn from SES research is that society often undervalues, in terms of prestige and pay, work that is essential for our individual and collective survival. In an effort to make the value of women's contribution to the economy more visible, for example, the International Women Count Network, a global grassroots feminist organization, has sought to give a monetary value to women's unpaid work. Besides providing symbolic recognition of women's contributions to society, it proposes that this value also be used to calculate pension and other benefits that are based on wages received. The United Nations has placed an $11-*trillion* price tag on unpaid labor by women, largely in child care, housework, and agriculture. In 2009, in order to ensure the full integration of women into the formal economy and to have their economic contributions considered in policy making, the United Nations Commission on the Status of Women called on governments to incorporate the value of unpaid work in the household into policies and budgets.

Using the results from a series of national surveys, sociologists have identified prestige rankings for more than 700 occupations. They created a scale with 0 as the lowest possible score and 100 as the highest, and ranked the occupations based on the results of their surveys. Physician, lawyer, dentist, and college professor were among the most highly regarded occupations, whereas bartender, farmworker, janitor, maid, and car washer were near the bottom. Sociologists have found a significant amount of stability in such rankings from 1925 to the present (J. Davis, Smith, and Marsden 2007). This suggests that we do confer status to people based on the positions they occupy. Someone with a higher status is more likely to get the benefit of the doubt because of the position she or he occupies, regardless of her or his individual characteristics, whereas the reverse is true for someone from a lower position.

INCOME AND WEALTH

Cultural capital and status provide a clearer picture of how we perceive social class, but income and wealth serve as its material foundation. **Income** refers to wages and salaries measured over some period, such as per hour or year. **Wealth** encompasses all of a person's material assets, including savings, land, stocks, and other types of property, minus his or her debts at a single point in time. If you were to sell everything you own and pay off all your debts, what you had left would be the value of your wealth. These material resources make our class-based lifestyles possible (Bourdieu 1986). As such, if we are to understand social classes in the United States, we need a clear picture of their distribution.

The Income Pie: Percentage Share of Total Income

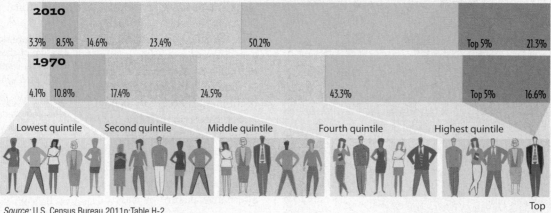

2010

3.3% | 8.5% | 14.6% | 23.4% | 50.2% | Top 5% | 21.3%

1970

4.1% | 10.8% | 17.4% | 24.5% | 43.3% | Top 5% | 16.6%

Lowest quintile | Second quintile | Middle quintile | Fourth quintile | Highest quintile

Top 5%

Source: U.S. Census Bureau 2011p:Table H-2.

Income Income inequality is a basic characteristic of a class system. In 2010, the median household income in the United States was $49,445, approximately the same as the previous year. In other words, half of all households had higher incomes in that year, and half had lower incomes. But this fact does not fully convey the income disparities in our society. We get some sense of income inequality by contrasting the median (middle) score with the mean (arithmetic average), which in 2010 was $67,530. The mean is so much higher because some people make a lot more money than others, which draws the mean up, making it a less useful statistic for describing "average" or typical income (DeNavas-Walt, Proctor, and Smith 2011).

We gain additional insight into this inequality by looking at the relative placement of households from bottom to top. One of the most common ways to present income dispersion is to line up all income-earning households from low to high and then break them into quintiles, or blocks of 20 percent. There are approximately 119 million households in the United States, so each quintile would include an equal number of about 23.7 million households. Doing so allows us to get a sense of what the average income is within each of these quintiles, along with the percentage of the total income pie that each quintile earns.

Mean Household Income by Quintile

$287,686

$169,633

$79,040

$49,309

$28,636

$11,034

Lowest quintile | Second quintile | Middle quintile | Fourth quintile | Highest quintile | Top 5%

Source: U.S. Census Bureau 2011p:Table H-3.

As we can see in the accompanying graphs, looking at the population in this way shows a significant degree of income inequality. Focusing on the extremes, the mean income for households in the lowest quintile is $11,034, while households in the top quintile average $169,633. Those households in the top 5 percent, the ones most responsible for bringing up the arithmetic mean, average $287,686. Those in the bottom quintile earn just 3.3 percent of the nation's total income, while those in the top quintile earn 50.2 percent. In fact, the top 5 percent earns a significantly greater percent of total income than the bottom 40 percent combined (DeNavas-Walt et al. 2011).

As we saw in Chapter 9, the Occupy Wall Street brought particular attention to the income advantages of the top 1 percent. Economists Thomas Piketty and Emmanuel Saez found that, in 2010, the average income for those in this group was $418,378. Even within this category, however, substantial income differences exist. At the top of the top, for example, the average income for the 15,617 families in the top 0.01 percent was $23.8 million. And, according to the IRS, the top 400 U.S. households had an average income of $271 million. On the other end of the scale, 163 million households reported incomes under $15,000 (DeNavas-Walt et al. 2011; Internal Revenue Service 2011; Piketty and Saez 2012).

Income inequality has increased steadily since 1970. Former Federal Reserve Board Chair Alan Greenspan was referring to this trend when he told Congress that the rising gap between the rich and the poor in the United States is a "very disturbing trend" that threatens democratic society (Greenspan 2005). Just how dramatic has this growth in inequality been? As the "Income Pie" chart, on the previous page shows, the share earned by each of the bottom quintiles has decreased since 1970, whereas the top quintile now earns almost one-half of total income. This represents the greatest degree of income inequality since before the Great Depression.

Americans do not appear to be seriously concerned about income and wealth inequality in the United States. In a comparison of opinions about social inequality in 27 different countries, respondents in the United States were less aware than those in other countries of the extent of inequality of the income distribution. Americans would prefer to "level down" the top of the nation's earning distribution, but compared to people in other countries, they are less concerned about reducing income differentials at the bottom of the distribution (Osberg and Smeeding 2006).

Wealth Wealth in the United States is even more unevenly distributed than income. The median wealth for households in 2009 was $106,000, but the mean was $554,500. This large difference is a consequence of the extreme amounts of wealth held by the richest households. We get a glimpse of that difference by comparing the top end to the bottom. On the low end, the mean wealth for the bottom 20 percent of households was −$27,000, meaning they owed more than they owned. The top 20 percent, in contrast, had a

Distribution of Wealth Owned, by Percentile

Wealth owned	Percentile of population
	99–100th
	95–99th
35.6%	90–95th
	80–90th
27.9%	60–80th
	40–60th
11.6%	20–40th
12.2%	
10.6%	0–20th
3.3%	
0.3%	
−1.4%	

Source: Allegretto 2011.

Did You Know?

... During the Great Recession of 2007–2009, the richest fifth of Americans lost 16 percent of their wealth, and the remaining 80 percent of households lost 25 percent. Although those at the bottom lost the highest percentage, households at the top lost the most money, including the top 1 percent, which lost $5.2 million.

Source: Allegretto 2011.

SOCTHINK

Why do you think that most Americans do not seem to be aware of or concerned about the degree of income inequality in the United States? To what extent might it be due to the power of the American Dream, the influence of the media, or the working of the dominant ideology?

mean wealth of $1.7 million per household (Allegretto 2011: Table 3).

Analysis of the percentage distribution of wealth illustrates the level of wealth inequality. The top 20 percent of households owns 87.2 percent of total wealth in the United States, and the bottom 80 percent split the remaining 12.8 percent. In fact, the top 1 percent owns 35.6 percent of all wealth—more than the bottom 90 percent combined—which works out to 225 times more than the household median. The concentration of ownership is even more extreme when it comes to stocks, with the top 1 percent owning 48.3 percent of the total value (Allegretto 2011). In fact, the only place where the bottom 50 percent comes close to matching its share of wealth relative to its portion of the population is with debt. The bottom 50 percent owes 52.8 percent of all installment debt and 43.1 percent of outstanding credit card debt (Kennickell 2009).

Middle-Class Struggles Even in an era of overall prosperity, those in the middle class often struggle just to make ends meet. Middle incomes have remained steady or even fallen over the past 40 years, while the income shares of those in the top quintile, and especially the top 5 percent, increased substantially. Health care costs have risen dramatically, and the cost of a college education, a critical resource for social mobility, has gone up even faster. As a result of the post-2008 economic downturn, many middle-class employees lost their jobs and the ripple effect led to increased bankruptcies and mortgage foreclosures. Whereas in the 1950s a single-income family could earn sufficient income to provide a middle-class lifestyle, most families now find they must rely on two incomes, an option not available for all families (Bucks et al. 2009; DeNavas-Walt et al. 2010; Lewin 2008).

Sociologists and other scholars have identified several factors that have contributed to the struggles middle-class families face:

- *Disappearing opportunities for those with little education.* Today, increasing numbers of jobs require formal schooling, yet fewer than a third of adults aged 25–29 have a college degree.
- *Global competition and rapid advances in technology.* These two trends, which began several decades ago, have rendered workers more replaceable than they once were. Increasingly, these trends are affecting the more complex jobs that were once the bread and butter of middle-class life.
- *Growing dependence on the temporary workforce.* For those workers who have no other job, these positions are tenuous at best, because they rarely offer health care coverage or retirement benefits.
- *The rise of new-growth industries and nonunion work-places.* In the past, workers in heavy industry were able to achieve middle-class incomes through the efforts of strong labor unions. But today, the

growth areas in the economy are in service jobs and large retail outlets. Though these industries have added employment opportunities, they are often nonunion jobs and at the lower end of the wage scale.

In response to these concerns, observers note that living standards in the United States are improving. Middle-class families want large homes, college degrees for their children, and high-quality health care—the cost of which has been rising faster than inflation. Accomplishing these goals, however, has often meant becoming a dual-income family, working longer hours, or taking multiple jobs (Leonhardt 2007; Massey 2007).

POVERTY

In 2010, 46.2 million people in the United States—15.1 percent of the population—were living in poverty. Based on official calculations, a family consisting of two adults and two children with a combined annual income of $22,113 or less fell below the poverty line. By contrast, a single

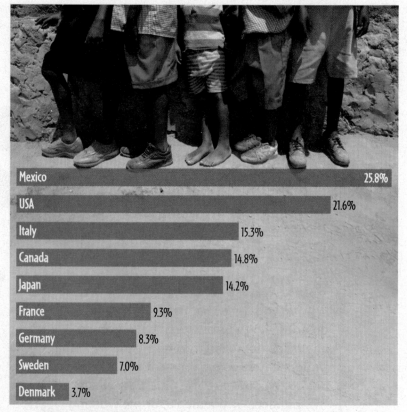

Going GLOBAL

The Poverty Rate in Households with Children, Selected Countries

Country	Rate
Mexico	25.8%
USA	21.6%
Italy	15.3%
Canada	14.8%
Japan	14.2%
France	9.3%
Germany	8.3%
Sweden	7.0%
Denmark	3.7%

Source: OECD 2011:Table EQ2.2.

person under the age of 65 must earn less than $11,344 annually to be officially considered poor (DeNavas-Walt et al. 2011).

Defining Poverty

Such figures make it seem like a simple matter to define who is living in poverty: You are either above the threshold or below it. Sociologists have found, however, that our conceptions of poverty vary. For example, we can define poverty in either absolute or relative terms.

Absolute poverty refers to a minimum level of subsistence that no family should be expected to live below. According to this definition, someone who is below the poverty level ultimately lacks sufficient resources to survive. Many nations, including the United States, use some form of this criterion as the basis of their definition of poverty. As we can see in the accompanying graph, a comparatively high proportion of children in U.S. households are poor, meaning that their families are unable to afford necessary consumer goods (food, shelter, and clothing). This cross-national comparison actually understates the extent of poverty in the United States because U.S. residents are likely to pay more for housing, health care, child care, and education than residents of other countries, where such expenses are often subsidized.

In contrast, **relative poverty** is a floating standard of deprivation by which people at the bottom of a society, whatever their lifestyles, are judged to be disadvantaged in comparison with the nation as a whole. For example, people who have sufficient food, clothing, and shelter might nonetheless be considered poor if they live in a wealthy nation such as the United States, because they can't afford to buy things the culture defines as important but are not essential for survival. Similarly, someone who would be considered poor by U.S. standards would be well-off by global standards of poverty; hunger and starvation are daily realities in many regions of the world. In addition, when viewed in historical terms, someone currently defined as poor may be better off in absolute terms than a poor person in the 1930s or 1960s.

The poverty line in the United States is calculated based on a formula established in 1964. President Lyndon B. Johnson had recently declared a War on Poverty, but at the time, no official measure of poverty existed. To enact an official measure, the Johnson administration turned to the work of Mollie Orshansky, a food economist at the research bureau of the Social Security Administration. Orshansky proposed combining two facts to establish a general poverty threshold. The first came from a study that found that families spend approximately one-third of their budget on food. The second was the estimated cost of a minimally nutritious diet established by U.S. Department of Agriculture dieticians. Orshansky combined these two pieces of information to establish the poverty threshold as three times the cost of the USDA diet. She assumed that families facing poverty would cut back on both food and nonfood expenditures at approximately the same rate so that the 3-to-1 ratio would hold (Fisher 1992, 2008; Orshansky 1965).

absolute poverty A minimum level of subsistence that no family should be expected to live below.

relative poverty A floating standard of deprivation by which people at the bottom of a society, whatever their lifestyles, are judged to be disadvantaged in comparison with the nation as a whole.

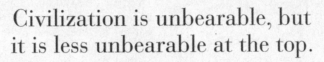

Civilization is unbearable, but it is less unbearable at the top.

Timothy Leary

There has been a long-standing debate about whether this approach to defining poverty in the United States measures the true nature of poverty. For example, critics argue that the measure is too simplistic, or that the multiplier should be higher because families now spend one-fourth or one-fifth of their budget on food. Recognizing the limits of the official definition, the U.S. government started calculating a supplemental measure of poverty in the fall of 2011. This more complex measure takes into account the actual costs of food, clothing, shelter, utilities, taxes, work expenses, and out-of-pocket medical costs. In addition to income, it counts food stamps and tax credits as available resources. And it is adjusted to reflect price differences across geographic regions (U.S. Census Bureau 2010b).

Who Are the Poor? One of the lessons we learn by analyzing those who fall below the poverty line is that our stereotypes about poverty are flawed. For example, many people in the United States believe that the vast majority of the poor are able to work but will not. Yet, of the 46.2 million people in poverty, 43 percent are either under age 18 or 65 years old or older. Many working-age adults who are poor do work outside the home, although often in part-time positions. In 2010, 2.6% million people worked full-time, year-round were in poverty. Of those poor adults who do not work, many are ill or disabled, or are occupied in maintaining a home. As we can see in the accompanying table, the likelihood of being in poverty is also shaped by factors such as age, race, ethnicity, and family type (DeNavas-Walt et al. 2011).

Since World War II, an increasing proportion of the poor people of the United States have been women, many of whom are divorced or never-married mothers. In 1959 female householders accounted for 23 percent of the nation's poor families; by 2010, that figure had risen to 51.5 percent. This alarming trend, known as the feminization of poverty, is evident not just in the United States but around the world (DeNavas-Walt et al. 2011).

About half of all women living in poverty in the United States are in transition, coping with an economic crisis caused by the departure, disability, or death of a husband. The other half tend to be economically dependent either on the welfare system or on friends and relatives living nearby. A major factor in the feminization of poverty has been the increase in families with women as single heads of household. In 2010, 31.6 percent of families headed by single mothers lived in poverty, compared to 15.8 percent for single-father households and 6.2 percent for married couples. Contributing to such rates are factors such as the difficulty in finding affordable child care and sex discrimination in the labor market (DeNavas-Walt et al. 2011).

In 2010, 42 percent of poor people in the United States were living in big cities. These urban residents are the focus of most governmental efforts to alleviate poverty. Yet, according to many observers, the plight of the urban poor is growing worse, owing to the devastating

Who Are the Poor in the United States?

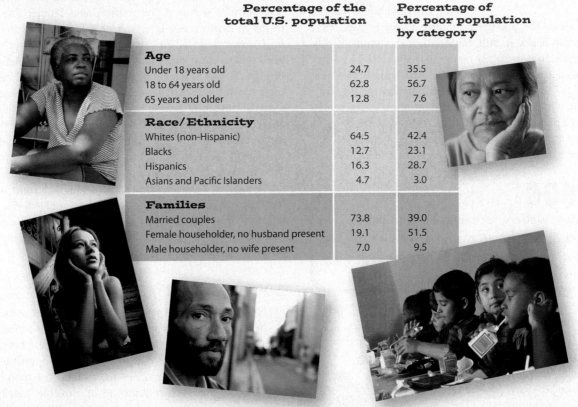

	Percentage of the total U.S. population	Percentage of the poor population by category
Age		
Under 18 years old	24.7	35.5
18 to 64 years old	62.8	56.7
65 years and older	12.8	7.6
Race/Ethnicity		
Whites (non-Hispanic)	64.5	42.4
Blacks	12.7	23.1
Hispanics	16.3	28.7
Asians and Pacific Islanders	4.7	3.0
Families		
Married couples	73.8	39.0
Female householder, no husband present	19.1	51.5
Male householder, no wife present	7.0	9.5

Note: Age and race ethnicity percents are based on total persons. Families percents are based on total families.

Source: DeNavas-Walt et al. 2011.

interplay of inadequate education and limited employment prospects. Traditional employment opportunities in the industrial sector are largely closed to the unskilled poor. Past and present discrimination heightens these problems for those low-income urban residents who are Black and Hispanic (DeNavas-Walt et al. 2011).

Along with other social scientists, sociologist William Julius Wilson (1987, 1996, 2008, 2009) used the term **underclass** to describe the long-term poor who lack training and skills. According to an analysis of census data, 7.9 million people live in high-poverty neighborhoods. About 30 percent of the population in these neighborhoods is Black, 29 percent Hispanic, and 24 percent White. In central cities, about 49 percent of the underclass is African American, 29 percent Hispanic, 17 percent White, and 5 percent "other" (Jargowsky and Yang 2006).

Analyses of people who are poor in general reveal that they are, however, not a static social class.

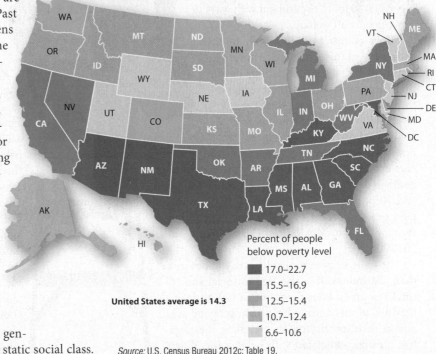

People below Poverty Level

United States average is 14.3

Percent of people below poverty level

- 17.0–22.7
- 15.5–16.9
- 12.5–15.4
- 10.7–12.4
- 6.6–10.6

Source: U.S. Census Bureau 2012c: Table 19.

underclass The long-term poor who lack training and skills.

The overall composition of the poor changes continually; some individuals and families move above the poverty level after a year or two, while others slip below it. Still, hundreds of thousands of people remain in poverty for many years at a time. In a study of Census data, researchers found that, over a three-year period, 28.9 percent of the U.S. population spent at least 2 months in poverty. The median duration for these episodes of poverty was 4.5 months. Of those who were in poverty at the beginning of the three-year study, 23 percent were in poverty for the whole time (Anderson 2011).

SOCTHINK

Should welfare recipients be required to work? If so, should the government subsidize preschool and afterschool care for their children while they are at work?

In 1996, in a historic shift in federal policy, Congress passed the Personal Responsibility and Work Opportunity Reconciliation Act, ending the long-standing federal guarantee of assistance to every poor family that meets eligibility requirements. The law sets a lifetime limit of five years of welfare benefits and requires all able-bodied adults to work after receiving two years of benefits (although hardship exceptions are allowed). The federal government gives block grants to the states to use as they wish in assisting poor and needy residents, and it permits states to experiment with ways to move people off welfare.

Other countries vary widely in their commitment to social service programs. But most industrialized nations devote higher proportions of their expenditures to housing, social security, welfare, health care, and unemployment compensation than the United States does. For example, in Cuba, 96 percent of health care expenditures are paid for by the government, compared to 82 percent in the United Kingdom and 70 percent in Canada. The U.S. government pays out 45 percent of health care expenditures, ranking close to Mexico and China (World Bank 2010a).

The issue of poverty is ultimately about more than just money. It is also tied to social and cultural resources. Poor people often lack the social network connections to help them get good jobs, not to mention having to overcome the negative prestige associated with being poor. When

it comes to cultural capital, they also often lack the same kind of educational credentials that can serve as a valuable cultural resource. Journalist David Shipler (2004), in his in-depth study titled *The Working Poor: Invisible in America,* referred to the combination of factors that poor people must overcome as the "interlocking deficits of poverty." As Shipler put it, "Breaking away and moving a comfortable distance from poverty seems to require a perfect lineup of favorable conditions. A set of skills, a good starting wage, and a job with the likelihood of promotion are prerequisites. But so are clarity of purpose, courageous self-esteem, a lack of substantial debt, freedom from mental illness or addiction, a functional family, a network of upstanding friends, and the right help from private or governmental agencies" (2004:4–5). To deal with poverty as a social problem, we must address all three of the major resource areas because mobility out of poverty is a difficult task.

SOCIAL MOBILITY

The belief in upward mobility is an important value in the United States. As we saw above, social class systems are more open than other stratification systems, but this does not mean that the principle of opportunity necessarily matches the practice of mobility. For such mobility to be possible, ascribed statuses and inherited positions, along with the resources to which they provide access, should not play a significant role in shaping outcomes.

Occupational Mobility Two classic sociological studies conducted a decade apart offered insight into the degree of mobility in the nation's occupational structure (Blau and Duncan 1967; Featherman and Hauser 1978). Taken together, these investigations lead to several noteworthy conclusions. First, occupational mobility (both intergenerational and intragenerational) has been common among males. Approximately 60–70 percent of sons are employed in higher-ranked occupations than their fathers. Second, although there is a great deal of mobility in the United States, much of it is minor. That is, people who reach an occupational level above or below that of their parents usually advance or fall back only one or two out of a possible eight occupational levels. Thus, the child of a laborer may become an artisan or a technician, but he or she is less likely to become a manager or professional. The odds of reaching the top are extremely low unless one begins from a relatively privileged position.

Income and Wealth More recent studies focusing on income and wealth mobility show much the same results (Corak 2010). Mobility does occur, but most people do not move very far. In comparing father's and son's income, researchers found that sons of low-income fathers have almost a 60 percent chance of rising above the lowest quintile, but only a 22.5 percent chance of reaching the median and a 4.5 percent chance of breaking into the top quintile (Mishel, Bernstein, and Shierholz 2009). Similarly, as we can see in the accompanying graph, when looking at wealth, 36 percent of children with parents in the lowest quintile end up there themselves while only 7 percent make it to the top quintile. On the other end of the scale, 36 percent of children with parents in the top wealth quintile stay there, whereas only 11 percent drop down into the bottom quintile (Haskins 2008:8). In fact, the likelihood of ending up in the same position as your parents has been rising since about 1980 (Aaronson and Mazumder 2007).

Education Studies also conclude that education plays a critical role in mobility. The impact of formal schooling on adult status is even greater than that of family background (although, as we have seen, family background influences the likelihood that one will receive higher education). Furthermore, education represents an important means of intergenerational mobility. A person who was born into a poor family but who graduates from college has a one in five chance of entering the top quintile of all income earners as an adult (Isaacs et al. 2008).

Education is a critical factor in the development of cultural capital. Thus, access to higher education plays an important role in social mobility. In 2009, 54.8 percent of high school students in the lowest income quintile enrolled

Did You Know?

... Although 67 percent of families make more money than their parents, only half of those earn enough to jump them into the next income quintile.

in college the following fall compared to 84.2 percent of those from the highest quintile (Aud et al. 2011:Table A-21). For students from families with the lowest incomes, the cost can be prohibitive. Only 11 percent of children

SOCTHINK

The percentage of financial aid in the form of grants has gone down while the percentage of loan aid has increased. Why do you think that has occurred? What are the consequences of such a shift for social mobility?

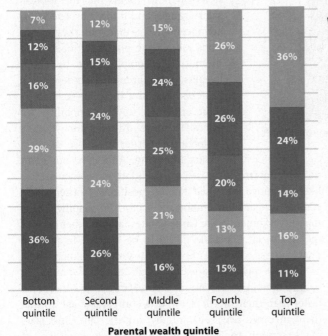

Wealth Mobility: Percentage of Children in Each Wealth Quintile Compared to Parental Wealth Quintile

Child wealth quintile
- Top
- Fourth
- Middle
- Second
- Bottom

Source: Haskins 2008.

Parental wealth quintile

	Bottom quintile	Second quintile	Middle quintile	Fourth quintile	Top quintile
Top	7%	12%	15%	26%	36%
Fourth	12%	15%	24%	26%	24%
Middle	16%	24%	25%	26%	14%
Second	29%	24%	21%	20%	16%
Bottom	36%	26%	16%	13%	11%
				15%	

from the poorest families in the United States have earned college degrees, compared to 53 percent of children from the top fifth of the population. Those moderate-income students who do graduate, and even those who fail to complete their degrees, are often saddled with heavy postgraduate debt (Isaacs et al. 2008).

The impact of education on mobility has diminished somewhat over the past decade. An undergraduate degree—a BA or BS—serves less as a guarantee of upward mobility now than it did in the past, simply because more and more entrants into the job market hold such a degree. Moreover, intergenerational mobility is declining because there is no longer such a stark difference between generations. In earlier decades, many high school–educated parents managed to send their children to college, but today's college students are increasingly likely to have college-educated parents (Economic Mobility Project 2007).

Race and Ethnicity Sociologists have long documented the fact that the class system is more rigid for African Americans than it is for members of other racial groups. Black men who have good jobs, for example, are less likely than White men to see their adult children attain the same status. The cumulative disadvantage of discrimination plays a significant role in the disparity between the two groups' experiences. Compared to White households, the relatively modest wealth of African American households means that adult Black children are less likely than adult White children to receive financial support from their parents. Indeed, young Black couples are much more likely than young White couples to be assisting their parents—a sacrifice that hampers their social mobility (Isaacs 2007c).

The African American middle class has grown over the past few decades owing to economic expansion and the benefits of the civil rights movement of the 1960s. Yet many of these middle-class households have little savings, a fact that puts them in danger during times of crisis. Studies have consistently shown that downward mobility is significantly higher for Blacks than it is for Whites (Isaacs 2007c; Oliver and Shapiro 1995).

The Latino population also faces substantial economic

life chances The opportunities people have to provide themselves with material goods, positive living conditions, and favorable life experiences.

Education Pays: Full-Time, Year-Round Workers, Ages 25–64

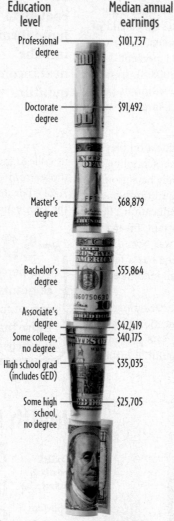

Education level	Median annual earnings
Professional degree	$101,737
Doctorate degree	$91,492
Master's degree	$68,879
Bachelor's degree	$55,864
Associate's degree	$42,419
Some college, no degree	$40,175
High school grad (includes GED)	$35,035
Some high school, no degree	$25,705

Source: U.S. Census Bureau 2011f: Part 28.

inequality. For example, in 2009 the median wealth for Hispanic households was $6,325. Comparatively, median wealth for White, non-Hispanic households was 15 times greater, representing the highest disparity since at least 1984. This gap has increased owing in part to the fact that the economic downturn affected groups differently. From 2005 to 2009 the median net worth for Hispanic families fell by 66 percent compared to a 16 percent decline for White, non-Hispanic households (Kochhar, Fry, and Taylor 2011).

Gender Studies of mobility, even more than those of class, have traditionally ignored the significance of gender, but some research findings are now available that explore the relationship between gender and mobility. Women's employment opportunities are much more limited than men's. Moreover, according to recent research, women whose skills far exceed the jobs offered them are more likely than men to withdraw entirely from the paid labor force. Their withdrawal violates an assumption common to traditional mobility studies: that most people will aspire to upward mobility and seek to make the most of their opportunities.

In contrast to men, women have a rather large range of clerical occupations open to them. But the modest salary ranges and limited prospects for advancement in many of these positions reduce the possibility of upward mobility. Self-employment as shopkeepers, entrepreneurs, independent professionals, and the like—an important road to upward mobility for men—is more difficult for women, who find it harder to secure the necessary financing. Although sons commonly follow in the footsteps of their fathers, women are less likely to move into their fathers' positions. Consequently, gender remains an important factor in shaping social mobility. Women in the United States (and in other parts of the world) are especially likely to be trapped in poverty, unable to rise out of their low-income status (Heilman 2001).

On the positive side, although today's women lag behind men in employment, their earnings have increased faster than their mothers' did at a comparable age so that their incomes are substantially higher. The one glaring exception to this trend involves the daughters of low-income parents. Because these women typically care for children—many as single parents—and sometimes for other relatives as well, their mobility is severely restricted (Isaacs 2007b).

>> Life Chances

One of the lessons we learn from sociology is that class matters. Max Weber saw class as being closely related to people's **life chances**—that is, their opportunities to provide themselves with material goods, positive living conditions, and favorable life experiences (Weber [1916] 1958a). Life chances are reflected in measures such as housing, education, and health. Occupying a higher position in a society improves individuals' life chances and brings greater access to social rewards. In contrast, people in the lower social classes are forced to devote a larger proportion of their limited resources to the necessities of life.

In fact, our very survival can be at stake. When the supposedly unsinkable British ocean liner *Titanic* hit an iceberg in 1912, it was not carrying enough lifeboats to accommodate all passengers. Plans had been made to evacuate only first- and second-class passengers. About 62 percent of the first-class passengers survived the disaster.

Despite a rule that women and children would go first, about a third of those passengers were male. In contrast, only 25 percent of the passengers in third class survived. The first attempt to alert them to the need to abandon ship came well after other passengers had been notified (D. A. Butler 1998; Crouse 1999).

digital divide The relative lack of access to the latest technologies among low-income groups, racial and ethnic minorities, rural residents, and the citizens of developing countries.

Class position also affects people's vulnerability to natural disasters. When Hurricane Katrina hit the Gulf Coast of the United States in 2005, affluent and poor people alike became its victims. However, poor people who did not own automobiles (100,000 of them in New Orleans alone) were less able than others to evacuate in advance of the storm. Those who survived its fury had no nest egg to draw on and thus were more likely than others to accept relocation wherever social service agencies could place them—some-times hundreds or even thousands of miles from home (Department of Homeland Security 2006; Fussell 2006).

Some people have hoped that the Internet revolution would help to level the playing field by making information and markets uniformly available. Unfortunately, however, not everyone can get onto the information superhighway, so yet another aspect of social inequality has emerged—the **digital divide**. The poor, minorities, and those who

Last Sunday's Count of Want Ads
Post-Dispatch.... 7149
All 6011
Post-Dispatch Gain 384

ST. LOUIS POST-DISPATCH

Only Evening Paper in St. Louis With the Associated Press News Service.

VOL. 64. NO. 240.   ST. LOUIS, TUESDAY EVENING, APRIL 16, 1912—28 PAGES.   PRICE ONE CENT

HOME EDITION

1302 LIVES LOST WHEN "TITANIC" SANK; 868 SAVED

Carpathia Steaming to New York With Survivors; None on Other Ships

NEW YORK, April 16.—Wireless from Capt. Roston of Carpathia, to Cunard line here, reads: "Proceeding to New York with about 800. Consulted with Mr. Ismay. So much ice about, considered New York best. Large number icebergs and twenty miles field-ice with bergs amongst."

MONTREAL, April 16.—The Allan Line issues the following statement: "We are in receipt of a Marconi via Cape Race, from Capt. Gambell of the Virginian, that he arrived on the scene of the disaster too late to be of service and is proceeding to Liverpool."

HALIFAX, N. S., April 16.—The Allan Liner Parisian reports by wireless, via Sable Island, that she has no passengers from the Titanic on board.

CAPE RACE, April 16.—Olympic reports by wireless "Carpathia reached Titanic position at daybreak FOUND BOATS AND WRECKAGE ONLY. Titanic sank about 2:20 a. m. in 41:16 n. 50:14w. ALL HER BOATS ACCOUNTED FOR, containing about 675 souls saved, crew and passengers included. Nearly all saved women and children. Californian remained searching exact position of disaster.

2-THIRDS WOMEN IN PARTIAL LIST OF THOSE RESCUED

Astor, Butt, Guggenheim and Many Other Famous Men Who Were on Board Not Mentioned Among Survivors---Money Loss Is $20,000,000.

7 ST. LOUISANS ARE REPORTED SAFE ON BOARD CARPATHIA

Mrs. Robert, Misses Madill and Allen, Hays and Wife Rescued and

... Researchers found that, by the age of three, children whose parents have professional jobs have heard 500,000 instances of praise and 80,000 of disapproval. In families receiving welfare, the ratio reverses; children have been praised 75,000 times and reprimanded 200,000 times.

Did You Know?

Source: Hart and Risley 1995.

live in rural communities and inner cities are not getting connected at home or at work. For example, as of August, 2011, 62 percent of households in the United States had broadband Internet access from home, but Internet access varies significantly by income. Only 41 percent of households making $30,000 or less have broadband access, compared to 89 percent of those with incomes of more than $75,000. Approximately 3 percent of adults still use a dial-up connection to access the Internet. Broadband access also varies significantly by age. Among those 65 years and older, 30 percent have broadband at home compared to 76% for those age 18–29 (Zickuhr and Smith 2012).

Wealth, status, and power may not ensure happiness, but they certainly provide additional ways of coping with problems and disappointments. For this reason, the opportunity for advancement—for social mobility—is of special significance to those at the bottom of society. People with limited resources want the chance to attain the rewards and privileges that are granted to high-ranking members of a culture.

If we are to better understand why we think and act the way we do, we must consider the impact of social class. The positions we occupy shape our access to material, social, and cultural resources, which in turn shape

SOC THINK

What factors have shaped your life chances? What kinds of resources have you inherited from others? What resources might you have lacked access to?

our future positions. In the United States, part of the American Dream is that anyone who is willing to work hard can get ahead. The principle of meritocracy—that we earn our positions—is at the heart of that faith, which represents a rejection of aristocracy in which positions are inherited. Class patterns in the United States call into question the degree to which principle and practice meet.

Roleplay! "Spent" is an online simulation game in which you have lost your job and your savings. Where will you live? What bills will you (not) pay? Can you make it through the month? Give it a try at www.playspent.org. The game is intended to create awareness and empathy for the homeless.

get involved!

For REVIEW

I. **What is social class?**
- Like slavery, caste, and estate, it is a stratification system in which people and groups are ranked, but it places them based primarily on economic position.

II. **How does social class operate?**
- Three categories of resources are key: material, including income and wealth; social, including social networks and prestige; and, cultural, including tastes, education, and knowledge. Power is based on access to and control over these resources.

III. **What are the consequences of social class?**
- Although class-based systems are more open than the others, our life chances are shaped by our inherited class position and the material, social, and cultural resources that go with it. For most people, the social mobility that does occur, whether in terms of occupation, income, or wealth, is of a relatively short distance.

Functionalist View

All societies have some degree of stratification in order to ensure that all of society's needs are met.

In a society with a complex **division of labor**, some positions will inevitably be more important or require more skill than others.

Those with more talent and determination fill the higher-paid and more prestigious positions, whereas those who do not develop their talents take the low-ranking jobs.

DIVISION OF LABOR, SOCIAL MOBILITY
KEY CONCEPTS

Conflict View

Stratification systems perpetuate unequal economic rewards and facilitate exploitation.

Social class standing is largely an **ascribed status**.

People in power maintain and spread their interests and influence through their hold on the **dominant ideology** in a society.

Income and wealth are **distributed unequally** in U.S. society, and the gap between the rich and the poor is steadily increasing.

STRATIFICATION, INEQUALITY, DOMINANT IDEOLOGY
KEY CONCEPTS

MAKE THE CONNECTION

After reviewing the chapter, answer the following questions:

Interactionist View

Social mobility results from interactions in which people attempt to better their place in the class system (for example, getting degrees, **networking**, acquiring cultural capital).

When we interact with others, we **exchange** our cultural capital resources, such as knowledge, tastes, attitudes, and ways of thinking.

Our social class helps determine our taste in clothes, food, music, TV shows, and many other everyday preferences.

NETWORKING, EXCHANGE
KEY CONCEPTS

1
Analyze social mobility from the point of view of the three perspectives (pp. 253–255). In what way might mobility be functional? How would conflict theory explain it? What role does interaction play in getting ahead?

2
How do the conflict and the interactionist perspectives intersect in Marx's concept of "false consciousness" (p. 243)?

3
How would a theorist from each perspective explain the distribution of material, social, and cultural resources in society?

4
Think about your own "life chances" (p. 258). Which perspective(s) helps you to see factors that shaped your opportunities and outcomes?

Pop Quiz

1. **Social inequality refers to**
   a. the structured ranking of entire groups of people that perpetuates unequal economic rewards and power in a society.
   b. social ranking based primarily on economic position.
   c. the positive or negative reputation an individual has in the eyes of others.
   d. a condition in which members of society have different amounts of wealth, prestige, or power.

2. **The stratification system in which hereditary ranks are usually religiously dictated is the**
   a. class system.
   b. estate system.
   c. caste system.
   d. slave system.

3. **A plumber whose father was a physician is an example of**
   a. downward intergenerational mobility.
   b. upward intergenerational mobility.
   c. downward intragenerational mobility.
   d. upward intragenerational mobility.

4. **According to Karl Marx, the class that owns the means of production is the**
   a. nobility.
   b. proletariat.
   c. Brahman.
   d. bourgeoisie.

5. **Which of the following were viewed by Max Weber as distinct components of stratification?**
   a. conformity, deviance, and social control
   b. class, status, and party
   c. class, caste, and age
   d. class, prestige, and esteem

6. **According to Pierre Bourdieu, our tastes, our education, the way we talk, and the things we like all represent forms of**
   a. social capital.
   b. esteem.
   c. cultural capital.
   d. intelligence.

7. **The term sociologists use to describe multiple measures of social position including income, education, and occupation is**
   a. prestige.
   b. esteem.
   c. socioeconomic status.
   d. ranking.

8. **Approximately how much wealth does the top I percent of families own in the United States?**
   a. 13 percent
   b. 36 percent
   c. 48 percent
   d. 87 percent

9. **Approximately what percentage of the U.S. population lived in poverty in 2009?**
   a. 3.3 percent
   b. 8.5 percent
   c. 15.1 percent
   d. 23.4 percent

10. **What term do sociologists use to describe the opportunities people have to provide themselves with material goods, positive living conditions, and favorable life experiences?**
    a. esteem
    b. wealth
    c. social mobility
    d. life chances

1. (d); 2. (c); 3. (a); 4. (d); 5. (b); 6. (c); 7. (c); 8. (b); 9. (c); 10. (d)

11

GLOBAL INEQ

UALITY

STRUGGLING TO SURVIVE IN A WORLD OF PLENTY

In summer of 2011 the eastern African nations of Somalia, South Sudan, Ethiopia, and Kenya were in the midst of Africa's worst famine in 60 years. More than 12 million people faced severe food shortages, and hundreds of thousands of people sought assistance in various camps established to provide humanitarian assistance. In southern Somalia alone it was estimated that more than 29,000 children under the age of 5 died from May through July (Gettleman 2011; Muhumed 2011). In spite of the severity of the crisis, and even though many more people were affected, donations for assistance were down substantially compared to other international crises such as the Indian Ocean tsunami in 2004, Hurricane Katrina in 2005, and the earthquake in Haiti in 2010 (Strom 2011).

Although crises such as these can raise awareness of the level of global inequality, daily struggles to find food are a long-term and ongoing problem around the world. In Haiti, for example, even before the massive 2010 earthquake, three-quarters of the population lived on less than $2 a day. Individuals such as Georges Jean Wesner would get up every day at 4:00 A.M. to walk two hours to get two small pails of rice and beans from a charity food kitchen—his only available source of food for his family. There are no available jobs from which to earn a living. Some even turn to eating patties made of mud, oil, and sugar, about which Olwich Louis Jeune, 24, says, "It's salty and it has butter, and you don't know you're eating dirt. . . . It makes your stomach quiet down" (Lacey 2008; Williams 2008).

Sociologically, to understand problems such as these, we must look beyond the lack of rain and the local availability of food to understand why people are dying of starvation. We must include analyses of the political and economic systems that affect the availability of resources. As Dominique Strauss-Kahn, the former managing director of the International Monetary Fund, stated during a previous food crisis, "There is enough food to feed the world . . . the problem is that prices have risen and many people cannot afford food. So we need to get food—or the money to buy food—to those most in need" (IMF 2008). In other words, we produce enough globally so that everyone can have enough, but we do not allocate resources in such a way that people now facing starvation can gain access to the food they need to survive.

As You READ

>>

- How did the global divide develop?
- How significant is global stratification?
- Why did the global movement for universal human rights develop?

>>The Global Divide

When it comes to resources, the global divide is immense. Millions of people struggle on the very edge of survival even as others around the world lead lives of relative comfort and leisure. A few centuries ago most people were poor. There was a substantial divide between the few who were extremely wealthy and the many who lacked significant resources, and not much of a middle class between the nobility and the peasants. In much of Europe, life was as difficult as it was in Asia or South America. This was true until the Industrial Revolution and increased agricultural productivity resulted in explosive economic growth. However, the ensuing rise in living standards was not evenly distributed across the world.

We get a glimpse of the global distribution of resources, and its consequences, by looking at differences between developing and industrial nations. For example, the likelihood of dealing with the death of a child or the burden of disease is much greater for those in developing nations. People living in the industrial nations of the world, even though they comprise a much smaller share of the total population, have much higher incomes and many more exports than the developing nations. They also are healthier, live longer, and have greater security due to what those nations spend on health care and the military (Sachs 2005a; Sutcliffe 2002). As we will see, the divide within countries in terms of income, wealth, poverty, and social mobility is also significant.

Average income varies significantly across the nations along a continuum from those that are the richest in economic resources to those that are the poorest. The contrast between those at the top and those at the bottom is stark. For example, in 2010, per capita gross national income

Before you finish eating breakfast in the morning,
you've depended on more than half of the world.

Martin Luther King, Jr.

Gross National Income per Capita

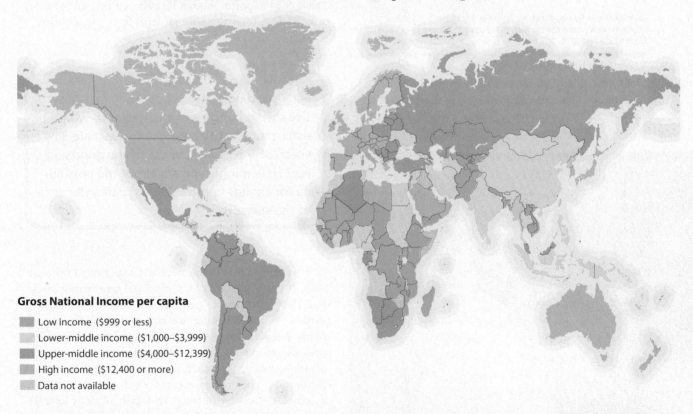

Gross National Income per capita

- Low income ($999 or less)
- Lower-middle income ($1,000–$3,999)
- Upper-middle income ($4,000–$12,399)
- High income ($12,400 or more)
- Data not available

Note: All data are from 2010 with the exception of Barbados, Burkina Faso, Dominican Republis, Greece, Honduras, Ireland, Liechtenstein, Myanmar, Namibia, Norway, Russian Federation, St. Lucia, Seychelles, and Uzbekistan, which are from 2009.

Source: World Bank 2012b.

Going *GLOBAL*

Measuring Global Inequality

Country	HDI
Niger	0.295
Ethiopia	0.363
Afghanistan	0.398
Haiti	0.454
India	0.547
Guatemala	0.574
China	0.687
Brazil	0.718
Russian Federation	0.755
United Arab Emirates	0.846
United States	0.910
Norway	0.943

Note: The Human Development Index combines data on health, education, and income to provide a snapshot for each of 187 countries. Scores range from 0 to 1. These data are for 2011.

(the total value of goods and services produced per citizen) in industrialized countries such as the United States, Canada, Switzerland, France, and Norway was more than

$40,000. By comparison, more than 30 countries, including Malawi, Ethiopia, Nepal, Rwanda, and Afghanistan, had a per capita gross national income of less than $1,000 (World Bank 2012b).

>>Perspectives on Global Stratification

To better understand how today's global system developed, and how its various parts fit together, theorists have taken a step back to look at the world from a top-down, macro perspective. We will focus on three major areas of analysis. These include the rise of modernization, the legacy of colonialism, and the growth of multinational corporations.

THE RISE OF MODERNIZATION

Many early sociologists assumed that society was progressing toward some common positive future. This was true for both Karl Marx and Émile Durkheim, who believed that all societies would evolve along a eventually common path, ending up in some shared version of the good society. For Durkheim this meant a future society with a natural balance between interdependence and individual freedom; for Marx it meant some form of socialism. Max Weber was not as hopeful, though he believed that all societies would move toward a rational-legal form of authority.

SOCTHINK

Early sociologists were optimistic that positive social change was inevitable. To what extent do you think people today share this vision of the inevitable rise of the good society? How might cynicism about the possibility for change contribute to the maintenance of the status quo?

This notion that the present was superior to the past, with its petty tyrannies and irrational superstitions, and that the future would unite us all, shaped how people viewed the world throughout much of the 20th century. Many people supposed that, through **modernization,** nations would move from traditional forms of social organization toward forms characteristic of post–Industrial Revolution societies. Features of the latter include a complex division of labor in which work is specialized; the separation of institutions including family, economy, government, education, and religion into specialized spheres, each with their own experts; the

THE PROGRESS OF THE CENTURY.

THE LIGHTNING STEAM PRESS.   THE ELECTRIC TELEGRAPH.   THE LOCOMOTIVE.   THE STEAMBOAT.

PUBLISHED BY CURRIER & IVES   Copyright 1876 by Currier & Ives, N.Y.   125 NASSAU ST NEW YORK

decline of the local and the rise of a societal or global orientation; the rise of rational decision making in the public sphere and a corresponding decline in public religious authority; and the spread of both cultural diversity, as more peoples from different backgrounds come into contact with each other, and a corresponding growth in egalitarianism as a value that embraces such diversity (Bruce 2000).

According to modernization theorists, countries such as China and India are in the process of becoming modern societies. Even if the transition from traditional to modern is difficult for many, the presupposition is that people will benefit from doing so in the long term. People in the United States and Europe experienced similar displacement and poverty in the early years of the Industrial Revolution, only later to lead more comfortable lives, and the same future awaits people in developing nations (Lipset 1959).

Critics of the modernization perspective suggest that terms such as *modernization* and even *development* contain an ethnocentric bias. They maintain that there is an implicit presupposition in this model that people in such nations are more "primitive" and that modern Western culture is more advanced, more "civilized." The unstated assumption is that what "they" (people living in developing countries) really want is to become more like "us"

(people in modern industrialized nations). From this perspective, "they" want "our" economic development and our cultural values, including democracy, freedom, and consumerism. Such modernization, according to critics, represents a form of cultural imperialism. Many groups around the world reject this modernization path, viewing such "development" as an attack on their way of life and a threat to their core values and norms (Césaire 1972).

> **modernization** The far-reaching process by which nations pass from traditional forms of social organization toward those characteristic of post–Industrial Revolution societies.
>
> **colonialism** The maintenance of political, social, economic, and cultural dominance over a people by a foreign power for an extended period.

THE LEGACY OF COLONIALISM

An alternative perspective to modernization focuses on colonialism as a model for better understanding the expansion of our interconnected world. **Colonialism** occurs when a foreign power maintains political, social, economic, and cultural domination over a people for an extended period. In simple terms, it is rule by outsiders. The long reign of the British Empire over much of North America, parts of Africa, and India is an example

When it comes to U.S. media portrayals of people from around the world, we frequently see negative stereotypes reinforced, perpetuating a sense of U.S. cultural superiority. In an analysis of more than 1,000 films, communications professor Jack Shaheen (2006, 2009) found that only 5 percent of Arab and Muslim characters were presented in a positive light. Arabs were repeatedly caricatured as villains, buffoons, lechers, incompetents, and terrorists. For example, Shaheen argues that Disney's *Aladdin* recycles Arab stereotypes, describing the fictional city of Agrabah as barbaric but home. The good news, he said, is that positive representations have risen to about 30 percent, thanks to films such as *Syriana* and *Babel*.

of colonial domination. The same can be said of French rule over Algeria, Tunisia, and other parts of North Africa. Theorists from this perspective maintain that relations between the colonial nation and the colonized people are similar to those between the dominant capitalist class and the proletariat, as described by Marx (Fanon 1963).

By the 1980s such global political empires had largely disappeared. Most of the nations that were colonies before World War I had achieved political independence and established their own governments. However, for many of these countries, the transition to genuine self-rule was not yet complete. Colonial domination had established patterns of economic exploitation that continued even after nationhood was achieved—in part because the former colonies were unable to develop their own industry and technology. Their dependence on more industrialized nations, including their former colonial masters, for managerial and technical expertise, investment capital, and manufactured goods kept the former colonies in a subservient position. Such continuing dependence and foreign domination are referred to as **neocolonialism**.

neocolonialism Continuing dependence of former colonies on foreign countries.

world systems analysis A view of the global economic system as one divided between certain industrialized nations that control wealth and developing countries that are controlled and exploited.

Sociologist Immanuel Wallerstein (2000, 2004, 2010) views the global economic system as being divided between nations that control wealth and nations from which resources are taken. Through his **world systems analysis,** Wallerstein has described the unequal economic and political relationships in which certain industrialized nations (among them the United States, Japan, and Germany) and their global corporations dominate the core of this system. At the semiperiphery of the system are countries with marginal economic status, such as China, Ireland, and India. Wallerstein suggests that the poor developing countries of Asia, Africa, and Latin America are on the periphery of the world economic system. The key to Wallerstein's analysis is the exploitative relationship of core nations toward noncore nations. Core nations and their corporations control and exploit noncore nations' economies. Unlike other nations, they are relatively independent of outside control (Hardt and Negri 2009).

The division between core and periphery nations is both significant and remarkably stable. A study by the International Monetary Fund (2000) found little change over the past century for the 42 economies studied. The only changes were Japan's movement up into the group of core nations and China's movement down toward the margins of the semiperiphery nations, a decline that has perhaps been reversed in recent years owing to economic changes there. Yet Wallerstein (2000, 2010) speculates that the world system as we currently understand it may soon undergo unpredictable changes. The world is becoming increasingly urbanized, a trend that is gradually eliminating the large pools of low-cost workers in rural areas. In the future, core nations will have to find other ways to

World Systems Analysis at the Beginning of the 21st Century

Core	Semiperiphery	Periphery
Canada	China	Afghanistan
France	India	Bolivia
Germany	Ireland	Chad
Japan	Mexico	Dominican Republic
United Kingdom	Pakistan	Egypt
United States	Panama	Haiti
		Philippines
		Vietnam

Note: Figure shows only a partial listing of countries.

Big Mac Index

Global average

Nairobi	
Jakarta	
Mexico City	
Budapest	
São Paulo	
Singapore	
Doha	
Shanghai	
Rome	
Johannesburg	
Moscow	
Paris	
Sydney	
Frankfurt	
New York	
London	
Toronto	
Tokyo	
Chicago	

0   20   40   60   80   100   120   140   160

Minutes

Note: Number of minutes it takes a worker with an average net wage to earn sufficient income to purchase a Big Mac, March 2009.

Sources: http://www.economist.com/daily/chartgallery/displayStory.cfm?story_id=14288808 and http://boingboing.net/2009/08/21/how-many-minutes-do.html.

reduce their labor costs. The exhaustion of land and water resources through clear-cutting and pollution is also driving up the costs of production.

Wallerstein's world systems analysis is the most widely used version of **dependency theory**. According to this theory, even as developing countries make economic advances, they remain weak and subservient to core nations and corporations in an increasingly intertwined global economy. This interdependency allows industrialized nations to continue to exploit developing countries for their own gain.

According to world systems analysis and dependency theory, a growing share of the human and natural resources of developing countries is being redistributed to the core industrialized nations. This redistribution happens in part because developing countries owe huge sums of money to industrialized nations as a result of foreign aid, loans, and trade deficits. The global debt crisis has intensified the Third World dependency rooted in colonialism, neocolonialism, and multinational investment. International financial institutions are pressuring indebted countries to take severe measures to meet their interest payments. The result

is that developing nations may be forced to devalue their currencies, freeze workers' wages, increase privatization of industry, and reduce government services and employment.

These trends are part of the larger process of *globalization*—the worldwide integration of government policies, cultures, social movements, and financial markets through trade and the exchange of ideas. Because the forces of world financial markets transcend governance by conventional nation-states, international organizations such as the World Bank and the International Monetary Fund have emerged as major players in the global economy. The function of these institutions, which are heavily funded and influenced by core nations, is to encourage trade and development and to ensure the smooth operation of international financial markets. As such, they are seen as promoters of globalization and defenders primarily of the interests of core nations. Critics call attention to a variety of related issues, including violations of workers' rights, the destruction of the environment, the loss of cultural identity, and discrimination against minority groups in periphery nations.

THE GROWTH OF MULTINATIONAL CORPORATIONS

Worldwide, corporate giants have played a key role in the rise of globalization. The term **multinational corporations** refers to commercial organizations that are headquartered in one country but do business around the world. Such private trade and lending relationships are not new; merchants have conducted business abroad for hundreds of years, trading gems, spices, garments, and other goods. Today's multinational giants are not merely buying and selling overseas; they are also producing goods all over the world (Wallerstein 1974, 2004). Through deindustrialization, corporate executives also have relocated production jobs around the globe.

> **dependency theory** An approach contending that industrialized nations continue to exploit developing countries for their own gain.

> **multinational corporation** A commercial organization that is headquartered in one country but does business throughout the world.

Increasingly, it is not just production jobs that are being relocated. Today's global factories may now have

SOCTHINK

Increasingly, we compete with workers around the world for jobs. What impact has the rise of globalization had on job prospects in your community and your country?

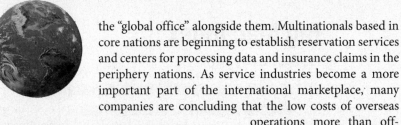

Going GLOBAL

Multinational Corporations Compared to Nations

Rank		
	▨ Corporate revenue	▨ Gross domestic product

Millions of dollars

Rank		
1	$421,849	Wal-Mart Stores
23	434,666	Saudi Arabia
2	$378,152	Royal Dutch Shell
26	379,069	Austria
3	$354,674	Exxon Mobil
28	363,910	South Africa
4	$308,928	BP
30	311,989	Denmark
5	$273,422	Sinopec Group
33	288,886	Colombia
6	$240,192	China National Petroleum
34	238,041	Finland
7	$226,294	State Grid
36	228,571	Portugal
8	$221,760	Toyota Motor
38	218,894	Egypt
9	$203,958	Japan Post Holdings
42	206,612	Ireland
10	$196,337	Chevron
45	192,032	Czech Republic

Note: Corporations are paired with comparably sized countries. Dollar amounts are in millions.

Sources: For corporate data, *Fortune* 2011; for GDP data, World Bank 2012c.

SOCTHINK

Multinational corporations have become so big that they have more economic resources than do some nations. What consequences arise from the fact that they can relocate their headquarters, offices, and production facilities anywhere in the world? How might this affect a nation's political power?

the "global office" alongside them. Multinationals based in core nations are beginning to establish reservation services and centers for processing data and insurance claims in the periphery nations. As service industries become a more important part of the international marketplace, many companies are concluding that the low costs of overseas operations more than off-set the expense of trans-mitting information around the world.

These multinational corporations are huge, with total revenues on a par with the total value of goods and services exchanged in entire nations. For-eign sales represent an important source of profit for multinational corporations, encouraging them to expand into other coun-tries (in many cases, the developing nations). The U.S. economy is heavily dependent on foreign com-merce, much of which is conducted by multinationals. In 2010 the combined value of U.S. exports and imports of goods and services was the equivalent of 28.6 percent of total economic output as measured by gross domestic product (Bureau of Economic Analysis 2011).

Modernization Consistent with the modernization approach, some analysts believe that the relationship between the corporation and the developing country is mutually beneficial. Multinational corporations can help the developing nations of the world by bringing indus-tries and jobs to areas where subsistence agriculture once served as the only means of survival. Multinationals also promote rapid development through the diffusion of inventions and innovations from industrial nations. The combination of skilled technology and management pro-vided by multinationals and the relatively cheap labor available in developing nations benefits the corporation. Multinationals can take maximum advantage of technol-ogy while reducing costs and boosting profits. Through their international ties, multinationals also make the nations of the world more interdependent. These ties may inhibit certain disputes from reaching the point of serious conflict. A country cannot afford to sever diplomatic rela-tions or engage in warfare with a nation that is the head-quarters for its main business suppliers or a key market for its exports.

Dependency Critics of multinational expansion chal-lenge this favorable evaluation of the impact of corpora-tions. They argue that multinationals exploit local workers to maximize profits. For example, Starbucks—the interna-tional coffee retailer based in Seattle—gets some of its cof-fee beans from farms in Ethiopia. It sold its "Black Apron Exclusives" coffee in a fancy black box for $26 per pound, but it paid Ethiopian workers who picked the beans 66 cents per day (Knudson 2007).

The pool of cheap labor in the developing world prompts multinationals to move factories out of core countries. Workers in these developing countries do not have the same kinds of legal protections and also lack unions to fight on their behalf. In industrialized countries, organized labor insists on decent wages and humane working conditions, but governments seeking to attract or keep multinationals may develop a "climate for investment," including repressive antilabor laws that restrict union activity and collective bargaining. If labor's demands become too threatening, the multinational firm will simply move its plant elsewhere, leaving a trail of unemployment behind. Nike, for example, has moved its factories from the United States to Korea to Indonesia to Vietnam in search of the lowest labor costs.

Workers in the United States and other core countries are beginning to recognize that their own interests are served by helping to organize workers in developing nations. As long as multinationals can exploit cheap labor abroad, they will be in a strong position to reduce wages and benefits in industrialized countries. With this in mind, starting in the 1990s labor unions, religious organizations, campus groups, and other activists began to mount public relations campaigns to pressure companies such as Nike, Starbucks, Reebok, Gap, and Wal-Mart to improve wages and working conditions in their overseas operations (Radovich 2006; Solidarity Center 2009).

Sociologists studying the effects of foreign investment by multinationals have found that, although it initially may contribute to a host nation's wealth, such investment eventually increases economic inequality within developing nations. This finding holds for both income and ownership. The upper and middle classes benefit most from economic expansion; the lower classes are less likely to benefit. And because multinationals invest in limited economic sectors and restricted regions of a nation, only some sectors benefit. The expansion of such sectors of the host nation's economy, such as hotels and high-end restaurants, appears

to retard growth in agriculture and other economic sectors. Moreover, multinational corporations often buy out or force out local entrepreneurs and companies, thereby increasing economic and cultural dependence (Kerbo 2009; Wallerstein 1979b, 2004).

Governments in developing nations are not always prepared to deal with the sudden influx of foreign capital and its effects on their economies. One particularly striking example of how unfettered capitalism can harm developing nations is found in the Democratic Republic of Congo (formerly Zaire). Congo has significant deposits of the metal columbite-tantalite—coltan, for short—which is used in the production of electronic circuit boards. Until the market for cell phones, pagers, and laptop computers heated up recently, U.S. manufacturers obtained most of their coltan from Australia. But at the height of consumer demand, they turned to miners in Congo to increase their supply.

Predictably, the escalating price of the metal—as much as $400 per kilogram at one point, or more than three times the average Congolese worker's yearly wages—attracted undesirable attention. Soon the neighboring countries of Rwanda, Uganda, and Burundi, at war with one another and desperate for resources to finance the conflict, were raiding Congo's national parks, slashing and burning to expose the coltan underneath the forest floor. In 2010 the U.S. Congress passed the Dodd-Frank Act, which included a provision requiring manufacturing companies to disclose whether they used any "conflict minerals," including colton, cassiterite, gold, wolframite, or their derivatives, originating from the Democratic Republic of Congo or adjoining nations. According to a UN report, the result has been reforms in how business and government operate in Congo (Lezhnev 2011; Wyatt 2012).

>>Stratification around the World

As these economic investments by multinationals suggest, at the same time the gap between rich and poor nations is widening, so too is the gap between rich and poor citizens within nations. As discussed previously, stratification in developing nations is closely related to their relatively weak and dependent position in the global economy. Local elites work hand in hand with multinational corporations and prosper from such alliances. At the same time, the economic system creates and perpetuates the exploitation of industrial and agricultural workers.

INCOME AND WEALTH

Global inequality is staggering. As the accompanying graphs demonstrate, wealth and income differences between the haves and have-nots are substantial.

Percent Shares of Global Household Wealth. 2011

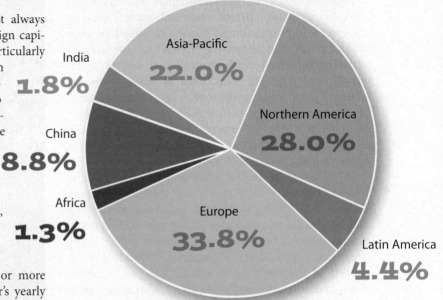

Source: Davies, et al. 2011: Table 2-4

Quintile Distribution of Income in Select Nations

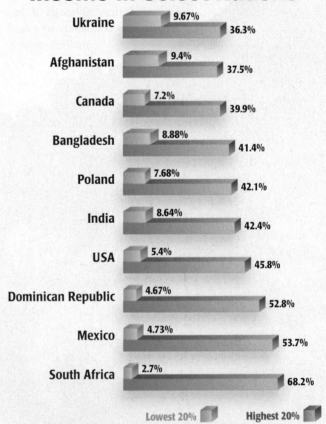

Note: Percentage of income earned by the top and bottom quintiles. Data are for the most recent year available.

Source: World Bank 2012d, 2012e.

Top
10%

Bottom
90%

72.0%
28.0%
Sweden

71.5%
28.5%
United
States

65.4%
34.6%
Indonesia

56%
44%
Ireland

Amount of Wealth Held by the Top 10 Percent

Source: Davies et al. 2011.

52.9%
47.1%
India

50.4%
49.6%
Canada

44.3%
55.7%
United
Kingdom

44%
56%
Chile

43.1%
56.9%
South
Korea

41.6%
58.4%
Spain

41.4%
58.6%
China

39.3%
60.7%
Japan

Focusing on high incomes, we see that there are at least 20 nations in which the top 10 percent of earners take home at least 40 percent of the country's income. The leader is Seychelles at 60 percent, but additional countries include Haiti, Colombia, Brazil, Namibia, Honduras, and Rwanda. Other countries have significantly less income inequality. For example, the top 10 percent in Ukraine, Afghanistan, Romania, and Austria earn less than 25 percent (World Bank 2012f).

The distribution for wealth is even more unequal. The top 10 percent of the world's population own 84.3 percent of global household wealth, and the top 1 percent own 44.2 percent. On the other end of the spectrum, the bottom 50 percent of the world's population combined own 1.2 percent of global wealth. Median household wealth globally is estimated to be $4,208 per

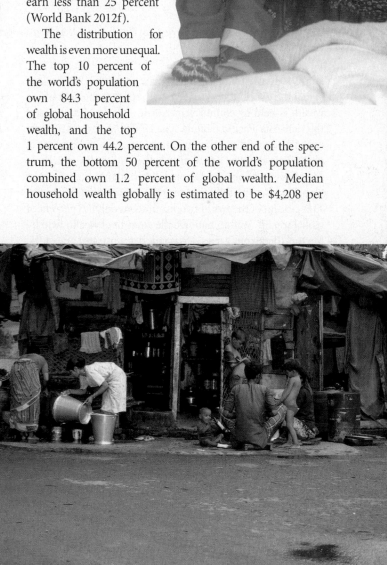

Mapping Global Poverty

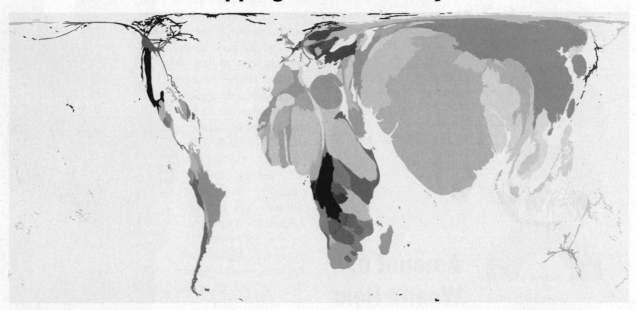

Note: The size of each country shows the proportion of the world population living in poverty there.

Source: www.worldmapper.org.

adult. To make it into the top 1 percent takes $712,233. Analyzing the distribution globally, one sees that the bulk of the wealth is held by countries in North America, Europe, and the rich Asia-Pacific nations. The United States has 5.2 percent of the world's adult population but owns 25.2 percent of global household wealth. Contrast this with India, which has 16.3 percent of the world's population but only 1.8 percent of global wealth. In addition, the entire continent of Africa has 11.5 percent of the world's population but only 1.3 percent of global wealth. Within nations, the amount of wealth held by the top 10 percent varies. Denmark demonstrates one of the highest levels of wealth inequality, with the top 10 percent of wealth holders there owning 76.4 percent of household wealth—significantly more than Japan, where the top 10 percent hold 39.3 percent of the wealth (Davies, Lluberas, and Shorrocks, 2011).

Women in developing countries often face significant obstacles, making it difficult for them to attain economic assets. Karuna Chanana Ahmed, a sociologist from India who has studied women in developing nations, calls women "the most exploited among the oppressed" (Anderson and Moore 1993). Beginning at birth, women face sex discrimination. They are commonly fed less than

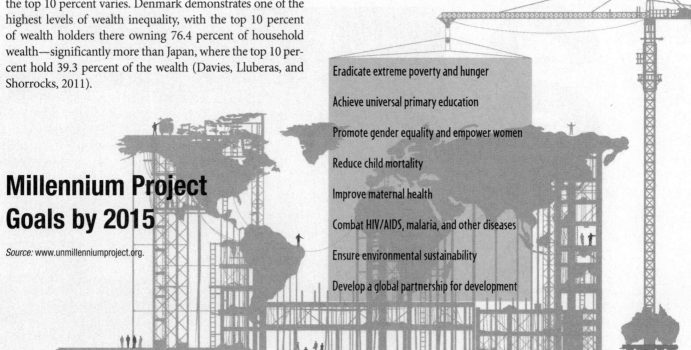

Millennium Project Goals by 2015

Source: www.unmillenniumproject.org.

Eradicate extreme poverty and hunger

Achieve universal primary education

Promote gender equality and empower women

Reduce child mortality

Improve maternal health

Combat HIV/AIDS, malaria, and other diseases

Ensure environmental sustainability

Develop a global partnership for development

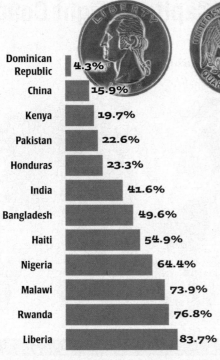

Percent of Population
Living on Less than $1.25 a Day

Country	Percent
Dominican Republic	4.3%
China	15.9%
Kenya	19.7%
Pakistan	22.6%
Honduras	23.3%
India	41.6%
Bangladesh	49.6%
Haiti	54.9%
Nigeria	64.4%
Malawi	73.9%
Rwanda	76.8%
Liberia	83.7%

Source: United Nations Development Programme 2011: Table 5.

male children, are denied educational opportunities, and often are hospitalized only when they are critically ill. In countries such as the United States, France, Colombia, Russia, Hungary, and Ethiopia, the proportion of the non-agricultural labor force made up by women approaches or exceeds 50 percent. In other nations the rate can be significantly lower: Yemen 6.2 percent, Bahrain 9.6 percent, Iraq 12.1 percent, Pakistan 12.6 percent, Saudi Arabia 14.6 percent, Iran 16.1 percent, Egypt 18.1 percent, and India 18.1 percent. In Afghanistan, it is illegal for a wife to step out of the house without her husband's

permission. In Saudi Arabia, women are prohibited from driving, walking alone in public, and socializing with men other than their families (International Labour Organization 2008; World Bank Al-Shihri 2011, 2011g).

POVERTY

In developing countries, any deterioration in the economic well-being of the least well-off threatens their

---

SOCTHINK

What are the major obstacles to accomplishing the Millennium Project's goals? To what extent are they economic, social, and/or cultural? Is it simply a matter of will?

---

very survival. Using the global poverty line established by the World Bank of $1.25 per day, 1.4 billion people in the world are considered poor, and 2.6 billion people consume less than $2 a day. In fact, 80 percent of the world's population lives on less than $10 a day (Chen and Ravallion 2008; Shah 2010).

Though poverty is a worldwide problem affecting billions of people, it is distributed unequally. As the world map above demonstrates, if we drew each country to scale based on its number of poor people, Africa and Asia would appear huge. The relatively affluent areas of North America and Europe would be quite small.

In an effort to reduce global poverty, the United Nations passed the Millennium Declaration in 2000, promising to "spare no effort to free our fellow men, women, and children from the abject and dehumanizing conditions of extreme poverty." They established 2015 as the target date for reaching specific, measurable goals to alleviate hunger and improve education, gender equality, and child mortality.

According to *The Millennium Development Goals Report 2011*, substantial progress has been made in a

5 Movies on GLOBAL INEQUALITY

Kinyarwanda
Resilience and reconciliation in Rwanda.

Slumdog Millionaire
A boy from the slums of Mumbai is accused of cheating on a game show.

Blood Diamond
A South African mercenary and a miner race to acquire a precious diamond.

Maria Full of Grace
A factory worker is forced to transport heroin to the United States.

A Separation
An Iranian couple's tale of love, loss, and family.

number of areas while challenges remain in others. The goal of cutting global poverty in half to 23 percent by 2015 is not only on track but also projected to reach 15 percent, largely driven by growth in China. Child mortality rates have fallen significantly, reducing the deaths of children under the age of 5 from 12.4 million in 1990 to 8.1 million in 2009, meaning 12,000 fewer children die per day. Increased access to immunization for measles alone accounts for one-fourth of that decline. The number of people dying from malaria and tuberculosis has dropped significantly. Access to drinking water improved for 1.8 billion people from 1990 to 2008, including a doubling of the number of people with access in Sub-Saharan Africa. In other areas, however, progress has been difficult. Almost one-fourth of children in the developing world remain underweight. Women around the world still face limited access to paid work. Progress toward universal primary education for children has slowed, reaching 89 percent in 2009, with substantially lower rates for children in poor countries affected by conflict. Although overall access to flush toilets or other forms of improved sanitation has improved, over 2.6 billion people still lack access to such facilities, and the rate has remained largely unchanged for the world's poorest 40 percent of households (United Nations 2011).

gross national income (GNI) The total value of a nation's goods and services.

To accomplish the project's goals, planners estimate that industrial nations must set aside 0.7 percent of their **gross national income (GNI)**—the total value of a nation's goods and services—for aid to developing nations. In 2010 only six countries were giving at least that much: Denmark, Luxembourg, the Netherlands, Norway, Belgium, and Sweden. The average level of official development assistance from developed countries was 0.47 percent, with the United States contributing 0.20 percent. Although the U.S. government delivers far more total aid dollars than any other nation, the rate of GNI it contributes ties it with Italy and Japan for last place among 22 industrialized nations such as the United Kingdom, France, and Germany (Deutscher 2010:Table 8.1).

SOCIAL MOBILITY

Although there is significant global inequality, perhaps sufficient social mobility exists to provide hope for those born without significant access to resources. As we saw in the previous chapter, mobility can and

Foreign Aid per Capita in Eight Countries

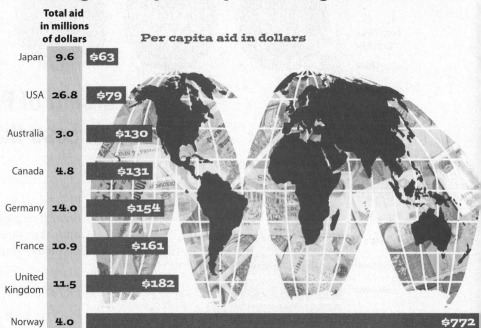

Per capita aid in dollars

Country	Total aid in millions of dollars	Per capita aid in dollars
Japan	9.6	$63
USA	26.8	$79
Australia	3.0	$130
Canada	4.8	$131
Germany	14.0	$154
France	10.9	$161
United Kingdom	11.5	$182
Norway	4.0	$772

Note: Data for bilateral aid in 2008 released by World Bank in 2010.
Source: Deutscher 2010:182, 187.

Intergenerational Earnings Mobility by Country

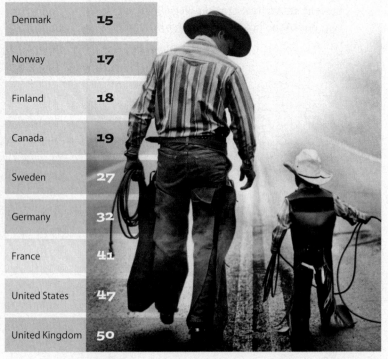

Country	Percentage of earning advantage passed from fathers to sons
Denmark	15
Norway	17
Finland	18
Canada	19
Sweden	27
Germany	32
France	41
United States	47
United Kingdom	50

Source: Corak 2006.

does happen in the United States, though the majority of such movement is over only short distances. Here we look at the possibility for mobility in both industrial nations and developing nations, and we consider the impact gender has on mobility.

Intergenerational Mobility across Nations

The likelihood of earning more or less than your parents varies across nations. Though Americans have more faith in their ability to get ahead than do those in other countries, their likelihood of doing so is lower than in most other industrialized nations (Isaacs 2008). As the table below shows, for example, when analyzing earnings, the amount of money fathers earn has a strong influence on the likely earnings of sons (Corak 2006). What this means, in contrast to the classic vision of the American Dream, is that there is less chance for inter-generational mobility in the United States than in those Scandinavian countries.

In developing nations, macrolevel social and economic changes often overshadow microlevel movement from one occupation to another. For example, there is typically a substantial wage differential between rural and urban areas, which leads to high levels of migration to the cities. Yet the urban industrial sectors of developing countries generally cannot provide sufficient employment for all those seeking work.

In large developing nations, the most socially significant mobility is the movement out of poverty. This type of mobility is difficult to measure and confirm, however, because economic trends can differ from one area of a country to another. For instance, China's rapid income growth has been accompanied by a growing disparity in income between urban and rural areas and among different regions. Similarly, in India during the economic development of the 1990s, poverty declined in urban areas but may have remained static at best in rural areas. Around the world, social mobility is also dramatically influenced by catastrophes such as crop failure and warfare (World Bank 2006).

Gender Differences and Mobility Only recently have researchers begun to investigate the effect of gender on the mobility patterns of developing nations. Many aspects of the development process—especially modernization in rural areas and the rural-to-urban migration just described—may result in modification or abandonment of traditional cultural practices and even marital systems. The effects on women's social standing and mobility are not necessarily positive. As a country develops and modernizes, women's vital role in food production deteriorates, jeopardizing both their autonomy and their material well-being. Moreover, the movement of families to the cities weakens women's ties to relatives who can provide food, financial assistance, and social support.

In the Philippines, however, women have moved to the forefront of the indigenous peoples' struggle to protect their ancestral land from exploitation by outsiders. Having established their right to its rich minerals and forests, members of indigenous groups had begun to feud among themselves over the way in which the land's resources should be developed. Aided by the United Nations Partners in Development Programme, women volunteers established the Pan-Cordillera Women's Network for Peace and Development, a coalition of women's groups dedicated to resolving local disputes. The women mapped boundaries, prepared development plans, and negotiated more than 2,000 peace pacts among community members. They have also run in elections, campaigned on issues related to social problems, and organized residents to work together for the common good (United Nations Development Programme 2000:87).

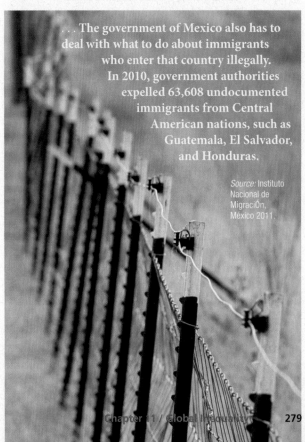

SOCIAL STRATIFICATION IN MEXICO

To get a more complete picture of these global stratification issues, it helps to look at a particular case. Here we will focus on the dynamics of stratification in Mexico, a country of 113 million people.

As we saw in Chapter 6, drug-related homicides have become a serious problem in Mexico. Although the reasons for this are historical and complex (Camp 2010a, 2010b), economic factors play a substantial role. The same is true for the hundreds of men, women, and children who die attempting to cross into the United States each year in search of opportunity. Though solid numbers are difficult to come by, the *Arizona Daily Star* (2011) has established a database of deaths in the Arizona-Sonora border region by gathering data from local medical examiners to gain a more accurate count. They report that 249 bodies were found in that region alone in 2010. The most common cause of death was heat exposure (Jimenez 2009).

Why do Mexicans turn to drug trafficking or risk their lives crossing the dangerous desert that lies between the two countries? The answer to this question can be found primarily in the income disparity between the two nations—one an industrial giant and the other a partially developed country still recovering from a history of colonialism and neocolonialism. Since the early 20th century, there has been a close cultural, economic, and political relationship between Mexico and the United States, one in which the United States is the dominant party. According to Immanuel Wallerstein's analysis, the United States is at the core while neighboring Mexico is still on the semiperiphery of the world economic system.

Mexico's Economy If we compare Mexico's economy to that of the United States, differences in the standard of living and in life chances are quite dramatic, even though Mexico is considered a semiperiphery nation. Gross national income is a commonly used measure of an average resident's economic well-being. In 2010 the gross national income per person in the United States came to $47,340; in Mexico, it was a mere $8,930. About 36.5 percent of adults in the United States have a bachelor's degree, compared to only 18.2 percent of those in Mexico. And fewer than 6.5 of every 1,000 infants in the United States die in the first year of life, compared to about 14.1 per 1,000 in Mexico (Snyder and Dillow 2011; World Bank 2012b, 2012h).

Not only is Mexico unquestionably a poor country, but the gap between its richest and poorest citizens is substantial. The top quintile earns 56.2 percent of total income while the bottom earns just 3.9 percent. The World Bank reports that 4.8 percent of Mexico's population survives on just $2 per day. At the same time, the wealthiest 10 percent of Mexico's people accounted for 41.4 percent of the nation's income. According to *Forbes* magazine, Mexico's Carlos Slim Helú again beat out Bill Gates as the world's richest person in 2011 with a fortune of $74 billion (*Fortune* 2011; World Bank 2011a, 2011d, 2011e, 2011f).

Political scientist Jorge Castañeda (1995:71), who later served as Mexico's foreign minister, called Mexico a "polarized society with enormous gaps between rich and poor, town and country, north and south, white and brown (or *criollos* and *mestizos*)." He added that the country is also divided along lines of class, race, religion, gender, and age. To better understand the nature of the stratification within Mexico, we examine race relations and the plight of Mexican Indians, the status of Mexican women, and immigration to the United States and its impact on the U.S.–Mexican borderlands.

Race Relations in Mexico: The Color Hierarchy

Mexico's indigenous Indians account for an estimated 14 percent of the nation's population. According to a United Nations report, more than 90 percent of Mexico's indigenous people (the ethnic group historically native to a region) live in extreme poverty. The literacy rate in Mexico as a whole is 92 percent, but it hovers around 50 percent among the indigenous population (Cevallos 2009; Minority Rights Group International 2007; United Nations Development Programme 2008).

The subordinate status of Mexico's Indians is but one reflection of the nation's color hierarchy, which links social class status to the appearance of racial purity. At the top of this hierarchy are the *criollos,* the 10 percent of the population who are typically White, well-educated members of the business and intellectual elites, with familial roots in Spain. In the middle is the large, impoverished *mestizo* majority, most of whom have brown skin and a mixed racial lineage as a result of intermarriage. At the bottom of the color hierarchy are the destitute, full-blooded Mexican Indian minority and a small number of Blacks, some descended from 200,000 African slaves brought to Mexico. This color hierarchy is an important part of day-to-day life—enough so that some Mexicans in the cities use hair dyes, skin lighteners, and blue or green contact lenses to appear White and European. Ironically, however, nearly all Mexicans are considered part Indian because of centuries of intermarriage (Castañeda 1995; Standish and Bell 2009).

—SOCTHINK—

How might racial categories in Mexico differ from those in the United States? Why might such differences arise?

Many observers take note of widespread denial of prejudice and discrimination against people of color in Mexico. Schoolchildren are taught that the election of Benito Juárez, a Zapotec Indian, as president of Mexico in the 19th century proves that all Mexicans are equal. Yet

Personal Sociology

Study Abroad

Central College, where I teach, started its first international program in 1965. It was a leader in establishing study abroad programs for students. It now operates programs around the world in places such as Merida in Mexico, Bangor in Wales, and Hangzhou in China. Central instituted these programs to provide students with a prolonged experience in another country in hopes that such exposure would enable them to go beyond being just a tourist and achieve a deeper understanding of another culture. And going abroad really does make a difference. My students are often nervous to go but come back with great stories. It is clear that the experience has changed how they understand both the world and themselves.

there has been a marked growth in the past decade of formal organizations and voluntary associations representing indigenous Indians (Escárcega 2008; Stavenhagen 1994; Utne 2003).

The Status of Women in Mexico Though the United Nations convened the first international conference on the status of women in Mexico in 1975, and opportunities there have improved, women still face significant obstacles. Women now constitute 45 percent of the labor force—an increase from 31 percent in 1980. Unfortunately, Mexican women are even more mired in the lowest-paying jobs than their counterparts in industrial nations, on average earning 42 percent less than men. Men are still typically viewed as heads of the household, making it difficult for women to obtain credit and technical assistance in many parts of the country and to inherit land in rural areas. As for education, the literacy rate for women in Chiapas (71 percent) and Oaxaca (73 percent), states with high levels of indigenous populations, is well below the national average (INEGI 2009; United Nations Development Programme 2008).

In the political arena, though they rarely occupy top decision-making positions, women have significantly increased their representation in the national legislature to 28 percent. Mexico now ranks 34th among 194 nations in female representation. In spite of this, the struggle for enforcement of legal rights continues. In February 2007, Mexico passed the General Law on Women's Access to a Life Free from Violence. States have not followed through with implementation of the law's basic requirements, such as establishing protocols to follow when claims of abuse are filed or constructing shelters for domestic violence victims. In fact, there are only 60 such shelters in all of

The Borderlands

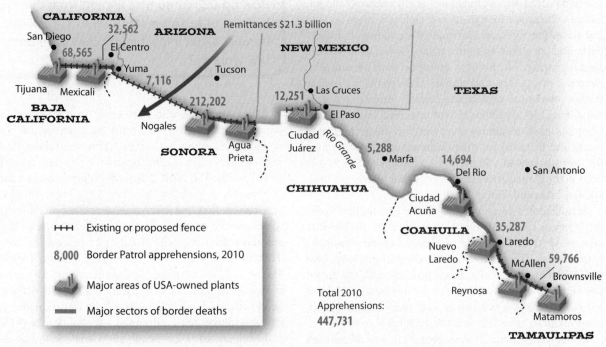

Source: Data from U.S. Customs and Border Protection 2011; Stevenson 2011.

Mexico (Amnesty International 2009a; Inter-Parliamentary Union 2011).

In recent decades, Mexican women have organized to address an array of economic, political, and health issues. For example, as far back as 1973, women in Monterrey—the nation's third-largest city—protested the continuing disruptions of the city's water supply. Through coordinated efforts, including delegations of politicians, rallies, and public demonstrations, they succeeded in improving Monterrey's water service, a major concern in developing nations. After being denied the opportunity to run for mayor in her hometown in 2007, Eufrosina Cruz organized QUIEGO (Queremos Unir Integrando por la Equidad y Género en Oaxaca, meaning "we want to come together for equity and gender in Oaxaca") to raise awareness about political rights for women in her home state and ultimately throughout Mexico (Bennett, Dávila-Poblete, and Rico 2005; Cevallos 2009).

borderlands The area of common culture along the border between Mexico and the United States.

remittances The monies that immigrants return to their families of origin. Also called *remesas*.

The Borderlands

Growing recognition of the borderlands reflects the increasingly close and complex relationship between Mexico and the United States. The term **borderlands** refers to the area of common culture along the border between Mexico and the United States. Legal and illegal emigration from Mexico to the United States, day laborers crossing the border regularly to go to work in the United States, the implementation of the North American Free Trade Agreement (NAFTA), the exchange of media across the border—all make the notion of separate Mexican and U.S. cultures obsolete in the borderlands.

The economic position of the borderlands is rather complicated, as demonstrated by the emergence of *maquiladoras*. These are foreign-owned factories, often located just across the border in Mexico, that are allowed to import parts and materials without tariffs. Typical jobs include manufacturing electronics, transportation equipment, electrical machinery, and textiles and apparel, as well as service jobs in call centers and coupon processing operations. The chief appeal for U.S. companies is less expensive labor. As of 2006 hourly compensation costs (including salary and benefits) for maquiladora manufacturing production workers was $2.64. This compares to $29.98 per hour in the United States (Bureau of Labor Statistics 2009a, 2009b; Cañas and Gilmer 2009).

Maquiladoras now employ more than 1.2 million workers. They account for about 40 percent of all Mexico's exports. Overall, 80 percent of Mexico's exports go to the United States. This makes Mexico's economy more sensitive to U.S. fluctuations, a significant problem with the recent economic downturn. Maquiladoras estimate a job loss of 163,000 for 2009, a rate two to four times higher than in other Mexican firms (Black 2009; Bogan et al. 2008).

Though the maquiladora program was established in 1965, it really took off after the North American Free Trade Agreement (NAFTA) was implemented in 1994, removing most barriers to trade between Mexico, the United States, and Canada. Things changed, however, with China's entry into the World Trade Organization in 2001. Labor costs were even lower there. As a result, jobs that had moved from the United States to Mexico, especially those requiring minimal skills, are now being transferred to China (Cañas and Gilmer 2009; Sargent and Matthews 2009).

Emigration to the United States The movement of people between Mexico and the United States significantly affects both nations. In 2010, 94,783 people who were born in Mexico became naturalized U.S. citizens, more than twice the number of any other country. Another 142,823 obtained legal permanent resident status in the United States, also more than twice as many as any other nation. However, 528,139 individuals from Mexico were classified as "deportable aliens" by U.S. immigration officials, which constituted 86% of that total (Homeland Security 2010, 2011).

From the Mexican point of view, the United States too often regards Mexico simply as a reserve pool of cheap labor, encouraging Mexicans to cross the border when workers are needed but discouraging and cracking down on them when they are not. Some people, then, see immigration more as a labor market issue than a law enforcement issue. Viewed from the perspective of world systems analysis and dependency theory, it is yet another example of a core industrialized nation exploiting a developing country.

SOCTHINK

How do U.S. consumers benefit from the buildup of factories along the U.S.–Mexican border? What impact might they have on U.S. workers?

Many Mexicans who have come to the United States send a portion of their earnings back across the border to family members in Mexico. This substantial flow of money, referred to as **remittances** (or *remesas*), amounted to $21.3 billion in 2010. It is second only to oil as a source of foreign revenue for Mexico. After years of growth, remittances sent to Mexico fell 3.6 percent in 2008, due to the economic downturn in the United States. The decline was more dramatic in 2009, falling 15 percent for the year. Though remittances still totaled $21.5 billion, it meant a loss of $3.8 billion to the Mexican economy. As a result of the weak economy, more Mexicans left the United States to head back to Mexico than entered the United States in the first quarter of 2009, a dramatic reversal of events (Barta and Millman 2009; Coronado and Cañas 2010; Passel and Cohn 2009; Stevenson 2011).

Mass grave site in Srebrenica, Bosnia-Herzegovina.

>>Universal Human Rights

As globalization has spread, affecting more and more peoples around the world, a movement toward ensuring universal human rights has arisen. Recognizing the harmful effects of such global expansion, activists in this movement fight to preserve and protect the interests of people who lack significant power or access to resources. The sheer size and economic might of multinational corporations, along with their freedom to move jobs and plants around the world without regard for the impact on national populations, encouraged the establishment of universal human rights as a countervailing source of power. The goal of human rights activists is to establish a nonnegotiable and inviolable foundation of rights that applies no matter where people are or which governments or multinational corporations are involved.

DEFINING HUMAN RIGHTS

The term **human rights** refers to universal moral rights that all people possess by virtue of being human. The most important elaboration of human rights appears in the Universal Declaration of Human Rights, adopted by the United Nations (UN) in 1948. This declaration prohibits slavery, torture, and degrading punishment; grants everyone the right to a nationality and its culture; affirms freedom of religion and the right to vote; proclaims the right to seek asylum in other countries to escape persecution; and prohibits arbitrary interference with one's privacy and the arbitrary seizure of a person's property. It also emphasizes that mothers and children are entitled to special care and assistance.

At first the United States opposed a binding obligation to the Universal Declaration of Human Rights. The government feared loss of national sovereignty—the right to rule over its people without external interference. This concern was driven in part by the existence of racial segregation laws that were still common at the time the UN issued the Universal Declaration and that violated the human rights principles. By the early 1960s, however, the United States had begun to use the declaration to promote democracy abroad (Forsythe 1990).

> **human rights** Universal moral rights possessed by all people because they are human.

In the 1990s concerns about human rights brought the term *ethnic cleansing* into the world's vocabulary as a euphemism for forcible expulsion and murder. In the former Yugoslavia, Serbs initiated a policy intended to "cleanse" Muslims from parts of Bosnia-Herzegovina and ethnic Albanians from the province of Kosovo. Hundreds of thousands of people were killed in fighting there, while many others were uprooted from their homes. Moreover, reports surfaced of Serbian soldiers raping substantial numbers of Muslim, Croatian, and Kosovar women. Regrettably, ethnic cleansing has since spread to other parts of the world, including East Timor, Iraq, Kenya, and Sudan.

An ongoing human rights concern is the transnational crime of trafficking in humans. Each year an estimated

Ongoing violence in East Timor has driven children like these to seek safety in refugee camps in the country.

Human Trafficking Report

Tier 1 Full Compliance	Tier 2 Significant Effort	Tier 2 Watch List Some Effort, but Trafficking Remains a Concern	Tier 3 Noncompliant, No Effort
Australia	Bahamas	Afghanistan	Burma
Canada	Brazil	Azerbaijan	Congo
Columbia	Cambodia	Chad	Cuba
Denmark	Greece	China	Dominican Republic
France	Hong Kong	Fiji	Eritrea
Germany	Israel	India	Iran
Italy	Japan	Iraq	Kuwait
Nigeria	Mexico	Malaysia	Mauritania
Norway	Pakistan	Niger	North Korea
Poland	Romania	Russia	Papua New Guinea
South Korea	Rwanda	Senegal	Saudi Arabia
Spain	Turkey	Syria	Sudan
	Zambia	Vietnam	Zimbabwe

Note: Table does not include all countries; each tier lists only a sampling of nations.

Source: U.S. Department of State 2010.

600,000–800,000 men, women, and children are transported across international borders for slavery or sexual exploitation. In 2000 Congress passed the Trafficking Victims Protection Act, which established minimum standards for the elimination of human trafficking. The act requires the State Department to monitor other countries' efforts to vigorously investigate, prosecute, and convict individuals who participate in trafficking—including government officials. Each year the department reports its findings, dividing countries into three groups, or tiers, depending on their level of compliance. Tier-1 countries are thought to be largely in compliance with the act. Tier-2 nations are making a significant effort to comply, while tier-2 "watch" nations are making efforts to comply, though trafficking remains a real concern. Tier-3 countries are not compliant (Kapstein 2006; Kempadoo and Doezema 1998; Ribando 2008).

PRINCIPLE AND PRACTICE

When it comes to human rights, the balance between principle and practice can be problematic. In the wake of the terrorist attacks of September 11, 2001, increased police personnel and surveillance at U.S. airports and border crossings caused some observers to wonder whether human rights were not being jeopardized in the name of security. At the same time, thousands of noncitizens of Arab and south Asian descent were questioned for no other reason than their ethnic and religious backgrounds. A few were placed in custody, sometimes without access to legal assistance. And as the war on terror moved overseas, human rights concerns escalated. In 2005 then Secretary-General Kofi Annan of the UN criticized the United States and Britain for equating people who were resisting the presence of foreign troops in Afghanistan and Iraq with terrorists (Parker 2004; Steele 2005).

What this points to is the significance of perspective even when it comes to something that appears to be a fundamental principle. Cultural insiders and outsiders can disagree about what constitutes a violation. For example, was India's caste system an inherent violation of human rights? What about the many cultures of the world that view the subordinate status of women as an essential element in their traditions? Should human rights be interpreted differently in different parts of the world?

SOCTHINK

To what extent do you think violations of human rights are excusable in a time of war? At such times, how might our perception of the balance between rights and security alter what we think of as universal?

We can consider, as an example, female genital mutilation, a practice that is common in more than 30 countries around the world but that has been condemned in Western nations as a human rights abuse. This controversial practice often involves removal of the clitoris, in the belief that its excision will inhibit a young woman's sex drive, making her chaste and thus more desirable to her future husband. Though some countries have passed laws against

the practice, they have gone largely unenforced. Emigrants from countries where genital mutilation is common often insist that their daughters undergo the procedure, to protect them from Western cultural norms that allow premarital sex (Religious Tolerance 2008). To what extent should outside nations have the power to dictate such internal laws? In this sense, the movement for universal human rights also represents a form of cultural imperialism.

In 1993 the United States opted for an absolute definition of human rights, insisting that the Universal Declaration of Human Rights set a single standard for acceptable behavior around the world. In practice, however, interpretation still plays a role. Some human rights activists have argued that the United States practices selective enforcement of human rights. Critics contend, for example, that officials in the United States are more likely to become concerned about human rights abuses when oil is at stake, as in the Middle East, or when military alliances come into play, as in Europe.

SOCTHINK

How active should the U.S. government be in addressing violations of human rights in other countries? At what point, if any, does concern for human rights turn into ethnocentrism through failure to respect the distinctive norms, values, and customs of another culture?

HUMAN RIGHTS ACTIVISM

Efforts to protect and ensure human rights seldom come from inside governments but arise out of social movements that organize to generate economic, social, and political pressure in an effort to force change. For example, in June 2008 Human Rights Watch (www.hrw.org), a premier international human rights organization, called for other African nations to impose sanctions on Zimbabwe after what they called the sham reelection of President Robert Mugabe. They monitor on human rights abuses around the world, including calling U.S. officials to end abuses against prisoners in the Guantanamo Bay detention camps.

In Sudan the Save Darfur Coalition (www.savedarfur .org) fights for justice and relief for refugees who were attacked, driven off their land and out of the country, and often killed by the Janjaweed, a group of armed gunmen backed by the Sudanese government. Their cause was helped significantly with the release of the film *The Devil Came on Horseback*—translated from the Janjaweed—in which ex-marine Brian Steidle, who was hired as a human rights observer by the African Union, documented genocide in Darfur with photos and video. He ultimately testified before Congress and at the UN, providing his documentation to support the genocide claims. In addition to numerous other organizational efforts, the Save Darfur Coalition also coordinated an agreement on May 28, 2008, in which presidential candidates Barack Obama, John McCain, and Hillary Clinton issued a joint statement demanding an end to the violence in Darfur. Though the Sudanese government maintains that the war is officially over, violence continues. In May 2010 Ibrahim Gambari, the head of UNAMID, the joint African Union–UN Mission in Darfur, put it this way: "Results have been mixed despite our best efforts. . . . In the area of security and the protection of civilians some progress has been made, but pockets of instability remain" (UN News Service 2010).

Médecins sans Frontières (Doctors Without Borders), the world's largest independent emergency medical aid organization, won the 1999 Nobel Peace Prize for its work in countries worldwide. Founded in 1971 and based in Paris, on any given day the organization has 27,000 doctors, nurses, and other expert volunteers working in more than 65 countries. "Our intention is to highlight current upheavals, to bear

> There can be no peace as long as there is grinding poverty, social injustice, inequality, oppression, environmental degradation, and as long as the weak and small continue to be trodden by the mighty and powerful.
>
> the Dalai Lama

United States, and other countries, including cases of torture, imprisonment, and extrajudicial execution. Later in 1994 the United States issued an order that would allow lesbians and gay men to seek political asylum in the United States if they could prove they had suffered government persecution in their home countries solely because of their sexual orientation (Amnesty International 2009b; Johnston 1994). One result of this policy change was that dozens of homosexual men and women from Mexico and other Latin American nations were granted asylum in the United States each year. As treatment of homosexuals has improved in those nations, the likelihood of receiving asylum has declined (Connolly 2008).

One of the things we learn from sociology is that we are embedded in larger networks in which decisions and events that happen far away, and about which we may know little or nothing, shape our daily life experiences. Ethnic cleansing in Sudan, human rights violations in Iraq and Afghanistan, increased surveillance in the name of counterterrorism, violence against women inside and outside the family, governmental persecution of lesbians and gay men—all of these are vivid reminders that social inequality can have life-and-death consequences. In each case, people recognized the consequences of global inequality, and individuals, groups, and nations took steps to address the problems. By developing a more fully formed sociological imagination, we can more readily see such issues and take necessary steps toward addressing them.

SOCTHINK

Should other nations and the UN have the power to force the United States to change its laws to comply with human rights principles?

witness to foreign tragedies and reflect on the principles of humanitarian aid," explains Dr. Rony Brauman, the organization's president (Doctors Without Borders 2010).

In the past few decades, awareness has been growing of lesbian and gay rights as an aspect of universal human rights. In 1994 Amnesty International (1994:2) published a pioneering report in which it acknowledged that "homosexuals in many parts of the world live in constant fear of government persecution." The report examined abuses in Brazil, Greece, Mexico, Iran, the

Donate! Give of your time and your money. It can be something as simple as going to www.freerice.com to donate rice to the UN World Food Program or giving clothes to a local shelter. Or perhaps it might include volunteering time at a local organization that works with international immigrants or donating money to organizations that seek to alleviate global poverty, such as OxFam.

get involved!

For REVIEW

I. **How did the global divide develop?**
   - Theorists emphasizing modernization argue that it is part of the natural evolution of societies as they pass through the effects of the Industrial Revolution and beyond. Dependency theorists argue that it is due to a fundamental power struggle between wealthy nations at the core and developing nations at the periphery.

II. **How significant is global stratification?**
   - Analyses of wealth, income, poverty, and social mobility demonstrate a wide gap both within and between nations.

III. **Why did the global movement for universal human rights develop?**
   - As global inequality became more apparent, activists worked to establish a foundational set of human rights that would protect people regardless of who or where they were.

Functionalist View

Through **modernization**, nations make the transition from traditional forms of organization to postindustrial societies for the benefit of all.

Globalization involves the worldwide **integration** of government policies, cultures, social movements, and financial markets through trade and exchange of ideas.

Multinational organizations create jobs and industries in developing countries, foster innovation, and make nations of the world **interdependent**.

Conflict View

There is significant **inequality** between the rich and the poor within as well as across nations, but the scourge of poverty is most evident in Africa and Asia.

According to world system analysis, modernization can result in political, economic, and cultural **imperialism**.

The economic success of core nations depends upon the extraction of raw materials and cheap labor from periphery nations.

Interactionist View

People undergoing modernization often experience a dramatic change in the established ways of working and interacting.

Encounters with people from different cultures open us up to alternative ways of thinking and acting.

Many women in developing nations face inequality in employment opportunities, education and health care, thus limiting their **social interaction** in the community.

KEY CONCEPTS
IMPERIALISM, INEQUALITY

KEY CONCEPTS
SOCIAL INTERACTION, ENCOUNTERS

MAKE THE CONNECTION

After reviewing the chapter, answer the following questions:

1

How might each perspective seek to better understand the situation in countries such as Haiti and Sudan (p. 261)?

2

How do the modernization and world systems theories fit with the functionalist and conflict perspectives (pp. 264–266)

3

How would each perspective provide insight into the situation of immigration between the United States and Mexico (p. 278)?

4

What ties do you have to a developing nation—perhaps as a tourist, or a second-generation immigrant, or an activist? Which perspective best fits those ties? Why?

Pop Quiz

1. Which of the following terms is used by contemporary social scientists to describe the far-reaching process by which nations pass from traditional forms of social organization toward those characteristic of post–Industrial Revolution societies?
   a. dependency
   b. globalization
   c. industrialization
   d. modernization

2. The maintenance of political, social, economic, and cultural domination over a people by a foreign power for an extended period of time is referred to as
   a. globalization.
   b. government-imposed stratification.
   c. colonialism.
   d. dependency.

3. Immanuel Wallerstein's world systems analysis focuses on
   a. the unequal access to and control of resources between core and periphery nations.
   b. the natural evolutionary development of all societies toward the modern ideal.
   c. the rise of multinational corporations.
   d. the global pattern of inequality faced by women.

4. Companies that are headquartered in one country but do business throughout the world are known as
   a. global corporations.
   b. multinational corporations.
   c. maquiladoras.
   d. international agencies.

5. Approximately how much of global household wealth is owned by households in North America?
   a. about one-tenth
   b. about one-quarter
   c. about one-third
   d. about one-half

6. How much of total global wealth do the bottom 50 percent of the world's population own?
   a. 1 percent
   b. 6 percent
   c. 23 percent
   d. 47 percent

7. Globally, approximately how many people subsist on less than $1.25 per day?
   a. 500 million
   b. 1.4 billion
   c. 3.2 billion
   d. 5 billion

8. Karuna Chanana Ahmed, a sociologist from India who has studied developing nations, calls which group the most exploited of oppressed people?
   a. children
   b. women
   c. the elderly
   d. the poor

9. Which of the following terms refers to the foreign-owned factories established just across the border in Mexico, where the companies that own them don't have to pay taxes or high wages, or provide insurance or benefits for their workers?
   a. *maquiladoras*
   b. *hombres*
   c. *mujeres*
   d. *remesas*

10. In what year did the United Nations adopt the Universal Declaration of Human Rights?
    a. 1865
    b. 1919
    c. 1948
    d. 1993

1. (d); 2. (c); 3. (a); 4. (b); 5. (b); 6. (a); 7. (b); 8. (b); 9. (a); 10. (c)

12

GENDER & SEXUALITY

QUOTIDIAN CRUELTIES

It was eleven thirty at night when a group of men came for Woineshet Zebene. She was in a deep sleep, but they took her from her home in the Ethiopian countryside and battered and raped her over the next two days. Afterward, it was expected that she would marry the man who led the assault. When she refused, she was again kidnapped, beaten, and raped. A court official to whom she pleaded for help advised her to "get over it" and marry her attacker. She was 13 years old. Though something like this is unlikely to happen to a typical teenage girl in the United States, sadly, halfway around the world, Woineshet's story is not uncommon.

Every day, women from all over the globe face systematic violence and discrimination. In their book *Half the Sky,* journalists Nicholas Kristof and Sheryl WuDunn (2009) tell the stories of many women and girls, including Woineshet, who are victims of such abuses. Women are particularly vulnerable to sex trafficking, gender-based violence (including honor killings and mass rape), and death or serious injury during childbirth due to inadequate medical care. For example, in Ghana, 21 percent of women report that their first sexual experience was by rape. Regarding inadequate health care, 1 in 7 women in Nigeria, 1 in 22 in sub-Saharan Africa, and 1 in 70 in India die during childbirth, compared to 1 in 4,800 in the United States.

Such practices often go unnoticed because they represent "quotidian cruelties"—the everyday practice of violence and discrimination that is largely invisible and considered inevitable or even natural. Fortunately, women around the world have successfully fought to change local attitudes and practices. In India, for example, Ruchira Gupta founded Apne Aap Women Worldwide, with its mission to end sex-trafficking (www.apneaap.org). In Pakistan, Mukhtar Mai used settlement money she received after having been gang raped to establish her School for Girls; she later expanded it to include a free legal clinic, a public library, and a women's shelter. And in Somaliland, former diplomat Edna Adan used her entire life's savings to establish the Edna Adan Maternity Hospital to provide medical care for women and children (www.ednahospital.org).

- How has our understanding of gender and sexuality shifted over time?
- How has opportunity for women in the United States changed over time?
- To what extent does gender still shape access to resources?

>>The Social Construction of Gender

When a baby is born, one of the first questions people ask is "Is it a boy or a girl?" The answer to this question represents one of the first and most powerful statuses we come to occupy. From those earliest days, it shapes how others will interact with us as newborns. Later it influences the clothes we wear, the friends we choose, the kinds of games we play, the college majors we consider, the types of jobs we have, the amount of money we are paid, and much more. And answering the question seems such a simple thing. Yet, from a sociological perspective, understanding what it means to be a boy or a girl—and later to become men and women—involves more than anatomy alone.

sex The biological differences between males and females.

gender The social and cultural significance that we attach to the biological differences of sex.

SEX AND GENDER

Historically, sociologists have drawn a distinction between sex and gender in order to differentiate between biology and culture. **Sex** refers to biological differences between males and females. **Gender** involves the social and cultural significance that we attach to those presumed biological

differences. Over time, even this distinction has become too limiting to fully depict our experiences as humans.

Sex emphasizes the differences between males and females that occur at the cellular, hormonal, and anatomical levels. From this perspective, we assume it is easy to tell the difference between males and females. Women have XX chromosome patterns, estrogen hormones, ovaries, and a vagina; men have XY chromosomes, androgen hormones, testicles, and a penis. The presupposition is that the dividing line is clear; there is no significant biological overlap between the sexes. This model is known as a simple two-sex, or dimorphic, model, in which the line between males and females is distinct and absolute (Fausto-Sterling 2000; Preves 2000).

The problem with such a simplistic division is that we find many exceptions to what is assumed to be the rule. Many people exhibit physical characteristics that we presume to belong to the "opposite" sex: women with facial hair, men with high voices, tall women and short men, women with narrow hips and broad shoulders, men who are slight of build or who have "breasts," women who experience "male pattern baldness," and so on. Differences go beyond these secondary sex characteristics to include people whose cellular, hormonal, and anatomical characteristics are sexually ambiguous. As geneticist Anne Fausto-Sterling (2000) points out in a critique of the simplistic male–female model, "On close inspection, absolute dimorphism disintegrates even at the level of basic biology. Chromosomes, hormones, the internal sex structures, the gonads and the external genitalia all vary more than most people realize" (p. 20).

We know, for example, that both

After she won the gold medal in the 800 meter race at the 2009 World Champions, questions were raised about South African runner Caster Semenya's sex. She was ordered to submit to a series of psychological, gynecological, and endocrine tests and was cleared for continued competition in international track and field events.

males and females have androgen and estrogen hormones and that sex hormone levels vary by individual.

Biologically, Fausto-Sterling (1993) suggests we have at least five sexes, not just two. In addition to male and female, we exhibit at least three intersexual categories. The first category includes "true hermaphrodites," who have one testis and one ovary. In other words, they are theoretically capable of producing both sperm and eggs. The second category includes "male pseudohermaphrodites." They have testes and what appear to be female genitalia, lacking a penis and ovaries. The third category includes "female pseudohermaphrodites," who have ovaries along with some male genitalia but no testes. She later suggested that even these five sexes present an overly simplistic model of the range of biological diversity, which better resembles a continuum (Fausto-Sterling 2000). Although it is difficult to know for certain how common such cases are, Fausto-Sterling (2000) estimates that about 1.7 percent of children are born intersexual in some way. Given a total U.S. population of roughly 300 million, that works out to approximately 5.1 million Americans who cannot easily be categorized as either male or female.

Sociologists initially distinguished gender from sex in part to account for the wide varieties of ways that we manifest differences based on sex across cultures and over time. This approach presupposed that gender is not narrowly defined by biology. We "socially construct" gender by attaching social and cultural significance to biological differences between the sexes. Whereas sex refers to who we are as males and females at birth, gender refers to what we become as men and women as displayed within various cultures and subcultures. This process of becoming occurs through socialization, in which we internalize the cognitive, normative, and material culture deemed appropriate or natural in our social worlds.

SOCTHINK

Why do most women in the United States assume that shaving their legs is natural? What role does it play as a rite of passage?

GENDER-ROLE SOCIALIZATION

Because we lack complex instincts that narrowly determine our behaviors, we construct our expressions of masculinity and femininity and reinforce those gender expressions through socialization. For example, the process of becoming boys and girls begins at birth:

> During the first six months of life, mothers tend to look at and talk to girl infants more than to boy infants, and mothers tend to respond to girls' crying more immediately than they do to boys'. In fact, these behaviors tend to be greater for girls over the first two years of life. Boys, on the other

An Experiment in Gender-Norm Violation by College Students

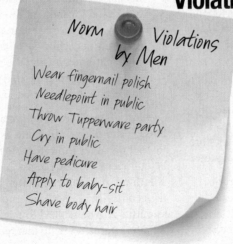

Norm Violations by Men

Wear fingernail polish
Needlepoint in public
Throw Tupperware party
Cry in public
Have pedicure
Apply to baby-sit
Shave body hair

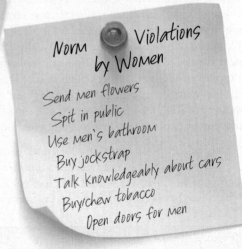

Norm Violations by Women

Send men flowers
Spit in public
Use men's bathroom
Buy jockstrap
Talk knowledgeably about cars
Buy/chew tobacco
Open doors for men

Source: Nielsen et al. 2000:287.

SOCstudies

hand, receive more touching, holding, rocking, and kissing than do girls in the first few months, but the situation is reversed by age six months. By one year, female infants are allowed and encouraged to spend significantly more time than males in touching and staying in close proximity to their mothers. The girls are encouraged to move away at later ages, but never as much as boys are. (Kimmel, 2004:130)

As children grow, we continue to reinforce male–female differences through our actions. Male babies get blue blankets; females get pink ones. Boys are expected to play with trucks, blocks, and toy soldiers; girls receive dolls and kitchen goods. Boys must be masculine—active, aggressive, tough, daring, and dominant—but girls must be feminine— soft, emotional, sweet, and submissive. An examination of the ads in any parenting magazine shows that these traditional gender-role patterns remain influential in the socialization of children in the United States (Kilbourne 2010).

Gender Displays Gender socialization never ends. In all of our interactions, we receive positive and negative feedback based on our gender performance. It is not hard to test how rigid gender-role socialization can be. Just try breaking some gender norm—say, by smoking a cigar in public if you are female, or wearing a skirt to work if you are male. Corrective feedback will likely follow. That was exactly the assignment given to sociology students at the University of Colorado and at Luther College in Iowa. Professors asked students to behave in ways that they thought violated the norms of how a man or woman should act. Over the years that this ongoing experiment has been performed, students consistently received clear signals— ranging from amusement to disgust—that their actions were inappropriate and that they should instead behave in ways defined as appropriate by dominant heterosexual gender norms (Nielsen, Walden, and Kunkel 2000).

Working out what it means to be feminine and masculine through our interactions with others is an ongoing project. Given the interactive nature of gender, it is helpful to look at being a man or a woman as something we *do* in our relationships with others, rather than as something we simply *are* (West and Zimmerman 1987).

When we interact with others, we usually display our gender clearly. When we find ourselves in situations lacking explicit gender cues, we are often unsure how to proceed. For example, sociologists Candace West and Don Zimmerman (1987) recount a meeting in a computer store where the sex of the person involved remained ambiguous:

The person who answered my questions was truly a *salesperson*. I could not categorize him/her as a woman or a man. What did I look for? (1) Facial hair: She/he was smooth skinned, but some men

When Emily and Eleanor were little, they covered our refrigerator with pictures they drew of our family. In the pictures, the girls wore dresses while I wore pants. They had long eyelashes and I did not. They had long hair, and I had what looked like a plate on my head. I asked Eleanor, "What about the women we know with short hair and the men we know with long hair?" She replied, "Yeah, but women have long hair and men have short hair." She knew there were people who didn't fit her hair theory, but she had already come to accept an image in which the line between men and women was obvious, important, and inevitable.

have little or no facial hair. (This varies by race; Native Americans and blacks often have none.) (2) Breasts: She/he was wearing a loose shirt that hung from his/her shoulders. And, as many women who suffered through a 1950s adolescence know to their shame, women are often flat-chested. (3) Shoulders: His/hers were small and round for a man, broad for a woman. (4) Hands: Long and slender fingers, knuckles a bit large for a woman, small for a man. (5) Voice: Middle range, unexpressive for a woman, not at all the exaggerated tones some gay males affect. (6) His/her treatment of me: Gave off no signs that would let me know if I were of the same or different sex as this person. There were not even any signs that he/she knew his/her sex would be difficult to categorize and I wondered about this even as I did my best to hide these questions so I would not embarrass him/her while we talked of computer paper. I left still not knowing the sex of my salesperson, and was disturbed by that unanswered question (child of my culture that I am). (pp. 133–134)

Most of the time we do not actually see the "parts" that biologically define someone as male or female; we rely instead on other indicators such as clothes and shapes to be sufficient. As sociologist Judith Lorber (1994) put it, "Clothing, paradoxically, often hides the sex but displays the gender" (p. 22). We depend on established cues (such as outfits and hairstyles) to recognize someone's sex when we interact, often taking that recognition for granted.

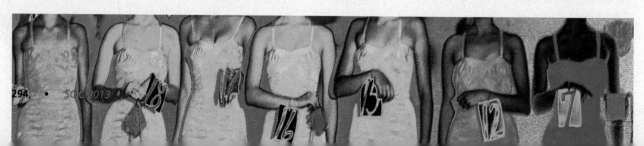

Women's Gender Roles

Parents, schools, friends, and the mass media all socialize us to internalize dominant gender norms. The positive and negative sanctions that we experience during such interactions shape the thoughts, actions, and appearances we accept as appropriate. Women, for example, continue to face pressure to be thin, beautiful, submissive, sexy, and maternal.

Films, television programs, and magazine ads all contribute to an idealized image of feminine beauty (Kilbourne 2010). As we saw in Chapter 6, this image, dubbed the "beauty myth" by Naomi Wolf (1992), is largely unattainable for most women. It contributes to millions of cosmetic procedures each year for those seeking it. And as noted in Chapter 2, even supermodels such as Cindy Crawford feel they cannot achieve their own idealized images. Part of the reason is that these images are often not real. Instead, they are altered with the assistance of computer programs

In 2009 Dove launched its ongoing Campaign for Real Beauty.

such as Photoshop (Gurari, Hetts, and Strube 2006). Attaining an idealized image can be particularly problematic for those who do not match the White and heterosexual assumptions upon which it is built (Milillo 2008; Reel et al. 2008; Tate 2009).

As we increasingly recognize the impact of such artificial images, attempts have been made to offer alternative images of women in the mass media. This includes magazines that have featured images of models or celebrities without makeup or photo retouching, as in the April 2010 issue of French *Elle*, which

Going GLOBAL

Satisfaction with Body Weight and Shape

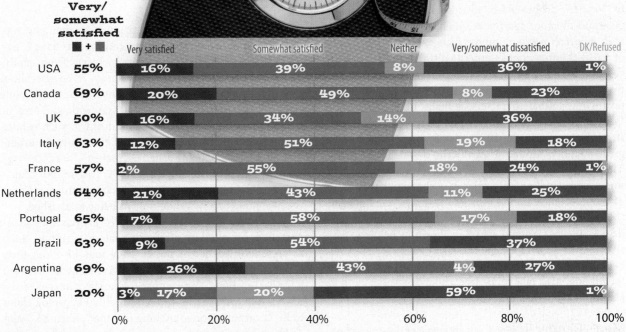

	Very/ somewhat satisfied ■+■	Very satisfied	Somewhat satisfied	Neither	Very/somewhat dissatisfied	DK/Refused
USA	55%	16%	39%	8%	36%	1%
Canada	69%	20%	49%	8%	23%	
UK	50%	16%	34%	14%	36%	
Italy	63%	12%	51%	19%	18%	
France	57%	2%	55%	18%	24%	1%
Netherlands	64%	21%	43%	11%	25%	
Portugal	65%	7%	58%	17%	18%	
Brazil	63%	9%	54%		37%	
Argentina	69%	26%	43%	4%	27%	
Japan	20%	3%	17%	20%	59%	1%

0%   20%   40%   60%   80%   100%

Source: Etcoff et al. 2004.

featured unretouched images of models and actresses without makeup. Similarly, Dove, as part of its Movement for Self-Esteem, provided curriculum that was used in hundreds of "Self-Esteem Weekend" programs for women and girls." (www.dove.us/social-mission). This program represents an extension of their earlier Campaign for Real Beauty, for which they hired academic researchers to conduct surveys of women around the world. Researchers found that only 2 percent of the women surveyed felt comfortable describing themselves as beautiful. This was in spite of the fact that these women distinguished between beauty (happiness, confidence, dignity, and humor) and physical attractiveness (how a person looks). Overall, just 13 percent of women said they were very satisfied with their weight and body shape. In the survey, 68 percent strongly agreed that "the media and advertising set an unrealistic standard of beauty that most women can't ever achieve." In response, Dove established its advertising campaign featuring a wide range of body types and highlighting expanded definitions of beauty. Researchers who have investigated such alternative image campaigns have called their effectiveness into question (Heiss 2011; Swami and Smith 2012).

Gendered messages about being a woman are about more than just beauty. They also project idealized images of "women's proper place," identifying some social status positions as more appropriate than others. Studies show that children's books reinforce such messages. One study of 5,618 children's books published throughout the 20th-century found that male characters were represented twice as often as females. The disparity was greatest when portraying animal characters as males or females. Little Golden Books were more unequal than other series they studied. Starting in the 1970s they found a trend toward greater equity, though a significant imbalance remains. The researchers conclude, "This widespread pattern of underrepresentation of females may contribute to a sense of unimportance among girls and privilege among boys" (McCabe et al: 221). Other studies have found similar gendered patterns. Women are often shown as helpless, passive, and in need of a male caretaker. Fathers, in a study of children's picture books, were significantly less likely to touch, hug, kiss, talk to, or feed children (Anderson and Hamilton 2005; Etaugh 2003; Hamilton et al. 2006).

Men's Gender Roles Conventional gender-role expectations also exist for men. For example, stay-at-home fathers are still relatively uncommon. Among married-couple families with children under 15, there are 28 times as many

stay-at-home moms than stay-at-home dads. Although it is still rare for men to stay home to care for their children, there is evidence that attitudes are changing. In a nationwide survey 69 percent of respondents said that if one parent stays home with the children, it makes no difference whether that parent is the mother or the father. Only 30 percent thought that the mother should be the one to stay home (Robison 2002; U.S. Census Bureau 2011k: Table SHP-1).

Did You Know?

Women in the United States are more likely to serve as volunteers than men. This is true regardless of age, education, or employment status. In 2011, 29.9 percent of women served as volunteers compared to 23.5 percent for men.

Source: Bureau of Labor Statistics.

While attitudes toward parenting may be changing, traditional gender-role expectations continue to have a significant impact. Men, too, receive messages from family, peers, and the media about what it means to be masculine. One of the most powerful expectations is to be tough, both physically and emotionally, in sports, at work, and even in relationships. Males who fail to conform to such gender norms face criticism and even humiliation. Boys, for example, run the risk of being called a "chicken," "sissy," or "fag" even by fathers or brothers (Katz 1999; Pascoe 2007). Such name-calling represents a form of social control that limits the likelihood of new gender norms being established.

We also see the effects of gendered expectations demonstrated by men in nontraditional occupations, such as preschool teacher or nurse. They may lie about their occupations when introduced to others in order to avoid negative reactions. For example, researchers interviewed a 35-year-old male nurse who reported that he would claim to be "a carpenter or something like that" when he "went clubbing," because women weren't interested in getting to know a male nurse. Subjects of the study made similar accommodations in casual exchanges with other men (Bagilhole and Cross 2006; Cross and Bagilhole 2002).

There may be a price to pay for such narrow conceptions of manhood. Boys who successfully adapt to cultural standards of masculinity may grow up to be inexpressive men who cannot share their feelings with others. They remain forceful and tough, but they are also closed and isolated. These traditional gender roles may be putting men at a disadvantage. Today girls outdo boys in high school, grabbing a disproportionate share of the leadership positions, from valedictorian to class president to yearbook editor—everything, in short, except captain of the boys' athletic teams. And their advantage continues after high school. In the 1980s, girls in the United States became more likely than boys to go to college. In 2010 women accounted for 57 percent of college students nationwide. And starting in 2005–2006, more women than men in the United States earned doctoral degrees (Aud et al. 2012:162, 284).

Increasing numbers of men in the United States have criticized the restrictive aspects of the traditional male gender role. Australian sociologist R. W. Connell (2002, 2005) has written about **multiple masculinities,** meaning that men learn and play a range of gender roles. These may include a nurturing-caring role, an effeminate-gay role, or their traditional role. Sociologist Michael Kimmel gave voice to this broader conception of what it means to be a man when he was sitting with his newborn son in the park. When a woman came up to him and said that he was expressing his "feminine side," he responded, "I'm not expressing anything of the sort, ma'am. I'm being tender and loving and nurturing toward my child. As far as I can tell, I'm expressing my *masculinity*" (Kimmel 2004:290–91).

GENDER ACROSS CULTURES

Though socialization into gender roles can narrow what we come to think of as appropriate behavior, examples such as Kimmel's suggest that what we define as appropriate does change over time. Gender expectations also differ across cultures. That gender expectations and performance vary across time and place suggests that masculinity and femininity are not strictly determined by our genes.

As we saw in the case of Woineshet Zebene at the beginning of the chapter, women face significant oppression, violence, and discrimination in nations around the globe. Whether in the form of sex trafficking, socially condoned rape, or denial of medical services, the simple fact of being a women is enough to justify such practices in some countries. Quotidian cruelties exist in these cultures because women are not seen as fully human (Kristof and WuDunn 2009).

Other cultures take dramatically different approaches toward gender. Some assume the existence of three or four gender categories. Judith Lorber (1994) notes that "male women," biological males who live for the most part as women, and "female men," biological females who live for the most part as men, can be found in various societies. "Female men" can be found in some African and Native American societies, and in Albania, where they take on male work and family roles. "Male women" include the *berdaches,* also known as two-spirit people, of the Native

Americans of the Great Plains, the *hijras* of India, and the *xanith* (Nanda 1997; Reddy 2005). Michael Kimmel (2004) describes the *xanith* of Oman in the Middle East:

> They work as skilled domestic servants, dress in men's tunics (but in pastel shades more associated with feminine colors), and sell themselves in passive homosexual relationships. They are permitted to speak with women on the street (other men are prohibited). At sex-segregated public events, they sit with the women. However, they can change their minds. (p. 65)

These gender categories are a well-accepted part of their social lives. Individuals who fill them are not simply tolerated or viewed as deviant. Two-spirit people for example, have high status because they are thought to have special powers (Kimmel, 2004; Roscoe 1997).

Beginning with the path-breaking work of Margaret Mead ([1935] 2001) and continuing through contemporary fieldwork, scholars have shown that gender roles can vary greatly from one physical environment, economy, and political system to the next. Peggy Reeves Sanday's (2002, 2008) work in West Sumatra, Indonesia, for example, describes the 4-million-member Minangkabau society as one in which men and women are not competitors but partners for the common good. This society is characterized by a nurturing approach to the environment, blended with Islamic religious ethics. Women control the land through inheritance; in the event of a divorce, the ex-husband leaves with only his clothes. The larger community may be governed by men, women, or both men and women working together. Sanday's findings, together with Mead's, confirm the influential role of culture and socialization in gender-role differentiation.

multiple masculinities The idea that men learn and play a full range of gender roles.

SOCTHINK

Given that our understandings of gender vary across time and place, why are we so committed to the notion that gender differences are narrowly determined by biology?

REIMAGINING SEX AND GENDER

When it comes to gender, many people assume that the patterns we observe are a given, that biology, as the old saying goes, is destiny. Or, more specifically, that our sex defines our experience as men and women in obvious and predictable ways. We hear echoes of this sentiment in places such as John Gray's best-selling book, *Men Are from Mars, Women Are from Venus* (1992). This powerful analogy presents men and women as aliens from different planets, implying that the chasm between them is natural, inevitable, and difficult, if not impossible, to bridge. A man behaves in certain ways because he is biologically male, and the same goes for women. There are, however, signs

"How It Works"

Source: XKCD.com/385.

that this assumption about the relationship between sex and gender is being called into question; sociologists have, in fact, identified numerous ways in which both sex and gender are social constructions.

Recognizing the limitations of a simple, dimorphic model of sex can then open up opportunities for both men and women. It suggests that the line between what anthropologist Lisa Peattie and sociologist Martin Rein refer to as the natural and the artificial shifts over time. When we say something is *natural,* what we mean is that it should be accepted as given and cannot be changed. For example, when people say that "men are more rational," or that "women are more nurturing," the assumption is that these stereotypes are determined by our biology and thus immutable. Analysis of how gender is expressed across cultures and over time suggests, however, that many such characteristics are really *artificial*—that is, they are social constructions subject to change (Peattie and Rein 1983).

Some major shifts in social life have been brought about by challenging what is considered "natural." Even into the 20th century it was thought that women's biological makeup justified their exclusion from schools, the workplace, and politics—social locations in which women's participation is now taken for granted. For example, women were once banned from colleges and universities in the United States, because it was presumed that they were biologically incapable of succeeding. At the Jefferson Medical College in Philadelphia in 1847, Professor Charles Meigs, in a famous speech delivered to an all-male class of gynecology students, said of women, "She has a head almost too small for intellect and just big enough for love. . . . She reigns in the heart . . . the household altar is her place of worship and service" (quoted in Collins 2003:89–90). In 1874, at Harvard University, Dr. Edward Clarke, a member of its board of overseers, wrote that women were too delicate to handle the rigors of college education. The increased effort needed for thinking would sap energy from a woman's uterus and ovaries, leading these reproductive organs to shrink (Clarke 1874). In fact, Harvard did not formally admit women to its undergraduate program until the early 1970s. When women were finally given the opportunity to attend college, a right they had to fight hard for to win, they excelled. They now have a higher overall grade point average, and they outnumber men among college graduates. What was once thought to be natural is now recognized to have been a social construction. It turns out that the problem wasn't biology; it was the socially constructed culture that denied opportunity. (Chee, Pino, and Smith 2005).

On the flip side, the notion that men just aren't as nurturing as women persists. It appears to grow out of the presumption that women, because they give birth and nurse babies, are naturally better at providing love, care, and protection. Yet research demonstrates that when men have the primary responsibility for raising children, they do the same things conventionally associated with "mothering." For example, sociologist Barbara Risman conducted research on single fathers and concluded that "when males take full responsibility for child care, when they meet expectations usually confined to females, they develop intimate and affectionate relationships with their children. Despite male sex-role training, fathers respond to the nontraditional role of single parent with strategies stereotypically considered feminine" (Risman 1986:101). Similarly, researchers looking at response patterns for nearly 30,000 parents found no significant differences between North American mothers and fathers on factors including nurturance, warmth, responsiveness, encouragement, interaction, or disciplinary strictness. Thus it is not strictly biology that determines nurturing; it is the social structure and a person's position within it (Barnett and Rivers 2004; Lytton and Romney 1991; Risman and Johnson-Sumerford 1998).

> Gender equality is more than a goal in itself. It is a precondition for meeting the challenge of reducing poverty, promoting sustainable development and building good governance.
>
> **Kofi Annan**

WOMAN MAY WEAR TROUSERS.

Attorney General of Kansas Rules There Is No Law Against It.

TOPEKA. Kan.. April 28.—Gov. Stubbs received a letter yesterday from a widow at Oswego asking permission to wear men's trousers while at work at her home. It said she was supporting a large family. which necessitated outside work, and that in wearing skirts she was badly handicapped.

The letter was turned over to the Attorney General. who ruled there was no law prohibiting a woman from wearing men's trousers. especially if she were the head of the house.

Source: Published: April 29, 1910. Copyright © The New York Times.

Identifying some aspect of our definitions of sex and gender as artificial reveals the complex relationship between the two. Questioning our conceptions of the natural, however, is never easy, as women who have worked for the right to vote and equal opportunity have discovered. Confronting these notions can look like an attempt to defy reality itself, but such defiance is necessary to enact significant social change.

>>Working for Change: Women's Movements

One of the lessons we learn from research on gender is that change is possible. As we saw with college education for women, past norms need not determine future practices. Change, however, seldom comes without conflict. People have fought against existing cultural assumptions about what is natural in order to advance opportunity for women in politics, the economy, and other spheres of public and private life. **Feminism** is the term for this belief in social, economic, and political equality for women.

THE FIRST WAVE

The feminist movement in the United States was born in upstate New York, in the town of Seneca Falls, in the summer of 1848. On July 19 the first women's rights convention began, attended by Elizabeth Cady Stanton, Lucretia Mott, and other pioneers in the struggle for women's rights. This first wave of feminists faced ridicule and scorn as they fought for legal and political equality for women. They were not afraid to risk controversy on behalf of their cause; in 1872, Susan B. Anthony was arrested for attempting to vote in that year's presidential election.

Ultimately, the early feminists won many victories. The pinnacle accomplishment of the first wave was the passage and ratification of the 19th Amendment to the Constitution, which granted women the right to vote in national elections beginning in 1920. After this peak, however, suffrage did not lead to other reforms related to women's social and economic position, and in the early and mid-20th century, the women's movement became a much less powerful force for social change.

> **feminism** The belief in social, economic, and political equality for women.

Did You Know?

. . . When the 19th Amendment finally passed in 1920, it did so by a single vote. Having passed the House and Senate in 1919, it still needed to win approval in 36 state legislatures. It reached this milestone when Tennessee legislator Harry T. Burn switched his vote and broke the tie after receiving a letter from his mother that said, "Don't forget to be a good boy and help Mrs. [Carrie Chapman] Catt put the 'Rat' in ratification."

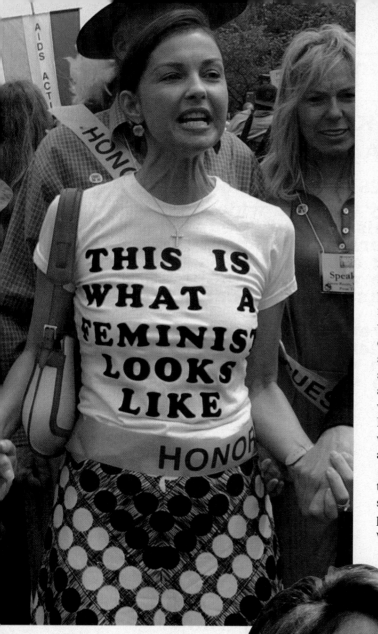

classmates about their lives. What she heard repeatedly from women like her was that they shared a sense of nameless, aching dissatisfaction that she famously labeled "the problem that has no name." Even though they were living what many considered the American Dream, something was missing. They mostly blamed themselves for this feeling of emptiness or incompleteness, and when they sought help, doctors and psychiatrists prescribed charity work, community activities, or perhaps tranquilizers.

In *The Feminine Mystique*, Friedan argued that the problem was not with women as individuals, but with the position they occupied in American society at the time. Friedan's realization that this was not a private trouble but a public issue represents a classic case of using the sociological imagination. Women were cut off from the public sphere, and their lack of access to valued economic, social, and cultural resources—including money and power in the workplace—was the real problem. (Friedan herself attributed part of her own relative happiness to the fact that she retained dual status as both journalist and housewife.) To challenge this structural problem, women had to fight against the cultural assumption that the primary and most "natural" goal for women was to be a wife and mother in the private sphere. As Friedan put it, "We can no longer ignore that voice within women that says, 'I want something more than my husband and my children and my home'" (1963:32).

In 1966, Friedan helped found the National Organization for Women (NOW) to fight for equality for women; she served as its president until 1970. In addition to political and legal battles, one of the organization's tools was "consciousness-raising groups." Among other goals, these groups sought to elevate awareness among women regarding the degree to which they shared "the problem that has no name." This shared consciousness could then lead to collective action and the development of a new structure with enhanced opportunities. Choice was a core value at the center of these efforts. The existing system limited options for women in many areas of social life. Feminists fought to open up structural opportunity and to ensure that women could make choices about going to college, pursuing a career based on ability rather than gender expectations, getting married or staying single, having children or remaining childless, and so on.

The question of whether women should have control over their reproductive rights and their bodies has also played a significant role in this movement.

Nancy Pelosi, Democrat from California, was the first female Speaker of the U.S. House of Representatives.

THE SECOND WAVE

What is called the second wave of feminism in the United States emerged in the 1960s and came into full force in the 1970s. Betty Friedan's book *The Feminine Mystique* played a crucial part, as did two other pioneering books that argued for women's rights: Simone de Beauvoir's *The Second Sex* (1952) and Kate Millett's *Sexual Politics* (1970). Friedan was an upper-middle class, White, suburban housewife who worked part-time as a freelance journalist in the 1950s. As part of a story she planned to write, she surveyed her college

A Woman's Proper Place?

Men

Women

60
50
40
30
20
10
0

1970 1974 1978 1982 1986 1990 1994 1998 2002 2006

Percentage of first-year college students who agree or strongly agree that "the activities of married women are best confined to the home and the family."
Source: Pryor et al. 2007.

In the United States, most people support a woman's right to a legal abortion, but with reservations. According to a 2012 national survey, 23 percent say that abortion should be legal in all cases and 31 percent say in most cases. Of those opposed, 16 percent say it should be illegal in all cases and 23 percent say in most (Pew Research Center 2012c). These percentages have stayed fairly steady for the past 35 years.

As more and more women identified existing cultural practices as sexist attitudes and practices—including attitudes they themselves had accepted through socialization into traditional gender roles—they began to challenge male dominance. A sense of sisterhood, much like the class consciousness that Marx hoped would emerge in the proletariat, became evident. Individual women identified their interests with women as a whole, and they rejected the principle that their happiness depended on their acceptance of submissive and subordinate roles.

SOCTHINK

What does it mean to be a feminist today?

THE THIRD WAVE

In the 1980s, partially because of second-wave successes in opening up opportunities and earning greater respect for women, a sense developed that the central goals of feminism had largely been accomplished. Some scholars argued that we had entered a postfeminist era. In the early 1990s, however, a new style of feminism arose that went beyond fighting the structural obstacles that motivated the first and second waves. It ventured into the cultural sphere to embrace a multiplicity of voices, expressions, and experiences. This third wave was part of a conceptual shift away from a singular focus on equality of persons, which it takes as a given, to a celebration of difference (Brooks 1997; Lotz 2007; Showden 2009).

The third wave arose in part as a generational shift; younger women were dissatisfied with the dominant image of feminism as stodgy and uptight. It also represented a shift in message toward a more varied and pluralistic understanding of what feminism is. This was evident in two early anthologies that played a pivotal role presenting the multiplicity of voices this movement represents: Rebecca Walker's *To Be Real: Telling the Truth and Changing the Face of Feminism* (1995) and Barbara Findlen's *Listen Up: Voices from the Next Feminist Generation* (1995). Previously, feminists were characterized as White, upper-middle class, and heterosexual. Third-wave feminists place greater emphasis on agency and subjectivity; are committed to personal empowerment; are more open about sexuality and sexual exploration; and celebrate diversity of gender, race, ethnicity, and class. Embracing a multiplicity of identities led to a commitment to social justice and a global perspective so that other voices have the opportunity to be heard (Baumgardner and Richards 2000; Groeneveld 2009; Lotz 2007; Zimmerman, McDermott, and Gould 2009).

There is in the third wave a bit of the postmodern idea of self-creation, according to which we can choose our identities from a buffet of possibilities and create our own realities. This fits with the notion that our sex is not narrowly determined by biology and that our expression of our gender need not be singular in nature but is open to our creativity and control. One result is a more playful or ironic element to the movement, especially when it comes to so-called girlie feminism, which seeks to reclaim things like lipstick, high heels, and more sexualized images of women as viable emblems of feminist empowerment. Critics have argued that this rhetoric of choice inappropriately minimizes the continued power of racial, sexual, and class positions in society (Munford 2007; Renegar and Sowards 2009; Showden 2009).

One of the outgrowths of this new feminist perspective was the recognition that defining others primarily by any one position may diminish the importance of the multiple positions we all occupy. To look at the social location of Hispanic women, for example, we must pay mind to both their gender and their ethnicity (as well as other factors). Two significant theoretical developments arising out of this multiple-identity approach are standpoint

standpoint theory Because our social positions shape our perceptions, a more complete understanding of social relations must incorporate the perspectives of marginalized voices.

intersectionality Gender, sexuality, race, ethnicity, and class must not be studied in isolation, because they have intermingled effects on our identity, knowledge, and outcomes.

sexuality Denotes our identities and activities as sexual beings.

sexual orientation The categories of people to whom we are sexually attracted.

theory and intersectionality. **Standpoint theory** maintains that our understanding of reality is shaped by the positions we occupy and the experiences we have. Given that the views of some (based on their gender, sexuality, race, ethnicity, or class) are privileged over others, this theory emphasizes the importance of listening to the voices of those who are in some way considered outsiders. Such attention provides a deeper and richer understanding of social systems (Collins 2000; Harding 2004; Hartsock 1983; Smith 1987). **Intersectionality** represents a second major development. According to this approach, we cannot speak of gender or race or class or sexuality as if they exist in isolation from each other. Rather, these combine within us in ways that make it difficult to separate the effects of each. Thus research must analyze the intermingled effects of multiple social statuses on identity, knowledge, and outcomes (Alimahomed 2010; Harding 2004; Shields 2008).

For both standpoint theory and intersectionality, a narrative approach in research, in which we hear the voices of those who are other to us, is critical.

>>The Social Construction of Sexuality

The shifts that occur in how sex and gender are defined—as more complex than simple binary categories of male and female or masculine and feminine—also apply to sexuality. In the United States, as a consequence of the dimorphic model of sex, the dominant ideology presumed heterosexual relationships, in which the idealized norm was chastity until marriage followed by lifelong faithfulness to a single partner. This vision reached perhaps its zenith in the 1950s television portrayal of families in programs such as *Leave It To Beaver* and *Father Knows Best*. Times have changed.

Sexuality denotes our identities and activities as sexual beings. In terms of identity, our sexuality represents an expression of who we are in a way similar to gender, race, ethnicity, and class. In terms of our sexual practices, sexuality shapes what we do (or do not do) and with whom.

SEXUALITY AND IDENTITY

Sexual expression is not simply a result of biological urges and instincts. It is situated within, and an outgrowth of, existing social, cultural, and historical processes. Though alternative expressions of sexuality have a long history in the United States, their existence and practice has not always been acknowledged (Duberman, Vicinus, and Chauncy 1989; Escoffier 1997). During the 1960s, experimentation with "free love" helped open the door to more widespread recognition of such expressions. At the same time organizations arose, such as the Gay Liberation Front in 1969 and the Gay Activist Alliance in 1970, that raised awareness that alternatives existed and sought to establish the legitimacy of alternative sexualities in the public consciousness. As a result, people became more aware of the concept of **sexual orientation**—the categories of people to whom we are sexually attracted—as a form of personal and community identity. Initially, in keeping with the dimorphic model of sex, the two major subcategories included

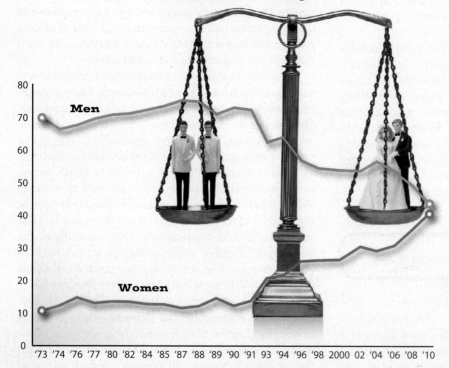

U.S. Attitudes about Homosexuality

Note: Responses are to the question "What about sexual relationship between two adults of the same sex - do you think it is always wrong, almost always wrong, wrong only sometimes, or worng at all?" Data are from the General Social Survey, a regularly administered national survey of the U.S. adult population.

Source: Smith, T. 2011

Thomas Beatie was born female and underwent sexual reassignment surgery to become male. He kept his female reproductive organs in hopes one day of becoming a parent. When his wife could not become pregnant, he conceived and gave birth to their first child in 2008.

existence and power (Brooks and Quina 2009; Crabtree 2009; Kinsey, Pomeroy, and Martin 1948; Kinsey, Pomeroy, and Gebhardt 1953; Waites 2009).

Though awareness of alternative forms of sexuality has increased, a cultural expectation of heterosexuality remains dominant in the United States. Sociologists use the term **heteronormativity** to describe the cultural presupposition that heterosexuality is the appropriate standard for sexual identity and practice and that alternative sexualities are deviant, abnormal, or wrong (Chambers 2007; Elia 2003). As an example of heteronormativity, a 1957 survey found that "four out of five people believed that anyone who preferred to remain single was 'sick,' 'neurotic,' or 'immoral'" (Coontz 2005:230). Additionally, homosexuality was categorized as a psychological disorder until 1972 in the American Psychiatric Association's official *Diagnostic and Statistical Manual of Mental Disorders* (DSM). A new edition of the DSM is due out in 2013, and debate centers on what are now called "gender identity disorders," including those who are transgender and transsexual. Some psychological professionals prefer not to identify these as disorders because doing so stigmatizes these identities. Others argue that it is important to maintain these diagnoses, because transgender people who seek gender reassignment surgery might not get proper diagnosis and treatment without such a designation (Drescher 2010, 2011; Melby 2009).

Heteronormativity is a form of ethnocentrism that generalizes a particular cultural ideal (heterosexuality) onto all

> **heterosexual** A category of sexual orientation that includes those who are sexually attracted to members of the opposite sex.
>
> **homosexual** A category of sexual orientation that includes those who are attracted to members of the same sex.
>
> **bisexual** A category of sexual orientation that includes those who are attracted to both men and women.
>
> **transgender** People who appear to be biologically one sex but who identify with the gender of another.
>
> **heteronormativity** A term that sociologists use to describe the cultural presupposition that heterosexuality is the appropriate standard for sexual identity and practice and that alternative sexualities are deviant, abnormal, or wrong.

heterosexual, those who were sexually attracted to members of the opposite sex, and **homosexual,** those who were attracted to members of the same sex. Homosexual men were identified as gay, and homosexual women were identified as lesbian. **Bisexual** was later added to these subcategories to include those who were attracted to both men and women.

This model of sexuality, even though it extended awareness of sexuality beyond the 1950s version, still presents the dividing lines as clear-cut and absolute. Classifying where you or others belong is presumed to be a simple matter of identifying your sexual practices and selecting the appropriate category. But people's experiences of sexuality are more complex and varied than that. For example, what about those who have had occasional homosexual experiences in their past but are now practicing heterosexuals? Or those who engage in same-sex practices but do not identify themselves as gay, lesbian, or bisexual? In an attempt to clarify just one of these definitions, historian David Halperin (2009) identified 13 different formulations of bisexuality, thus highlighting the ambiguity in drawing these lines.

Over time, in response to the limitations of this approach, a new model presented sexuality as a continuum rather than an either-or designation. A key component of this approach is the recognition of people who are **transgender**—those who appear to be biologically one sex but who identify with the gender of another—as an additional category. Such recognition highlights the socially constructed nature of sexuality as opposed to its biological element, and creates more space for alternative expressions of sexuality. This is particularly true if transgender is defined even more broadly, as historian Susan Stryker (2007) suggests, "as anything that disrupts or denaturalizes normative gender, and which calls our attention to the process through which normativity is produced" (p. 60). From this perspective, transgender involves transgressions of dominant gender norms in ways that enable us to recognize their

other populations, thus denying legitimacy to those outside it (Chambers 2007). It can be maintained in subtle, often invisible ways during our everyday interactions. The television series *Glee* captured just such a moment in an encounter between Kurt, a gay high school student, and his father, Burt, who is generally understanding and supportive of Kurt's sexuality. Kurt was saddened at the seeming ease with which his dad talked sports with Finn, the school's star quarterback. His father tries to reassure him by saying, "Kurt, I love you. And I am sympathetic to all your stuff. But come on, buddy, we've got a deal here, right? I don't try to change you; you don't try to change me. You are my son, and a little guy talk with some other kid isn't going to change that." Kurt replies, "Guy talk? I'm a guy." It is precisely at moments such as this, when a person becomes invisible as a guy because he does not conform to the dominant gender expectations, that heteronormativity is at work.

SOCTHINK

How is heteronormativity reinforced in the current top-rated songs and television programs? Can you think of any exceptions?

Socialization plays a key role in determining our sexual identity (Parker 2009). Just as was the case with gender, we face significant pressure to obey dominant norms for masculinity and femininity. In her book *Dude You're a Fag*, sociologist C. J. Pascoe (2007) set out to understand how heteronormativity is reproduced. She conducted an ethnographic study of boys in a working-class high school. She found that one of the ways they reinforced existing masculinity norms was by casually using the term "fag" to call out anyone who deviates from the dominant masculine ideal. According to Pascoe, calling someone a fag was not so much an antigay act (though she admits it was that, too) as it was a means of keeping guys in line. Whereas it was possible to be a homosexual and still be masculine, being a fag represented a form of failed masculinity. The threat of being a fag hangs over boys like a specter or ghost that could possess them at any time; only eternal vigilance keeps it at bay. Pascoe argues that rejecting this role also represented a repudiation of femininity. So not only did this discourse support existing heteronormative standards, it also reinforced traditional conceptions of gender. Other researchers found similar results in a study of "hogging", in which men have sex with overweight or obese women not as a means of establishing a relationship with them but as a game to prove their masculinity to other guys (Prohaska and Gailey 2010).

Such examples point to the fact that differences in sexuality are not just matters of orientation and alternative preferences; they are connected to larger systems of power in which some statuses are privileged over others (Brickell 2009). We construct our sexual identities, making sense of who we are, within the contexts of our social structures.

Within these worlds, not all paths are accepted as equally legitimate. In the United States, establishing a sexual identity as something other than heterosexual has been difficult owing to the meanings attached to such identities and the lack of broader cultural support for them. These power differences contribute to discrimination and threats of violence. According to the FBI, for example, 19.1 percent of the 7,690 hate crime offenses reported in 2010 involved sexual orientation (U.S. Department of Justice 2011c).

SOCTHINK

How does gendered name-calling, such as joking that a guy is a fag, function to maintain clear-cut gender boundaries? What consequences does it have for gays, lesbians, or heterosexual girls?

In an effort to ensure the civil, political, and social rights of those in lesbian, gay, bisexual, and transgender (LGBT) communities around the world, a group of human rights experts gathered in Indonesia in 2006 to establish the Yogyakarta Principles (www.yogyakartaprinciples.org/). The principles are built on the supposition of universal human rights and seek to extend these rights to include sexual orientation and gender identity. They identify 29 basic principles including the right to equality and nondiscrimination, the right to work, and the right to found a family. This movement arose in part because homosexuality remains a crime in many nations; in some it is punishable by death.

In places where there has been more openness about sexuality, increasingly, sexual preference may not necessarily be the primary mode of identification, but it exists in combination with gender, race, ethnicity, nationality, and class (Stein 2010). As alternative expressions of sexuality become more accepted and less alternative, their role as master status through which all identity is filtered may become less powerful. Instead, in keeping with the intersectionality perspective, sexuality may become but one significant piece of identity that shapes who we are and the paths we are likely to pursue (Gomez 1997).

SEXUALITY IN ACTION

While our sexuality shapes our conception of who we are, it also has consequences for what we do. In sociological terms, as suggested by the Thomas theorem (see p. 15), our self-esteem is shaped by our interactions with others. We then act on the basis of those perceptions. In our everyday lives, our perceptions of ourselves and our sexual practices often reinforce each other. Working out our sexuality in practice includes the types of sex acts we perform and the types of sexual relationships we establish with others.

Because such topics are generally considered to be taboo, people are often both ignorant and curious about actual

Alfred C. Kinsey, with the help of his team of researchers, provided unprecedented insight into people's sexual practices in the United States.

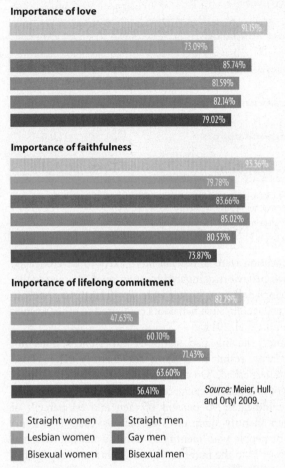

Relationship Values by Gender and Sexual Identity

Importance of love

91.15%
73.09%
85.74%
81.59%
82.14%
79.02%

Importance of faithfulness

93.36%
79.78%
83.66%
85.02%
80.53%
73.87%

Importance of lifelong commitment

82.79%
47.63%
60.10%
71.43%
63.60%
56.41%

Source: Meier, Hull, and Ortyl 2009.

☐ Straight women	☐ Straight men
☐ Lesbian women	☐ Gay men
☐ Bisexual women	☐ Bisexual men

sexual practices. The Kinsey Reports (*Sexual Behavior in the Human Male* [1948] and *Sexual Behavior in the Human Female* [1953]) provided the earliest in-depth research studies on people's sexual practices. Compiled by American biologist Alfred C. Kinsey and his colleagues, the reports, particularly their finding that 8 percent of men had been in predominantly homosexual relationships for at least three years between ages 16 and 55, were considered shocking at the time. Both volumes became best sellers. Their studies opened the door for others to conduct additional research (Bullough 1998; Laumann et al. 1994; Smith 2006).

The National Survey of Family Growth (NSFG) provides recent data and includes detailed information on actual sexual practices. It is conducted by the National Center for Health Statistics (NCHS) and the Centers for Disease Control and Prevention (CDC), and is based on a national sample of more than 13,000 respondents (Chandra, Mosher, Copen, and Sionean 2011). Summarizing the results of heterosexual relationship patterns, the NSFG researchers report:

> Among adults aged 25–44, about 98% of women and 97% of men ever had vaginal intercourse, 89% of women and 90% of men ever had oral sex with an opposite-sex partner, and 36% of women and 44% of men ever had anal sex with an opposite-sex partner. (p. 1)

They also investigated the numbers of opposite-sex partners people age 25–44 had in their lifetime, finding that, among women, 32 percent report they have had 1 or 2 male partners, 36 percent say 3 to 6, and 10 percent

report they have had 15 or more. For men the numbers are 19 percent with 1 or 2 partners, 29 percent say 3 to 6, and 28 percent report 15 or more. The median number of partners was 3.6 for women and 6.1 for men. Among married couples, 3.9 percent of married men and 2.2 percent of married women reported more than one opposite-sex partner in the previous 12 months. Among those cohabitating, 15 percent of men and 13 percent of women reported more than one opposite-sex partner within the previous year (Chandra et al. 2011).

One contentious question in such studies is the percentage of homosexuals in the U.S. population. A commonly used figure (derived from the Kinsey Reports) estimates that approximately 10 percent of the population is homosexual. The NSFG study distinguished between having had same-sex experiences and identifying with particular sexual orientations. The researchers found that, among men aged 25–44, 5.8 percent have had same-sex sexual contact in their lifetime. Among women of the same age, 12.0 percent have had same-sex sexual contact in their lifetime Likelihoods of engaging in same-sex sexual behavior varied by educational attainment. Men with higher levels

Sexuality Self-Identification, Ages 18–44

	Men	Women
Heterosexual	95.7	93.7
Homosexual	1.7	1.1
Bisexual	1.1	3.5
Something else	0.2	0.6
No response	1.3	1.1

Note: Percent is in response to the question "Do you think of yourself as heterosexual, homosexual, bisexual, or something else?"

Source: Chandra et al. 2011.

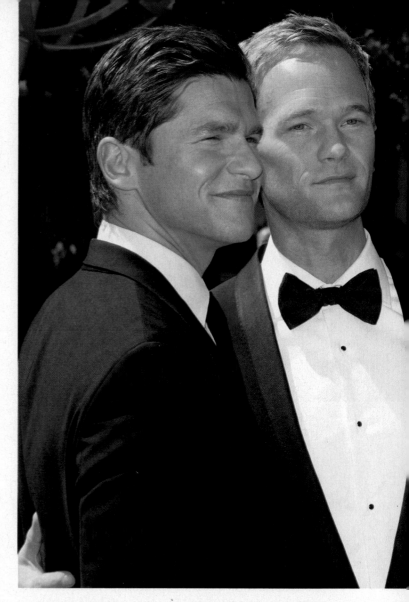

of education were somewhat *more* likely to have engaged in such behaviors compared to other men. Women with a bachelor's degree or higher were significantly *less* likely to have engaged in such behaviors compared to other women (Chandra et al. 2011).

Simply having had same-sex experiences does not necessarily result in a same-sex identity. The NSFG researchers asked, "Do you think of yourself as a heterosexual, homosexual, bisexual, or something else?" As the table above indicates, 96 percent of men and 94 percent of women identify themselves as heterosexual. The numbers of people who identify as homosexual and bisexual are lower than the numbers of those who have engaged in such practices. Overall, the percentage of men and women aged 18–44 who identify themselves as either homosexual or bisexual is less than 4 percent. This finding is consistent with other recent national studies on sexual behavior in the United States (Chandra et al. 2011; Gates 2010; Indiana University Center for Sexual Health Promotion 2010).

The age at which people have their first sexual experiences has historically been an additional interest of researchers. In terms of opposite-sex experiences, the percentage of teens that have had sexual intercourse rises with each subsequent year. At age 15, 23 percent of girls and 21 percent of boys have had vaginal sexual intercourse; by age 17, it is 44 percent for both girls and boys; among 18–19 year olds, it is 62 percent for females and 66 percent for males. Of those aged 15–17, approximately 6.7 percent of girls and 9.8 percent of boys had engaged in oral sex but had not had vaginal intercourse (Chandra et al. 2011).

One of the concerns about those who have sex at a young age is sexual coercion. In fact, among girls who had their first sexual intercourse before age 14, 18 percent said that they really didn't want it to happen at the time. Another 52 percent had mixed feelings about whether they wanted sex or not. For boys who were the same age, 8.9 percent didn't want it to happen and 34 percent had mixed feelings. Put another way, among those who had sex before age 20, 41 percent of females and 63 percent of males really

wanted it to happen at the time (Martinez, Copen, and Abma 2011:Table 9).

When it comes to same-sex experiences among those who are younger, females have a higher likelihood of having had same-sex contact. Among those aged 15–19, 11 percent of women and 2.5 percent of men report having had some form of sexual contact with a member of the same sex. Of those aged 20–24, 15.8 percent of women and 5.6 percent of men report such contact. When it comes to self-identification, women aged 18–19 are the most likely to identify as something other than heterosexual, with 5.8 percent selecting bisexual and 1.9 percent choosing homosexual. By contrast, men of the same age report at 1.1 percent and 1.6 percent, respectively (Chandra et al. 2011).

One of the most significant developments in the history of human sexuality was the invention of the birth control pill. It was approved for use in the United States in 1960 and helped spark the sexual revolution. Together with other modern forms of birth control, the pill made it possible to engage in sex without significant risk of getting pregnant. It gave women greater control over their sexuality and their careers by allowing them to control their fertility. Effective birth control also resulted in debates about how sex should be viewed, whether primarily for procreation

increases their opportunities for self-determination. It also increases the likelihood of extending basic human rights and protections to women in countries around the world (Inglehart, Norris, and Welzel 2002; Kristof and WuDunn 2009; United Nations 2011g).

SOCTHINK

How might economic, social, and cultural factors influence a society's pattern of birth control use? How might these factors influence a society's attitudes about gender?

(that is, having babies) or recreation (for pleasure, love, and commitment) or both. Religious groups, including the Roman Catholic Church, continue to struggle with these issues (Benagiano and Mori 2009).

Internationally, birth control practices vary significantly from country to country. The overall global average for use of modern forms of birth control—condoms, the pill, and sterilization—is 56 percent among people aged 15–44. For Europe as a whole, 59 percent of people use a modern form

SOCTHINK

Why are young women the most likely category to both engage in same-sex practices and embrace alternative sexual identities?

of birth control. The rate jumps to 77 percent in the countries of northern Europe (such as Norway and the United Kingdom) and 69 percent in western Europe (including France and Germany). In Asia, China's rate is 86 percent, Japan's is 44 percent, and India's is 49 percent. Compare these countries with Africa, where the overall rate is 22 percent (though there is substantial variation between countries). Some African nations have extremely low rates (for example, Somalia at 1 percent, Chad at 2 percent, and Guinea at 4 percent). Others have rates higher than the global average (for example, Zimbabwe at 58 percent, Egypt at 58 percent, and South Africa at 60 percent). Just as was the case for women in the United States, greater control over fertility by women internationally

>>Gender and Inequality

Although the work of early sociologists such as Harriet Martineau, Charlotte Perkins Gilman, and Ida B. Wells-Barnett highlighted the significance of gender inequality, in the 1950s sociologists Talcott Parsons and Robert Bales (1955) argued that families need both an instrumental and an expressive leader. The **instrumental leader** is the person in the family who bears responsibility for completion of tasks, focuses on distant goals, and manages the external relationship between the family and other social institutions. The **expressive leader** is the person in the family who bears responsibility for the maintenance of harmony and internal emotional affairs. According to their theory, women's interest in expressive goals frees men for instrumental tasks, and vice versa.

instrumental leader The person in the family who bears responsibility for the completion of tasks, focuses on distant goals, and manages the external relationship between one's family and other social institutions.

expressive leader The person in the family who bears responsibility for the maintenance of harmony and internal emotional affairs.

Trends in U.S. Women's Participation in the Paid Labor Force

Proportion of adult women in paid labor force (percentage)

Single women

Married women

Year: 1890 1900 1910 1920 1930 1940 1950 1960 1970 1980 1990 2000 2009 2010

Source: U.S. Census Bureau 1975, 2011h:Table 597.

SEXISM AND DISCRIMINATION

Sociologists are interested in understanding the "consequences of difference," that is, the impact the social structures we build have on the distribution of valued resources. When it comes to gender, sociologists investigate the degree of sexism that exists within social systems. **Sexism** is the ideology that claims one sex is superior to the other. The term generally refers to male prejudice and discrimination against women. It is not enough, however, to understand gender inequality only by looking at the attitudes and practices of individuals, such as sexist remarks and acts of aggression. We must analyze it as a characteristic of the social system itself. Sociologists refer to such patterns of treatment that, as part of a society's normal operations, systematically deny a group access to resources and opportunities as **institutional discrimination.**

All the major institutions in the United States—including the government, the armed forces, large corporations, the media, universities, and the medical establishment—are controlled by men. Analysis of patterns of distribution allow for some assessment of the degree to which institutional sexism exists.

sexism The ideology that one sex is superior to the other.

institutional discrimination A pattern of treatment that systematically denies a group access to resources and opportunities as part of society's normal operations.

Women become naturally anchored in the family as wives, mothers, and household managers; men become anchored in the occupational world outside the home.

As a result of insights from feminist theorists and findings from further research, sociologists now argue that such separate abilities are not innate but are instead social constructs. The key sociological task is to analyze how gender expectations are created and maintained—for example, through gender-role socialization—and then to investigate the consequences of such constructs.

WOMEN IN THE UNITED STATES

More than 35 years ago, the U.S. Commission on Civil Rights (1976) concluded that the phrase in the Declaration of Independence proclaiming that "all men are created equal" had been taken literally for too long. It found that women in the United States experienced a consistent pattern of inequality. Looking at the workplace, income, housework, politics, and more, we can see that their concern is still valid.

Labor Force Participation The labor market has

Women's Representation in U.S. Occupations

Underrepresented		Overrepresented	
Firefighters	3.6	High school teachers	57.0
Aircraft pilots	5.2	Cashiers	73.7
Civil engineers	9.7	Social workers	80.8
Police officers	13.0	Elementary teachers	81.8
Printers	17.3	File clerks	82.0
Clergy	17.5	Librarians	82.8
Chefs and head cooks	19.0	Tellers	88.0
Dentists	25.5	Registered nurses	91.1
Computer scientists	30.5	Word processors and typists	92.5
Lawyers	31.5	Receptionists	92.7
Physicians	32.3	Child care workers	94.7
Mail carriers	37.7	Dental hygienists	95.1

Note: Women constitute 47.2 percent of the entire labor force. These data are for 2010. The elementary teacher category includes middle school teacher.

Source: Bureau of Labor Statistics 2011f: Table 11.

opened up significantly since Betty Friedan published *The Feminine Mystique* in 1963. Today, millions of women—married or single, with or without children, pregnant or recently having given birth—are in the labor force. Overall, 58.6 percent of adult women in the United States were in the labor force in 2010, compared to 43 percent in 1970. By contrast, in 2010, 71.2 percent of adult men in the United States were in the labor force, compared to 80 percent in 1970. Among married mothers, 62 percent of those with children under age 6 were in the labor force in 2010, compared to 30 percent in 1970 (U.S. Census Bureau 2011h:Table 599; Bureau of Labor Statistics 2011f:Table 2).

Still, women entering the job market find their options restricted in important ways. Particularly damaging is occupational segregation, or confinement to sex-typed "women's jobs." For example, in 2010, women accounted for 95 percent of all dental hygienists and 83 percent of all librarians. Entering such sex-typed occupations often places women in "service" roles that parallel the traditional gender-role standard (Bureau of Labor Statistics 2011f: Table 11).

Women are underrepresented in occupations historically defined as "men's jobs," which often offer much greater financial rewards and prestige than women's jobs. For example, in 2010, women accounted for 47.2 percent of the paid labor force of the United States, yet they constituted only 5.2 percent of aircraft pilots, 9.7 percent of civil engineers, 25.5 percent of all dentists, and 32.3 percent of physicians. Sixty-nine percent of professional women are in health care or education (Bureau of Labor Statistics 2011f:Table 11; 2011g:2).

When it comes to getting promotions, women sometimes encounter attitudinal or organizational bias that prevents them from reaching their full potential. The term **glass ceiling** refers to an invisible barrier that blocks the promotion of a qualified individual in a work environment because of the individual's gender, race, or ethnicity. In 2011 women held 16.1 percent of the seats on the boards of directors of the 500 largest corporations in the United States. Only 18 of those corporations had a female board Chair, whereas 482 had a male in that prestigious post (Catalyst 2012a; 2011a).

Income Today we claim to value "equal pay for equal work," meaning that someone's sex (along with race, ethnicity, or age) shouldn't matter in determining what the person earns; the only characteristic that should matter is job performance. But in practice, women do not earn as much on average as men, even in the same occupations. When comparing individuals who worked full-time, year-round in 2010, the median income for men was $47,715, and the median for women was $36,931 (DeNavas-Walt et al. 2011). In other words, women earned 77 cents for every dollar that men earned overall.

Taking occupational segregation into account does not explain away the wage gap. Women are often more concentrated in occupations with lower average wages than men (child care worker or receptionist versus physician or civil engineer). In 2009, out of 108 specific jobs for which there were sufficient data, there were only four in which women earned more on average than men: teacher assistants, bakers, "life, physical, and social science technicians," and "dining room and cafeteria attendants and bartender helpers." Significant wage gaps exist within occupations across the board. For example, wage gaps persist in the three occupations for which women receive the highest average pay: pharmacist (76 percent of men's earnings), lawyer (75 percent), and chief executive (75 percent). Of course, in some occupations the wage gap is significantly wider, including insurance agent (62 percent), financial manager (67 percent), and physician/surgeon (64 percent) (Bureau of Labor Statistics 2010c:Table 18).

> **glass ceiling** An invisible barrier that blocks the promotion of a qualified individual in a work environment because of the individual's gender, race, or ethnicity.

Even in occupations where women are more likely to be concentrated, they still earn less on average than do men in the same field. Examples include social worker (91 percent), elementary or middle school teacher (91 percent), and registered nurse (87 percent). Observers of the labor force have termed this advantage for men in female-dominated occupations the "glass escalator," in contrast to the glass ceiling (Bureau of

Gender Wage Gap by Age

Woman's median weekly earnings as a percent of men's

Age (years)
16–19	94.6%
20–24	93.8%
25–34	90.8%
35–44	79.9%
45–54	76.5%
55–64	75.2%
65+	75.7%

Note: Wage gap is women's median weekly earnings as a percent of men's. Overall weekly earnings wage gap is 81.2 percent.

Source: Bureau of Labor Statistics 2011g:Table 1.

Did You Know?

. . . Married mothers spend about twice as much time per week on child care and housework as married fathers. Mothers spend about 12 hours per week on child care and 18 hours on housework compared to 6 and 9, respectively, for fathers.

Source: Krantz-Kent 2009.

second shift The double burden—work outside the home followed by child care and housework—that many women face and few men share equitably.

in the same occupation? The Census Bureau studied the following characteristics of men and women in the same occupation:

- Age and degree of formal education
- Marital status and the presence of children at home
- Specialization within the occupation (for example, family practice versus surgical practice)
- Years of work experience
- Hours worked per year

Taking all these factors into consideration reduced the pay gap between men and women by only 2 cents. Even taking such factors into account, women still earned 79 cents for every dollar earned by men. In sum, the disparity in pay between men and women cannot be explained by pointing to women's career choices (Correll, Benard, and Paik 2007; Government Accountability Office 2003; Weinberg 2007).

Home and Work Today, many women face the challenge of trying to juggle work and family. Who does the housework when women become productive wage earners? In households where both work full-time, wives do on average 28 hours of housework while husbands do 16. This approximate 2:1 ratio holds across social class levels. Even in households where she works and he does not, wives still do more housework (Belkin 2008).

Sociologist Arlie Hochschild (1989, 1990, 2005) has used the phrase **second shift** to describe the double burden—work outside the home followed by child care and housework—that many women face and few men share equitably. On the basis of interviews with and observations of 52 couples over an eight-year period, Hochschild reported that the wives (and not their husbands) drive home from the office while planning domestic schedules and playdates for children—and then begin their second shift. Drawing on national studies, she concluded that women spend 15 fewer hours each week in leisure activities than their husbands. In a year, these women work an extra month of 24-hour days because of the second shift; over a dozen years, they work an extra year of 24-hour days. Hochschild found that the married couples she studied were fraying at the edges, and so were their careers and their marriages. With such reports in mind, many feminists have advocated greater governmental and corporate support for child care, more flexible family leave policies, and other reforms designed to ease the burden on the nation's families (Mann Sullivan, and Gershuny 2011; Moen, and Roehling 2005).

Labor Statistics 2011g:Table 2; Cognard-Black 2004).

What accounts for these wage gaps between men and women

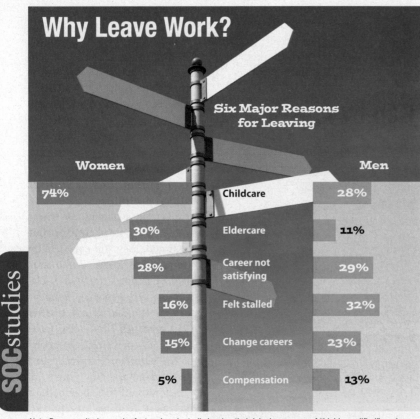

Why Leave Work?

Six Major Reasons for Leaving

Women		Men
74%	Childcare	28%
30%	Eldercare	11%
28%	Career not satisfying	29%
16%	Felt stalled	32%
15%	Change careers	23%
5%	Compensation	13%

SOCstudies

Note: Reasons cited as major factors in voluntarily leaving their jobs in a survey of "highly qualified" workers, age 28-55, defined as those with a graduate degree, a professional degree, or a bachelor's degree with honors.

Source: Hewlett, Foster, Sherbin, Shiller, and Sumberg 2010.

Politics Turning to political involvement, after years of struggle, women won the right to vote with the passage of the

19th Amendment in 1920. Looking at voter participation rates, we can see that they have taken advantage of that opportunity. In fact, a higher percentage of women turn out to vote than do men. This has been true in every presidential election since 1980. In the 2008 presidential election, for example, 65.7 percent of voting-age women reported having voted, compared with 61.5 percent of men (Lopez and Taylor 2009).

When it comes to holding elected office, however, we find the same kind of underrepresentation in positions of power by women as is evident in the workplace. Even though women make up slightly more than half of the population, they make up a significantly smaller proportion of elected officials. In 2010, for example, only 6 of the nation's 50 states had a female governor (Arizona, New Mexico, North Carolina, Oklahoma, South Carolina, and Washington).

Women have made slow but steady progress in certain political arenas. In 1981, out of 535 members of Congress, only 21 were women: 19 in the House of Representatives and 2 in the Senate. By 2010, 17 percent of the members of Congress were women: 72 in the House and 17 in the Senate. Yet even when Nancy Pelosi served as Speaker of the House from 2007 to 2011—the first woman ever to serve in that role—the membership and leadership of Congress remained overwhelmingly male. Since 1789, 11,743 men have served as members of Congress compared to only 270 women—a mere 2.2 percent of the total (Center for American Women and Politics 2011a, 2011b).

At the Supreme Court, Sandra Day O'Connor became the nation's first female justice in 1981 (and retired in 2006). She was joined by Ruth Bader Ginsberg in 1993. In August 2009, Sonia Sotomayor became the third woman and first Hispanic on the Court. In August 2010 Elena Kagan was sworn in to the Court, making it the first time three women have ever served as justices on the Court at the same time.

In the executive branch, no woman has ever been elected either president or vice president of the United States, although Hillary Clinton and Sarah Palin challenged that barrier in 2008.

Violence against Women As the story of Woineshet Zebene suggests, violence against women is a global problem. The full extent of such violence, both in the United States and abroad, is unknown because such crimes often go unreported and unrecognized. In a global survey, researchers found the likelihood of experiencing physical or sexual violence varied significantly from place to place. For example, they found that 15 percent of women in Japan had been victims of sexual or physical violence by an intimate partner, compared to 71 percent in Ethiopia and 69 percent in Peru (García-Moreno et al. 2005).

Violence against women in the United States remains a significant problem. According to the National Crime Victimization Survey (see Chapter 6), there were 188,380 rapes and sexual assaults in 2010. Among female victims, 73 percent of the offenses were committed by someone familiar to them (such as a friend, acquaintance, intimate partner, or other relative). Overall, only 50 percent of these rapes and sexual assaults were reported to police (Truman and Rand 2010). Other studies suggest that the likelihood of reporting such acts to police may be significantly lower.

5 Movies on GENDER AND SEXUALITY

The Kids Are All Right
Two children of a lesbian couple look for their biological father.

Beginners
A young man's father comes out of the closet at age 75.

Jennifer's Body
A feminist take on horror films.

Fight Club
An outsized exploration of modern masculinity.

Transamerica
A male-to-female transsexual travels the country with her son.

Young Women and Men Voters (18–29) in Presidential Elections

	Women	Men
1992	54%	50%
1996	43%	36%
2000	43%	38%
2004	52%	46%
2008	55%	47%

Source: Kirby and Kawashima-Ginsberg 2009.

Research shows that women and girls of all ages are subject to acts of violence. Among high school girls, 9.3 percent had been hit, slapped, or physically hurt on purpose by their boyfriend or girlfriend in the previous year, and 10.5 percent had been physically forced to have sexual intercourse when they did not want to (Centers for Disease Control and Prevention 2010:Table 12). In a survey of college women, 19 percent experienced either an attempted or completed sexual assault while in college. Overall, 3.4 percent of college women had been forcibly raped and 8.5 percent had been raped while incapacitated—drunk, passed out, drugged, or asleep. Among college women who were victims of a forced sexual assault, only 13 percent reported it to police or campus security, though 69 percent disclosed the incident to a family member or friend (Krebs et al. 2007). In a national survey of adult women in the United States, researchers found that 18 percent had been raped at some point in their lifetime. Only 16 percent of these women had reported it to law enforcement officials (Kilpatrick et al. 2007). And in the most extreme form of

Bineta Diop, founder of Femmes Africa SolidaritØ, which focuses on women-led peace building, was one of Time magazine's 100 Most Influential People In The World in 2011.

violence, 2,340 women were murdered by their intimate partners in 2007 (Catalano et al. 2009).

The likelihood of violence against women is shaped in part by cultural attitudes about women, along with the relative power women possess in society. As Kristof and WuDunn (2009) put it, "People get away with enslaving village girls for the same reason that people got away with enslaving blacks two hundred years ago: The victims are perceived as discounted humans" (p. 24). Increased education and opportunity for women, they suggest, leads to a curtailing of violence. In the United States, the fight for self-determination by women has had a substantial effect on opportunity for women in politics, the workplace, and relationships.

Going GLOBAL

Gender Inequality in Industrial Nations

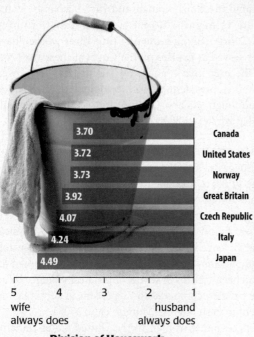

	Division of Housework	Empowerment
Canada	3.70	0.81
United States	3.72	0.68
Norway	3.73	1.00
Great Britain	3.92	0.46
Czech Republic	4.07	0.28
Italy	4.24	0.26
Japan	4.49	0.13

5   4   3   2   1
wife always does   husband always does

0   0.20   0.40   0.60   0.80   1.00
least equality   most equality

Division of Housework
(includes laundry, grocery shopping, dinner preparation, and care for sick family members)

Empowerment
(includes the proportions of women in parliament, in management, and in professional/technical positions)

Striking differences exist in women's empowerment—that is, the percentage of women in leadership positions—from one country to the next (right). Yet there is much less difference in the division of housework, even in the same countries (left).

Source: Adapted from Fuwa 2004:757.

WOMEN AROUND THE WORLD

Globally, women grow half the world's food, but they rarely own land. They constitute one-third of the world's paid labor force but frequently hold the lowest-paying jobs. Women workers often toil long hours for low pay, contributing significantly to their families' incomes, and still bear the responsibility for the majority of unpaid labor in society (OECD 2011; Quisumbing, Meinzen-Dick, and Bassett 2008; UNCTAD 2009).

Opportunities for women vary significantly around the world. In an attempt to quantify the degree of global gender inequality, the World Economic Forum releases an annual report ranking nations in four areas: the economy, education, health, and politics. The resulting Gender Gap Index score for each country ranges from 0 to 1. In 2010 only four countries—Iceland, Norway, Finland, and Sweden—scored above 0.8. The United States ranked 19th, with a score of 0.74, behind nations such as the Philippines, the United Kingdom, South Africa, and Sri Lanka. The bottom 13 nations, including Saudi Arabia, Turkey, Pakistan, and Egypt, scored below 0.6. Considering each of the four indicators, there were 22 nations that had achieved equality on educational attainment and 37 that had reached virtual equality in health and survival with scores of 0.98. Scores for economic participation and opportunity were lower with no country scoring above 0.9, and those for political empowerment were the lowest of the four with none above 0.7. Countries in the Middle East and in Africa had the lowest average rankings, primarily because of their low scores on economic and political indicators (Hausmann, Tyson, and Zahidi 2010).

Although people in most nations agree that women should have equal rights, significant variation exists. For example, in Egypt, 45 percent of men agree, compared to 76 percent for women, a gap of 31 percent. In Nigeria the gap is 21 percent, and in Kenya it is 20. Similar gaps exist in Egypt, Pakistan, and Jordan regarding whether a woman should be able to work outside the home. On the question of education, in Egypt, Pakistan, and India, at least 50 percent believe that a university education is more important for a boy than for a girl (Pew Research Center 2010f).

Globally, when it comes to housework and child care, women spend 2.5 more hours per day doing unpaid labor than do men, according to a study of 29 countries. In some nations, including Mexico, the average is as high as 5 hours more per day (OECD 2011). Sociologist Makiko Fuwa (2004) found that countries that placed greater emphasis on empowerment for women tended to have more balanced housework loads between men and women.

Change is possible. In an effort to address some of the structural inequality that exists, legislators in Norway established minimum quotas for the number of female members of boards of directors for companies. As the architects of the plan put it, "Instead of assuming what people *can't* do at work, provide opportunities for employees to prove what they can do." Norway now has the highest average percentage of female board members of any nation: 39.5 percent. Only three nations—Norway, Sweden, and Finland—have averages over 16 percent (Catalyst 2011b; Norwegian Ministry of Children and Equality 2009).

Sociology often confronts us with things that can make us uncomfortable, such as gender inequality. The point of doing so is a more complete understanding of what we do and why we do it. Such knowledge can lead us to new and better practices that provide greater understanding, fairness, equality, and opportunity. Through practicing the sociological imagination, as Betty Friedan did in the case of gender, we can make the world a better place.

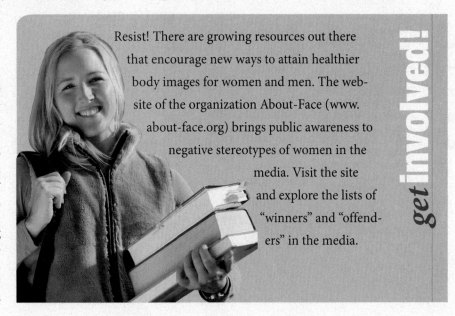

get involved!

Resist! There are growing resources out there that encourage new ways to attain healthier body images for women and men. The website of the organization About-Face (www.about-face.org) brings public awareness to negative stereotypes of women in the media. Visit the site and explore the lists of "winners" and "offenders" in the media.

For REVIEW

I. How has our understanding of gender and sexuality shifted over time?

- The presumption that gender and sexuality are narrowly determined by our biology has given way to an understanding of both as socially constructed, complex, and multidimensional.

II. How has opportunity for women in the United States changed over time?

- In the 1950s women's primary roles were wife and mother. Since that time, largely because of the efforts of the second wave of the women's movement, their labor force participation and income have risen significantly.

III. To what extent does gender still shape access to resources?

- Women continue to be paid less than men in the same occupations, tend to be segregated into a narrower range of female-dominated occupations, bear greater responsibility for housework, and are underrepresented as elected officials

Functionalist View

Gender roles establish the proper behavior, attitudes, and activities expected of men and women for a stable society.

Shifts in sexuality are a consequence of changes in what modern societies need, especially in terms of reproduction, to maintain social order.

Families need both an **instrumental leader** and an **expressive leader**; historically, women's natural gravitation to expressive goals freed men for instrumental tasks, and vice versa.

GENDER ROLES, INSTRUMENTAL LEADER, EXPRESSIVE LEADER
KEY CONCEPTS

Conflict View

The presumption that gender is determined by nature results in a belief that biology is destiny, an ideology that reinforces the existing system of gender inequality.

Heteronormativity is a form of power that limits alternative expressions of sexuality and contributes to discrimination.

Even after the feminist movements produced substantial changes, women still face significant **discrimination** in wages, occupations, and politics.

IDEOLOGY, DISCRIMINATION, SEXISM
KEY CONCEPTS

MAKE THE CONNECTION

After reviewing the chapter, answer the following questions:

Interactionist View

Our conceptions of gender and sexuality are not determined by biology but, rather, are the consequences of historical, social, and cultural practices over time.

Male–female differences and heterosexual preferences get reinforced through **everyday interaction**, such as giving trucks to boys and dolls to girls.

The negative responses people have when gender and sexuality norms are broken—reinforce existing dominant roles.

SOCIAL CONSTRUCTION, GENDER NORMS, ROLES
KEY CONCEPTS

1

How would each of the perspectives seek to explain the experiences of women around the world, such as Woineshet Zebene, who face significant violence and discriminations (pp. 293–294)?

2

How would each of the three perspectives look at the supposition that differences between men and women are "natural" and always have been?

3

How would the macro approaches of the conflict and functionalist perspectives study gender and sexuality differently than the micro approach of the interactionist perspective?

4

How does each perspective contribute to your understanding of your own gender-role socialization?

Pop Quiz

1. **What term do sociologists use to describe the biological differences between males and females?**
   a. gender
   b. sexism
   c. anatomy
   d. sex

2. **What term does geneticist Anne Fausto-Sterling use to describe those who have biological characteristics typically associated with both males and females?**
   a. sex
   b. gender
   c. intersexual
   d. gender displays

3. **When college students conducted an experiment in which they violated expected gender norms, they demonstrated the power of**
   a. gender-role socialization.
   b. biological determinism.
   c. instrumental leadership.
   d. the glass ceiling.

4. **What is the expression used when claiming that gender for men is not narrowly limited to traditional conceptions of masculinity?**
   a. intersexual
   b. gender modification
   c. sex
   d. multiple masculinities

5. **What do groups such as the *berdaches, hijras,* and *xanith* reveal about the nature of sex and gender?**
   a. All societies share the same dimorphic, male–female model of sex.
   b. The number of sex and gender categories varies across cultures.
   c. Socialization plays a significant role in modern societies, but a more limited role in traditional societies.
   d. Sex categories vary across cultures, but expressions of gender are universal.

6. **The primary accomplishment of the first wave of the women's movement was**
   a. making women citizens.
   b. gaining the right to an abortion.
   c. earning the right to nondiscrimination in the workplace.
   d. winning the right to vote.

7. **What term describes the categories of people to whom we are sexually attracted?**
   a. heteronormativity
   b. sexual orientation
   c. sexuality
   d. sexual displays

8. **According to early sociologists Talcott Parsons and Robert Bales, which type of leader bears responsibility for completion of tasks, focuses on more-distant goals, and manages the external relationship between the family and other social institutions?**
   a. expressive
   b. charismatic
   c. instrumental
   d. traditional

9. **Overall, when comparing full-time, year-round workers, how much do women earn compared to every dollar men earn?**
   a. 42 cents
   b. 63 cents
   c. 77 cents
   d. 92 cents

10. **The expression "second shift" refers to**
    a. doing the emotional work of maintaining family relationships.
    b. maintaining the household including housework in addition to a job outside the home.
    c. having a work shift ranging approximately between 4:00 P.M. and midnight.
    d. doing paid labor at the workplace.

1. (d); 2. (c); 3. (c); 4. (d); 5. (b); 6. (d); 7. (b); 8. (c); 9. (c); 10. (b)

13

RACE AND ETHNICITY

COMING TO AMERICA

On May 12, 2008, Santiago Cordero was on a high school field trip when he received an urgent text message. The Immigration and Customs Enforcement agency (ICE) had raided Agriprocessors, Inc., the meat packing plant where his mother worked. ICE had arrested 389 people, and his mom was one of them. She now faced the prospect of deportation back to Mexico (Fuson 2008).

Santiago's immigration story is not uncommon. His dad came to the United States first and was able to obtain the necessary legal documents to secure a job as a school custodian in Postville, Iowa, the small town where the meat processing plant is located. With a foothold having been established for the family, Santiago, his mother, and his siblings arrived a year or so later. They had no legal papers. As a result, even though they were trying to live the American Dream, their situation was always precarious.

In high school Santiago did everything right. He served as an interpreter for student–teacher conferences, started on the varsity football team, and organized the school's first soccer team, which included 28 students from five nationalities. As a senior he won the class volunteer award and received two scholarships. And yet, unlike most model students in the United States, when he walked across the stage to receive his high school diploma, he faced the possibility of immediate arrest and deportation (Fuson 2008).

Places like Postville symbolize the immigrant story for many in the United States (Bloom 2000). Meat processing plants in such towns serve as a magnet for a steady stream of people from other countries looking for jobs. The German immigrants who had settled the town generations ago gave way to Mexican and Bosnian immigrants a decade or so ago. Of the 389 workers arrested in the 2008 raid, 295 were from Guatemala (Leys 2008). Other plants in similar towns are increasingly employing immigrants from Somalia and Sudan. People leave their homelands where jobs are scarce and come to the United States in hope of a better future. And sometimes they take substantial risks to do so.

In a small community like this, face-to-face interaction with people from other cultures is inevitable. Such contact can break down some barriers and lead to greater understanding on all sides. As Postville's school superintendent, David Strudthoff, put it, "It's harder than hell to hate people when you get to know them" (quoted in Fuson 2008).

As You READ

>>

- How do sociologists define race and ethnicity?
- What are prejudice and discrimination, and how do they operate?
- What are the consequences of race and ethnicity for opportunity?

>>Racial and Ethnic Groups

Freedom, equality, and justice are core values in the story of the United States as the land of opportunity. The election of Barack Obama as the first African American president was yet another milestone in the gradual expansion of that ideal over time. All over the country, there were reports of children from various racial and ethnic backgrounds, both boys and girls, saying that anyone could grow up to be president. And, yet, the fact that his election was news indicates that there may still be a ways to go until principle and practice meet.

Throughout American history, struggles over race and ethnicity have repeatedly been at the heart of the struggle toward equality and opportunity. Since European colonists established their first settlement in Jamestown in 1607 with the help of the native Powhatan tribe, intergroup relations based on ethnic and racial background have played a powerful role in shaping both interaction and opportunity in the United States. A **minority group** is a subordinate group whose members have significantly less control or power over their own lives than the members of the dominant or majority group have over theirs. Sociologists consider groups that lack power to be minority groups even if they represent a numeric majority of the population in a society.

Race and ethnicity historically have served as markers of minority group status. The term **racial group** describes a group that is set apart from others because of physical

minority group A subordinate group whose members, even if they represent a numeric majority, have significantly less control or power over their own lives than the members of a dominant or majority group have over theirs.

racial group A group that is set apart from others because of physical differences that have taken on social significance.

ethnic group A group that is set apart from others primarily because of its national origin or distinctive cultural patterns.

Did You Know?

. . . In 2010, 46.5 percent of U.S. public school students were members of a racial or ethnic minority. This represents an increase from 22 percent in 1972.

Source: Aud et al. 2012:26; Planty et al. 2008:10.

differences that have taken on social significance. Whites, African Americans, and Asian Americans are all considered racial groups in the United States. Although the construct of race emphasizes the significance of external physical differences, it is the culture of a particular society that identifies and attaches social significance to those differences. An **ethnic group** is one that is set apart from others primarily because of its national origin or distinctive cultural patterns. In the United States, Puerto Ricans, Jews, and Polish Americans are all categorized as ethnic groups. As a nation composed primarily of immigrants and their descendants, the United States has a significant amount of racial and ethnic diversity.

RACE

Historically in the United States, it was presumed that racial categorization was a simple matter: Race was biologically determined in straightforward ways, and the dividing lines between groups were clear. It was also assumed that, for the most part, a person's parents would both be of the same race, so identifying a child's racial makeup was

Racial and Ethnic Groups in the United States

Classification	Number in Thousands	Percentage of Total Population
Racial Groups		
Whites (non-Hispanic)	196,929	63.7%
Blacks/African Americans	37,898	12.3
Asian American	14,566	4.7
Chinese	3,457	1.1
Asian Indians	2,765	0.9
Filipinos	2,513	0.8
Vietnamese	1,625	0.5
Koreans	1,456	0.5
Japanese	775	0.3
Native Hawaiian/Pacific Islanders	508	0.2
Native Americans, Alaskan Native	2,554	0.8
Ethnic Groups		
White ancestry (single or mixed, non-Hispanic)		
Germans	47,902	15.5
Irish	34,670	11.2
English	25,926	8.4
Italians	17,236	5.6
Poles	9,569	3.1
French	8,761	2.8
Scottish and Scots-Irish	8,718	2.8
Hispanic (or Latinos)	50,740	16.4
Mexican Americans	32,930	10.6
Puerto Ricans	4,692	1.5
Cubans	1,874	0.6
Salvadorans	1,830	0.6
Dominicans	1,509	0.5
Total (all groups)	**309,350**	

Source: U.S. Census Bureau 2011q: Table S0201

also a simple matter. Of course there were times when people from different racial groups had children. In the 19th century, potential ambiguity was resolved in the United States by establishing the "one-drop rule." In that case, if a person had any ancestors who were Black, no matter how many generations back, the person was labeled Black, even if he or she appeared to be White.

The one-drop rule represented a biased attempt at keeping racial classification simple and pure, but biological analysis demonstrates that no clear boundaries exist between the entrenched racial categories. When considering race, one does not need to question whether biological variation exists—it certainly does. The key is whether or not such differences justify the division of the human population into clear and distinct groups.

When it comes to genetic variation, the biological differences within what we think of as racial groups are actually greater than the differences between those groups. Genetic researchers Luca Cavalli-Sforza, Paolo Menozzi, and Alberto Piazza (1994), for example, point out that people from northeast China are genetically closer to Europeans, Eskimos, and North American Indians than they are to people from south China (p. 84). In fact, the overall degree of human genetic variation is quite small when compared with genetic variation among other large mammals—due primarily to the fact that communities of human beings have always interacted and reproduced, even across great distances (MacEachern 2003:20).

Scientists working on the Human Genome Project (HGP) have mapped all the genes of human beings, providing us with the most detailed description of our biological makeup available. They concluded that race as we understand it does not exist. Craig Venter (2000), one of the project's lead scientists, declared in his presentation of the HGP results that "the concept of race has no genetic or scientific basis," and in a later interview, he said, "Race is a social concept, not a scientific one" (quoted in Angier 2000). The researchers found that all humans share the same basic genetic material, and physical manifestations such as skin color represent different combinations, in greater or lesser degrees, of the same shared genes.

Social Construction of Race To understand race, we must move beyond biology to understand the ways in which we socially construct racial categories. If we look cross-culturally, we see that different groups define racial categories in different ways at different times. Each society defines which differences are important while ignoring other characteristics that could serve as a basis for social differentiation. In the United States, we see differences in both skin color and hair color, yet people learn that differences in skin color have a dramatic social and political meaning whereas differences in hair color do not.

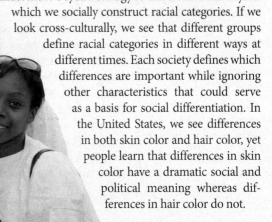

When observing skin color, many people in the United States tend to lump others rather casually into the traditional categories of "Black," "White," and "Asian." More-subtle differences in skin color often go unnoticed. In many nations of Central America and South America, by contrast, people recognize color gradients on a continuum from light to dark skin color. Brazil has approximately 40 color groupings, and in other countries people may be described as "Mestizo Honduran," "Mulatto Colombian," or "African Panamanian." What people see as "obvious" differences, then, are subject to each society's social definitions.

We develop our understanding of racial categories through the process of what sociologists Michael Omi and Howard Winant (1994) have called **racial formation**—a sociohistorical process in which racial categories are created, inhibited, transformed, and destroyed. Omi and Winant argue that race is neither fundamentally biological nor an illusion that can simply be ignored. To understand race, one must pay careful attention to the social, economic, and political forces that have established it as a basic distinction among human beings. Historically, those in positions of power have categorized whole groups of people as fundamentally distinct from each other (for example, when the one-drop rule was instituted) and then used their control over resources to treat people differently based on those distinctions. The result is a social structure that reinforces presumed racial differences and justifies unequal treatment on the basis of race. The creation of a reservation system for Native Americans in the late 1800s is one example of racial formation. Federal officials combined what were distinctive tribes into a single racial group, which we refer to today as Native Americans.

Given that our understanding of race was rooted in particular historical circumstances, it has shifted over time as those circumstances changed. For example, the massive influx of immigrants in the 19th century, from places such as Ireland, Germany, China, Italy, and eastern Europe, complicated the supposed simplicity of the Black–White divide. These immigrant groups were often judged to be biologically beneath White citizens. For instance, both the Irish and the Italians were regarded as members of another race inferior to Whites. Many African Americans of the time regarded being Irish as lower socially than being Black. Over time, both the Irish and the Italians came to be seen as two White ethnic groups. This was accomplished in part by positioning themselves as distinct from African Americans in order to identify more closely with the White majority (Guglielmo 2003; Ignatiev 1995; Roediger 2005).

Even though these differences are socially constructed, their consequences are no less real. Race is often used to justify unequal access to economic, social, and cultural resources based on the assumption that such inequality is somehow "natural." This can happen through the use of **stereotypes,** for example, which are unreliable generalizations about all members of a group that do not recognize individual differences within the group. Anthropologist Ashley Montagu (1997), who was at the forefront of the movement to use scientific evidence to demonstrate the socially constructed nature of race, suggested that "the very word (*race*) is racist; that the idea of 'race,' implying the existence of significant biologically determined mental

Did You Know?

In the 2010 Census, the number of Americans who checked both "Black" and "White" as their race rose 134 percent compared to the 2000 Census. Barack Obama was **not** one of them. He self-identified as Black.

Source: Cohn 2011.

racial formation A sociohistorical process in which racial categories are created, inhibited, transformed, and destroyed.

stereotype An unreliable generalization about all members of a group that does not recognize individual differences within the group.

SOCTHINK

To what extent do race and ethnicity influence the opportunities you have and obstacles you face? How conscious are you of your race and ethnicity and their possible influences on your life?

differences rendering some populations inferior to others, is wholly false" (p. 35).

Multiple Identities As the number of people who are biracial or multiracial grows, the limits of our racial categories are becoming increasingly apparent. Prominent figures have helped to bring this trend into the limelight. Tiger Woods, the world's best-known golfer, provides a classic example. Woods created his own racial category, referring to himself as "Cablinasian," a combination of his Caucasian, Black, American Indian, and Asian (Chinese and Thai) ancestry. Other examples include President Barack Obama, who had a Black father originally from Kenya and a White mother originally from Kansas, and Academy Award–winning actress Halle Berry, who had an African American father and a White, British-born mother.

In recognition of the growing diversity of the U.S. population, and the growing numbers of interracial marriages, for the first time in 2000 and again in 2010 the Census allowed people to select more than one category when identifying their race. People can now choose from five major race categories—White, Black, Asian, Native American, and Native Hawaiian or Other Pacific Islander—in addition to "Some other race." Considering all the combinations people might select, a total of 57 race categories are now possible (Humes et al. 2011).

In the 2010 Census more than 9 million people in the United States, 2.9 percent overall, reported that they were of two or more races. Of these, 20.4 percent chose both Black and White, the most frequent combination. Within racial categories, more than half of those who chose Native Hawaiian or Other Pacific Islander also selected another race, whereas those who self-identified as White were least likely to do so (Humes et al. 2011).

This expansion of possible racial categories is part of the Census Bureau's ongoing effort to provide a snapshot of race as it is understood at various points in U.S. history. As the table on page 322 demonstrates, racial categories used by the Census Bureau have shifted over time. The most recent expansion to allow multiracial identification is a direct consequence of the limitations of using fewer categories to reflect an increasingly diverse society. To get an accurate count, the Census Bureau needs categories that are mutually exclusive, meaning that each individual fits in one place and one place only. To do so, it must expand the number of available options beyond the three- or five-race models that often seemed, by common sense, to be sufficient.

ETHNICITY

An ethnic group is set apart from others explicitly because of its national origin or cultural patterns. Distinctive characteristics can include language, diet, sports, and religious beliefs, along with various traditions, norms, and values. Among the ethnic groups in the United States are peoples with a Spanish-speaking background, referred to collectively as Latinos or Hispanics, such as Puerto Ricans, Mexican Americans, and Cuban Americans. Other ethnic groups in this country include Jewish, Irish, Italian, and Norwegian Americans.

Puerto Rican Day Parade, New York City.

U.S. Race Categories, 1790–2010

Year	Race Categories
1790	Free white males Free white females All other free persons Slaves
1890	White Black Mulatto Chinese Indian
1940	White Negro Indian Chinese, Japanese, Filipino, Hindu, Korean Other
1990	White Black or Negro American Indian Eskimo Aleut Asian or Pacific Islander, Chinese, Filipino, Hawaiian, Korean, Vietnamese, Japanese, Asian Indian, Samoan, Guamanian, other Asian or Pacific Islander Other race
2010	White Black, African American, or Negro American Indian or Alaskan Native (print name of tribe) Asian: Asian Indian, Chinese, Filipino, Japanese, Korean, Vietnamese, Other Asian Native Hawaiian, Guamanian or Chamorro, Samoan, or Other Pacific Islander Some other race (print race)

Source: Nobles 2000:1739; U.S. Census Bureau 2010c.

The distinction between race and ethnicity is not always clear-cut. While the conventional approach views race as biological and ethnicity as cultural, racial groups express their identity in cultural ways (including language, norms, values, diet, and so on.). Alternatively, ethnic groups may self-identify as a race. The Census Bureau runs into this difficulty in its attempt to catalog each. It treats race and ethnicity as separate items, but in its ethnicity question, the only category recognized is "Hispanic, Latino, or Spanish origin." This situation creates difficulties for groups that see themselves as a distinct ethnicity and find the race options inadequate to describe who they are. In such circumstances, many people choose "Some other race" and then write in an ethnicity or nationality (such as Mexican, Iranian, or Saudi Arabian) as their race. In the 2010 Census, of those who selected "other," 97 percent also selected Hispanic as their ethnicity. In fact, 41 percent of those who self-identified as Hispanic also selected "Some other race" (Humes et al. 2011; U.S. Commission on Civil Rights 2009:4).

The Census has continued to try to make these categories clear. In an attempt to clarify confusion about the relationship between race and ethnicity, the 2010 Census included the line "For this census, Hispanic origins are not races" (U.S. Census Bureau 2010c). It also considered, but did not implement, collapsing race and ethnicity into a single question, effectively making Hispanic into a racial category (consistent with the way many Hispanics, especially Mexican Hispanics, view themselves). It also contemplated dropping the "Some other race" category to reduce confusion, effectively forcing people to choose from the existing categories. To address the limitations of the ethnicity question, the 2010 Census also studied the possibility of expanding it to include additional options (for example, German, French, Italian) to more fully reflect people's self-identified ethnic origin (U.S. Commission on Civil Rights 2009). As currently practiced, the Census further complicates things by including some ethnic nationalities

Did You Know?

. . . Of the Muslims in the United States, 65 percent are foreign born. Of those who were born here, about one-half are African American. Approximately one-fourth of all U.S. Muslims are third generation.

as examples within racial categories (for example, Japanese and Chinese as examples in the Asian category) but does not do so for others (for instance, White or Black). Such examples highlight the fact that race and ethnicity are more complex in practice than the commonsense models we may believe.

Although we will look at various ethnic and racial groups in more detail later in the chapter, it is important to understand the significance such categories have in society. As we have already seen, often they are used to justify exclusion from critical resources. This exclusion is rooted in both values and norms, that is, in how we think and how we act. When it comes to race and ethnicity, the terms that describe such practices are *prejudice* and *discrimination*.

>>Prejudice and Discrimination

In recent years, college campuses across the United States have been the scene of bias-related incidents. Student-run newspapers and radio stations have ridiculed racial and ethnic minorities; threatening literature has been stuffed under the doors of minority students; and graffiti endorsing the views of White supremacist organizations such as the Ku Klux Klan have been scrawled on university walls.

In some cases, there have even been violent clashes between groups of White and Black students. Such acts grow out of attitudes people have about other groups (Perry 2010; Schmidt 2008).

PREJUDICE

Prejudice is a negative attitude toward an entire category of people, often an ethnic or racial minority. If you resent your roommate because he or she is sloppy, you are not necessarily guilty of prejudice. However, if you immediately stereotype your roommate on the basis of such characteristics as race, ethnicity, or religion, that is a form of prejudice. Prejudice tends to perpetuate false definitions of individuals and groups.

Sometimes prejudice results from *ethnocentrism*—the tendency to assume that one's own culture and way of life represent the norm or are superior to all others. Ethnocentric people judge other cultures by the standards of their own group without taking into account the perspectives and experiences of others. This often leads to prejudice against cultures they view as inferior.

One important and widespread ideology that reinforces prejudice is **racism**—the belief that one race is supreme and all

> **prejudice** A negative attitude toward an entire category of people, often an ethnic or racial minority.
>
> **racism** The belief that one race is supreme and all others are innately inferior.

Before passage of the Civil Rights Act in 1964, segregation of public accommodations was the norm throughout the South.

Categorization of Hate Crime Incidents

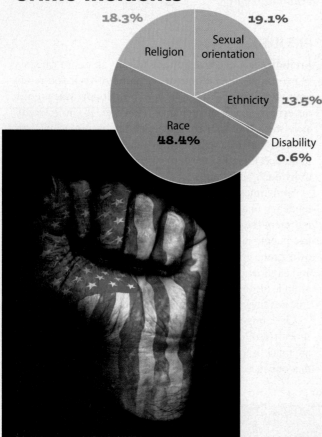

Religion 18.3%

Sexual orientation 19.1%

Ethnicity 13.5%

Race 48.4%

Disability 0.6%

Source: U.S. Department of Justice 2010c:Table1.

Some sociologists suggest that **color-blind racism,** which uses the principle of race neutrality to perpetuate a racially unequal status quo, is at work (Bonilla-Silva 2010). In such cases, commitment to the principle of equality actually serves to perpetuate inequality. In a system where inequality based on race and ethnicity is built into the structure of society, unwillingness to address these issues explicitly in those terms serves to perpetuate the status quo. Although the practice might seem counter to the principle of equality, some nations have established quotas in political representation and hiring to force the social structure to provide greater opportunity, a practice that is controversial in the United States.

DISCRIMINATION

Prejudice often leads to **discrimination**—the denial of opportunities and equal rights to individuals and groups because of prejudice or other arbitrary reasons. Whereas prejudice is a way of thinking, discrimination involves action. Imagine that a White corporate president with a prejudice against Asian Americans has to fill an executive position and that the most qualified candidate for the job is a Vietnamese American. If the president refuses to hire this candidate and instead selects an inferior White candidate, she or he is engaging in an act of racial discrimination.

Discriminatory Behavior Prejudiced attitudes should not be equated with discriminatory behavior Although the two are generally related, they are not identical; either condition can be present without the other. A prejudiced person does not always act on his or her biases. The White president, for example, might choose—despite her or his prejudices—to hire the Vietnamese American because that person is the most qualified. That would be prejudice without discrimination. On the other hand, a White corporate president with a completely respectful view of Vietnamese Americans might refuse to hire them for executive posts out of fear that biased clients would take their business elsewhere. In that case, the president's action would constitute discrimination without prejudice.

To better track the scope of overt racist acts in the United States, Congress passed the Hate Crimes Statistics

others are innately inferior. Such beliefs may exist even if they are not explicitly stated as part of a society's dominant values. Over the past three generations, nationwide surveys have consistently shown growing support among Whites for integration, interracial dating, and the election of minority group members to public office—including even the presidency of the United States. Nevertheless, there are persistent patterns of unequal treatment. People claim not to be prejudiced, affirming principles such as equal opportunity, yet many fail to put these ideals into practice.

color-blind racism The use of race-neutral principles to perpetuate a racially unequal status quo.

discrimination The denial of opportunities and equal rights to individuals and groups because of prejudice or other arbitrary reasons.

Members of the Ku Klux Klan, masked in white robes and hoods, used nighttime cross-burnings to instill terror.

Act in 1990. A **hate crime** is a criminal offense committed because of the offender's bias against an individual based on race, religion, ethnicity, national origin, or sexual orientation. The act was amended in 2009 to also include gender and gender identity. In 2010 alone, 7,690 hate crime offenses were reported to authorities. Overall, 61.9 percent of those crimes involved racial or ethnic bias (Department of Justice 2011c: Table 1). Offenses include crimes against individuals (including murder, rape, and assault) and crimes against property (such as vandalism, theft, and arson).

In sociologist Devah Pager's experiments investigating racial discrimination in hiring (see Chapter 2), a White job applicant with a prison record received slightly more callbacks than a Black applicant with no criminal record. Over time, the cumulative impact of such differential behavior contributes to significant differences in access to critical resources. As the adjacent graph shows, income varies significantly based on race and ethnicity in the United States (Pager and Shepherd 2008; Pager et al. 2009a, 2009b).

The Glass Ceiling Discrimination persists even for the most educated and qualified minority group members. Recall that the term *glass ceiling* refers to an invisible barrier that blocks the promotion of a qualified individual in a work environment because of the individual's gender, race, or ethnicity. In 1995 the Federal Government's Glass Ceiling Commission offered the first comprehensive study of barriers to promotion in the United States. They found that prejudice plays a substantial role in hiring decisions. They also concluded that the supply of viable minority group candidates for top-level positions is constrained owing to the cumulative effects of previous discrimination, which limits candidates' access to the training and experiences necessary for such jobs (Glass Ceiling Commission 1995; Jackson and O'Callaghan 2009).

Patterns of inequality persist. For example, in 2010, 78 percent of the members on the boards of directors for Fortune 500 companies were White men, compared to 13 percent White women, 7 percent minority males,

U.S. Median Income by Race, Ethnicity, and Gender

Median income (thousands of dollars)

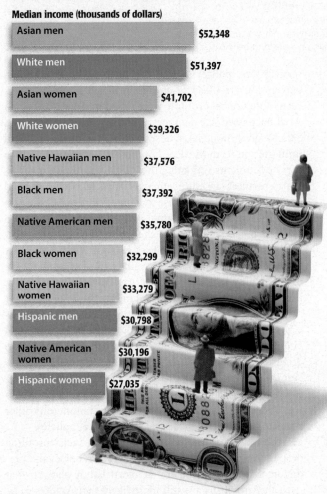

Asian men	$52,348
White men	$51,397
Asian women	$41,702
White women	$39,326
Native Hawaiian men	$37,576
Black men	$37,392
Native American men	$35,780
Black women	$32,299
Native Hawaiian women	$33,279
Hispanic men	$30,798
Native American women	$30,196
Hispanic women	$27,035

Note: Includes only people working full-time, year-round, 16 years and older. White refers to non-Hispanic Whites.

Source: U.S. Census Bureau 2010:Table B20017.

and 3 percent minority females (Catalyst 2011a). In fact, the glass ceiling appears to harm firms. Researchers have found that having more diversity increases performance in groups; firms with more diverse boards also are more profitable than those that are more homogeneous (Phillips, Liljenquist, and Neale 2009; Virtcom 2009).

> **hate crime** A criminal offense committed because of the offender's bias against an individual based on race, gender, religion, ethnicity, national origin, or sexual orientation.

Federal troops were needed to support the Supreme Court decision that led to the integration of schools in the 1950s.

Racial Profiling Another form of discrimination involves **racial profiling,** which is any arbitrary action initiated by an authority based on race, ethnicity, or national origin rather than on a person's behavior. Generally, racial profiling occurs when law enforcement officers, including customs officials, airport security, and police, assume that people who fit a certain description are likely to engage in illegal activities. Concerns about racial profiling were raised in April 2010 when Arizona passed the Support Our Law Enforcement and Safe Neighborhoods Act, designed to crack down on illegal immigration from Mexico. The law requires immigrants to carry documents validating their legal immigration status. It also requires law enforcement officials who have stopped someone for another offense to request evidence of the person's legal immigration status "where reasonable suspicion exists that the person is an alien who is unlawfully present in the United States" (State of Arizona 2010). Concerns were also expressed about the effect the law would have on the ability of local police officers to conduct effective investigations in Hispanic communities. To protest the law, numerous groups and organizations—such as the National Council of La Raza, the Service Employees International Union, and the Los Angeles City Council—decided not to do further business in Arizona, resulting in millions of dollars in lost revenue for the state. Although its more controversial provisions were banned by a court ruling, which was upheld in April 2011, the law inspired numerous other states to push for much stricter immigration policies.

> **racial profiling** Any police-initiated action based on race, ethnicity, or national origin rather than on a person's behavior.

Today, authorities continue to rely on racial profiling despite overwhelming evidence that race is not a valid predictor of criminal behavior. A recent study showed that African Americans are still more likely than Whites to be frisked and handled with force when they are stopped. Yet Whites are more likely than Blacks to possess weapons, illegal drugs, and stolen property (Ridgeway 2007).

Racial profiling occurs as a consequence of fear and suspicion. For example, after the September 11, 2001 terrorist attacks on the United States, federal authorities

Did You Know?

. . . Blacks and Whites have significantly different perceptions of local law enforcement. In a 2007 survey, when asked how much confidence they had in local police, 42 percent of Whites and 14 percent of Blacks had a "great deal," while 31 percent of Blacks and 10 percent of Whites had "very little."

subjected foreign students from Arab countries to special questioning, and they scrutinized legal immigrants identified as Arab or Muslim for possible illegal activity. They also prosecuted Arab and Muslim detainees for violations that were routinely ignored among immigrants of other ethnicities and faiths (Withrow 2006).

THE PRIVILEGES OF THE DOMINANT

One often-overlooked aspect of discrimination is the privileges that dominant groups enjoy at the expense of others. For instance, we tend to focus more on the difficulty women have balancing career and family than on the ease with which men avoid household chores and advance in the workplace. Similarly, we concentrate more on discrimination against racial and ethnic minorities than on the advantages members of the White majority enjoy. Indeed, most White people rarely think about their "Whiteness," taking their status for granted. However, sociologists and other social scientists are becoming increasingly interested in what it means to be "White," because White privilege is the other side of the proverbial coin of racial discrimination (Painter 2010).

Feminist scholar Peggy McIntosh (1988) became interested in White privilege after noticing that most men would not acknowledge the privileges attached to being male—even if they would agree that being female had its disadvantages. She wondered whether White people suffer from a similar blind spot regarding their own racial privilege. Intrigued, McIntosh began to list all the ways in which she benefited from her Whiteness. She soon realized that the list of unspoken advantages was long and significant.

McIntosh found that as a White person, she rarely needed to step out of her comfort zone, no matter where she went. If she wished to, she could spend most of her time with people of her own race. She could find a good place to live in a pleasant neighborhood, buy the foods she liked to eat from almost any grocery store, and get her hair styled in almost any salon. She could attend a public meeting without feeling that she did not belong or that she was different from everyone else.

McIntosh discovered, too, that her skin color opened doors for her. She could cash checks and use credit cards without suspicion, and she could browse through stores without being shadowed by security guards. She could be seated without difficulty in a restaurant. If she asked to see the manager, she could assume he or she would be of her own race. If she needed help from a doctor or a lawyer, she could get it.

McIntosh also realized that her Whiteness made the job of parenting easier. She did not need to worry about protecting her children from people who didn't like them because of their race. She could be sure that their books would show pictures of people who looked like them and that their history texts would describe White people's achievements. She knew that the television programs they watched would include White characters.

Finally, McIntosh had to admit that others did not constantly evaluate her in racial terms. When she appeared in public, she didn't need to worry that her clothing or behavior might reflect poorly on White people. If she was recognized for an achievement, it was seen as her own accomplishment, not that of an entire race. And no one ever assumed that the personal opinions she voiced should be those of all White people. Because McIntosh blended in with the people around her, she wasn't always onstage.

> ## Whites of course have the privilege of not caring, of being colorblind. Nobody else does.
>
> Ursula K. LeGuin

These are not all the privileges White people take for granted as a result of their membership in the dominant racial group in the United States. As Devah Pager's study showed, White job seekers enjoy a tremendous advantage over equally well-qualified—even better-qualified—Blacks. Whiteness *does* carry privileges—to a much greater extent than most White people realize.

INSTITUTIONAL DISCRIMINATION

Such persistent patterns of inequality suggest that discrimination is practiced not only by individuals in one-to-one encounters but also by institutions in their daily operations. Social scientists are particularly concerned with the ways in which structural factors, such as employment, housing, health care, and government operations, maintain the social significance of race and ethnicity. *Institutional discrimination* refers to the denial of opportunities and equal rights to individuals and groups that results from the normal operations of a society. This kind of discrimination consistently affects certain racial and ethnic groups more than others.

The response to the September 11, 2001 terrorist attacks on the United States provides an example of institutional discrimination. Under pressure to prevent terrorist takeovers of commercial airplanes, Congress passed the Aviation and Transportation Security Act, which was intended to strengthen airport screening procedures. The law stipulated that all airport screeners must be U.S. citizens. Nationally, 28 percent of all airport screeners were legal residents but not citizens of the United States; as a group, they were disproportionately Latino, Black, and Asian. Many observers noted that other airport and airline workers, including pilots, cabin attendants, and even armed National Guardsmen stationed at airports, need not be citizens. Though a Circuit Court of Appeals judge issued a court order in 2002 allowing qualified noncitizen airport screeners to retain or reapply for their jobs, in 2003 a California district court dismissed the case. Even well-meant legal measures can have disastrous consequences for racial and ethnic minorities (H. Weinstein 2002).

SOCTHINK

McIntosh recommends that we all step back and consider unearned advantages we inherit owing to the positions we may occupy. What would be on your list? What disadvantages might you inherit?

SOCTHINK

Why might institutional discrimination be an even greater concern than interpersonal discrimination?

In some cases, even seemingly neutral institutional standards can have discriminatory effects. African American

students at a midwestern state university protested a policy under which fraternities and sororities that wanted to use campus facilities for a dance were required to post a $150 security deposit to cover possible damages. The Black students complained that the policy had a discriminatory impact on minority student organizations. Campus police countered that the university's policy applied to all student groups interested in using the facilities. However, because the overwhelmingly White fraternities and sororities at the school had their own houses, which they used for dances, the policy indeed affected only African American and other minority organizations.

Attempts have been made to eradicate or compensate for discrimination in the United States. The 1960s saw the passage of many pioneering civil rights laws, including the landmark 1964 Civil Rights Act, which prohibits discrimination in public accommodations and publicly owned facilities on the basis of race, color, creed, national origin, and gender. In two important rulings in 1987, the Supreme Court held that federal prohibitions against racial discrimination protect members of all ethnic minorities—including Hispanics, Jews, and Arab Americans—even though they may be considered White.

For more than 40 years, government, schools, and industry have instituted affirmative action programs to overcome past discrimination. **Affirmative action** refers to positive efforts to recruit minority group members or women for jobs, promotions, and educational opportunities. Many people resent these programs, arguing that advancing one group's cause merely shifts the discrimination to another group. By giving priority to African Americans in admissions, for

affirmative action Positive efforts to recruit minority group members or women for jobs, promotions, and educational opportunities.

example, schools may deny more academically qualified White candidates. In many parts of the country and many sectors of the economy, affirmative action is being rolled back, even though it was never fully implemented.

Discriminatory practices continue to pervade nearly all areas of life in the United States. In part, that is because various individuals and groups actually benefit from racial and ethnic discrimination in terms of money, status, and influence. Discrimination permits members of the majority to enhance their wealth, power, and prestige at the expense of others. Less qualified people get jobs and

promotions simply because they are members of the dominant group. Such individuals and groups will not surrender these advantages easily.

>>Sociological Perspectives on Race and Ethnicity

Sociologists seek to understand and explain why prejudice and discrimination develop and persist and what might be done to address them. As we have seen, often such negative characteristics exist because they serve certain interests. Here we look at how prejudice and discrimination contribute to the maintenance of the existing social order by reinforcing the dominant culture.

SOCIAL ORDER AND INEQUALITY

One of the ways we see such beliefs and practices perpetuated is through acceptance of the dominant ideology that supports them. Prejudice and discrimination are rooted in fundamental beliefs about the natural order of the world. Such values provide a moral justification for maintaining an unequal society that routinely deprives minority groups of their rights and privileges. In the 19th century, Southern Whites, for example, justified slavery by asserting that Africans were physically and spiritually subhuman and devoid of souls. It is easy in retrospect to find such beliefs appalling, but they became part of what people assumed was natural and were therefore difficult to challenge.

This does not mean, however, that certain groups do not intentionally promote such beliefs at the expense of others. Prejudice and discrimination help to preserve the existing system of inequality. **Exploitation theory,** for example, argues that such practices are a basic part of the capitalist economic system (Blauner 1972; Cox 1948; Hunter 2000). Racism keeps minorities in low-paying jobs, thereby supplying the capitalist ruling class with a pool of cheap labor. Moreover, by forcing racial minorities to accept low wages, capitalists can restrict the wages of all members of the proletariat. Business owners can always replace workers from the dominant group who demand higher wages with minorities who have no choice but to accept low-paying jobs. This increases the likelihood that working-class members of the majority group will develop racist attitudes toward working-class members of minority groups, whom they view as threats to

SOCTHINK

What are the cost and benefits of establishing hiring quotas based on race, ethnicity, or gender to ensure greater opportunity?

Perceptions of Discrimination

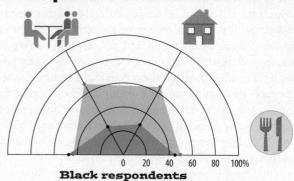

Black respondents

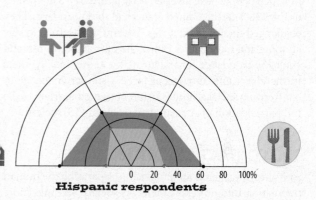

Hispanic respondents

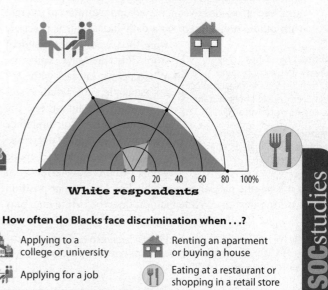

White respondents

How often do Blacks face discrimination when . . . ?

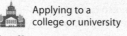 Applying to a college or university

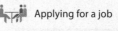 Applying for a job

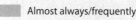 Almost always/frequently

Renting an apartment or buying a house

Eating at a restaurant or shopping in a retail store

Not often/hardly ever

Source: Pew Research Center 2007:30.

their jobs. As a result, they direct their hostilities not toward the capitalists but toward other workers, thereby not challenging the structure of the existing system.

Maintaining these practices, however, comes at significant cost to society. For

> **exploitation theory** A belief that views racial subordination in the United States as a manifestation of the class system inherent in capitalism.

example, a society that practices discrimination fails to use the resources of all individuals. Discrimination limits the search for talent and leadership to the dominant group. Advocates for the children whose parents were caught up in the Postville immigration raid, for example, bemoaned the loss of creativity and talent that those kids would take with them when they left the country with their deported parents. Discrimination also aggravates social problems such as poverty, delinquency, and crime. Such effects require the investment of a good deal of time and money in which the primary goal is to maintain barriers to the full participation of all members (Rose 1951).

Challenging prejudice and discrimination, however, involves questioning taken-for-granted views of the world in which people have invested their faith and trust. Women in the 1950s in the United States had to do just that. They challenged the idea that it was "natural" for women to stay at home and have babies rather than get an education and enter the paid labor force. During the same time, workers in the civil rights movement faced a similar challenge in confronting social attitudes that represented barriers to the full participation of African Americans in U.S. society.

THE CONTACT HYPOTHESIS

At its heart, racism is about division, separating the human population into us versus them. As society becomes more global and interdependent, more people from diverse cultural backgrounds have increased opportunities to interact with others unlike them on a daily basis. This is precisely what the school superintendent from Postville gave voice to. When people interact with others as people, rather than as stereotypes or distant others, the possibility arises for prejudice and discrimination to decrease.

Take, for example, a Hispanic woman who is transferred from a job on one part of an assembly line to a similar position working next to a White man. At first, the White man may be patronizing, assuming that she must be incompetent. For her part, the Latina is cold and resentful; even when she needs assistance, she refuses to admit it. After a week, the growing tension between the two leads to a bitter quarrel. Yet over time, each slowly comes to appreciate the other's strengths and talents. A year after they begin working together, these two workers become respectful friends. This example represents an example of the contact hypothesis in action.

The **contact hypothesis** states that in cooperative circumstances, interracial contact between people of equal status will cause them to become less prejudiced and to abandon old stereotypes. People begin to see one another as individuals and to discard the broad generalizations characteristic of stereotyping. Note the phrases "equal status" and "cooperative circumstances." In our assembly-line example, if the two workers had been competing for one vacancy as a supervisor, the racial hostility between them might have worsened, highlighting the significance of power and position when it comes to the issue of racism (Allport 1979; Fine 2008).

As Latinos and other minorities slowly gain access to better-paying and higher-responsibility jobs, the contact hypothesis may take on even greater significance. The trend in our society is toward increasing contact between individuals from dominant and subordinate groups. That may be one way of eliminating—or at least reducing—racial and ethnic stereotyping and prejudice. Another may be the establishment of interracial coalitions, an idea suggested by sociologist William Julius Wilson (1999). To work, such coalitions would obviously need to provide an equal role for all members.

PATTERNS OF INTERGROUP RELATIONS

The possibility of equal status, however, is shaped by how societies handle racial and ethnic differences. Some societies are more open to diverse groups maintaining their cultural traditions. Others pressure groups to abandon their beliefs and practices in favor of those of the dominant society. We will focus on six characteristic patterns of intergroup relations: genocide, expulsion, amalgamation, assimilation, segregation, and pluralism. Each pattern defines the dominant group's actions and the minority group's responses. The first two are relatively rare, though their consequences are extreme; the final four are more common.

Genocide The most devastating pattern of intergroup relations is **genocide**—the deliberate, systematic killing of an entire people or nation. This is precisely what happened when Turkish authorities killed 1 million Armenians beginning in 1915. The term is most commonly associated with Nazi Germany's extermination of 6 million European Jews, along with gays, lesbians, and the Romani people ("Gypsies"), during World War II. The term also describes the United States' policies toward Native Americans in the 19th century. In 1800 the Native American (or American

contact hypothesis The theory that in cooperative circumstances interracial contact between people of equal status will reduce prejudice.

genocide The deliberate, systematic killing of an entire people or nation.

Civil rights activist Rosa Parks being fingerprinted upon her arrest in 1955 for her act of civil disobedience in refusing to give up her seat on a bus to a White man.

Indian) population of the United States was about 600,000; by 1850 warfare with the U.S. cavalry, disease, and forced relocation to inhospitable environments had reduced it to 250,000.

Expulsion Another extreme response is **expulsion**—the systematic removal of a group of people from society. In 1979 Vietnam expelled nearly 1 million ethnic Chinese, partly as a result of centuries of hostility between Vietnam and neighboring China. Similarly, Serbian forces began a program of "ethnic cleansing" in 1991,

As part of their annual study of the top 100 films, researchers at USC's Annenberg School for Communication and Journalism found that, out of the 4,016 speaking roles they identified, only 4.9 percent went to Hispanic characters. They also found that only 6 of the top 100 were directed by African Americans. In those films, 63 percent of the characters with speaking roles were Black, compared to only 11 percent in the 94 films with non–African American directors (Smith and Choueiti 2011).

in the newly independent states of Bosnia and Herzegovina. Throughout the former Yugoslavia, the Serbs drove more than 1 million Croats and Muslims from their homes. Some they tortured and killed; others they abused and terrorized, in an attempt to "purify" the land (Cigar 1995; Petrovic 1994). More recently, the government of Sudan has pushed people off their land and out of the country in Darfur (Steidle 2007).

Amalgamation When a majority group and a minority group combine to form a new group, **amalgamation** results. This often occurs through intermarriage over several generations. This pattern can be expressed as $A + B + C \rightarrow D$, where A, B, and C represent different groups in a society, and D signifies the end result, a unique cultural-racial group unlike any of the initial groups (Newman 1973).

The belief in the United States as a "melting pot" became compelling in the early 20th century, particularly since that image suggested that the nation had an almost divine mission to amalgamate various groups into one people. In actuality, however, many residents were not willing to include Native Americans, Jews, Blacks, Asians, and Irish Roman Catholics in the melting pot. Therefore, this pattern does not adequately describe dominant-subordinate relations in the United States.

Assimilation In India, many Hindus complain about Indian citizens who emulate the traditions and customs of the British. In France, people of Arab and African origin, many of them Muslim, complain they are treated as second-class citizens—a charge that provoked riots in 2005. In Australia, Aborigines who have become part of the dominant society refuse to acknowledge their darker-skinned grandparents on the street. All these cases are examples of the effects of **assimilation**—the process through which a person forsakes his or her own cultural tradition to become part of a different culture. Generally, it is practiced by minority group members who want to conform to the standards of the dominant group. Assimilation can be described as a pattern in which $A + B + C \rightarrow A$. The majority, A, dominates in such a way that members of minorities B and C imitate it and attempt to become indistinguishable from it (Newman 1973).

Assimilation can strike at the very roots of a person's identity. In the United States, some immigrants have changed their ethnic-sounding family names to names that better fit into the dominant White Protestant culture. Jennifer

> **expulsion** The systematic removal of a group of people from society.
>
> **amalgamation** The process through which a majority group and a minority group combine to form a new group.
>
> **assimilation** The process through which a person forsakes his or her own cultural tradition to become part of a different culture.

Anastassakis, for example, changed her name to Jennifer Aniston, Ralph Lipschitz became Ralph Lauren, Natalie Portman switched from Natalie Hershlag, and the Academy Award–winning British actress Helen Mirren gave up her birth name of Ilyena Vasilievna Mironova. Name changes, switches in religious affiliation, and the dropping of native languages can obscure one's roots and heritage. Especially across generations, assimilation can lead to the virtual death of a culture in that family's history. It is not uncommon for grandchildren of immigrants who have not learned the language or the cultural traditions of their ancestors to regret this loss.

Segregation

Separate schools, separate seating on buses and in restaurants, separate washrooms, even separate drinking fountains—these were all part of the lives of African Americans in the South when segregation ruled early in the 20th century. **Segregation** refers to the physical separation of two groups of people in terms of residence, workplace, and social events. Generally, a dominant group imposes this pattern on a minority group. Segregation is rarely complete, however. Intergroup contact inevitably occurs, even in the most segregated societies.

Former South African President Nelson Mandela oversaw that country's transition from a segregated society.

Composition of Neighborhoods by Racial and Ethnic Groups June 6–25, 2005			
	% of non-Hispanic Whites who say there are "many" of each group in area	% of Blacks who say there are "many" of each group in area	% of Hispanics who say there are "many" of each group in area
Whites	86%	45%	52%
Blacks	28%	66%	32%
Hispanics	32%	26%	61%
Asians	12%	6%	13%
Recent immigrants	14%	18%	30%

From 1948 (when it received its independence) to 1990, the Republic of South Africa severely restricted the movement of Blacks and other non-Whites by means of a wide-ranging system of segregation known as **apartheid.** Apartheid even included the creation of separate homelands where Blacks were expected to live. However, decades of local resistance to apartheid, combined with international pressure, led to marked political changes in the 1990s. In 1994 a prominent Black activist, Nelson Mandela, became South Africa's president in the first election in which Blacks (the majority of the nation's population) were allowed to vote. Mandela had spent almost 28 years in South African prisons for his anti-apartheid activities. His election was widely viewed as the final blow to South Africa's oppressive policy of segregation.

Long-entrenched social patterns are difficult to change, however. A recent analysis of living patterns in U.S. metropolitan areas shows that, despite federal laws that forbid housing discrimination, residential segregation is still the norm. Even though 65 percent of Americans say they prefer to live in a racially diverse community, across the nation, neighborhoods remain divided along both racial and ethnic lines. The average White person lives in an area that is at least 83 percent White, whereas the average African American lives in a neighborhood that is mostly Black. The typical Latino lives in an area that is 42 percent Hispanic. Overall, segregation flourishes at the community and neighborhood levels, despite the increasing diversity of the nation as a whole (Bolt, Ozuekren, and Phillips 2010; Taylor and Morin 2008).

Pluralism In a pluralistic society, a subordinate group does not have to forsake its lifestyle and traditions. **Pluralism** is based on mutual respect for one another's cultures among the various groups in a society. This pattern allows a minority group to express its own culture and still participate without prejudice in the larger society. Earlier, we described amalgamation as A + B + C → D, and assimilation as A + B + C → A. Using this same approach, we can conceive of pluralism as A + B + C → A + B + C; that is, all the groups coexist in the same society (Newman 1973).

In the United States, pluralism is more of an ideal than a reality. There are distinct instances of pluralism—the ethnic neighborhoods in major cities, such as Koreatown, Little Tokyo, Andersonville (Swedish Americans), and Spanish Harlem—yet there are also limits to cultural freedom. To survive, a society must promote a certain consensus among its members regarding basic ideals, values, and beliefs. Thus, if a Romanian immigrant to the United States wants to move up the occupational ladder, he or she cannot avoid learning English.

Switzerland exemplifies the modern pluralistic state. There the absence of both a national language and a dominant religious faith leads to a tolerance for cultural diversity. In addition, various political devices safeguard the interests of ethnic groups in a way that has no parallel in the United States. By contrast, Great Britain has had difficulty achieving cultural pluralism in a multiracial society. East Indians, Pakistanis, and Blacks from the Caribbean and Africa experience prejudice and discrimination within the dominant White society there. Some British advocate cutting off all Asian and Black immigration, and a few even call for expulsion of those non-Whites currently living in Britain.

>>Race and Ethnicity in the United States

Few societies have a more diverse population than the United States. The nation is truly a multiracial, multiethnic society and is becoming more so. According to results from the 2010 Census, 92 percent of the population growth in the United States over the previous decade was due to increased numbers of racial and ethnic minorities, with Hispanics accounting for 56 percent overall (Passel, Cohn, and Lopez 2011).

> **pluralism** Mutual respect for one another's cultures among the various groups in a society, which allows minorities to express their own cultures without experiencing prejudice.

RACIAL GROUPS

The largest racial minorities in the United States are African Americans, Native Americans, and Asian Americans.

African Americans "I am an invisible man," wrote Black author Ralph Ellison in his novel *Invisible Man* (1952:3). "I am a man of substance, of flesh and bone, fiber and liquids—and I might even be said to possess a mind. I am invisible, understand, simply because people refuse to see me."

Almost six decades later, many African Americans still feel invisible. Despite their large numbers, they have long been treated as second-class citizens. As of 2010, according to official government statistics, 27.4 percent of African Americans were in poverty compared to 9.9 percent for non-Hispanic Whites (DeNavas-Walt et al. 2011).

Racial and Ethnic Groups in the United States, 1790–2050 (Projected)

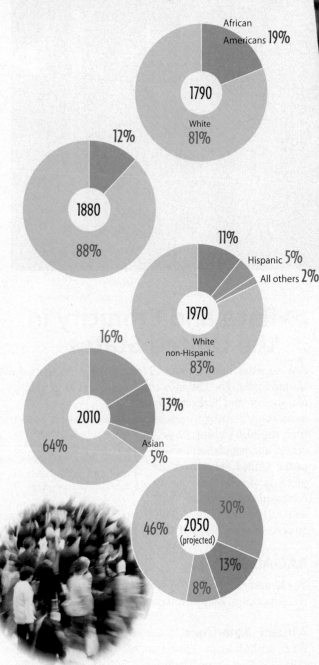

1790
African Americans 19%
White 81%

1880
12%
88%

1970
11%
Hispanic 5%
All others 2%
White non-Hispanic 83%

2010
16%
13%
64%
Asian 5%

2050 (projected)
30%
46%
13%
8%

Note: U.S. Census categories vary over time.

Source: Gibson and Jung 2002: Table 1; Humes et al. 2011; Ortman and Guarneri 2008.

Contemporary institutional discrimination and individual prejudice against African Americans are rooted in the history of slavery in the United States. Many other subordinate groups had little wealth and income, but as

sociologist W. E. B. Du Bois (1909) and others have noted, enslaved Blacks were in an even more oppressive situation because they could not own property legally and could not pass on the benefits of their labor to their children. In spite of generations of slavery with its long-term economic consequences, African Americans never received slave reparations to compensate for the historical injustices of forced servitude (Williams and Collins 2004).

The end of the Civil War did not bring genuine freedom and equality for Blacks. Whites were able to maintain their dominance formally through legalized segregation and informally by means of vigilante terror and violence. The southern states passed "Jim Crow" laws to enforce official segregation, and the Supreme Court in the case of *Plessy v. Ferguson* upheld them as constitutional in 1896. In

Poverty Rates by Race and Ethnicity

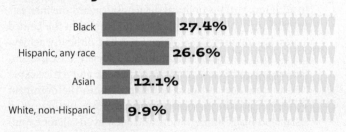

Black	**27.4%**
Hispanic, any race	**26.6%**
Asian	**12.1%**
White, non-Hispanic	**9.9%**

Source: DeNavas-Walt et al. 2011: Table 4.

addition, Blacks faced the danger of lynching campaigns, often led by the Ku Klux Klan, during the late 1800s and early 1900s (Franklin and Moss 2000).

During the 1950s and 1960s, a vast civil rights movement emerged, with many competing factions and strategies for change. The Southern Christian Leadership Conference (SCLC), founded by Dr. Martin Luther King Jr., used nonviolent civil disobedience to oppose segregation. The National Association for the Advancement of Colored People (NAACP) favored use of the courts to press for equality for African Americans. Many younger Black leaders, most notably Malcolm X, turned toward an ideology of Black power. Proponents of **Black power** rejected the goal of assimilation into White middle-class society. They defended the beauty and dignity of Black and African cultures and supported the creation of Black-controlled political and economic institutions (Ture and Hamilton 1992).

Despite numerous courageous actions to achieve Black civil rights, Black and White citizens are still separate, still unequal. The median household income for African American households is $32,068, compared to $54,620 for non-Hispanic Whites. The majority of Black children from middle-income families end up earning less than their parents, whereas 68 percent of children in middle-income White families earn more. And in part because of unequal access to health care, the life expectancy of African Americans is shorter than that of Whites (DeNavas-Walt et al. 2011; Isaacs 2008).

Substantial variation exists in the types of occupations African Americans occupy. Overall, African Americans make up 10.8 percent of persons employed in the labor force. Using this number as a baseline, it is possible to highlight jobs in which African Americans are over- and under-represented. For example, African Americans comprise only 1 percent of dentists, 1.6 percent of architects, 2.7 percent of CEOs, 4.3 percent of computer programmers, and 5.3 percent of physicians. By contrast, they constitute 22.8 percent of social workers, 26.4 percent of postal clerks, 26.7 percent of taxi drivers, 27.7 percent of barbers, and 33.1 percent of nurses aids (Bureau of Labor Statistics 2012f: Table 11).

In politics, though African Americans remain underrepresented, progress in the number of

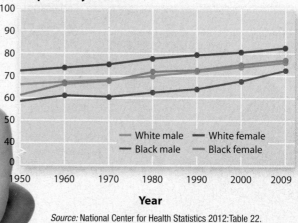

Life Expectancy by Race and Sex, 1950–2009

Life expectancy at birth

Legend: — White male — White female — Black male — Black female

Source: National Center for Health Statistics 2012:Table 22.

elected officials has improved over time. Between 1969 and 2012, the number of African Americans in Congress rose from 6 to a record of 42, and the election of Barack Obama as president represents a major breakthrough in the glass ceiling. However, African Americans still make up only 8.2 percent of Congress. Such lack of progress is especially distressing in view of sociologist W. E. B. Du Bois's observation over a century ago that Blacks could not expect to achieve equal social and economic opportunity without first gaining political rights (Manning 2011).

Native Americans Today about 2.6 million Native Americans represent a diverse array of cultures distinguishable by language, family organization, religion, and livelihood. The outsiders who came to the United States—European settlers and their descendants—came to know these native peoples' forebears as "American Indians." By the time the Bureau of Indian Affairs (BIA) was organized as part of the War Department in 1824, Indian–White relations had featured three centuries of hostility that had led to the virtual elimination of native peoples. During the 19th century, many bloody wars

> **Black power** A political philosophy, promoted by many younger Blacks in the 1960s, that supported the creation of Black-controlled political and economic institutions.

Did You Know?

... With the release of *The Princess and the Frog* in 2009, Princess Tiana became Disney's first African American princess in a feature film. At the same time, Disney was criticized for drawing on racial stereotypes of 1920s New Orleans in the film.

Major Asian American Groups in the United States

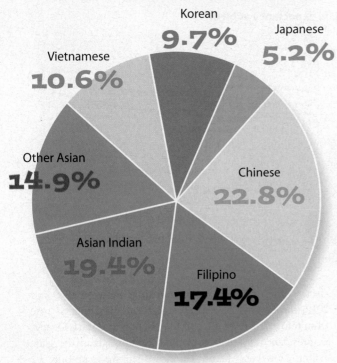

Korean **9.7%**

Japanese **5.2%**

Vietnamese **10.6%**

Other Asian **14.9%**

Chinese **22.8%**

Asian Indian **19.4%**

Filipino **17.4%**

Source: U.S. Census Bureau 2011d:Table DP-1.

wiped out a significant part of the nation's Indian population. By the end of the century, schools for Indians—operated by the BIA or by church missions—prohibited the practice of Native American cultures. Yet at the same time, such schools did little to make the children effective competitors in White society (Humes et al. 2011).

model or ideal minority A subordinate group whose members supposedly have succeeded economically, socially, and educationally despite past prejudice and discrimination.

Life remains difficult for members of the 562 tribal groups in the United States, whether they live in urban areas or on reservations. For example, one Native American teenager in six has attempted suicide—a rate four times higher than the rate for other teenagers. Over time, some Native Americans have chosen to assimilate and abandon all vestiges of their tribal cultures to escape certain forms of prejudice. However, by the 1990s, an increasing number of people in the United States were openly claiming a Native American identity. Since 1960 the federal government's count of Native Americans has quadrupled. According to the 2010 Census, the Native American population increased 18 percent during the 2000s. Demographers believe that more and more Native Americans who previously concealed their identity are no longer trying to pass as White (Grieco and Cassidy 2001; Humes et al. 2011).

The introduction of gambling on Indian reservations has transformed the lives of some Native Americans. Native Americans got into the gaming industry in 1988, when

Congress passed the Indian Gambling Regulatory Act. The law stipulates that states must negotiate agreements with tribes interested in commercial gaming; they cannot prevent tribes from engaging in gambling operations even if state law prohibits such ventures. The income from these lucrative operations is not evenly distributed, however. About two-thirds of recognized Indian tribes are not involved in gambling ventures. And those tribes that earn substantial revenues from gambling constitute only a small fraction of Native Americans (J. Taylor and Kalt 2005).

Asian Americans Asian Americans are a diverse group, one of the fastest-growing segments of the U.S. population. Among the many groups of Americans of Asian descent are Vietnamese Americans, Chinese Americans, Japanese Americans, and Korean Americans.

Asian Americans are often held up as a **model** or **ideal minority** group, supposedly because they have succeeded economically, socially, and educationally despite past prejudices and discrimination. Yet this representation minimizes the degree of diversity among Asian Americans. For example, 80 percent of Vietnamese children in the United States speak a language other than English at home, and 25 percent of them speak English with difficulty. Contrast this with Filipino children, 34 percent of whom speak another language at home and 8 percent of whom have difficulty with English. Educational attainment also varies significantly between groups. The likelihood of having completed at least a bachelor's degree among 25- to 29-year-olds ranges from 80 percent for those of Asian Indian descent and 70 percent for Chinese to 45 percent for Vietnamese and 36 percent for Other Asian nationalities. Poverty rates also vary. The rate for Filipino children is 5 percent, and for Asian Indians it is 7.5 percent. Among Vietnamese children, in contrast, it is 15.2, and for those of Other Asian nationalities it is 19.9 percent (Aud, Fox, and KewalRamani 2010).

Examples such as these highlight the limitations of viewing people of Asian descent in the United States as a singular group. But even given high overall levels of attainment in education and income, those of Asian descent can still face a glass ceiling. For example, in 2010 only 2.1 percent of Board of Directors seats at Fortune 500 companies were held by those of Asian or Pacific Islander descent (Catalyst 2011a).

Vietnamese Americans Each Asian American group has its own history and culture. Vietnamese Americans, for instance, came to the United States primarily during and after the Vietnam War—especially after the U.S. withdrawal from the region in 1975—and currently number 1.6 million. Assisted by local agencies, refugees from communist Vietnam settled throughout the United States, tens of thousands of them in small towns. Over time, Vietnamese Americans have gravitated toward the larger urban areas, establishing ethnic enclaves featuring Vietnamese restaurants and grocery stores.

In 1995 the United States resumed normal diplomatic relations with Vietnam. Gradually, the *Viet Kieu,* or Vietnamese living abroad, began to return to their old country to visit, but usually not to take up permanent residence. Today, almost 40 years after the end of the Vietnam War, sharp differences of opinion remain among Vietnamese Americans, especially the older ones, concerning the war and the present government of Vietnam (Pfeifer 2008).

Chinese Americans Unlike African slaves and Native Americans, the Chinese were initially encouraged to immigrate to the United States. From 1850 to 1880, thousands of Chinese immigrated to this country, lured by job opportunities created by the discovery of gold, including the building of the transcontinental railroad. However, as employment possibilities decreased and competition for jobs grew, the Chinese became the target of a bitter campaign to limit their numbers and restrict their rights. Chinese laborers were exploited, then discarded.

> One day our descendants will think it incredible that we paid so much attention to things like the amount of melanin in our skin or the shape of our eyes or our gender instead of the unique identities of each of us as complex human beings.
>
> Franklin Thomas

In 1882 Congress en-acted the Chinese Exclusion Act, which prevented Chinese immigration and even forbade Chinese in the United States to send for their families. As a result, the Chinese population declined steadily until after World War II. More recently, the descendants of the 19th-century immigrants have been joined by a new influx from Hong Kong and Taiwan. These groups may contrast sharply in their degree of assimilation, desire to live in Chinatowns, and feelings about this country's relations with the communist People's Republic of China.

Currently, 3.5 million Chinese Americans live in the United States. Some Chinese Americans have entered lucrative occupations, yet many immigrants struggle to survive under living and working conditions that belie the model minority stereotype. In major U.S. cities, including New York and San Francisco, Chinatown districts contain illegal sweatshops in which recent immigrants—many

The Image of Diversity

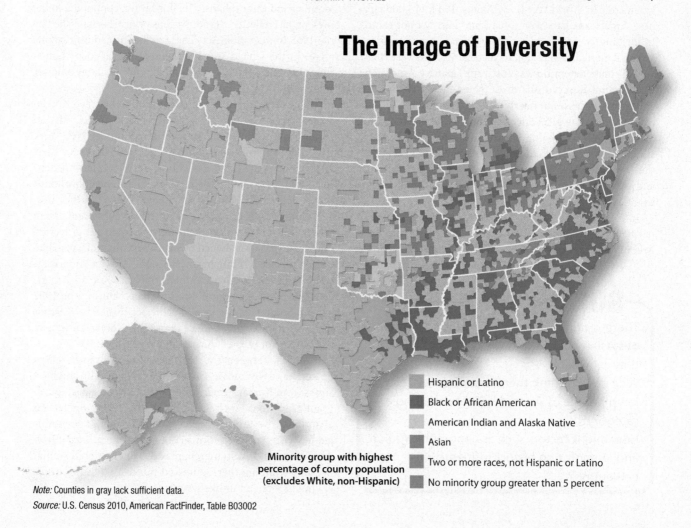

Minority group with highest percentage of county population (excludes White, non-Hispanic)

- Hispanic or Latino
- Black or African American
- American Indian and Alaska Native
- Asian
- Two or more races, not Hispanic or Latino
- No minority group greater than 5 percent

Note: Counties in gray lack sufficient data.

Source: U.S. Census 2010, American FactFinder, Table B03002

of them Chinese women—work for minimal wages. Even in legal factories in the garment industry, hours are long and rewards are limited. (Greenhouse 2008; Louie 2001; Shi 2008; Shipler 2004).

Japanese Americans Approximately 775,000 Japanese Americans live in the United States. As a people, they are relatively recent arrivals. In 1880 only 148 Japanese lived in the United States, but by 1920 there were more than 110,000. Japanese immigrants—called the *Issei*, or first generation—were usually males seeking employment opportunities. Many Whites saw them (along with Chinese immigrants) as a "yellow peril" and subjected them to prejudice and discrimination.

In 1941 the attack on Hawaii's Pearl Harbor by Japan had severe repercussions for Japanese Americans. The federal government decreed that all Japanese Americans on the West Coast had to leave their homes and report to "evacuation camps." Japanese Americans became, in effect, scapegoats for the anger that other people in the United States felt concerning Japan's role in World War II. By August 1943, 113,000 Japanese Americans had been forced into hastily built camps. In striking contrast, only a few German Americans and Italian Americans were sent to such camps (Neiwert 2005).

This mass detention was costly for Japanese Americans. The Federal Reserve Board estimates their total income and property losses at nearly half a billion dollars. Moreover, the psychological effect on these citizens—including the humiliation of being labeled "disloyal"—was immeasurable. Eventually, children born in the United States to the *Issei*, called *Nisei*, were allowed to enlist in the army and serve in Europe in a segregated combat unit. Others resettled in the East and Midwest to work in factories.

In 1983 a federal commission recommended government payments to all surviving Japanese Americans who had been held in detention camps. The commission reported that the detention was motivated by "race prejudice, war hysteria, and a failure of political leadership." It added that "no documented acts of espionage, sabotage, or fifth-column activity were shown to have been committed" by Japanese Americans. In 1988 President Ronald Reagan signed the Civil Liberties Act, which required the federal government to issue individual apologies for all violations of Japanese Americans' constitutional rights and established a $1.6 billion trust fund to pay reparations to the approximately 82,250 surviving Japanese Americans who had been detained (U.S. Department of Justice 1999). Each person who applied and was eligible received $20,000 with payments starting in 1990.

> *A fully functional multiracial society cannot be achieved without a sense of history and open, honest dialogue.*
>
> Cornel West

Korean Americans At 1.5 million, the population of Korean Americans exceeds that of Japanese Americans. Yet Korean Americans are often overshadowed by other groups from Asia. Today's Korean American community is the result of three waves of immigration. The initial wave arrived between 1903 and 1910, when Korean laborers migrated to Hawaii. The second wave followed the end of the Korean War in 1953; most of those immigrants were wives of U.S. servicemen and war orphans. The third wave, continuing to the present, has reflected the admissions priorities established by the 1965 Immigration Act. These well-educated immigrants arrive in the United States with professional skills, though they often must settle, at least initially, for positions of lower responsibility than those they held in Korea.

In the early 1990s, the apparent friction between Korean Americans and another minority racial group, African Americans, attracted nationwide attention. In New York City, Los Angeles, and Chicago, Korean American merchants confronted Blacks who were allegedly threatening them or robbing their stores. Black neighborhoods responded with hostility to what they perceived as the disrespect and arrogance of Korean American entrepreneurs. In South Central Los Angeles, the only places to buy groceries, liquor, and gas were owned by Korean immigrants, who had largely replaced White businesspeople. African Americans were well aware of the dominant role that Korean Americans played in their local retail markets. During the 1992 riots in South Central, small businesses owned by Koreans were a particular target. More than 1,800 Korean businesses were looted or burned during the riots (Kim 1999).

Conflict between the two groups was dramatized in Spike Lee's 1989 movie *Do the Right Thing*. The situation stems from Korean Americans' position as the latest immigrant group to cater to the needs of inner-city populations abandoned by those who have moved up the economic ladder. This type of friction is not new; generations of Jewish, Italian, and Arab merchants have encountered similar hostility from another oppressed minority that to outsiders might seem an unlikely source.

SOCTHINK

There is significant variation among numerous Asian nations and the billions of people they represent.

Why do you think there is a tendency to lump people of Asian descent into a single category?

How might factors such as geographic region and immigration history influence this perception?

Arab Americans Arab Americans are immigrants and their descendants who hail from the 22 nations of the Arab world. As defined by the League of Arab States, these are the nations of North Africa and what is commonly known as the Middle East. Not all residents of those countries are Arab; for example, the Kurds of northern Iraq are not Arab. And some Arab Americans may have immigrated to the United States from non-Arab countries such as Great Britain or France, where their families have lived for generations.

The Arabic language is the single most unifying force among Arabs, although not all Arabs, and certainly not all Arab Americans, can read and speak Arabic. Moreover, the language has evolved over the centuries so that people in different parts of the Arab world speak different dialects. The fact that the Muslim holy book the Qur'an (or Koran) was originally written in Arabic gives the language special importance to Muslims.

Estimates of the size of the Arab American community differ widely. According to the U.S. Census, 1.6 million people of Arab ancestry now reside in the United States. (U.S. Census Bureau 2011q: Table DP02). Iraq, Egypt, Lebanon, and Jordan were the top four Arab countries of origin for the foreign-born population in the United States (U.S. Census Bureau 2011q: Table B05006). As with other racial and ethnic groups, the Arab American population is concentrated in certain areas of the United States. Their rising numbers have led to the development of Arab retail centers in several cities, including Dearborn and Detroit,

Michigan; Los Angeles; Chicago; New York City; and Washington, D.C. (David 2008).

As a group, Arab Americans are extremely diverse. Many families have lived in the United States for several generations; others are foreign born. Despite the stereotype, most Arab Americans are *not* Muslim, and not all practice religion. The majority of Arab Americans are Christian. Nor can Arab Americans be characterized as having a specific family type, gender role, or occupational pattern (Arab American Institute 2008; David 2004).

For years, airport personnel and law enforcement authorities used appearance and ethnic-sounding names to identify Arab Americans and search their belongings. After the terrorist attacks of September 2001, criticism of this practice declined as concern for the public's safety mounted.

ETHNIC GROUPS

Many different ethnic groups have come together in the United States resulting in a shifting mosaic of cultures. Three major groupings include Hispanics (Latinos), Jews, and White ethnics.

Hispanics Together Hispanics make up the largest minority group in the United States. According to the 2010 Census, there were 50.5 million Hispanics, an increase of 43 percent since 2000. This includes 32 million Mexican Americans, 4.6 million Puerto Ricans, 1.8 million Cubans, 1.6 Salvadorans, 1.4 million Dominicans, and more from other countries. The fastest growing subgroups are those who come from the Central American nations of El Salvador, Honduras, and Guatemala (Humes et al. 2011). The majority of the overall Hispanic population increase is due not to immigration, however, but to higher birthrates within the Hispanic population (Johnson and Lichter 2010).

Though the growth in the Hispanic population has been a national phenomenon, more than half resides in California, Texas, and Florida. Major urban areas have also experienced substantial expansion. Hispanics now outnumber African Americans in 8 of the 10 largest U.S. cities. Even Chicago and Philadelphia, the two exceptions, are among the cities with the largest Hispanic populations (see graph on page 340). In these cities, the proportion of the Latino population varies from 29 percent for New York City to 81 percent in El Paso, Texas (Ennis, Ríos-Vargas, and Albert 2011; U.S. Census Bureau 2010j:Table DP-5).

The various Latino groups share a heritage of Spanish language and culture, which can cause serious problems in their assimilation. An intelligent student whose first language is Spanish may be presumed to be slow or even unruly by English-speaking schoolchildren, and frequently by English-speaking teachers as well. The labeling of Latino children as underachievers, as learning disabled, or as emotionally disturbed can act as a self-fulfilling prophecy for some children. Bilingual education aims at

Arab American Religious Affiliation

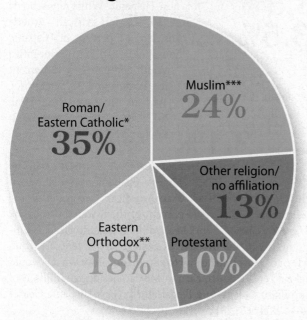

*Catholic includes Roman Catholic, Maronite, and Melkite (Greek Catholic).

**Orthodox includes Antiochian, Syrian, Greek, and Coptic.

***Muslim includes Sunni, Shi'a, and Druze.

Source: Arab American Institute 2008.

U.S. Cities with Highest Numbers of Hispanics

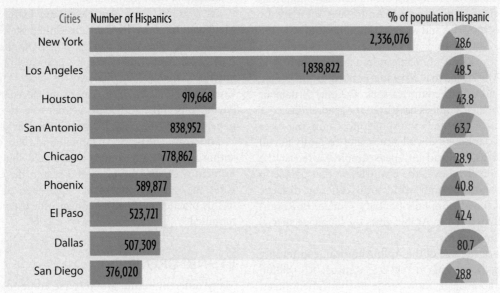

Cities	Number of Hispanics	% of population Hispanic
New York	2,336,076	28.6
Los Angeles	1,838,822	48.5
Houston	919,668	43.8
San Antonio	838,952	63.2
Chicago	778,862	28.9
Phoenix	589,877	40.8
El Paso	523,721	42.4
Dallas	507,309	80.7
San Diego	376,020	28.8

Source: Ennis et al. 2011.

easing the educational difficulties experienced by Hispanic children and others whose first language is not English.

The educational challenges facing Latinos is reflected in the fact that 72 percent of Hispanics aged 25–29 have completed high school, compared to 94 percent for non-Hispanic Whites. At the college level, 39 percent of Whites have a bachelor's degree, whereas only 13 percent of Hispanics have the same. The average income for Hispanic households is $37,759, which is 69 percent as much as non-Hispanic White households. In terms of wealth, in 2009, Hispanic households had a median net worth of $6,325 compared to $113,149 for non-Hispanic White households and $5,677 for African Americans, and 31 percent of Hispanic households had zero or negative wealth compared to 15 percent for Whites and 35 percent for African Americans (Aud et al. 2012: 286; DeNavas- Walt 2011; Kochar, Fry, and Taylor 2011).

Major Hispanic Groups in the United States

Other Hispanic **6.8%**

Other Central and South American **8.1%**

Dominican **2.8%**

Salvadoran **3.3%**

Cuban **3.5%**

Puerto Rican **9.6%**

Guatemalan **2.1%**

Mexican **63.0%**

Source: Ennis et al. 2011:Table1.

Mexican Americans The largest Hispanic population in the United States is Mexican American (see graph on the left). Approximately 64 percent of them were born in the United States. Of the 11.2 million unauthorized immigrants living in the Unites States, 58 percent are from Mexico. The opportunity to earn in one hour what it would take an entire day to earn in Mexico has drawn millions of immigrants, legal and illegal, north (Pew Hispanic Center 2011a:Table 7; 2011b).

Aside from the family, the most important social institution in the Mexican American community is the church—specifically, the Roman Catholic Church. This strong identification with the Catholic faith has reinforced the already formidable barriers between Mexican Americans and their predominantly White and Protestant neighbors in the Southwest. At the same time, the Catholic Church helps many immigrants to develop a sense of identity and assists their assimilation into the dominant culture of the United States. The complexity of the Mexican American community is underscored by the fact that Protestant churches—especially those that endorse expressive, open worship—have attracted increasing numbers of Mexican Americans (Pew Hispanic Center 2011).

Puerto Ricans

The second-largest segment of Latinos in the United States is Puerto Ricans. Since 1917 residents of Puerto Rico have held the status of American citizens; many have migrated to New York and other eastern cities. Puerto Ricans have experienced serious poverty both in the United States and on the island. Those who live in the continental United States earn barely half the family income of Whites. As a result, a reverse migration began in the 1970s, with more Puerto Ricans leaving for the island than coming to the mainland (Torres 2008).

Politically, Puerto Ricans in the United States have not been as successful as Mexican Americans in organizing for their rights. For many mainland Puerto Ricans—as for many residents of the island—the paramount political issue is the destiny of Puerto Rico itself. Should it continue in its present commonwealth status, petition for admission to the United States as the 51st state, or attempt to become an independent nation? This question has divided Puerto Rico for decades and remains a central issue in Puerto Rican elections. In a 1998 referendum, for example, voters supported a "none of the above" option, effectively favoring continuation of the commonwealth status over statehood or independence.

Cuban Americans

Cuban immigration to the United States dates back as far as 1831, but it began in earnest following Fidel Castro's seizure of power in the Cuban revolution of 1959. The first wave of 200,000 Cubans included many professionals with relatively high levels of schooling; these men and women were largely welcomed as refugees from communist tyranny. However, more recent waves of immigrants have aroused growing concern, partly because they were less likely to be skilled professionals. After Castro's revolution, the United States severed formal relations with Cuba, preventing all trade and banning travel. In recent years there has been some softening of that relationship, facilitated in part when Castro stepped down from the presidency in 2008. In April 2009, President Obama signed a bill easing both economic and travel restrictions.

Jewish Americans

Jews constitute about 2.1 percent of the population of the United States. They play a prominent role in the worldwide Jewish community because the United States has the world's largest concentration of Jews. Like the Japanese, many Jewish immigrants came to this country and became white-collar professionals in spite of prejudice and discrimination.

Anti-Semitism—that is, anti-Jewish prejudice—has often been vicious in the United States, although rarely so widespread and never so formalized as in Europe. In many cases, Jews have been used as scapegoats for other people's failures. Given such attitudes, Jews continue to face discrimination. Despite high levels of education and professional training, they are still conspicuously absent from the top management of large corporations (except for the few firms founded by Jews). Until the late 1960s, many prestigious universities maintained restrictive quotas that limited Jewish enrollment. Private social clubs and fraternal groups frequently limit membership to gentiles (non-Jews), a practice upheld by the Supreme Court in the 1964 case *Bell v. Maryland.*

> **anti-Semitism** Anti-Jewish prejudice.

The Anti-Defamation League (ADL) of B'nai B'rith funds an annual tally of reported anti-Semitic incidents. Although the number has fluctuated, the 1994 tabulation reached the highest level in the 20 years the ADL had been recording them. In 2010, the total reported incidents of harassment, threats, vandalism, and assaults came to 1,239, which represented a 2.3 percent increase over 2009. Some incidents were inspired and carried out by neo-Nazi skinheads—groups of young people who champion racist and anti-Semitic ideologies. Such threatening behavior only intensifies the fears of many Jewish Americans, who remember the Holocaust—the extermination of 6 million Jews by Nazi Germany during World War II (Anti-Defamation League 2011).

As is true for other minorities in the United States, Jewish Americans face the choice of maintaining ties to their long religious and cultural heritage or becoming as indistinguishable as possible from gentiles. Many Jews have tended to assimilate, as is evident from the rise in the rate of marriages between Jews and Christians. A study of 50 Jewish communities in the United States found a median intermarriage rate of 33 percent. Many people in the Jewish community worry that intermarriage will lead to a rapid decline in those who identify themselves as "Jewish." Yet, when asked which was the greater threat to Jewish life in the United States—intermarriage or anti-Semitism—only 33 percent of respondents chose intermarriage; 62 percent selected anti-Semitism (American Jewish Committee 2005; Sheskin and Dashefsky 2007).

White Ethnics Overall, 69.1 percent of the U.S. population is composed of non-Hispanic Whites. The nation's White ethnic population includes about 48 million people who claim at least partial German ancestry, 35 million Irish Americans, almost 17 million Italian Americans, and 10 million Polish Americans, as well as immigrants from other European nations. Some of these people continue to live in close-knit ethnic neighborhoods, whereas others have largely assimilated and left the "old ways" behind (U.S. Census Bureau 2011q: Table S0201; Hixson, Hepler, and Kim 2011).

Many White ethnics today identify only sporadically with their heritage. **Symbolic ethnicity** refers to an emphasis on concerns such as ethnic food or political issues rather than on deeper ties to one's ethnic heritage. It is reflected in the occasional family trip to an ethnic bakery, the celebration of a ceremonial event such as St. Joseph's Day among Italian Americans, or concern about the future of Northern Ireland among Irish Americans. Except in cases in which new immigration reinforces old traditions, symbolic ethnicity tends to decline with each passing generation (Anagnostou 2009a, 2009b; Gans 2009; Waters 2009).

Whites increasingly feel excluded and even threatened by efforts to embrace multiculturalism and expand diversity (Plaut, Garnett, Buffardi, and Sanchez-Banks 2011). According to a national survey, Whites now perceive the level of anti-White bias to be greater than bias against Blacks. Greater numbers of Whites now believe that opportunity for Blacks comes at the expense of Whites (Norton and Sommers 2011).

In many respects, the plight of White ethnics involves the same basic issues as that of other subordinate people in the United States. How ethnic can people be—how much can they deviate from an essentially White, Anglo-Saxon, Protestant norm—before society responds to their desire to be different? The United States does seem to reward people for assimilating. Yet, as we have seen, assimilation is no easy process. In the years to come, more and more people will face the challenge of fitting in, not only in the United States, but also around the world as the flow of immigrants from one country to another continues to increase.

symbolic ethnicity An ethnic identity that emphasizes concerns such as ethnic food or political issues rather than deeper ties to one's ethnic heritage.

>>Immigration

According to a United Nations report, there are 191 million international immigrants in the world, or 3 percent of the global population. This includes 38.5 million foreign-born

individuals in the United States. Of these, 53 percent are from Latin America, 28 percent from Asia, 13 percent from Europe, and 4 percent from Africa (United Nations 2009; U.S. Census Bureau 2010:Table DP-2). The constantly increasing numbers of immigrants and the pressure they put on employment opportunities and welfare capabilities in the countries they enter raise difficult questions for many of the world's economic powers. Who should be allowed in? At what point should immigration be curtailed (Bloemraad, Korteweg, and Yurdakal 2008)?

> Race hate isn't human nature; race hate is the abandonment of human nature.
>
> Orson Welles

IMMIGRATION TRENDS

The migration of people is not uniform across time or space. At certain times, war or famine may precipitate large movements of people, either temporarily or permanently. Temporary dislocations occur when people wait until it is safe to return to their home areas. However, more and more migrants who cannot eke out an adequate living in their home nations are making permanent moves to developed nations. The major migration streams flow into North America, the oil-rich areas of the Middle East, and the industrial economies of western Europe and Asia. Currently, seven of the world's wealthiest nations (including Germany, France, the United Kingdom, and the United States) shelter about one-third of the world's migrant population but less than one-fifth of the world's total

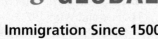

Going GLOBAL

World Immigration Since 1500

Source: J. Allen 2008.

population. As long as disparities in job opportunities exist among countries, there is little reason to expect this international trend to reverse.

Even though the sending nation loses a significant source of labor and talent due to emigration, the process does contribute to its economy. For example, it reduces the size of the population that an economy with limited resources has a difficult time supporting, and it leads to an economic infusion in the form of remittances—monies that immigrants send back to their home nations. Worldwide, immigrants send more than $300 billion a year back home to their relatives—an amount that represents a major source of income for developing nations. In Guatemala, for example, the home country of the majority of workers at the Postville meat packing plant, $4.3 billion was sent back home in 2008, representing 11 percent of Guatemala's economy (*Guatemala Times* 2009; Leys 2008). (Because of the economic downturn, remittances to Guatemala fell in 2009 but rebounded in 2010).

Immigrants continue to face obstacles owing to their relative lack of resources. Immigrant women, for example, face all the challenges that immigrant men do, plus some additional ones. Typically, they bear the responsibility for obtaining services for their families, particularly their children. Women are often left to navigate the bureaucratic tangle of schools, city services, and health care, as well as the unfamiliar stores and markets they must shop at to feed their families. Women who need special medical services or are victims of domestic violence are often reluctant to seek outside help. Finally, because many new immigrants view the United States as a dangerous place

to raise a family, women must be especially watchful over their children's lives (Hondagneu-Sotelo 2003).

One consequence of global immigration has been the emergence of transnationals—people or families who move across borders multiple times in search of better jobs and education. The industrial tycoons of the early 20th century, whose power outmatched that of many nation-states, were among the world's first transnationals. Today, however, millions of people, many of very modest means, move back and forth between countries much as commuters do between city and suburbs. More and more of these people have dual citizenship. Rather than being shaped by allegiance to one country, their identity is rooted in their struggle to survive—and in some instances prosper—by transcending international borders (Croucher 2004; Sassen 2005).

SOCTHINK

Birthrates in the United States, as in many industrialized nations, are low. Populations in many states face natural decrease and will shrink without immigration to compensate for those low birthrates. Given this, why does immigration still cause such tension among many communities in the United States? Might this change as people in such states realize they need those immigrants?

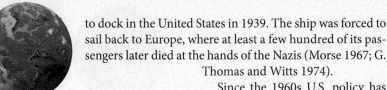

Going GLOBAL

Legal Migration to the United States, 1820–2010

Millions of immigrants

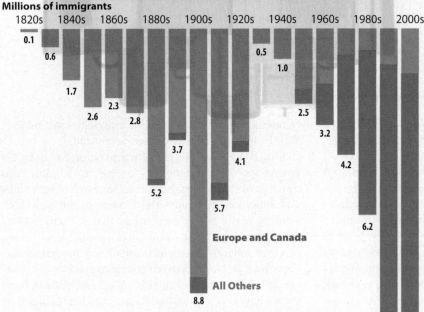

1820s	1840s	1860s	1880s	1900s	1920s	1940s	1960s	1980s	2000s
0.1	0.6	1.7	2.3	3.7	4.1	0.5	2.5	6.2	
		2.6	2.8	5.2	5.7	1.0	3.2	9.7	9.7
				8.8			4.2		10.2

Europe and Canada

All Others

Source: Author's estimates for the period 2000–2010; Office of Immigration Statistics 2007.

IMMIGRATION POLICIES

Countries that have long been a destination for immigrants, such as the United States, usually have policies to determine who has preference to enter. Often, clear racial and ethnic biases are built into these policies. In the 1920s U.S. policy gave preference to people from western Europe while making it difficult for residents of southern and eastern Europe, Asia, and Africa to enter the country. During the late 1930s and early 1940s, the federal government refused to loosen restrictive immigration quotas in order to allow Jewish refugees to escape the terror of Nazi Germany. In line with this policy, the SS *St. Louis,* with more than 900 Jewish refugees on board, was denied permission to dock in the United States in 1939. The ship was forced to sail back to Europe, where at least a few hundred of its passengers later died at the hands of the Nazis (Morse 1967; G. Thomas and Witts 1974).

Since the 1960s U.S. policy has encouraged the immigration of relatives of U.S. residents and of people who have desirable skills. This policy has significantly altered the pattern of sending nations. Previously, Europeans dominated, but for the past 40 years, immigrants have come primarily from Latin America and Asia. Thus, an ever-growing proportion of the U.S. population will be Asian or Hispanic. To a large extent, fear and resentment of racial and ethnic diversity is a key factor in opposition to immigration. In many nations, people are concerned that the new arrivals do not reflect and will not embrace their own cultural and racial heritage. Others fear that immigrants represent an economic threat, because they increase the supply of available workers. In 1986 Congress approved the Immigration Reform and Control Act which, for the first time, outlawed the hiring of undocumented immigrants and subjected employers to fines and even imprisonment if they violated the law. Arizona's controversial immigration law in 2010, mentioned earlier, was another outgrowth of these cultural and economic concerns.

Under the George W. Bush administration, numerous high profile workplace raids occurred—like the one in Postville—to send a very public message that they were serious about cracking down on illegal immigration. Since the election of Barack Obama, the number of such raids declined, although the number of people exported has gone up (Homeland Security 2010). They have been replaced by what are sometimes called "silent raids," in which ICE focuses instead on inspecting employers' hiring paperwork to see whether their workers have the legal documentation necessary for employment. In doing this, they target sectors that have historically hired immigrant undocumented laborers such as the garment industry, fast food chains, and agricultural companies. The effect is that these workers lose their jobs. After one such raid, the clothing maker American Apparel laid off 1,500 workers, approximately a quarter of its workforce. The goal of this approach is to shut down the supply of jobs for workers who lack legal documentation, thus discouraging illegal immigration. Companies who employ these workers, however, are not entirely pleased, because it means that they will have to pay more to attract applicants to these difficult and often tedious jobs (Jordan 2011). Even given this change in tactics, there has still been a substantial increase in the number of individuals deported under the Obama administration than under Bush (Preston 2011).

Battles over immigration continue. Immigrants have staged massive marches to pressure Congress to speed the naturalization process and develop ways for illegal immigrants to gain legal residency. Opponents of illegal immigration have called for more resources with which to track down and deport illegal immigrants and close up the U.S.–Mexican border. Numerous states, including Georgia, Alabama, and Texas, are also considering legislation patterned after the 2010 Arizona law. Despite this widespread public dissatisfaction with the nation's immigration policy, little progress has been made. Congress has had difficulty reaching a bipartisan compromise that pleases both sides.

The intense debate over immigration reflects deep value conflicts in the cultures of many nations. One strand of U.S. culture, for example, has traditionally emphasized egalitarian principles and a desire to help people in time of need. At the same time, hostility to potential immigrants and refugees—whether the Chinese in the 1880s, European Jews in the 1930s and 1940s, or Mexicans, Haitians, and Arabs today—reflects not only racial, ethnic, and religious prejudice but also a desire to maintain the dominant culture of the in-group by excluding those viewed as outsiders.

get Involved!

Investigate! Most immigrant groups have museums dedicated to preserving their heritage. Find one in your area and learn the local immigrant story. If a local museum is not available, take advantage of online museums that preserve that history.

For REVIEW

I. **How do sociologists define race and ethnicity?**

- Race is defined by the social significance that groups attach to external physical characteristics. Ethnicity is rooted in cultural and national traditions that define a population. Sociologists emphasize the significance of culture and its consequences for both.

II. **What are prejudice and discrimination, and how do they operate?**

- Prejudice involves attitudes and beliefs whereas discrimination involves actions. In both cases, they represent a negative response to a group of people that denies them full equality as persons. Institutional discrimination is built into the structure of society itself, systematically denying some groups access to key resources.

III. **What are the consequences of race and ethnicity for opportunity?**

- Racial and ethnic groups in the United States—including African Americans, Native Americans, Asian Americans, Hispanic Americans, Jewish Americans, and White ethnic Americans—face differing levels of opportunity based on their relative position in society. Groups within each of these categories continue to face significant structural inequality.

Functionalist View

Historically, race and ethnicity have contributed to **social integration** and **identity** by providing clear boundaries between groups.

Amalgamation, assimilation, and pluralism function to bring **order** to society. Immigration is functional for the host nation if it gains needed workers and for the sending nation when remittances are sent back.

INTEGRATION, IDENTITY, ORDER
KEY CONCEPTS

Conflict View

Prejudice, discrimination, ethnocentrism, stereotyping, racism, and hate crimes are all manifestations of perceived **superiority** of a dominant group over subordinate minority groups.

Institutional discrimination denies opportunities and equal rights to individuals and groups as part as the normal operations of society.

Exploitation theory holds that prejudice and discrimination help preserve inequality in the economic system as a whole.

KEY CONCEPTS
DISCRIMINATION, EXPLOITATION, RACISM

MAKE THE CONNECTION

After reviewing the chapter, answer the following questions:

Interactionist View

According to the **contact hypothesis**, interracial contact between people in cooperative circumstances will lessen prejudice and stereotyping.

Racial **profiling** occurs when arbitrary actions are taken by authorities based on a person's perceived racial or ethnic identity.

Being White in the United States represents an often unacknowledged form of privilege in everyday encounters.

KEY CONCEPTS
CONTACT, INTERACTION

1

Examine the story of the Postville immigrants from the point of view of each perspective (p. 317).

2

How would each perspective explain stereotyping (p. 320)?

3

How do the functionalist and conflict perspectives intersect in both color-blind racism (p. 324) and affirmative action (p. 328)?

4

Using the interactionist perspective, describe an example of interracial contact you have experienced along with its consequences.

Pop Quiz

1. A group that is set apart because of its national origin or distinctive cultural patterns is a(n)
   a. assimilated group.
   b. ethnic group.
   c. minority group.
   d. racial group.

2. According to the findings of the Human Genome Project, race
   a. determines intellectual ability.
   b. is a biological, not a social, concept.
   c. explains significant social outcomes.
   d. has no genetic or scientific basis.

3. Starting with the 2000 Census, there were a total of ____ possible race combinations you could choose from to identify yourself.
   a. 3
   b. 6
   c. 27
   d. 57

4. Suppose that a White employer refuses to hire a Vietnamese American and selects an inferior White applicant. This decision is an act of
   a. prejudice.
   b. ethnocentrism.
   c. discrimination.
   d. stigmatization.

5. The term that Peggy McIntosh uses to describe the unearned advantages that those in the majority take for granted is
   a. privilege.
   b. discrimination.
   c. racism.
   d. institutional discrimination.

6. Working together as computer programmers for an electronics firm, a Hispanic woman and a Jewish man overcome their initial prejudices and come to appreciate each other's strengths and talents. This scenario is an example of
   a. the contact hypothesis.
   b. a self-fulfilling prophecy.
   c. amalgamation.
   d. reverse discrimination.

7. Intermarriage over several generations, resulting in various groups combining to form a new group, would be an example of
   a. pluralism.
   b. assimilation.
   c. segregation.
   d. amalgamation.

8. Jennifer Anastassakis changed her name to Jennifer Aniston. Her action was an example of
   a. expulsion.
   b. assimilation.
   c. segregation.
   d. pluralism.

9. Which of the following is the largest overall minority group in the United States?
   a. African Americans
   b. Asian Americans
   c. Latinos
   d. Arab Americans

10. Which of the following approaches to immigration enforcement has become most common in the Obama administration?
    a. high profile workplace raids
    b. relaxed enforcement reducing the number of deportations
    c. targeting community organizations that provide services to immigrants
    d. silent raids focusing on employers and documentation

1. (b); 2. (d); 3. (d); 4. (c); 5. (a); 6. (a); 7. (d); 8. (b); 9. (c); 10. (d)

14

POPULATION, HEAL
ENVI

DEEP WATERS

On April 20, 2010, an explosion at the Deepwater Horizon oil drilling platform approximately 40 miles off the coast of Louisiana in the Gulf of Mexico marked the beginning of an environmental catastrophe. Workers had just completed a series of pressure tests to ensure the well's integrity when methane gas entered the drill column and erupted out of the well. The blowout protector, designed to automatically seal the well in such cases, failed. Eleven members of the 126-person crew aboard the oil rig were killed in the resulting explosion. At the wellhead on the Gulf floor, as many as 62,000 barrels of oil per day began gushing into the water.

A year earlier, as part of the oil-drilling approval process, BP, the corporation that owns the rights to the well, filed an exploration plan with the Minerals Management Service (MMS), an agency of the U.S. Department of the Interior. In that report, BP repeatedly minimized both the likelihood of an accident and any possible impact should one occur, reporting that, "in the event of an unanticipated blowout resulting in an oil spill, it is unlikely to have an impact" (BP Exploration & Production Inc. 2009). BP maintained that any effects would likely be "sublethal" to fish, marine mammals, turtles, and birds. It also argued that the well's distance from shore would ensure minimal impact on beaches, wildlife refuges, and wilderness areas in the event of an oil spill. And the corporation expressed confidence in its ability to contain, recover, and remove any spill. Having filed this report, BP received an exemption from the MMS, freeing it from conducting a detailed environmental impact analysis.

After conducting nearly a year-long investigation, the United States Coast Guard (2011) released a report finding that a convergence of factors, including flawed technology, inadequate maintenance, systemic failures in the company's safety management system, and lax government oversight, brought about this disastrous result. Just as the natural environment consists of an interdependent web of relationships, so also does the social environment. We must develop a more complete understanding of both to avoid catastrophic outcomes like this one in the future.

TH, AND
RONMENT

As You READ

>>

- What role do population dynamics play in shaping our lives?
- What does sociology contribute to something as seemingly biological as health?
- What environmental lessons do we learn from sociology?

  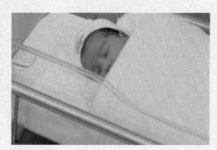

One of the advantages of the sociological imagination is that it provides us with a better understanding of the big picture of society and where we fit in it. It does so by contextualizing our beliefs and practices within a larger social framework, one that is often invisible to us. We have already seen this at work with regard to various components of social structure, including family, religion, education, economy, and politics. In sociology, place matters. This is no less true when it comes to the topics of population, health, and environment. Approaching these issues in a way that takes into account a big-picture perspective allows us to see how our individual outcomes are shaped by the positions we occupy.

>>Population

Today there are more than 7 billion people on Earth, and billions more are expected in the next few decades. Every single one of us must live off the limited resources the planet provides. To better understand our life chances, as well as those of others, we must take into account the direction that population trends are heading. **Demography**—the statistical study of population dynamics—is the discipline committed to studying such patterns. It focuses on how populations change over time, with particular attention to whether or not they are growing, shrinking, or staying the same. It also includes analysis of the composition of those populations—particularly age and sex—especially to the extent that a group's makeup influences their likelihood for population change. For example if the population is young, there is more potential for women to bear children, increasing the possibility for future population growth.

> **demography** The statistical study of population dynamics.
>
> **fertility** The number of children born in a given period of time.

In their analysis, demographers begin by specifying the population to be studied. They might select a city, county, state, or, most often, a nation—though they could choose any group with a specified population boundary. They then gather data about that group over some specified period of time, usually per year, to see how many new members join and how many existing members leave. New arrivals come via birth and immigration, while departures occur through death and emigration. Demographers can then use their results to show how a population changes from one point in time to another or to contrast differences between populations.

BIRTH

Births are the primary means by which a population replaces its members from one generation to the next. Yet the likelihood of each of our births was shaped by population dynamics above and beyond the desires of our biological parents. The rate at which women give birth varies significantly over time and place. To better understand these patterns—whether studying England in the Middle Ages, the United States in the late 19th century, or Afghanistan today—demographers analyze trends in **fertility,** the number of children born in a given period of time. The two primary measures they use to do so are the crude birth rate and the total fertility rate.

World Population Clock, 2012

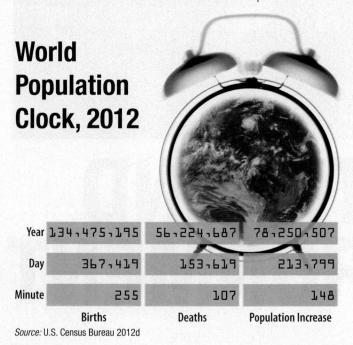

	Births	Deaths	Population Increase
Year	134,475,195	56,224,687	78,250,507
Day	367,419	153,619	213,799
Minute	255	107	148

Source: U.S. Census Bureau 2012d

A population's **crude birth rate** refers to the number of live births per 1,000 people in the population in a given year. It is described as crude because it provides a simple measure, without taking additional factors into consideration, thus allowing for straightforward comparisons between populations. In the United States, for example, the crude birth rate dropped from 23.7 in 1960 to 15.7 in 1985 to 14 in 2010, suggesting the long-term possibility of declining population size. Contrast this with the 2010 rates in a variety of other nations, such as Niger at 48.5, Afghanistan at 43.6, China at 12.1, and Germany at 8.3 and a global rate of 19.6 (World Bank 2012i). One variable in isolation, however, is not sufficient to understand the full scope of population change.

A second indicator is a population's **total fertility rate,** which measures the average number of children a woman would have during her lifetime given current birth rates and assuming she survives through her child-bearing years. This indicator is, in some ways, easier to understand because we may already be familiar with the notion that "the average family has 2.5 children." To provide a more precise count, rather than tying the indicator to particular family situations that are subject to change, this benchmark measures it per woman regardless of her family status. Doing so provides a more universally comparable statistic. In the United States the average number of children a woman had in her lifetime in 1965 was 3.65. By 1985 the rate was cut in half to 1.84 before rising again to 2.1 in 2010. This rate varies widely by country, with Niger at 7.1, Afghanistan at 6.3, India at 2.63, and Bosnia and Herzegovina at 1.15 in 2010 (World Bank 2012j).

To sustain a population over time—apart from the addition of immigrants who join from the outside—the total fertility rate must fall no lower than approximately 2.1, which is known as the **replacement fertility rate.** This is considered the minimum number of children a woman would need to average in her lifetime to reproduce the population in the next generation. The reason for this number is fairly simple. Because men can't have babies, the average woman must have at least two children so that two parents are replaced in the next generation by two children. The number is boosted a bit to account for the fact that not all females survive through their child-bearing years and because the ratio between males and females is not exactly 50/50. The global total fertility rate has fallen from 4.91 in 1960 to 2.45 in 2010, suggesting a slowing in the overall population growth rate and, if trends continue, the possibility of zero population growth, or even global population decline, at some point in the future (World Bank 2012j).

DEATH

Just as new arrivals occur through birth, departures occur through death. And just as with birth, demographers use a simple measure of mortality to allow for comparisons between populations. The **crude death rate** is a measure of the number of deaths per 1,000 people in a population in a given year. In the United States the crude death rate fell from 9.5 in 1960 to 8 in 2010. That rate compares with a high of 16.7 in Guinea-Bissau and a low of 1.3 in United Arab Emirates (World Bank 2012k). Overall, this measure

Total Fertility Rates

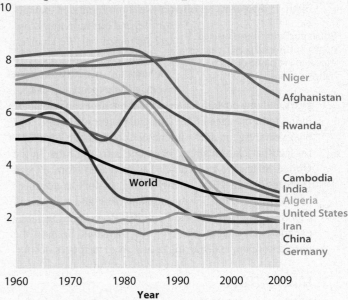

Average number of births per woman*

* If the woman survives to the end of her childbearing years

Source: Google 2011a

is more difficult to interpret, because it is influenced by the age composition of the population. For example, in a society in which the population is on average older, the death rate may be higher, even though people are living longer. Because of this, demographers often turn to two additional measures: infant mortality and life expectancy.

A population's **infant mortality rate** measures the number of deaths in infants less than one year old per 1,000 live births per year. It is considered a major indicator of the overall well-being of a population, because it is a reflection of available health care, economic opportunity, and inequality. The fact that the numbers vary substantially also suggests that actions can be taken to improve the likelihood that a baby survives infancy. The rate in the United States in 1960 was 25.9. It fell to 10.7 by 1985 and then to 6.5 in 2010 owing to improved prenatal care and medical innovations. Internationally the global rate was 50 in 2010. Sierra Leone had the top rate at 113.7, followed closely by the Democratic Republic of Congo (111.7), Somalia (108.3), and Central African Republic (106). At the other end of the scale, Iceland had the lowest rate at 1.6. Other nations with rates of less than 2.5 included Japan, Sweden, and Singapore (World Bank 2012h).

> **crude birth rate** The number of live births per 1,000 people in the population in a given year.
>
> **total fertility rate** The average number of children a woman would have during her lifetime given current birth rates and assuming she survives through her child-bearing years.
>
> **replacement fertility rate** The minimum number of children a woman would need to average in her lifetime to reproduce the population in the next generation.
>
> **crude death rate** The number of deaths per 1,000 people in a population in a given year.
>
> **infant mortality rate** The number of deaths in infants less than one year old per 1,000 live births per year.

The mortality statistic that is perhaps easiest for us to identify with is **life expectancy,** the projected number of years a person can expect to live based on his or her year of birth. It represents an often unwelcome reminder that factors beyond our individual control influence our life chances. For example, a baby born in Afghanistan in 2010 has an average life expectancy of 48.3 years, but one born in Japan at the same time can anticipate living until the age of 82.9. The global average in 2010 was 69.6 years. Again, such differences point to the sociological fact that place matters. The same is true of time. In the United States life expectancy has increased from 69.8 in 1960 to 78.2 in 2010, owing to such factors as advances in health care, reductions in smoking rates, and increases in exercise and fitness (World Bank 2012l). As life expectancy expands, population size typically increases, because the number of people departing in any given year goes down.

> **life expectancy** The projected number of years a person can expect to live based on his or her year of birth.

MIGRATION

In addition to birth and death, arrivals and departures also occur through **migration,** the movement of people from one population group to another. **Immigration** occurs when someone joins a population group of which they were not previously a member. **Emigration** occurs when a member of a population leaves that group. In other words, an immigrant is someone who arrives, and an emigrant is someone who departs.

Reasons for joining or leaving a population group can be varied. Sometimes an immigrant joins a new group because of the opportunities that doing so provides. This might include new job opportunities, connections with families, freedom of religious expression, or other factors that make migration appealing. Such influences are known as *pull* factors, because they serve as a sort of magnet attracting the immigrant to the new place. Other times people leave locations, because they seek to get away from unappealing features in their home country including violence, oppression, and lack of jobs. These are known as *push* factors, because they encourage the emigrant to leave.

> **migration** The movement of people from one population group to another.
>
> **immigration** When individuals join a population group of which they were not previously a member.
>
> **emigration** When members of a population leaves that group.

As we saw in Chapter 13, immigration is a global phenomenon. From 1950 to 2010, 92 million people departed what the United Nation classifies as less-developed regions, including various nations in Asia, Latin America and the Caribbean, and Africa and migrated to more developed regions (see accompanying Global Migration, 1950–2010

graph). The nation that saw the greatest net number of departures during that period was Mexico, with 13.8 million, followed by Bangladesh at 12.1 million and China with 8.9 million. If we control for the effect of population size, countries among those with the lowest net migration rates from 2005 to 2010, meaning they were most likely to lose people, included Samoa, Zimbabwe, and El Salvador, whereas those with the highest rates of joiners included Qatar, United Arab Emirates, and Bahrain. The single most common destination location, receiving the greatest net number of migrants from 1950 to 2010, was the United States, with 43.4 million (United Nations 2011a, 2011b).

In the United States, 12.5 percent of the population is foreign born, of which one-half arrived from Latin America and more than one-quarter came from Asia (see accompanying Foreign-Born Population graph). As indicated in Chapter 13, Mexico leads the way as the source country, accounting for approximately 30 percent, followed by China at 5.2 percent, Philippines at 4.5, and India at 4.3. California is the most common destination for these immigrants, with 26 percent of the foreign-born population living there. New York, Texas, and Florida are also common destinations, each accounting for approximately 10 percent of the foreign-born population (Greico and Trevelyan 2010).

Immigrants in the United States are classified into four major categories by the Department of Homeland Security (2011). Legal permanent residents are those who have been granted lawful permanent residence in the United States. Sometimes referred to as having received their "Green

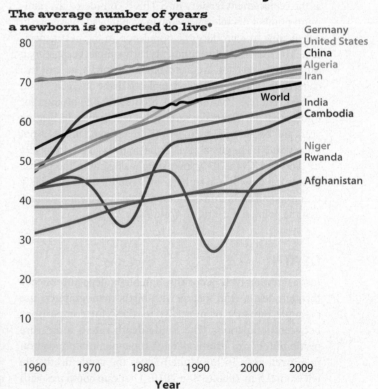

Life Expectancy

The average number of years a newborn is expected to live*

Germany, United States, China, Algeria, Iran, World, India, Cambodia, Niger, Rwanda, Afghanistan

Year

* If current mortality patterns remain the same

Source: Google 2011b

SOCTHINK

What factors may have influenced those in your family to migrate (whether recently or generations ago)? What roles did push and pull play?

Global Migration, 1950–2010

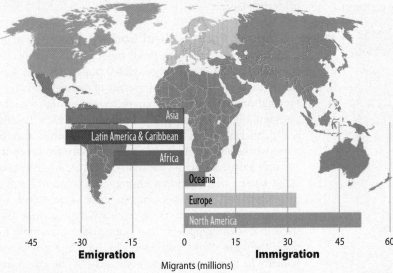

Emigration — Immigration
Migrants (millions)

Source: United Nations 2011a

Globally, the world's population increases each year, because the overall birth rate exceeds the overall death rate. From 2005 to 2010, the world's population grew an average of 1.16 percent per year. This rate represents a decline from the 2.07 percent annual increase during the late 1960s, but it is still significantly higher than the projected annual rate of 0.06 percent by the year 2100. In other words, even though the population will continue to rise by several billion over the next several decades, projections show a substantial decline in the rate of the overall population increase (United Nation 2011c). This prediction of a leveling off of total population after generations of growth is consistent with the population model known as the demographic transition.

Card," they can legally get a job, attend public schools or colleges, and even join the military. In 2010 there were 1 million such recipients, two-thirds of whom were family-sponsored immigrants, meaning they were direct relatives of U.S. citizens (Monger and Yankay 2011). Naturalization, the second category, includes foreign citizens or nationals who become U.S. citizens. In 2010 there were 620,000 new naturalized citizens, 41 percent of whom came from Asia (Lee 2011). The third category consists of those who have been granted formal refuge in the United States owing to persecution, or its imminent threat, in their home country. In 2010 approximately 73,000 people living outside the country were granted refugee status enabling admission into the United States, and another 21,000 people who were already in the country were granted asylum status. The three top countries from which refugees came were Iraq, Burma, and Bhutan. China, Ethiopia, and Haiti were the leading sources of asylees (Martin 2011). The final category includes immigrants who lack legal status to remain in the country but are living in the U.S. In 2010, 387,000 people were removed from the country via court order, approximately half of whom had been convicted of a crime, and another 476,000 were simply returned to their home country without a court order, often having been apprehended by border patrol agents (Homeland Security 2011).

By combining data on births, deaths, and migration, it is possible to create a single indicator that provides a more complete picture of population dynamics. One such measure is a population's **growth rate,** which represents the overall percent change in a population per year. It is important to consider this overall rate in conjunction with the other measures, because the internal population dynamics at any given time can vary. For example, birth rates and death rates might both rise or fall over a given time period, or one might go up while the other goes down, and migration rates can be similarly variable. The growth rate measure provides a snapshot of whether or not the population as a whole is growing or shrinking.

DEMOGRAPHIC TRANSITION

The most defining characteristic of population dynamics in the past 100 years or so is its explosive growth. Throughout most of human history, global population levels were relatively stable. The world's total population 2,000 years ago was approximately 300 million people. It took 1,500 years for it to reach the 500 million mark and another 300 years to surpass 1 billion in 1804. At that point population growth began accelerating rapidly (see accompanying World Population Growth graph). From 1927 to 2012 the population grew from 2 billion to 7 billion and is projected to top the 10 billion mark in 2083 (United Nations 1999, 2011d).

> **growth rate** The overall percent change in a population per year.

Perhaps the best known attempt to come to terms with the population explosion was offered early on by English economist Thomas Malthus (1766–1834). In 1798 he published the first edition of his book *An Essay on the Principle of Population,* in which he argued that there are natural limits to the number of people the environment can sustain. He claimed that, even though total food production expands to provide for a growing population, it does so at an arithmetic rate (1→2→3→4→5). The problem is that population grows at a geometric rate (1→2→4→8→16). Ultimately, population will grow so fast there won't be sufficient land to provide enough food for everyone. Crises would inevitably occur—including poverty, famine, disease, and war—and people would die as a result, reducing the population size to a more sustainable level. For Malthus, history is a never-ending struggle over resources in which people attempt to escape want, a battle that those who control resources are more likely to win. As a result, the burden of this misery falls more heavily on the poor. Though he did argue that people could and should exercise moral restraint to rein in population growth by delaying marriage and practicing celibacy, ultimately, Malthus's emphasis was on control of population through the increased mortality rates that result from crises over resources (Malthus 1878).

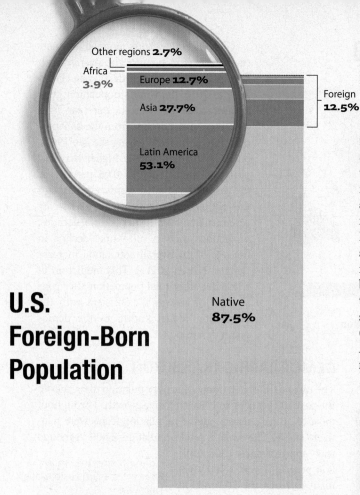

U.S. Foreign-Born Population

Other regions **2.7%**

Africa **3.9%**

Europe **12.7%**

Asia **27.7%**

Foreign **12.5%**

Latin America **53.1%**

Native **87.5%**

Source: Grieco and Trevelyan 2010

and long life spans as virtually inevitable (Bongaarts 2009; Kirk 1996; Myrskylä et al. 2009). This transition has four primary stages.

Stage 1: Preindustrial Society This is the stage humans occupied throughout most of our history. As is evident in the graph below, global population size was steady for a very long time. In terms of demographic factors, nations at this stage are characterized by high fertility rates and high death rates. The economies of such nations are primarily agricultural, and more children means more workers to produce the food necessary for survival. Because infant and child mortality rates are high in this stage, having more children ensures that some will make it to adulthood. Life expectancy in such nations tends to be short. To provide a visual representation of this distribution, demographers use population pyramids to show the ratio of the population by both age groupings (usually in 5-year increments) and sex. As the graph for Afghanistan on page 355 demonstrates, pyramids for nations at this stage tend to have a wide base, indicating a

An alternative, and somewhat less dismal, model of population change is known as the **demographic transition.** According to this model, as societies transform from preindustrial to postindustrial, their population size shifts from small but stable, with high birth and death rates, through a period of significant population growth, to large but stable, when both birth and death rates are low (Notestein 1945; Thompson 1929, 1948). Unlike Malthus, theorists here do not see elevated death rates through disease and war as inevitable checks on population growth. Instead, they argue that a natural decline in fertility rates occurs owing to technological, social, and economic changes. In basic terms, they portray the transition of a population with large families but short life spans to one with small families

demographic transition As societies transform from preindustrial to postindustrial, their population size shifts from small but stable with high birth and death rates, through a period of significant population growth, to large but stable, when both birth and death rates are low.

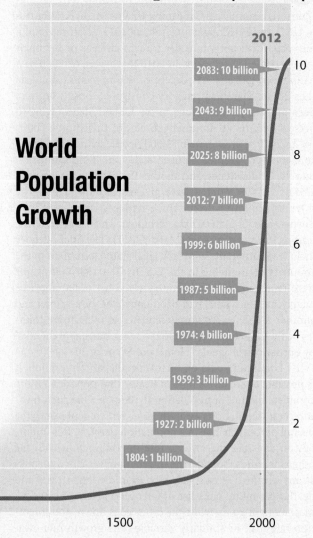

World Population Growth

World Population (billions)

2012

2083: 10 billion — 10

2043: 9 billion —

2025: 8 billion — 8

2012: 7 billion —

1999: 6 billion — 6

1987: 5 billion —

1974: 4 billion — 4

1959: 3 billion —

1927: 2 billion — 2

1804: 1 billion —

Year — 0   50   1000   1500   2000

Source: United Nations 1999, 2011d

large percentage of children in the population, and to narrow quickly at the top, showing the relatively small percentage of those who are elderly.

Stage 2: Early Industrial Society In this stage, death rates fall while birth rates remain high. More babies survive infancy and additional children make it to adulthood. Because there are more young adults, and the birth rate stays high, even more babies are born. On top of that, overall life expectancy increases. The result is a population explosion. This occurs as a consequence of innovations taking place in the society. Advances in technology lead to increased food supplies, cleaner water, improved sanitation, and better medical care. Developments in agricultural technology and techniques, such as crop rotation, are particularly important. In population pyramid terms, the base widens as the total number of children grows and the top both expands and gets taller owing to more people living longer. Historically, nations that entered this phase early on in the Industrial Revolution, such as the United States or Germany, saw slower population growth rates during this stage than have more recent developing nations. Gaining access to existing advances in medical technology often plays a critical role for developing nations, because it can dramatically decrease death rates (Bongaarts 2010).

Stage 3: Late Industrial Society Over time, fertility rates also begin to drop. People start to realize that, with mortality rates falling, having many children is no longer necessary to ensure that some survive into adulthood. Additionally, as the economy transitions away from agriculture, children are no longer needed as workers to assist in food production. In fact, especially with the establishment of child labor laws, children can become a liability rather than an asset. They are no longer primarily producers who

contribute, becoming instead consumers whose needs must be met. Advances in contraception technology facilitate this choice to have fewer children. One effect of declining fertility rates is increased opportunity for women. As they spend less time bearing children, women are freed up to play expanded roles in the public spheres of politics and the economy. Because the adult population is relatively young, without an overwhelming number of children or elderly people to support, the economy often thrives, creating what is sometimes referred to as a demographic dividend (Bongaarts 2010).

Stage 4: Postindustrial Society Eventually the demographic transition is complete and population size becomes stable once again. This occurs because birth rates and death rates both reach low levels. Globally this takes a long time, but within a country the amount of time can vary: longer in early industrializing nations but less time for more recent developing nations. Total fertility rates reached replacement levels in Europe and Northern America by 1980 and are anticipated to do so in Asia and Latin America by 2020 (Bongaarts 2009). As a result of these changes, the population pyramid develops sides that are more vertical before they angle in to its pinnacle (see Global Population Pyramid on page 356). According to this theory, as these trends spread it is just a matter of time, perhaps by the end of this century, until we reach a global population peak and stability (Scherbov, Lutz, and Sanderson 2011).

Some demographers have suggested that the demographic transition model needs to be extended to include additional stages to adequately describe recent demographic trends. In a possible Stage 5, fertility rates would continue falling below replacement levels, contributing to population decline. This has already occurred in numerous nations, including Germany and China (Bloom et al. 2010; Hvistendahl 2010; Myrskylä, Kohler, and Billari 2009). In such cases, as the number of people who retire increases relative to the working-age population, questions arise about how to care for the needs of an aging population. In the United States ongoing political struggles over health care are driven, to some extent, by concerns about the ability to pay for increased Medicare costs caused by the demographic surge in retirees in the coming years (OASDI 2011). Some countries, such as Japan, have begun taking steps to boost fertility by establishing programs, such as extended paid maternity leave and subsidized day care, that encourage people to have more children (Suzuki 2009).

In recent years, some of these nations with below-replacement birth rates have experienced a fertility rebound,

Afghanistan Population Pyramid, 2010

Age (years)

Males   Females

100+
95–99
90–94
85–89
80–84
75–79
70–74
65–69
60–64
55–59
50–54
45–49
40–44
35–39
30–34
25–29
20–24
15–19
10–14
5–9
0–4

3   2   1   0   0   1   2   3

Population (millions)

? Did You Know

Chinese officials instituted a one-child policy in 1979 and claim their one-child policy reduced the current population by 400 million. Demographers counter that total fertility rates would have fallen substantially even without the policy, as they have in other nations.
Source: Cai 2010; Hvistendahl 2010.

Global Population Pyramid

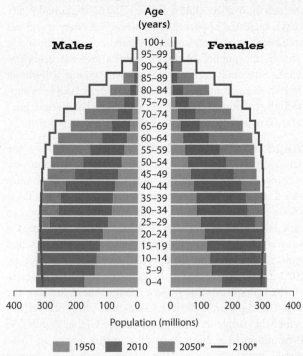

Age (years)

Males	**Females**

100+
95–99
90–94
85–89
80–84
75–79
70–74
65–69
60–64
55–59
50–54
45–49
40–44
35–39
30–34
25–29
20–24
15–19
10–14
5–9
0–4

400 300 200 100 0   0 100 200 300 400

Population (millions)

■ 1950   ■ 2010   ■ 2050*   — 2100*

*Numbers for 2050 & 2100 are projections based on existing birth and death rate trends.

Source: United Nations 2011f

a possible Stage 6 of the demographic transition model. Demographers suggest that this is most likely to occur in countries with the highest scores on the United Nations Human Development Index (HDI). As we saw in Chapter 11, this index ranges from 0 to 1 and is based on three societal dimensions, including health, education, and income. Countries with an HDI score of greater than 0.86, such as the United States and Norway, are most likely to experience this rebound (Myrskylä et al. 2009). Parents in such countries can worry less about having sufficient individual and collective resources to provide for the needs of their children.

Studying population dynamics is important, because the world into which we are born is not of our own choosing, yet it shapes our life chances. When we were born, how long we live, and our likelihood for migration are all part of larger social trends. Understanding the nature and direction of these patterns can empower us to create new pathways in hopes of a better future. Such informed innovation has contributed to advances in health care, education, and environmental protection, substantially improving the life chances of people all around the world.

Anorexia is not a new disease, though it is discussed much more openly today. Victoria Beckham is one of several celebrities who have spoken publicly about struggling with an eating disorder.

┌─ **SOC**THINK ──────────────────────┐
What factors do you think might explain the fertility rebound in countries with high HDI scores?
└──────────────────────────────────┘

>>Sociological Perspectives on Health and Illness

To understand health, we cannot focus on biology alone. We must consider relationships, contexts, and the significance and impact of culture and society. Whether we are considered "healthy" or "ill" is not our decision alone to make. Family, friends, co-workers, physicians, and others all shape how we perceive the state of our health. A sociological understanding must take into account how society defines health and illness, what the consequences of such definitions are, and how social position and access to resources shape health outcomes.

CULTURE, SOCIETY, AND HEALTH

Our conceptions of what it means to be healthy vary from place to place. In an attempt to provide a more universally applicable definition, the World Health Organization (WHO), in the preamble to

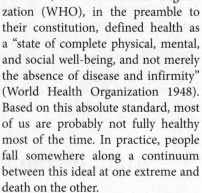

their constitution, defined health as a "state of complete physical, mental, and social well-being, and not merely the absence of disease and infirmity" (World Health Organization 1948). Based on this absolute standard, most of us are probably not fully healthy most of the time. In practice, people fall somewhere along a continuum between this ideal at one extreme and death on the other.

Where we live influences where along that continuum we might fall. For example, the care we receive and the risks we face vary based upon whether we live in the city or the country. In rural areas, people may have to travel many miles to see a doctor or specialist. And in cities, urban dwellers face stresses, threats, and environmental risks different from those facing people living in the country. Another variable is cultural attitudes toward health care treatments. For example, in Japan, organ transplants are rare. The Japanese do not generally favor harvesting organs from brain-dead donors. As a result, they forgo the benefits that such transplants provide.

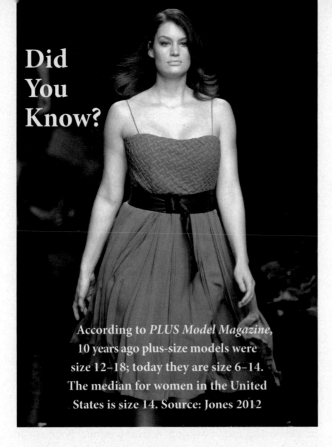

Did You Know?

According to *PLUS Model Magazine*, 10 years ago plus-size models were size 12–18; today they are size 6–14. The median for women in the United States is size 14. Source: Jones 2012

Researchers have shown that diseases, too, are rooted in the shared meanings of particular cultures. The term **culture-bound syndrome** refers to a disease or illness that cannot be understood apart from some specific social context. This means that there is something particular about the culture—how it is organized, what it believes, what is expected of members—that contributes to that malady (Buckle et al. 2007; Nicolas et al. 2006; U.S. Surgeon General 1999).

In the United States, a culture-bound syndrome known as anorexia nervosa has received increasing attention in recent decades. First described in England in the 1860s, this condition is characterized by an intense fear of becoming obese and a distorted image of one's body. Those who suffer from anorexia nervosa (primarily young women in their teens or 20s) lose weight drastically through self-induced semistarvation. Anorexia nervosa is best understood in the context of Western culture, which typically views the slim, youthful individual as healthy and beautiful, and the fat person as ugly and lacking in self-discipline.

Throughout most of the 20th century, U.S. researchers dealt with the concept of culture-bound syndromes only in cross-cultural studies. However, recent increases in immigration, especially after the Immigration and Nationality Act of 1965 opened the doors to more immigrants, along with efforts by the medical establishment to reach out to immigrant communities, have led to a belated recognition that not everyone views medicine in the same way. Medical practitioners are now being trained to recognize cultural beliefs that are related to medicine. For example, people from Central America may consider pain a consequence of the imbalance of nature, and Muslim women are particularly concerned about personal modesty. Health care professionals are increasingly incorporating such knowledge into their practices.

ILLNESS AND SOCIAL ORDER

Illness represents a threat to the social order. If too many people are sick at the same time, it not only presents a problem for those who are ill but also undercuts our collective ability to perform tasks necessary for the continued operation of society. This can result in debates over what constitutes being "sick enough" to be considered truly ill. At what point, for example, do we stay home from school or work due to illness, and who gets to decide? All of us have likely faced this dilemma, sometimes dragging ourselves out of bed and going anyway because we felt we needed to be there, whether for the sake of ourselves or for others.

When people cross the line into illness, they take on what sociologists call the **sick role,** a term that refers to societal expectations about the attitudes and behavior of a person labeled as ill (Parsons 1951, 1975). Fit members of society exempt those who are sick from typical, day-to-day responsibilities and generally do not blame them for their condition. Yet the sick members of society are obligated to attempt recovery, which includes seeking competent professional care. This obligation arises from the sense of responsibility we have to perform our normal roles in society, whether as student, worker, parent, or more. It also is motivated by the reality that we may well face sanctions from others for failing to return to those normal roles quickly. In fact, especially in the context of competitive work environments, we often look down on those who seem to get sick too easily or frequently, suspecting that they are either lazy or weak. Such attitudes present significant difficulties for those facing chronic health problems.

> **culture-bound syndrome** A disease or illness that cannot be understood apart from some specific social context.
>
> **sick role** Societal expectations about the attitudes and behavior of a person viewed as being ill.

Personal Sociology

Health Care Fortunes

While working on revisions for this chapter, my retina detached and I went blind in one eye. Fortunately, I had access to experts, especially my retina specialist Dr. Heilskov, all of whom provided me with the best possible advice and care. Three operations later, my sight has largely been restored. And, (again) fortunately, I had health insurance to help pay those sizable medical bills. Had I been in the position of the majority of the world's population—lacking access to such care and coverage—I would have remained blind in that eye for life. To me, this ordeal affirmed one of the most basic lessons of sociology: Our life chances are shaped by the social positions we occupy.

Physicians and nurses have the power to label people as healthy or sick and, thus, to function as gatekeepers for the sick role. For example, instructors often require students to get a note from a health care professional to verify a claim of illness as a legitimate excuse for missing a paper or an exam. The ill person becomes dependent on the doctor or nurse, because physicians and nurses control the resources that patients need, whether it be a note for a professor or a prescription for medication. We look to such professionals to solve our health care needs, trusting that they have sufficient expertise and experience to diagnose and treat our problems.

Factors such as gender, age, social class, and ethnic group all influence patients' judgments regarding their own state of health. Younger people may fail to detect the warning signs of a dangerous illness, and the elderly may focus too much on the slightest physical malady. People who are employed are less willing to assume the sick role for fear of consequences they might face at work. Similarly, from an early age, athletes learn to define certain ailments as "sports injuries" and so do not regard themselves as "sick" when suffering from such maladies.

POWER, RESOURCES, AND HEALTH

The faith we place in physicians to heal what ails us has helped them attain significant levels of prestige and power. Sociologist Eliot Freidson (1970:5) has likened the status of medicine today to that of state religions in the past—it has an officially approved monopoly on the right to define health and to treat illness. Theorists use the phrase "medicalization of society" to refer to the growing role of medicine as a major institution of social control (Conrad 2007; Zola 1972, 1983).

The Medicalization of Society Social control involves techniques and strategies for regulating behavior in order to enforce the distinctive norms and values of a culture. How does medicine manifest its social control? First, medicine has greatly expanded its domain of expertise in recent decades. Physicians now examine a wide range of issues in addition to basic health, among them sexuality, old age, anxiety, obesity, child development, alcoholism, and drug addiction. We tolerate this expansion of the boundaries of medicine because we hope that these experts can provide factual and effective cures to complex human problems, as they have to various infectious diseases.

The social significance of this expanding medicalization is that once a problem is viewed from a medical model framework—once medical experts become influential in proposing and assessing relevant public policies—it becomes more difficult for common people to join the discussion and exert influence on decision making. It also becomes more difficult to view these issues as being shaped by social, cultural, or psychological factors rather than simply by physical or medical factors (Caplan 1989; Davis 2006; Starr 1982).

A second way that medicine serves as an agent of social control is by retaining absolute jurisdiction over many health care procedures. The medical industry has even attempted to guard its jurisdiction by placing health care professionals such as chiropractors and nurse-midwives outside the realm of acceptable medicine. Despite the fact that midwives first brought professionalism to child delivery, they have been portrayed by doctors as having invaded the "legitimate" field of obstetrics, in both the United States and Mexico. Nurse-midwives have sought licensing as a way to achieve professional respectability, but physicians continue to exert power to ensure that midwifery remains a subordinate occupation (Scharnberg 2007).

Inequities in Health Care Another serious concern regarding power and resources in the context of contemporary medicine involves the glaring inequities that exist in health care. Around the world, poor areas tend to be underserved because medical services concentrate where the wealth is. The United States, for example, has 24.2 physicians per 10,000 people, whereas African nations average 2.2 per 10,000 (World Health Organization 2012).

The supply of health care in poorer countries is further reduced by what is referred to as **brain drain**—the immigration to the United States and other industrialized nations of skilled workers, professionals, and technicians who are needed in their home countries. As part of this brain drain, physicians, nurses, and other health care professionals have come to the United States from developing countries such as India, Pakistan, and various African states. Their emigration represents yet another way in which the world's core industrialized nations enhance their quality of life at the expense of developing countries (List 2009).

Such inequities in health care have clear life-and-death consequences. For example, as we saw earlier, there are dramatic differences in infant mortality rates between developing countries such as Afghanistan, Sierra Leone, and Pakistan and industrial nations such as Iceland, Japan, and Australia. Such differences in infant mortality reflect unequal distribution of health care resources based on the wealth or poverty of various nations as seen, for example, in prenatal nutrition, delivery procedures, and infant screening measures. Surprisingly, despite its national wealth and the huge amounts spent on health care in the United States, more than 40 nations have lower infant mortality rates, including Canada, Cuba, and the United Kingdom. An additional way that developing countries suffer the consequences of health care inequality is in reduced life expectancy. Average life expectancy in sub-Saharan African nations is 54 compared to 80 in European Union nations. By comparison, in the United States it is nearly 79 years (World Bank 2012h; 2012l).

Labeling and Power Sometimes the power to label and the power to oppress go hand in hand. A historical example illustrates perhaps the ultimate extreme in labeling social behavior as a sickness. As enslavement of Africans in the United States came under increasing attack in the 19th century, medical authorities provided new rationalizations for the oppressive practice. Noted physicians published articles stating that the skin color of Africans deviated from "healthy" white skin coloring because Africans suffered from congenital leprosy. Moreover, physicians classified the continuing efforts of enslaved Africans to escape from their White masters as an example of the "disease" of drapetomania (or "crazy runaways"). In 1851 the prestigious *New Orleans Medical and Surgical Journal* suggested that the remedy for this "disease" was to treat slaves kindly, as one might treat children. Apparently, these medical authorities would not entertain the view that it was healthy and sane to flee slavery or join in a slave revolt (Szasz 1971).

> **brain drain** The immigration to the United States and other industrialized nations of skilled workers, professionals, and technicians who are needed in their home countries.

Globally, the power of one particular label—"HIV positive"— has become quite evident. This label often functions as a master status that overshadows all other aspects of a person's life. Once someone is told that he or she has tested positive for HIV, the virus associated with AIDS, that person is forced to confront immediate and difficult questions: Should I tell my family members? My sex partners? My friends? My coworkers? My employer? How will these people respond? People's intense fear of the disease has led to prejudice and discrimination—even social ostracism—against those who have (or are suspected of having) AIDS. A person who has AIDS must deal not only with the serious medical consequences of the disease, but also with the distressing social consequences associated with the label.

AIDS caught major social institutions— particularly the government, the health care system, and the economy—by surprise when it was first noticed by medical practitioners in the 1970s. It has since spread around the world, with the first U.S. cases of AIDS reported in 1981. Rather than being a distinct disease, AIDS is actually a predisposition to various diseases that is caused by a virus, the human immunodeficiency virus (HIV). The virus gradually destroys the body's immune system, leaving the carrier vulnerable to infections such as pneumonia that those with healthy immune systems generally can resist.

Although the numbers of new cases and deaths have recently shown some evidence of decline, approximately 1.2 million people in the United States were living with AIDS or HIV as of 2009. Globally, an estimated

5 Movies on HEALTH AND MEDICINE

The Diving Bell and the Butterfly
A man suddenly becomes completely paralyzed.

My Sister's Keeper
Cancer puts a strain on family relationships.

Living in Emergency
Volunteers for Doctors Without Borders provide medical care under extreme conditions.

Sicko
A documentary criticizing the U.S. health care system.

Life, Above All
A 12-year-old girl uncovers her community's unspoken struggle with AIDS.

33.3 million people are now infected; however, the disease is not evenly distributed. Those areas least equipped to deal with it—the developing nations of sub-Saharan Africa, where 5.0 percent of the adult population is infected—face the greatest challenge (UNAIDS 2010).

Going GLOBAL

Infant Mortality Rates in Selected Countries

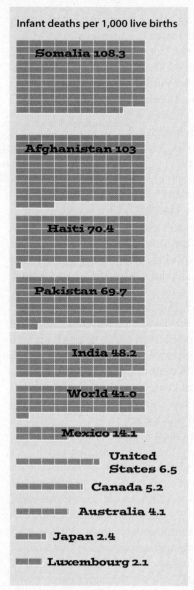

Infant deaths per 1,000 live births

Somalia 108.3

Afghanistan 103

Haiti 70.4

Pakistan 69.7

India 48.2

World 41.0

Mexico 14.1

United States 6.5

Canada 5.2

Australia 4.1

Japan 2.4

Luxembourg 2.1

Source: World Bank 2012h.

In the United States, because those in high-risk groups—gay men and IV drug users—were comparatively powerless, and labeled as such, policy makers were slow to respond to the AIDS crisis. Over time and with increased education and advocacy, however, the response has improved, and today people with HIV or AIDS who receive appropriate medical treatment are living longer than they did in the past. The high cost of drug treatment programs has generated intensive worldwide pressure on the major pharmaceutical companies to lower the prices to patients in developing nations, especially in sub-Saharan Africa. Bowing to this pressure, several of the companies have agreed to make the combination therapies available at cost. As a result, the accessibility of HIV treatment has increased steadily, though inequalities remain. Globally, the proportion of adults and children with advanced HIV infection receiving antiretroviral therapy rose from 7 percent in 2003 to percent in 44 percent in 2009, and there were 20% fewer AIDS-related deaths in sub-Saharan Africa in 2009 than 2004 after treatment dramatically expanded (Mahy et al. 2010; UNAIDS 2010).

According to labeling theorists, we can view a variety of life experiences as illnesses or not. Recently, the medical community has recognized premenstrual syndrome, posttraumatic disorders, and hyperactivity as medical disorders. Probably the most noteworthy medical example of labeling is the case of homosexuality. For years, psychiatrists classified being gay or lesbian not as a lifestyle but as a mental disorder subject to treatment. This official sanction by the psychiatry profession became an early target of the growing gay and lesbian rights movement in the United States. In 1974 members of the American Psychiatric Association voted to drop homosexuality from the standard manual on mental disorders (Conrad 2007).

Going GLOBAL

HIV/AIDS Cases

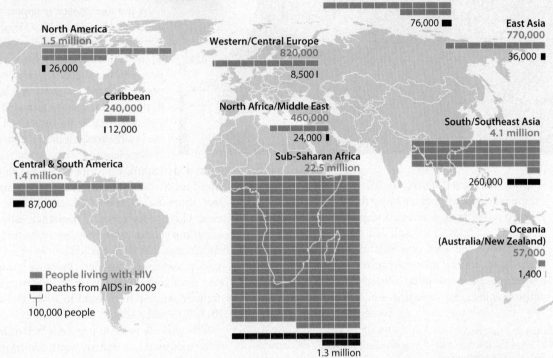

Eastern Europe/Central Asia
1.4 million
76,000 ■

North America
1.5 million
■ 26,000

East Asia
770,000
36,000 ■

Western/Central Europe
820,000
8,500 |

Caribbean
240,000
| 12,000

North Africa/Middle East
460,000
24,000 ■

South/Southeast Asia
4.1 million
260,000 ■■■■

Central & South America
1.4 million
■ 87,000

Sub-Saharan Africa
22.5 million
1.3 million

**Oceania
(Australia/New Zealand)**
57,000
1,400 |

■ People living with HIV
■ Deaths from AIDS in 2009
⌐ 100,000 people

Source: UNAIDS 2010.

Note: Total number of adults and children living with HIV, 33.3 million; total number of estimated adult and child deaths during 2009, 1.8 million.

NEGOTIATING CURES

In practice, we seek to strike a balance between the authority of the physician and the agency of the patient. Physicians use cues to reinforce their prestige and power. According to medical sociologist Brenda Beagan (2001, 2003), the technical language students learn in medical school becomes the basis for the script they follow as novice physicians. The familiar white coat and stethoscope is their costume—one that helps them to appear confident and professional at the same time that it identifies them as doctors to patients and other staff members. Beagan found that many medical students struggle to project the appearance of competence they think their role demands, but over time most become accustomed to expecting respect and deference.

Patients, however, are not passive. Active involvement in health care can have positive or negative consequences. Sometimes, patients play an active role in health care by failing to follow a physician's advice. For example, some patients stop taking medications long before they should. Some decrease or increase the dosage on purpose (because they think they know better what they need), and others never even fill their prescriptions. Such noncompliance results in part from the prevalence of self-medication in our society; many people are accustomed to self-diagnosis and self-treatment.

Patients' active involvement in their health care can have very positive consequences. Some patients consult books, magazines, and websites about preventive health care techniques, attempt to maintain a healthful and nutritious diet, carefully monitor any side effects of medication, and adjust the dosage based on perceived side effects. Recognizing this change, pharmaceutical firms are advertising their prescription drugs directly to potential customers. For their part, medical professionals are understandably suspicious of these new sources of information. Studies, including one published in the *Journal of the American Medical Association,* found that health information on the Internet can be incomplete and inaccurate, even on the best sites. Nevertheless, there is little doubt that Internet research is transforming patient–physician encounters (Adams and de Bont 2007; Arora et al. 2008; Berland 2001).

>>Social Epidemiology

By looking at patterns of health and illness throughout society, we can better understand which factors are at work in shaping health outcomes. **Social epidemiology** is the study of disease distribution, impairment, and general health status across a population. Initially, epidemiology concentrated on the scientific study of epidemics, focusing on how they started and spread. Contemporary social epidemiology is much broader in scope, concerned not only with epidemics but also with nonepidemic diseases, injuries, drug addiction and alcoholism,

> **social epidemiology** The study of the distribution of disease, impairment, and general health status across a population.

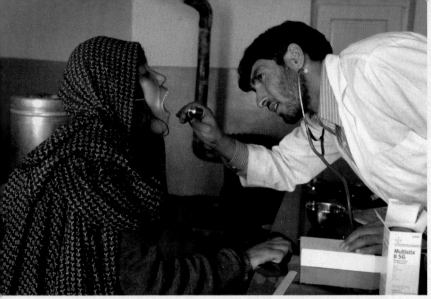

classes have higher rates of mortality and disability than those in higher classes. One study concluded that Americans with 12 years or less of schooling could expect to die seven years sooner than those with more than 12 years of schooling (Meara, Richards, and Cutler 2008; Pear 2008).

A number of factors appear to influence the effect class has on health. Crowded living conditions, substandard housing, poor diet, and stress all contribute to the ill health of many low-income people in the United States. In certain instances, poor education may lead to a lack of awareness of measures necessary to maintain good health. Financial strains are certainly a major factor in the health problems of less affluent people.

People who are poor—many of whom belong to racial and ethnic minorities—are less able than others to afford quality medical care (see the accompanying graph). Not surprisingly, those with high incomes are significantly more likely to have health insurance, either because they can afford it or because they have jobs that provide it. The middle class has been particularly hard hit by the decision of companies to eliminate employer-provided coverage (the most common form of health insurance). Such rates declined steadily from 2000 to 2010 (DeNavas-Walt et al. 2011; E. Gould 2008).

The ultimate price to pay for a lack of health insurance is the increased risk of early death. Uninsured women who develop breast cancer tend to be diagnosed later—when treatment is less effective—than insured women. Uninsured men who develop high blood pressure are more likely than others to forgo screenings and medication, a decision that

suicide, and mental illness. In 2001 epidemiologists took on the new role of tracking bioterrorism. They mobilized to trace an anthrax outbreak and prepare for any terrorist use of smallpox or other lethal microbes. Epidemiologists draw on the work of a wide variety of scientists and researchers, among them physicians, sociologists, public health officials, biologists, veterinarians, demographers, anthropologists, psychologists, and meteorologists.

incidence The number of new cases of a specific disorder that occur within a given population during a stated period.

prevalence The total number of cases of a specific disorder that exist at a given time.

morbidity rate The incidence of disease in a given population.

mortality rate The incidence of death in a given population.

To describe how widespread a disease is and how fast it is spreading, social epidemiologists report on rates of prevalence and incidence. **Prevalence** refers to the total number of cases of a specific disorder that exist at a given time. **Incidence** refers to the number of new cases of a specific disorder that occur within a given population during a specified period of time, usually a year. Using AIDS as an example, in terms of prevalence, there were 1.2 million people in the United States and 33.3 million globally who were living with HIV in 2009. Turning to incidence, there were 54,000 new cases in the United States and 2.6 million globally in 2009. From 2001 to 2009, incidence rates fell by more than 25 percent in 33 countries (UNAIDS 2010).

When disease incidence figures are presented as rates—for example, the number of reports per 100,000 people—they are called **morbidity rates.** This is distinct from the **mortality rate,** which refers to the incidence of death in a given population. Sociologists find morbidity rates useful because they can reveal whether a specific disease occurs more frequently among one segment of a population than another. As we shall see, social class, race, ethnicity, gender, and age can all affect a population's morbidity rates (Barr 2008).

SOCIAL CLASS

Social class is clearly associated with differences in morbidity and mortality rates. Studies in the United States and other countries have consistently shown that people in the lower

Did You Know?

... In research looking at how social class operates, sociologist Annette Lareau (2003) found that middle-class parents and children were more likely to engage with physicians, asking questions and questioning diagnoses. Working-class patients were more deferential to the doctor's authority.

Percentage of People without Health Insurance

Household income

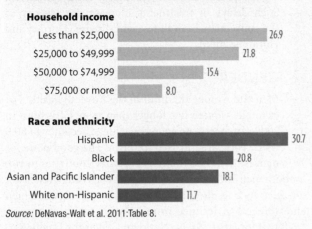

Less than $25,000	26.9
$25,000 to $49,999	21.8
$50,000 to $74,999	15.4
$75,000 or more	8.0

Race and ethnicity

Hispanic	30.7
Black	20.8
Asian and Pacific Islander	18.1
White non-Hispanic	11.7

Source: DeNavas-Walt et al. 2011:Table 8.

jeopardizes their health. According to a 2009 Harvard Medical School study, approximately 45,000 deaths per year are associated with lack of health insurance (Wilper et al. 2009).

What is particularly troubling about social class differences is that they appear to be cumulative. Little or no health care in childhood or young adulthood is likely to mean more illness later in life. The longer that low income presents a barrier to adequate health care, the more chronic and difficult to treat illness becomes (Prus 2007).

Karl Marx would have argued, and some contemporary sociologists agree, that capitalist societies such as the United States care more about maximizing profits than they do about the health and safety of industrial workers. As a result, government agencies do not take forceful action to regulate conditions in the workplace, and workers suffer many preventable job-related injuries and illnesses. As we will see later in this chapter, research also shows that the lower classes are more vulnerable to environmental pollution, another consequence of capitalist production, than are the affluent, not only where they work but where they live as well.

> It is a lot harder to keep people well than it is to just get them over a sickness.
>
> DeForest Clinton Jarvis

RACE AND ETHNICITY

The health profiles of many racial and ethnic minorities reflect the social inequality evident in U.S. society. The poor economic and environmental conditions of groups such as African Americans, Hispanics, and Native Americans are manifested in high morbidity and mortality rates for these groups. It is true that some afflictions, such as sickle-cell anemia among Blacks, are influenced by genetics, but in most instances, environmental factors contribute to the differential rates of disease and death.

As noted earlier, infant mortality is regarded as a primary indicator of health care. There is a significant gap in the United States between the infant mortality rates of African Americans and Whites. On average, the rate of infant death is more than twice as high among Blacks. Non-Hispanic African Americans account for 14.5 percent of all live births in the nation but 28.6 percent of infant deaths. Hispanics and Asians have rates that are lower than those of non-Hispanic Whites (Mathews and MacDorman 2011).

Considering mortality rates, Blacks have higher death rates from heart disease, pneumonia, diabetes, and cancer than do Whites. The death rate from stroke is twice as high among African Americans. Such epidemiological findings are related to the social class effects noted previously—the fact that average income for African Americans is lower than that for Whites. The effect of these factors can be seen in terms of life expectancy. According to statistics from the Centers for Disease Control, overall life expectancy in the United States is 78.5 years, but for Whites it is 78.8 years compared to 74.5 years for Blacks. This gap is lower than the high of 7.1 years in 1989 (National Center for Health Statistics 2012: Table 22).

The medical establishment is not exempt from institutional discrimination. There is evidence that minorities receive inferior care even when they are insured. Despite having access to care, Blacks, Latinos, and American Indians are treated unequally as a result of differences in the quality of various health care plans. Furthermore, national clinical studies have shown that even allowing for differences in income and insurance coverage, racial and ethnic minorities are less likely than other groups to receive both standard health care and life-saving treatment (Dressler, Oths, and Gravlee 2005; A. Green et al. 2007).

Numerous examples in the history of African American health care demonstrate that such institutional discrimination has been around for a long time. For example, in a study conducted from 1992 to 1997, researchers sought to determine whether there is a biological or genetic basis for violent behavior. They intentionally misled the parents of young subjects, all of whom were Black males, by telling them that

Infant Mortality Rates in the United States

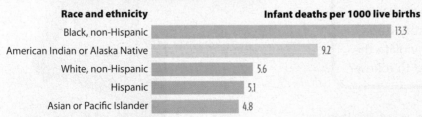

Race and ethnicity	Infant deaths per 1000 live births
Black, non-Hispanic	13.3
American Indian or Alaska Native	9.2
White, non-Hispanic	5.6
Hispanic	5.1
Asian or Pacific Islander	4.8

Note: Rates represent the number of infant deaths per 1,000 live births.
Source: Mathews and MacDorman 2011.

the children would undergo a series of tests and questions. In fact, the boys were given potentially risky doses of the same drug found in the now-banned Fen-phen weight-loss pill, which causes heart irregularities (Washington 2006; R. Williams 2007).

Having to deal with the effects of racism may itself contribute to the medical problems of Blacks. The stress that results from racial prejudice and discrimination helps to explain the higher rates of hypertension found among African Americans (and Hispanics) compared to Whites. Hypertension—twice as common in Blacks as in Whites—is believed to be a critical factor in Blacks' high mortality rates from heart disease, kidney disease, and stroke (Fiscella and Holt 2008).

Mexican Americans and many other Latinos adhere to cultural beliefs that make them less likely to use the established medical system. They may interpret their illnesses according to traditional Latino folk medicine, or **curanderismo**—a form of holistic health care and healing. *Curanderismo* influences how one approaches health care and even how one defines illness. Although most Hispanics use folk healers, or *curanderos,* infrequently, perhaps 20 percent rely on home remedies. Some define such illnesses as *susto* (fright sickness) and *atague* (fighting attack) according to folk beliefs. Because these complaints often have biological bases, sensitive medical practitioners need to deal with them carefully to diagnose and treat illnesses accurately (Tafur, Crowe, and Torres 2009).

curanderismo Latino folk medicine, a form of holistic health care and healing.

SOCTHINK

Studies such as the one on violence and genetics mentioned above seem to clearly violate ethical principles of research. How do you think that researchers justify studies involving race that appear to violate the ethical guidelines they are bound to follow?

Also affecting Latino morbidity rates is the fact that Latinos are much more likely to wait to seek treatment.

Partly because of a lack of health insurance, they seek treatment for pressing medical problems at clinics and emergency rooms rather than receiving regular preventive care through a family physician. Such delays in treatments increase the severity of the consequences of illness and disease (Durden and Hummer 2006).

GENDER

Men and women do differ in their overall health. For example, women live longer than men. Girls born in 2009 can anticipate an average life expectancy of 80.9 years, compared to 76.0 for boys. The good news for men is that, though life expectancy continues to rise for both men and women, rates have been rising even faster for men. As a result, the life expectancy gap between men and women has declined from 7.6 years for those born in 1970 to 4.9 years in 2009 (National Center for Health Statistics 2012: Table 22).

Greater longevity for women appears to be tied to lifestyle differences between men and women that grow out of gendered norms. Historically, women's lower rate of cigarette smoking (reducing their risk of heart disease, lung cancer, and emphysema), lower consumption of alcohol (reducing the risk of auto accidents and cirrhosis of the

Smoking Rates by Gender

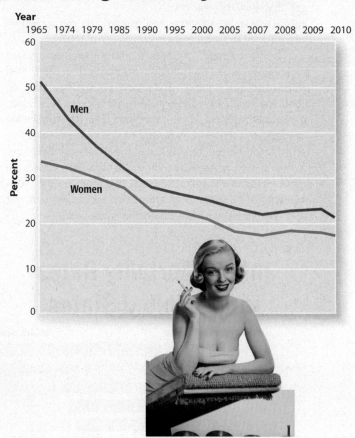

Source: National Center for Health Statistics 2012:Table 60.

liver), and lower rate of employment in dangerous occupations explain about one-third of their greater longevity than men. Researchers argue that women are much more likely than men to seek treatment, to be diagnosed as having a disease, and thus to have their illnesses reflected in the data examined by epidemiologists (National Center for Health Statistics 2010). Changes in lifestyle do matter. The declining gap in smoking rates between men and women accounts for some of reduction in the difference in life expectancy between men and women.

With everything from birth to beauty being treated in an increasingly medical context, women have been particularly vulnerable to the medicalization of society. Ironically, even given the increased power of the medical establishment in women's lives, medical researchers have often excluded them from clinical studies. Female physicians and researchers charge that sexism lies at the heart of such research practices and insist there is a desperate need for studies of female subjects (Pinnow et al. 2009; Rieker and Bird 2000).

AGE

Health is the overriding concern of the elderly. Most older people in the United States report having at least one chronic illness, but only some of those conditions are potentially life threatening or require medical care. The quality of life among older people is of particular concern in the face of potentially escalating health problems. A substantial number of older people in the United States are troubled by arthritis and other chronic diseases, and many have visual or hearing impairments that can interfere with the performance of everyday tasks (Hootman et al. 2006; National Center for Health Statistics 2010).

Older people are also especially vulnerable to certain mental health problems. Alzheimer's disease, the leading cause of dementia in the United States, afflicts an estimated 5.1 million (13 percent) of people aged 65 years and older. While some individuals with Alzheimer's exhibit only mild symptoms, the risk of severe problems resulting from this disease rises substantially with age (Alzheimer's Association 2010).

Because of their increased health risks, the rate at which older people in the United States (ages 75 and older) use health services is more than three times greater than that for younger people (ages 15–24). This heightened use level is tied to health insurance coverage, with people over age 65 the most likely to be covered (see adjacent graph). The disproportionate use of the U.S. health care system by older people is a critical factor in all discussions about the cost of health care and possible reforms of the health care system (U.S. Census Bureau 2009f:Table 162).

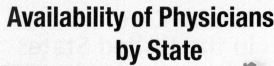

Availability of Physicians by State

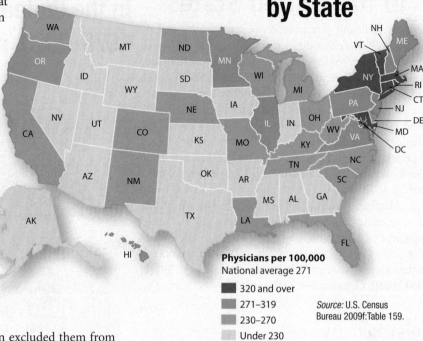

Physicians per 100,000
National average 271

- 320 and over
- 271–319
- 230–270
- Under 230

Source: U.S. Census Bureau 2009f:Table 159.

A person's odds of good health are shaped by her or his class, race and ethnicity, gender, and age. Even geography matters, as there are significant differences in the number of physicians from one state to the next. Health care professionals and program advisors need to take such differential effects into account when considering what constitutes equitable health care coverage. Any attempts to do so, however, are constrained by the cost of health care.

Health Insurance Rates by Age

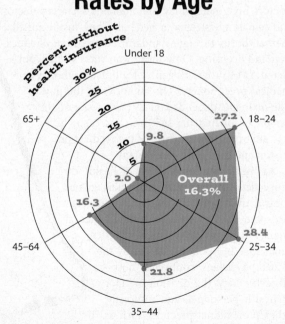

Source: DeNavas-Walt et al. 2011:Table 8.

>>Health Care in the United States

The costs of health care have skyrocketed in the past 40 years. In 1997 total expenditures for health care in the United States crossed the trillion-dollar threshold—more than four times the 1980 figure. In 2000 the amount spent on health care equaled what we spent on education, defense, prisons, farm subsidies, food stamps, and foreign aid combined. By the year 2019, total expenditures for health care in the United States are expected to exceed 4.6 trillion or $13,709 per person. The United States devotes a greater proportion of its total spending to health care, 17.6 percent as measured by GDP, than does any other country in the world except Marshall Islands. Contrast the U.S. rate with those in countries such as Canada (11.4), France (11.9), United Kingdom (9.8), Sweden (10.0), or Japan (9.5). Health care in the United States has become a major economic concern (Centers for Medicare and Medicaid Services 2012a, 2011b; World Health Organization 2012:Table 7).

A HISTORICAL VIEW

Today, state licensing and medical degrees confer a widely recognized level of authority on medical professionals. This was not always the case. The "popular health movement" of the 1830s and 1840s emphasized preventive care and what is termed "self-help." It voiced strong criticism of "doctoring" as a paid occupation. New medical philosophies or sects established their own medical schools and challenged the authority and methods of traditional doctors. By the 1840s most states had repealed medical licensing laws, and the health care field was largely unregulated (Porter 1998, 2004).

In response, through the leadership of the American Medical Association (AMA), founded in 1848, "regular" doctors marginalized lay practitioners, sectarian doctors, and female physicians in general. They institutionalized their authority through standardized programs of education and licensing. Only those who successfully completed AMA programs gained legitimate authority as medical practitioners. The authority of the physician no longer depended on lay attitudes or on the person occupying the sick role; increasingly, it was built into the structure of the medical profession and the health care system.

As the institutionalization of health care proceeded, the medical profession gained control over both the market for its services and the various organizational hierarchies that govern medical practice, financing, and policy making. By the 1920s physicians controlled hospital technology, the division of labor of health personnel, and indirectly, other professional practices such as

Total Health Care Expenditures in the United States, 1970–2020 (projected)

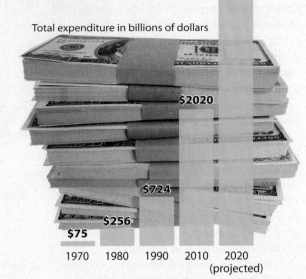

Total expenditure in billions of dollars

$4,630

$2020

$724

$256

$75

| 1970 | 1980 | 1990 | 2010 | 2020 |
| | | | | (projected) |

Source: Centers for Medicare and Medicaid Services 2012a:Table 1; 2012b:Table 1.

nursing and pharmaceutical services (Coser 1984; Starr 1982; Whorton 2002).

THE ROLE OF GOVERNMENT

Not until the 20th century did health care receive federal aid in conjunction with the expansion of medicine as a social institution. The first significant government involvement was the 1946 Hill-Burton Act, which provided subsidies for building and improving hospitals, especially in rural areas. An even more important development was the enactment in 1965 of two wide-ranging government assistance programs: Medicare, which is essentially a compulsory health insurance plan for the elderly, and Medicaid, which is a noncontributory federal and state insurance plan for the poor. These programs greatly expanded federal involvement in health care financing for needy men, women, and children.

While health care costs were rising, a growing portion of the U.S. population (49.9 million in 2010) remained uninsured. An inability to afford coverage was a major factor. In 1993 the Clinton administration proposed health care reform designed to provide universal coverage, but the legislation failed to pass. Throughout the George W. Bush administration, the United States remained the only wealthy, industrialized nation that did not provide some form of universal coverage (DeNavas-Walt et al. 2011).

By 2009 there was widespread political agreement that the existing system, with its projected escalating costs, was not sustainable. From 1999 to 2008, for example, the cost of health insurance premiums rose 119 percent, while wages rose only 34 percent (Kaiser Family Foundation 2009). The Obama administration pledged to enact reform that would both contain costs and expand coverage. Though there was general consensus regarding these aims, there were significant disagreements on how best to accomplish them. Some supported a single-payer system in which the government is the primary source of health care funding. Others continued to support market-based reforms that minimize government involvement. A significant intervening position focused on whether or not the government should provide a "public option," allowing people to choose a government-funded plan among many private company plans.

In March 2010 Congress passed, and President Obama signed into law, the Patient Protection and Affordable Care Act and the Health Care and Education Reconciliation Act. Though implementation will take years to complete, key provisions include:

- Young adults will be able to stay on their parents' health care plans until age 26.
- Coverage for checkups and other preventive care will not require co-pays.
- Annual caps and lifetime limits on the cost of benefits patients can receive will be eliminated.
- People with preexisting conditions cannot be denied coverage, and companies will no longer be able to cut employees from a plan when they get sick.
- Most Americans will be required to purchase some form of health insurance.
- Tax credits for the purchase of insurance will be available for individuals and families between 100 and 400 percent of the poverty level.
- Companies with more than 50 employees will be required to provide an employer-sponsored health plan that provides a mandated level of minimal coverage.
- Small businesses will be eligible to receive tax credits to assist them in providing coverage.

- State-based insurance exchanges will offer a choice of plans for small businesses and people who lack employer-supplied coverage.
- Insurance companies will be required to provide greater transparency regarding spending on overhead costs.

The acts passed Congress with virtually no bipartisan support. Republicans continued to prefer market-based solutions arguing that free market capitalism would lead to greater efficiency and cost control. Though most liberal Democrats voted for the legislation, many of them were also critical of the bill. They argued that reform did not go far enough to ensure universal coverage and cost reduction, and they expressed displeasure about the lack of a public option. In the end, however, the legislation represented a substantial shift in the history of health care in the United States.

> **holistic medicine** Therapies in which the health care practitioner considers the person's physical, mental, emotional, and spiritual characteristics.

COMPLEMENTARY AND ALTERNATIVE MEDICINE

In modern forms of health care, people rely on physicians and hospitals for the treatment of illness. Yet a significant proportion of adults in the United States attempt to maintain good health or respond to illness through the use of alternative health care techniques. For example, in recent decades, interest has been growing in holistic medical principles, first developed in China. **Holistic medicine** refers to therapies in which the health care practitioner considers the person's physical, mental, emotional, and spiritual characteristics. The individual is regarded as a totality rather than a collection of interrelated organ systems. Treatment methods include massage, chiropractic medicine, acupuncture, respiratory exercises, and the use of herbs as remedies. Nutrition, exercise, and visualization may also be used to treat ailments (Barnes, Bloom, and Nahin 2008; Stratton and McGivern-Snofsky 2008).

Practitioners of holistic medicine do not necessarily function totally outside the traditional health care system. Some have medical degrees and rely on X-rays and EKG machines for diagnostic assistance. Others who staff holistic clinics, often referred to as wellness clinics, reject the use of medical technology. The recent resurgence of holistic medicine comes amid widespread

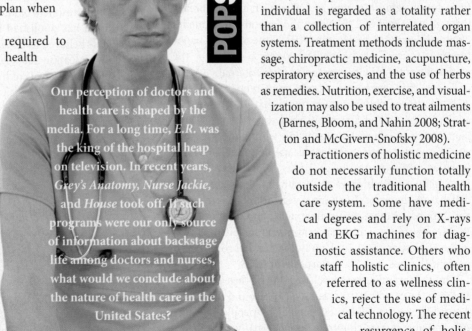

POPSOC

Our perception of doctors and health care is shaped by the media. For a long time, *E.R.* was the king of the hospital heap on television. In recent years, *Grey's Anatomy*, *Nurse Jackie*, and *House* took off. If such programs were our only source of information about backstage life among doctors and nurses, what would we conclude about the nature of health care in the United States?

Rising Medicare Expenses

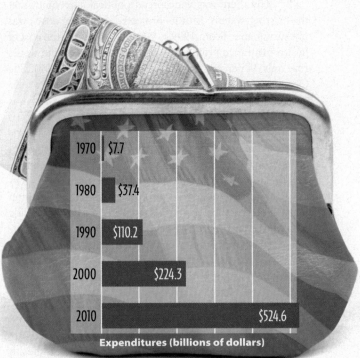

1970	$7.7
1980	$37.4
1990	$110.2
2000	$224.3
2010	$524.6

Expenditures (billions of dollars)

Source: Centers for Medicare and Medicaid Services 2012a:Table 3.

recognition of the value of nutrition and the dangers of over reliance on prescription drugs—especially those used to reduce stress, such as Valium (Baer and Coulter 2008).

SOCTHINK

What do you think about alternative medicine? Would you be willing to get assistance from a holistic healer? What background factors, such as age, race and ethnicity, or gender, might play a role in your willingness or unwillingness to do so?

The medical establishment—professional organizations, research hospitals, and medical schools—continues to zealously protect its authority. However, a major breakthrough occurred in 1992 when the federal government's National Institutes of Health (NIH)—the nation's major funding source for biomedical research—opened the National Center for Complementary and Alternative Medicine and empowered it to accept grant requests. A 2007 NIH-sponsored national study found that 38.3 percent of adults in the United States had used some form of complementary or alternative medicine within the previous year. Examples of practices include use of natural products (such as echinacea or omega-3 fatty acids), deep breathing, meditation, chiropractic treatment, massage, yoga, diet-based therapies (including vegetarian, macrobiotic, and Atkins), homeopathic treatment, and acupuncture. When private or communal prayer was included as part of the NIH-sponsored 2002 study, the number rose to 62.1 percent (Barnes et al. 2004; Barnes et al. 2008).

On the international level, the WHO has begun to monitor the use of alternative medicine around the world. According to the WHO, 80 percent of people in some African and Asian countries use alternative medicine, from herbal treatments to the services of a faith healer. In most countries, these treatments are largely unregulated, even though some of them can be fatal. For example, kava

kava, an herbal tea used in the Pacific Islands to relieve anxiety, can be toxic to the liver in concentrated form. Other alternative treatments have been found to be effective in the treatment of serious diseases, such as malaria and sickle-cell anemia. The WHO's goal is to compile a list of such practices, as well as to encourage the development of universal training programs and ethical standards for practitioners of alternative medicine. To date the organization has published findings on about 100 of the 5,000 plants believed to be used as herbal remedies (World Health Organization 2005, 2008a).

Sociological analysis of health and illness suggests that if we are to understand sickness we must look beyond

Complementary and Alternative Medicine Use

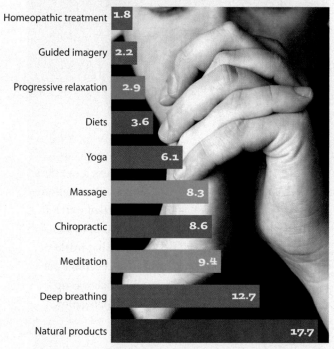

- Homeopathic treatment: 1.8
- Guided imagery: 2.2
- Progressive relaxation: 2.9
- Diets: 3.6
- Yoga: 6.1
- Massage: 8.3
- Chiropractic: 8.6
- Meditation: 9.4
- Deep breathing: 12.7
- Natural products: 17.7

Source: Barnes et al. 2008.

biology. Society and culture, family and friends, the medical profession, and social position all help shape medical outcomes. Given the increasing costs of health care, and the fact that different groups experience different outcomes, this issue becomes one of equality and fairness. To what extent, for example, are we willing to accept that a child will live or die due to his or her income, race, or ethnicity? Or that one's life expectancy is shaped by such factors? It is precisely such concerns that drive debates about the expansion of health care coverage as a social right.

>>Sociological Perspectives on the Environment

We have seen that the environment people live in has a noticeable effect on their health. Those who live in stressful, overcrowded places suffer more from disease than those who do not. Likewise, people have a noticeable effect on their environment. Around the world, increases in population, together with the economic development that accompanies them, have had serious environmental consequences. We can see signs of despoliation almost everywhere: our air, our water, and our land are being polluted, whether we live in St. Louis; Mexico City; or Lagos, Nigeria. Although environmental problems may be easy to identify, devising socially and politically acceptable solutions to them is much more difficult. Sociologists provide

us with some models to better understand the issues we must consider (Sutton 2007).

HUMAN ECOLOGY

Human ecology is an area of study that is concerned with interrelationships between people and their environment. As biologist and environmentalist Barry Commoner (1971:39) put it during the early stages of the modern environmental movement, "Everything is connected to everything else." Human ecologists focus on how the physical environment shapes people's lives and on how people influence the surrounding environment.

> **human ecology** The area of study concerned with the interrelationships between people and their environment.

In an application of the human ecological perspective, sociologists and environmentalists have identified several relationships between the environment and people. Among them are the following:

- *The environment provides the resources essential for life.* These include air, water, and materials used to create shelter, transportation, and needed products. If human societies exhaust these resources—for example, by polluting the water supply or cutting down rain forests—the consequences could be dire.
- *The environment serves as a waste repository.* More so than other living species, humans produce a huge quantity and variety of waste products—bottles, cans, boxes, paper, sewage, garbage, and so on. Various types of pollution have become more common because human societies are generating more wastes than the environment can safely absorb.
- *The environment "houses" our species.* It is our home, our living space, the place where we reside, work, and play. At times we take this truism for granted, but not when day-to-day living conditions become unpleasant

Did You Know?

. . . In a 2008 Arctic expedition, scientists found high levels of toxic contaminants including mercury, PBDEs (flame retardants used in upholstery, textiles, and plastics), pesticides (including DDT and HCH), and PCBs.

and problematic. If our air is polluted, if our tap water turns brown, or if toxic chemicals seep into our neighborhood, we remember why it is vital to live in a healthful environment.

There is no shortage of illustrations of the interconnectedness of humans and the environment. For example, scientific research has linked pollutants in the environment to people's health and behavior. The increasing prevalence of asthma, lead poisoning, and cancer has been tied to human alterations to the environment. Similarly, the rise in melanoma (skin cancer) diagnoses has been linked to global climate change. And ecological changes in our food and diet have been related to childhood obesity and diabetes.

With its view that "everything is connected to everything else," human ecology stresses the trade-offs inherent in every decision that alters the environment. In facing the environmental challenges of the 21st century, government policy makers and environmentalists must determine how they can fulfill humans' pressing needs for food, clothing, and shelter while preserving the environment as a source of resources, a waste repository, and a home.

POWER, RESOURCES, AND THE ENVIRONMENT

Analyzing environmental issues from a world systems approach allows us to better understand the global consequences of differential access to resources. This approach highlights the difference in relative power between core nations, which control wealth and so dominate the global economy, and developing countries, which lack control and whose resources are exploited. This process only intensifies

Did You Know?

. . . In 2010, Americans drank more than 8.8 billion gallons of bottled water at a total cost of $10.7 billion. That works out to 28.3 gallons per person, which was up from less than 6 gallons in 1987.

Source: Rodwan 2011.

the destruction of natural resources in poorer regions of the world. Less affluent nations are being forced to exploit their mineral deposits, forests, and fisheries in order to meet their debt obligations. People in developing nations often end up turning to the only means of survival available to them, including plowing mountain slopes, burning sections of tropical forests, and overgrazing grasslands (Palm et al. 2005; Pollini 2009).

Brazil exemplifies this interplay between economic troubles and environmental destruction. Each year more than 4.3 million acres of rain forest are cleared for crops and livestock. The elimination of the rain forest affects worldwide weather patterns, heightening the gradual warming of the earth. These socioeconomic patterns, with their harmful environmental consequences, are evident not only in Central and South America, but also in many regions of Africa and Asia (INPE 2010).

Although destruction of the rain forest has long been a concern, only in the past few decades have policy makers begun to listen to the indigenous peoples who live in these areas. Preservation of the rain forests may make sense at the global level, but for many local peoples, it limits their ability to cultivate crops or graze cattle. Even though it harms the global environment, they feel they have no choice but to take advantage of their available resources. In 2008 native peoples from Brazil to the Congo to Indonesia convened to make the case that wealthier countries should compensate them for conservation of the tropical rain forests (Barrionuevo 2008).

There is, in fact, a certain amount of ethnocentrism involved when people in industrialized countries insist

Did You Know?

An average of 17,454 square kilometers (4.3 million acres) of Brazilian rain forest was lost each year from 2001 to 2009. The rate has recently slowed with 7,464 square kilometers (1.8 million acres) lost in 2009.

Source: INPE 2010.

that those developing nations change their practices to save the planet. In calling for the poverty-stricken and "food-hungry" populations of the world to sacrifice, they should also consider the lifestyle consequences for the "energy-hungry" nations. The industrialized nations of North America and Europe account for only 12 percent of the world's population but are responsible for 60 percent of worldwide consumption. The money their residents spend on ocean cruises each year could provide clean drinking water for everyone on the planet. Ice cream expenditures in Europe alone could be used to immunize every child in the world. The global consumer represents a serious environmental threat, but it is often difficult to look in the mirror and blame ourselves because our individual contribution to the problem seems so small. Collectively, however, the choices we make have a significant global impact (Diamond 2008; Gardner, Assadourian, and Sarin 2004).

The rise in global consumption is tied to a capitalist system that depends upon growth for its survival. Capitalism creates a "treadmill of production" (Baer 2008; Schnaiberg 1994). Cutting back on consumption means cutting back on purchases, which leads to reduced production and the loss of profits and jobs. This treadmill necessitates creating an increasing demand for products, obtaining natural resources at minimal cost, and manufacturing products as quickly and cheaply as possible—no matter what the long-term environmental consequences.

> ## Suburbia is where the developer bulldozes out the trees, then names the streets after them.
>
> **Bill Vaughn**

and scholars have identified other environmental disparities that break along racial and social class lines. In general, poor people and people of color are much more likely than others to be victimized by the everyday consequences of economic development, including air pollution from expressways and incinerators (Sandler and Pezzullo 2007).

Sociologists Paul Mohai and Robin Saha (2007) examined more than 600 hazardous waste treatment, storage, and disposal facilities in the United States. They found that non-Whites and Latinos make up 43 percent of the people who live within one mile of these dangerous sites. There are two possible explanations for this finding. One is that racial and ethnic minorities possess less political power than others, so they cannot prevent toxic sites from being located in their backyards. The other is that they end up settling near the sites after they are constructed, because economics and the forces of discrimination push them into the least desirable living areas.

Following reports from the Environmental Protection Agency (EPA) and other organizations documenting the discriminatory location of hazardous waste sites, President Bill Clinton issued an executive order in 1994 requiring all federal agencies to ensure that low-income and minority communities have access to better information about their environment, as well as an opportunity to participate in shaping government policies that affect their health. Initial efforts to implement the

> **environmental justice** A legal strategy based on claims that racial minorities are subjected disproportionately to environmental hazards.

ENVIRONMENTAL JUSTICE

In autumn 1982 nearly 500 African Americans participated in a six-week protest against a hazardous waste landfill containing cancer-causing chemicals in Warren County, North Carolina. Their protests and legal actions continued until 2002, when decontamination of the site finally began. This 20-year battle can be seen as yet another "not-in-my-backyard" (NIMBY) event in which people desire the benefits of growth but want someone else to pay for its negative effects. In any event, the Warren County struggle is viewed as a transformative moment in contemporary environmentalism: the beginning of the environmental justice movement (Bullard 2000; McGurty 2007; North Carolina Department of Environment and Natural Resources 2008).

Environmental justice is a legal strategy based on claims that racial minorities are subjected disproportionately to environmental hazards. Some observers have heralded environmental justice as the "new civil rights of the 21st century" (Kokmen 2008:42). Since the advent of the environmental justice movement, activists

Should Environmental Issues Be Top Priorities of Congress?

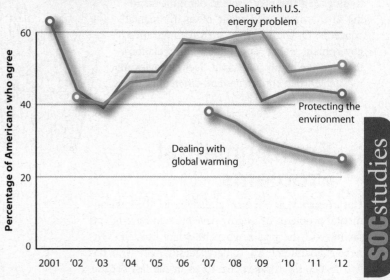

Source: Pew Research Center 2012.

policy, along with increased activity by the environmental justice movement, aroused widespread opposition because of the delays the policy imposes in establishing new industrial sites. Some observers question the wisdom of an order that slows economic development in areas that are in dire need of employment opportunities. Others counter that such businesses employ few unskilled or less skilled workers and only make the environment less livable (Stretesky 2006; D. Taylor 2000).

Meanwhile, the poor and oppressed continue to bear the brunt of environmental pollution. In the 1990s the federal government, unable to find a disposal site for spent nuclear fuel, turned to tribal reservations. Agents eventually persuaded a tiny band of Goshute Indians in Skull Valley, Utah, to accept more than 44,000 barrels of the highly radioactive substance, which will remain dangerous for an estimated 10,000 years. The government dropped the plan only after opposition from surrounding towns and cities, whose residents objected to the movement of the material through their communities. This was not the first time the government had attempted to persuade the impoverished tribe to accept environmentally objectionable installations. The military's nerve-gas storage facility resides on or near the reservation, along with the Intermountain Power Project, which generates coal-fired electrical power for consumers in California (Eureka County 2006; Foy 2006).

In considering environmental issues, sociologists have emphasized the interconnectedness of humans and the environment, as well as the divisiveness of race and social class. Scientific findings can also play a role in our understanding of the nature and scope of environmental concerns. Of course, when such findings affect government policy and economic regulations, they become highly politicized. Such struggles are inevitable when core values and differential access to resources are at stake.

>>Environmental Problems

Unfortunately, as we have already seen, the environmental problems caused by development have effects far beyond the places where they are created. Witness Muhammad Ali, a Bangladeshi man who has had to flee floodwaters five times in the last decade. Scientists believe that global warming is to blame

both for worsening monsoons and for the raging waters of the Iamuna River, swollen by abnormally high glacier melt from the

Movies on THE ENVIRONMENT

Avatar
Strife erupts between humans and Na'vi over Pandora's natural resources.

An Inconvenient Truth
The truth about global warming.

Food, Inc.
The effects of the food manufacturing industry on the environment.

No Impact Man
A man attempts to have zero impact on the environment for a year.

WALL-E
A robot in the year 2700 discovers his destiny.

5

Himalayas. Every time the river floods, Ali tears down his house, made of tin and bamboo, and moves to higher ground. But he is running out of land to move to. "Where we are standing, in five days it will be gone," he says. "Our future thinking is that if this problem is not taken care of, we will be swept away" (Goering 2007).

In 2011, 41 years after the first Earth Day celebration in the United States, public polls reflected historically low levels of public concern about the environment. The percentage of people who considered themselves to be either active participants in, or sympathetic to the environmental movement declined to 62 percent from 71 percent in 2000. In 2010 the percentage of people who believed the environmental movement had done more harm than good rose to 36 from 21 percent in 2000. And, for the first time since they started polling on this question in 2000, more people placed a higher priority on economic development (even if it harms the environment) than did those who said environmental protection should be given priority. That percentage rose even higher in 2011, which may be driven in part by concerns about the weak economy (Gallup 2011).

AIR POLLUTION

Worldwide, more than 1 billion people are exposed to potentially health-damaging levels of air pollution. Unfortunately, in cities around the world, residents have come to accept polluted air as normal. Urban air pollution is caused primarily by emissions from automobiles and secondarily by emissions from electric power plants and heavy industries. Air pollution not only limits visibility, but also can lead to health problems as uncomfortable as eye irritation and as deadly as lung cancer. Such problems are especially severe in developing countries. The WHO estimates that up to 2 million premature deaths per year could be prevented if pollutants were brought down to safer levels (World Health Organization 2008b).

People are capable of changing their behavior, but they are also often unwilling to make such changes permanent. During the 1984 Olympics in Los Angeles, authorities asked residents to carpool and stagger their work hours to relieve traffic congestion and improve the quality of the air athletes would breathe. These changes resulted in a remarkable 12 percent drop in ozone levels. After the Olympics ended, however, people reverted to their normal behavior, and the ozone levels climbed once again. Similarly, China took drastic action to ensure that Beijing's high levels of air pollution did not mar the 2008 Olympic Games. Construction work in the city ceased, polluting factories and power plants closed down, and workers swept roads and sprayed them with water several times a day. This temporary solution, however, has not solved China's ongoing pollution problem (*The Economist* 2008b).

WATER POLLUTION

Throughout the United States, waste materials dumped by industries and local governments have polluted streams, rivers, and lakes. Consequently, many bodies of water have become unsafe for fishing and swimming, let alone

Reprinted with the permission of Mike Luckovich and Creators Syndicate.

Projected Emissions of Greenhouse Gases, 2025

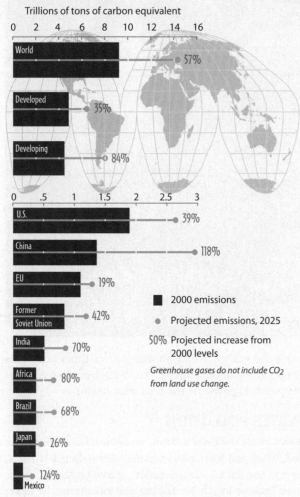

Trillions of tons of carbon equivalent

World — 57%
Developed — 35%
Developing — 84%

U.S. — 39%
China — 118%
EU — 19%
Former Soviet Union — 42%
India — 70%
Africa — 80%
Brazil — 68%
Japan — 26%
Mexico — 124%

■ 2000 emissions

● Projected emissions, 2025

50% Projected increase from 2000 levels

Greenhouse gases do not include CO₂ from land use change.

In 2000 the United States was the largest emitter of CO_2 from fossil fuels. China is expected to take the lead by 2025.

Sources: Baumert, Herzog, and Pershing 2005.

drinking. Around the world, pollution of the oceans is an issue of growing concern. The Deepwater Horizon spill in the Gulf of Mexico represents the ripple effects that such accidents can have on the environment, including the impact on birds, fish, mammals, and their habitats. The impact of the spill on various species has been substantial. For example, in the two years following its

occurrence, 675 dolphins were stranded in the northern Gulf of Mexico compared to an annual rate of 74, deepwater corals experienced significant stress, the nitrogen cycle for microorganisms was inhibited, and 102 species of birds were harmed (National Geographic 2012).

This incident is one among many water-based accidents that have resulted in significant environmental harm. When the oil tanker *Exxon Valdez* ran aground in Prince William Sound, Alaska, in 1989, its cargo of 11 million gallons of crude oil spilled into the sound and washed onto the shore, contaminating 1,285 miles of shoreline. Altogether, about 11,000 people joined in a massive cleanup effort that cost more than $2 billion. Globally, oil spills occur regularly. In 2002 the oil tanker *Prestige* spilled twice as much fuel as the *Valdez*, greatly damaging coastal areas in Spain and France (ITOPF 2006).

Less dramatic than large-scale accidents or disasters, but more common in many parts of the world, are problems with the basic water supply. Worldwide, more than 884 million people lack safe and adequate drinking water, and 2.6 billion lack access to improved sanitation facilities—a problem that further threatens the quality of water supplies. The health costs of unsafe water are enormous (World Health Organization and UNICEF 2010).

Given such water shortages, it should not come as a surprise that water is now a highly contested commodity in many parts of the world. In the United States, competition over water is intense, especially in booming Las Vegas and the Southwest. In the Middle East, the immense political challenges posed by ethnic and religious conflict are often complicated by battles over water. There, competing nations accuse each other of taking unfair advantage of existing water supplies, and water tanks are a likely target for both military forces and terrorists (Carmichael 2007).

GLOBAL CLIMATE CHANGE

The scientific evidence for global climate change is clear, consistent, and compelling, yet public opinion polls show that people remain skeptical. Global warming, the term most frequently associated with climate change, refers to the

Threatened and Endangered Species, 2011

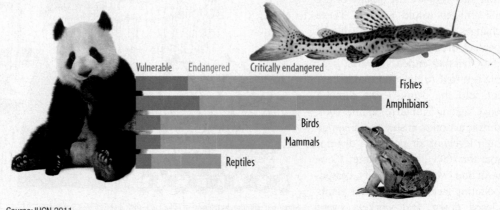

Vulnerable Endangered Critically endangered

Fishes
Amphibians
Birds
Mammals
Reptiles

Source: IUCN 2011.

significant rise in the earth's surface temperatures that occurs when industrial gases such as carbon dioxide turn the planet's atmosphere into a virtual greenhouse. Even one additional degree of warmth in the planet's average temperature increases the likelihood of wildfires, shrinking rivers and lakes, desert expansion, and torrential downpours, including typhoons and hurricanes. Despite the potential catastrophic risks, 48 percent of Americans believe that the seriousness of global warming is generally exaggerated (Newport 2010).

Scientists now track carbon dioxide emissions around the world and can map the current and projected contribution each country makes (see the graph on p. 374). Such analyses show the sizable and growing contribution made by the United States (Lymas 2008). For some politicians, however, the problem seems too abstract and distant. Others recognize that effective solutions demand a difficult-to-manage multinational response, and they fear that their nation may bear too much of the cost. The Kyoto Protocol, established in 1997 and enacted in 2005, was intended to provide a unified response in which the nations of the world would take collective responsibility to reduce global emissions of greenhouse gases. As of 2010, 187 countries have signed the accord, but the United States, which produces 19 percent of the world's carbon dioxide, has failed to ratify it. Opponents of the Kyoto Protocol argue that doing so would place the nation at a disadvantage in the global marketplace (Energy Information Administration 2008; United Nations Framework Convention on Climate Change 2010a).

We can again draw on world systems analysis when it comes to seeing who pays the highest price for global climate changes. Historically, core nations have been the major emitters of greenhouse gases. Today, much manufacturing has moved to semiperiphery and periphery nations, where greenhouse gas emissions are escalating. Ironically, many of those who are now calling for a reduction in the human activity that contributes to global climate change are located in core nations, which have contributed disproportionately to the problem. We want our hamburgers, but we decry the destruction of the rain forests to create grazing land for cattle. We want inexpensive clothes and toys, but we condemn developing countries for depending on coal-fired power plants, the number of which are expected to increase 46 percent by

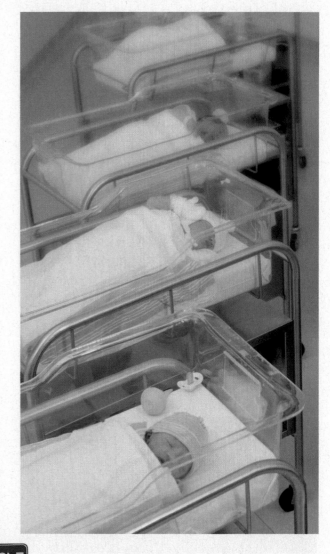

2030. The challenge of global climate change, then, is closely tied to global inequality (M. Jenkins 2008; Leonard 2010; Roberts, Grines, and Manale 2003).

In addition to the environmental costs of supporting global population increase, technological advances also contribute to environmental concerns. At least since the Industrial Revolution and the invention of the steam engine, the automobile, coal-burning power plants, and more, the environmental effects of technological innovation have been extreme. Biologist and environmentalist Barry Commoner argued that additional contributors to the problem include plastics, detergents,

Perceptions of Global Climate Change

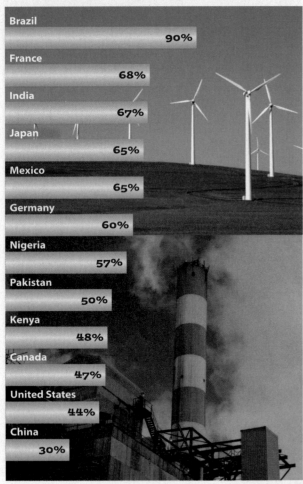

Brazil: 90%
France: 68%
India: 67%
Japan: 65%
Mexico: 65%
Germany: 60%
Nigeria: 57%
Pakistan: 50%
Kenya: 48%
Canada: 47%
United States: 44%
China: 30%

Note: Percentage of people citing climate change as a very serious problem.

Source: Pew Research Center 2009e.

synthetic fibers, pesticides, herbicides, and chemical fertilizers. We appreciate the lifestyles that such innovations allow us to experience, but we pay a significant price for their benefits (Commoner 1971, 1990; Ehrlich 1968).

THE GLOBAL RESPONSE

Globalization can be both good and bad for the environment. On the negative side, it can create a race to the bottom as polluting companies relocate to countries with less stringent environmental standards. Also of concern is that globalization allows multinationals to exploit the resources of developing countries for short-term profit. From Mexico to China, the industrialization that often accompanies globalization has increased pollution of all types.

Yet globalization can have a positive impact as well. As barriers to the international movement of goods, services, and people fall, multinational corporations have an incentive to carefully consider the cost of natural resources. As the establishment of the Kyoto Protocol demonstrated, countries around the world can come together on a global level to take action that makes a significant difference. For example, as of 2010, the industrialized nations that agreed to the Kyoto Protocol were on track to meet their emission reduction targets. In December 2009, nations around the world came together in Copenhagen to begin work on a new set of global environmental targets, a process that continued in Bonn, Germany, in June 2010. The goal was to work toward establishing a new global climate change treaty (United Nations Framework Convention on Climate Change 2010b).

Overusing or wasting resources makes little sense, especially when they are in danger of depletion (Kwong 2005). Perhaps, as Émile Durkheim might have argued long ago, by recognizing our mutual interdependence, we will take the steps necessary to bring about positive social change. There are signs that individuals, countries, and corporations are beginning to do just that. For example, individuals are taking greater responsibility for their global impact by recycling and switching to fluorescent light bulbs (Morales 2010). Increasing numbers of corporations are "going green" and even finding profits in doing so. Sociology helps us to better see the ways we are interconnected by highlighting the significance of the system as a whole, as well as raising awareness about the inequalities that are a consequence of the global system we have constructed. Such analysis can prepare us to more effectively respond to the global challenges we face.

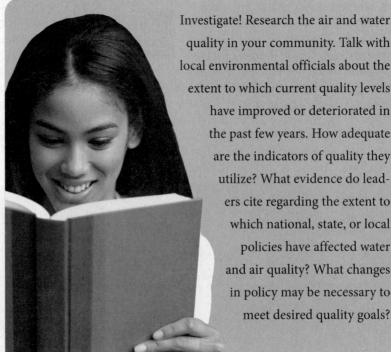

get involved!

Investigate! Research the air and water quality in your community. Talk with local environmental officials about the extent to which current quality levels have improved or deteriorated in the past few years. How adequate are the indicators of quality they utilize? What evidence do leaders cite regarding the extent to which national, state, or local policies have affected water and air quality? What changes in policy may be necessary to meet desired quality goals?

For REVIEW

I. **What role do population dynamics play in shaping our lives?**

- Population dynamics provide a context within which we are born, live, move, and even die, and population trends vary significantly across time and between nations, shaping our life chances.

II. **What does sociology contribute to something as seemingly biological as health?**

- Our understanding of what counts as health and illness is shaped by the society to which we belong. Similarly, our social position and control over resources shape our likelihood of exposure to illness and our access to health care.

III. **What environmental lessons do we learn from sociology?**

- The natural environment represents our human home, within which all social interaction occurs, and the way we organize our social relations influences the effects we have on the environment. Countries that control a larger amount of resources have a bigger impact and therefore bear a greater responsibility for those effects.

Functionalist View

Over time, population levels naturally reach a balance that maximizes social order.

Health care is a social institution that provides for our health and welfare and thus preserves **social order.**

As we become more socially, economically, and environmentally **interdependent**, new, more global conscious, norms and values arise.

SOCIAL ORDER, INTERCONNECTEDNESS
KEY CONCEPTS

Conflict View

Popula-tion crises are driven more by battles over resources than by natural processes.

Core nations **exploit** the natural resources of developing nations on the periphery without taking responsibility for the consequences.

Poor people and minorities suffer disproportionately from **inequities** in health care and exposure to environmental hazards, such as toxic waste and air and water pollution.

CONTROL, INEQUALITY, EXPLOITATION
KEY CONCEPTS

MAKE THE CONNECTION

After reviewing the chapter, answer the following questions:

Interactionist View

Changes in population trends show the importance of the choices we make in shaping society.

Patients can play an **active role** in their health both by seeking out a physician's services and by choosing whether or not to follow a doctor's orders.

The degree to which we think significant environmental problems exist is a consequence of **socialization** by family, friends, teachers, television, and so on.

ACTIVITY, INTERACTION
KEY CONCEPTS

1

How would each perspective approach the study of the Deep Horizon oil spill in the Gulf of Mexico (p. 349)?

2

How would each of the perspectives approach the demographic transition model, and how would their insights differ?

3

What insights would we gain from each perspective regarding the current state of health care in the United States, including recent health care reform efforts (p. 366)?

4

Look at your experience with the medical world from an interactionist perspective. What were your interactions with the doctors and nurses like? Have you taken an active role or a passive role as a patient?

Pop Quiz

1. **How is the total fertility rate defined?**
   a. number of children born over a given period of time
   b. number of live births per 1,000 people in the population in a given year
   c. average number of children a woman would have during her lifetime given current birth rates and assuming she survives through her child-bearing years
   d. minimum number of children a woman would need to average in her lifetime to reproduce the population in the next generation

2. **What term is used when people leave a population group to which they had belonged?**
   a. immigration
   b. replacement
   c. emigration
   d. transition

3. **What was the relationship between birth rates and death rates throughout most of human history as described by the demographic transition model?**
   a. Both were low.
   b. Death rates were low; birth rates were high.
   c. Birth rates were low; death rates were high.
   d. Both were high.

4. **A disease that cannot be understood apart from its specific social context is an example of**
   a. human ecology.
   b. culture-bound syndrome.
   c. the sick role.
   d. holistic medicine.

5. **Which one of these nations has the lowest infant mortality rate?**
   a. United States
   b. Sierra Leone
   c. Canada
   d. Japan

6. **In the area of social epidemiology, what does prevalence refer to?**
   a. the rate at which key indicators change over time
   b. the total number of cases of a specific disorder that exist at a given period of time
   c. the likelihood that a disease or illness will be labeled as such in a given cultural context
   d. the number of new cases of a specific disorder that occur within a given population during a stated period

7. **The age group that is most likely to be covered by some form of health insurance is**
   a. under 18.
   b. 18–34.
   c. 35–64.
   d. 65 and older.

8. **Compared to other nations around the world, how much does the United States spend on health care (as measured by GDP)?**
   a. near the bottom
   b. about in the middle or median
   c. at about the 75th percentile
   d. more than virtually all other nations

9. **The industrialized nations of North America and Europe account for 12 percent of the world's population. What percentage of worldwide consumption are they responsible for?**
   a. 15 percent
   b. 30 percent
   c. 45 percent
   d. 60 percent

10. **What is the international treaty that sought to reduce global emissions of greenhouse gases?**
    a. Valdez Treaty
    b. Kyoto Protocol
    c. Port Huron Statement
    d. Gore Accord

1. (c); 2. (c); 3. (d); 4. (b); 5. (d); 6. (b); 7. (d); 8. (d); 9. (d); 10. (b)

15

CHANGING THE WORLD ONE CAMPUS AT A TIME

In the summer of 1964, college students traveled to Mississippi to change the world. As volunteers in Freedom Summer, their goal was to make a difference in the lives of African Americans who had been systematically denied the right to vote, quality education, and legal and political representation. The volunteers—mostly upper-middle-class White students from northern colleges—registered Black voters, established Freedom Schools, and provided legal advice and medical assistance. By the end of the summer, they had registered 17,000 voters and taught 3,000 children. In 1964, 6.7 percent of voting-age African Americans in Mississippi were registered, but by 1967, 66.5 percent were registered (Colby 1986; McAdam 1988).

From April 18 to May 8, 2001, students at Harvard University occupied Massachusetts Hall, the location of the president's and provost's offices, as part of their Living Wage Campaign. The city of Cambridge, where Harvard is located, had passed a living-wage ordinance ensuring a minimum wage of $10 per hour, adjustable for inflation. Students argued that a school with a multibillion-dollar endowment could do better than the $6.50 many employees were receiving. After numerous attempts at negotiation, students decided to make a statement. During the sit-in, students organized daily pickets and rallies involving thousands of people. After three weeks, the administration agreed to establish a committee to implement living wage principles (Progressive Student Labor Movement 2008).

In 2007 students at Middlebury College in Vermont convinced their trustees to build a $12-million biomass power plant in keeping with their campus commitment to carbon neutrality. The plant began operation in February 2009. While a student at Cornell University in New York, Catherine McEachern was involved in a similar student movement. She says, "Global warming has been neglected by the previous generation, and we see it as an injustice that needs to be changed" (quoted in James 2008).

College students continue to fight for and bring about significant change on campuses around the world. Max Weber argued that all of us have the potential power to change our world. In fact, change will happen whether we like it or not. A key question is this: will we be active agents seeking the change we desire or passive recipients who accept the change enacted by others?

As You READ >>

- How and why does social change happen?
- What factors shape the success of a social movement?
- What does it mean to practice sociology?

>>Global Social Change

We are at a truly dramatic era in history in terms of global social change. Within the past few decades, we have witnessed the computer revolution and the explosion of Internet connectivity; the collapse of communism; major regime changes and severe economic disruptions in Africa, the Middle East, and Eastern Europe; the spread of AIDS; the first verification of the cloning of a complex animal, Dolly the sheep; and the first major terrorist attack on U.S. soil. Today we continue to face global challenges including international terrorism, a global economic meltdown, and climate change, along with other threats.

One of the most significant transformations so far in the 21st century is the emergence of the Arab Spring. This term refers to the substantial political upheaval that occurred in a number of northern African and Arabian Peninsula nations from 2010 through 2012. To supporters, these changes represented the beginning of new life, although it was a death that helped trigger them.

The protests started in Tunisia on December 18, 2010 after Mohamed Bouazizi, a 26-year-old street vendor whose vegetable cart had been confiscated by local police and who had grown tired of years of humiliation and corruption, set himself on fire as a form of both protest and resignation. He died 18 days later. Bouazizi's act became a symbol of the frustration felt by many others in the region.

Facilitated by text messaging and social networking sites, word spread quickly, helping to spawn huge protests in Tunisia, which sparked rallies in numerous countries including Egypt (where Tahrir Square became a rallying place), Libya, Yeman, Syria, Bahrain, and others. Many of those who participated were young, well-educated, and technologically savvy. They sought economic and political reforms, greater opportunities for self-determination, and hope for a better life. As a result of the protests, in addition to many other consequences, Tunisian President Zine El Abidine Ben Ali was ousted after 23 years in power. Egyptian President Hosni Mubarak, who had been in power for nearly 30 years, resigned. Libyan leader Colonel Muammar el-Qaddafi, who ruled for 42 years, was overthrown and killed, and Yemeni President Ali Abdullah Saleh stepped down after 33 years in power (Gelvin 2012; Noueihed and Warren 2012; Raghavan 2011; Shenker et al. 2011).

Part of what makes the Arab Spring movement significant is that it represented the overthrow of entrenched and repressive political regimes and the promise of greater empowerment and opportunity in the hands of the people. Those in positions of power are frequently able to use their control over valued resources to reinforce the status quo, yet these protests demonstrate the power of agency and engaged social action. Time will tell to what extent the new regimes in the various countries are able to live up to their

Did You Know?

"... When the first call for protesters for Occupy Wall Street went out, organizers made an explicit reference to Arab Spring protests in Egypt. They wrote, 'Are you ready for a Tahrir moment? On Sept 17, protesters flood into lower Manhattan, set up tents, kitchens, peaceful barricades and occupy Wall Street.'"

ideals, given their economic, social, and cultural challenges (Amnesty International 2011; Fisher 2012).

Sociology helps us to understand such shifts by paying attention both to large-scale, or macro, shifts that alter the basic landscape of society and the relationships among groups, and to the small-scale, or micro, changes in social interaction within which decisions are made that can alter the course of history. We construct society through our everyday actions. As such, we have the power to change society by altering the choices we make. Of course, some people, because of their control over valued resources, have more power than do others. Sociology can better focus our attention so that we might understand which direction change might follow.

>>Sociological Perspectives on Social Change

As humans, we are creative beings. We continually innovate and experiment, developing new technologies, ideas, and ways of doing things. Each innovation represents an example of **social change,** which involves significant alteration over time in behavior patterns and culture. Social change can occur so slowly as to be almost undetectable to those it affects, but it can

> **social change** Significant alteration over time in behavior patterns and culture, including norms and values.

The United States: A Changing Nation

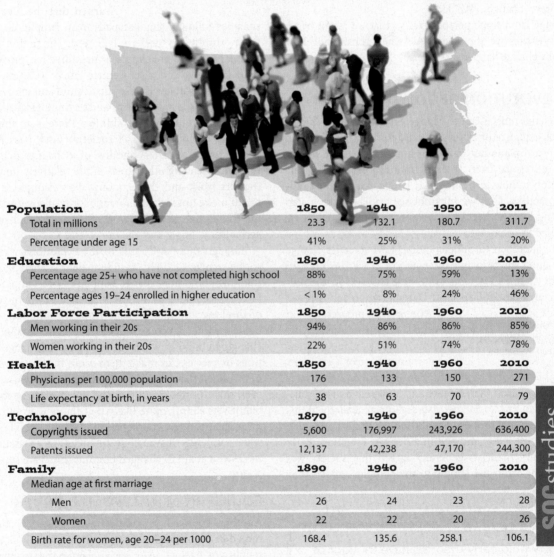

Population	1850	1940	1950	2011
Total in millions	23.3	132.1	180.7	311.7
Percentage under age 15	41%	25%	31%	20%

Education	1850	1940	1960	2010
Percentage age 25+ who have not completed high school	88%	75%	59%	13%
Percentage ages 19–24 enrolled in higher education	< 1%	8%	24%	46%

Labor Force Participation	1850	1940	1960	2010
Men working in their 20s	94%	86%	86%	85%
Women working in their 20s	22%	51%	74%	78%

Health	1850	1940	1960	2010
Physicians per 100,000 population	176	133	150	271
Life expectancy at birth, in years	38	63	70	79

Technology	1870	1940	1960	2010
Copyrights issued	5,600	176,997	243,926	636,400
Patents issued	12,137	42,238	47,170	244,300

Family	1890	1940	1960	2010
Median age at first marriage				
Men	26	24	23	28
Women	22	22	20	26
Birth rate for women, age 20–24 per 1000	168.4	135.6	258.1	106.1

SOCstudies

Note: Data are comparable, although definitions vary somewhat across time. Education rate for 1850 is for those over age 70. Earliest birthrate is from 1905.

Source: Bureau of Labour Statistics 2011e; Carter et al. 2006: vol.1: 28–29, 401–402, 440, 541, 685, 697, 709, vol. 2: 441–442, vol. 3: 422–425, 427–428; National Center for Health Statistics 2011:Table 106; Snyder and Dillow 2011:Table 8.11; U.S. Census Bureau 2010f: Tables 80:2011a:Table MS-2; 2011h:Tables 778, 780 World Bank 2011l.

also happen with breathtaking rapidity. In the past century or so, for example, the U.S. population has more than doubled, the percentage of people finishing high school and attending college has skyrocketed, women have entered the paid labor force in significant numbers, life expectancy has risen, technological innovation has exploded, men and women have been marrying later, and family size has shrunk. In our global, interdependent world, there is no reason to suspect that such changes will cease, and many future changes will be difficult to predict.

Explaining social change is clearly a challenge in the diverse and complex world we inhabit. Nevertheless, sociologists have sought to analyze, interpret, and explain social change. In some instances, they have examined historical events to arrive at a better understanding of contemporary changes. We look at change from three perspectives so that we might better identify issues we should include when considering how and why change happens.

> ## All change is not growth, as all movement is not forward.
>
> Ellen Glasgow

THE EVOLUTION OF SOCIETIES

All societies must adapt to change. Sometimes that change is a consequence of external forces, for example, from an act of war by another nation or a natural disaster. Sometimes it results from internal innovation, such as the invention of new technologies. Change can also be gradual, something that we may not see until we take a step back and look. Other times it can come quickly, when we are called to respond to a crisis.

One approach to understanding how societies change draws upon the principle of evolution. It was inspired, in part, by Charles Darwin's (1809–1882) work on the biological evolution of species. Darwin's approach stresses a continuing progression of successive generations of life forms as they adapt to their environment. For example, human beings came at a later stage of evolution than reptiles and represent a more complex form of life. Social theorists seeking an analogy to this biological model proposed **evolutionary theory,** in which society is viewed as moving in a definite direction. Early evolutionary theorists generally agreed that society was progressing from the simple to the complex, which they assumed was superior.

evolutionary theory A theory of social change that holds that society is moving in a definite direction.

SOCTHINK

Why would early theorists have thought of traditional societies as "primitive"? How is this a reflection of the evolutionary theoretical paradigm they adopted?

Early sociologists and anthropologists believed it was possible to study what they referred to at that time as simple or "primitive" societies for clues about the essential building blocks that serve as the foundation for all societies. Auguste Comte (1798–1857), a founder of sociology, was an evolutionary theorist of change. He saw human societies as moving forward in their thinking, from mythology to the scientific method. Similarly, Émile Durkheim ([1893]1933) maintained that society progressed from simple to complex forms of social organization. Both Comte and Durkheim believed that by gaining a rational understanding of the principles of order and change in such societies, we would be able to more effectively shape the direction our modern, more complex societies would take.

Since that time, we have learned that the idea that all societies follow a singular path from simple to complex, from primitive to modern, is flawed. The notion that traditional societies are simple or primitive has proven to be both incorrect and ethnocentric. Such societies demonstrate significant levels of sophistication and innovation, in terms of both social relations and technological adaptation to their environments. In addition, there is no single path of social evolution that all societies must pass through. Social change can affect one area of social life, such as politics, while leaving other areas of life relatively unchanged, such as work and the economy. For example, a society might move toward a democratic form of government, but the traditional nature of work, primarily small-scale and agricultural, might stay the same.

Though there are limits to the evolutionary model of social change, it does provide a helpful metaphor when thinking about how change happens. For example, we can look to past practices to better understand where new ways of thinking and acting come from. In addition, it highlights the role that context or environment plays in shaping change. In biology, when the environment changes, mutations in species can make them more fit to survive in that new context than were past generations. For Darwin, however, this did not mean that the new was superior to the old; it was simply more likely that the new would survive given changed environmental circumstances. The danger when applying this analogy to society is to assume that those who adapt to changed circumstances are superior.

EQUILIBRIUM AND SOCIAL ORDER

Another approach to understanding social change is rooted in the principle that societies naturally seek to attain stability or balance. Any social change that occurs represents necessary adjustments as society seeks to return to that state of equilibrium. For example, sociologist Talcott Parsons (1902–1979), an advocate of this approach, viewed even prolonged labor strikes or civilian riots as temporary disruptions in the status quo rather than as significant alterations in the social structure. According to his **equilibrium model,** as changes occur in one part of society, adjustments must be made in other parts. If not, society's equilibrium will be threatened and strains will occur.

Parsons (1966) maintained that four processes of social change are inevitable. The first, differentiation, refers to the increasing complexity of social organization. We see this in the form of job specialization as is evident in bureaucratic systems. The transition from a healer—a single person who handles all of your health care needs—to a series of positions, including physician, anesthetist, nurse, and pharmacist, is an illustration of differentiation in the field of medicine. This process is accompanied by adaptive upgrading, in which social institutions become more specialized in their purposes. The division of physicians into obstetricians, internists, surgeons, and so forth is an example of adaptive upgrading.

The third process Parsons identified is the inclusion of groups that were previously excluded because of their gender, race, ethnicity, and social class. In the past two decades or so, medical schools have practiced inclusion by admitting increasing numbers of women and African Americans. Finally, Parsons contended that societies experience value generalization—the development of new values that legitimate a broader range of activities. The acceptance of preventive and alternative medicine is an example of value generalization: society has broadened its view of health care. All four processes identified by Parsons stress consensus—societal agreement on the nature of social organization and values (Gerhardt 2002).

One of the sources of potential strain that can lead to such social adaptation involves technological innovation.

SOCTHINK

Why might the equilibrium model have a difficult time addressing such issues as inequality and poverty as social problems to be solved?

As we saw in Chapter 3, sociologist William F. Ogburn (1922) distinguished between material and nonmaterial aspects of culture. Material culture includes inventions, artifacts, and technology; nonmaterial culture encompasses ideas, norms, communications, and social organization. Ogburn pointed out that technology often changes faster than do the ideas and values with which we make sense of such change. Thus, the nonmaterial culture, including values and norms, typically must respond to changes in the material culture. Ogburn introduced the term *cultural lag* to refer to the period of adjustment when the nonmaterial culture is still struggling to adapt to new material conditions. One example is the Internet, which spread quickly but now raises serious questions about personal privacy.

In certain cases, the changes in the material culture can strain the relationships between social institutions. For example, the invention of the birth control pill in 1960, along with other modern forms of birth control, led to significant social changes. It helped to reduce family size at a time when large families were no longer necessary—and were even a constraint to mobility—given the shift from agricultural to industrial and service economies. It provided greater opportunity for women to pursue careers and maintain control over their fertility. In so doing, it challenged our conceptions about ideal family size and the role of women in society and the economy. The birth control pill also affected religious faith (among Roman Catholics, for example), because it challenged beliefs about the role of God and the value of human life in reproduction (Tentler 2004).

From Parsons's point of view, such tensions represent little more than normal adjustments needed to maintain the inevitable balance that is the natural state of all societies. Though his approach explicitly incorporates the evolutionary notion of continuing progress, the dominant theme in this model is stability. Society may change, but it remains stable through new forms of integration. For example, in place of the kinship ties that provided social cohesion in the past, people develop laws, judicial processes, and new values and belief systems. Parsons and other theorists would argue that those parts of society that persist, even including crime, terrorism, and poverty, do so because they contribute to

> **equilibrium model** The view that society tends toward a state of stability or balance.

social stability. Critics note, however, that his approach virtually disregards the use of coercion by the powerful to maintain the illusion of a stable, well-integrated society (Gouldner 1960).

RESOURCES, POWER, AND CHANGE

Such theories are helpful, but it is not enough to look at change as part of the natural evolution or equilibrium of societies. Some groups in society, because they control valued resources, are able either to inhibit or to facilitate social change more effectively than are others. Although Karl Marx, for example, accepted the evolutionary argument that societies develop along a particular path, he did not view each successive stage as an inevitable improvement over the previous one. History, according to Marx, proceeds through a series of stages, and within each stage, those who control the means of production exploit an entire class of people. Thus, ancient society exploited slaves, the estate system of feudalism exploited serfs, and modern capitalist society exploits the working class. Ultimately, through a socialist revolution led by the proletariat, human society would move toward the final stage of development: a classless communist society, or "community of free individuals," as Marx described it in 1867 in *Das Kapital* (Marx [1867] 2000:478).

> **vested interests** Those people or groups who will suffer in the event of social change and who have a stake in maintaining the status quo.

Marx argued that conflict is a normal and desirable aspect of social change. In fact, change must be encouraged if social inequality is to be eliminated. In his view, people are not restricted to a passive role in responding to inevitable cycles or changes in the material culture. Rather, Marxist theory offers a tool for those who wish to seize control of the historical process and gain their freedom from injustice. Efforts to promote social change are, however, likely to meet with resistance.

Certain individuals and groups have a stake in maintaining the existing state of affairs. Social economist Thorstein Veblen (1857–1929) coined the term **vested interests** to refer to those people or groups who will suffer in the event of social change. For example, historically the American Medical Association (AMA) has taken strong stands against national health insurance and the professionalization of midwifery. National health insurance was seen as a threat to physicians' income and authority, and a rise in the status of midwives could threaten the preeminent position of doctors as deliverers of babies. In general, those with a disproportionate share of society's wealth, status, and power, such as members of the AMA, have a vested interest in preserving the status quo (Furedi 2006; Scelfo 2008; Veblen 1919).

Economic factors play an important role in resistance to social change. For example, it can be expensive for manufacturers to meet mandated standards for the safety of products and workers and for the protection of the environment. In the pursuit of both profit and survival, many firms seek to avoid the costs of meeting strict safety and environmental standards. If they have sufficient power in society, they can effectively pass the costs of such practices on to others who must bear the consequences. To battle against such influence requires countervailing sources of power. Government regulations, for example, force all companies to bear the common burden of such costs, and labor unions can present the unified power of workers as a group.

Communities, too, protect their vested interests, often in the name of "protecting property values." The abbreviation NIMBY stands for "not in my backyard," a cry often heard when people protest landfills, prisons, nuclear power facilities, and even bike trails and group homes for people with developmental disabilities. The targeted community may not challenge the need for the facility, but may simply insist that it be located elsewhere. The NIMBY attitude has become so common that it is almost impossible for policy makers to find acceptable locations for facilities such as

hazardous waste dumps. Unfortunately, it is often those with the fewest resources who end up on the losing end of such battles (Lambert 2009; Schelly and Stretesky 2009).

In today's world, change is inevitable. From sociology we learn that we need to watch for the ways in which change evolves out of existing practices. We also must be aware of the ways in which societies perpetuate existing social order by seeking an acceptable level of balance between stability and change. Finally, we recognize the role that power and control over resources plays in shaping what changes do or do not occur. In all these cases, because of the ways it both enables and constrains, we must be aware of the role that technology plays in affecting the nature and direction of social change.

>>Technology and the Future

As discussed in Chapter 3, technology is a form of culture in which humans modify the natural environment to meet our wants and needs. Technological advances—the telephone, the automobile, the airplane, the television, the atomic bomb, and more recently, the computer, digital media, and the cellular phone—have brought striking changes to our culture, our patterns of socialization, our social institutions, and our day-to-day social interactions. Technological innovations are, in fact, emerging and being accepted with remarkable speed.

In the past generation alone, industrial countries have seen a major shift in consumer technologies. We no longer buy electronic devices to last for 10 years. Increasingly, we buy them with the expectation that within three years or less, we will need to upgrade to an entirely new technology, whether it be a handheld device or a home computer. These technologies have both positive and negative consequences. They enable us to communicate with almost anyone, almost anywhere, at almost any time. Yet they also facilitate outsourcing and globalization, resulting in the loss of local jobs and the decline of communities.

Adopting Technology

Omnivores: 8% of American adults constitute the most active participants in the information society, consuming information goods and services at a high rate and using them as a platform for participation and self-expression.

The Connectors: 7% of the adult population surround themselves with technology and use it to connect with people and digital content. They get a lot out of their mobile devices and participate actively in online life.

Lackluster Veterans: 8% of American adults make up a group who are not at all passionate about their abundance of modern information and communication technologies (ICTs). Few like the intrusiveness their gadgets add to their lives and not many see ICTs adding to their personal productivity.

Productivity Enhancers: 9% of American adults happily get a lot of things done with information technology, both at home and at work.

Mobile Centrics: 10% of the general population are strongly attached to their cell phones and take advantage of a range of mobile applications.

Connected but Hassled: 9% of American adults fit into this group. They have invested in a lot of technology, but the connectivity is a hassle for them.

Inexperienced Experimenters: 8% of adults have less ICT on hand than others. They feel competent in dealing with technology, and might do more with it if they had more.

Light but Satisfied: 15% of adults have the basics of information technology, use it infrequently, and do not consider it to be an important part of their lives.

Indifferents: 11% of adults have a fair amount of technology on hand, but it does not play a central role in their daily lives.

Off the Net: 15% of the population, mainly older Americans, are off the modern information network.

Note: From a Pew Internet and American Life Project Survey conducted in April 2006.
Source: Horrigan 2007:vii.

COMPUTER TECHNOLOGY

In the past decade, computer access has gone global, and Internet access along with it. While the revolutions in transportation and communication have brought us together since the Industrial Revolution, the Internet provides a potential for immediate global connection that previously was virtually and physically impossible. In 2012, the Internet reached 2.3 billion users, or 32.7 percent of the world's population (Internet World Stats 2012a).

The Internet evolved from a computer system built in 1962 by the U.S. Defense Department to enable scholars and military researchers to continue their government work, even if part of the nation's communications system were destroyed by nuclear attack. For years, it was difficult to gain access to the Internet without holding a position at a university or a government research laboratory. Today, however, virtually anyone with sufficient resources can reach the Internet with a wireless-enabled computer or a smartphone. People buy and sell cars, trade stocks, auction off items, research new medical remedies, vote, connect with friends, and coordinate social movements, to mention just a few of the thousands of possibilities (Shirky 2008).

If we look at global Internet use, the regions with the greatest number of users are Asia and Europe. Asia alone represents more than 1 billion users. However, in terms of access, a larger proportion of the population in North America—about 79 percent—can connect to the Internet than in any other continent. Even though Asia has the greatest number of users, only about 26 percent of the population there has Internet access. Another sign of the global nature of this expansion has been the increase in languages used on the Internet. While English continues to lead, the number of Chinese-speaking users increased 1,277 percent between 2000 and 2010, and Arabic speakers increased 2,501 percent, compared to 281 percent for English speakers (Internet World Stats 2012a, 2011b).

Unfortunately, a digital divide persists, and not everyone can get onto the information highway, especially not the less affluent. Moreover, this pattern of inequality is global. In Africa, for example, only 8.7 percent of the population has access to the Internet. The core nations that Immanuel Wallerstein described in his world systems analysis have a virtual monopoly on information technology; the peripheral nations of Asia, Africa, and Latin America depend on the core nations both for technology and for

Internet Use and Penetration by World Region

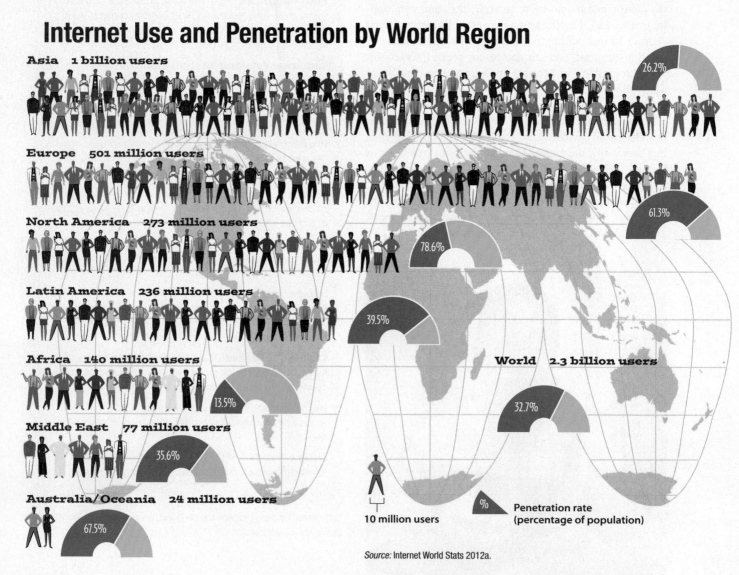

Asia 1 billion users — 26.2%

Europe 501 million users — 61.3%

North America 273 million users — 78.6%

Latin America 236 million users — 39.5%

Africa 140 million users — 13.5%

Middle East 77 million users — 35.6%

Australia/Oceania 24 million users — 67.5%

World 2.3 billion users — 32.7%

10 million users

% Penetration rate (percentage of population)

Source: Internet World Stats 2012a.

the information it provides. For example, North America, Europe, and a few industrialized nations in other regions possess almost all the world's Internet hosts—computers that are connected directly to the worldwide network.

One way to address this divide is to provide computers to people around the world who do not have them. The One Laptop per Child (OLPC) campaign, which originated at the Massachusetts Institute of Technology, is one example of a program seeking to do just that (www.laptop .org). Established in January 2005 by Nicholas Negroponte, MIT media technology professor and co-founder of MIT's Media Lab, its mission is "to create educational opportunities for the world's poorest children by providing each child with a rugged, low-cost, low-power, connected laptop with content and software designed for collaborative, joyful, self-empowered learning" (OLPC 2010). The organization designed and built durable, yet inexpensive laptop computers (called the XO-1) that can connect wirelessly with one another and share an Internet connection to provide access to the wider world. Negroponte's vision is to persuade individuals, foundations, and governments in industrial nations to fund the purchase and distribution of

the laptops, making them available to children for free. As of July 2011, OLPC had distributed 2.1 million computers to children and teachers around the world in places such as Peru, Haiti, Cambodia, Rwanda, Iraq, and Mongolia.

PRIVACY AND CENSORSHIP IN A GLOBAL VILLAGE

In addition to the digital divide, sociologists have also raised concerns about threats to privacy and the possibility of censorship. Recent advances have made it increasingly easy for business firms, government agencies, and even

SOCTHINK

From a purely business point of view, what would be the pros and cons of giving a free XO-1 to every needy child in the developing world? Would the social benefits of doing so outweigh the business costs and benefits?

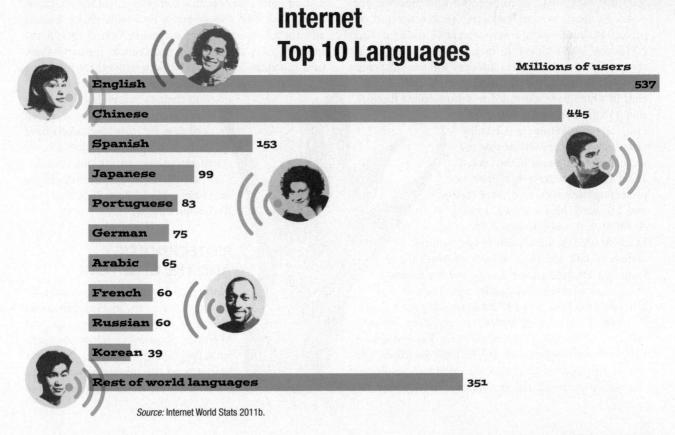

Internet
Top 10 Languages

Millions of users

Language	Users
English	537
Chinese	445
Spanish	153
Japanese	99
Portuguese	83
German	75
Arabic	65
French	60
Russian	60
Korean	39
Rest of world languages	351

Source: Internet World Stats 2011b.

criminals to retrieve and store information about everything from our buying habits to our Web-surfing patterns. In public places, at work, and on the Internet, surveillance devices now track our every move, be it a keystroke or an ATM withdrawal. As technology spreads, so does the exposure to risk. In 2006, for example, the theft of a laptop computer from the home of an employee of the Veterans Administration compromised the names, Social Security numbers, and dates of birth of up to 26.5 million veterans.

At the same time that these innovations have increased others' power to monitor our behavior, they have raised fears that they might be misused for undemocratic purposes. In short, new technologies threaten not just our privacy but our freedom from surveillance and censorship (O'Harrow 2005). There is, for example, the danger that the most powerful groups in a society will use technology to violate the privacy of the less powerful. Indeed, officials in China have attempted to censor online discussion groups and web postings that criticize the government. Civil liberties advocates remind us that the same abuses can occur in the United States if citizens are not vigilant in protecting their right to privacy (Liang and Lu 2010; Moyer 2010). Indeed, in April 2010, it was discovered that officials in a Pennsylvania school district had captured almost 58,000 webcam pictures of students, including images in their homes and bedrooms, using school-issued Macbook laptops. The case was ultimately resolved with a $1.2 million settlement.

In the United States, legislation regulating the surveillance of electronic communications has not always upheld citizens' right to privacy. In 1986 the federal government passed the Electronic Communications Privacy Act, which outlawed the surveillance of telephone calls except with the permission of both the U.S. attorney general and a federal judge. Telegrams, faxes, and email did not receive the same degree of protection, however. In 2001, one month after the terrorist attacks of September 11, Congress passed the USA PATRIOT Act, which relaxed existing legal checks on surveillance by law enforcement officers. Federal agencies are now freer to gather data electronically, including credit card receipts and banking records (Etzioni 2007; Singel 2008; Zetter 2009).

In the early days of Internet expansion, many people were quite concerned about sharing any personal information online for fear that someone might use it against them. Now, with the advent of Facebook, Flickr, Twitter, and a whole host of other social networking sites, many Internet users see no such risk. People regularly share their thoughts, feelings, and actions with others, including total strangers. But Facebook's frequent privacy setting changes and selling of customers' personal information raised red flags for many, and others have learned the hard way that schools and employers can use this information to make decisions about discipline and hiring (Finder 2006; Relerford et al. 2008; Solove 2008).

BIOTECHNOLOGY AND THE GENE POOL

Another field in which technological advances have spurred global social change is biotechnology. Sex selection of fetuses, genetically engineered organisms, the cloning of animals—these have been among the significant yet controversial scientific advances in the field of

Cloning Milestones

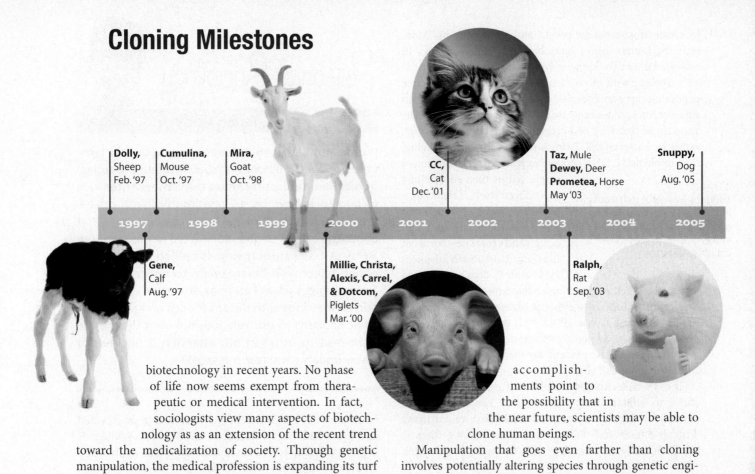

Dolly, Sheep Feb. '97

Cumulina, Mouse Oct. '97

Mira, Goat Oct. '98

CC, Cat Dec. '01

Taz, Mule
Dewey, Deer
Prometea, Horse May '03

Snuppy, Dog Aug. '05

1997 | 1998 | 1999 | 2000 | 2001 | 2002 | 2003 | 2004 | 2005

Gene, Calf Aug. '97

Millie, Christa, Alexis, Carrel, & Dotcom, Piglets Mar. '00

Ralph, Rat Sep. '03

biotechnology in recent years. No phase of life now seems exempt from therapeutic or medical intervention. In fact, sociologists view many aspects of biotechnology as as an extension of the recent trend toward the medicalization of society. Through genetic manipulation, the medical profession is expanding its turf still further (Clarke et al. 2003).

One area of genetic modification that has raised concern involves genetically modified (GM) food. This issue arose in Europe but has since spread to other parts of the world, including the United States. The idea behind the technology is to increase food production and make agriculture more efficient and economical. But critics use the term *frankenfood* (as in Frankenstein) to refer to everything from breakfast cereals made from genetically engineered grains to "fresh" GM tomatoes. Members of the antibiotech movement object to tampering with nature and are concerned about the possible health effects of GM food. Supporters of GM food include not just biotech companies but also those who see the technology as a way to help feed the growing populations of Africa and Asia (Bovis 2007; Schurman 2004).

Even as the genetic modification of plants continues to be a concern, the debate about the genetic manipulation of animals escalated in 1997 when scientists in Scotland announced that they had cloned a sheep, which they named Dolly. After many unsuccessful attempts, they were finally able to replace the genetic material of a sheep's egg with DNA from an adult sheep, creating a lamb that was a cloneof the adult. Shortly thereafter, Japanese researchers successfully cloned cows. Since then many other species have been successfully cloned (see the timeline above), and it is now even possible to get your pet cat or dog cloned, and scientists have begun work on cloning the extinct wooly mammoth with a goal of giving birth to a mammoth baby by 2016 (Grossman 2012). Such accomplishments point to the possibility that in the near future, scientists may be able to clone human beings.

Manipulation that goes even farther than cloning involves potentially altering species through genetic engineering. Fish and plant genes have already been mixed to create frost-resistant potato and tomato crops. More recently, human genes have been implanted in pigs to provide humanlike kidneys for organ transplants. Geneticists working with mouse fetuses have managed to disable genes that carry an undesirable trait and replace them with genes carrying a desirable trait. And in May 2010 scientists announced that they had created the first self-replicating, synthetic bacterial cell. Using a process similar to cloning, they implanted a DNA sequence created by humans into a single cell; it then successfully reproduced itself. This accomplishment was seen as a major step forward in our ability to design and create new forms of life (*Edge* 2010). Such advances raise ethical concerns related to applying such engineering to humans to eliminate disease or infirmities or to enhance physical abilities such as sight or strength (Avise 2004). This concern is shared by most Americans, 84 percent of whom say cloning humans is morally wrong; 62 percent say the same about cloning animals (Gallup 2011b).

Luddites Rebellious craft workers in 19th-century England who destroyed new factory machinery as part of their resistance to the Industrial Revolution.

Today's biotechnology holds itself out as totally beneficial to human beings, but it is in constant need of monitoring. Biotechnological advances have raised many difficult ethical and political questions. Among them is the desirability of tinkering with the gene pool, which

SOCTHINK

If you could modify your children's genes to protect them from genetic diseases, would you do it? How about enhancing their abilities such as eyesight, strength, or intelligence?

Five Questions to Ask When Adopting New Technology

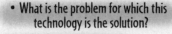

- What is the problem for which this technology is the solution?
- Whose problem is it?
- What new problems might be created because we solve the problem?
- Which people and institutions might be most seriously harmed?
- Which people and institutions might acquire special economic and political power?

Source: Postman 1988.

Personal Sociology

Technology and Society

I confess to having mixed emotions about new technology. I love my iPhone and couldn't resist the appeal of the iPad. Yet I worry about the consequences such technologies have on my relationships with others. We are quick to adopt the latest gadgets, but what about the effects of abandoning old norms? I'm sure all of us have encountered that iPod-wearing cell-phone talker who barely seems to notice we exist. Technologies such as Facebook do enable us to maintain connections with distant friends and family. But what happens to our relationships with the people right next to us when our attention is diverted to status updates and text messages?

could alter our environment and ourselves in unexpected and unwanted ways (McKibben 2003). Even William F. Ogburn could not have anticipated the extent of such scientific developments when he first proposed the problem of culture lag in the 1920s.

RESISTANCE TO TECHNOLOGY

Given such consequences, it should come as no surprise that, through the ages, there have been those who questioned whether such technological innovation equals progress. Inventions that grew out of the Industrial Revolution, for example, led to strong resistance in some countries. In England, beginning in 1811, masked craft workers took extreme measures: They mounted nighttime raids on factories and destroyed some of the new machinery. The government hunted these rebels, known as **Luddites,** and ultimately banished or hanged them. In a similar effort in France, angry workers threw their wooden shoes (sabots) into factory machinery to destroy it, giving rise to the term *sabotage.* Although the resistance of the Luddites and the French workers was short-lived and unsuccessful, they have come to symbolize resistance to technology.

It would be a mistake, however, to simply dismiss the actions of the Luddites and French workers as antitechnology or irrational. Their primary concern was with the impact such technology had on their employment, their communities, and their way of life. They recognized that it would undercut taken-for-granted norms and values and fought against such threats. While it is easy to write such groups and individuals off as being against progress— or even as technophobes that fear change—their bigger concern is the impact adoption of technologies has on society. The Amish, for example, are often dismissed as backward, when, in fact, they are quite rational and deliberative about adopting technology. They carefully weigh the benefits new technologies would provide against the potential costs adoption would have on family and community life. They do not assume that, simply because something makes work easier or faster, it is necessarily better. For the Amish, working together in community is more highly valued than working more quickly in isolation (Hostetler 1993; Hurst and McConnell 2010).

Sociologist Jacques Ellul (1964, 1980, 1990) argued that the key factor to consider when analyzing our modern technological society is not simply the *technology,* by which he meant the physical tools we create as we modify our material environment, but what he referred to more generally as *technique.* By this he meant our systemic commitment to maximizing efficiency and increasing productivity in all areas of human endeavor. Success, whether in business, education, or love, is increasingly measured in quantitative terms. That which cannot be measured is suspect. For example, we see evidence of this at work in the No Child Left Behind education reforms. Performance on particular kinds of tests, in a narrow range of subjects, is becoming the primary indicator of learning. Although living in a technique-focused system has the advantage of technical progress, we lose something human in the process—art, beauty, and qualitative, as opposed to quantitative, values. Ellul's concerns echo those of Max Weber about the dehumanizing consequences of bureaucracy.

Most of us today automatically adopt the latest technologies without taking time to step back and ask what consequences they might have for social order and meaning. Communications professor Neil Postman (1988, 1993, 1999) argues that, instead of passively accepting technological innovations, we should critically examine whether or not we really need them and investigate what consequences adoption might have on ourselves, our relationships, and our society (see Postman's five questions on page 392). In a sense, Postman is calling us to recognize ways in which our choices are influenced by the technological system within which we live. Doing so enables us to resist unconscious acceptance and exercise greater freedom in the choices that we make.

>>Social Movements

We do have the power to resist change even when it seems inevitable. More than that, we also have the power to bring about positive social change. Although factors such as the physical environment, population, technology, and social inequality serve as sources of change, it is the collective effort of individuals organized in social movements that ultimately leads to change. Sociologists use the term **social movements** to refer to organized collective activities to bring about or resist fundamental change in an existing group or society. Herbert Blumer (1955:19) recognized the special importance of social movements when he defined them as "collective enterprises to establish a new order of life."

In many nations, including the United States, social movements have had a dramatic impact on the course of history and the evolution of the social structure. Consider the actions of abolitionists, suffragists, civil rights workers, and anti–Vietnam War activists. Members of each social movement stepped outside traditional channels for bringing about social change, yet they had a noticeable influence on public policy. In the Arab Spring protests, equally dramatic collective efforts helped to topple repressive regimes in a largely peaceful manner, in nations that many observers had thought were "immune" to such social change.

social movement An organized collective activity to bring about or resist fundamental change in an existing group or society.

Social movements change how we think and act. Even if they initially fail to accomplish their explicit goals, social movements can influence cultural attitudes and expectations in ways that open people up to future change. Initially, people viewed the ideas of Margaret Sanger and other early advocates of birth control as radical, yet contraceptives are now widely available in the United States. Similarly, protests—whether against the practices of multinational corporations, same-sex marriage, the unethical treatment of animals, environmental destruction, or war—challenge us to question our taken-for-granted understandings of what is happening and why. This holds true even if we never formally participate ourselves or do not fully subscribe to all the beliefs and practices of the protestors.

At least since the work of Karl Marx, sociologists have studied how and why social movements emerge. Obviously,

Did You Know?

... In 1916 Margaret Sanger opened a family planning and birth control clinic. Nine days later, it was raided by police, and she served 30 days in jail as a result. She was undeterred and continued working to dispense birth control information.

one factor is that people become discontented with the way things are. To explain how this develops and is transformed into action, sociologists rely on two primary explanations: relative deprivation and resource mobilization.

RELATIVE DEPRIVATION

Those members of a society who feel most frustrated with and disgruntled by social and economic conditions are not necessarily the worst off in an objective sense. Social scientists have long recognized that what is most significant is how people perceive their situation. As Marx pointed out, although the misery of the workers was important to their perception of their oppressed state, so was their position in relation to the capitalist ruling class (McLellan 2000).

The term **relative deprivation** refers to the conscious feeling of a negative discrepancy between legitimate expectations and present actualities. In other words, things aren't as good as one hoped they would be. Such a state may be characterized by scarcity rather than a complete lack of necessities. A relatively deprived person is dissatisfied because he or she feels downtrodden relative to some appropriate reference group. Thus, blue-collar workers who live in two-family houses on small plots of land—though hardly destitute—may nevertheless feel deprived in comparison to corporate managers and professionals who live in lavish homes in exclusive suburbs (Stewart 2006).

In addition to the feeling of relative deprivation, however, two other elements must be present before discontent will be channeled into a social movement. First, people must feel that they have a right to their goals, that they deserve better than what they have. For example, the struggle against European colonialism in Africa intensified when growing numbers of Africans decided that it was legitimate for them to have political and economic independence. Second, the disadvantaged group must perceive that its goals cannot be attained through conventional means. This belief may or may not be correct. In any case, the group will not mobilize into a social movement unless there is a shared perception that members can end their relative deprivation only through collective action (Walker and Smith 2002).

Critics of this approach have noted that people don't need to feel deprived to be moved to act. In addition, this approach fails to explain why certain feelings of deprivation are transformed into social movements, whereas in other, similar situations, no collective effort is made to reshape society. Consequently, in recent years, sociologists have paid increasing attention to the forces needed to bring about the emergence of social movements (Finkel and Rule 1987; Ratner 2004).

relative deprivation The conscious feeling of a negative discrepancy between legitimate expectations and present actualities.

resource mobilization The ways in which a social movement utilizes such resources as money, political influence, access to the media, and personnel.

> I cannot say whether things will get better if we change; what I can say is they must change if they are to get better.
>
> George Christoph Lichtenberg

SOCTHINK

Are there any issues on your campus or in your community that people persistently complain about? If so, what factors might inhibit them from organizing to bring about social change?

RESOURCE MOBILIZATION APPROACH

It takes more than desire to start a social movement. It helps to have money, political influence, access to the media, and personnel. The term **resource mobilization** refers to the ways in which a social movement utilizes such resources. The success of a movement for change will depend in good part on what resources it has and how effectively it mobilizes them (Balch 2006; J. Jenkins 2004; Ling 2006).

Sociologist Anthony Oberschall (1973:199) has argued that to sustain social protest or resistance, there must be an "organizational base and continuity of leadership." As people become part of a social movement, norms develop to guide their behavior. Members of the movement may be expected to attend regular meetings of organizations, pay dues, recruit new adherents, and boycott "enemy" products or speakers. In forming a distinct identity, an emerging social movement may give rise to special language or new words for familiar terms. In recent years, social movements have been responsible for new terms of self-reference such as *Blacks* and *African Americans* (to replace *Negroes*), *senior citizens* (to replace *old folks*), *gays* (to replace *homosexuals*), and *people with disabilities* (to replace *the handicapped*).

Leadership is a central factor in the mobilization of the discontented into social movements. Often, a movement will be led by a charismatic figure, such as occurred in the civil rights movement with Dr. Martin Luther King, Jr. Charisma alone, however, may not be enough. If a group is to succeed, coordinated action is essential. As they grow, such organizations may find they need to take advantage of the efficiency that bureaucratic structures provide. This can result in their taking on some of the characteristics of the groups they were organized to protest. For example, leaders

might dominate the decision-making process without directly consulting followers. The bureaucratization of social movements is not inevitable, however. More radical movements that advocate major structural change in society and embrace mass actions tend not to be hierarchical or bureaucratic (Fitzgerald and Rodgers 2000; Michels [1915] 1949). Innovations in social networking technologies, including Facebook and Twitter, facilitate the organization of mass protests, as was evidenced in the 2011 Arab Spring uprisings and in the London riots in August 2011.

One of the tasks such movements face is to raise consciousness among those who would be inclined to support the movement but who may lack the language or the sense of solidarity with others to mount a systematic critique of the existing system. Marx, for example, recognized the importance of recruitment when he called on workers to become aware of their oppressed status and to develop a class consciousness. Like theorists of the resource mobilization approach, Marx held that a social movement would require leaders to sharpen the awareness of the oppressed. They would need to help workers to overcome feelings of *false consciousness*—attitudes that do not reflect workers' objective position—in order to organize a revolutionary movement (see Chapter 10).

GENDER AND SOCIAL MOVEMENTS

Betty Friedan's publication of *The Feminine Mystique* in 1963 gave voice to a sense (that many women had at the time) that something was wrong, but they did not know that others felt the same way. The book alone, however, was not enough. One of the challenges faced by women's liberation activists of the late 1960s and early 1970s was to convince women that they were being deprived of their rights and of socially valued resources. Consciousness-raising groups represented a critical tool used by women's liberation activists in the 1960s and 1970s. In these groups, women gathered to discuss topics relevant to their experience in the home, at work, in politics, and more. This helped to create a popular base that contributed to significant political and social change (Morgan 2009; Sarachild 1978).

Sociologists point out that gender continues to be an important element in understanding social movements. In our male-dominated society, women continue to find themselves cut off from leadership positions in social movement organizations. Though women often serve disproportionately as volunteers in these movements, their contributions are not always recognized, nor are their voices as easily heard as men's. Gender bias causes the real extent of their influence

to be overlooked. Indeed, traditional examination of the sociopolitical system tends to focus on such male-dominated corridors of power as legislatures and corporate boardrooms, to the neglect of more female-dominated domains such as households, community-based groups, and faith-based networks. But efforts to influence family values, child rearing, relationships between parents and schools, and spiritual values are clearly significant to a culture and society (Ferree and Merrill 2000; Kuumba 2001; V. Taylor 1999, 2004).

Before the June 2009 presidential election in Iran, women's social movement organizations foresaw an opportunity for change and organized to take advantage of it. Almost 40 equal rights groups combined to form an organization called the "Coalition of Women's Movements to Advocate Electoral Demands." Noushin Ahmadi Khorasani (2009), a key leader of the women's rights movement in Iran, described the opportunity this way: "We could grasp this relatively short and transient moment with both hands, with hope and motivation (and looking forward to tomorrow) in order to voice our demands." During the government crackdown on the protests that followed the election, women continued to fight for change. Perhaps the most visible symbol of their fight was Neda Agha-Soltan, a protestor who was shot and bled to death in the street. The violent image was caught on video and quickly spread around the world (Gheytanchi 2009; Ravitz 2009). Women continue to play a substantial role in social movements, as demonstrated by their leadership in many of the democratic uprisings during the 2011 Arab Spring protests (Ghitis 2011).

> **new social movement** An organized collective activity that addresses values and social identities, as well as improvements in the quality of life.

NEW SOCIAL MOVEMENTS

Beginning in the late 1960s, European social scientists observed a change in both the composition and the targets of emerging social movements. Previously, traditional social movements had focused on economic issues, often led by labor unions or by people who shared the same occupation. However, many social movements that have become active in recent decades—including the second and third waves of feminism, the peace movement, and the environmental movement—do not have the social class roots typical of the labor movements in the United States and Europe over the past century (Carty and Onyett 2006).

The term **new social movements** refers to organized collective activities that address values and social identities, as well as improvements in the quality of life. These movements may be involved in developing collective identities. Many have complex agendas that go beyond a single issue and even cross national boundaries. Educated, middle-class people are significantly represented in some of these new social movements, such as the women's movement and the movement for lesbian and gay rights (Tilly 1993, 2004).

New social movements generally do not view government as their ally in the struggle for a better society. They typically do not seek to overthrow the government, but they may criticize, protest, or harass public officials. Researchers have found that members of new social movements call into question the legitimacy of arguments made by established authorities. Even scientific or technical claims, they argue, do not simply represent objective facts, but often serve specific interests. This characteristic is especially evident in the environmental and antinuclear power movements, whose activists present their own experts to counter those of government or big business (Clammer 2009; Jamison 2006; Rootes 2007).

The environmental movement is one of many new social movements with a worldwide focus. In their efforts

SOCTHINK

Online sites such as changemakers.net serve as information clearinghouses and networking hubs for social activists. How might the existence of such resources shape social activism both positively and negatively?

to reduce air and water pollution, curtail global climate change, and protect endangered animal species, environmental activists have realized that strong regulatory measures within a single country are not sufficient. Similarly, labor union leaders and human rights advocates cannot adequately address exploitative sweatshop conditions in a developing country if a multinational corporation can simply move the factory to another country, where workers earn even less. Whereas traditional views of social movements tended to emphasize resource mobilization on a local level, new social movement theory offers a broader, global perspective on social and political activism (Obach 2004).

Stephen Colbert worked for several years as a sarcastic correspondent on *The Daily Show* on Comedy Central, but he became famous for spoofing TV talking heads on his show, *The Colbert Report.* He was quite serious, however, when he gave advice in a 2006 commencement speech at Knox College. He challenged students not to give in to cynicism, telling them, "Cynicism masquerades as wisdom, but it is the farthest thing from it. Because cynics don't learn anything. Because cynicism is a self-imposed blindness, a rejection of the world because we are afraid it will hurt us or disappoint us. Cynics always say 'no.' But saying 'yes' begins things. Saying 'yes' is how things grow. Saying 'yes' leads to knowledge. 'Yes' is for young people. So for as long as you have the strength to, say 'yes.' "

COMMUNICATION AND THE GLOBALIZATION OF SOCIAL MOVEMENTS

Although technological advances have contributed to some of the problems people in social movements have raised,

new technologies also facilitate activism and social movement formation. Using social networking technologies, social activists can reach a large number of people around the world almost instantaneously, with relatively little effort and expense. For example, Facebook and Twitter allow organizers of social movements to enlist like-minded people without face-to-face contact or simultaneous interaction. In fact, significant social action can occur without the participants ever having met in person (Kavada 2005; Shirky 2008).

The potential power of new communication technologies was made apparent during Iran's June 2009 post-presidential-election protests, which may have served as a precursor and inspiration for the Arab Spring uprisings. A majority of Iran's population is under 30 and technologically well connected. Before the election, young people used their online social networking skills to coordinate campaign events and raise support for candidates. After President Ahmadinejad's reelection was declared, technologies such as Twitter, Facebook, and texting became critical tools for sharing information, coordinating actions, and documenting abuses by government forces. It was possible to organize rallies without revealing their location until the last minute, making it more difficult for the government to have troops in place to disperse the crowd.

Equally significant, these networking tools also were used to send stories, pictures, and video to the wider world, revealing the brutality of the government's crackdown. The result was an outpouring of global sympathy for the protestors. Iranian authorities sought to shut down wireless phone service and restrict Internet access, including blocking sites such as YouTube and Facebook. In spite of this, people were able to use various technological hacks to get around such restrictions and spread the word (Bray 2009; Quirk 2009; Stelter and Stone 2009).

>>Sociology Is a Verb

Ultimately, social change happens because we begin to act in new ways. It involves our stepping off expected paths and, in doing so, creating new sets of norms. Although external changes in our technological and environmental contexts do influence social change, it still takes people willing to do things differently to bring about such shifts.

Sociology is a tool that helps open up new pathways for us. By enabling us to see things we might have missed before, it helps us to view ourselves and the world around us differently. Sociology allows us to recognize how the distribution of social, cultural, and material resources gives advantage to some and disadvantage to others. It helps us to understand whether the things we do are consistent with what we claim to believe. It can inform our conversation of whether we are headed where we want to go. It does these things by getting us to pay attention to the world around us in a new way.

We need to move from thinking of sociology as only something we learn about to thinking of sociology as something we *do*. In our daily lives, sociology can help us to better understand our own individual actions and the actions of those around us. In the context of our larger society and the world, it also enables us to better appreciate the forces at work shaping outcomes—knowledge that we can then use to act in ways that make the world a better place. In both our personal and public lives, we need to practice sociology in the same way that doctors practice medicine.

public sociology The process of bringing the insights gained through sociological observation and analysis into the public sphere, thereby seeking to bring about positive social change.

PERSONAL SOCIOLOGY

Sociology can help us in our everyday lives to better understand our beliefs and actions and to make more informed choices. We learn from sociology that we are in society and society is in us. Self and society are not two separate things. Being an individual necessitates understanding the importance of place, of position, of connection, and of interaction. Though we like to believe that any choice is available to us, in reality, our options are limited.

Practicing sociology means asking uncomfortable questions and not settling for easy answers. It means taking into account the significance of both the individual and society, of both action and structure, of both freedom and constraint. It means recognizing the significance of power and the impact that access to material, social, and cultural resources has on the choices available to us. In short, as we saw in Chapter 1, doing *personal sociology* means recognizing the impact our individual position has on who we are and how we think and act,

and taking responsibility for the impacts our actions have on others.

From the beginning, sociologists wanted to understand our constraints so that we might be able to change them. As sociologist Pierre Bourdieu (1998b) put it, "To those who always tax the sociologist with determinism and pessimism, I will only say that if people became fully aware of them, conscious action aimed at controlling the structural mechanisms that engender moral failure would be possible" (p. 56). In other words, we need to be honest with ourselves about the degree to which society limits our choices so that we might be empowered to make choices that are more informed and therefore more effective in helping us to attain our goals.

As individuals, we need to learn to see the degree to which we follow visible and invisible rules. We need to ask whether our current paths represent the values, norms, and goals that we really want to follow. As we have seen, the shows we watch, the things we buy, our likelihood for suicide, our chances of facing a wage gap, our perception of reality, our very selves—all are shaped by the positions we occupy. Understanding these influences empowers us to change.

> Another world is not only possible, she is on her way. On a quiet day, I can hear her breathing.

— Arundhati Roy

PUBLIC SOCIOLOGY: TOOLS FOR CHANGE

Beyond providing a more informed understanding of why we as individuals act and think the way we do, sociology calls on us to look beyond ourselves to the world around us and ask, What might we do to make the world a better place? Sociologists since the very beginning have sought to understand and explain social processes for the purpose of shaping the future of society. **Public sociology** involves bringing the insights gained through sociological observation and analysis into the public sphere, thereby seeking to bring about positive social change. As Michael Burawoy, former president of the American Sociological Association, put it, public sociology seeks to speak to a wide audience, aiming to "enrich public debate about moral and political issues by infusing them with sociological theory and research" (Burawoy 2004:1603).

Because we construct the existing social structures through our collective and recurring actions, we bear responsibility for their consequences. Existing systems—the structure and culture we create—are not inevitable.

Citizen Activities in a Democratic Society

PRIVATE LIFE	CIVIC LIFE	
Individual activity	**Civic engagement activities**	
	Nonpolitical activities	Political participation
Family School Work	Recycling Fellowship meetings Service activities	Voting Attending political meetings Political campaigning
Cultivates personal relationships, serves individual needs—e.g., getting an education, earning a living	Provides community services and acts as a training ground for political participation	Fulfills demands of democratic citizenship

Functions

We can choose to change them; we can act differently, as the accompanying table suggests. It can be difficult to step off the "paths of least resistance" that support the existing system (Johnson 1997), and the consequences for action and belief that run counter to the status quo can be severe. But we can do so.

What we cannot do is absolve ourselves of responsibility for the systems we end up with. In fact, to not act differently is to support the existing system of inequality. As sociologist Scott Schaffer (2004) points out, we can no longer ignore practices that violate our basic beliefs, trying to wash our hands of responsibility:

> Our hands are already dirty; the question I leave here is whether our hands will be dirtied through action intended to bring concrete, actual, enacted freedom into the world, or through our choice to preserve ourselves at the cost of all others in the here and now and in the future. (pp. 271–272)

Our cynicism and resignation only reinforce systems of oppression and violence. To not act to bring about positive change still represents a choice, and our hands are dirty either way.

By helping us to see why we think and act as we do, by helping us to clarify the relationship between belief and practice, and by helping us to better understand the consequences of difference, personal and public sociology can encourage discussion that can lead to a better future. We can use the tools of sociology to allow ourselves to enter into conversations in which we share our stories with others (both positive and negative), clarifying places where we agree and disagree, and opening ourselves up to our blind spots. We often want to avoid uncomfortable conflict, opting instead for polite discourse, but to fail to be more genuinely engaged in our cultural and structural differences virtually ensures a lack of progress toward implementing our core principles (Schaffer 2004).

PRACTICING SOCIOLOGY

Change comes because people continue not only to believe that it is possible but also to act on their hopes and dreams (see the figure below). As ethnographer Studs Terkel (2003) put it, "In all epochs, there were at first doubts and the fear of stepping forth and speaking out, but the attribute that spurred the warriors on was hope. And the *act*" (p. xviii).

Do You Believe You Can Effect Political Change?

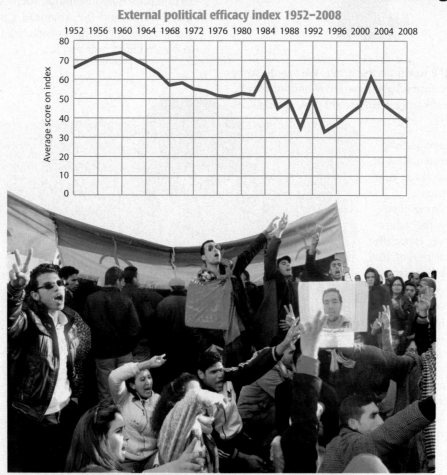

Source: American National Election Studies 2010:Table 5B.1.

themselves; they aren't just facts but are embedded in networks and systems that have their own interests.

- *Vote.* Elected leaders in a democracy, whether local, state, or national, are chosen by voters. It may not seem like your individual vote is significant, but the simple fact is that all those votes still add up to a winner. And even if your candidate cannot win, you can still make a statement; for example, if you don't think any of the candidates would make a good choice, write in someone who would.

- *Participate in local politics.* Think of politics as a contact sport: Go to rallies, protests, school board meetings, city council meetings, and more. You might be surprised how much of a difference a single voice can make, especially on the local level.

- *Run for office.* Don't assume that such positions of leadership are only for others who are somehow better or more informed than you. We need more people to believe that they can lead so that we get more diversity in our leaders.

- *Volunteer.* There are local organizations in every community seeking to bring about positive social change. You might contact a local school to see if you can read to kids, work at a homeless shelter, or help build houses with Habitat for Humanity.

- *Join.* There are many organizations that provide long-term outreach opportunities, such as AmeriCorps, the Peace Corps, and the American Red Cross, in which you provide assistance to people with varieties of needs, in communities near and far.

We can change the world for the better. We can do so by becoming more informed about ourselves and others and then acting on that knowledge. Here are some possibilities for action:

- *Practice personal sociology.* Become more conscious of the factors that shape your beliefs and actions.

- *Become more aware of privilege.* Identify the advantages you have, especially relative to the rest of the world; you likely have sufficient food, clothes, and shelter; you can read this; you can plan for the future; and so on.

- *Become more informed.* We have access to more information about our world now than ever. Seek it out; find out what's going on.

- *Interpret what you learn.* Analyze the information you receive. Remember that data never speak for

Investigate. Learn. Vote. Organize. Run for office. Fight for change. Practice sociology. Make a difference.

get involved!

- *Organize.* Work to bring about the world you envision; there are undoubtedly others out there who share your views. Find them and work with them, both inside and outside existing institutions, to bring about change.
- *Fight for change.* Regardless of where you are, whether in your relationships, your family, your workplace, your community, or elsewhere, work to bring about positive social change. We have the power to change the world; we can't do so in a vacuum, but if sociologists are at all correct about the social construction of reality, things could be otherwise.

As Comte wrote at sociology's very founding, "Science leads to foresight, and foresight leads to action" (quoted in Bourdieu 1998b:55). It is only by seeing those things that limit us that we can move toward freedom.

We learn a lesson from sociology that is reminiscent of the one Ebenezer Scrooge learns in Charles Dickens's *A Christmas Carol,* written in 1843. Scrooge, a miserly businessman, thinks only of himself, caring little if anything for others, including his employee, his family, and the poor. But on Christmas Eve, he is visited by three ghosts: the Ghost of Christmas Past, the Ghost of Christmas Present, and the Ghost of Christmas Yet to Come. After each of these spirits shows him visions of their time, Scrooge repents, promising to live "an altered life" in which he will reaffirm relationships and reconnect to those around him. What is particularly interesting sociologically is the way he phrases his promise: "I will live in the Past, the Present, and the Future! The Spirits of all Three shall strive within me."

At its core, Scrooge's resolution represents what we are called to do by the sociological imagination. Just as history and biography intersect, so also do we need to understand that the past, created by the actions of ourselves and those who came before us, has shaped who we are now. As American novelist and essayist James Baldwin ([1965] 1985) wrote, "The great force of history comes from the fact that we carry it within us, are unconsciously controlled by it in many ways, and history is literally *present* in all that we do" (p. 410). Further, our present actions shape the future directions of both our lives and the lives of others in the worlds around us and of those yet to come. Like Scrooge, we can reject the myth of the isolated individual and affirm the significance of relationships and companionship (to return to one of the root word meanings of sociology). By simultaneously holding the past, present, and future together in our minds, we can act to make the world a better place to live.

Sociology is more than just a noun. Sociology is a verb. It is something we do, not something we possess. Our over-reliance on individualistic models, and our failure to appreciate the impact of social forces, presents a distorted picture of our freedom. An appreciation of the relationship between self and society and of the consequences of difference allows us to make more informed choices and to shape the future. It allows us to provide answers to the questions "Why do we think the way we think?" and "Why do we act the way we act?" Sociology shouldn't be something confined to college classrooms. It shouldn't be left only to professionals. We are all sociologists now, and there is work to be done.

For REVIEW

I. **How and why does social change happen?**
- Social change evolves out of past social practices; it represents a response by those in society to maintain social order by seeking an acceptable level of balance between stability and change; and it is influenced by the distribution of power and control over resources, which shapes what changes do or do not occur. Technological innovation has played a powerful role causing social change.

II. **What factors shape the success of a social movement?**
- There needs to be a sense of relative deprivation in which people have a sense that injustice exists that can and should be challenged. In addition, people must have the capacity to mobilize resources to bring about the change they seek.

III. **What does it mean to practice sociology?**
- Personal sociology involves better understanding the influence social factors have on our thoughts and actions and using this information to our advantage. Public sociology means taking responsibility for the collective impacts our individual actions have in shaping society and opportunity and working for positive social change.

Functionalist View

Social change is a way for society to make adjustments in order to return to a state of **stability** or balance.

The four processes of social change identified by Parsons—differentiation, adaptive upgrading, inclusion, and value generalization—stress **consensus** in society.

Social movements and protests enable us to see the dysfunctions of the existing system, and thus facilitate positive social change.

EQUILIBRIUM, CONSENSUS, STABILITY
KEY CONCEPTS

Conflict View

Groups in society that **control** valued resources can either inhibit or facilitate social change more effectively than other groups.

Though new technology can provide tools that facilitate greater freedom, those in positions of power can use it to exert greater control and surveillance.

Social change should be encouraged as a way of eliminating **inequality** and correcting social **injustice**.

CONTROL, SURVEILLANCE, VESTED INTERESTS
KEY CONCEPTS

Interactionist View

Every individual has the power to change society through the everyday **choices** he or she makes and **actions** he or she takes (i.e., words we use, relationships we build, voting, volunteering, organizing for change).

Technological innovations in communication allow us to **connect** and interact with people around the world but may also cut us off from those right next to us.

Social movements consist of the **collective activities** of individuals in search of change.

ACTION, ORGANIZATION, CONNECTION
KEY CONCEPTS

MAKE THE CONNECTION

After reviewing the chapter, answer the following questions:

1

How would each perspective explain the activism of college students described in the opening vignette (p. 381)?

2

Why does "culture lag" occur (p. 385)? Why might the interactionist perspective be particularly helpful to explain it?

3

According to each perspective, what effects have new communication technologies (for example the Internet, cell phones, and so on) had on our interactions, relationships, and communities?

4

How would drawing an insight from each perspective enable you to more effectively bring about social change?

Pop Quiz

1. **According to the definition, what is social change?**
   a. tumultuous, revolutionary alterations that lead to changes in leadership
   b. a significant alteration over time in behavior patterns and culture
   c. regular alterations in a consistent social frame of reference
   d. subtle alterations in any social system

2. **Nineteenth-century theories of social change reflect the pioneering work in biological evolution done by**
   a. Albert Einstein.
   b. Harriet Martineau.
   c. James Audubon.
   d. Charles Darwin.

3. **According to Talcott Parsons's equilibrium model, during which process do social institutions become more specialized in their purposes?**
   a. differentiation
   b. adaptive upgrading
   c. inclusion
   d. value generalization

4. **Which of the following did William F. Ogburn use to describe the period of maladjustment during which the nonmaterial culture is still struggling to adapt to new material conditions?**
   a. economic shift
   b. political turmoil
   c. social change
   d. culture lag

5. **The One Laptop per Child campaign was designed to overcome the problem of**
   a. relative deprivation.
   b. social change.
   c. the digital divide.
   d. vested interests.

6. **You are a student and do not own a car. All your close friends who are attending your college or university have vehicles of their own. You feel downtrodden and dissatisfied. You are experiencing**
   a. relative deprivation.
   b. resource mobilization.
   c. false consciousness.
   d. depression.

7. **It takes more than desire to start a social movement; it helps to have money, political influence, access to the media, and workers. The ways in which a social movement uses such things are referred to collectively as**
   a. relative deprivation.
   b. false consciousness.
   c. resource mobilization.
   d. economic independence.

8. **Karl Marx held that leaders of social movements must help workers overcome feelings of**
   a. class consciousness.
   b. false consciousness.
   c. socialist consciousness.
   d. surplus value.

9. **Organized collective activities that promote autonomy and self-determination, as well as improvements in the quality of life, are referred to as**
   a. new social movements.
   b. social revolutions.
   c. resource mobilizations.
   d. crazes.

10. **Recognizing the impact our individual position has on who we are and how we think and act and taking responsibility for the effects our actions have on others is known as**
   a. resource mobilization.
   b. false consciousness.
   c. public sociology.
   d. personal sociology.

1. (b); 2. (d); 3. (b); 4. (d); 5. (c); 6. (a); 7. (c); 8. (b); 9. (a); 10. (d)

A

Absolute poverty   A minimum level of subsistence that no family should be expected to live below.   *250*

Achieved status   A social position that is within our power to change.   *104*

Activity theory   A theory of aging that suggests that those elderly people who remain active and socially involved will have an improved quality of life.   *95*

Adoption   In a legal sense, a process that allows for the transfer of the legal rights, responsibilities, and privileges of parenthood to a new legal parent or parents.   *165*

Affirmative action   Positive efforts to recruit minority group members or women for jobs, promotions, and educational opportunities.   *328*

Ageism   Prejudice and discrimination based on a person's age.   *96*

Agency   The freedom individuals have to choose and to act.   *7*

Agrarian society   The most technologically advanced form of preindustrial society. Members are engaged primarily in the production of food, but they increase their crop yields through technological innovations such as the plow.   *122*

Alienation   Loss of control over our creative human capacity to produce, separation from the products we make, and isolation from our fellow producers.   *116*

Amalgamation   The process through which a majority group and a minority group combine to form a new group.   *331*

Anomie   Durkheim's term for the loss of direction felt in a society when social control of individual behavior has become ineffective.   *13*

Anticipatory socialization   Processes of socialization in which a person "rehearses" for future positions, occupations, and social relationships.   *89*

Anti-Semitism   Anti-Jewish prejudice.   *341*

Apartheid   A former policy of the South African government, designed to maintain the separation of Blacks and other non-Whites from the dominant Whites.   *332*

Applied sociology   The use of the discipline of sociology with the specific intent of yielding practical applications for human behavior and organizations.   *19*

Argot   Specialized language used by members of a group or subculture.   *63*

Ascribed status   A social position assigned to a person by society without regard for the person's unique talents or characteristics.   *104*

Assimilation   The process through which a person forsakes his or her own cultural tradition to become part of a different culture.   *331*

Authority   Power that is recognized as legitimate by the people over whom it is exercised.   *214*

Avatar   A person's online representation as a character, whether in the form of a 2D or 3D image or simply through text.   *113*

B

Bilateral descent   A kinship system in which both sides of a person's family are regarded as equally important.   *155*

Bisexual   A category of sexual orientation that includes those who are attracted to both men and women.   *303*

Black power   A political philosophy, promoted by many younger Blacks in the 1960s, that supported the creation of Black-controlled political and economic institutions.   *335*

Borderlands   The area of common culture along the border between Mexico and the United States.   *282*

Bourgeoisie   Karl Marx's term for the capitalist class, comprising the owners of the means of production.   *243*

Brain drain   The immigration to the United States and other industrialized nations of skilled workers, professionals, and technicians who are needed in their home countries.   *359*

Bureaucracy   A component of formal organization that uses rules and hierarchical ranking to achieve efficiency.   *115*

Bureaucratization   The process by which a group, organization, or social movement increasingly relies on technical-rational decision making in the pursuit of efficiency.   *119*

C

Capitalism   An economic system based on private property, in which profit-seeking individuals, companies, and corporations compete in the marketplace.   *216*

Caste   A hereditary rank, usually religiously dictated, that tends to be fixed and immobile.   *239*

Causal logic   A relationship exists between variables in which change in one brings about change in the other.   *28*

Charismatic authority   Power made legitimate by a leader's exceptional personal or emotional appeal to his or her followers.   *215*

Class   A group of people who have a similar level of economic resources.   *244*

Class consciousness   In Karl Marx's view, a subjective awareness held by members of a class regarding their common vested interests and need for collective political action to bring about social change.   *243*

Class system   A social ranking based primarily on economic position in which achieved characteristics can influence social mobility.   *240*

Classical theory   An approach to the study of formal organizations that views workers as being motivated almost entirely by economic rewards.   *120*

Clinical sociology   The use of the discipline of sociology with the specific intent of altering social relationships or restructuring social institutions.   *20*

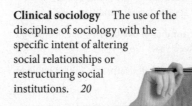

Closed system   A social system in which there is little or no possibility of individual social mobility.   *241*

Coalition   A temporary or permanent alliance geared toward a common goal.   *110*

Code of ethics   The standards of acceptable behavior developed by and for members of a profession.   *40*

Cognitive theory of development   The theory that children's thought progresses through four stages of development.   *79*

Cohabitation   The practice of a man and a woman living together in a sexual relationship without being married.   *169*

Colonialism   The maintenance of political, social, economic, and cultural dominance over a people by a foreign power for an extended period.   *269*

Color-blind racism   The use of race-neutral principles to perpetuate a racially unequal status quo.   *324*

Conflict perspective   A sociological approach that assumes that social behavior is best understood in terms of tension between groups over power or the allocation of resources, including housing, money, access to services, and political representation.   *17*

Conformity   The act of going along with peers—individuals of our own status who have no special right to direct our behavior.   *131*

Contact hypothesis   The theory that in cooperative circumstances interracial contact between people of equal status will reduce prejudice.   *330*

Content analysis   The systematic coding and objective recording of data, guided by some rationale.   *39*

Control group   The subjects in an experiment who are not introduced to the independent variable by the researcher.   *36*

Control theory   A view of conformity and deviance that suggests that our connection to members of society leads us to systematically conform to society's norms.   *135*

Control variable   A factor that is held constant to test the relative impact of an independent variable.   *31*

Correlation   A relationship between two variables in which a change in one coincides with a change in the other.   *29*

Correspondence principle   The tendency of schools to promote the values expected of individuals in each social class and to prepare students for the types of jobs typically held by members of their class.   *186*

Counterculture   A subculture that deliberately opposes certain aspects of the larger culture.   *64*

Credentialism   An increase in the lowest level of education required to enter a field.   *187*

Crime   A violation of criminal law for which some governmental authority applies formal penalties.   *137*

Crude birth rate   The number of live births per 1,000 people in the population in a given year   *351*

Crude death rate   The number of deaths per 1,000 people in a population in a given year   *351*

Cultural capital   Our tastes, knowledge, attitudes, language, and ways of thinking that we exchange in interaction with others.   *245*

Cultural relativism   The viewing of people's behavior from the perspective of their own culture.   *66*

Cultural transmission   A school of criminology that argues that criminal behavior is learned through social interactions.   *144*

Cultural universal   A common practice or belief shared by all societies.   *50*

Culture   Everything humans create in establishing our relationships to nature and with each other.   *48*

Culture lag   A period of adjustment when the nonmaterial culture is still struggling to adapt to new material conditions.   *54*

Culture shock   The feelings of disorientation, uncertainty, and even fear that people experience when they encounter unfamiliar cultural practices.   *65*

Culture-bound syndrome   A disease or illness that cannot be understood apart from some specific social context.   *357*

Curanderismo   Latino folk medicine, a form of holistic health care and healing.   *364*

D

Degradation ceremony   An aspect of the socialization process within some total institutions, in which people are subjected to humiliating rituals.   *91*

Deindustrialization   The systematic, widespread withdrawal of investment in basic aspects of productivity, such as factories and plants.   *211*

Democracy   In a literal sense, government by the people.   *221*

Demographic transition   As societies transform from preindustrial to post industrial, their population size shifts from small but stable with high birth and death rates, through a period of significant population growth, to large but stable, when both birth and death rates are low.   *354*

Demography   The statistical study of population dynamics.   *350*

Denomination   A large, organized religion that is not officially linked to the state or government.   *197*

Dependency theory   An approach that contends that industrialized nations continue to exploit developing countries for their own gain.   *271*

Dependent variable   The variable in a causal relationship that is subject to the influence of another variable.   *28*

Deviance   Behavior that violates the standards of conduct or expectations of a group or society.   *135*

Dictatorship   A government in which one person has nearly total power to make and enforce laws.   *221*

Differential association   A theory of deviance that holds that violation of rules results from exposure to attitudes favorable to criminal acts.   *144*

Differential justice   Differences in the way social control is exercised over different groups.   *147*

Diffusion   The process by which a cultural item spreads from group to group or society to society.   *52*

Digital divide   The relative lack of access to the latest technologies among low-income groups, racial and ethnic minorities, rural residents, and the citizens of developing countries.   *259*

Discovery   The process of making known or sharing the existence of an aspect of reality.   *52*

Discrimination   The denial of opportunities and equal rights to individuals and groups because of prejudice or other arbitrary reasons.   *324*

Disengagement theory   A theory of aging that suggests that society and the aging individual mutually sever many of their relationships.   *93*

Domestic partnership   Two unrelated adults who share a mutually caring relationship, reside together, and agree to be jointly responsible for their dependents, basic living expenses, and other common necessities.   *171*

Dominant ideology   A set of cultural beliefs and practices that legitimates existing powerful social, economic, and political interests.   *62*

Downsizing   Reductions in a company's workforce as part of deindustrialization.   *211*

Dramaturgical approach   A view of social interaction in which people are seen as actors on a stage, attempting to put on a successful performance.   *78*

E

Ecclesia   A religious organization that claims to include most or all members of a society and is recognized as the national or official religion.   *196*

Economy   A social institution dedicated to the production, distribution, and consumption of goods and services.   *210*

Education   A social institution dedicated to the formal process of transmitting culture from teachers to students.   *180*

Egalitarian family   An authority pattern in which spouses are regarded as equals.   *160*

Elite model   A view of society as being ruled by a small group of individuals who share a common set of political and economic interests.   *224*

Emigration   When members of a population leaves that group.   *352*

Endogamy   The restriction of mate selection to people within the same group.   *161*

Environmental justice   A legal strategy based on claims that racial minorities are subjected disproportionately to environmental hazards.   *371*

Equilibrium model   The view that society tends toward a state of stability or balance.   *385*

Established sect   A religious group that is the outgrowth of a sect, yet remains isolated from society.   *198*

Estate system   A system of stratification under which peasants were required to work land leased to them by nobles in exchange for military protection and other services. Also known as *feudalism*.   *240*

Esteem   The reputation that a specific person has earned within an occupation.   *248*

Ethnic group   A group that is set apart from others primarily because of its national origin or distinctive cultural patterns.   *318*

Ethnocentrism   The tendency to assume that one's own culture and way of life represent what's normal or are superior to all others.   *65*

Ethnography   The study of an entire social setting through extended systematic observation.   *35*

Evolutionary theory   A theory of social change that holds that society is moving in a definite direction.   *384*

Exogamy   The requirement that people select a mate outside certain groups.   *162*

Experiment   An artificially created situation that allows a researcher to manipulate variables.   *36*

Experimental group   The subjects in an experiment who are exposed to an independent variable introduced by a researcher.   *36*

Exploitation theory   A belief that views racial subordination in the United States as a manifestation of the class system inherent in capitalism.   *329*

Expressive leader   The person in the family who bears responsibility for the maintenance of harmony and internal emotional affairs.   *307*

Expulsion   The systematic removal of a group of people from society.   *331*

Extended family   A family in which relatives—such as grandparents, aunts, or uncles—live in the same household as parents and their children.   *156*

F

Face-work   The efforts people make to maintain a proper image and avoid public embarrassment.   *79*

False consciousness   A term used by Karl Marx to describe an attitude held by members of a class that does not accurately reflect their objective position.   *243*

Familism   Pride in the extended family, expressed through the maintenance of close ties and strong obligations to kinfolk outside the immediate family.   *164*

Feminism   The belief in social, economic, and political equality for women.   *299*

Fertility   The number of children born in a given period of time.   *350*

Folkway   Norms governing everyday behavior, whose violation raises comparatively little concern.   *59*

Force   The actual or threatened use of coercion to impose one's will on others.   *214*

Formal norm   A norm that generally has been written down and that specifies strict punishments for violators.   *59*

Formal social control   Social control that is carried out by authorized agents, such as police officers, judges, school administrators, and employers.   *133*

Functionalist definition of families   A definition of families that focuses on how families provide for the physical, social, and emotional needs of individuals and of society as a whole.   *158*

Functionalist perspective   A sociological approach that emphasizes the way in which the parts of a society are structured to maintain its stability.   *16*

Fundamentalism Rigid adherence to core religious doctrines, often accompanied by a literal application of scripture or historical beliefs to today's world. *195*

G

Gemeinschaft A close-knit community, often found in rural areas, in which strong personal bonds unite members. *121*

Gender The social and cultural significance that we attach to the biological differences of sex. *292*

Gender role Expectations regarding the proper behavior, attitudes, and activities of males or females. *82*

Generalized other The attitudes, viewpoints, and expectations of society as a whole that a child takes into account in his or her behavior. *78*

Genocide The deliberate, systematic killing of an entire people or nation. *330*

Gerontology The study of the sociological and psychological aspects of aging and the problems of the aged. *93*

Gesellschaft A community, often urban, that is large and impersonal, with little commitment to the group or consensus on values. *121*

Glass ceiling An invisible barrier that blocks the promotion of a qualified individual in a work environment because of the individual's gender, race, or ethnicity. *309*

Globalization The worldwide integration of government policies, cultures, social movements, and financial markets through trade and the exchange of ideas. *20*

Goal displacement Overzealous conformity to official regulations of a bureaucracy. *117*

Gross national income (GNI) The total value of a nation's goods and services. *278*

Group Any number of people with shared norms, values, and goals who interact with one another on a regular basis. *107*

H

Hate crime A criminal offense committed because of the offender's bias against an individual based on race, religion, ethnicity, national origin, or sexual orientation. *325*

Hawthorne effect The unintended influence that observers of experiments can have on their subjects. *36*

Health As defined by the World Health Organization, a state of complete physical, mental, and social well-being, not merely the absence of disease and infirmity. *346*

Heteronormativity A term that sociologists use to describe the cultural presupposition that heterosexuality is the appropriate standard for sexual identity and practice and that alternative sexualities are deviant, abnormal, or wrong. *303*

Heterosexual A category of sexual orientation that includes those who are sexually attracted to members of the opposite sex. *303*

Hidden curriculum Standards of behavior that are deemed proper by society and are taught subtly in schools. *185*

Holistic medicine Therapies in which the health care practitioner considers the person's physical, mental, emotional, and spiritual characteristics. *367*

Homogamy The conscious or unconscious tendency to select a mate with personal characteristics and interests similar to one's own. *162*

Homosexual A category of sexual orientation that includes those who are attracted to members of the same sex. *303*

Horizontal mobility The movement of an individual from one social position to another of the same rank. *242*

Horticultural society A preindustrial society in which people plant seeds and crops rather than merely subsist on available foods. *122*

Hospice care Treatment of the terminally ill in their own homes, or in special hospital units or other facilities, with the goal of helping them to die comfortably, without pain. *97*

Human ecology The area of study concerned with the interrelationships between people and their environments. *369*

Human relations approach An approach to the study of formal organizations that emphasizes the role of people, communication, and participation in a bureaucracy and tends to focus on the informal structure of the organization. *120*

Human rights Universal moral rights possessed by all people because they are human. *283*

Hunting-and-gathering society A preindustrial society in which people rely on whatever foods and fibers are readily available in order to survive. *122*

Hypothesis A testable statement about the relationship between two or more variables. *27*

I

I The acting self that exists in relation to the Me. *76*

Ideal type An abstract model of the essential characteristics of a phenomenon. *116*

Immigration When individuals join a population group of which they were not previously a member. *352*

Impression management The altering of the presentation of the self in order to create distinctive appearances and satisfy particular audiences. *79*

Incest taboo The prohibition of sexual relationships between certain culturally specified relatives. *162*

Incidence The number of new cases of a specific disorder that occur within a given population during a stated period. *362*

Income Wages and salaries measured over some period of time, such as per hour or year. *249*

Independent variable The variable in a causal relationship that causes or influences a change in a second variable. *28*

Index crimes The eight types of crime reported annually by the FBI in the *Uniform Crime Reports:* murder, forcible rape, robbery, aggravated assault, burglary, larceny-theft, motor vehicle theft, and arson. *137*

Industrial society A society that depends on mechanization to produce its goods and services. *123*

Infant mortality rate The number of deaths of infants under one year old per 1,000 live births in a given year. *351*

Informal economy   Transfers of money, goods, or services that are not reported to the government.   *219*

Informal norm   A norm that is generally understood but not precisely recorded.   *59*

Informal social control   Social control that is carried out casually by ordinary people through such means as laughter, smiles, and ridicule.   *133*

In-group   A category of people who share a common identity and sense of belonging.   *109*

Innovation   The process of introducing a new idea or object to a culture through discovery or invention.   *51*

Institutional discrimination   The denial of opportunities and equal rights to individuals and groups that results from the normal operations of a society.   *308*

Instrumental leader   The person in the family who bears responsibility for the completion of tasks, focuses on distant goals, and manages the external relationship between one's family and other social institutions.   *307*

Interactionist perspective   A sociological approach that generalizes about everyday forms of social interaction in order to explain society as a whole.   *17*

Intergenerational mobility   Changes in the social position of children relative to their parents.   *242*

Intersectionality   Gender, sexuality, race, ethnicity, and class must not be studied in isolation, because they have intermingled effects on our identity, knowledge, and outcomes.   *302*

Interview   A face-to-face or telephone questioning of a respondent to obtain desired information.   *34*

Intragenerational mobility   Changes in social position within a person's adult life.   *242*

Invention   The combination of existing cultural items into a form that did not exist before.   *52*

Iron law of oligarchy   The principle that all organizations, even democratic ones, tend to develop into bureaucracies ruled by an elite few.   *119*

K

Kinship   The state of being related to others.   *155*

L

Labeling theory   An approach to deviance that attempts to explain why certain people are viewed as deviants while others engaged in the same behavior are not.   *146*

Laissez-faire   The principle that people should be able to compete freely, without government interference, in the capitalist marketplace.   *217*

Language   A system of shared symbols; it includes speech, written characters, numerals, symbols, and nonverbal gestures and expressions.   *54*

Law   Formal norms enforced by the state.   *59*

Liberation theology   Use of a church, primarily Roman Catholicism, in a political effort to eliminate poverty, discrimination, and other forms of injustice from a secular society.   *203*

Life chances   The opportunities people have to provide themselves with material goods, positive living conditions, and favorable life experiences.   *258*

Life course approach   A research orientation in which sociologists and other social scientists look closely at the social factors that influence people throughout their lives, from birth to death.   *89*

Life expectancy   The projected number of years a person can expect to live based on his or her year of birth.   *352*

Looking-glass self   A theory that we become who we are based on how we think others see us.   *76*

Luddites   Rebellious craft workers in 19th-century England who destroyed new factory machinery as part of their resistance to the Industrial Revolution.   *394*

M

Machismo   A sense of virility, personal worth, and pride in one's maleness.   *164*

Macrosociology   Sociological investigation that concentrates on large-scale phenomena or entire civilizations.   *15*

Master status   A status that dominates others and thereby determines a person's general position in society.   *105*

Material culture   The physical or technological aspects of our daily lives.   *53*

Matriarchy   A society in which women dominate in family decision making.   *159*

Matrilineal descent   A kinship system in which only the mother's relatives are significant.   *156*

McDonaldization   The process by which the principles of efficiency, calculability, predictability, and control shape organization and decision making, in the United States and around the world.   *119*

Me   The socialized self that plans actions and judges performances based on the standards we have learned from others.   *76*

Mean   A number calculated by adding a series of values and then dividing by the number of values.   *34*

Mechanical solidarity   Social cohesion based on shared experiences, knowledge, and skills in which things function more or less the way they always have, with minimal change.   *121*

Median   The midpoint, or number that divides a series of values into two groups of equal numbers of values.   *34*

Microsociology   Sociological investigation that stresses the study of small groups and the analysis of our everyday experiences and interactions.   *15*

Midlife crisis   A stressful period of self-evaluation that begins at about age 40.   *91*

Migration   The movement of people from one population group to another.   *352*

Minority group   A subordinate group whose members, even if they represent a numeric majority, have significantly less control or power over their own lives than the members of a dominant or majority group have over theirs.   *318*

Mixed economy   An economic system that combines elements of both capitalism and socialism.   *218*

Mode The single most common value in a series of scores. *35*

Model or ideal minority A subordinate group whose members supposedly have succeeded economically, socially, and educationally despite past prejudice and discrimination. *336*

Modernization The far-reaching process by which nations pass from traditional forms of social organization toward those characteristic of post–Industrial Revolution societies. *269*

Monarchy A form of government headed by a single member of a royal family, usually a king, queen, or some other hereditary ruler. *220*

Monogamy A form of marriage in which one woman and one man are married only to each other. *156*

Monopoly Control of a market by a single business firm. *217*

Morbidity rate The incidence of disease in a given population. *362*

Mores Norms deemed highly necessary to the welfare of a society. *59*

Mortality rate The incidence of death in a given population. *362*

Multinational corporation A commercial organization that is headquartered in one country but does business throughout the world. *271*

Multiple masculinities The idea that men learn and play a full range of gender roles. *297*

N

Natural science The study of the physical features of nature and the ways in which they interact and change. *9*

Neocolonialism Continuing dependence of former colonies on foreign countries. *270*

New religious movement (NRM) or cult A small, alternative faith community that represents either a new religion or a major innovation in an existing faith. *198*

New social movement An organized collective activity that addresses values and social identities, as well as improvements in the quality of life. *396*

Nonmaterial culture Ways of using material objects, as well as customs, ideas, expressions, beliefs, knowledge, philosophies, governments, and patterns of communication. *53*

Nonverbal communication The use of gestures, facial expressions, and other visual images to communicate. *57*

Norm An established standard of behavior maintained by a society. *59*

Nuclear family A married couple and their unmarried children living together. *156*

O

Obedience Compliance with higher authorities in a hierarchical structure. *131*

Observation A research technique in which an investigator collects information through direct participation and/or by closely watching a group or community. *35*

Offshoring The transfer of work to foreign contractors. *211*

Oligarchy A form of government in which a few individuals rule. *220*

Open system A social system in which the position of each individual is influenced by his or her achieved status. *241*

Operational definition Transformation of an abstract concept into indicators that are observable and measurable. *27*

Organic solidarity Social cohesion based on mutual interdependence in the context of extreme division of labor. *121*

Organized crime The work of a group that regulates relations among criminal enterprises involved in illegal activities, including prostitution, gambling, and the smuggling and sale of illegal drugs. *140*

Out-group A category of people who do not belong or do not fit in. *109*

P

Party The capacity to organize to accomplish some particular goal. *245*

Patriarchy A society in which men dominate in family decision making. *159*

Patrilineal descent A kinship system in which only the father's relatives are significant. *156*

Peace The absence of war, or, more broadly, a proactive effort to develop cooperative relations among nations. *232*

Personal sociology The process of recognizing the impact our individual position has on who we are and how we think and act, and of taking responsibility for the impacts our actions have on others. *118*

Pluralism Mutual respect for one another's cultures among the various groups in a society, which allows minorities to express their own cultures without experiencing prejudice. *333*

Pluralist model A view of society in which many competing groups within the community have access to government, so that no single group is dominant. *226*

Political system The social institution that is founded on a recognized set of procedures for implementing and achieving society's goals. *220*

Politics The competition between individuals or groups over the allocation of valued resources. *220*

Polyandry A form of polygamy in which a woman may have more than one husband at the same time. *157*

Polygamy A form of marriage in which an individual may have several husbands or wives simultaneously. *157*

Polygyny A form of polygamy in which a man may have more than one wife at the same time. *157*

Postindustrial society A society whose economic system is engaged primarily in the processing and control of information. *123*

Postmodern society A technologically sophisticated, pluralistic, interconnected, globalized society. *123*

Power The ability to exercise one's will over others even if they resist. *211*

Power elite A small group of military, industrial, and government leaders who control the fate of the United States. *224*

Prejudice A negative attitude toward an entire category of people, often an ethnic or racial minority. *323*

Prestige The respect and admiration that an occupation holds in a society. *248*

Prevalence The total number of cases of a specific disorder that exist at a given time. *362*

Primary group A small group characterized by intimate, face-to-face association and cooperation. *108*

Private troubles Problems we face in our immediate relationships with particular individuals in our personal lives. *5*

Profane The ordinary and commonplace elements of life, as distinguished from the sacred. *193*

Proletariat Karl Marx's term for the working class in a capitalist society who lack ownership of the means of production. *243*

Protestant ethic Max Weber's term for the disciplined commitment to worldly labor driven by a desire to bring glory to God, shared by followers of Martin Luther and John Calvin. *202*

Public issues Problems we face as a consequence of the positions we occupy within the larger social structure. *5*

Public sociology The process of bringing the insights gained through sociological observation and analysis into the public sphere, thereby seeking to bring about positive social change. *398*

Q

Qualitative research Research that relies on what is seen in field or naturalistic settings more than on statistical data. *35*

Quantitative research Research that collects and reports data primarily in numerical form. *34*

Questionnaire A printed, written, or computerized form used to obtain information from a respondent. *34*

R

Racial formation A sociohistorical process in which racial categories are created, inhibited, transformed, and destroyed. *320*

Racial group A group that is set apart from others because of physical differences that have taken on social significance. *318*

Racial profiling Any police-initiated action based on race, ethnicity, or national origin rather than on a person's behavior. *326*

Racism The belief that one race is supreme and all others are innately inferior. *323*

Random sample A sample for which every member of an entire population has the same chance of being selected. *30*

Rational-legal authority Authority based on formally agreed upon and accepted rules, principles, and procedures of conduct that are established in order to accomplish goals in the most efficient manner possible. *216*

Reference group Any group that individuals use as a standard for evaluating themselves and their own behavior. *110*

Relative deprivation The conscious feeling of a negative discrepancy between legitimate expectations and present actualities. *394*

Relative poverty A floating standard of deprivation by which people at the bottom of a society, whatever their lifestyles, are judged to be disadvantaged in comparison with the nation as a whole. *253*

Reliability The extent to which a measure produces consistent results. *31*

Religion A social institution dedicated to establishing a shared sense of identity, encouraging social integration, and offering believers a sense of meaning and purpose. *192*

Religious belief A statement to which members of a particular religion adhere. *194*

Religious experience The feeling or perception of being in direct contact with the ultimate reality, such as a divine being, or of being overcome with religious emotion. *196*

Religious ritual A practice required or expected of members of a faith. *195*

Remittances The monies that immigrants return to their families of origin. Also known as *remesas*. *282*

Representative democracy A system of government in which citizens elect political leaders to make decisions on behalf of the people. *221*

Research design A detailed plan or method for obtaining data scientifically. *32*

Resocialization The process of discarding former behavior patterns and accepting new ones as part of a transition in one's life. *90*

Resource mobilization The ways in which a social movement utilizes such resources as money, political influence, access to the media, and personnel. *394*

Rite of passage A ritual marking the symbolic transition from one social position to another. *88*

Role conflict The situation that occurs when incompatible expectations arise from two or more social statuses held by the same person. *105*

Role exit The process of disengagement from a role that is central to one's self-identity in order to establish a new role and identity. *106*

Role strain The difficulty that arises when the same social status imposes conflicting demands and expectations. *106*

Role taking The process of mentally assuming the perspective of another and responding from that imagined viewpoint. *77*

S

Sacred Elements beyond everyday life that inspire respect, awe, and even fear. *193*

Sample A selection from a larger population that is statistically representative of that population. *30*

Sanction A penalty or reward for conduct concerning a social norm. *61*

Sandwich generation   The generation of adults who simultaneously try to meet the competing needs of their parents and their children.   *91*

Sapir-Whorf hypothesis   The idea that the language a person uses shapes his or her perception of reality and therefore his or her thoughts and actions.   *56*

Science   The body of knowledge obtained by methods based on systematic observation.   *9*

Scientific management approach   Another name for the classical theory of formal organizations.   *120*

Scientific method   A systematic, organized series of steps that ensures maximum objectivity and consistency in researching a problem.   *26*

Secondary analysis   A variety of research techniques that make use of previously collected and publicly accessible information and data.   *37*

Secondary group   A formal, impersonal group in which there is little social intimacy or mutual understanding.   *108*

Second shift   The double burden—work outside the home followed by child care and housework—that many women face and few men share equitably.   *310*

Sect   A relatively small religious group that has broken away from some other religious organization to renew what it considers the original vision of the faith.   *197*

Secularization   Religion's diminishing influence in the public sphere, especially in politics and the economy.   *199*

Segregation   The physical separation of two groups of people in terms of residence, workplace, and social events; often imposed on a minority group by a dominant group.   *332*

Self   Our sense of who we are, distinct from others, and shaped by the unique combination of our social interactions.   *76*

Serial monogamy   A form of marriage in which a person may have several spouses in his or her lifetime, but only one spouse at a time.   *156*

Sex   The biological differences between males and females.   *292*

Sexism   The ideology that one sex is superior to the other.   *308*

Sexual orientation   The categories of people to whom we are sexually attracted.   *298*

Sexuality   Denotes our identities and activities as sexual beings.   *302*

Sick role   Societal expectations about the attitudes and behavior of a person viewed as being ill.   *357*

Significant other   An individual who is most important in the development of the self, such as a parent, friend, or teacher.   *77*

Single-parent family   A family in which only one parent is present to care for the children.   *166*

Slavery   A system of enforced servitude in which some people are owned by others as property.   *239*

Social change   Significant alteration over time in behavior patterns and culture, including norms and values.   *383*

Social control   The techniques and strategies for preventing deviant human behavior in any society.   *130*

Social disorganization theory   The theory that attributes increases in crime and deviance to the absence or breakdown of communal relationships and social institutions, such as the family, school, church, and local government.   *145*

Social epidemiology   The study of the distribution of disease, impairment, and general health status across a population.   *361*

Social inequality   A condition in which members of society have different amounts of wealth, prestige, or power.   *9*

Social institution   An organized pattern of beliefs and behavior centered on basic social needs.   *113*

Social interaction   A reciprocal exchange in which two or more people read, react, and respond to each other.   *102*

Social mobility   Movement of individuals or groups from one position in a society's stratification system to another.   *241*

Social movement   An organized collective activity to bring about or resist fundamental change in an existing group or society.   *393*

Social network   A series of social relationships that links individuals directly to others, and through them indirectly to still more people.   *110*

Social role   A set of expected behaviors for people who occupy a given social status.   *105*

Social science   The study of the social features of humans and the ways in which they interact and change.   *9*

Social structure   The underlying framework of society consisting of the positions people occupy and the relationships between them.   *103*

Socialism   An economic system under which the means of production and distribution are collectively owned.   *217*

Socialization   The lifelong process through which people learn the attitudes, values, and behaviors appropriate for members of a particular culture.   *72*

Societal-reaction approach   Another name for *labeling theory*.   *146*

Society   The structure of relationships within which culture is created and shared through regularized patterns of social interaction.   *49*

Sociobiology   The systematic study of how biology affects human social behavior.   *50*

Socioeconomic status (SES)   A measure of class that is based on income, education, occupation, and related variables.   *249*

Sociological imagination   An awareness of the relationship between who we are as individuals and the social forces that shape our lives.   *4*

Sociology   The systematic study of the relationship between the individual and society and of the consequences of difference.   *4*

Standpoint theory   Because our social positions shape our perceptions, a more complete understanding of social relations must incorporate the perspectives of marginalized voices.   *302*

Status   The social positions we occupy relative to others.   *103*

Status group   People who share the same preceived level of prestige.   *244*

Stereotype An unreliable generalization about all members of a group that does not recognize individual differences within the group. *320*

Stigma A label used to devalue members of certain social groups. *136*

Strain theory of deviance Robert Merton's theory of deviance as an adaptation of socially prescribed goals or of the means governing their attainment, or both. *143*

Stratification A structured ranking of entire groups of people that perpetuates unequal economic rewards and power in a society. *238*

Subculture A segment of society that shares a distinctive pattern of mores, folkways, and values that differs from the pattern of the larger society. *63*

Substantive definition of the family A definition of the family based on blood, meaning shared genetic heritage, and law, meaning social recognition and affirmation of the bond including both marriage and adoption. *155*

Survey A study, generally in the form of an interview or questionnaire, that provides researchers with information about how people think and act. *32*

Symbol A gesture, object, or word that forms the basis of human communication. *77*

Symbolic ethnicity An ethnic identity that emphasizes concerns such as ethnic food or political issues rather than deeper ties to one's ethnic heritage. *342*

T

Teacher-expectancy effect The impact that a teacher's expectations about a student's performance may have on the student's actual achievements. *185*

Technology A form of culture in which humans modify the natural environment to meet our wants and needs. *54*

Terrorism The use or threat of violence against random or symbolic targets in pursuit of political aims. *231*

Theory In sociology a set of statements that seeks to explain problems, actions, or behavior. *10*

Total fertility rate The average number of children a woman would have during her lifetime given current birth rates and assuming she survives through her child-bearing years. *351*

Total institution An institution that regulates all aspects of a person's life under a single authority, such as a prison, the military, a mental hospital, or a convent. *90*

Totalitarianism Virtually complete government control and surveillance over all aspects of a society's social and political life. *221*

Tracking The practice of placing students in specific curriculum groups on the basis of their test scores and other criteria. *186*

Traditional authority Legitimate power conferred by custom and accepted practice. *215*

Trained incapacity The tendency of workers in a bureaucracy to become so specialized that they develop blind spots and fail to notice potential problems. *116*

Transgender People who appear to be biologically one sex but who identify with the gender of another. *303*

Transnational crime Crime that occurs across multiple national borders. *141*

U

Underclass The long-term poor who lack training and skills. *256*

V

Validity The degree to which a measure or scale truly reflects the phenomenon under study. *30*

Value A collective conception of what is considered good, desirable, and proper—or bad, undesirable, and improper—in a culture. *57*

Value neutrality Max Weber's term for objectivity of sociologists in the interpretation of data. *42*

Variable A measurable trait or characteristic that is subject to change under different conditions. *42*

Vertical mobility The movement of an individual from one social position to another of a different rank. *242*

Vested interests Those people or groups who will suffer in the event of social change and who have a stake in maintaining the status quo. *386*

Victimization survey A questionnaire or interview given to a sample of the population to determine whether people have been victims of crime. *138*

Victimless crime A term used by sociologists to describe the willing exchange among adults of widely desired, but illegal, goods and services. *140*

W

War Conflict between organizations that possess trained combat forces equipped with deadly weapons. *229*

Wealth The total of all a person's material assets, including savings, land, stocks, and other types of property, minus their debt at a single point in time. *249*

White-collar crime Illegal acts committed by affluent, "respectable" individuals in the course of business activities. *139*

World systems analysis A view of the global economic system as one divided between certain industrialized nations that control wealth and developing countries that are controlled and exploited. *270*

References

A

Aaronson, Daniel, and Bhashkar Mazumder. 2007. "Intergenerational Economic Mobility in the U.S., 1940 to 2000." FRB Chicago Working Paper No. WP 2005–12, revised February 2007. Federal Reserve Bank of Chicago. Accessed June 21, 2008 (http://ssrn.com/abstract=869435).

Abercrombie, Nicholas, Stephen Hill, and Bryan S. Turner. 1980. *The Dominant Ideology Thesis.* London: George Allen and Unwin.

———. 1990. *Dominant Ideologies.* Cambridge, MA: Unwin Hyman.

———. 2006. *The Penguin Dictionary of Sociology,* 5th ed. New York: Penguin Books.

Aberle, David E., A. K. Cohen, A. K. Davis, M. J. Leng Jr., and F. N. Sutton. 1950. "The Functional Prerequisites of a Society." *Ethics* 60 (January): 100–111.

Abma, Joyce C., Gladys M. Martinez, and Casey E. Copen. 2010. "Teenagers in the United States: Sexual Activity, Contraceptive Use, and Childbearing, National Survey of Family Growth 2006–2008." National Center for Health Statistics. *Vital and Health Statistics* 23 (30). Accessed August 9, 2011 (www.cdc.gov/nchs/data/series/sr_23/sr23_030.pdf).

Abma, Joyce C., Gladys M. Martinez, William D. Mosher, and Brittany S. Dawson. 2004. "Teenagers in the United States: Sexual Activity, Contraceptive Use, and Childbearing, 2002." National Center for Health Statistics. *Vital and Health Statistics* 23 (24). Accessed May 12, 2010 (http://www.cdc.gov/nchs/data/series/sr_23/sr23_024.pdf).

Adair-Toteff, Christopher. 2005. "Max Weber's Charisma." *Journal of Classical Sociology* 5 (2): 189–204.

Adams, Jimi. 2007. "Stained Glass Makes the Ceiling Visible: Organizational Opposition to Women in Congregational Leadership." *Gender and Society* 21 (February): 80–115.

Adams, Samantha, and Antoinette de Bont. 2007. "Information Rx: Prescribing Good Consumerism and Responsible Citizenship." *Health Care Analysis* 15 (4): 273–290.

Adbusters. 2011. "#OCCUPYWALLSTREET." Adbusters Blog July 12. Accessed May 28, 2012 (http://www.adbusters.org/blogs/adbusters-blog/occupywallstreet.html).

Addams, Jane. 1910. *Twenty Years at Hull-House.* New York: Macmillan.

———. 1930. *The Second Twenty Years at Hull-House.* New York: Macmillan.

Adler, Patricia A., and Peter Adler. 1985. "From Idealism to Pragmatic Detachment: The Academic Performance of College Athletes." *Sociology of Education* 58 (October): 241–250.

———. 1996. "Preadolescent Clique Stratification and the Hierarchy of Identity." *Sociological Inquiry* 66 (2): 111–142.

———. 2004. *Paradise Laborers: Hotel Work in the Global Economy.* Ithaca, NY: Cornell University Press.

———. 2007. "The Demedicalization of Self-Injury: From Psychopathology to Sociological Deviance." *Journal of Contemporary Ethnography* 36 (October): 537–570.

Adler, Patricia A., and Peter Adler. 2011. The Tender Cut: Inside the Hidden World of Self-Injury. New York: NYU Press.

Adler, Patricia A., Peter Adler, and John M. Johnson. 1992. "Street Corner Society Revisited." *Journal of Contemporary Ethnography* 21 (April): 3–10.

Adler, Patricia A., Steve J. Kless, and Peter Adler. 1992. "Socialization to Gender Roles: Popularity Among Elementary School Boys and Girls." *Sociology of Education* 65 (July): 169–187.

Administration for Children and Families. 2010. "Head Start Program Fact Sheet." Washington, DC: U.S. Department of Health and Human Services. Accessed June 3, 2011 (http://www.acf.hhs.gov/programs/ohs/about/fy2010.html).

Alimahomed, Sabrina. 2010. "Thinking Outside the Rainbow: Women of Color Redefining Queer Politics and Identity." *Social Identities* 16 (2): 151–168.

Allen, John L. 2008. *Student Atlas of World Politics,* 8th ed. New York: McGraw-Hill.

Allegretto, Sylvia A. 2011. "The State of Working America's Wealth, 2011: Through Volatility and Turmoil, the Gap Widens." Accessed June 9, 2011 (http://www.epi.org/page/-/BriefingPaper292.pdf?nocdn=1).

Allport, Gordon W. 1979. *The Nature of Prejudice,* 25th anniversary ed. Reading, MA: Addison-Wesley.

Alter, Alexandria. 2007. "Is This Man Cheating on His Wife?" *The Wall Street Journal,* August 10, p. W1. Accessed June 3, 2008 (http://online.wsj.com/article/SB118670164592393622.html).

Amato, Paul R., and Alan Booth. 1997. *A Generation at Risk.* Cambridge, MA: Harvard University Press.

American Academy of Cosmetic Surgery. 2010. "American Academy of Cosmetic Surgery 2009 Procedural Census." Prepared by RH Research, February. Accessed April 9, 2010 (http://www.cosmeticsurgery.org/media/2009_full_report.pdf).

American Bar Association. 2009. "Death Penalty Moratorium Implementation Project." ABA Section of Individual Rights and Responsibilities. Accessed May 20, 2009 (http://www.abanet.org/moratorium/home.html).

American Federation of Teachers. 2008. "Survey and Analysis of Teacher Salary Trends 2007." Washington, DC: American Federation of Teachers, AFL-CIO. Accessed April 19, 2010 (http://archive.aft.org/salary/2007/download/AFT2007SalarySurvey.pdf).

American Jewish Committee. 2005. "2005 Annual Survey of American Jewish Opinion." Accessed June 3, 2010 (http://www.ajc.org/site/apps/nlnet/content3.aspx?c=ijIT12PHKoG&b=846741&ct=1740283).

American National Election Studies. 2010. "The ANES Guide to Public Opinion and Electoral Behavior." Center for Political Studies, Ann Arbor, MI. Accessed July 1, 2011 (http://www.electionstudies.org/nesguide/gd-index.htm).

American Society of Plastic Surgeons. 2012. "2011 Plastic Surgery Statistics Report." ASPS National Clearing House of Plastic Surgery Procedural Statistics. Arlington Heights, IL: ASPS. Accessed April 23, 2012 (http://www.plasticsurgery.org/Documents/news-resources/statistics/2011-statistics/2011_Stats_Full_Report.pdf).

American Sociological Association. 1997. *Code of Ethics.* Washington, DC: ASA (www.asanet.org/members/ecoderev.html).

———. 2006a. *Careers in Sociology with an Undergraduate Degree in Sociology,* 7th ed. Washington, DC: ASA.

———. 2006b. "What Can I Do with a Bachelor's Degree in Sociology?" *A National Survey of Seniors Majoring in Sociology: First Glances: What Do They Know and Where Are They Going?* Washington, DC: ASA. Accessed August 2, 2008 (http://www.asanet.org/galleries/default-file/b&b_first_report_final.pdf).

Amnesty International. 1994. *Breaking the Silence: Human Rights Violations Based on Sexual Orientation.* New York: Amnesty International.

———. 2009a. "Mexico: Two Years On: The Law to Protect Women Has Had No Impact at State Level." Accessed June 15, 2009 (www.amnesty.org/en/for-media/press-releases/mexico-two-years-law-protect-women-has-had-no-impact-state-level-2009012).

———. 2009b. "Sexual Orientation and Gender Identity." Accessed June 15, 2009 (www.amnesty.org/en/sexual-orientation-and-gender-identity).

Amnesty International. 2011. "Annual Report 2011: The State of the World's Human Rights." Accessed May 28, 2012 (http://www.amnesty.org/en/annual-report/2011).

Anagnostou, Yiorgos. 2009a. "A Critique of Symbolic Ethnicity: The Ideology of Choice?" *Ethnicities* 9 (1): 94–122.

———. 2009b. "About Facts and Fictions: Reply to Herbert Gans and Mary Waters." *Ethnicities* 9 (1).

Anderson, David, and Mykol C. Hamilton. 2005. "Gender Role Stereotyping of Parents in Children's Picture Books: The Invisible Father." *Sex Roles* 52: 145–151.

Anderson, John Ward, and Molly Moore. 1993. "Born Oppressed: Women in the Developing World Face Cradle-to-Grave Discrimination, Poverty." *Washington Post,* February 14, p. A1.

Anderson, Robin J., "Dynamics of Economic Well-being: Poverty, 2004–2006." Current Population Reports, P70–123, U.S. Census

Bureau, Washington, DC, 2011. Accessed June 9, 2011 (http://www.census.gov/prod/2011pubs/p70-123.pdf).

Anderson, Terry H. 2007. *The Sixties*, 3rd ed. Englewood Cliffs, NJ: Prentice Hall.

Andrees, Beate, and Patrick Belser, eds. 2009. *Forced Labor: Coercion and Exploitation in the Private Economy*. Geneva: International Labour Organization.

Angier, Natalie. 2000. "Do Races Differ? Not Really, Genes Show." *New York Times*, August 22, p. F6. Accessed June 30, 2008 (http://query.nytimes.com/gst/fullpage.html?res=9E07E7DF1E3EF931A1575BC0A9669C8B63&scp=2&sq=natalie+angier&st=nyt).

Anti-Defamation League. 2011. "2010 Audit of Anti-Semitic Incidents." Anti-Defamation League, New York, NY, October 4. Accessed May 27, 2012 (http://www.adl.org/main_Anti_Semitism_Domestic/2010_Audit).

Arab American Institute. 2008. "Arab Americans: Demographics." Accessed July 1, 2008 (http://www.aaiusa.org/arab-americans/22/demographics).

Archibold, Randal C. 2011. "In Mexico, Massacres and Claims of Progress." *New York Times*, February 1. Accessed May 27, 2011 (http://www.nytimes.com/2011/02/02/world/americas/02mexico.html).

Arizona Daily Star. 2011. "Border Deaths Database." *Arizona Daily Star*, March 31. Accessed June 12, 2011 (http://azstarnet.com/online/databases/html_c104ad38-3877-11df-aa1a-001cc4c002e0.html).

Arora, Neeraj K., Bradford W. Hesse, Barbara K. Rimer, K. Viswanath, Marla L. Clayman, and Robert T. Croyle. 2008. "Frustrated and Confused: The American Public Rates Its Cancer-Related Information-Seeking Experiences." *Journal of General Internal Medicine* 23 (3): 223–228.

Atchley, Robert C. 1976. *The Sociology of Retirement*. New York: Wiley.

Aud, Susan, Mary Ann Fox, and Angelina KewalRamani. 2010. "Status and Trends in the Education of Racial and Ethnic Groups." National Center for Education Statistics, U.S. Department of Education, Washington, DC, NCES 2010-015. Accessed June 20, 2011 (http://nces.ed.gov/pubsearch/pubsinfo.asp?pubid=2010015).

Aud, Susan, William Hussar, Grace Kena, Kevin Bianco, Lauren Frohlich, Jana Kemp, Kim Tahan. 2011. The Condition of Education 2011. NCES 2011-033. National Center for Education Statistics, Institute for Education Sciences, U.S. Department of Education, Washington, DC. Accessed June 4, 2011 (http://nces.ed.gov/pubs2011/2011033.pdf).

Aud, Susan, William Hussar, Grace Kena, Erin Roth, Eileen Manning, Xiaolei Wang, and Jijun Zhang. 2012. *The Condition of Education 2012*. NCES Report 2012-045. National Center for Education Statstics, U.S. Department of Education, Washington, DC, May 24. Accessed May 25, 2012 (http://nces.ed.gov/pubs2012/2012045.pdf).

Auritt, Elizabelth S. 2012. "Harvard Accepts Record Low of 5.9 Percent to the Class of 2016." *The Harvard Crimson* March 29. Accessed May 16, 2012 (http://www.thecrimson.com/article/2012/3/29/admissions-harvard-rate-2016/).

Avise, John C. 2004. *The Hope, Hype, and Reality of Genetic Engineering: Remarkable Stories from Agriculture, Industry, Medicine, and the Environment*. New York: Oxford University Press.

B

Baby Name Wizard. 2012. "NameVoyager: Explore Name Trends Letter by Letter." Accessed March 14, 2012 (http://www.babynamewizard.com/voyager#).

Badoo. 2011. "Three Quarters of European Princes Marry Commoners." Badoo Trading Limited, April 26. Accessed May 30, 2011 (http://corp.badoo.com/entry/press/23/).

Baer, Hans. 2008. "Global Warming as a By-product of the Capitalist Treadmill of Production and Consumption—The Need for an Alternative Global System." *Australian Journal of Anthropology* 19 (1): 58–62.

Baer, Hans, and Ian Coulter. 2008. "Introduction—Taking Stock of Integrative Medicine: Broadening Biomedicine or Co-option of Complementary and Alternative Medicine?" *Health Sociology Review* 17 (4): 331–341.

Bagilhole, Barbara, and Simon Cross. 2006. "'It Never Struck Me as Female': Investigating Men's Entry into Female-Dominated Occupations." *Journal of Gender Studies* 15 (1): 35–48.

Bahr, Peter Riley. 2008. "*Cooling Out* in the Community College: What Is the Effect of Academic Advising on Students' Chances of Success?" *Research in Higher Education* 49: 704–732.

Bainbridge, William Sims. 2007. "The Scientific Research Potential of Virtual Worlds." *Science* 317 (July 27): 472–476.

Balch, Robert W. 2006. "The Rise and Fall of Aryan Nations: A Resource Mobilization Perspective." *Journal of Political & Military Sociology* 34 (1): 81–113.

Baldwin, James. [1965] 1985. "White Man's Guilt." pp. 409–414 in *The Price of the Ticket: Collected Nonfiction, 1948–1985*. New York: St. Martin's Press.

Balfour, Gillian. 2006. "Re-imagining a Feminist Criminology." *Canadian Journal of Criminology & Criminal Justice* 48 (5): 735–752.

Banks, Pauline and Maggie Lawrence. 2006. "The Disability Discrimination Act, a Necessary, but Not Sufficient Safeguard for People with Progressive Conditions in the Workplace? The Experiences of Younger People with Parkinson's Disease." *Disability and Rehabilitation* 28 (1): 13–24.

Banks, Duren and Tracey Kyckelhahn. 2011. "Characteristics of Suspected Human Trafficking Incidents, 2008–2010." April, NCJ 233732. Bureau of Justice Statistics, Office of Justice Programs, U.S. Department of Justice. Accessed June 8, 2011 (http://bjs.ojp.usdoj.gov/content/pub/pdf/cshti0810.pdf).

Banerjee, Neela. 2006. "Clergywomen Find Hard Path to Bigger Pulpit." *New York Times*, August 26, pp. A1, A11.

Barna Group. 2001. "Religious Beliefs Vary Widely by Denomination." Ventura, CA: The Barna Group. Accessed June 1, 2009 (http://www.barna.org/barna-update/article/5-barna-update/53-religious-beliefs-vary-widely-by-denomination).

Barnes, Patricia M., Barbara Bloom, and Richard L. Nahin. 2008. "Complementary and Alternative Medicine Use Among Adults and Children: United States, 2007." *National Health Statistics Reports* 12. Hyattsville, MD: National Center for Health Statistics. Accessed May 20, 2010 (http://nccam.nih.gov/news/2008/nhsr12.pdf).

Barnes, Patricia M., Eve Powell-Griner, Kim McFann, and Richard L. Nahin. 2004. *Complementary and Alternative Medicine Use Among Adults, United States, 2002*. Advance Data from *Vital and Health Statistics* 343. Hyattsville, MD: National Center for Health Statistics. Accessed July 5, 2008 (http://nccam.nih.gov/news/camsurvey_fs1.htm).

Barnett, Rosalind, and Caryl Rivers. 2004. *Same Difference: How Gender Myths Are Hurting Our Relationships, Our Children, and Our Jobs*. New York: Basic Books.

Barr, Donald A. 2008. *Health Disparities in the United States: Social Class, Race, Ethnicity, and Health*. Baltimore: Johns Hopkins University Press.

Barrett, David B., Todd M. Johnson, and Peter F. Crossing. 2011. "The 2010 Annual Megacensus of Religions." pp. 508-509 in *Time Almanac 2011*. Chicago: Encyclopædia Britannica.

Barrionuevo, Alexei. 2008. "Amazon's 'Forest Peoples' Seek a Role in Striking Global Climate Agreements." *New York Times*, April 6, p. 6.

Barta, Patrick, and Joel Millman. 2009. "The Great U-Turn." *The Wall Street Journal*, June 6. Accessed June 15, 2009 (http://online.wsj.com/article_email/SB124424701106590613-lMyQjAxMDI5NDA0NzIwNDc3Wj.html).

Basso, Keith H. 1972. "Ice and Travel Among the Fort Norman Slave: Folk Taxonomies and Cultural Rules." *Language in Society* 1 (March): 31–49.

Baudrillard, Jean. [1981] 1994. *Simulacra and Simulation*. Ann Arbor: University of Michigan Press.

Baumert, Kevin, Timothy Herzog, and Jonathan Pershing. 2005. *Navigating the Numbers: Greenhouse Gas Data and International Climate Policy*. Washington, DC: World Resources Institute. Accessed August 6, 2009 (http://pdf.wri.org/navigating_numbers.pdf).

Baumgardner, Jennifer, and Amy Richards. 2000. *Manifesta: Young Women, Feminism and the Future*. New York: Farrar, Straus, and Giroux.

BBC. 2006. "Madrid Bans Waifs from Catwalks." September 13. Accessed June 7, 2008 (http://news.bbc.co.uk/2/hi/europe/5341202.stm).

BBC News. 2005. "Indonesian Village Report: January 12, 2005." Accessed January 19 (www.theworld.org).

Beagan, Brenda. 2003. "Teaching Social and Cultural Awareness to Medical Students: 'It's All Very Nice to Talk About It in Theory, but Ultimately It Makes No Difference.'" *Academic Medicine* 78 (6): 605–614.

Beagan, Brenda L. 2001. "'Even If I Don't Know What I'm Doing I Can Make It Look Like I Know What I'm Doing': Becoming a Doctor in the 1990s." *Canadian Review of Sociology and Anthropology* 38: 275–292.

Bearman, Peter S., James Moody, and Katherine Stovel. 2004. "Chains of Affection: The Structure of Adolescent Romantic and Sexual Networks." *American Journal of Sociology* 110 (July): 44–91.

Beauvoir, Simone de. 1952. *The Second Sex*. New York: Knopf.

Becker, Howard S. 1963. *The Outsiders: Studies in the Sociology of Deviance*. New York: Free Press.

———. ed. 1964. *The Other Side: Perspectives on Deviance*. New York: Free Press.

Beeghley, Leonard. 2007. *The Structure of Social Stratification in the United States,* 5th ed. Boston: Allyn & Bacon.

Belkin, Lisa. 2008. "When Mom and Dad Share It All." *New York Times,* June 15. Accessed June 17, 2009 (www.nytimes.com /2008/06/15/magazine/15parenting-t.html).

Bell, Daniel. 1953. "Crime as an American Way of Life." *Antioch Review* 13 (Summer): 131–154.

———. 1999. *The Coming of Post-industrial Society: A Venture in Social Forecasting*. With new foreword. New York: Basic Books.

———. 2001. *Liberation Theology After the End of History: The Refusal to Cease Suffering*. New York: Routledge.

Benagiano, Giuseppe, and Maurizio Mori. 2009. "The Origins of Human Sexuality: Procreation or Recreation?" *Reproductive BioMedicine Online* 18 (S1): 50–59.

Bendick Jr., Marc, Charles W. Jackson, and J. Horacio Romero. 1993. *Employment Discrimination Against Older Workers: An Experimental Study of Hiring Practices*. Washington, DC: Fair Employment Council of Greater Washington.

Benhorin, Shira, and Susan D. McMahon. 2008. "Exposure to Violence and Aggression: Protective Roles of Social Support Among Urban African American Youth." *Journal of Community Psychology* 36 (6): 723–743.

Bennett, Drake. 2010. "This Will Be on the Midterm. You Feel Me? Why So Many Colleges Are Teaching *The Wire*." *Slate,* March 24. Accessed April 9, 2010 (http://www.slate.com/id/2245788/).

Bennett, V., S. Dávila-Poblete, and M. N. Rico, eds. 2005. *Opposing Currents: The Politics of Water and Gender in Latin America*. Pittsburgh, PA: University of Pittsburgh Press.

Benschop, Yvonne. 2009. "The Micro-politics of Gendering in Networking." *Gender, Work & Organization* 16 (2): 217–237.

Berenson, Alex, and Diana B. Henriques. 2008. "Look at Wall St. Wizard Finds Magic Had Skeptics." *New York Times,* December 12. Accessed May 21, 2009 (http://www.nytimes.com/2008/12/13 /business/13fraud.html).

Bergen, Raquel Kennedy. 2006. *Marital Rape: New Research and Directions*. Harrisburg, PA: VAW Net.

Berger, Peter. 1969. *The Sacred Canopy: Elements of a Sociological Theory of Religion*. Garden City, NY: Anchor Books.

Berger, Peter, and Thomas Luckmann. 1966. *The Social Construction of Reality*. New York: Doubleday.

Berland, Gretchen K. 2001. "Health Information on the Internet: Accessibility, Quality, and Readability in English and Spanish." *Journal of the American Medical Association* 285 (March 23): 2612–2621.

Berlin, Brent, and Paul Kay. 1991. *Basic Color Terms: Their Universality and Evolution*. Berkeley: University of California Press.

Bernasek, Anna. 2006. "A Poverty Line That's Out of Date and Out of Favor." *New York Times,* August 14, p. 8.

Bernburg, Jón Gunnar, Marvin D. Krohn, and Craig Rivera. 2006. "Official Labeling, Criminal Embeddedness, and Subsequent Delinquency: A Longitudinal Test of Labeling Theory." *Journal of Research in Crime & Delinquency* 43 (1): 67–88.

Bhrolcháin, Máire Ní. 2001. "'Divorce Effects' and Causality in the Social Sciences." European Sociological Review 17(1): 33–57.

Bianchi, Suzanne M., John P. Robinson, and Melissa A. Milkie. 2006. *Changing Rhythms of American Family Life*. New York: Sage.

Bisi, Simonetta. 2002. "Female Criminality and Gender Difference." *International Review of Sociology* 12 (1): 23–43.

Black, Donald. 1995. "The Epistemology of Pure Sociology." *Law and Social Inquiry* 20 (Summer): 829–870.

Black, Thomas. 2009. "Mexican Factories May Cut Fewer Jobs than in 2001." *Bloomberg News,* June 1. Accessed June 15, 2009 (www.bloomberg.com/apps/news?pid=20601086&sid=aFT3Y. rFittM&refer=news).

Blaine, Tasha. 2009. *Just Like Family: Inside the Lives of Nannies, the Parents They Work for, and the Children They Love*. Boston: Houghton Mifflin Harcourt.

Blau, Peter M., and Otis Dudley Duncan. 1967. *The American Occupational Structure*. New York: Wiley.

Blauner, Robert. 1972. *Racial Oppression in America*. New York: Harper and Row.

Bligh, Michelle C., and Jeffrey C. Kohles. 2009. "The Enduring Allure of Charisma: How Barack Obama Won the Historic 2008 Presidential Election." *Leadership Quarterly* 20 (3): 483–492.

Bloemraad, Irene, Anna Korteweg, and Gökçe Yurdakul. 2008. "Citizenship and Immigration: Multiculturalism, Assimilation, and Challenges to the Nation-State." *Annual Review of Sociology* 34: 153–179.

Bloom, David E., David Canning, Günther Fink, and Jocelyn E. Finlay. 2010. "The Cost of Low Fertility in Europe." European Journal of Population 26: 141–158.

Bloom, Stephen G. 2000. *Postville: A Clash of Cultures in Heartland America*. New York: Harcourt.

Blossfeld, Hans-Peter. 2009. "Educational Assortative Marriage in Comparative Perspective." *Annual Review of Sociology* 35 (1): 513–530.

Blumer, Herbert. 1955. "Collective Behavior." pp. 165–198 in *Principles of Sociology,* 2nd ed., ed. Alfred McClung Lee. New York: Barnes and Noble.

Boaz, Rachel Floersheim. 1987. "Early Withdrawal from the Labor Force." *Research on Aging* 9 (December): 530–547.

Bogan, Jesse, Kerry A. Dolan, Christopher Helman, and Nathan Vardi. 2008. "Failing State." *Forbes,* December 22. Accessed June 15, 2009 (www.forbes.com/global/2008/1222/058.html).

Bohn, Roger E., and James E. Short. 2010. *How Much Information? 2009 Report on American Consumers*. San Diego: Global Information Industry Center.

Bolt, Gideon, A. Sule Ozuekren, and Deborah Phillips. 2010. "Linking Integration and Residential Segregation." *Journal of Ethnic & Migration Studies* 36 (2): 169–186.

Bonilla-Silva, Eduardo. 2010. *Racism Without Racists: Color-Blind Racism and the Persistence of Racial Inequality in America,* 3rd ed. Lanham, MD: Rowman & Littlefield.

Bongaarts, John. 2009. "Human Population Growth and the Demographic Transition." Philosophical Transactions of the Royal Society, Series B, Biological Sciences 364: 2985–2990.

Booth, Alan, and Paul R. Amato. 2001. "Parental Predivorce Relations and Offspring Postdivorce Well-Being." *Journal of Marriage and the Family* 62: 197–212.

Booth, William. 2009. "In Mexico, the U.S. Downturn Hits Home." *Washington Post,* June 14. Accessed June 15, 2009 (www .washingtonpost.com/wp-dyn/content/story/2009/06/14/ST2009 061400169.html).

Bortolotti, Dan. 2006. *Hope in Hell: Inside the World of Doctors Without Borders*. Buffalo, NY: Firefly Books.

Bouis, Howarth E. 2007. "The Potential of Genetically Modified Food Crops to Improve Human Nutrition in Developing Countries." *Journal of Development Studies* 43 (1): 79–96.

Bourdieu, Pierre. 1962. *The Algerians*. Preface by Raymond Aron. Boston: Beacon Press.

———. 1984. *Distinction: A Social Critique of the Judgment of Taste*. Cambridge, MA: Harvard University Press.

———. 1986. "The Forms of Capital." pp. 241–258 in *Handbook of Theory and Research for the Sociology of Education,* ed. J.G. Richardson. New York: Greenwood Press.

———. 1998a. *Acts of Resistance: Against the Tyranny of the Market.* New York: New Press.

———. 1998b. *On Television.* New York: New Press.

Boushey, Heather. 2009. "Gender and the Recession: Recession Hits Traditionally Male Jobs Hardest." Center for American Progress, Washington, DC. Accessed June 4, 2009 (www.americanprogress.org/issues/2009/05/gender_recession.html).

Bowles, Samuel, and Herbert Gintis. 1976. *Schooling in Capitalistic America: Educational Reforms and the Contradictions of Economic Life.* New York: Basic Books.

BP Exploration & Production Inc. 2009. *Initial Exploration Plan: Mississippi Canyon Block 252.* OCS-G 32306, February. Accessed May 19, 2010 (http://www.gomr.mms.gov/PI/PDFImages/PLANS/29/29977.pdf).

Brand, Jennie E., and Yu Xie. 2010. "Who Benefits Most from College? Evidence for Negative Selection in Heterogeneous Economic Returns to Higher Education." *American Sociological Review* 75 (2): 273–302.

Brandon, Emily. 2012. "The New Ideal Retirement Age: 67." Planning to Retire, Money, *U.S. News & World Report*, May 8. Accessed May 22, 2012 (http://money.usnews.com/money/blogs/planning-to-retire/2012/05/08/the-new-ideal-retirement-age-67).

Brannigan, Augustine, and William Zwerman. 2001. "The Real 'Hawthorne Effect.'" *Society* 38 (January/February): 55–60.

Bray, Hiawatha. 2009. "Finding a Way Around Iranian Censorship." *Boston Globe,* June 19. Accessed July 1, 2009 (www.boston.com/business/technology/articles/2009/06/19/activists_utilizing_twitter_web_proxies_to_sidestep_iranian_censorship/).

Brewer, Cynthia A., and Trudy A. Suchan. 2001. *Mapping Census 2000: The Geography of U.S. Diversity.* Washington, DC: U.S. Government Printing Office.

Brewer, Rose M., and Nancy A. Heitzeg. 2008. "The Racialization of Criminal Punishment." *American Behavioral Scientist* 51 (January): 625–644.

Brewin, Bob. 2011. "Army Taps Second Life for Troop and Family Support." NextGov, February 3. Accessed May 25, 2011 (http://www.nextgov.com/nextgov/ng_20110203_6055.php).

Brickell, Chris. 2009. "Sexuality and the Dimensions of Power." *Sexuality & Culture* 13 (2): 57–74.

Bricker, Jesse, Brian Bucks, Arthur Kennickell, Traci Mach, and Kevin Moore. 2011. "Surveying the Aftermath of the Storm: Changes in Family Finances from 2007 to 2009." Paper No. 2011–17. Finance and Economics Discussion Series, Divisions of Research & Statistics and Monetary Affairs, Federal Reserve Board, Washington, D.C. Accessed June 9, 2011 (http://www.federalreserve.gov/Pubs/feds/2011/201117/201117pap.pdf).

Brooks, Ann. 1997. *Postfeminisms: Feminism, Cultural Theory, and Cultural Forms.* New York: Routledge.

Brooks, Kelly D., and Kathryn Quina. 2009. "Women's Sexual Identity Patterns: Differences Among Lesbians, Bisexuals, and Unlabeled Women." *Journal of Homosexuality* 56 (8): 1030–1045.

Brown, David K. 2001. "The Social Sources of Educational Credentialism: Status Cultures, Labor Markets, and Organizations." *Sociology of Education* 74 (Extra Issue): 19–34.

Brown, George M. 2006. "Degrees of Doubt: Legitimate, Real and Fake Qualifications in a Global Market." *Journal of Higher Education Policy & Management* (1): 71–79.

Brown, Meta, Andrew Haughwout, Donghoon Lee, Maricar Mabutas, and Wilbert van der Klaauw. 2012. "Grading Student Loans." Federal Reserve Bank of New York, March 5. Accessed May 22, 2012 (http://libertystreeteconomics.newyorkfed.org/2012/03/grading-student-loans.html).

Brown, Robert McAfee. 1980. *Gustavo Gutierrez.* Atlanta: John Knox.

Brownfield, David, Ann Marie Sorenson, and Kevin M. Thompson. 2001. "Gang Membership, Race, and Social Class: A Test of the Group Hazard and Master Status Hypotheses." *Deviant Behavior* 22 (1): 73–89.

Bruce, Steve. 2000. *Choice and Religion: A Critique of Rational Choice Theory.* New York: Oxford University Press.

Buckle, Chris, Y. M. Lisa Chuah, Calvin S. Fones, and Albert H. C. Wong. 2007. "A Conceptual History of Koro." *Transcultural Psychiatry* 44 (1): 27–43.

Bucks, Brian K., Arthur B. Kennickell, Traci L. Mach, and Kevin B. Moore. 2009. "Changes in U.S. Family Finances from 2004 to 2007: Evidence from the Survey of Consumer Finances." *Federal Reserve Bulletin* 95 (February): A1–A55.

Bullard, Robert. 2000. *Dumping in Dixie: Race, Class, and Environmental Quality,* 3rd ed. Boulder, CO: Westview Press.

Bulle, Wolfgang F. 1987. *Crossing Cultures? Southeast Asian Mainland.* Atlanta: Centers for Disease Control and Prevention.

Bullough, Vern L. 1998. "Alfred Kinsey and the Kinsey Report: Historical Overview and Lasting Contributions." *Journal of Sex Research* 35 (2): 127–131.

Burawoy, Michael. 2004. "Public Sociologies: Contradictions, Dilemmas, and Possibilities." *Social Forces* 82: 1603–1618.

Bureau of Economic Analysis. 2011. "Gross Domestic Product: Fourth Quarter and Annual 2010 (Third Estimate)." New Release, BEA 11–13, March 25. U.S. Department of Commerce, Washington, DC. Accessed June 11, 2011 (http://www.bea.gov/newsreleases/national/gdp/2011/pdf/gdp4q10_3rd.pdf).

Bureau of the Census. 2007b. "American Community Survey 2006" (www.census.gov).

———. 2008. *Statistical Abstract of the United States.* Washington, DC: U.S. Government Printing Office.

Bureau of Labor Statistics. 2007. "Labor Force (Demographic) Data." February 13. Accessed February 28, 2007 (www.bls.gov).

———. 2008a. "Employment Characteristics of Families in 2007." Accessed May 26, 2009 (http://www.bls.gov/news.release/famee.toc.htm).

———. 2008b. "Number of Jobs Held, Labor Market Activity, and Earnings Growth Among the Youngest Baby Boomers: Results from a Longitudinal Survey." *BLS News,* June 27. Accessed May 6, 2009 (http://www.bls.gov/news.release/pdf/nlsoy.pdf).

———. 2008c. "Highlights of Women's Earnings in 2007." U.S. Department of Labor, October, Report 1008. Accessed June 17, 2009 (www.bls.gov/cps/cpswom2007.pdf).

———. 2009b. "International Comparisons of Hourly Compensation Costs in Manufacturing, 2007." *Bureau of Labor Statistics News,* March 26. Accessed June 14, 2009 (www.bls.gov/news.release/pdf/ichcc.pdf).

———. 2009c. "Employment Characteristics of Families in 2008." Accessed April 11, 2010 (http://www.bls.gov/news.release/famee.toc.html).

———. 2010a. "Civilian Labor Force, 2008–2018." Employment Projections, Labor Force (Demographic) Data. Accessed April 20, 2010 (http://www/bls.gov/emp/ep_data_labor_force.htm).

———. 2010b. "Civilian Labor Force, 2019–2050." Employment Projections, Labor Force (Demographic) Data. Accessed April 20, 2010 (http://www/bls.gov/emp/ep_data_labor_force.htm).

———. 2010c. "Women in the Labor Force: A Databook." December, Report 1026. Accessed June 14, 2011 (http://www.bls.gov/cps/wlf-databook2010.htm).

———. 2011e. "Labor Force Statistics." Current Population Survey, Databases, Tables & Calculators by Subject. Washington, DC: United States Department of Labor. Accessed July 1, 2011 (http://www.bls.gov/data/#employment).

———. 2011f. "Women in the Labor Force: A Databook." Report 1034, December. Accessed May 26, 2012 (http://www.bls.gov/cps/wlf-databook-2011.pdf).

———. 2011g. "Highlights of Women's Earnings in 2010." U.S. Department of Labor, July. Accessed May 26, 2012 (http://www.bls.gov/cps/cpswom2010.pdf).

Bureau of Labor Statistics. 2012a. "Unemployment: Rates & Levels—Labor Force Statistics including the National Unemployment Rate." Current Population Survey, Databases, Tables & Calculators by Subject. Washington, DC: United States Department of Labor. Accessed March 10, 2012 (http://www.bls.gov/data/#unemployment).

———. 2012b. "Employment Characteristics of Families—2011." U.S. Department of Labor, USDL-12-0771. Accessed May 3, 2012 (http://www.bls.gov/news.release/pdf/famee.pdf).

———. 2012c. "College Enrollment and Work Activity of 2011 High School Graduates." United States Department of Labor, 12-0716. Accessed May 15, 2012 (http://www.bls.gov/news.release/pdf/hsgec.pdf).

———. 2012d. "2012 Employment & Earnings Online: Household Survey Data." United States Department of Labor. Accessed May 16, 2012 (www.bls.gov/opub/ee/2012/cps/annual.htm).

———. 2012e. "Volunteering in the United States —2011." U.S. Department of Labor, February 22, Report 12-0329. Accessed May 25, 2012 (http://www.bls.gov/news.release/pdf/volun.pdf).

———. 2012f. "Annual Average Household Data." Household Survey Data, 2012 Employment & Earnings Online, Office of Publications & Special Studies. Accessed May 26, 2012 (http://www.bls.gov /opub/ee/2012/cps/annual.htm).

Burgoon, Judee K., Laura K. Guerrero, and Kory Floyd. 2010. *Nonverbal Communication.* New York: Allyn & Bacon.

Burkitt, Laurie. 2012. "Starbucks Price Increase Stirs China's Netizens." *The Wall Street Journal* February 1. Accessed March 24, 2012 (http://blogs.wsj.com/chinarealtime/2012/02/01/starbucks-price-increase-stirs-chinas-netizens/).

Butler, Daniel Allen. 1998. *Unsinkable: The Full Story.* Mechanicsburg, PA: Stackpole Books.

Butler, Robert N. 1990. "A Disease Called Ageism." *Journal of American Geriatrics Society* 38 (February): 178–180.

C

Call, V. R., and J. D. Teachman. 1991. "Military Service and Stability in the Family Life Course." *Military Psychology* 3: 233–250.

Callaway, Ewen. 2008. "Polygamy Is the Key to a Long Life." *New Scientist,* August 19. Accessed May 26, 2009 (http://www.newscientist .com/article/dn14564-polygamy-is-the-key-to-a-long-life.html).

Camp, Roderic Ai. 2010a. The Metamorphosis of Leadership in a Democratic Mexico. New York: Oxford University Press.

———. 2010b. Armed Forces and Drugs: Public Perceptions and Institutional Challenges. pp. 291–325 in Shared Responsibility: U.S.-Mexico Policy Options for Confronting Organized Crime, ed. Eric L. Olson, David A. Shirk, and Andrew Selee. San Diego: University of San Diego Trans-Border Institute.

Cañas, Jesus, and Robert W. Gilmer. 2009. "The Maquiladora's Changing Geography." Federal Reserve Bank of Dallas, *Southwest Economy*: Second Quarter. Accessed June 14, 2009 (http://dallasfed.org /research/swe/2009/swe0902c.cfm).

Caplan, Ronald L. 1989. "The Commodification of American Health Care." *Social Science and Medicine* 28 (11): 1139–1148.

Caplow, Theodore, and Louis Hicks. 2002. *Systems of War and Peace,* 2nd ed. Lanham, MD: University Press of America.

Cai, Yong. 2010. "China's Below-Replacement Fertility: Government Policy or Socioeconomic Development?" Population and Development Review 36: 419–440.

Carey, Anne R., and Elys A. McLean. 1997. "Heard It Through the Grapevine?" *USA Today,* September 15, p. B1.

Carmichael, Mary. 2007. "Troubled Waters." *Newsweek* 149 (June 4): 52–56.

Carr, Deborah. 2007. "Baby Blues." *Contexts* (Spring): 62.

Carr, Nicholas. 2010. The Shallows: What the Internet Is Doing to Our Brains. New York: W. W. Norton & Company.

Carson, Rachel. 1962. *Silent Spring.* Boston: Houghton Mifflin.

Carter, Susan B., Scott Sigmund Gartner, Michael R. Haines, Alan L. Olmstead, Richard Sutch, and Gavin Wright. 2006. *Historical Statistics of the United States: Earliest Times to the Present, Millennial Edition.* 5 vols. Cambridge: Cambridge University Press.

Carty, Victoria, and Jake Onyett. 2006. "Protest, Cyberactivism and New Social Movements: The Reemergence of the Peace Movement Post 9/11." *Social Movement Studies* 5 (3): 229–249.

Castañeda, Jorge G. 1995. "Ferocious Differences." *Atlantic Monthly* 276 (July): 68–69, 71–76.

Castells, Manuel. 1997. *The Power of Identity.* Vol. 1 of *The Information Age: Economy, Society and Culture.* London: Blackwell.

———. 1998. *End of Millennium.* Vol. 3 of *The Information Age: Economy, Society and Culture.* London: Blackwell.

———. 2000. *The Information Age: Economy, Society and Culture* (3 vols.), 2nd ed. Oxford and Malden, MA: Blackwell.

Catalano, Shannan, Erica Smith, Howard Snyder, and Michael Rand. 2009. "Female Victims of Violence." Bureau of Justice Statistics, Selected Findings, September, NCJ 228356. Accessed June 2, 2010 (http://bjs.ojp.usdoj.gov/content/pub/pdf/fvv.pdf).

Catalyst. 2007. *2007 Catalyst Census of Women Board Directors, Corporate Officers, and Top Earners.* New York: Catalyst.

Catalyst 2011a. "2011 Catalyst Census: Fortune 500 Women Board Directors." Catalyst, The Prout Group, The Executive Leadership Council, the Hispanic, Association on Corporate Responsibility, and Leadership Education for Asian Pacifics, Inc. Accessed May 26, 2012 (http:// www.catalyst.org/file/533/2011_fortune_500_census_wbd.pdf).

Catalyst 2012a. "Women CEOs of the Fortune 1000." Catalyst, The Prout Group, The Executive Leadership Council, the Hispanic, Association on Corporate Responsibility, and Leadership Education for Asian Pacifics, Inc. Accessed May 26, 2012 (http://catalyst .org/publication/271/women-ceos-of-the-fortune-1000).

Cavalli-Sforza, L. Luca, Paolo Menozzi, and Alberto Piazza. 1994. *The History and Geography of Human Genes.* Princeton, NJ: Princeton University Press.

CBS News. 1979. Transcript of *Sixty Minutes* segment "I Was Only Following Orders." March 31, pp. 2–8.

Center for American Women and Politics. 2011a. "Women in Elective Office 2011." CAWP Fact Sheet, Eagleton Institute of Politics, Rutgers University, New Brunswick, NJ. Accessed June 14, 2011 (http://www.cawp.rutgers.edu/fast_facts/levels_of_office /documents/elective.pdf).

———. 2011b. "Historical Information about Women in Congress." Eagleton Institute of Politics, Rutgers University, New Brunswick, NJ. Accessed June 14, 2011 (http://www.cawp.rutgers.edu/fast _facts/levels_of_office/Congress-HistoricalInfo.php).

Centers for Disease Control and Prevention. 2008. "Youth Risk Behavior Surveillance—United States, 2007." Surveillance Summaries, June 6. *Morbidity and Mortality Weekly Report* 57 (SS-4). Accessed June 1, 2010 (http://www/cdc.gov/mmwr/PDF/ss/ss5704.pdf).

———. 2010. "Youth Risk Behavior Surveillance—United States, 2009." Surveillance Summaries, June 4. MMWR 59 (SS-5). Accessed June 15, 2011 (http://www.cdc.gov/mmwr/pdf/ss/ss5905.pdf).

Centers for Medicare and Medicaid Services. 2010a. "National Health Expenditure Web Tables." U.S. Department of Health and Human Services. Accessed May 20, 2010 (https://www.cms.gov /NationalHealthExpendData/downloads/tables.pdf).

———. 2010b. "National Health Expenditure Projections 2009–2019." U.S. Department of Health and Human Services. Accessed May 20, 2010 (https://www.cms.gov/NationalHealthExpendData /downloads/proj2009.pdf).

Centers for Medicare and Medicaid Services. 2012a. "National Health Expenditure Tables." U.S. Department of Health and Human Services. Accessed May 28, 2012 (http://www.cms.gov/Research-Statistics-Data-and-Systems/Statistics-Trends-and-Reports /NationalHealthExpendData/Downloads/tables.pdf).

———. 2012b. "National Health Expenditure Projections 2010–2020." U.S. Department of Health and Human Services. Accessed May 28, 2012 (https://www.cms.gov/Research-Statistics-Data-and-Systems /Statistics-Trends-and-Reports/NationalHealthExpendData /downloads/proj2010.pdf).

Césaire, Aimé. 1972 *Discourse on Colonialism.* New York: Monthly Review Press.

Cevallos, Diego. 2009. "Indigenous Woman Fights for Rights." *Inter Press Service,* April 1. Accessed June 15, 2009 (www.ips.org/mdg3 /mexico-indigenous-woman-on-the-offensive/#more-21).

Chambers, Samuel. 2007. " 'An Incalculable Effect': Subversions of Heteronormativity." *Political Studies* 55 (3): 656–679.

Chambliss, William. 1973. "The Saints and the Roughnecks." *Society* 11 (November/December): 24–31.

Chandra, Anjani, William D. Mosher, Casey Copen, and Catlainn Sionean. 2011. "Sexual Behavior, Sexual Attraction, and Sexual Identity in the United States: Data from the 2006–2008 National Survey of Family Growth." National Center for Health Statistics.

National Health Statistics Reports 36, March 3. Accessed August 9, 2011 (www.cdc.gov/nchs/data/nhsr/nhsr036.pdf).

Charter, David, and Jill Sherman. 1996. "Schools Must Teach New Code of Values." *London Times*, January 15, p. 1.

Chee, Kyong Hee, Nathan W. Pino, and William L. Smith. 2005. "Gender Differences in the Academic Ethic and Academic Achievement." College Student Journal 39 (3): 604–618.

Chen, Shaohua, and Martin Ravallion. 2008. "The Developing World Is Poorer Than We Thought, but No Less Successful in the Fight Against Poverty." Policy Research Working Paper 4703, World Bank Development Research Group, August 2008. Accessed June 13, 2009 (www-wds.worldbank.org/external/default/WDS Content-Server/IW3P/IB/2008/08/26/000158349_20080826113239 /Rendered/PDF/WPS4703.pdf).

———. 2009. "The Impact of the Global Financial Crisis on the World's Poorest." April 30. Accessed June 13, 2009 (www.voxeu .org/index.php?q=node/3520).

Cheng, Shu-Ju Ada. 2003. "Rethinking the Globalization of Domestic Service." *Gender and Society* 17 (2): 166–186.

Cherlin, Andrew. 2004. "The Deinstitutionalization of American Marriage." *Journal of Marriage and Family* 66: 848–861.

———. 2006. "On Single Mothers 'Doing' Family." *Journal of Marriage and Family* 68 (November): 800–803.

———. 2008a. "Can the Left Learn the Lessons of Welfare Reform?" *Contemporary Sociology* 37 (March): 101–104.

———. 2008b. *Public and Private Families: An Introduction,* 5th ed. New York: McGraw-Hill.

———. 2009. *The Marriage-Go-Round: The State of Marriage and the Family in America Today.* New York: Knopf.

Chesney-Lind, Meda. 1989. "Girls' Crime and Women's Place: Toward a Feminist Model of Female Delinquency." *Crime and Delinquency* 35: 5–29.

Chesney-Lind, Meda, and Lisa Pasko. 2004. *The Female Offender: Girls, Women, and Crime,* 2nd ed. Thousand Oaks, CA: Sage.

Chu, Henry. 2011. "Britain Celebrates the Royal Wedding." *Los Angeles Times,* April 29. Accessed May 30, 2011 (http://articles.latimes. com/2011/apr/29/world/la-fg-royal-wedding-20110430).

Chun, Helen, Maria I. Tavarez, Grace E. Dann, and Michael P. Anastario. 2011. "Interviewer Gender and Self-Reported Sexual Behavior and Mental Health among Male Military Personnel." *International Journal of Public Health* 56 (2): 225:229.

Christian, Joseph. 2009. "Coffee Culture: A Symbol of Middle-Class Lifestyle." *China Daily,* November 3. Accessed April 1, 2010 (http:// www.chinadaily.com.cn/cndy/2009–11/03/content_8903174.htm).

Cigar, Norman. 1995. *Genocide in Bosnia: The Policy of "Ethnic Cleansing."* College Station: Texas A&M University Press.

Circle. 2011. "The Youth Vote in 2010: Final Estimates Based on Census Data." The Center for Information & Research on Civic Learning & Engagement, April 15. Medford, MA: Tufts University. Accessed June 8, 2011 (http://www.civicyouth.org/wp-content /uploads/2011/04/The-CPS-youth-vote-2010-FS-FINAL1.pdf).

Clammer, John. 2009. "Sociology and Beyond: Towards a Deep Sociology." *Asian Journal of Social Science* 37 (3): 332–346.

Clark, Burton. 1960. "The 'Cooling-Out' Function in Higher Education." *American Journal of Sociology* 65: 569–576.

———. 1980. "The 'Cooling-Out' Function Revisited." *New Directions for Community Colleges* 32: 15–31.

Clark, Burton, and Martin Trow. 1966. "The Organizational Context." pp. 17–70 in *The Study of College Peer Groups,* ed. Theodore M. Newcomb and Everett K. Wilson. Chicago: Aldine.

Clarke, Adele E., Janet K. Shim, Laura Maro, Jennifer Ruth Fusket, and Jennifer R. Fishman. 2003. "Bio Medicalization: Technoscientific Transformations of Health, Illness, and U.S. Biomedicine." *American Sociological Review* 68 (April): 161–194.

Clarke, Edward H. 1874. *Sex in Education; or, A Fair Chance for Girls.* Boston: James R. Osgood.

Clemons, Steve. 2011. "GOP an Oligarchy or Democracy? It Matters." *The Atlantic,* July 6. Accessed July 22, 2011 (www.theatlantic.com /national/archive/2011/07/gop-an-oligarchy-or-democracy-it-matters/241506/).

Clinard, Marshall B., and Robert F. Miller. 1998. *Sociology of Deviant Behavior,* 10th ed. Fort Worth, TX: Harcourt Brace.

CNN. 2006. "Skinny Models Banned from Catwalk." September 13. Accessed June 7, 2008 (http://www.cnn.com/2006/WORLD/ europe/09/13/spain.models/index.html).

———. 2008. "Exit Polls." CNN Election Center 2008. Accessed May 27, 2009 (http://www.cnn.com/ELECTION/2008/results /polls/#val=USP00p3).

Cognard-Black, Andrew J. 2004. "Will They Stay, or Will They Go? Sex-Atypical Work Among Token Men Who Teach?" *Sociological Quarterly* 45: 113–139.

Cohn, D'Vera. 2011. "Multi-Race and the 2010 Census." Pew Research Center April 6. Accessed June 18, 2011 (http://pewresearch.org /pubs/1953/multi-race-2010-census-obama).

Cohn, D'Vera, Jeffrey S. Passel, Wendy Wang and Gretchen Livingston. 2012. "Barely Half of U.S. Adults Are Married—A Record Low." A Social & Demographic Trends Report, Pew Research Center, December 14. Accessed May 2, 2012 (http://www .pewsocialtrends.org/files/2011/12/Marriage-Decline.pdf).

Colby, David C. 1986. "The Voting Rights Act and Black Registration in Mississippi." *Publius* 16 (Fall): 123–137.

Cole, Elizabeth S. 1985. "Adoption, History, Policy, and Program." pp. 638–666 in *A Handbook of Child Welfare,* ed. John Laird and Ann Hartman. New York: Free Press.

Coleman, James William. 2006. *The Criminal Elite: Understanding White-Collar Crime,* 6th ed. New York: Worth.

Collins, Gail. 2003. *America's Women.* New York: HarperCollins.

Collins, Patricia Hill. 2000. *Black Feminist Thought,* 2nd ed. New York: Routledge.

Commission for the Status of Women. 2009. "The Fifty-Third Session of the Commission on the Status of Women." Division for the Advancement of Women, Department of Economic and Social Affairs. March 2–13, Washington, DC. Accessed June 6, 2009 (http://www.un.org/womenwatch/daw/csw/53sess.htm).

Commission on Civil Rights. 1976. *A Guide to Federal Laws and Regulations Prohibiting Sex Discrimination.* Washington, DC: U.S. Government Printing Office.

Commoner, Barry. 1971. *The Closing Circle.* New York: Knopf.

———. 1990. *Making Peace with the Planet.* New York: Pantheon Books.

Connell, R. W. 2002. *Gender.* Cambridge, UK: Polity Press.

———. 2005. *Masculinities,* 2nd ed. Berkeley: University of California Press.

Connolly, Ceci. 2008. "As Latin Nations Treat Gays Better, Asylum Is Elusive." *Washington Post,* August 12. Accessed May 28, 2010 (http://www.washingtonpost.com/wp-dyn/content/article/2008 /08/11/AR2008081102038.html).

Conrad, Peter. 2007. *The Medicalization of Society: On the Transformation of Human Conditions into Treatable Disorders.* Baltimore: Johns Hopkins University Press.

Cooley, Charles. H. 1902. *Human Nature and the Social Order.* New York: Scribner.

Coontz, Stephanie. 1992. *The Way We Never Were: American Families and the Nostalgia Trap.* New York: Basic Books.

———. 2005. *Marriage, a History: From Obedience to Intimacy or How Love Conquered Marriage.* New York: Viking.

———. 2006. "A Pop Quiz on Marriage." *New York Times,* February 19, p. 12.

———. 2008. "The Future of Marriage." *Cato Unbound,* January 14. Accessed August 2, 2010 (http://www.cato-unbound .org/2008/01/14/stephanie-coontz/the-future-of-marriage).

———. 2011. *A Strange Stirring: The Feminine Mystique and American Women at the Dawn of the 1960s.* New York: Basic Books.

Cooper, Bruce S., and John Sureau. 2007. "The Politics of Homeschooling: New Developments, New Challenges." *Educational Policy* 21 (January and March): 110–131.

Cooper, K., S. Day, A. Green, and H. Ward. 2007. "Maids, Migrants and Occupational Health in the London Sex Industry. *Anthropology and Medicine* 14 (April): 41–53.

Cooperstone, Josie. 2011. "Japan Relief Fundraiser Press Release." Amaretto Breedable, April 18. Accessed May 25, 2011 (http:// amarettobreedables.com/blogs/5/28/japan-relief-fundraiser-press).

References

Corak, Miles. 2006. "Do Poor Children Become Poor Adults? Lessons from a Cross Country Comparison of Generational Earnings Mobility." Institute for the Study of Labor (IZA) Discussion Paper No. 1993, March. Accessed June 24, 2008 (http://papers.ssrn.com /sol3/papers.cfm?abstract_id=889034).

———. 2010. "Chasing the Same Dream, Climbing Different Ladders: Economic Mobility in the United States and Canada." Economic Mobility Project: An Initiative of the Pew Charitable Trusts. Accessed April 26, 2010 (http://www.economicmobility.org/assets /pdfs/PEW_EMP_US-CANADA.pdf).

Corbett, Christianne, Catherine Hill, and Andresse St. Rose. 2008. *Where the Girls Are: The Facts About Gender Equity in Education.* Washington, DC: AAUW. Accessed May 29, 2009 (http://www .aauw.org/research/upload/whereGirlsAre.pdf).

Correll, Shelley J., Stephen Benard, and In Paik. 2007. "Getting a Job: Is There a Motherhood Penalty?" *AJS* 112 (5): 1297–1338.

Coser, Rose Laub. 1984. "American Medicine's Ambiguous Progress." *Contemporary Sociology* 13 (January): 9–13.

Côté, James E. 2000. *Arrested Adulthood: The Changing Nature of Identity and Maturity in the Late World.* New York: New York University.

Cox, Oliver C. 1948. *Caste, Class, and Race: A Study in Social Dynamics.* Detroit: Wayne State University Press.

Crabtree, Catherine. 2009. "Rethinking Sexual Identity." *Existential Analysis* 20 (2): 248–261.

Croucher, Sheila L. 2004. *Globalization and Belonging: The Politics of Identity in a Changing World.* Lanham, MD: Rowman & Littlefield.

Crouse, Kelly. 1999. "Sociology of the Titanic." *Teaching Sociology Listserv,* May 24.

CTIA. 2011. "Background on CTIA's Semi-Annual Wireless Industry Survey." CTIA–the Wireless Association. Accessed March 24, 2012 (http://files.ctia.org/pdf/CTIA_Survey_MY_2011_Graphics.pdf).

Cullen, Lisa Takevchi. 2007. "Till Work Do Us Part." *Time,* October 8, pp. 63–64.

Cumming, Elaine, and William E. Henry. 1961. *Growing Old: The Process of Disengagement.* New York: Basic Books.

Currie, Elliot. 1985. *Confronting Crime: An American Challenge.* New York: Pantheon Books.

———. 1998. *Crime and Punishment in America.* New York: Metropolitan Books.

Curtiss, Susan. 1977. *Genie: A Psycholinguistic Study of a Modern Day "Wild Child."* New York: Academic Press.

D

Dahl, Robert A. 1961. *Who Governs?* New Haven, CT: Yale University Press.

Daisey, Mike. 2002. *21 Dog Years: Doing Time @ Amazon.com.* New York: Free Press.

Dalla, Rochelle L., and Wendy C. Gamble. 2001. "Teenage Mothering and the Navajo Reservation: An Examination of Intergovernmental Perceptions and Beliefs." *American Indian Culture and Research Journal* 25 (1): 1–19.

Dao, James. 1995. "New York's Highest Court Rules Unmarried Couples Can Adopt." *New York Times,* November 3, pp. A1, B2.

Darwin, Charles. 1859. *On the Origin of Species.* London: John Murray.

David, Gary. 2004. "Scholarship on Arab Americans Distorted Past 9/11." *Al Jadid* (Winter/Spring): 26–27.

———. 2008. "Arab Americans." pp. 84–87 in *Encyclopedia of Race, Ethnicity, and Society,* vol. 1, ed. Richard T. Schaefer. Thousand Oaks, CA: Sage.

Davidov, Eldad, Peter Schmidt, and Shalom H. Schwartz. 2008. "Bringing Values Back In." *Public Opinion Quarterly* 72 (3): 420–445.

Davies, James, Rodrigo Lluberas, and Anthony Shorrocks. 2011. "Global Wealth Databook 2011." Credit Suisse Research Institute, October. Accessed May 18, 2012 (https://infocus.credit-suisse. com/data/_product_documents/_shop/324292/2011_global _wealth_report_databook.pdf).

Davis, Darren W. and Brian D. Silver. 2003. "Stereotype Threat and Race of Interviewer Effects in a Survey on Political Knowledge." *American Journal of Political Science* 47(1): 33–45.

Davis, Gerald. 2003. *America's Corporate Banks Are Separated by Just Four Handshakes.* Accessed August 2, 2010 (http://www .ns.umich.edu/index.html?Releases/2002/Dec02/chr121002).

———. 2004. "American Cronyism: How Executive Networks Inflated the Corporate Bubble." *Contexts* (Summer): 34–40.

Davis, James A., Tom W. Smith, and Peter V. Marsden. 2007. *General Social Surveys, 1972–2006: Cumulative Codebook.* Chicago: National Opinion Research Center.

Davis, Joseph E. 2006. "How Medicalization Lost Its Way." *Society* 43 (6): 51–56.

Davis, Kingsley. 1940. "Extreme Social Isolation of a Child." *American Journal of Sociology* 45 (January): 554–565.

———. 1947. "A Final Note on a Case of Extreme Isolation." *American Journal of Sociology* 52 (March): 432–437.

Davis, Kingsley, and Wilbert E. Moore. 1945. "Some Principles of Stratification." *American Sociological Review* 10 (April): 242–249.

Dawson, Lorne. 2009. "Church-Sect-Cult: Constructing Typologies of Religious Groups." pp. 525–544 in *The Oxford Handbook of the Sociology of Religion,* ed. Peter B. Clarke. New York: Oxford University Press.

Death Penalty Information Center. 2012. "Facts about the Death Penalty." Washington, DC, April 20. Accessed April 24, 2012 (http:// www.deathpenaltyinfo.org/documents/FactSheet.pdf).

DeCarlo, Scott. 2012. "America's Highest Paid CEOs." *Forbes* April 4. Accessed May 16, 2012 (http://www.forbes.com/sites /scottdecarlo/2012/04/04/americas-highest-paid-ceos/).

Deflem, Mathieu. 2005. "'Wild Beasts Without Nationality': The Uncertain Origins of Interpol, 1898–1910." pp. 275–285 in *Handbook of Transnational Crime and Justice,* ed. Philip Rerchel. Thousand Oaks, CA: Sage.

Deflem, Mathieu. 2008. *Sociology of Law: Visions of a Scholarly Tradition.* Cambridge: Cambridge University Press.

DeMott, Benjamin. 1990. *The Imperial Middle: Why Americans Can't Think Straight About Class.* New York: Morrow.

———. 2009b. "Income, Poverty, and Health Insurance Coverage in the United States: 2008." *Current Population Reports* pp. 60–233. Washington, DC: U.S. Government Printing Office.

DeNavas-Walt, Carmen, Bernadette D. Proctor, and Jessica C. Smith. 2011. "Income, Poverty, and Health Insurance Coverage in the United States: 2010." *Current Population Reports* pp. 60–239. Washington, DC: U.S. Government Printing Office. Accessed March 14, 2012 (http://www.census.gov/prod/2011pubs/pp.60-239.pdf).

Denzin, Norman K. 2009. *The Research Act: A Theoretical Introduction to Sociological Methods.* Piscataway, NJ: Transaction Publishers.

Department of Defense. 2012. "Military Personnel Statistics." Statistical Information Analysis Division, Washington, DC. Accessed May 24, 2012 (http://siadapp.dmdc.osd.mil/personnel /MILITARY/miltop.htm).

Department of Health and Human Services. 2007. "HIV/AIDS Surveillance Report." Cases of HIV Infection and AIDS in the United States and Dependent Areas, vol. 19. Centers for Disease Control and Prevention, Atlanta. Accessed June 25, 2009 (www .cdc.gov/hiv/topics/surveillance/resources/reports/2007report /pdf/2007SurveillanceReport.pdf).

Department of Homeland Security. 2006. *The Federal Response to Hurricane Katrina: Lessons Learned.* Washington, DC: U.S. Government Printing Office.

Deutscher, Eckhard. 2010. *Development Co-operation Report 2010.* An Organisation for Economic Co-operation and Development report, April 23. Paris: OECD Publishing. Accessed April 29, 2010 (http://www.oecd.org/dac/dcr).

Devitt, James. 1999. *Framing Gender on the Campaign Trail: Women's Executive Leadership and the Press.* New York: Women's Leadership Conference.

Diamond, Jared. 2008. "What's Your Consumption Factor?" *New York Times,* January 2. Accessed May 21, 2010 (http://www.nytimes .com/2008/01/02/opinion/02diamond.html).

Dickens, Charles. 1843. *A Christmas Carol*. London: Chapman and Hall. Accessed July 7, 2008 (www.gutenberg.org/dirs/4/46/46-h/46-h.htm).

Doctors Without Borders. 2010. "What Is Doctors Without Borders?" Accessed April 29, 2010 (http://www.doctorswithoutborders.org/aboutus/factsheets/What-is-MSF.pdf).

Domhoff, G. William. 1978. *Who Really Rules? New Haven and Community Power Reexamined*. New Brunswick, NJ: Transaction.

———. 2006. *Who Rules America?* 5th ed. New York: McGraw-Hill.

———. 2009. "The Power Elite and Their Challengers: The Role of Nonprofits in American Social Conflict." *American Behavioral Scientist* 52 (7): 955–973.

Doress, Irwin, and Jack Nusan Porter. 1977. *Kids in Cults: Why They Join, Why They Stay, Why They Leave*. Brookline, MA: Reconciliation Associates.

Drescher, Jack. 2010. "Queer Diagnoses: Parallels and Contrasts in the History of Homosexuality, Gender Variance, and the Diagnostic and Statistical Manual." *Archives of Sexual Behavior* 39 (2): 427–460.

Drescher, Jack. 2011. "The Removal of Homosexuality from the DSM: Its Impact on Today's Marriage Equality Debate." *Journal of Gay & Lesbian Mental Health* 16 (2): 124–135.

Dressler, William W., Kathryn S. Oths, and Clarence C. Gravlee. 2005. "Race and Ethnicity in Public Health Research: Models to Explain Health Disparities." pp. 231–252 in *Annual Review of Anthropology 2005*, ed. William H. Durham. Palo Alto, CA: Annual Reviews.

Duberman, Martin Bauml, Martha Vicinus, and George Chauncy Jr., eds. 1989. *Hidden from History: Reclaiming the Gay and Lesbian Past*. New York: New American Library.

Dubner, Stephen J. 2007. "Everything You Always Wanted to Know About Street Gangs (but Didn't Know Whom to Ask)." Freakanomics blog, *New York Times*, August 6. Accessed June 10, 2008 (http://freakanomics.blogs.nytimes.com/2007/08/06/everything-you-always-wanted-to-know-about-street-gangs-but-didnt-know-whom-to-ask/).

Du Bois, W.E.B. [1903] 1994. *The Souls of Black Folk*. New York: Dover.

———. [1909] 1970. *The Negro American Family*. Cambridge, MA: MIT Press.

———. [1940] 1968. *Dusk of Dawn*. New York: Schocken Books.

Dukes, Richard L., Tara M. Bisel, Karoline N. Burega, Eligio A. Lobato, and Matthew D. Owens. 2003. "Expression of Love, Sex, and Hurt in Popular Songs: A Content Analysis of All-Time Greatest Hits." *Social Science Journal*, pp. 643–650.

Duneier, Mitchell. 1994a. "On the Job, but Behind the Scenes." *Chicago Tribune*, December 26, pp. 1, 24.

———. 1994b. "Battling for Control." *Chicago Tribune*, December 28, pp. 1, 8.

———. 1999. *Sidewalk*. New York: Farrar, Straus and Giroux.

Durden, T. Elizabeth, and Robert A. Hummer. 2006. "Access to Health-care Among Working-Age Hispanic Adults in the United States." *Social Science Quarterly* 87 (December): 1319–1343.

Durkheim, Émile. [1887] 1972. "Religion and Ritual." pp. 219–238 in *Émile Durkheim: Selected Writings*, ed. A. Giddens. Cambridge: Cambridge University Press.

———. [1893] 1933. *Division of Labor in Society*, trans. George Simpson. New York: Free Press.

———. [1895] 1964. *The Rules of Sociological Method*, trans. Sarah A. Solovay and John H. Mueller. New York: Free Press.

———. [1897] 1951. *Suicide*, trans. John A. Spaulding and George Simpson. New York: Free Press.

———. [1925] 1961. *Moral Education: A Study in the Theory and Application of the Sociology of Education*. Glencoe, IL: Free Press.

Dye, Jane Lawler. 2010. "Fertility of American Women: June 2008." Current Population Reports P20–563. Washington, DC: U.S. Census Bureau. Accessed June 1, 2011 (http://www.census.gov/prod/2010pubs/p20–563.pdf).

E

Ebaugh, Helen Rose Fuchs. 1988. *Becoming an Ex: The Process of Role Exit*. Chicago: University of Chicago Press.

Eckert, Penelope and Sally McConnell-Ginet. 2003. *Language and Gender*. New York: Cambridge University Press.

Economic Mobility Project. 2007. *Economic Mobility of Immigrants in the United States*. Washington, DC: Pew Charitable Trusts.

The Economist. 2008a. "Maharishi Mahesh Yogi." (February 16): 95.

———. 2008b. "A Ravenous Dragon: A Special Report on China's Quest for Resources." (March 15): 1–22.

Edge. 2010. "On 'Creation of a Bacterial Cell Controlled by a Chemically Synthesized Genome' by Venter et al." *Edge* 318 (May 20). Accessed May 24, 2010 (http://www.edge.org/documents/archive/edge318.html#rc).

Edin, Kathryn and Maria Kefalas. 2005. *Promises I Can Keep: Why Poor Women Put Motherhood Before Marriage*. Berkeley: University of California Press.

EEOC. 2011. "Age Discrimination in Employment Act (includes concurrent charges with Title VII, ADA and EPA): FY 1997 - FY 2010." Washington, DC: U.S. Equal Employment Opportunity Commission. Accessed May 23, 2011 (http://www.eeoc.gov/eeoc/statistics/enforcement/adea.cfm).

Ehrlich, Paul R. 1968. *The Population Bomb*. New York: Ballantine Books.

Elgin, Suzette Haden. 1984. *Native Tongue*. New York: Feminist Press.

———. 1988. *A First Dictionary and Grammar of Láadan*, 2nd ed. Madison, WI: Society for the Furtherance and Study of Fantasy and Science Fiction.

Elia, John P. 2003. "Queering Relationships: Toward a Paradigmatic Shift." *Journal of Homosexuality* 45 (2–4): 61–86.

Elish, Jill. 2010. "Failed College Dreams Don't Spell Depression, Study Finds." *Florida State News*, March 19. Accessed April 19, 2010 (http://www.fsu.edu/news/2010/03/19/failed.dreams/).

Elliott, Michael. 2005. "Hopelessly Devoted: Being a Fan Is Like Having Your Own Personal Time Machine." *Time*, June 20, p. 76.

Ellison, Brandy. 2008. "Tracking." pp. 301–304 in *Encyclopedia of Race, Ethnicity, and Society*, vol. 2, ed. Richard T. Schaefer. Thousand Oaks, CA: Sage.

Ellison, Ralph. 1952. *Invisible Man*. New York: Random House.

Ellul, Jacques. 1964. *The Technological Society*. New York: Knopf.

———. 1990. *The Technological Bluff*. Grand Rapids, MI: Eerdmans.

———. 1980. *The Technological System*. New York: Continuum.

Ely, Robin J. 1995. "The Power of Demography: Women's Social Construction of Gender Identity at Work." *Academy of Management Journal* 38 (3): 589–634.

Emerson, Michael O., David Hartman, Karen Cook, and Douglas Massey. 2006. "The Rise of Religious Fundamentalism." *Annual Review of Sociology* 32: 127–144.

Energy Information Administration. 2008. "Emissions of Greenhouse Gases in the United States 2007." Office of Integrated Analysis and Forecasting, U.S. Department of Energy, Washington, DC. Accessed June 28, 2009 (www.eia.doe.gov/oiaf/1605/ggrpt/pdf/0573(2007).pdf).

Engels, Friedrich [1884] 1959. "The Origin of the Family, Private Property, and the State." pp. 392–394 in *Marx and Engels: Basic Writings on Politics and Philosophy*, ed. Lewis Feuer. Garden City, NY: Anchor Books.

Ennis, Sharon R., Merarys Ríos-Vargas, and Nora G. Albert. 2011. "The Hispanic Population: 2010." 2010 Census Briefs, C2010BR-04, May. Accessed June 20, 2011 (http://www.census.gov/prod/cen2010/briefs/c2010br-04.pdf).

Escárcega, Sylvia. 2008. "Mexico." pp. 898–902 in *Encyclopedia of Race, Ethnicity, and Society*, vol. 2, ed. Richard T. Schaefer. Thousand Oaks, CA: Sage.

Escoffier, Jeffrey. 1997. "Homosexuality and the Sociological Imagination: The 1950s and 1960s." pp. 248–261 in *A Queer World: The Center for Lesbian and Gay Studies Reader*, ed. Martin Duberman. New York: New York University Press.

Etaugh, Claire. 2003. "Witches, Mothers and Others: Females in Children's Books." *Hilltopics* (Winter): 10–13.

Etcoff, Nancy, Susie Orbach, Jennifer Scott, and Heidi D'Agostino. 2004. "The Real Truth About Beauty: A Global Report—Findings of the Global Study on Women, Beauty and Well-Being." Commissioned by Dove, a Unilever Beauty Brand. Accessed June 28, 2008 (http://www.campaignforrealbeauty.com/uploadedfiles /DOVE_white_paper_final.pdf).

Etzioni, Amitai. 1965. *Political Unification*. New York: Holt, Rinehart and Winston.

———. 2007. "Are New Technologies the Enemy of Privacy?" *Knowledge, Technology & Policy* 20 (2): 115–119.

Eureka County. 2006. "EPA Hears Testimony on Proposed Radiation Rule." *Nuclear Waste Office Newsletter* 11 (Winter). Eureka County Yucca Mountain Information Office.

ExecuNet. 2009. "2009 Executive Job Market Intelligence Report— Executive Summary." Accessed May 12, 2009 (http://www .execunet.com/promo/pdf/EUN2009Survey_summary.pdf).

ExecuNet. 2011. "2011 Executive Job Market Intelligence Report." Accessed April 9, 2012 (http://www.execunet.com/promo/pdf /ExecuNet_Executive_Job_Market_Intelligence_Report_2011.pdf).

F

Faith, Nazila. 2005. "Iranian Cleric Turns Blogger in Campaign for Reform." *New York Times,* January 16, p. 4.

Fanon, Frantz. 1963. *The Wretched of the Earth*. New York: Grove.

Farley, Melissa, and Victor Malarek. 2008. "The Myth of the Victimless Crime." *New York Times,* March 12. Accessed May 20, 2009 (http:// www.nytimes.com/2008/03/12/opinion/12farley.html).

Farr, Grant M. 1999. *Modern Iran*. New York: McGraw-Hill.

Fausto-Sterling, Anne. 1993. "The Five Sexes: Why Male and Female Are Not Enough." *The Sciences* (July/August): 18–23.

———. 2000. "The Five Sexes, Revisited." *The Sciences* (July/August): 18–23.

Fearon, James D., and David D. Laitin. 2003. "Ethnicity, Insurgency, and Civil War." *American Political Science Review* 97 (March): 75–90.

Featherman, David L., and Robert M. Hauser. 1978. *Opportunity and Change*. New York: Aeodus.

Federal Bureau of Investigation. 2012. "Organized Crime." Accessed April 24, 2012 (http://www.fbi.gov/about-us/investigate /organizedcrime).

Felson, David, and Akis Kalaitzidis. 2005. "A Historical Overview of Transnational Crime." pp. 3–19 in *Handbook of Transnational Crime and Justice,* ed. Philip Reichel. Thousand Oaks, CA: Sage.

Ferree, Myra Marx, and David A. Merrill. 2000. "Hot Movements, Cold Cognition: Thinking About Social Movements in Gendered Frames." *Contemporary Society* 29 (May): 454–462.

Fields, Jason. 2004. "America's Families and Living Arrangements: 2003." *Current Population Reports* P20-553. Washington, DC: U.S. Government Printing Office.

Finder, Alan. 2006. "For Some, Online Persona Undermines a Résumé." *New York Times,* June 11. Accessed June 30, 2009 (www .nytimes.com/2006/06/11/us/11recruit.html).

Findlen, Barbara, ed. 1995. *Listen Up: Voices From the Next Feminist Generation*. Seattle, WA: Seal Press.

Fine, Gary C. 2008. "Robbers Cave." pp. 1,163–1,164 in *Encyclopedia of Race, Ethnicity, and Society,* vol. 3, ed. Richard T. Schaefer. Thousand Oaks, CA: Sage.

Finkel, Steven E., and James B. Rule. 1987. "Relative Deprivation and Related Psychological Theories of Civil Violence: A Critical Review." *Research in Social Movements* 9: 47–69.

Fiscella Kevin, and Kathleen Holt. 2008. "Racial Disparity in Hypertension Control: Tallying the Death Toll." *Annals of Family Medicine* 6: 497–502.

Fisher, Gordon M. 1992. "The Development and History of the Poverty Thresholds." *Social Security Bulletin* 55 (4): 3–14. Accessed April 25, 2010 (http://www.ssa.gov/history/fisheronpoverty.html).

———. 2008. "Remembering Mollie Orshansky—the Developer of the Poverty Thresholds." *Social Security Bulletin* 68 (3): 79–83.

Accessed April 25, 2010 (http://www.ssa.gov/policy/docs/ssb /v68n3/v68n3p79.pdf).

Fisher, Max. 2012. "The Middle East Didn't Really Get Any Freer in 2011." *The Atlantic* January 19. Accessed May 28, 2012 (http://www.theatlantic.com/international/archive/2012/01 /the-middle-east-didnt-really-get-any-freer-in-2011/251653/).

Fishman, Charles. 2006. *The Wal-Mart Effect: How the World's Most Powerful Company Really Works—and How It's Transforming the American Economy*. New York: Penguin Books.

Fitzgerald, Kathleen J., and Diane M. Rodgers. 2000. "Radical Social Movement Organization: A Theoretical Model." *Sociological Quarterly* 41 (4): 573–592.

Forbes. 2011. "The World's Billionaires." *Forbes,* March. Accessed June 12, 2011 (http://www.forbes.com/wealth/billionaires/list).

Force, W. R. 2011. "Another Two Cents on England (and Crawley): Masculinity, Culture, and Tucson." Sociology Lens, The Society Pages April 26. Accessed March 10, 2012 (http://thesocietypages .org/sociologylens/2011/04/26/another-two-cents-on-england- and-crawley-masculinity-culture-and-tucson/).

Forsythe, David P. 1990. "Human Rights in U.S. Foreign Policy: Retrospect and Prospect." *Political Science Quarterly* 105 (3): 435–454.

Forte, Maximilian. 2011. "The Human Terrain System and Anthropology: A Review of Ongoing Public Debates." *American Anthropologist* 113 (1): 149–153.

Fortune. 2011. "Global 500: World's Largest Corporations." *Fortune* July 25. Accessed May 18, 2012 (http://money.cnn.com /magazines/fortune/global500/2011/full_list/).

Foy, Paul. 2006. "Interior Rejects Goshute Nuclear Waste Stockpile." *Indian Country Today* 20 (September 18): 1.

Franklin, John Hope, and Alfred A. Moss. 2000. *From Slavery to Freedom: A History of African Americans,* 8th ed. Upper Saddle River, NJ: Prentice Hall.

Freidson, Eliot. 1970. *Profession of Medicine*. New York: Dodd, Mead.

French, Howard W. 2000. "The Pretenders." *New York Times Magazine,* December 3, pp. 86–88.

Freudenburg, William R. 2005. "Seeing Science, Courting Conclusions: Reexamining the Intersection of Science, Corporate Cash, and the Law." *Sociological Forum* 20 (March): 3–33.

Fry, Richard and D'Vera Cohn. 2010. "Women, Men and the New Economics of Marriage." A Social & Demographic Trends Report, Pew Research Center January 19. Accessed June 2, 2011 (http:// pewsocialtrends.org/files/2010/11/new-economics-of-marriage.pdf).

Fry, Richard and D'Vera Cohn. 2011. "Living Together: The Economics of Cohabitation." A Social & Demographic Trends Report, Pew Research Center, June 27. Accessed May 8, 2012 (http://www .pewsocialtrends.org/files/2011/06/pew-social-trends- cohabitation-06-2011.pdf).

Friedan, Betty. 1963. *The Feminine Mystique*. New York: Dell.

Friman, H. Richard. 2004. "The Great Escape? Globalization, Immigrant Entrepreneurship and the Criminal Economy." *Review of International Political Economy* 11 (1): 98–131.

Furedi, Frank. 2006. "The End of Professional Dominance." *Society* 43 (6): 14–18.

Furman, Nelly, David Goldberg, and Natalia Lusin. 2007. "Enrollments in Languages Other Than English in United States Institutions of Higher Education, Fall 2006." Modern Language Association, November 13. Accessed May 3, 2009 (http://www .mla.org/pdf/06enrollmentsurvey_final.pdf).

Furstenberg, Frank F. 2007. "The Making of the Black Family: Race and Class in Qualitative Studies in the Twentieth Century." *Annual Review of Sociology* 33: 429–448.

Furstenberg Jr., Frank F. 2010 "On a New Schedule: Transitions to Adulthood and Family Change." *The Future of Children* 20 (1): 67–87.

Fuson, Ken. 2008. "Raid Mars Future for 3 Graduating Today from Postville." *Des Moines Register,* May 25. Accessed June 29, 2008 (http:// www.desmoinesregister.com/apps/pbcs.dll/article?AID=/20080525 /NEWS/805250327/1001&theme=POSTVILLE_ICE_RAID).

Fussell, Elizabeth. 2006. "Leaving New Orleans: Social Stratification, Networks, and Hurricane Evacuation." Understanding

Katrina: Perspectives from the Social Sciences, Social Science Research Council, Brooklyn, NY. Accessed June 10, 2009 (http://understandingkatrina.ssrc.org/Fussell).

Fussell, Paul. 1992. *Class: A Guide Through the American Status System.* New York: Touchstone.

Fuwa, Makiko. 2004. "Macro-level Gender Inequality and the Division of Household Labor in 22 Countries." *American Sociological Review* 69 (December): 751–767.

G

Gabler, Neal. 2006. *Walt Disney: The Triumph of the American Imagination.* New York: Knopf.

Gallup. 2008a. "Abortion." Accessed March 6, 2008 (www.gallup.com).

———. 2008b. "Homosexual Relations." Accessed March 6, 2008 (www.gallup.com).

———. 2008c. "Religion." Accessed March 14, 2008 (www.gallup.com).

———. 2008d. "Environment." Accessed March 18, 2008 (www.gallup.com).

Gallup. 2011. "Environment." Washington, DC: Gallup, Inc. Accessed June 30, 2011 (http://www.gallup.com/poll/1615/environment.aspx).

———. 2011b. "Doctor-Assisted Suicide Is Moral Issue Dividing Americans Most." Washington, DC: Gallup, Inc. Accessed August 12, 2011 (www.gallup.com/poll/147842/Doctor-Assisted-Suicide-Moral-Issue-Dividing-Americans.aspx).

———. 2011c. "Record-High 50% of Americans Favor Legalizing Marijuana Use." *Gallup Politics* October 17. Accessed April 23, 2012 (http://www.gallup.com/poll/150149/Record-High-Americans-Favor-Legalizing-Marijuana.aspx).

Gallup. 2012. "Military and National Defense." Washington, DC: Gallup, Inc. Accessed May 24, 2012 (http://www.gallup.com/poll/1666/military-national-defense.aspx).

Gans, Herbert. 1971. "The Uses of Poverty: The Poor Pay All." *Social Policy,* July/August, pp. 20–24.

———. 2009. "Reflections on Symbolic Ethnicity: A Response to Y. Anagnostou." *Ethnicities* 9 (1): 123–130.

GAO. 2012. "Unemployment Insurance: Economic Circumstances of Individuals Who Exhausted Benefits." United States Government Accounting Office, GAO-12-408, February 17. Accessed May 22, 2012 (http://www.gao.gov/assets/590/588680.pdf).

García-Moreno, Claudia, Henrica A.F.M. Jansen, Mary Ellsberg, Lori Heise, and Charlotte Watts. 2005. *WHO Milti-Country Study on Women's Health and Domestic Violence Against Women: Initial Results on Prevalence, Health Outcomes and Women's Responses.* Geneva: World Health Organization. Accessed June 2, 2010 (http://www.who.int/gender/violence/who_multicountry_study/en/index.html).

Gardner, Gary. 2008. "Microfinance Surging." *World Watch* 21 (November/December): 30.

Gardner, Gary, Erik Assadourian, and Radhika Sarin. 2004. "The State of Consumption Today." pp. 3–21 in *State of the World 2004,* ed. Brian Halweil and Lisa Mastny. New York: Norton.

Garfinkel, Harold. 1956. "Conditions of Successful Degradation Ceremonies." *American Journal of Sociology* 61 (March): 420–424.

Garrett, Ruth Irene. 2003. Crossing Over: One Woman's Escape from Amish Life. New York: HarperOne.

Gates, Gary J. 2010. "Sexual Minorities in the 2008 General Social Survey: Coming Out and Demographic Characteristics." The Williams Institute, UCLA, October. Accessed August 9, 2011 (www3.law.ucla.edu/williamsinstitute/pdf/Sexual-Minorities-2008-GSS.pdf).

Gaviria, Marcela, and Martin Smith. 2009. "The Madoff Affair." *PBS Frontline,* May 12. Accessed May 21, 2009 (http://www.pbs.org/wgbh/pages/frontline/madoff).

Gelvin, James L. 2012. *The Arab Uprisings: What Everyone Needs to Know.* New York: Oxford University Press.

Gendell, Murray. 2008. "Older Workers: Increasing Their Labor Force Participation and Hours of Work." *Monthly Labor Review,* January, pp. 41–54.

Gentleman, Amelia. 2007. "Police Ignore Serial Killings in Delhi Slum, Exposing Unequal Justice for India's Poor." *New York Times,* January 7, p. 8.

Gerhardt, Uta. 2002. *Talcott Parsons: An Intellectual Biography.* New York: Cambridge University Press.

Gerth, H. H., and C. Wright Mills. 1958. *From Max Weber: Essays in Sociology.* New York: Galaxy.

Gettleman, Jeffrey. 2011. "Somalis Waste Away as Insurgents Block Escape from Famine." *New York Times,* August 1. Accessed August 8, 2011 (www.nytimes.com/2011/08/02/world/africa/02somalia.html).

Gheytanchi, Elham. 2009. "Iranian Women Lead the Protests." *San Francisco Chronicle,* June 29. Accessed June 30, 2009 (www.sfgate.com/cgi-bin/article.cgi?f=/c/a/2009/06/29/ED8618EMUC.DTL).

Ghitis, Frida. 2011. "Women of Arab Spring Still Fighting for Liberation." *Salt Lake Star Tribune,* June 21. Accessed August 12, 2011 (www.startribune.com/opinion/otherviews/124292204.html).

Gibson, Campbell, and Kay Jung. 2002. "Historical Census Statistics on Population Totals by Race, 1790 to 1990, and by Hispanic Origin, 1970 to 1990, for the United States, Regions, Divisions, and States." Population Division, U.S. Census Bureau, Washington, DC, September, Working Paper Series No. 56. Accessed May 17, 2010 (http://www.census.gov/population/www/documentation/twps0056/twps0056.html).

Giordano, Peggy C. 2003. "Relationships in Adolescence." pp. 257–281 in *Annual Review of Sociology, 2003,* ed. Karen S. Cook and John Hagan. Palo Alto, CA: Annual Reviews.

Giroux, Henry A. 1988. *Schooling and the Struggle for Public Life: Critical Pedagogy in the Modern Age.* Minneapolis: University of Minnesota Press.

Gitlin, Todd. 1993. *The Sixties: Years of Hope, Days of Rage.* New York: Bantam Books.

Glass Ceiling Commission. 1995. "Good for Business: Making Full Use of the Nation's Human Capital—The Environmental Scan." A Fact-Finding Report of the Federal Glass Ceiling Commission, Washington, DC. Accessed June 19, 2011 (http://www.dol.gov/oasam/programs/history/reich/reports/ceiling.pdf).

Glassner, Barry. 2010. "Still Fearful." *Chronicle of Higher Education* 56 (January 22): B11–B12.

Glaze, Lauren E. 2011. "Correctional Populations in the United States, 2010." *Bureau of Justice Statistics Bulletin,* December, NCJ 236319. Accessed April 23, 2012 (http://bjs.ojp.usdoj.gov/content/pub/pdf/cpus10.pdf).

Glenn, David. 2007. "Anthropologists in a War Zone: Scholars Debate Their Role." *Chronicle of Higher Education* 54 (September 30): A1, A10–A12.

Goering, Laurie. 2007. "The First Refugees of Global Warming." *Chicago Tribune,* May 2, pp. 1, 25.

Goffman, Erving. 1959. *The Presentation of Self in Everyday Life.* New York: Doubleday.

———. 1961. *Asylums: Essays on the Social Situation of Mental Patients and Other Inmates.* Garden City, NY: Doubleday.

———. 1963. *Stigma: Notes on Management of Spoiled Identity.* Englewood Cliffs, NJ: Prentice Hall.

———. 1979. *Gender Advertisements.* Cambridge, MA: Harvard University Press.

Goldscheider, Frances, Gayle Kaufman, and Sharon Sassler. 2010. "Navigating the 'New' Marriage Market: How Attitudes Toward Partner Characteristics Shape Union Formation." *Journal of Family Issues* 30 (6): 719–737.

Goldstein, Melvyn C., and Cynthia M. Beall. 1981. "Modernization and Aging in the Third and Fourth World: Views from the Rural Hinterland in Nepal." *Human Organization* 40 (Spring): 48–55.

Gomez, Jewelle L. 1997. "The Event of Becoming." pp. 17–23 in *A Queer World: The Center for Lesbian and Gay Studies Reader,* ed. Martin Duberman. New York: New York University Press.

González, Roberto J. 2008. "Human Terrain." *Anthropology Today* 24 (1): 21–26.

Goodwin Paula Y., William D. Mosher, and Anjani Chandra. 2010. "Marriage and Cohabitation in the United States: A Statistical Portrait Based on Cycle 6 (2002) of the National Survey of Family Growth." *Vital and Health Statistics,* 23 (28). National Center for Health Statistics, Washington, DC.

Google. 2011a. "Fertility Rate." World Bank Development Indicators, Public Data Visualization Program. Accessed May 27, 2012 (http://www.google.com/publicdata/explore?ds=wb-wdi&met_y=sp_dyn_tfrt_in&idim=country:USA&dl=en&hl=en&q=fertility+rate#ctype=l&strail=false&nselm=h&met_y=sp_dyn_tfrt_in&scale_y=lin&ind_y=false&rdim=country&idim=country:USA:AFG:CHN:IND:NER:DZA:KHM:IRN:DEU:RWA&tdim=true&hl=en&dl=en).

———. 2011b. "Life Expectancy." World Bank Development Indicators, Public Data Visualization Program. Accessed May 27, 2012 (http://www.google.com/publicdata/explore?ds=wb-wdi&met_y=sp_dyn_le00_in&idim=country:USA&dl=en&hl=en&q=life+expectancy#ctype=l&strail=false&nselm=h&met_y=sp_dyn_le00_in&scale_y=lin&ind_y=false&rdim=country&idim=country:USA:AFG:DZA:KHM:CHN:DEU:IND:IRN:NER:RWA&tdim=true&hl=en&dl=en).

Gottfredson, Michael, and Travis Hirschi. 1990. *A General Theory of Crime.* Palo Alto, CA: Stanford University Press.

Gottlieb, Lori. 2006. "How Do I Love Thee?" *Atlantic Monthly,* March, pp. 58, 60, 62–68, 70.

Gould, Elise. 2008. "The Erosion of Employer-Sponsored Health Insurance: Declines Continue for the Seventh Year Running." EPI Briefing Paper No. 223, October 9. Washington, DC: Economic Policy Institute. Accessed June 26, 2009 (http://epi.3cdn.net/d1b4356d96c21c91d1_ilm6b5dua.pdf).

Gould, Larry A. 2002. "Indigenous People Policing Indigenous People: The Potential Psychological and Cultural Costs." *Social Science Journal* 39: 171–188.

Gouldner, Alvin. 1960. "The Norm of Reciprocity." *American Sociological Review* 25 (April): 161–177.

———. 1970. *The Coming Crisis of Western Sociology.* New York: Basic Books.

Government Accountability Office. 2003. *Women's Earnings: Work Patterns Partially Explain Difference Between Men's and Women's Earnings.* Washington, DC: U.S. Government Printing Office.

Gramsci, Antonio. 1929. *Selections from the Prison Notebooks,* ed. and trans. Quintin Hoare and Geoffrey Nowell Smith. London: Lawrence and Wishort.

Gray, John. 1992. *Men Are from Mars, Women Are from Venus: A Practical Guide for Improving Communication and Getting What You Want in Your Relationships.* New York: Harper Collins.

Green, Alexander R., Dana R. Carney, Daniel J. Pallin, Long H. Ngo, Kristal L. Raymond, Lisa I. Iezzoni, and Mahzarin R. Banaji. 2007. "Implicit Bias Among Physicians and Its Prediction of Thrombolysis Decisions for Black and White Patients." *Journal of General Internal Medicine* 9 (September): 1231–1238.

———. 2008. "Queens Factory Is Found to Owe Workers $5.3 Million." *New York Times,* July 23. Accessed June 20, 2009 (http://cityroom.blogs.nytimes.com/2008/07/23/a-queens-sweatshop-found-to-owe-workers-53-million/).

Greenspan, Alan. 2005. "Testimony." Hearing Before the Committee on Banking, Housing, and Urban Affairs, United States Senate One Hundred Ninth Congress, S. Hrg. 109–204. Accessed June 6, 2009 (http://frwebgate.access.gpo.gov/cgi-bin/getdoc.cgi?dbname=109_senate_hearings&docid=f:24852.pdf).

Grieco, Elizabeth M. and Edward N. Trevelyan. 2010. "Place of Birth of the Foreign-Born Population: 2009." American Community Survey Briefs, ACSBR/09-15, October. Accessed June 26, 2011 (http://www.census.gov/prod/2010pubs/acsbr09-15.pdf).

Grieco, Elizabeth M., and Rachel C. Cassidy. 2001. "Overview of Race and Hispanic Origin." *Current Population Reports,* Ser. CENBR/01–1. Washington, DC: U.S. Government Printing Office.

Groeneveld, Elizabeth. 2009. "'Be a Feminist or Just Dress Like One': BUST, Fashion and Feminism as Lifestyle." *Journal of Gender Studies* 18 (2): 179–190.

Gross, Jane. 2005. "Forget the Career. My Parents Need Me at Home." *New York Times,* November 24, pp. A1, A20.

Grossman, Samantha. 2012. "The Wooly Mammoth's Return? Scientists Plan to Clone Extinct Creature." *Time* NewsFeed, March 14. Accessed May 29, 2012 (http://newsfeed.time.com/2012/03/14/the-woolly-mammoths-return-scientists-plan-to-clone-extinct-creature/).

Groza, Victor, Scott Ryan, and Sara Thomas. 2008. "Institutionalization, Romanian Adoptions and Executive Functioning." *Child & Adolescent Social Work Journal* 25 (3): 185–204.

Guatemala Times. 2009. "Increase of Guatemala Remittances in 2008." *Guatemala Times,* January 9. Accessed May 17, 2010 (http://www/guatemala-times.com/news/guatemala/629-increase-of-guatemala-remittances-in-2008.html).

Guglielmo, Jennifer. 2003. "White Lies, Dark Truths." pp. 1–14 in *Are Italians White? How Race Is Made in America,* ed. Jennifer Guglielmo and Salvatore Salerno. New York: Routledge.

Gurari, Inbal, John Hetts, and Michael Strube. 2006. "Beauty in the 'I' of the Beholder: Effects of Idealized Media Portrayals on Implicit Self-Image." *Basic & Applied Social Psychology* 28 (3): 273–282.

Gutiérrez, Gustavo. 1990. "Theology and the Social Sciences." pp. 214–225 in *Liberation Theology at the Crossroads: Democracy or Revolution?* ed. Paul E. Sigmund. New York: Oxford University Press.

H

Halle, David. 1993. *Inside Culture: Art and Class in the American Home.* Chicago: University of Chicago Press.

Halperin, David M. 2009. "Thirteen Ways of Looking at a Bisexual." *Journal of Bisexuality* 9 (3/4): 451–455.

Hamilton, Mykol C., David Anderson, Michelle Broaddus, and Kate Young. 2006. "Gender Stereotyping and Underrepresentation of Female Characters in 200 Popular Children's Books: A Twenty-first Century Update." *Sex Roles* 55 (11/12): 757–765.

Hampton, Keith N., Lauren F. Sessions, Eun Ja Her, and Lee Rainie. 2009. "Social Isolation and New Technology: How the Internet and Mobile Phones Impact Americans' Social Networks." Pew Internet and American Life Project, November. Accessed May 23, 2011 (http://www.pewinternet.org/Reports/2009/18--Social-Isolation-and-New-Technology.aspx).

Harding, Sandra. 2004. "Introduction: Standpoint Theory as a Site of Political, Philosophic, and Scientific Debate." pp. 1–16 in *The Feminist Standpoint Theory Reader: Intellectual and Political Controversies,* ed. Sandra Harding. New York: Routledge.

Harding, Sandra, ed. 2003. *The Feminist Standpoint Theory Reader: Intellectual and Political Controversies.* New York: Routledge.

Hardt, Michael, and Antonio Negri. 2009. *Commonwealth.* Cambridge, MA: Belknap Press.

Harlow, Harry F. 1971. *Learning to Love.* New York: Ballantine Books.

Harrington, Michael. 1962. *The Other America: Poverty in the United States.* Baltimore: Penguin Books.

———. 1980. "The New Class and the Left." pp. 123–138 in *The New Class,* ed. B. Bruce Briggs. New Brunswick, NJ: Transaction.

Harris Interactive. 2009. "Firefighters, Scientists and Doctors Seen as Most Prestigious Occupations." The Harris Poll #86, August 4. Accessed June 9, 2011 (http://www.harrisinteractive.com/vault/Harris-Interactive-Poll-Research-Pres-Occupations-2009-08.pdf).

Hart, Betty, and Todd R. Risley. 1995. *Meaningful Differences in the Everyday Experience of Young American Children.* Baltimore: Paul H. Brookes.

Hart, Zachary P., Vernon D. Miller, and John R. Johnson. 2003. "Socialization, Resocialization and Communication Relationships in the Context of an Organizational Change." *Communication Studies* 54 (4): 483–495.

Hartsock, Nancy C. M. 1983. "The Feminist Standpoint: Developing the Ground for a Specifically Feminist Historical Materialism." pp. 283–310 in *Discovering Reality: Feminist Perspectives in Epistemology, Methodology, and Philosophy of Science,* ed. Sandra Harding and Merrill B. Hintikka. Dordrect: Reidel.

Haskins, Ron. 2008. "Wealth and Economic Mobility." Chap. 4 in *Getting Ahead or Losing Ground: Economic Mobility in America.* Washington, DC: Pew Charitable Trusts. Accessed August 2, 2010 (http://economicmobility.org/assets/pdfs/EMP_WealthandEconomicMobility_ChapterIV.pdf).

Hausmann, Ricardo, Laura D. Tyson, and Saadia Zahidi. 2010. The Global Gender Gap Report 2010. Geneva: World Economic

Forum. Accessed June 15, 2011 (http://www.weforum.org/issues/global-gender-gap).

Haviland, William A., Harald E. L. Prins, Dana Walrath, and Bunny McBride. 2005. *Cultural Anthropology: The Human Challenge,* 11th ed. Belmont, CA: Wadsworth.

Hayden, H. Thomas. 2004. "What Happened at Abu Ghraib." Accessed September 19, 2011 (http://www.military.com/NewContent/0,13190,Hayden_090704,00.html).

He, Wan, Manisha Sengupta, Victoria A. Velkoff, and Kimberly A. DeBarros. 2005. "65+ in the United States: 2005." *Current Population Reports* P23–209. Washington, DC: U.S. Government Printing Office.

Heatherton, Todd F., and James Sargent. 2009. "Does Watching Smoking in Movies Promote Tennage Smoking?" *Current Directions in Psychological Science* 18 (2): 63–67.

Heilman, Madeline E. 2001. "Description and Prescription: How Gender Stereotypes Prevent Women's Ascent up the Organizational Ladder." *Journal of Social Issues* 57 (4): 657–674.

Heiss, Sarah N. 2011. "Locating the Bodies of Woman and Disability in Definitions of Beauty: An Analysis of Dove's Campaign for Real Beauty." *Disability Studies Quarterly* 31 (1). Accessed May 25, 2012 (http://dsq-sds.org/article/view/1367/1497).

Henderson, Anita. 2003. "What's in a Slur?" *American Speech* 78 (1): 52–74.

Henriques, Diana B., and Jack Healy. 2009. "Madoff Goes to Jail After Guilty Pleas." *New York Times,* March 12. Accessed May 21, 2009 (http://www.nytimes.com/2009/03/13/business/13madoff.html).

Herek, Gregory M. 2004. "Beyond 'Homophobia.' Thinking About Sexual Prejudice and Stigma in the Twenty-first Century." *Sexuality Research & Social Policy* 1 (2): 6–24.

———. 2007. "Confronting Sexual Stigma and Prejudice: Theory and Practice." *Journal of Social Issues* 63 (4): 905–925.

Herman, Charlie. 2010. "Amid Rising Demand, Price Of Coffee Beans Soars." NPR, November 25. Accessed May 20, 2011 (http://www.npr.org/2010/11/25/131594733/price-of-coffee-beans-on-the-rise).

Hertz, Rosanna. 2006. *Single by Chance. Mothers by Choice.* New York: Oxford University Press.

Hetherington, E. Mavis, and John Kelly. 2002. *For Better or for Worse: Divorce Reconsidered.* New York: Norton.

Hewlett, Sylvia Ann, Diana Foster, Laura Sherbin, Peggy Shiller, and Karen Sumberg. 2010. *Off-Ramps and On-Ramps Revisited.* New York: Center for Work-Life Policy.

Higgins, George E., Richard Tewksbury, and Elizabeth Mustaine. 2007. "Sports Fan Binge Drinking: An Examination Using Low Self-Control and Peer Association." *Sociological Spectrum* 27 (4): 389–404.

Higgins, Michelle. 2008. "No Shoes, No Shirt, No Worries." *New York Times,* April 27. Accessed August 5, 2009 (http://travel.nytimes.com/2008/04/27/travel/27nude.html).

Hirschi, Travis. 1969. *Causes of Delinquency.* Berkeley: University of California Press.

Hirschman, Charles, and Irina Voloshin. 2007. "The Structure of Teenage Employment: Social Background and the Jobs Held by High School Seniors." *Research in Social Stratification and Mobility* 25: 189–203.

Hixson, Lindsay, Bradford B. Hepler, and Myoung Ouk Kim. 2011r. "The White Population: 2010." 2010 Census Briefs, Report C2010BR-05, September. Accessed May 27, 2012 (http://www.census.gov/prod/cen2010/briefs/c2010br-05.pdf).

Hochschild, Arlie Russell. 1989. *The Second Shift: Working Parents and the Revolution at Home.* New York: Viking Press.

———. 1990. "The Second Shift: Employed Women Are Putting in Another Day of Work at Home." *Utne Reader* 38 (March/April): 66–73.

Hochschild, Arlie Russell. 1997. *The Time Bind: When Work Becomes Home and Home Becomes Work.* New York: Henry Holt and Company.

———. 2005. *The Commercialization of Intimate Life: Notes from Home and Work.* Berkeley: University of California Press.

Holden, Constance. 1980. "Identical Twins Reared Apart." *Science* 207 (March 21): 1323–1328.

———. 1987. "The Genetics of Personality." *Science* 257 (August 7): 598–601.

Holder, Kelly. 2006. "Voting and Registration in the Election of November 2004." *Current Population Reports* P20–556. Washington, DC: U.S. Government Printing Office.

Hollingshead, August B. 1975. *Elmtown's Youth and Elmtown Revisited.* New York: Wiley.

Holmes, Mary. 2006. "Love Lives at a Distance: Distance Relationships over the Lifecourse." *Sociological Research Online* 11 (3).

Homans, George C. 1979. "Nature Versus Nurture: A False Dichotomy." *Contemporary Sociology* 8 (May): 345–348.

Home School Legal Defense Association. 2005. "State Laws" and "Academic Statistics on Homeschooling." Accessed August 2, 2010 (www.hslda.org).

Homeland Security. 2010. 2009 Yearbook of Immigration Statistics. Office of Immigration Statistics, August 2010. U.S. Department of Homeland Security, Washington, DC. Accessed June 13, 2011 (http://www.dhs.gov/files/statistics/publications/yearbook.shtm).

Homeland Security. 2011. "Immigration Enforcement Actions: 2010." Office of Immigration Statistics, Annual Flow Report, March. Accessed June 26, 2011 (http://www.dhs.gov/xlibrary/assets/statistics/publications/enforcement-ar-2010.pdf).

Homeland Security. 2011. *2010 Yearbook of Immigration Statistics.* Office of Immigration Statistics. U.S. Department of Homeland Security, Washington, DC. Accessed May 18, 2012 (http://www.dhs.gov/files/statistics/publications/yearbook.shtm).

Hondagneu-Sotelo, Pierrette, ed. 2003. *Gender and U.S. Immigration: Contemporary Trends.* Berkeley: University of California Press.

Hootman, J., J. Bolen, C. Helmick, and G. Langmaid. 2006. "Prevalence of Doctor-Diagnosed Arthritis and Arthritis-Attributable Activity Limitation—United States, 2003–2005." *Morbidity and Mortality Weekly Report* 55 (40): 1089–1092.

Horowitz, Helen Lefkowitz. 1987. *Campus Life.* Chicago: University of Chicago Press.

Horrigan, John B. 2007. *A Typology of Information and Communication Technology Users.* Washington, DC: Pew Internet and American Life Project.

Hostetler, John A. 1993. *Amish Society,* 4th ed. Baltimore: Johns Hopkins University Press.

Hout, Michael, and Claude S. Fischer. 2002. "Why More Americans Have No Religious Preference: Politics and Generations." *American Sociological Review* 67 (April): 165–190.

Howard, Russell D., and Reid L. Sawyer. 2003. *Terrorism and Counterterrorism: Understanding the New Security Environment.* Guilford, CT: McGraw-Hill/Dushkin.

Howden, Lindsay M. and Julie A. Meyer. 2011. "Age and Sex Composition: 2010." 2010 Census Briefs C2010BR-03. Washington, DC: U.S. Government Printing Office. Accessed April 6, 2012 (http://www.census.gov/prod/cen2010/briefs/c2010br-03.pdf).

Huang, Gary. 1988. "Daily Addressing Ritual: A Cross-Cultural Study." Paper presented at the annual meeting of the American Sociological Association, Atlanta.

Hughes, Everett. 1945. "Dilemmas and Contradictions of Status." *American Journal of Sociology* 50 (March): 353–359.

Human Rights Campaign. 2009. "Maps of State Laws & Policies." Accessed May 27, 2009 (http://www.hrc.org/about_us/state_laws.asp).

———. 2010. "Marriage Equality & Other Relationship Recognition Laws." Human Rights Campaign, Washington, DC, April 2. Accessed April 14, 2010 (http://www.hrc.org/documents/Relationship_Recognition_Laws_Map.pdf).

Human Rights Campaign. 2012. "Same-Sex Relationship Recognition Laws: State by State." Human Rights Campaign, Washington, DC, March 23. Accessed May 8, 2012 (http://www.hrc.org/resources/entry/same-sex-relationship-recognition-laws-state-by-state).

Humes, Karen R., Nicholas A. Jones, and Roberto R. Ramirez. 2011. "Overview of Race and Hispanic Origin: 2010." 2010 Census Briefs, C2010BR-02, March. Accessed June 18, 2011 (http://www.census.gov/prod/cen2010/briefs/c2010br-02.pdf).

Hunter, Herbert M., ed. 2000. *The Sociology of Oliver C. Cox: New Perspectives: Research in Race and Ethnic Relations,* vol. 2. Stamford, CT: JAI Press.

Hurst, Charles E., and David L. McConnell. 2010. *An Amish Paradox: Diversity and Change in the World's Largest Amish Community.* Baltimore: Johns Hopkins University Press.

Hussar, William J., and Tabitha M. Bailey. 2011. *Projections of Education Statistics to 2020.* NCES 2011-026. National Center for Education Statistics, Institute of Education Sciences, U.S. Department of Education, Washington, DC. Accessed May 16, 2012 (http://nces.ed.gov/pubs2011/2011026.pdf).

Hvistendahl, Mara. 2010. "Has China Outgrown the One-Child Policy?" Science 329 (September 17): 1458-1461.

I

Ignatiev, Noel. 1995. *How the Irish Became White.* New York: Routledge.

Igo, Sarah E. 2007. *The Average American: Surveys, Citizens, and the Making of a Mass Public.* Cambridge, MA: Harvard University Press.

Illinois State Board of Education. 2012. "eReportcard Public Site." Assessment Division. Accessed May 15, 2012 (http://webprod.isbe .net/ereportcard/publicsite/getsearchcriteria.aspx).

Indiana University Center for Sexual Health Promotion. 2010. "Special Issue: Findings from the National Survey of Sexual Health and Behavior (NSSHB)." *Journal of Sexual Medicine* 7 (Supplement 5).

INEGI. 2009. "Mujeres y Hombres en México 2005. Anexo estadístico." Instituto Nacional de Estadística y Geografía. Accessed June 14, 2009 (www.inegi.org.mx/inegi/contenidos /espanol/bvinegi/productos/integracion/sociodemografico /mujeresyhombres/2005/anexo_2005.xls).

Inglehart, Ronald, Pippa Norris, and Christian Welzel. 2002. "Gender Equality and Democracy." *Comparative Sociology* 1 (3/4): 321–346.

Innocence Project. 2012. "Facts on Post-Conviction DNA Exonerations." Accessed April 24, 2012 (http://www.innocenceproject.org /Content/Facts_on_PostConviction_DNA_Exonerations.php).

INPE. 2010. "Specific Data of PRODES/INPE Confirms the Range of the Amazon Deforestation." Instituto Nacional de Pesquisas Espaciais, April 29. Accessed May 21, 2010 (http://www.inpe.br/ingles /news/news_dest117.php).

Institute of International Education. 2012. "*Open Doors 2011* Fast Facts." New York City: Institute of International Education, Inc. Accessed May 15, 2012 (http://www.iie.org/en /Research-and-Publications/Open-Doors/Data/Fast-Facts).

Instituto Nacional de Migración, México. 2011. "Extranjeros Alojados y Devueltos, Cuadro 3.2.1 (xls)." Boletín Estadístico 2010. Gobierno Federal, México. Accessed June 13, 2011 (http://www .inm.gob.mx/index.php/page/Boletin_Estadistico_2010).

Internal Revenue Service. 2011. "The 400 Individual Income Tax Returns Reporting the Highest Adjusted Gross Incomes Each Year, 1992–2008." Accessed June 9, 2011 (http://www.irs.gov/pub /irs-soi/08intop400.pdf).

International Centre for Prison Studies. 2012. "Entire world—Prison Population Rates per 100,000 of the National Population." In partnership with the University of Essex, London. Accessed April 24, 2012 (http://www.prisonstudies.org/info/worldbrief/wpb_stats .php?area=all&category=wb_poprate).

International Institute for Democracy and Electoral Assistance. 2009. "Voter Turnout Database." Accessed June 2, 2009 (www.idea.int /vt/view_data.cfm).

———. 2011. "Voter Turnout Database." Accessed June 8, 2011 (http:// www.idea.int/vt/view_data.cfm).

International Institute for Democracy and Electoral Assistance. 2012. "Voter Turnout Database." Accessed May 23, 2012 (http://www .idea.int/vt/viewdata.cfm).

International Labour Organization. 2008. *World of Work Report 2008: Income Inequalities in the Age of Financial Globalization.* Geneva International Institute for Labour Studies. Accessed June 12, 2009 (www.ilo.org/public/english/bureau/inst/download/world08.pdf).

International Monetary Fund. 2000. *World Economic Outlook: Asset Prices and the Business Cycle.* Washington, DC: IMF.

———. 2008. "IMF Helping Countries Respond to Food Price Crisis." *IMF Survey Magazine: In the News,* June 3. Washington, DC: IMF. Accessed August 2, 2010 (http://www.imf.org/external/pubs/ft /survey/so/2008/NEW060308A.htm).

International Telecommunications Union. 2010. *Measuring the Information Society 2010.* Geneva: International Telecommunications Union.

International Telecommunications Union. 2012. "ICT Statistics Database." ITU ICT Eye. Accessed April 5, 2012 (http://www.itu.int /ITU-D/ICTEYE/Indicators/Indicators.aspx).

Internet World Stats. 2012a. "Internet Usage Statistics: The Internet Big Picture." Accessed May 28, 2012 (http://www.internetworldstats .com/stats.htm).

———. 2012b. "Internet World Users by Language: Top 10 Languages." Accessed May 28, 2012 (http://www.internetworldstats.com /stats7.htm).

Inter-Parliamentary Union. 2011. "Women in Parliament in 2011: The Year in Perspective." Geneva, Switzerland. Accessed May 24, 2012 (http://www.ipu.org/pdf/publications/wmnpersp11-e.pdf).

Inter-Parliamentary Union. 2012. "Women in National Parliaments: Situation as of 31 March 2012." Geneva, Switzerland. Accessed May 24, 2012 (http://www.ipu.org/wmn-e/classif.htm).

Ionescu, Carmiola. 2005. "Romania's Abandoned Children Are Still Suffering." *Lancet* 366 (9497): 1595–1596.

Isaacs, Julia B. 2007a. *Economic Mobility of Families Across Generations.* Washington, DC: Economic Mobility Project, Pew Charitable Trusts.

———. 2007b. *Economic Mobility of Men and Women.* Washington, DC: Economic Mobility Project.

———. 2007c. *Economic Mobility of Black and White Families.* Washington, DC: Economic Mobility Project.

———. 2008. "Economic Mobility of Black and White Families." *Economic Mobility Project,* Pew Charitable Trusts, November. Accessed June 21, 2009 (www.brookings.edu/reports/2008/~ /media/Files/rc/reports/2008/02_economic_mobility_sawhill /02_economic_mobility_sawhill_ch6.pdf).

Isaacs, Julia B., Isabel V. Sawhill, and Ron Haskins. 2008. *Getting Ahead or Losing Ground: Economic Mobility in America.* Washington, DC: Pew Charitable Trust.

ITOPF. 2006. "Statistics: International Tanker Owners Pollution Federation Limited." Accessed May 2, 2007 (www.itopf.com /stats.html).

IUCN. 2011. "Table 2: Changes in Numbers of Species in the Threatened Categories (CR, EN, VU) from 1996 to 2011 for the Major Taxonomic Groups on the Red List." IUCN Red List of Threatened Species, Version 2011.1. Cambridge, U.K.: International Union for Conservation of Nature and Natural Resources. Accessed June 30, 2011 (http://www.iucnredlist.org/documents/summarystatistics /2011_1_RL_Stats_Table_2.pdf).

J

Jackson, Jerlando, and Elizabeth O'Callaghan. 2009. "What Do We Know About Glass Ceiling Effects? A Taxonomy and Critical Review to Inform Higher Education Research." *Research in Higher Education* 50 (5): 460–482.

Jacobs, David, Zhenchao Qian, Jason T. Carmichael, and Stephanie L. Kent. 2007. "Who Survives on Death Row? An Individual and Contextual Analysis." *American Sociological Review* 72 (August): 610–632.

James, Susan Donaldson. 2008. "Students Use Civil Rights Tactics to Combat Global Warming." *ABC News,* January 19. Accessed August 2, 2010 (http://abcnews.go.com/Technology /GlobalWarming/story?id=2805553&page=1).

———. 2008a & 2008b. "Wild Child Speechless After Tortured Life: Abandoned by Doctors and Mother, Abused in Foster Care, 'Genie' Regressed." *ABC News Online,* May 19. Accessed May 5, 2009 (http://abcnews.go.com/Health/Story?id=4873347 &page=1).

Jamison, Andrew. 2006. "Social Movements and Science: Cultural Appropriations of Cognitive Praxis." *Science as Culture* 15 (1): 45–59.

Jargowsky, Paul A., and Rebecca Yang. 2006. "The 'Underclass' Revisited: A Social Problem in Decline." *Journal of Urban Affairs* 28 (1): 55–70.

Jenkins, J. Craig. 2004. "Social Movements: Resource Mobilization Theory." pp. 14,368–14,371 in *International Encyclopedia of the Social and Behavioral Sciences*, ed. Neil J. Smelser and Paul B. Baltes. New York: Elsevier.

Jenkins, Matt. 2008. "A Really Inconvenient Truth." *Miller-McCure* 1 (March/April): 38–41.

Jenness, Valerie, David A. Smith, and Judith Stepan-Norris. 2006. "Pioneer Public Sociologist C. Wright Mills, 50 Years Later." *Contemporary Sociology* 35 (6): 7–8.

Jimenez, Maria. 2009. "Humanitarian Crisis: Migrant Deaths at the U.S.—Mexico Border." A joint report of the American Civil Liberties Union of San Diego and Imperial Counties and Mexico's National Commission of Human Rights, October 1. Accessed June 12, 2011 (http://www.aclu.org/immigrants-rights /humanitarian-crisis-migrant-deaths-us-mexico-border).

Johnson, Allan G. 1997. *The Forest and the Trees: Sociology as Life, Practice, and Promise.* Philadelphia: Temple University Press.

Johnson, Kenneth M. and Daniel T. Lichter. 2010. "Growing Diversity among America's Children and Youth: Spatial and Temporal Dimensions." Population and Development Review 36(1): 151–176.

Johnson, Tallese D. 2008. "Maternity Leave and Employment Patterns: 2001–2003." *Current Population Reports*, P70–113. Washington, DC: U.S. Census Bureau.

Johnston, David Cay. 1994. "Ruling Backs Homosexuals on Asylum." *New York Times*, June 12, pp. D1, D6.

Jones. David D. 2011. "Oligarchy in the Making: Is Our Democracy Doomed?" July 17. Accessed July 22, 2011 (www.phillyburbs .com/news/local/courier_times_news/opinion/guest/oligarchy-in-the-making-is-our-democracy-doomed/article_b1cf7f12-0b30-5ff6-81c6-547a8727eee2.html).

Jones, Madeline. 2012. "Plus Size Bodies, What Is Wrong With Them Anyway?" *PLUS Model Magazine*, January 8. Accessed May 27, 2012 (http://www.plus-model-mag.com/2012/01 /plus-size-bodies-what-is-wrong-with-them-anyway/).

Joseph, Jay. 2004. *The Gene Illusion: Genetic Research in Psychiatry and Psychology Under the Microscope.* New York: Algora Books.

Josephson Institute of Ethics. 2011. "The Ethics of American Youth: 2010." Josephson Institute's 2010 Report Card on the Ethics of American Youth. Accessed May 20, 2011 (http://charactercounts .org/programs/reportcard/index.html).

Jordan, Miriam. 2011. "More 'Silent Raids' Over Immigration." The *Wall Street Journal*, June 16. Accessed June 21, 2011 (http://online .wsj.com/article/SB10001424052702304186404576387843087137 216.html).

Jost, Kenneth. 2008. "Women in Politics."*CQ Researcher* 18 (March 21).

Juergensmeyer, Mark. 2003. *Terror in the Mind of God: The Global Rise of Religious Violence*, 3rd ed. Berkeley: University of California Press.

K

Kaiser Family Foundation. 2005. *Sex on TV: 2005.* Santa Barbara, CA: Kaiser Family Foundation.

———. 2009. "Trends in Health Care Costs and Spending." Kaiser Family Foundation Publication #7692–02, March, Menlo Park, CA. Accessed June 26, 2009 (www.kff.org/insurance /upload/7692_02.pdf).

Kalev, Alexandria, Frank Dobbin, and Erin Kelly. 2006. "Best Practices or Best Guesses? Assessing the Efficacy of Corporate Affirmative Action and Diversity Policies." *American Sociological Review* 71: 589–617.

Kalish, Richard A. 1985. *Death, Grief, and Caring Relationships,* 2nd ed. Monterey, CA: Brooks/Cole.

Kalita, S. Mitra. 2006. "On the Other End of the Line." *Washington Post National Weekly Edition,* January 9, pp. 20–21.

Kalmijn, Matthijs. 1991. "Status Homogamy in the United States." *American Journal of Sociology* 97 (2): 496–523.

———. 1998. "Intermarriage and Homogamy: Causes, Patterns, Trends." *Annual Review of Sociology* 24: 395–412.

Kamp, Marianne. 2008. *The New Woman in Uzbekistan.* Seattle: University of Washington Press.

Kanter, Rosabeth Moss. 1993. *Men and Women of the Corporation.* New York: Basic Books.

Kapstein, Ethan B. 2006. "The New Global Slave Trade." *Foreign Affairs* 85 (November/December): 103–115.

Karney, Benjamin R., and John S. Crown. 2007. "Families Under Stress: An Assessment of Data, Theory, and Research on Marriage and Divorce in the Military." Santa Monica, CA: RAND Corporation.

Kasavin, Greg. 2003. "Real Life: The Full Review." GameSpot, July 11. Accessed June 3, 2008 (http://www.gamespot.com/gamespot /features/all/gamespotting/071103minusworld/1.html).

Katz, Jason. 1999. *Tough Guise: Violence, Media, and the Crisis in Masculinity.* Video. Directed by Sut Jhally. Northampton, MA: Media Education Foundation.

Kavada, Anastasia 2005. "Exploring the Role of the Internet in the 'Movement for Alternative Globalization': The Case of the Paris 2003 European Social Forum." *Westminster Papers in Communication and Culture* 2 (1): 72–95.

Kempadoo, Kamala, and Jo Doezema, eds. 1998. *Global Sex Workers: Rights, Resistance, and Redefinition.* New York: Routledge.

Kennickell, Arthur B. 2009. "Ponds and Streams: Wealth and Income in the U.S., 1989 to 2007." Finance and Economics Discussion Series, Divisions of Research & Statistics and Monetary Affairs, Federal Reserve Board, Washington, DC. Accessed June 7, 2009 (www.federalreserve.gov/pubs/feds/2009/200913/200913pap.pdf).

Kentor, Jeffrey, and Yong Suk Jang. 2004. "Yes, There Is a (Growing) Transnational Business Community." *International Sociology* 19 (September): 355–368.

Kerbo, Harold R. 2009. *Social Stratification and Inequality: Class Conflict in Historical, Comparative, and Global Perspective*, 7th ed. New York: McGraw-Hill.

Khorasani, Noushin Ahmadi. 2009. "How Social Movements Can Change Iran." *The Mark,* June 11. Accessed June 30, 2009 (www.themarknews.com/articles/290-how-social-movements-can-change-iran).

Kilbourne, Jean. 2010. *Killing Us Softly 4: Advertising's Image of Women.* Video. Produced and directed by Sut Jhally. Northampton, MA: Media Education Foundation.

Kilpatrick, Dean G., Heidi S. Resnick, Kenneth J. Ruggiero, Lauren M. Conoscenti, and Jenna McCauley. 2007. "Drug-Facilitated, Incapacitated, and Forcible Rape: A National Study." National Institute of Justice Grant No. 2005-Wg-BX-0006. Accessed June 1, 2010 (http://www.ncjrs.gov/pdffiles1/nij/grants/219181.pdf).

Kim, Kwang Chung. 1999. *Koreans in the Hood: Conflict with African Americans.* Baltimore: Johns Hopkins University Press.

Kimmel, Michael. 2004. *The Gendered Society,* 2nd ed. New York: Oxford University Press.

Kinsella, Kevin, and David R. Phillips. 2005. "Global Aging: The Challenge of Success." *Population Bulletin* 60 (March).

Kinsey, Alfred C., Wardell B. Pomeroy, and Paul H. Gebhard. 1953. *Sexual Behavior in the Human Female.* Philadelphia: Saunders.

Kinsey, Alfred C., Wardell B. Pomeroy, and Clyde E. Martin. 1948. *Sexual Behavior in the Human Male.* Philadelphia: Saunders.

Kirby, Emily Hoban, and Kei Kawashima-Ginsberg. 2009. "The Youth Vote in 2008." Fact Sheet, Center for Information & Research on Civic Learning & Engagement, April. Accessed June 18, 2009 (www .civicyouth.org/PopUps/FactSheets/FS_youth_Voting_2008.pdf).

Kirk, Dudley. 1996. "Demographic Transition Theory." Population Studies 50: 361–387.

Kitchener, Richard F. 1991. "Jean Piaget: The Unknown Sociologist." *British Journal of Sociology* 42 (September): 421–442.

Klein, Stefan. 2006. *The Science of Happiness: How Our Brains Make Us Happy—And What We Can Do to Get Happier.* New York: Marlowe.

Kleinknecht, William. 1996. *The New Ethnic Mobs: The Changing Face of Organized Crime in America.* New York: Free Press.

Kliewer, Wendy, and Terri N. Sullivan. 2009. "Community Violence Exposure, Threat Appraisal, and Adjustment in Adolescents." *Journal of Clinical Child & Adolescent Psychology* 37 (4): 860–873.

Kline, Susan L. and Shuangyue Zhang. 2009. "The Role of Relational Communication Characteristics and Filial Piety in Mate Preferences: Cross-cultural Comparisons of Chinese and US College Students." *Journal of Comparative Family Studies* 40 (3): 325–353.

Klinenberg, Eric. 2002. *Heat Wave: A Social Autopsy of Disaster in Chicago.* Chicago: University of Chicago Press.

Knapp, Laura G., Janice E. Kelly-Reid, and Scott A. Grinder. 2012. *Enrollment in Postsecondary Institutions, Fall 2010; Financial Statistics, Fiscal Year 2010; and Graduation Rates, Selected Cohorts, 2002–07.* U.S. Department of Education, NCES 2012–280. Washington, DC: National Center for Education Statistics. Accessed June 5, 2011 (http://nces.ed.gov/pubs2012/2012280.pdf).

Knudson, Tom. 2006. "Promises and Poverty: Starbucks Calls Its Coffee Worker-Friendly—but in Ethiopia, a Day's Pay Is a Dollar." *Sacramento Bee,* September 23. Accessed June 12, 2009 (www.sacbee.com/502/story/393917.html).

———. 2007. "Investigative Report: Promises and Poverty." *Sacramento Bee,* September 23. Accessed August 6, 2009 (www.sacbee.com/502/story/393917.html).

Kochhar, Rakesh. 2004. *The Wealth of Hispanic Households: 1996 to 2002.* Washington, DC: Pew Hispanic Center.

Kochhar, Rakesh, Richard Fry, and Paul Taylor. 2011. "Wealth Gaps Rise to Record Highs between Whites, Blacks, and Hispanics." *Social & Demographic Trends, Pew Research Center,* July 26. Accessed August 6, 2011 (http://pewsocialtrends.org/2011/07/26/wealth-gaps-rise-to-record-highs-between-whites-blacks-hispanics/).

———. 2011. "Wealth Gaps Rise to Record Highs Between Whites, Blacks and Hispanics." *Social & Demographic Trends,* Pew Research Center, July 26. Accessed September 19, 2011 (http://pewsocialtrends.org/files/2011/07/SDT-Wealth-Report_7-26-11_FINAL.pdf).

Kochhar, Rakesh, Ana Gonzalez-Barrera, and Daniel Dockterman. 2009. "Through Boom and Bust: Minorities, Immigrants and Homeownership." Pew Hispanic Center, May 12. Accessed June 22, 2009 (http://pewhispanic.org/files/reports/109.pdf).

Kochar, Rakesh, Richard Fry, and Paul Taylor. 2011. "Wealth Gaps Rise to Record Highs Between Whites, Blacks, and Hispanics." A Social & Demographic Trends Report, Pew Research Center, July. Accessed May 27, 2012 (http://www.pewsocialtrends.org/files/2011/07/SDT-Wealth-Report_7-26-11_FINAL.pdf).

Koerner, Brendan I. 2003. "What Does a 'Thumbs Up' Mean in Iraq?" *Slate,* March 28. Accessed May 3, 2009 (http://www.slate.com/id/2080812).

Kokmen, Leyla. 2008. "Environmental Justice for All." *Utne Reader,* March/April, pp. 42–46.

Korczyk, Sophie M. 2002. *Back to Which Future? The U.S. Aging Crisis Revisited.* Washington, DC: AARP.

Kosmin, Barry A., and Ariela Keysar. 2009. *American Religious Identification Survey: ARIS 2008 Summary Report.* Hartford, CT: Trinity College. Accessed June 1, 2009 (http://b27.cc.trincoll.edu/weblogs/AmericanReligionSurvey-ARIS/reports/ARIS_Report_2008.pdf).

Kottak, Conrad. 2004. *Anthropology: The Explanation of Human Diversity.* New York: McGraw-Hill.

Kozol, Jonathan. 2005. *The Shame of the Nation: The Restoration of Apartheid Schooling in America.* New York: Crown.

Krantz-Kent, Rachel. 2009. "Measuring Time Spent in Unpaid Household Work: Results from the American Time Use Survey." *Monthly Labor Review* July: 46–59.

Kraybill, Donald. 2001. *The Riddle of Amish Culture,* rev. ed. Baltimore: Johns Hopkins University Press.

Krebs, Christopher P., Christine H. Lindquist, Tara D. Warner, Bonnie S. Fisher, and Sandra L. Martin. 2007. "The Campus Sexual Assault (CSA) Study, Final Report." National Institute of Justice Grant No. 2004-WG-BX-0010. Accessed June 1, 2010 (http://www.ncjrs.gov.pdffiles1/nij/grants/221153.pdf).

Kreider, Rose M. 2008. "Living Arrangements of Children: 2004." *Current Population Reports,* No. 114. Washington, DC: U.S. Government. Printing Office.

———. 2010. "Increase in Opposite-sex Cohabiting Couples from 2009 to 2010 in the Annual Social and Economic Supplement (ASEC) to the Current Population Survey (CPS)." Housing and Household Economic Statistics Division Working Paper. Washington, DC: U.S. Bureau of the Census. Accessed June 1, 2011 (http://www.census.gov/population/www/socdemo/Inc-Opp-sex-2009-to-2010.pdf).

Kreider, Rose M. and Renee Ellis. 2011. "Number, Timing, and Duration of Marriages and Divorces: 2009." *Current Population Reports,* P70–125. Washington, DC: U.S. Census Bureau. Accessed September 19, 2011 (http://www.census.gov/prod/2011pubs/p70–125.pdf).

Kristof, Nicholas D., and Sheryl WuDunn. 2009. *Half the Sky: Turning Oppression into Opportunity for Women Worldwide.* New York: Knopf.

Kroll, Luisa, and Allison Fass. 2006. "The World's Billionaires." *Forbes,* March 9.

Kronstadt, Jessica, and Melissa Favreault. 2008. "Families and Economic Mobility." Washington, DC: Economic Mobility Project. Accessed August 13, 2008 (www.economicmobility.org/reports_and_research/literature_reviews?id=0004).

Kruttschnitt, Candace, and Kristin Carbone-Lopez. 2006. "Moving Beyond the Stereotypes: Women's Subjective Accounts of Their Violent Crime." *Criminology* 44 (2): 321–352.

Kübler-Ross, Elisabeth. 1969. *On Death and Dying.* New York: Macmillan.

Kuhl, Patricia K. 2004. "Early Language Acquisition: Cracking the Speech Code." *Nature Reviews Neuroscience* 5: 831–843.

Kuumba, M. Bahati. 2001. *Gender and Social Movements.* Lanham, MD: AltaMira Press.

Kwong, Jo. 2005. "Globalization's Effects on the Environment." *Society* 42 (January/February): 21–28.

Kyckelhahn, Tracey, Allen J. Beck, and Thomas H Cohen. 2009. "Characteristics of Suspected Human Trafficking Incidents, 2007–08." Bureau of Justice Statistics, Special Reports, January, NCJ 224526. Accessed June 2, 2010 (http://bjs.ojp.usdoj.gov/content/pub/pdf/cshti08.pdf).

L

Lacey, Marc. 2008. "Hunger in Haiti Increasing Rapidly." *International Herald Tribune,* April 17. Accessed August 12, 2008 (http://www.iht.com/articles/2008/04/17/news/Haiti.php).

Ladner, Joyce. 1973. *The Death of White Sociology.* New York: Random Books.

Laidlaw, Ken, DaHua Wang, Claudia Coelho, and Mick Power. 2010. "Attitudes to Ageing and Expectations for Filial Piety across Chinese and British Cultures: A Pilot Exploratory Evaluation." *Aging & Mental Health* 14 (3): 283–292.

Lambert, Emily. 2009. "Nimby Wars." *Forbes* 183 (February 16): 98–101. Accessed June 29, 2009 (www.forbes.com/forbes/2009/0216/098.html).

Landale, Nancy S., and R. S. Oropesa. 2007. "Hispanic Families: Stability and Change." *Annual Review of Sociology* 33: 381–405.

Langhout, Regina D., and Cecily A. Mitchell. 2008. "Engaging Contexts: Drawing the Link Between Student and Teacher Experiences of the Hidden Curriculum." *Journal of Community & Applied Social Psychology* 18 (6): 593–614.

Lareau, Annette. 2003. *Unequal Childhoods: Class, Race, and Family Life.* Berkeley: University of California Press.

Larson, Edward J. 2006. *Summer for the Gods: The Scopes Trial and America's Continuing Debate over Science and Religion.* New York: Basic Books.

Lasker, John. 2008. "Inside Africa's PlayStation War." *Toward Freedom,* July 8. Accessed June 3, 2009 (http://towardfreedom.com/home/content/view/1352/1).

Laumann, Edward O., John H. Gagnon, Robert T. Michael, and Stuart Michaels. 1994. *The Social Organization of Sexuality: Sexual Practices in the United States.* Chicago: University of Chicago Press.

Le Bon, Gustav. 1895. *The Crowd: A Study of the Popular Mind.* New York: Macmillan.

Lee, James. 2011. "U.S. Naturalization: 2010." Homeland Security, Office of Immigration Statistics, Annual Flow Report, March. Accessed June 26, 2011 (http://www.dhs.gov/xlibrary/assets /statistics/publications/natz_fr_2010.pdf).

Lefevre, Romana. 2011. *Rude Hand Gestures of the World: A Guide to Offending without Words.* San Francisco: Chronicle Books.

Lengermann, Patricia Madoo, and Jill Niebrugge-Brantley. 1998. *The Women Founders: Sociology and Social Theory, 1830–1930.* Boston: McGraw-Hill.

Leonard, Annie. 2010. *The Story of Stuff: How Our Obsession with Stuff Is Trashing the Planet, Our Communities, and Our Health—and a Vision for Change.* New York: Free Press.

Leonhardt, David. 2007. "Middle-Class Squeeze Comes with Nuances." *New York Times,* April 25, pp. C1, C12.

Levanon, Gad, Vivian Chen and Ben Chang. 2012. "Feeling the Pain: Wage Growth in the United States during and after the Great Recession." Executive Action Series, The Conference Board, New York, April.

Levine, Kenneth J., and Cynthia A. Hoffner. 2006. "Adolescents' Conceptions of Work: What Is Learned from Different Sources During Anticipatory Socialization?" *Journal of Adolescent Research* 21 (6): 647–669.

Levitt, Steven D., and Stephen J. Dubner. 2005. *Freakonomics: A Rogue Economist Explores the Hidden Side of Everything.* New York: Morrow.

Lewin, Tamar. 2008. "College May Become Unaffordable for Most in U.S." *New York Times,* December 3. Accessed May 19, 2010 (http://www.nytimes.com/2008/12/03/education/03college.html).

Leys, Tony. 2008. "New Faces Endure Same Struggle." *Des Moines Register,* May 18, pp. 1, 11.

Lezhnev, Sasha. 2011. "New U.N. Report: U.S. Conflict Minerals Law Having Impact in Congo." *Enough,* June 16. Accessed August 8, 2011 (www.enoughproject.org/blogs/ new-un-report-us-conflict-minerals-law-having-impact-congo).

Lim, Dawn. 2011. "Real-Life *Inception*: Army Looks to 'Counteract Nightmares' with Digital Dreams." *Wired: Danger Room* Octorber 21. Accessed April 9, 2012 (http://www.wired.com /dangerroom/2011/10/real-life-inception/).

Liang, Bin, and Hong Lu. 2010. "Internet Development, Censorship, and Cyber Crimes in China." *Journal of Contemporary Criminal Justice* 26 (1): 103–120.

Linden, BK. 2011. "Q1 2011 Linden Dollar Economy Metrics Up, Users and Usage Unchanged." Second Life Blog: Featured News. San Francisco: Linden Research, Inc. Accessed May 25, 2011 (http://community.secondlife.com/t5/Featured-News /Q1-2011-Linden-Dollar-Economy-Metrics-Up-Users-and-Usage /ba-p/856693).

Ling, Peter. 2006. "Social Capital, Resource Mobilization and Origins of the Civil Rights Movement." *Journal of Historical Sociology* 19 (2): 202–214.

Lino, Mark. 2008a. "Damages Cut Against Exxon in *Valdez* Case." *New York Times,* June 26. Accessed April 27, 2009 (http://www.nytimes .com/2008/06/26/washington/26punitive.html).

———. 2008b. "From One Footnote, a Debate over the Tangles of Law, Science and Money." *New York Times,* June 26. Accessed April 27, 2009 (http://www.nytimes.com/2008/11/25/washington/25bar.html).

Lino, Mark, and Andrea Carlson. 2009. *Expenditures on Children by Families, 2008.* Center for Nutrition Policy and Promotion, Miscellaneous Publication No. 1528-2008. U.S. Department of Agriculture, Washington, DC. Accessed April 13, 2010 (http://www.cnpp .usda.gov/Publications/CRC/crc2008.pdf).

Lino, Mark. 2011. *Expenditures on Children by Families, 2010.* Center for Nutrition Policy and Promotion, Miscellaneous Publication No. 1528-2010. U.S. Department of Agriculture, Washington, DC. Accessed May 8, 2012 (http://www.cnpp.usda.gov/Publications /CRC/crc2010.pdf).

Lipset, Seymour Martin. 1959. "Some Social Requisites of Democracy: Economic Development and Political Legitimacy." *American Political Science Review* 53: 69–105

List, Justin M. 2009. "Justice and the Reversal of the Healthcare Worker 'Brain-Drain.'" *American Journal of Bioethics* 9 (3): 10–12.

Lofquist, Daphne, Terry Lugaila, Martin O'Connell, and Sarah Feliz. 2012. "Households and Families: 2010." 2010 Census Brief, C2010BR-14, April. Washington, DC: U.S. Census Bureau. Accessed May 8, 2012 (http://www.census.gov/prod/cen2010 /briefs/c2010br-14.pdf).

Logue, Susan. 2009. "Poll: More Newlyweds Met Online." *Voice of America News,* March 27. Accessed May 26, 2009 (http://www .voanews.com/english/archive/2009-03/2009-03-27-voa17.cfm).

Lopata, Helena Znaniecki. 1971. *Occupation: Housewife.* New York: Oxford University Press.

Lopez, Mark Hugo, and Paul Taylor. 2009. "Dissecting the 2008 Electorate: Most Diverse in U.S. History." Pew Research Center, Washington, DC, April 30. Accessed June 18, 2009 (http:// pewresearch.org/assets/pdf/dissecting-2008-electorate.pdf).

Lorber, Judith. 1994. *Paradoxes of Gender.* New Haven, CT: Yale University Press.

Lotz, Amanda D. 2007. "Theorising the Intermezzo: The Contributions of Postfeminism and Third Wave Feminism." pp. 71–85 in *Third Wave Feminism: A Critical Exploration,* expanded 2nd ed., ed. Stacy Gillis, Gillian Howie, and Rebecca Munford. New York: Palgrave Macmillan.

Louie, Miriam Ching Yoon. 2001. *Sweatshop Warriors: Immigrant Women Workers Take on the Global Factory.* Cambridge, MA: South End Press.

Lovgren, Stefan. 2006. "Can Cell-Phone Recycling Help African Gorillas?" *National Geographic News,* January 20. Accessed June 3, 2009 (http://news.nationalgeographic.com/news/2006/01/0120 _060120_cellphones.html).

Lucal, Betsy. 2010. "Better Informed, Still Skeptical: Response to Machalek and Martin." *Teaching Sociology* 38 (1): 46–49.

Lukács, Georg. 1923. *History and Class Consciousness.* London: Merlin.

Lumpe, Lora. 2003. "Taking Aim at the Global Gun Trade." *Amnesty Now* (Winter): 10–13.

Lundquist, Jennifer Hickes. 2006. "Choosing Single Motherhood." *Contexts* 5 (Fall): 64–67.

Lyall, Sarah. 2002. "For Europeans, Love, Yes; Marriage, Maybe." *New York Times,* March 24, pp. 1–8.

Lymas, Mark. 2008. *Six Degrees: Our Future on a Hotter Planet.* Washington, DC: National Geographic.

Lynn, Barry C. 2003. "Trading with a Low-Wage Tiger." *The American Prospect* 14 (February): 10–12.

Lytton, Hugh, and David M. Romney. 1991. "Parents' Differential Socialization of Boys and Girls: A Meta-analysis." *Psychological Bulletin* 109 (2): 267–296.

M

MacEachern, Scott. 2003. "The Concept of Race in Anthropology." pp. 10–35 in *Race and Ethnicity: An Anthropological Focus on the United States and the World,* ed. R. Scupin. Upper Saddle River, NJ: Prentice Hall.

MacFarquhar, Neil. 2008. "Resolute or Fearful, Many Muslims Turn to Home Schooling." *New York Times,* March 26, p. A1.

Machalek, Richard, and Michael W. Martin. 2010. "Evolution, Biology, and Society: A Conversation for the 21st-Century Classroom." *Teaching Sociology* 38 (1): 35–45.

Maher, Timothy M. 2008. "Police Chiefs' Views on Police Sexual Misconduct." *Police Practice & Research* 9 (3): 239–250.

Mahy, Mary, Jean-Michel Tassie, Peter D. Ghys, John Stover, Michel Beusenberg, Priscilla Akwara, and Yves Souteyrand. 2010. "Estimation of Antiretroviral Therapy Coverage: Methodology and Trends." *Current Opinion in HIV and AIDS* 5 (1): 97–102.

Malacrida, Claudia. 2005. "Discipline and Dehumanization in a Total Institution: Institutional Survivors' Descriptions of Time-Out Rooms." *Disability & Society* 20 (5): 523–537.

Malcolm X, with Alex Haley. 1964. *The Autobiography of Malcolm X.* New York: Grove.

Malthus, Thomas R. 1878. An Essay on the Principle of Population: Or, A View of Its Past and Present Effects on Human Happiness, with an Inquiry into Our Prospects Respecting the Future Removal or Mitigation of the Evils which it Occasions. 8th edition. London: Reeves and Turner.

Mandel, Stephen. 2008. *Debt Relief as if Justice Mattered.* London: New Economics Foundation.

Mangan, Katherine. 2006. "Survey Finds Widespread Cheating in M.B.A. Programs." *Chronicle of Higher Education,* September 19. Accessed June 6 (http://chronicle.com/ daily/2006/09 /2006091902n.htm).

Mangum, Garth L., Stephen L. Mangum, and Andrew M. Sum. 2003. *The Persistence of Poverty in the United States.* Baltimore: Johns Hopkins University Press.

Mann, Horace. [1848] 1957. "Report No. 12 of the Massachusetts School Board." pp. 79–97 in *The Republic and the School: Horace Mann on the Education of Free Men,* ed. L. A. Cremin. New York: Teachers College.

Mann Yee Kan, Oriel Sullivan, and Jonathan Gershuny. 2011. "Gender Convergence in Domestic Work: Discerning the Effects of Interactional and Institutional Barriers from Large-scale Data." Sociology 45 (2): 234–251.

Manning, Jennifer E. 2011. "Membership of the 112th Congress: A Profile." A Congressional Research Service Report for Congress, Washington, DC, March 1. June 8, 2011 (www.senate.gov /reference/resources/pdf/R41647.pdf).

Mapel, Tim. 2007. "The Adjustment Process of Ex-Buddhist Monks to Life After the Monastery." *Journal of Religion & Health* 46 (1): 19–34.

Marijuana Policy Project. 2008. "State-by-State Medical Marijuana Laws: 2008." Washington, DC: Marijuana Policy Project. Accessed May 19, 2009 (http://www.mpp.org/assets/pdfs/download-materials/SBSR_NOV2008.pdf).

———. 2011. "The Sixteen States and One Federal District with Effective Medical Marijuana Laws." Washington, DC: Marijuana Policy Project. Accessed May 26, 2011 (http://www.mpp.org/assets/pdfs /17EffectiveLawsPlusMaryland.pdf).

Marshall, T. H. 1950. *Citizenship and Social Class and Other Essays.* Cambridge: Cambridge University Press.

Martin, Daniel C. 2011. "Refugees and Asylees: 2010." Homeland Security, Office of Immigration Statistics, Annual Flow Report, March. Accessed June 26, 2011 (http://www.dhs .gov/xlibrary/assets/statistics/publications/ois_rfa_fr_ 2010.pdf).

Martineau, Harriet. [1837] 1962. *Society in America.* Edited, abridged, with an introductory essay by Seymour Martin Lipset. Garden City, NY: Doubleday.

———. [1838] 1989. *How to Observe Morals and Manners.* Philadelphia: Leal and Blanchard. Sesquentennial edition, ed. M. R. Hill. New York: Transaction.

Martinez Gladys, Casey Copen, and Joyce C. Abma. "Teenagers in the United States: Sexual Activity, Contraceptive Use, and Childbearing, 2006–2010." National Survey of Family Growth, National Center for Health Statistics. *Vital and Health Statistics* 23 (31). Accessed May 26, 2012 (http://www.cdc.gov/nchs/data/series /sr_23/sr23_031.pdf).

Marx, Karl. [1845] 2000. "German Ideology." pp. 175–208 in *Karl Marx: Selected Writings,* 2nd ed., ed. David McLellan. New York: Oxford University Press.

———. [1867] 2000. "Capital." pp. 452–546 in *Karl Marx: Selected Writings,* 2nd ed., ed. David McLellan. New York: Oxford University Press.

Marx, Karl, and Friedrich Engels. [1847] 1955. *Selected Work in Two Volumes.* Moscow: Foreign Languages Publishing House.

———. [1848] 1998. *The Communist Manifesto: A Modern Edition.* New York: Verso.

Massey, Douglas S. 2007. *Categorically Unequal: The American Stratification System.* New York: Sage.

Mather, Mark and Diana Lavery. 2010. "In U.S., Proportion Married at Lowest Recorded Levels." Population Reference Bureau September. Accessed June 1, 2011 (http://www.prb.org/Articles/2010 /usmarriagedecline.aspx).

Mathews, T. J., and Marian F. MacDorman. 2010. "Infant Mortality Statistics from the 2006 Period Linked Birth/Infant Death Data Set." *National Vital Statistics Reports* 58 (17). Hyattsville, MD: National Center for Health Statistics. Accessed May 20, 2010 (http://www.cdc.gov/nchs/data/nvsr/nvsr58/nvsr58_17.pdf).

Mathews, T. J. and Marian F. MacDorman. 2011. "Infant Mortality Statistics From the 2007 Period Linked Birth/Infant Death Data Set." *National Vital Statistics Report* 59 (6). Hyattsville, MD: National Center for Health Statistics. Accessed May 28, 2012 (http://www .cdc.gov/nchs/data/nvsr/nvsr59/nvsr59_06.pdf).

Mayeux, Lara, Marlene J. Sandstrom, and Antonius H. N. Cillessen. 2008. "Is Being Popular a Risky Proposition?" *Journal of Research on Adolescence* 18 (1): 49–74.

Mayo, Elton. 1933. *The Human Problems of an Industrial Civilization.* London: Macmillan.

McAdam, Doug. 1988. *Freedom Summer.* New York: Oxford University Press.

McCabe, Donald L., Kenneth D. Butterfield, and Linda Klebe Treviño. 2006. "Academic Dishonesty in Graduate Business Programs: Prevalence, Causes, and Proposed Action." *Academy of Management Learning & Education* 5 (3): 294–305.

McCabe, Janice. 2005. "What's in a Label? The Relationship Between Feminist Self-Identification and 'Feminist' Attitudes Among U.S. Women and Men." *Gender & Society* 19 (4): 480–505.

McCabe, Janice, Emily Fairchild, Liz Grauerholz, Bernice A. Pescosolido and Daniel Tope. 2011. "Gender in Twentieth-Century Children's Books: Patterns of Disparity in Titles and Central Characters." Gender & Society 25 (2): 197–226.

McCoy, Adrian. 2011. "Reliving History: Virtual World Lets IUP Students Participate in Critical Civil Rights Battles." Pittsburg Post-Gazette, February 9. Accessed May 25, 2011 (http://www .post-gazette.com/pg/11040/1123965-51.stm).

McConnell-Ginet, Sally. 2011. *Gender, Sexuality, and Meaning: Linguistic Practice and Politics.* New York: Oxford University Press.

McDonald, Michael. 2009. "Election of a Century?" United States Elections Project. Accessed June 2, 2009 (http://elections.gmu.edu /Election_of_a_Century.html).

McDowell, David J., and Ross D. Parke. 2009. "Parental Correlates of Children's Peer Relations: An Empirical Test of a Tripartite Model." *Developmental Psychology* 45 (1): 224–235.

McGue, Matt, and Thomas J. Bouchard Jr. 1998. "Genetic and Environmental Influence on Human Behavioral Differences." pp. 1–24 in *Annual Review of Neurosciences.* Palo Alto, CA: Annual Reviews.

McGurty, Eileen. 2007. *Transforming Environmentalism: Warren County, PCBs, and the Origins of Environmental Justice.* Piscataway, NJ: Rutgers University Press.

McIntosh, Peggy. 1988. "White Privilege and Male Privilege: A Personal Account of Coming to See Correspondence Through Work and Women's Studies." Working Paper No. 189, Wellesley College Center for Research on Women, Wellesley, MA.

McKibben, Bill. 2003. *Enough: Staying Human in an Engineered Age.* New York: Henry Holt.

McKown, Clark, and Rhona S. Weinstein. 2008. "Teacher Expectations, Classroom Context, and the Achievement Gap." *Journal of School Psychology* 46 (3): 235–261.

McLaughlin, Emma, and Nicola Kraus. 2002. *The Nanny Diaries: A Novel.* New York: St. Martin's Press.

McLellan, David, ed. 2000. *Karl Marx, Selected Writings,* rev. ed. New York: Oxford University Press.

Mead, George H. 1934. *Mind, Self and Society,* ed. Charles W. Morris. Chicago: University of Chicago Press.

———. 1964a. *On Social Psychology,* ed. Anselm Strauss. Chicago: University of Chicago Press.

———. 1964b. "The Genesis of the Self and Social Control." pp. 267–293 in *Selected Writings: George Herbert Mead,* ed. Andrew J. Reck. Indianapolis: Bobbs-Merrill.

Mead, Margaret. [1935] 2001. *Sex and Temperament in Three Primitive Societies.* New York: Perennial, HarperCollins.

Meara Ellen R., Seth Richards, and David M. Cutler. 2008. "The Gap Gets Bigger: Changes in Mortality and Life Expectancy, by Education, 1981–2000." *Health Affairs* 27 (2): 350–360.

Mehl, Matthias R., Simine Vazire, Nairán Ramírez-Esparza, Richard B. Slatcher, and James W. Pennebacker. 2007. "Are Women Really More Talkative than Men?" *Science* 317 (July 6): 82.

Meier, Robert F., and Gilbert Geis. 1997. *Victimless Crime? Prostitution, Drugs, Homosexuality, Abortion.* Los Angeles: Roxbury Books.

Melby, Todd. 2007. "Exploring Why We Have Sex." *Contemporary Sexuality* 41 (October): 1, 4–6.

———. 2009. "Creating the DSM-V." *Contemporary Sexuality* 43 (3): 1, 4–6.

Mendez, Jennifer Bickman. 1998. "Of Mops and Maids: Contradictions and Continuities in Bureaucratized Domestic Work." *Social Problems* 45 (February): 114–135.

Merton, Robert. 1948. "The Bearing of Empirical Research upon the Development of Social Theory." *American Sociological Review* 13 (October): 505–515.

———. 1968. *Social Theory and Social Structure.* New York: Free Press.

Merton, Robert K., and Alice S. Kitt. 1950. "Contributions to the Theory of Reference Group Behavior." pp. 40–105 in *Continuities in Social Research: Studies in the Scope and Methods of the American Soldier,* ed. Robert K. Merton and Paul L. Lazarsfeld. New York: Free Press.

Meston, Cindy M., and David M. Buss. 2007. "Why Humans Have Sex." *Archives of Sexual Behavior* 36: 477–507.

———. 2009. *Why Women Have Sex: Understanding Sexual Motivations—From Adventure to Revenge (and Everything in Between).* New York: Henry Holt.

Michels, Robert. [1915] 1949. *Political Parties.* Glencoe, IL: Free Press.

Milgram, Stanley. 1963. "Behavioral Study of Obedience." *Journal of Abnormal and Social Psychology* 67 (October): 371–378.

———. 1975. *Obedience to Authority: An Experimental View.* New York: Harper & Row.

Milillo, Diana. 2008. "Sexuality Sells: A Content Analysis of Lesbian and Heterosexual Women's Bodies in Magazine Advertisements." *Journal of Lesbian Studies* 12 (4): 381–392.

Miller, David L., and JoAnne DeRoven Darlington. 2002. "Fearing for the Safety of Others: Disasters and the Small World Problem." Paper presented at the annual meeting of the Midwest Sociological Society, Milwaukee, WI.

Millett, Kate. 1970. *Sexual Politics.* Garden City, NY: Doubleday.

Mills, C. Wright. [1956] 2000. *The Power Elite.* New edition with afterword by Alan Wolfe. New York: Oxford University Press.

———. [1959] 2009. *The Sociological Imagination.* New York: Oxford University Press.

Milner Jr., Murray. 2006. *Freaks, Geeks, and Cool Kids: American Teenagers, Schools, and the Culture of Consumption.* New York: Routledge.

Miniño, Arialdi M., Sherry L. Murphy, Jiquan Xu, and Kenneth D. Kochanek 2011. "Deaths: Final Data for 2008." *National Vital Statistics Reports* 59 (10). Hyattsville, MD: National Center for Health Statistics. Accessed March 10, 2012.

Minnesota Center for Twin and Family Research. 2012. "Research at the MCTFR." Minneapolis: University of Minnesota. Accessed April 4, 2012 (http://mctfr.psych.umn.edu/).

Minority Rights Group International. 2007. "World Directory of Minorities and Indigenous Peoples–Mexico: Overview." Geneva: United Nations High Commissioner for Refugees. Accessed June 14, 2009 (www.unhcr.org/refworld/docid/4954ce409a.html).

Mirapaul, Matthew. 2001. "How the Net Is Documenting a Watershed Moment." *New York Times,* October 15, p. E2.

Mishel, Lawrence, Jared Bernstein, and Heide Shierholz. 2009. *The State of Working America 2008/2009.* Ithaca, NY: ILR Press.

Mizruchi, Mark S. 1996. "What Do Interlocks Do? An Analysis, Critique, and Assessment of Research on Interlocking Directorates." pp. 271–298 in *Annual Review of Sociology,* ed. John Hagan and Karen Cook. Palo Alto, CA: Annual Reviews.

Moen, Phyllis, and Patricia Roehling. 2005. *The Career Mystique: Cracks in the American Dream.* Lanham, MD: Rowman & Littlefield.

Mohai, Paul, and Robin Saha. 2007. "Racial Inequality in the Distribution of Hazardous Waste: A National-Level Reassessment." *Social Problems* 54 (3): 343–370.

Monaghan, Peter. 2012. "'Our Storehouse of Knowledge About Social Movements…Is Going to Be Left Bare.'" *The Chronicle of Higher Education* February 19. Accessed March 14, 2012 (http://chronicle.com/article/5-Minutes-With-a-Sociologist/130849/).

Montagu, Ashley, 1997. *Man's Most Dangerous Myth: The Fallacy of Race,* 6th ed., abridged student ed. Walnut Creek, CA: AltaMira Press.

Moore, David W. 2002. "Americans' View of Influence of Religion Settling Back to Pre–September 11 Levels." *Gallup Poll Tuesday Briefing,* December 31.

Moore, Molly. 2006. "Romance, but Not Marriage." *Washington Post National Weekly Edition,* November 27, p. 18.

Moore, Robert B. 1976. *Racism in the English Language: A Lesson Plan and Study Essay.* New York: The Racism and Sexism Resource Center for Educators.

Moore, Wilbert E. 1968. "Occupational Socialization." pp. 861–883 in *Handbook of Socialization Theory and Research,* ed. David A. Goslin. Chicago: Rand McNally.

Monger, Randall and James Yankay. 2011. "U.S. Legal Permanent Residents: 2010." Homeland Security, Office of Immigration Statistics, Annual Flow Report, March. Accessed June 26, 2011 (http://www.dhs.gov/xlibrary/assets/statistics/publications/lpr_fr_2010.pdf).

Morales, Lymari. 2010. "Green Behaviors Common in U.S., but Not Increasing." Washington, DC: Gallup, Inc., April 9. Accessed May 21, 2010 (http://www.gallup.com/poll/127292/Green-Behaviors-Common-Not-Increasing.aspx).

Morgan, Sue. 2009. "Theorising Feminist History: A Thirty-Year Retrospective." *Women's History Review* 18 (3): 381–407.

Morse, Arthur D. 1967. *While Six Million Died: A Chronicle of American Apathy.* New York: Ace.

Morselli, Carlo, Pierre Tremblay, and Bill McCarthy. 2006. "Mentors and Criminal Achievement." *Criminology* 44 (1): 17–43.

Mortimer, Jeylan T., and Michael J. Shanahan, eds. 2006. *Handbook of the Life Course.* New York: Springer Science and Business Media.

Mosher, William D., Anjani Chandra, and Jo Jones. 2005. "Sexual Behavior and Selected Health Measures: Men and Women 15–44 Years of Age, United States, 2002." *Advance Data from Vital and Health Statistics* 362. Hyattsville, MD: National Center for Health Statistics.

Moss, Michael, and Ford Fessenden. 2002. "New Tools for Domestic Spying, and Qualms." *New York Times,* December 10, pp. A1, A18.

Moyer, Michael. 2010. "Internet Ideology War." *Scientific American* 302 (4): 14–16.

Ms. 2006. "The *Ms.* Poll: Support High for Being a Feminist." *Ms.* 16 (3): 44.

Muhumued, Malkhadir M. 2011. "Malnourished Somali Baby Thriving as Rare Success." *Associated Press,* August 6. Accessed August 8, 2011 (www.boston.com/news/world/africa/articles/2011/08/06/doctor_malnourished_somali_baby_doing_well/).

Munford, Rebecca. 2007. "'Wake Up and Smell the Lipgloss': Gender, Generation, and the (A)Politics of Girl Power." pp. 266–279 in *Third Wave Feminism: A Critical Exploration,* expanded 2nd ed., Stacy Gillis, Gillian Howie, and Rebecca Munford. New York: Palgrave Macmillan.

Murdock, George P. 1945. "The Common Denominator of Cultures." pp. 123–142 in *The Science of Man in the World Crisis,* ed. Ralph Linton. New York: Columbia University Press.

———. 1949. *Social Structure.* New York: Macmillan.

———. 1957. "World Ethnographic Sample." *American Anthropologist* 59 (August): 664–687.

Myrskylä, Mikko, Hans-Peter Kohler and Francesco C. Billari. 2009. "Advances in Development Reverse Fertility Declines." *Nature* 460 (August 6): 741–743.

N

Nanda, Serena. 1997. "The Hijras of India." pp. 82–86 in *A Queer World: The Center for Lesbian and Gay Studies Reader,* ed. Martin Duberman. New York: New York University Press.

Naples, Nancy. 2003. *Feminism and Method: Ethnography, Discourse Analysis, and Activist Research.* New York: Routledge.

NAEP. 2011. "Main NAEP." NAEP Data Explorer, National Center for Education Statistics, Institute of Education Sciences, U.S. Department of Education. Accessed June 3, 2011 (http://nces.ed.gov /nationsreportcard/naepdata/).

El Nasser, Haya and Paul Overberg. 2011. "Fewer Couples Embrace Marriage; More Live Together." *USA Today,* May 26. Accessed June 1, 2011 (http://www.usatoday.com/news/nation/census /2011-05-26-census-unmarried-couples_n.htm).

National Cancer Institute. 2008. *The Role of the Media in Promoting and Reducing Tobacco Use.* Tobacco Control Monograph No. 19. National Institutes of Health, National Cancer Institute, NIH Pub. No. 07-6242. Bethesda, MD: U.S. Department of Health and Human Services.

National Center for Health Statistics. 2010. Health, United States, 2010: With Special Feature on Death and Dying. Hyattsville, MD. Acccessed June 20, 2011 (http://www.cdc.gov/nchs/data/hus /hus10.pdf).

———. 2011. Health, United States, 2010: With Special Feature on Death and Dying. Hyattsville, MD. Acccessed May 23, 2011 (http://www.cdc.gov/nchs/data/hus/hus10.pdf).

———. 2011. Health, United States, 2010: With Special Feature on Death and Dying. Hyattsville, MD. Accessed June 30, 2011 (http:// www.cdc.gov/nchs/data/hus/hus10.pdf).

National Center for Health Statistics. 2012. *Health, United States, 2011: With Special Feature on Socioeconomic Status and Health.* Hyattsville, MD. Accessed May 26, 2012 (http://www.cdc.gov/nchs/data /hus/hus11.pdf).

National Counterterrorism Center. 2011. "Worldwide Incidents Tracking System." Report generated for incidents between January 1, 2010, and December 31, 2010. June 8, 2011 https://wits.nctc.gov /FederalDiscoverWITS/index.do?t=Reports&Rcv=Incident&Nf=p _IncidentDate|GTEQ+20100101||p_IncidentDate|LTEQ+20101231 &N=0).

National Geogrphic. 2012. "Gulf Spill Pictures: Ten New Studies Show Impact on Coast. *National Geopraphic* April. Accessed May 28, 2012 (http://news.nationalgeographic.com/news/energy/2012/04 /pictures/120420-gulf-oil-spill-impact-studies/).

National Institute of Justice. 2007. "Transnational Organized Crime." U.S. Department of Justice. Accessed May 20, 2009 (http://www .ojp.usdoj.gov/nij/topics/crime/transnational-organized-crime /welcome.htm).

NCAA. 2011. "NCAA Sports Sponsorship and Participation Rates Report: 1981–82—2010–2011." Indianapolis, IN: The National Collegiate Athletic Association. Accessed May 16, 2012 (http://www.ncaapublications.com/productdownloads /PR2012.pdf).

NEA. 2010. "Rankings & Estimates: Rankings of the States 2010 and Estimates of School Statistics 2011." NEA Research, National Education Association, December. Accessed June 4, 2011 (http://www.nea.org/assets/docs/HE/NEA_Rankings_and _Estimates010711.pdf).

Neiwert, David A. 2005. *Strawberry Days: How Internment Destroyed the Japanese Community.* New York: Palgrave Macmillan.

Neumark, David. 2008. "Reassessing the Age Discrimination in Employment Act." Washington, DC: AARP Public Policy Institute. Accessed June 27, 2009 (http://www.aarp.org/research/work /agediscrim/2008_09_adea.html).

Newman, William M. 1973. *American Pluralism: A Study of Minority Groups and Social Theory.* New York: Harper & Row.

Newport, Frank. 2010. "Americans' Global Warming Concerns Continue to Drop." Washington, DC: Gallup, Inc. March 11. Accessed May 21, 2010 (http://www.gallup.com/poll/126560 /Americans-Global-Warming-Concerns-Continue-Drop.aspx).

Newport, Frank. 2011. "For First Time, Majority of Americans Favor Legal Gay Marriage." Gallup Politics, May 20. Accessed May 25, 2012 (http://www.gallup.com/poll/147662/first-time-majority- americans-favor-legal-gay-marriage.aspx).

Newton, Michael. 2002. *Savage Girls and Wild Boys: A History of Feral Children.* London: Faber and Faber.

New York Times. 2006. "Questions Couples Should Ask (or Wish They Had) Before Marrying." *New York Times,* December 17. Accessed August 6, 2009 (www.nytimes.com/2006/12/17/fashion /weddings/17FIELDBOX.html).

NFHS. 2011. "2010–11 High School Athletics Participation Survey." National Federation of State High School Associations, Indianapolis, IN. Accessed May 16, 2012 (http://www.nfhs.org/content .aspx?id=3282).

NHPCO. 2012. "NHPCO Facts and Figures: Hospice Care in America." 2011 Edition. Alexandria, VA: National Hospice and Palliative Care Organization. Accessed April 6, 2012 (http://www.nhpco.org /files/public/Statistics_Research/2011_Facts_Figures.pdf).

Nicolas, Guerda, Angela M. DeSilva, Kathleen S. Grey, and Diana Gonzalez-Eastep. 2006. "Using a Multicultural Lens to Understand Illnesses Among Haitians Living in America." *Professional Psychology: Research & Practice* 37 (6): 702–707.

Nielsen, Joyce McCarl, Glenda Walden, and Charlotte A. Kunkel. 2000. "Gendered Heteronormativity: Empirical Illustrations in Everyday Life." *Sociological Quarterly* 41 (2): 283–296.

Nielsen. 2012a. "State of the Media: The Cross-Platform Report— Quarter 3, 2011." Accessed April 5, 2012 (http://www.nielsen.com /us/en/insights/reports-downloads/2012/cross-platform-report- q3-2011.html).

———. 2012b. "State of the Media: U.S. Digital Consumer Report— Q3-Q4 2011." Accessed April 5, 2012 (http://www.nielsen.com /content/dam/corporate/us/en/reports-downloads/2012-Reports /Digital-Consumer-Report-Q4-2012.pdf).

Nobles, Melissa. 2000. "History Counts: A Comparative Analysis of Racial/Color Categorization in U.S. and Brazilian Censuses." *American Journal of Public Health* 90: 1738–1745.

Nofziger, Stacey, and Hye-Ryeon Lee. 2006. "Differential Associations and Daily Smoking of Adolescents: The Importance of Same-Sex Models." *Youth & Society* 37 (4): 453–478.

Nolan, Patrick, and Gerhard Lenski. 2006. *Human Societies: An Introduction to Macrosociology,* 10th ed. Boulder, CO: Paradigm.

Norris, Pippa, and Ronald Inglehart. 2004. *Sacred and Secular: Religion and Politics Worldwide.* Cambridge: Cambridge University Press.

North Carolina Department of Environment and Natural Resources. 2008. "Warren County PCB Landfill Fact Sheet." Accessed April 9, 2008 (www.wastenotnc.org/WarrenCo_Fact_Sheet.htm).

Norton, Michael I. and Samuel R. Sommers. 2011. "Whites See Racism as a Zero-Sum Game That They Are Now Losing." *Perspectives on Psychological Science* 6(3): 215–218.

Norwegian Ministry of Children and Equality. 2009. "Women in Norwegian Politics." Norway, the Official Site in the United States. Accessed June 18, 2009 (www.norway.org/policy/gender/politics /politics.htm).

Notestein, Frank. 1945. "Population: The Long View." pp. 36–57 in Food for the World, edited by Theodore W. Schultz. Chicago: University of Chicago Press.

Noueihed, Lin and Alex Warren. 2012. *The Battle for the Arab Spring: Revolution, Counter-Revolution and the Making of a New Era.* New Haven: Yale University Press.

O

Oakes, Jeannie. 2008. "Keeping Track: Structuring Equality and Inequality in an Era of Accountability." *Teachers College Record* 110 (3): 700–712.

OASDI. 2011. "The 2011 Annual Report of the Board of Trustees of the Federal Old-Age and Survivors Insurance and Federal Disability Insurance Trust Funds." Social Security Administration,

66–327, May 13. Washington, DC: U.S. Government Printing Office. Accessed June 29, 2011 (http://www.ssa.gov/oact /TR/2011/).

Obach, Brian K. 2004. *Labor and the Environmental Movement: The Quest for Common Ground*. Cambridge, MA: MIT Press.

Oberschall, Anthony. 1973. *Social Conflict and Social Movements*. Englewood Cliffs, NJ: Prentice Hall.

O'Connell, Martin, and Daphne Lofquist. 2009. "Counting Same-Sex Couples: Official Estimates and Unofficial Guesses." Annual meeting of the Population Association of America, Detroit, April 30–May 2, 2009. Accessed May 27, 2009 (http://www.census.gov /population/www/socdemo/files/counting-paper.pdf).

O'Connell, Martin and Sarah Feliz. 2011. "Same-sex Couple House-hold Statistics from the 2010 Census." Social, Economic and Hous-ing Statistics Division, U.S. Bureau of the Census, SEHSD Working Paper Number 2011-26, September 27. Accessed May 2, 2012 (www.census.gov/hhes/samesex/files/ss-report.doc).

O'Connor, Anne-Marie. 2004. "Time of Blogs and Bombs." *Los Angeles Times*, December 27, pp. E1, E14–E15.

OECD. 2011. "Society at a Glance 2011-OECD Social Indicators." Paris: Organisation for Economic Co-operation and Development. Accessed June 9, 2011 (http://www.oecd.org/els/social/indicators /SAG).

———. 2010. "Development Aid Rose in 2009 and Most Donors Will Meet 2010 Aid Targets." Organization for Economic Co-operation and Development, April 14. Accessed April 28, 2010. (http://www.oecd.org/document/11/0,3343,en_2649 _34487_44981579_1_1_1_1,00.html).

Office of Immigration Statistics. 2007. "2006 Yearbook of Immigra-tion Statistics." Washington, DC: U.S. Department of Homeland Security.

Ogburn, William F. 1922. *Social Change with Respect to Culture and Original Nature*. New York: Huebsch (reprinted 1966, New York: Dell).

Ogburn, William F., and Clark Tibbits. 1934. "The Family and Its Functions." pp. 661–708 in *Recent Social Trends in the United States*, ed. Research Committee on Social Trends. New York: McGraw-Hill.

O'Harrow Jr., Robert. 2005. "Mining Personal Data." *Washington Post National Weekly Edition* (February 6), pp. 8–10.

Okrent, Arika. 2009. *In the Land of Invented Languages: Esperanto Rock Stars, Klingon Poets, Loglan Lovers, and the Mad Dreamers Who Tried to Build a Perfect Language*. New York: Spiegel and Grau.

———. 2010. "The New Klingon Without So Much as a Dictionary, Avatar Fans Are Learning How to Speak Na'vi." *Slate*, March 24. Accessed March 31, 2010 (http://www.slate.com/id/2248683/).

Okun, Arthur. 1975. *Equality and Efficiency: The Big Tradeoff*. Wash-ington, DC: The Brookings Institution.

Oliver, Melvin L., and Thomas M. Shapiro. 1995. *Black Wealth /White Wealth: New Perspectives on Racial Inequality*. New York: Routledge.

OLPC. 2010. "One Laptop per Child: Vision." One Laptop per Child, Cambridge, MA. Accessed May 23, 2010 (http://laptop.org/en /vision/index.shtml).

Omi, Michael, and Howard Winant. 1994. *Racial Formation in the United States: From the 1960s to the 1990s*, 2nd ed. New York: Routledge.

Onishi, Norimitso. 2003. "Divorce in South Korea: Striking a New Attitude." *New York Times*, September 21, p. 19.

Orshansky, Mollie. 1965. "Counting the Poor: Another Look at the Poverty Profile." *Social Security Bulletin* 28 (1): 3–29.

Ortman, Jennifer M., and Christine E. Guarneri. 2008. "United States Population Projections: 2000 to 2050." 2009 National Population Projections, U.S. Census Bureau. Accessed May 17, 2010 (http:// www.census.gov/population/www/projections/analytical-document09.pdf).

Osberg, Lars, and Timothy Smeeding. 2006. "'Fair' Inequality? Attitudes Toward Pay Differentials: The United States in Comparative Perspective." *American Sociological Review* 71 (June): 450–473.

P

Padian, Kevin. 2007. "The Case of Creation." *Nature* 448 (July 19): 253–254.

Pager, Devah. 2003. "The Mark of a Criminal Record." *American Journal of Sociology* 108 (March): 937–975.

Pager, Devah, and Hana Shepherd. 2008. "The Sociology of Discrimi-nation: Racial Discrimination in Employment, Housing, Credit, and Consumer Markets." *Annual Review of Sociology* 34: 181–209.

Pager, Devah, Bruce Western, and Bart Bonikowski. 2009. "Dis-crimination in a Low Wage Labor Market: A Field Experiment." American Sociological Review 74: 777–799.

Pager, Devah, Bruce Western, and Naomi Sugie. 2009. "Sequencing Disadvantage: Barriers to Employment Facing Young Black and White Men with Criminal Records." Annals of the American Academy of Political and Social Sciences 623: 195–213.

Panagopoulos, Costas. 2009. "Polls and Elections: Preelection Poll Accuracy in the 2008 General Elections." *Presidential Studies Quarterly* 39 (4): 896–907.

Painter, Nell Irvin. 2010. *The History of White People*. New York: Norton.

Palm, Cheryl, Stephen A. Vosti, Pedro A. Sanchez, and Polly J. Ericksen, eds. 2005. *Slash-and-Burn Agriculture: The Search for Alternatives*. New York: Columbia University Press.

Park, Kristin. 2005. "Choosing Childlessness: Weber's Typology of Action and Motives of the Voluntarily Childless." *Sociological Inquiry*, August, pp. 372–402.

Park, Robert E. 1922. *The Immigrant Press and Its Control*. New York: Harper.

Parker, Alison. 2004. "Inalienable Rights: Can Human-Rights Law Help to End U.S. Mistreatment of Noncitizens?" *American Prospect*, October, pp. A11–A13.

Parker, Richard. 2009. "Sexuality, Culture and Society: Shifting Para-digms in Sexuality Research." *Culture, Health & Sexuality* 11 (3): 251–266.

Parsons, Talcott. 1951. *The Social System*. New York: Free Press.

———. 1966. *Societies: Evolutionary and Comparative Perspectives*. Englewood Cliffs, NJ: Prentice Hall.

———. 1975. "The Sick Role and the Role of the Physician Recon-sidered." *Milbank Medical Fund Quarterly Health and Society* 53 (Summer): 257–278.

Parsons, Talcott, and Robert Bales. 1955. *Family: Socialization, and Interaction Process*. Glencoe, IL: Free Press.

Pascoe, C. J. 2007. *Dude You're a Fag: Masculinity and Sexuality in High School*. Berkeley: University of California Press.

Passel, Jeffrey S., D'Vera Cohn, and Mark Hugo Lopez. 2011. "His-panics Account for More than Half of Nation's Growth in Past Decade." Pew Hispanic Center, A Pew Research Center Project, March 24. Accessed June 20, 2011 (http://pewhispanic.org /reports/report.php?ReportID=140).

Patten, Eileen and Kim Parker. 2012. "A Gender Reversal On Career Aspirations: Young Women Now Top Young Men in Valuing a High-Paying Career." A Social & Demo-graphic Trends Report, Pew Research Center, April 19. Accessed May 2, 2012 (http://www.pewsocialtrends. org/2012/04/19/a-gender-reversal-on-career-aspirations/).

Patterson, Thomas E. 2003. *We the People*, 5th ed. New York: McGraw-Hill.

Pattillo, Mary. 2005. "Black Middle-Class Neighborhoods." *Annual Review of Sociology* 31: 305–329.

Paxton, Pamela, Sheri Kunovich, and Melanie M. Hughes. 2007. "Gen-der in Politics." pp. 263–285 in *Annual Review of Sociology 2007*. Palo Alto, CA: Annual Reviews.

Pear, Robert. 2008. "Gap in Life Expectancy Widens for the Nation." *New York Times*, March 23. Accessed June 26, 2009 (www .nytimes.com/2008/03/23/us/23health.html).

Pearson, Allison. 2011. "Citizen Kate." Newsweek April 3. Accessed May 30, 2011 (http://www.newsweek.com/2011/04/03 /citizen-kate.html).

Peattie, Lisa, and Martin Rein. 1983. *Women's Claims: A Study in the Political Economy.* New York: Oxford University Press.

Peel, Lilly. 2008. "Matchmaker, Matchmaker Make Me a Match . . . If the Algorithms Agree." *Times Online,* October 6. Accessed May 26, 2009 (http://business.timesonline.co.uk/tol/business /industry_sectors/technology/article4887501.ece).

Perrow, Charles. 1986. *Complex Organizations,* 3rd ed. New York: Random House.

Perry, Barbara. 2010. "'No Biggie': The Denial of Oppression on Campus." Education, Citizenship and Social Justice 5 (3): 265–279.

Pershing, Jana L. 2003. "Why Women Don't Report Sexual Harassment: A Case Study of an Elite Military Institution." *Gender Issues* 21 (4): 3–30.

Peterson, Karen S. 2003. "Unmarried with Children: For Better or Worse." *USA Today,* August 18, pp. 1A, 8A.

Petrovic, Drazen. 1994. "Ethnic Cleansing—an Attempt at Methodology." *EJIL* 5: 1–19.

Pew Charitable Trusts. 2012. "A Year or More: The High Cost of Long-Term Unemployment—Addendum." Pew Fiscal Analysis Initiative, May 2. Accessed May 22, 2012 (http://www.pewtrusts .org/uploadedFiles/wwwpewtrustsorg/Reports/Fiscal_Analysis /Addendum_Long-Term_Unemployment_May2012.pdf).

Pew Hispanic Center. 2011a. "Statistical Portrait of Hispanics in the United States, 2009." A Pew Research Center Project, February 17. Accessed June 21, 2011 (http://pewhispanic.org/factsheets /factsheet.php?FactsheetID=70).

Pew Hispanic Center. 2007. "Changing Faiths: Latinos and the Transformation of American Religion." Washington, DC: The Pew Forum on Religion & Public Life, Pew Research Center. Accessed June 21, 2011 (http://pewhispanic.org/reports/report .php?ReportID=75).

Pew Hispanic Center. 2011b. "Unauthorized Immigrant Population: National and State Trends, 2010." Pew Research Center, February 1. Accessed June 21, 2011 (http://pewhispanic.org/reports/report .php?ReportID=133).

Pew Research Center. 2006. "More Americans Discussing—and Planning—End-of-Life Treatment." Pew Research Center for the People & the Press, Washington, DC, January 5. Accessed June 18, 2009 (http://people-press.org/reports/pdf/266.pdf).

———. 2007. "Optimism About Black Progress Declines: Blacks See Growing Values Gap Between Poor and Middle Class." Washington, DC: Pew Research Center. Accessed July 1, 2008 (http://pewsocialtrends.org/assets/pdf/Race.pdf).

Pew Research Center. 2008a. "U.S. Religious Landscape Survey." Pew Forum on Religion in Public Life. Washington, DC: Pew Research Center. Accessed June 14, 2008 (http://religions.pewforum.org /pdf/report-religious-landscape-study-full.pdf).

———. 2008b. "Election-Year Economic Ratings Lowest Since '92: An Even More Partisan Agenda for 2008." Pew Research Center for the People & the Press. Washington, DC: Pew Research Center. Accessed July 4, 2008 (http://people-press.org/reports/display .php3?ReportID=388).

———. 2009a. "Independents Take Center Stage in Obama Era." Pew Research Center for the People & the Press, May 21. Accessed June 2, 2009 (http://people-press.org/report/?pageid=1516).

———. 2009c. "Majority Continues to Support Civil Unions: Most Still Oppose Same-Sex Marriage." Pew Research Center for the People & the Press, Washington, DC, October 9. Accessed April 14, 2010 (http://people-press.org/reports/pdf/553.pdf).

———. 2009d. "The Stronger Sex—Spiritually Speaking." Pew Forum on Religion & Public Life, February 26. Accessed April 19, 2010 (http://pewforum.org/docs/?DocID=403).

———. 2009e. "End of Communism Cheered but Now with More Reservations: Two Decades After the Wall's Fall." Pew Global Attitudes Project, November 2. Accessed April 23, 2010 (http:// pewglobal.org/reports/pdf/267.pdf).

———. 2010. "Public's Priorities for 2010: Economy, Jobs, Terrorism." Pew Research Center for the People & the Press, January 25. Accessed May 21, 2010 (http://people-press.org/reports/pdf /584.pdf).

———. 2010a. "Millennials: A Portrait of Generation Next." Pew Research Publications, February. Accessed April 8, 2010 (http:// pewsocialtrends.org/assets/pdf/millennials-confident-connected-open-to-change.pdf).

———. 2010b. "Broad Public Support for Legalizing Medical Marijuana." Pew Research Center for the People & the Press, Washington, DC, April 1. Accessed April 9, 2010 (http:// pewresearch.org/pubs/1548/broad-public-support-for-legalizing-medical-marijuana).

———. 2010c. "Trust in Government Database: 1958–2010." Accessed April 23, 2010 (http://people-press.org/trust/trust-database.xls).

———. 2010e. "The Decline of Marriage and Rise of New Families." Social & Demographic Trends Project, Pew Research Center. Accessed May 31, 2011 (http://pewsocialtrends.org/2010/11/18 /the-decline-of-marriage-and-rise-of-new-families/).

———. 2010f. "Gender Equality Universally Embraced, but Inequalities Acknowledged." Global Attitudes Project, July 1. Accessed June 15, 2011 (http://pewglobal.org/files/pdf/Pew-Global-Attitudes-2010-Gender-Report.pdf).

———. 2011a. "Opinion of the United States: Do You Have a Favorable or Unfavorable View of the U.S.?" Key Indicators Database. Pew Global Attitudes Project. Accessed May 23, 2011 (http:// pewglobal.org/database/?indicator=1&survey=12).

———. 2011c. "Economy Dominates Public's Agenda, Dims Hopes for the Future." The Pew Research Center for the People & the Press, January 20. Accessed June 30, 2011 (http://people-press.org/files /legacy-pdf/696.pdf).

———. 2011d. "The American-Western European Values Gap: American Exceptionalism Subsides." Pew Global Attitudes Project November 17. Accessed March 25, 2012 (http://www.pewglobal .org/files/2011/11/Pew-Global-Attitudes-Values-Report-FINAL-November-17-2011-10AM-EST1.pdf).

———. 2011e. "Global Digital Communication: Texting, Social Networking Popular Worldwide." Global Attitudes Project December 20. Accessed April 9, 2012 (http://www.pewglobal.org /files/2011/12/Pew-Global-Attitudes-Technology-Report-FINAL-December-20-20111.pdf).

———. 2011f. "Obama Leadership Image Takes a Hit, GOP Ratings Decline." A For the People & the Press Report, August 25." Accessed May 24, 2012 (http://www.people-press.org/files /legacy-pdf/8-25-11%20Political%20Release.pdf).

Pew Research Center. 2012a. "More Support for Gun Rights, Gay Marriage than in 2008, 2004." The Pew Research Center for the People & the Press, April 25. Accessed May 8, 2012 (http://www .people-press.org/files/legacy-pdf/4-25-12%20Social%20Issues.pdf).

———. 2012b. "Young, Underemployed and Optimistic: Coming of Age, Slowly, in a Tough Economy." A Social & Demographic Trends Report, February 9. Accessed May 22, 2012 (http://www .pewsocialtrends.org/files/2012/02/young-underemployed-and-optimistic.pdf).

———. 2012c. "More Support for Gun Rights, Gay Marriage than in 2008, 2004." A For The People & The Press Report, April 25. Accessed May 25, 2012 (http://www.people-press.org/files /legacy-pdf/4-25-12%20Social%20Issues.pdf).

———. 2012d. "Public Priorities: Deficit Rising, Terrorism Slipping." A For The People & The Press Report, January 23. Accessed May 28, 2012 (http://www.people-press.org/files/legacy-pdf /1-23-12%20Priorities%20Release.pdf).

Pfeifer, Mark. 2008. "Vietnamese Americans." pp. 1,365–1,368 in *Encyclopedia of Race, Ethnicity, and Society,* vol. 3, ed. Richard T. Schaefer. Thousand Oaks, CA: Sage.

Phillips, Katherine A., Katie A. Liljenquist, and Margaret A. Neale. 2009. "Is the Pain Worth the Gain? The Advantages and Liabilities of Agreeing with Socially Distinct Newcomers." *Personality and Social Psychology Bulletin* 35 (3): 336–350.

Piaget, Jean. 1954. *The Construction of Reality in the Child,* trans. Margaret Cook. New York: Basic Books.

Piketty, Thomas and Emmanuel Saez. 2012. "Tables and Figures Updated to 2010 in Excel Format, March 2012 for 'Income Inequality in the United States, 1913–1998,' *The Quarterly Journal*

of Economics, February, 2003." Accessed May 17, 2012 (http://elsa
.berkeley.edu/~saez/TabFig2010.xls).

Pinderhughes, Dianne. 1987. *Race and Ethnicity in Chicago Politics: A
Reexamination of Pluralist Theory.* Urbana: University of Illinois
Press.

Pinkerton, James P. 2003. "Education: A Grand Compromise." *Atlantic
Monthly* 291 (January/February): 115–116.

Pinnow, Ellen, Pellavi Sharma, Ameeta Parekh, Natalie Gevorkian,
and Kathleen Uhl. 2009. "Increasing Participation of Women in
Early Phase Clinical Trials Approved by the FDA." *Women's Health
Issues* 19 (2): 89–92.

Planty, M., W. Hussar, T. Snyder, G. Kena, A. Kewal-Ramani,
J. Kemp, K. Bianco, and R. Dinkes. 2009. *The Condition of Education 2009.* NCES 2009-081. Washington, DC: National Center for
Education Statistics, Institute of Education Sciences, U.S. Department of Education. Accessed May 29, 2009 (http://nces.ed.gov
/pubs2009/2009081.pdf).

Planty, M., W. Hussar, T. Snyder, S. Provasnik, G. Kena, R. Dinkes, A.
Kewal-Ramani, and J. Kemp. 2008. *The Condition of Education
2008.* NCES 2008-031. Washington, DC: National Center for Education Statistics, Institute of Education Sciences, U.S. Department
of Education. Accessed June 14, 2008 (http://nces.ed.gov
/pubs2008/2008031.pdf).

Plaut, Victoria C., Flannery G. Garnett, Laura E. Buffardi, and Jeffrey
Sanchez-Burks. 2011. "'What About Me?' Perceptions of Exclusion
and Whites' Reactions to Multiculturalism." *Journal of Personality
and Social Psychology* 101(2): 337–353.

Pollini, Jacques. 2009. "Agroforestry and the Search for Alternatives
to Slash-and-Burn Cultivation: From Technological Optimism to
a Political Economy of Deforestation." *Agriculture, Ecosystems &
Environment* 133 (1/2): 48–60.

Pollster.com. 2012. "National Party Identification (Registered and
Likely Voters Only)." Accessed May 24, 2012 (http://www.pollster
.com/polls/us/party-id.php).

Popenoe, David, and Barbara Dafoe Whitehead. 1999. *Should We Live
Together? What Young Adults Need to Know About Cohabitation
Before Marriage.* Rutgers, NJ: National Marriage Project.

Population Reference Bureau. 2009. *2009 World Population Data
Sheet.* Washington, DC. Accessed May 20, 2010 (http://www.prb
.org/Publications/Datasheets.aspx).

Population Reference Bureau. 2011. *2011 Word Population Data Sheet.*
Washington, DC: Population Reference Bureau. Accessed April 5,
2012 (http://www.prb.org/pdf11/2011population-data-sheet_eng.pdf).

Porter, Roy. 1998. *The Greatest Benefit to Mankind: A Medical History
of Humanity.* New York: HarperCollins.

———. 2004. *Blood and Guts: A Short History of Medicine.*
New York: Norton.

Postman, Neil. 1988. "Questioning the Media." Video. The January
Series, January 12. Grand Rapids, MI: Calvin College.

———. 1993. *Technopoly: The Surrender of Culture to Technology.* New
York: Vintage Books.

———. 1999. *Building a Bridge to the 18th Century: How the Past Can
Improve Our Future.* New York: Knopf.

Potts, John. 2009. *A History of Charisma.* New York: Palgrave
Macmillan.

Preves, Sharon S. 2000. "Negotiating the Constraints of Gender
Binarism: Intersexuals' Challenge to Gender Categorization."
Current Sociology 48 (3): 27–50.

ProCon.org. 2009. "Medical Marijuana: Votes and Polls, National."
Accessed May 19, 2009 (http://medicalmarijuana.procon.org
/viewadditionalresource.asp?resourceID=000151).

Progressive Student Labor Movement. 2008. "A Brief History of the
Living Wage Debate at Harvard." Accessed July 7 (http://www.hcs
.harvard.edu/~pslm/livingwage/timeline.html).

Project on Student Debt. 2011. "Student Debt and the Class of 2010."
The Institute for College Access and Success, November. Accessed
May 22, 2012 (http://projectonstudentdebt.org/files/pub
/classof2010.pdf).

Prohaska, Ariane, and Jeannine Gailey. 2010. "Achieving Masculinity Through Sexual Predation: The Case of Hogging." *Journal of
Gender Studies* 19 (1): 13–25.

Preston, Julia. 2011. "Latinos and Democrats Press Obama to Curb
Deportations." *New York Times,* April 20. Accessed June 21, 2011
(http://www.nytimes.com/2011/04/21/us/politics/21immigration
.html).

Provasnik, S., and Planty, M. 2008. *Community Colleges: Special
Supplement to the Condition of Education 2008.* NCES 2008-
033. Washington, DC: National Center for Education Statistics,
Institute of Education Sciences, U.S. Department of Education.
Accessed May 31, 2009 (http://nces.ed.gov/pubs2008/2008033
.pdf).

Prus, Steven G. 2007. "Age, SES, and Health: A Population-Level
Analysis of Health Irregularities over the Lifecourse." *Sociology of
Health and Illness* 29 (March): 275–296.

Pryor, John H., Sylvia Hurtado, Victor B. Saenz, José Luis Santos,
and William S. Korn. 2007. *The American Freshman: Forty-Year
Trends.* Los Angeles: Higher Education Research Institute, UCLA.

Pryor, John H., Linda DeAngelo, Laura Palucki Blake, Sylvia Hurtado,
and Serge Tran. 2011. *The American Freshman: National Norms
Fall 2011.* Los Angeles: Higher Education Research Institute,
UCLA. Accessed March 25, 2012 (http://heri.ucla.edu/PDFs/pubs
/TFS/Norms/Monographs/TheAmericanFreshman2011.pdf).

Q

Quinney, Richard. 1970. *The Social Reality of Crime.* Boston: Little,
Brown.

———. 1974. *Criminal Justice in America.* Boston: Little, Brown.

———. 1979. *Criminology,* 2nd ed. Boston: Little, Brown.

———. 1980. *Class, State and Crime,* 2nd ed. New York: Longman.

Quirk, Patrick W. 2009. "Iran's Twitter Revolution." *The Epoch Times,*
June 24. Accessed July 1, 2009 (www.theepochtimes.com/n2
/content/view/18593).

Quisumbing, Agnes, Ruth Meinzen-Dick, and Lucy Bassett. 2008.
"Helping Women Respond to the Global Food Price Crisis." IFPRI
Policy Brief 7, October. Accessed June 18, 2009 (www.ifpri.org
/pubs/bp/bp007.pdf).

QuotaProject. 2012. "Global Database of Quotas for Women." International IDEA, Stockholm University and Inter-Parliamentary
Union. Accessed May 24, 2012 (http://www.quotaproject.org
/system.cfm).

R

Radovich, Sasha. 2006. *The Global Alliance for Workers and Communities: Lessons Learned About Partnership Goverance and Accountability from a Milti-stakeholder Initiative.* London: AccountAbility.
Accessed May 28, 2010 (http://info.worldbank.org/etools/docs
/library/238370/The%2520Global%2520Alliance%2520for%2520
Workers%2520and%2520Communities.pdf).

Raghavan, Sudarsan. 2011. "Inspired by Tunisia and Egypt, Yemenis
Join in Anti-government Protests." Washington Post January 27.
Accessed May 28, 2012 (http://www.washingtonpost.com/wp-dyn
/content/article/2011/01/27/AR2011012702081.html).

Rainie, Lee. 2001. *The Commons of the Tragedy.* Washington, DC: Pew
Internet and American Life Project.

Rand, Robert. 2006. *Tamerlane's Children: Dispatches from Contemporary Uzbekistan.* Oxford: Oneworld Publications.

Ratner, Carl. 2004. "A Cultural Critique of Psychological Explanations
of Terrorism." *Cross-Cultural Psychology Bulletin* 38 (1/2): 18–24.

Ravitz, Jessica. 2009. "Neda: Latest Iconic Image to Inspire." *CNN,*
June 24. Accessed June 30, 2009 (www.cnn.com/2009/WORLD
/meast/06/24/neda.iconic.images/).

Ray, Julie, and Rajesh Srinivasan. 2010a. "Afghans More Skeptical of
U.S. Leadership, Troops in 2009." Washington, DC: Gallup, Inc.
Accessed March 28, 2010 (http://www.gallup.com/poll/125537
/Afghans-Skeptical-Leadership-Troops-2009.aspx).

———. 2010b. "Taliban Increasingly Unpopular in Pakistan."
Washington, DC: Gallup, Inc. Accessed March 28, 2010

(http://www.gallup.com/poll/126602/Taliban-Increasingly-Unpopular-Pakistan.aspx).

Rayner, Gordon. 2011. "Royal Wedding: Kate Middleton Will Be 'Oldest Bride'." The Telegraph November 16. Accessed May 31, 2011 (http://www.telegraph.co.uk/news/uknews/theroyalfamily /8136788/Royal-wedding-Kate-Middleton-will-be-oldest-bride .html)

Reddy, Gayatri. 2005. *With Respect to Sex: Negotiating Hijra Identity in South India.* Chicago: University of Chicago Press.

Reel, Justine J., Sonya SooHoo, Julia Franklin Summerhays, and Diane Gill. 2008. "Age Before Beauty: An Exploration of Body Image in African-American and Caucasian Adult Women." *Journal of Gender Studies* 17 (4): 321–330.

Reid, Luc. 2006. *Talk the Talk: The Slang of 65 American Subcultures.* Cincinnati: Writer's Digest Books.

Reinharz, Shulamit. 1992. *Feminist Methods in Social Research.* New York: Oxford University Press.

Rein, Shaun. 2012. "Why Starbucks Succeeds in China." *USA Today* February 10. Accessed March 24, 2012 (http://www .usatoday.com/money/industries/food/story/2012-02-12 /cnbc-starbucks-secrets-of-china-success/53040820/1).

Reitman, Meredith. 2006. "Uncovering the White Place: Whitewashing at Work." *Social & Cultural Geography* 7 (2): 267–282.

Reitzes, Donald C., and Elizabeth J. Mutran. 2004. "The Transition to Retirement: Stages and Factors that Influence Retirement Adjustment." *International Journal of Aging & Human Development* 59 (1): 63–84.

Relerford, Patrice, Chao Xiong, Michael Rand, and Curt Brown. 2008. "42 Students Questioned, 13 Disciplined." *Minneapolis Star-Tribune,* January 10. Accessed June 30, 2009 (www.startribune .com/local/west/13663951.html).

Religious Tolerance. 2008. "Female Genital Mutilation (FGM): Informational Materials." Accessed March 1, 2008 (www .religioustolerance.org).

Renegar, Valerie R., and Stacey K. Sowards. 2009. "Contradiction as Agency: Self-Determination, Transcendence, and Counterimagination in Third Wave Feminism." *Hypatia* 24 (2): 1–20.

Reynolds, John R., and Chardie L. Baird. 2010. "Is There a Downside to Shooting for the Stars? Unrealized Educational Expectations and Symptoms of Depression." *American Sociological Review* 75 (1): 151–172.

Ribando, Clare M. 2008. *CRS Report for Congress: Trafficking in Persons.* Washington, DC: Congressional Research Service.

Richtel, Matt. 2006. "The Long-Distance Journey of a Fast-Food Order." *New York Times,* April 11. Accessed May 13, 2009 (http:// www.nytimes.com/2006/04/11/technology/11fast.html).

Rideout, Victoria, Donald F. Roberts, and Ulla G. Foehr. 2005. *Generation M: Media in the Lives of 8–18-Year-Olds.* Menlo Park, CA: Kaiser Family Foundation.

Rideout, Victoria J., Ulla G. Foehr, and Donald F. Roberts. 2010. *Generation M2: Media in the Lives of 8–18-Year-Olds.* Kaiser Family Foundation Study, Menlo Park, CA, January. Accessed April 30, 2010 (http://www.kff.org/entmedia/8010.cfm).

Ridgeway, Greg. 2007. "Analysis of Racial Disparities in the New York Police Department's Stop, Question, and Frisk Practices." Santa Monica, CA: RAND Corporation.

Rieker, Patricia R., and Chloe E. Bird. 2000. "Sociological Explanations of Gender Differences in Mental and Physical Health." pp. 98–113 in *Handbook of Medical Sociology,* ed. Chloe Bird, Peter Conrad, and Allan Fremont. New York: Prentice Hall.

Risman, Barbara J. 1986. "Can Men 'Mother'? Life as a Single Father." *Family Relations* 35: (1): 95–102.

Risman, Barbara J., and Danette Johnson-Sumerford. 1998. "'Doing It Fairly: A Study of Postgender Marriages." *Journal of Marriage and Family* 60 (1): 23–40.

Ritzer, George. 2008. *The McDonaldization of Society 5.* Thousand Oaks, CA: Sage.

Roberson, Debi, Ian Davies, and Jules Davidoff. 2000. "Color Categories Are Not Universal: Replications and New Evidence from Stone Age Culture." *Journal of Experimental Psychology* 129 (3): 369–398.

Roberts, J. Timmons, Peter E. Grines, and Jodie L. Manale. 2003. "Social Roots of Global Environmental Change: A World-Systems Analysis of Carbon Dioxide Emissions." *Journal of World-Systems Research* 9 (Summer): 277–315.

Robison, Jennifer. 2002. "Should Mothers Work?" Gallup, Inc., August 27. Accessed June 17, 2009 (www.gallup.com/poll/6676 /Should-Mothers-Work.aspx).

Rodriguez, Richard. 2002. *Brown: The Last Discovery of America.* New York: Penguin Books.

Rodwan, John, Jr. 2011. "Bottled Water 2010: The Recovery Begins." Bottled Water Reporter 51 (April/May): 10–17. Accessed June 30, 2011 (http://www.bottledwater.org/content/455 /bottled-water-reporter).

Roediger, David R. 2005. *Working Toward Whiteness: How America's Immigrants Became White.* New York: Basic Books.

Rootes, Christopher. 2007. "Acting Locally: The Character, Contexts and Significance of Local Environmental Mobilisations." *Environmental Politics* 16 (5): 722–741.

Roscigno, Vincent J. 2010. "Ageism in the American Workplace." *Contexts* 9 (1):16–21.

Roscoe, Will. 1997. "Gender Diversity in Native North America: Notes Toward a Unified Analysis." pp. 65–81 in *A Queer World: The Center for Lesbian and Gay Studies Reader,* ed. Martin Duberman. New York: New York University Press.

Rose, Arnold. 1951. *The Roots of Prejudice.* Paris: UNESCO.

Rosen, William. 2010. *The Most Powerful Idea in the World: A Story of Steam, Industry, and Invention.* New York: Random House.

Rosenfeld, Michael J. 2008. "Racial, Educational and Religious Endogamy in the United States: A Comparative Historical Perspective." *Social Forces* 87 (1): 1–33.

Rosenthal, Robert, and Lenore Jacobson. 1968. *Pygmalion in the Classroom.* New York: Holt.

Rosenwald, Michael S. 2010. "Second Life's Virtual Money Can Become Real-Life Cash." *Washington Post,* March 8. Accessed April 8, 2010 (http://www.washingtonpost.com/wp-dyn/content /article/2010/03/07/AR2010030703524.html).

Rosin, Hanna. 2007. *God's Harvard: A Christian College on a Mission to Save America.* New York: Harcourt.

Rossi, Alice S. 1968. "Transition to Parenthood." *Journal of Marriage and the Family* 30 (February): 26–39.

———. 1984. "Gender and Parenthood." *American Sociological Review* 49 (February): 1–19.

Rossides, Daniel W. 1997. *Social Stratification: The Interplay of Class, Race, and Gender,* 2nd ed. Upper Saddle River, NJ: Prentice Hall.

Rothenberg, Stuart. 2011. "Are We Headed for Four Wave Elections in a Row?" The Rothenberg Political Report February 3. Accessed June 7, 2011 (http://rothenbergpoliticalreport.com/news/article /are-we-headed-for-four-wave-elections-in-a-row).

Rothstein, Richard. 2009. "Equalizing Opportunity: Dramatic Differences in Children's Home Life and Health Mean that Schools Can't Do It Alone." *American Educator* 33 (2): 4–7, 45–46. Accessed April 26, 2010 (http://archive.aft.org/pubs-reports /american_educator/issues/summer2009/equalizingopportunity .pdf).

Rowland, Christopher, ed. 2007. *The Cambridge Companion to Liberation Theology,* 2nd ed. New York: Cambridge University Press.

Rubie-Davies, Christine M. 2010. "Teacher Expectations and Perceptions of Student Attributes: Is There a Relationship?" *British Journal of Educational Psychology* 80 (1): 121–135.

Rubin, Alissa J. 2003. "Pat-Down on the Way to Prayer." *Los Angeles Times,* November 25, pp. A1, A5.

Rutter, Michael. 2010. "Gene Environment Interplay." *Depression and Anxiety* 27: 1–4.

Rutter, Michael, Terrie E. Moffitt, and Avshalom Caspi. 2006. "Gene-Environment Interplay and Psychopathology: Multiple Varieties but Real Effects." *Journal of Child Psychology and Psychiatry* 47 (3/4): 226–261.

Rymer, Russ. 1993. *Genie: An Abused Child's Flight from Science.* New York: HarperCollins.

S

Saad, Lydia. 2004. "Divorce Doesn't Last." *Gallup Poll Tuesday Briefing*, March 30 (www.gallup.com).

Sachs, Jeffrey D. 2005a. *The End of Poverty: Economic Possibilities for Our Time.* New York: Penguin Books.

———. 2005b. "Can Extreme Poverty Be Eliminated?" *Scientific American* 293 (September): 56–65.

Sacks, Peter. 2007. *Tearing Down the Gates: Confronting the Class Divide in American Education.* Berkeley: University of California Press.

Saez, Emmanuel. 2012. Strking it Richer: The Evolution of Top Incomes in the United States (Updated with 2009 and 2010 estimates)." Center for Equitable Growth, March 2. Accessed May 22, 2012 (http://elsa.berkeley.edu/~saez/saez-UStopincomes-2010.pdf).

Samuelson, Paul A., and William D. Nordhaus. 2005. *Economics*, 18th ed. New York: McGraw-Hill.

Sanday, Peggy Reeves. 2002. *Women at the Center: Life in a Modern Matriarchy.* Ithaca, NY: Cornell University Press.

———. 2008. Homepage. Accessed March 15 (www.sas.upenn.edu/~psanday).

Sandler, Ronald, and Phaedra C. Pezzullo, eds. 2007. *Environmental Justice and Environmentalism: The Social Justice Challenge to the Environmental Movement.* Cambridge: MIT Press.

Sanyal, Paromita. 2009. "From Credit to Collective Action: The Role of Microfinance in Promoting Women's Social Capital and Normative Influence." *American Sociological Review* 74 (4): 529–550.

Sarachild, Kathie. 1978. "Consciousness-Raising: A Radical Weapon." pp. 144–150 in *Feminist Revolution.* New York: Random House. Accessed June 30, 2009 (http://scriptorium.lib.duke.edu/wlm/fem/sarachild.html).

Sargent, John, and Linda Matthews. 2009. "China Versus Mexico in the Global EPZ Industry: Maquiladoras, FDI Quality, and Plant Mortality." *World Development* 37 (6): 1,069–1,082.

Sassen, Saskia. 2005. "New Global Classes: Implications for Politics." pp. 143–170 in *The New Egalitarianism*, ed. Anthony Giddens and Patrick Diamond. Cambridge, U.K.: Polity Press.

Sawhill, Isabel V. 2006. "Teenage Sex, Pregnancy, and Nonmarital Births." *Gender Issues* 23 (4): 48–59.

Scarce, Rik. 1994. "(No) Trial (but) Tribulations: When Courts and Ethnography Conflict." *Journal of Contemporary Ethnography* 23 (July): 123–149.

———. 1995. "Scholarly Ethics and Courtroom Antics: Where Researchers Stand in the Eyes of the Law." *American Sociologist* 26 (Spring): 87–112.

———. 2005. "A Law to Protect Scholars." *Chronicle of Higher Education*, August 12, p. 324.

———. 2005. *Contempt of Court: A Scholar's Battle for Free Speech from Behind Bars.* Lanham, MD: AltaMira Press.

Scelfo, Julie. 2008. "Baby, You're Home." *New York Times*, November 12. Accessed June 29, 2009 (www.nytimes.com/2008/11/13/garden/13birth.html).

Schachtman, Tom. 2006. *Rumspringa: To Be or Not to Be Amish.* New York: North Point Press.

Schaefer, Richard T. 1998a. "Differential Racial Mortality and the 1995 Chicago Heat Wave." Paper presented at the annual meeting of the American Sociological Association, August, San Francisco.

———. 1998b. *Alumni Survey.* Chicago: Department of Sociology, De Paul University.

———. 2009. *Sociology: A Brief Introduction*, 8th ed. New York: McGraw-Hill.

Schaefer, Richard T., and William W. Zellner. 2007. *Extraordinary Groups*, 8th ed. New York: Worth.

Schaffer, Scott. 2004. *Resisting Ethics.* New York: Palgrave Macmillan.

Scharnberg, Kirsten. 2007. "Black Market for Midwives Defies Bans." *Chicago Tribune*, November 25, pp. 1, 10.

Schelly, David, and Paul B. Stretesky. 2009. "An Analysis of the 'Path of Least Resistance' Argument in Three Environmental Justice Success Cases." *Society & Natural Resources* 22 (4): 369–380.

Scherbov, Sergei, Wolfgang Lutz, and Warren C. Sanderson. 2011. "The Uncertain Timing of Reaching 7 Billion and Peak Population." International Institute for Applied Systems Analysis, Interim Report IR-11-002, February 21. Accessed June 29, 2011 (http://www.iiasa.ac.at/Admin/PUB/Documents/IR-11-002.pdf).

Schmeeckle, Maria. 2007. "Gender Dynamics in Stepfamilies: Adult Stepchildren's Views." *Journal of Marriage and Family* 69 (February): 174–189.

Schmeeckle, Maria, Roseann Giarrusso, Du Feng, and Vern L. Bengtson. 2006. "What Makes Someone Family? Adult Children's Perceptions of Current and Former Stepparents." *Journal of Marriage and Family* 68 (August): 595–610.

Schmidt, Peter. 2008. "A University Examines Underlying Problems After Racist Incidents." *Chronicle of Higher Education* 54 (March 14): A18–A21.

Schnaiberg, Allan. 1994. *Environment and Society: The Enduring Conflict.* New York: St. Martin's Press.

Schur, Edwin M. 1965. *Crimes Without Victims: Deviant Behavior and Public Policy.* Englewood Cliffs, NJ: Prentice Hall.

———. 1985. "'Crimes Without Victims: A 20-Year Reassessment.'" Paper presented at the annual meeting of the Society for the Study of Social Problems.

Schurman, Rachel. 2004. "Fighting 'Frankenfoods': Industry Opportunity Structures and the Efficacy of the Anti-biotech Movement in Western Europe." *Social Problems* 51 (2): 243–268.

Schwartz, Shalom H., and Anat Bardi. 2001. "Value Hierarchies Across Cultures: Taking a Similarities Perspective." *Journal of Cross-Cultural Perspective* 32 (May): 268–290.

Scott, Greg. 2005. "Public Symposium: HIV/AIDS, Injection Drug Use and Men Who Have Sex with Men." pp. 38–39 in *Scholarship with a Mission*, ed. Susanna Pagliaro. Chicago: De Paul University.

Second Life. "2009 End of Year Second Life Economy Wrap-Up (Including Q4 Economy in Detail)." Blogpost, January 19. San Francisco: Linden Research. Accessed April 8, 2010 (https://blogs.secondlife.com/community/features/blog/2010/01/19/2009-end-of-year-second-life-economy-wrap-up-including-q4-economy-in-detail).

———. 2011. "The Second Life Economy in Q3 2011." Linden Research, Inc., October 14. Accessed April 9, 2012 (http://community.secondlife.com/t5/Featured-News/The-Second-Life-Economy-in-Q3-2011/ba-p/1166705).

Sedivy, Julie. 2012. "Is Your Language Making You Broke and Fat? How Language Can Shape Thinking and Behavior (and How It Can't)." *Discover Magazine* February 27. Accessed March 24, 2012 (http://blogs.discovermagazine.com/crux/2012/02/27/is-your-language-making-you-broke-and-fat-how-language-can-shape-thinking-and-behavior-and-how-it-cant/).

Shah, Anup. 2010. "Poverty Facts and Stats." *Global Issues*, March 22. April 28, 2010 (http://www.globalissues.org/article/26/poverty-facts-and-stats).

Shaheen, Jack. 2006. *Reel Bad Arabs: How Hollywood Vilifies a People.* Video. Directed by Sut Jhally. 50 minutes. Northampton, MA: Media Education Foundation.

———. 2009. *Reel Bad Arabs: How Hollywood Vilifies a People*, 2nd ed. New York: Olive Branch Press.

Shapiro, Samantha M. 2009. "Can the Muppets Make Friends in Ramallah?" *New York Times*, October 4. Accessed April 6, 2010 (http://www.nytimes.com/2009/10/04/magazine/04sesame-t.html).

Sharp, Gwen. 2011. "Two News Stories about Gabrielle Giffords . . . and Husband." *Sociological Images* Jan 9. Accessed March 10, 2012 (http://thesocietypages.org/socimages/2011/01/09/two-news-stories-about-gabrielle-giffords-shooting-and-husband/).

Shaw, Clifford R., and Henry D. McKay. 1969. *Juvenile Delinquency and Urban Areas.* Chicago: University of Chicago Press.

Shenk, David. 2010. *The Genius in All of Us: Why Everything You've Been Told About Genetics, Talent, and IQ Is Wrong.* New York: Doubleday.

Shenker, Jack, Angelique Chrisafis, Lauren Williams, Tom Finn, Giles Tremlett, and Martin Chulov. 2011. "Young Arabs Who Can't Wait to Throw Off Shackles of Tradition." *The Guardian* February 14. Accessed May 28, 2012 (http://www.guardian.co.uk/world/2011/feb/14/young-arabs-throw-off-shackles-tradition).

Sherkat, Darren E. 2004. "Religious Intermarriage in the United States: Trends, Patterns, and Predictors." *Social Science Research* 33 (4): 606–625.

Sheskin, Ira M., and Arnold Dashefsky. 2007. "Jewish Population of the United States, 2006." In *American Jewish Year Book 2006*, ed. David Singer and Lawrence Grossman. New York: American Jewish Committee.

Shi, Yu. 2008. "Chinese Immigrant Women Workers: Everyday Forms of Resistance and 'Coagulate Politics.'" *Communication and Critical/Cultural Studies* 5 (4): 363–382.

Shields, Stephanie A. 2008. "Gender: An Intersectionality Perspective." *Sex Roles* 59 (5/6): 301–311.

Al-Shihri, Abdullah. 2011. "Saudi Woman Held by Police–for Driving." *The Independent*, May 22. Accessed June 12, 2011 (http://www.independent.co.uk/news/world/middle-east/saudi-woman-held-by-police-ndash-for-driving-2287650.html).

Shipler, David K. 2004. *The Working Poor: Invisible in America*. New York: Knopf.

Shirky, Clay. 2008. *Here Comes Everybody: The Power of Organizing Without Organizations*. New York: Penguin Books.

Shostak, Arthur B. 2002. "Clinical Sociology and the Art of Peace Promotion: Earning a World Without War." pp. 325–345 in *Using Sociology: An Introduction from the Applied and Clinical Perspectives*, ed. Roger A. Straus. Lanham, MD: Rowman & Littlefield.

Showden, Carisa R. 2009. "What's Political About the New Feminisms?" *Frontiers: A Journal of Women Studies* 30 (2): 166–198.

Shupe, Anson D., and David G. Bromley. 1980. "Walking a Tightrope." *Qualitative Sociology* 2: 8–21.

Silver, Ira. 1996. "Role Transitions, Objects, and Identity." *Symbolic Interaction* 10 (1): 1–20.

Simmons, Robin. 2009. "Entry to Employment: Discourses of Inclusion and Employability in Work-Based Learning for Young People." *Journal of Education & Work* 22 (2): 137–151.

Simmons, Tavia, and Martin O'Connell. 2003. "Married-Couple and Unmarried-Partner Households: 2000." *Census 2000 Special Reports*, CENBR-5. Washington, DC: U.S. Government Printing Office.

Singel, Ryan. 2008. "FBI Tried to Cover Patriot Act Abuses with Flawed, Retroactive Subpoenas, Audit Finds." *Wired*, March 13. Accessed June 30, 2009 (www.wired.com/threatlevel/2008/03/fbi-tried-to-co).

Sisson, Carmen K. 2007. "The Virtual War Family." *Christian Science Monitor*, May 29.

Skerrett, Delaney Michael. 2010. "Can the Sapir–Whorf Hypothesis Save the Planet? Lessons from Cross-cultural Psychology for Critical Language Policy." *Current Issues in Language Planning* 11 (4): 331–340.

Smiley, Tavis and Cornel West. 2012. "America's New Working Poor." *Salon*, May 1. Accessed May 22, 2012 (http://www.salon.com/2012/05/01/working_in_poverty/).

Smith, Adam. [1776] 2003. *The Wealth of Nations*. New York: Bantam Classics.

Smith, Craig. 2006a. "Romania's Orphans Face Widespread Abuse, Group Says." *New York Times*, May 10, p. A3.

———. 2006b. "Warm and Fuzzy TV, Brought to You by Hamas." *New York Times*, January 18. Accessed April 5, 2010 (http://www.nytimes.com/2006/01/18/international/middleeast/18hamas.html).

Smith, Denise. 2003. "The Older Population in the United States: March 2002." U.S. Census Bureau, *Current Population Reports*, P20–546. Washington, DC. Accessed June 18, 2009 (www.census.gov/prod/2003pubs/p20–546.pdf).

Smith, Dorothy E. 1987. *The Everyday World as Problematic: A Feminist Sociology*. Boston: Northeastern University Press.

Smith, James H. 2011. "Tantalus in the Digital Age: Coltan Ore, Temporal Dispossession, and 'Movement' in the Eastern Democratic Republic of the Congo." American Ethnologist 38: 17–35.

Smith, Stacy L., and Marc Choueiti. 2011. "Black Characters in Popular Film: Is the Key to Diversifying Cinematic Content Held in the Hand of the Black Director?" Annenberg School for Communication & Journalism, University of Southern California. Accessed June 20, 2011(http://annenberg.usc.edu/Faculty/Communication%20and%20Journalism/~/media/BlackCharacters_KeyFindings.ashx).

Smith, Tom W. 2003. *Coming of Age in 21st Century America: Public Attitudes Toward the Importance and Timing of Transition to Adulthood*. Chicago: National Opinion Research Center.

———. 2004. "Coming of Age in Twenty-first Century America: Public Attitudes Towards the Importance and Timing of Transitions to Adulthood." *Ageing International* 29 (2): 136–148.

———. 2006. "American Sexual Behavior: Trends, Socio-Demographic Differences, and Risk Behavior." National Opinion Research Center, University of Chicago, GSS Topical Report No. 25. Updated March, 2006. Accessed May 12, 2010 (http://www.norc.org/NR/rdonlyres/2663F09F-2E74-436E-AC81-6FFBF288E183/0/AmericanSexualBehavior2006.pdf).

Smith, Tom W. "Public Attitudes toward Homosexuality." NORC/University of Chicago, September. Accessed May 26, 2012 (http://www.norc.org/PDFs/2011%20GSS%20Reports/GSS_Public%20Attitudes%20Toward%20Homosexuality_Sept2011.pdf).

Snyder, T.D., and S.A. Dillow, 2011. Digest of Education Statistics 2010. NCES 2011-015. Washington, DC: National Center for Education Statistics, Institute of Education Sciences, U.S. Department of Education. Accessed May 2, 2011 (http://nces.ed.gov/pubs2011/2011015.pdf).

Social Security Administration. 2008. "Fast Facts & Figures About Social Security, 2008." SSA Publication No. 13–11785. Social Security Administration, Office of Research, Evaluation, and Statistics, Washington, DC. Accessed June 18, 2009 (www.ssa.gov/policy/docs/chartbooks/fast_facts/2008/fast_facts08.pdf).

Soderstrom, Melanie. 2007. "Beyond Babytalk: Re-Evaluating the Nature and Content of Speech Input to Preverbal Infants." *Developmental Review* 27: 501–532.

Solidarity Center. 2009. *2009 Annual Report*. Solidarity Center, AFL-CIO, Washington, DC. Accessed May 28, 2010 (http://www.solidaritycenter.org/files/pubs_annual_report_2009.pdf).

Solove, Daniel J. 2008. "Do Social Networks Bring the End of Privacy?" *Scientific American* 299 (September): 100–106. Accessed June 30, 2009 (www.scientificamerican.com/article.cfm?id=do-social-networks-bring).

Sommers: See Norton & Sommers above.

Sorokin, Pitirim A. [1927] 1959. *Social and Cultural Mobility*. New York: Free Press.

Spalter-Roth, Roberta, and Nicole Van Vooren. 2008a. "What Are They Doing with a Bachelor's Degree in Sociology?" American Sociological Association Department of Research and Development. Washington, DC: Association. Accessed March 25, 2010 (http://www.asanet.org/images/research/docs/pdf/What%20Are%20They%20Doing%20with%20BA%20in%20Soc.pdf).

———. 2008b. "Pathways to Job Satisfaction." American Sociological Association Department of Research and Development. Washington, DC: Association. Accessed March 25, 2010 (http://www.asanet.org/images/research/docs/pdf/Pathways%20to%20Job%20Satisfaction.pdf).

———. 2009. "Idealists vs. Careerists: Graduate School Choices of Sociology Majors." American Sociological Association Department of Research and Development. Washington DC: ASA. Accessed March 25, 2010 (http://www.asanet.org/images/research/docs/pdf/Idealist%20vs%20Careerisst.pdf).

Spalter-Roth, Roberta, and Nicole Van Vooren. 2010. "Mixed Success: Four Years of Experiences of 2005 Sociology Graduates." American Sociological Association Department of Research and Development. Washington, DC: American Sociological Association. Accessed May 5, 2011 (http://www.asanet.org/research/BBMixedSuccessBrief.pdf).

Spencer, Malia. 2011. "Pittsburgh Filmmaker Works in Virtual World." *Pittsburgh Business Times*, February 18. Accessed May 25, 2011 (http://www.bizjournals.com/pittsburgh/print-edition/2011/02/18/filmmaker-works-in-virtual-world.html).

Sprague, Joey. 2005. *Feminist Methodologies for Critical Research: Bridging Differences*. Lanham, MD: AltaMira Press.

Squire, Peverill. 1988. "Why the 1936 *Literary Digest* Poll Failed." *Public Opinion Quarterly* 52: 125–133.

Stack, Carol. 1974. *All Our Kin: Strategies for Survival in a Black Community.* New York: Harper & Row.

Stafford, Laura. 2010. "Geographic Distance and Communication during Courtship." Communication Research 37 (2): 275–297.

Standish, Peter, and Steven Bell. 2008. *Culture and Customs of Mexico.* Santa Barbara, CA: Greenwood Press.

Stark, Rodney, and William Sims Bainbridge. 1979. "Of Churches, Sects, and Cults: Preliminary Concepts for a Theory of Religious Movements." *Journal for the Scientific Study of Religion* 18 (June): 117–131.

———. 1985. *The Future of Religion.* Berkeley: University of California Press.

Starr, Paul. 1982. *The Social Transformation of American Medicine.* New York: Basic Books.

State of Arizona. 2010. "Senate Bill 1070: Support Our Law Enforcement and Safe Neighborhoods Act." Forty-ninth Legislature, Second Regular Session. Accessed May 16, 2010 (http://www.azleg.gov/legtext/49leg/2r/bills/sb1070s.pdf).

Stavenhagen, Rodolfo. 1994. "The Indian Resurgence in Mexico." *Cultural Survival Quarterly* (Summer/Fall): 77–80.

Steele, Jonathan. 2005. "Annan Attacks Britain and U.S. over Erosion of Human Rights." *Guardian Weekly,* March 16, p. 1.

Steidle, Brian. 2007. *The Devil Came on Horseback: Bearing Witness to the Genocide in Darfur.* New York: PublicAffairs.

Stein, Arlene. 2010. "The Incredible Shrinking Lesbian World and Other Queer Conundra." *Sexualities* 13 (1): 21–32.

Stelter, Brian, and Brad Stone. 2009. "Web Pries Lid of Iranian Censorship." *New York Times,* June 22. Accessed July 1, 2009 (www.nytimes.com/2009/06/23/world/middleeast/23censor.html).

Stenning, Derrick J. 1958. "Household Viability Among the Pastoral Fulani." pp. 92–119 in *The Developmental Cycle in Domestic Groups,* ed. John R. Goody. Cambridge: Cambridge University Press.

Steward, Samuel M. 1990. *Bad Boys and Tough Tattoos: A Social History of the Tattoo with Gangs, Sailors, and Street-Corner Punks.* Binghamton, NY: Harrington Park Press.

Stewart, Quincy Thomas. 2006. "Reinvigorating Relative Deprivation: A New Measure for a Classic Concept." *Social Science Research* 35 (3): 779–802.

Stewart, Susan D. 2007. *Brave New Stepfamilies: Diverse Paths Toward Stepfamily Living.* Thousand Oaks, CA: Sage.

Stitt, Carmen, and Dale Kunkel. 2008. "Food Advertising During Children's Television Programming on Broadcast and Cable Channels." *Health Communication* 23: 573–584.

Stone, Charley, Carl Van Horn, and Cliff Zukin. 2012. "Chasing the American Dream: Recent College Graduates and the Great Recession." WorkTrends: Americans' Attitudes about Work, Employers, and Government, John J. Heldrich Center for Workforce Development, Rutgers University, May 2012. Accessed May 22, 2012 (http://www.heldrich.rutgers.edu/sites/default/files/content/Chasing_American_Dream_Report.pdf).

Stratton, Terry D., and Jennifer L. McGivern-Snofsky. 2008. "Toward a Sociological Understanding of Complementary and Alternative Medicine Use." *Journal of Alternative and Complementary Medicine* 14 (6): 777–783.

Strauss, Gary. 2002. "'Good Old Boys' Network Still Rules Corporate Boards." *USA Today,* November 1, pp. B1, B2.

Streib, Jessi. 2011. "Class Reproduction by Four Year Olds." Qualitative Sociology 34 (2): 337–352.

Stretesky, Paul B. 2006. "Corporate Self-Policing and the Environment." *Criminology* 44 (3): 671.

Stevenson, Mark. 2011. "Money Sent Home By Mexican Migrants Holds Steady." *Chron,* February 1. Accessed June 13, 2011 (http://www.chron.com/disp/story.mpl/business/7408082.html).

Strier, Roni. 2010. "Women, Poverty, and the Microenterprise: Context and Discourse." *Gender, Work & Organization* 17 (2): 195–218.

Strom, Stephanie. 2011. "Off Media Radar, Famine Garners Few Donations." *New York Times,* August 1. Accessed August 8, 2011 (www.nytimes.com/2011/08/02/world/africa/02donate.html).

Stryker, Susan. 2007. "Transgender Feminism: Queering the Woman Question." pp. 59–70 in *Third Wave Feminism: A Critical Exploration,* expanded 2nd ed., Stacy Gillis, Gillian Howie, and Rebecca Munford. New York: Palgrave Macmillan.

Sudan Tribune. 2008. "Darfur's Poorest Squeezed by Ration Cuts." June 22. Accessed August 12, 2008 (http://www.sudantribune.com/spip.php?article27608).

Suitor, J. Jill, Staci A. Minyard, and Rebecca S. Carter. 2001. "'Did You See What I Saw?' Gender Differences in Perceptions of Avenues to Prestige Among Adolescents." *Sociological Inquiry* 71 (Fall): 437–454.

Sullivan, Kevin. 2006. "In War-Torn Congo, Going Wireless to Reach Home." *Washington Post,* July 9. Accessed May 6, 2009 (http://www.washingtonpost.com/wp-dyn/content/article/2006/07/08/AR2006070801063.html).

Sumner, William G. 1906. *Folkways.* New York: Ginn.

Sun, Yongmin, and Yuanzhang Li. 2008. "Stable Postdivorce Family Structures During Late Adolescence and Socioeconomic Consequences in Adulthood." *Journal of Marriage & Family* 70 (1): 129–143.

Sutherland, Edwin H. 1940. "White-Collar Criminality." *American Sociological Review* 5 (February): 1–11.

———. 1949. *White Collar Crime.* New York: Dryden.

———. 1983. *White Collar Crime: The Uncut Version.* New Haven, CT: Yale University Press.

Sutherland, Edwin H., Donald R. Cressey, and David F. Luckenbill. 1992. *Principles of Criminology,* 11th ed. New York: Rowman & Littlefield.

Sutton, Philip W. 2007. *The Environment: A Sociological Introduction.* Malden, MA: Polity Press.

Suzuki, Toru. 2009. "Fertility Decline and Governmental Interventions in Eastern Asian Advanced Countries." The Japanese Journal of Population 7 (1): 47–56.

Swami, Viren and Joanna-Marie Smith. 2012. "How *Not* to Feel Good Naked? The Effects of Television Programs That Use 'Real Women' on Female Viewers' Body Image and Mood." *Journal of Social and Clinical Psychology* 31 (2): 151–168.

Swatos Jr., William H. 2011. "Encyclopedia of Religion and Society." Hartford Institute for Religion Research, Hartford Seminary, Hartford, Connecticut. Accessed June 6, 2011 (http://hirr.hartsem.edu/ency/).

Swatos Jr., William H., ed. 1998. *Encyclopedia of Religion and Society.* Lanham, MD: AltaMira Press.

Swidler, Ann. 1986. "Culture in Action: Symbols and Strategies." *American Sociological Review* 51 (April): 273–286.

Szasz, Thomas S. 1971. "The Same Slave: An Historical Note on the Use of Medical Diagnosis as Justificatory Rhetoric." *American Journal of Psychotherapy* 25 (April): 228–239.

T

Tafur, Maritza Montiel, Terry K. Crowe, and Eliseo Torres. 2009. "A Review of Curanderismo and Healing Practices Among Mexicans and Mexican Americans." *Occupational Therapy International* 16 (1): 82–88.

Taha, T. A. 2007. "Arabic as 'A Critical-Need' Foreign Language in Post–9/11 Era: A Study of Students' Attitudes and Motivation." *Journal of Instructional Psychology* 34 (3): 150–160.

Takahashi, Dean. 2012. "Zynga Accounted for $445M, or 12 percent of Facebook's Revenue, in 2011." VentureBeat February 1. Accessed April 9, 2012 (http://venturebeat.com/2012/02/01/zynga-accounted-for-12-percent-of-facebooks-revenue-in-2011/).

Tate, Shirley Anne. 2009. *Black Beauty: Aesthetics, Stylization, Politics.* Burlington, VT: Ashgate.

Taylor, Dorceta E. 2000. "The Rise of the Environmental Justice Paradigm." *American Behavioral Scientist* 43 (January): 508–580.

Taylor, Frederick Winslow. 1911. *The Principles of Scientific Management.* New York: Harper & Brothers Publishers.

Taylor, Jonathan B., and Joseph P. Kalt. 2005. *American Indians on Reservations: A Data Book of Socioeconomic Change Between the 1990 and 2000 Censuses.* Cambridge, MA: Harvard Project on American Indian Development.

Taylor, Paul, and Richard Morin. 2008. "Americans Say They Like Diverse Communities; Election, Census Trends Suggest Otherwise." Pew Research Center Report, December 2. Accessed May 17, 2010 (http://pewsocialtrends.org/assets/pdf/diverse-political-communities.pdf).

Taylor, Paul, Rich Morin, Kim Parker, D'Vera Cohn, and Wendy Wang. 2009. *Growing Old in America: Expectations vs. Reality.* Pew Research Center Social & Demographic Trends Project, January. Accessed April 5, 2010 (http://pewsocialtrends.org/assets/pdf/Getting-Old-in-America.pdf).

Taylor, Paul. 2011. "Is College Worth It? College Presidents, Public Assess Value, Quality and Mission of Higher Education." A Pew Research Center Social & Demographic Trends Report, May 16. Accessed May 22, 2012 (http://www.pewsocialtrends.org/files/2011/05/higher-ed-report.pdf).

Taylor, Verta. 1999. "Gender and Social Movements: Gender Processes in Women's Self-Help Movements." *Gender and Society* 13: 8–33.

———. 2004. "Social Movements and Gender." pp. 14,348–14,352 in *International Encyclopedia of the Social and Behavioral Sciences,* ed. Neil J. Smelser and Paul B. Baltes. New York: Elsevier.

Tejada-Vera, Betzaida, and Paul D. Sutton. 2009. "Births, Marriages, Divorces, and Deaths: Provisional Data for 2008." *National Vital Statistics Reports* 57 (19). Hyattsville, MD: National Center for Health Statistics. Accessed April 11, 2010 (http://www.cdc.gov/nchs/data/nvsr/nvsr57/nvsr57_19.pdf).

———. 2010. "Births, Marriages, Divorces, and Deaths: Provisional Data for July 2009." *National Vital Statistics Reports* 58 (15). Hyattsville, MD: National Center for Health Statistics. Accessed April 14, 2010 (http://www.cdc.gov/nchs/data/nvsr/nvsr58/nvsr58_15.pdf).

———. 2010. "Births, Marriages, Divorces, and Deaths: Provisional Data for 2009." *National Vital Statistics Reports* 58 (25). Hyattsville, MD: National Center for Health Statistics. Accessed May 28, 2011 (http://www.cdc.gov/nchs/data/nvsr/nvsr58/nvsr58_25.pdf).

Tentler, Leslie Woodcock. 2004. *Catholics and Contraception: An American History.* Ithaca, NY: Cornell University.

Terkel, Studs. 2003. *Hope Dies Last: Keeping the Faith in Difficult Times.* New York: New Press.

Terry, Sara. 2000. "Whose Family? The Revolt of the Child-Free." *Christian Science Monitor,* August 29, pp. 1, 4.

Tertilt, Michèle. 2005. "Polygyny, Fertility, and Savings." *Journal of Political Economy* 113 (6): 1341–1370.

Thernsrom, Melanie. 2005. "The New Arranged Marriage." *New York Times,* February 13. Accessed April 14, 2010 (http://www.nytimes.com/2005/02/13/magazine/13MATCHMAKING.html).

Thomas, Adam, and Isabel Sawhill. 2002. "For Richer and Poorer: Marriages as an Antipoverty Strategy." *Journal of Policy Analysis and Management* 21 (4): 587–599.

Thomas, Gordon, and Max Morgan Witts. 1974. *Voyage of the Damned.* Greenwich, CT: Fawcett Crest.

Thomas, William I., and Dorothy Swain Thomas. 1928. *The Child in America: Behavior Problems and Programs.* New York: Knopf.

Thompson, Warren S. 1929. "Population." *American Journal of Sociology* 34 (6): 959–975.

———. 1948. *Plenty of People: The World's Population Pressures, Problems and Policies and How They Concern Us, Revised Edition.* New York: Ronald Press.

Thomson, Elizabeth, and Eva Bernhardt. 2010. "Education, Values, and Cohabitation in Sweden." *Marriage & Family Review* 46 (1/2): 1–21.

Thornberg, Robert. 2008. "'It's Not Fair!'—Voicing Pupils' Criticisms of School Rules." *Children & Society* 22 (6): 418–428.

Tierney, John. 2003. "Iraqi Family Ties Complicate American Efforts for Change." *New York Times,* September 28, pp. A1, A22.

Tilly, Charles. 1993. *Popular Contention in Great Britain 1758–1834.* Cambridge, MA: Harvard University Press.

———. 2004. *Social Movements, 1768–2004.* Boulder, CO: Paradigm.

Tolbert, Kathryn. 2000. "In Japan, Traveling Alone Begins at Age 6." *Washington Post National Weekly Edition* 17, May 15, p. 17.

Tonkinson, Robert. 1978. *The Mardudjara Aborigines.* New York: Holt.

Tönnies, Ferdinand. [1887] 1988. *Community and Society.* New Brunswick, NJ: Transaction.

Toossi, Mitra. 2007. "Labor Force Projections to 2016: More Workers in Their Golden Years." *Monthly Labor Review,* November, pp. 33–52.

Torres, Lourdes. 2008. "Puerto Rican Americans" and "Puerto Rico." pp. 1,082–1,089, vol. 3, in *Encyclopedia of Race, Ethnicity, and Society,* ed. Richard T. Schaefer. Thousand Oaks, CA: Sage.

Traugott, Michael W. 2005. "The Accuracy of the National Preelection Polls in the 2004 Presidential Election." *Public Opinion Quarterly* 69 (5): 642–654.

Truman, Jennifer L. 2011. "Criminal Victimization, 2010: National Crime Victimization Survey." *Bureau of Justice Statistics Bulletin* September, NCJ 235508. Accessed April 24, 2012 (http://bjs.ojp.usdoj.gov/content/pub/pdf/cv10.pdf).

Tully, Shawn. 2012. "The 2011 Fortune 500: The Big Boys Rack Up Record-Setting Profits." CNNMoney, May 7. Accessed May 22, 2012 (http://www.dailyfinance.com/2012/05/07/the-2011-fortune-500-the-big-boys-rack-up-record-setting-profit/).

Ture, Kwame, and Charles Hamilton. 1992. *Black Power: The Politics of Liberation,* rev. ed. New York: Vintage Books.

Turkle, Sherry. 2011. *Alone Together: Why We Expect More from Technology and Less from Each Other.* New York: Basic Books.

Twitchell, James B. 2000. "The Stone Age." pp. 44–48 in *Do Americans Shop Too Much?* ed. Juliet Schor. Boston: Beacon Press.

U

UN News Service. 2010. "Darfur: Security Council Warned of 'Significant Challenges' to Peace Process." UN News Centre, May 20. Accessed May 28, 2010 (http://www.un.org/apps/news/story.asp?NewsID=34761&Cr=&Crl=).

UNAIDS. 2010. *Global Report: UNAIDS report on the Global AIDS Epidemic.* Geneva: Joint United Nations Programme on HIV/AIDS. Accessed May 28, 2012 (http://www.unaids.org/globalreport/documents/20101123_GlobalReport_full_en.pdf).

UNCTAD. 2009. "Mainstreaming Gender in Trade Policy." United Nations Conference on Trade and Development, March 10–11, Geneva. Accessed June 18, 2009 (www.unctad.org/Templates/WebFlyer.asp?intItemID=4760&lang=1.)

———. 2009a. *International Migration Report 2006: A Global Assessment.* Department of Economic and Social Affairs, Population Division. Accessed June 21, 2009 (www.un.org/esa/population/publications/2006_MigrationRep/report.htm).

———. 2009b. *World Marriage Data 2008.* UN Department of Economic and Social Affairs, Population Division, POP/DB/Marr/Rev2008. Accessed April 11, 2010 (http://www.un.org/esa/population/publications/WMD2008/Main.html).

———. 2010. *Special Rapporteur on Contemporary Forms of Slavery.* Office of the High Commissioner for Human Rights, Geneva. Accessed April 24, 2010 (http://www2.ohchr.org/english/issues/slavery/rapporteur/index.htm).

UNESCO. 2010. *Atlas of the World's Languages in Danger.* 3rd Edition. Paris: UNESCO Publishing.

United Nations. 1999. "The World at Six Billion." Population Division, Department of Economic and Social Affairs, United Nations Secretariat, October. Accessed June 28, 2011 (http://www.un.org/esa/population/publications/sixbillion/sixbillion.htm).

———. 2010. *The Millennium Development Goals* Report: 2010. New York: United Nations. Accessed June 12, 2011 (http://www.un.org/millenniumgoals/reports.shtml).

———. 2011. *The Millennium Development Goals* Report 2011. New York: United Nations. Accessed August 8, 2011 (www.un.org/millenniumgoals/reports.shtml).

———. 2011a. "Net Number of Migrants (Both Sexes Combined) by Major Area, Region and Country, 1950–2100 (Thousands)." World

Population Prospects: The 2010 Revision. Department of Economic and Social Affairs, Population Division. Accessed June 27, 2011 (http://esa.un.org/unpd/wpp/Excel-Data/migration.htm).

———. 2011b. "Net Migration Rate by Major Area, Region and Country, 1950-2100 (Per 1,000 Population)." World Population Prospects: The 2010 Revision. Department of Economic and Social Affairs, Population Division. Accessed June 27, 2011 (http://esa.un.org/unpd/wpp/Excel-Data/migration.htm).

———. 2011c. "Average Annual Rate of Population Change by Major Area, Region and Country, 1950-2100 (Percentage)." World Population Prospects: The 2010 Revision. Department of Economic and Social Affairs, Population Division. Accessed June 27, 2011 (http://esa.un.org/unpd/wpp/Excel-Data/population.htm).

———. 2011d. "Total Population (Both Sexes Combined) by Major Area, Region and Country, Annually for 1950-2100 (Thousands)." World Population Prospects: The 2010 Revision. Department of Economic and Social Affairs, Population Division. Accessed June 28, 2011 (http://esa.un.org/unpd/wpp/Excel-Data/population.htm).

———. 2011e. "World Population to Reach 10 Billion by 2100 if Fertility in All Countries Converges to Replacement Level." World Population Prospects: The 2010 Revision. Department of Economic and Social Affairs, Population Division. Accessed June 30, 2011 (http://esa.un.org/unpd/wpp/Other-Information/Press_Release_WPP2010.pdf).

———. 2011f. "Population by Age Groups," World Population Prospect, the 2010 Revision." World Population Prospects: The 2010 Revision. Department of Economic and Social Affairs, Population Division. Accessed June 30, 2011 (http://esa.un.org/unpd/wpp/Excel-Data/population.htm).

———. 2011g. "World Contraceptive Use 2010." Department of Economic and Social Affairs, Population Division. Accessed May 26, 2012 (http://www.un.org/esa/population/publications/wcu2010/WCP_2010/Data.html).

United Nations Development Programme. 2000. *Poverty Report 2000: Overcoming Human Poverty.* Washington, DC: UNDP.

———. 2008. *Human Development Indices: A Statistical Update 2008.* New York: UNDP. Accessed June 7, 2009 (http://hdr.undp.org/en/media/HDI_2008_EN_Complete.pdf).

———. 2011. *Sustainability and Equity: A Better Future for All.* Human Development Report 2011. New York: The United Nations Development Programme. Accessed May 17, 2012 (http://hdr.undp.org/en/media/HDR_2011_EN_Complete.pdf).

United Nations Framework Convention on Climate Change. 2010a. "Status of Ratification of the Kyoto Protocol." Accessed June 8, 2010 (http://unfccc.int/playground/items/5524.php).

———. 2010b. "Bonn Climate Change Talks—June 2010." Accessed June 8, 2010 (http://unfccc.int/2860.php).

United Nations Population Division. 2005. *World Fertility Report 2003.* New York: UNPD.

United States Coast Guard. 2011. "Report of Investigation into the Circumstances Surrounding the Explosion, Fire, Sinking and Loss of Eleven Crew Members Aboard the Mobile Offshore Drilling Unit Deepwater Horizon in the Gulf of Mexico April 20–22, 2010." MISLE Activity Number: 3721503. Accessed June 30, 2011 (http://www.uscg.mil/history/docs/USCGDeepwaterHorizon3721503.pdf).

UNODC. 2010. *The Globalization of Crime: A Transnational Organized Crime Threat Assessment.* Vienna: United Nations Office on Drugs and Crime. Accessed April 24, 2012 (http://www.unodc.org/documents/data-and-analysis/tocta/TOCTA_Report_2010_low_res.pdf).

Urbina, Ian. 2004. "Disco Rice, and Other Trash Talk." *New York Times,* July 31, p. A11.

U.S. Census Bureau. 1975. *Historical Statistics of the United States, Colonial Times to 1970.* Washington, DC: U.S. Government Printing Office.

———. 1994. *Statistical Abstract of the United States: 1994* (114th ed.). Washington, DC: U.S. Government Printing Office. Accessed April 13, 2010 (http://www2.census.gov/prod2/statcomp/documents/1994-01.pdf).

———. 1998. "Interracial Tables." Washington, DC: U.S. Census Bureau. Accessed April 12, 2010 (http://www.census.gov/population/www/socdemo/interrace.html).

———. 2004. "Current Population Survey (CPS)—Definitions and Explanations." Washington, DC: U.S. Census Bureau. Accessed June 8, 2008 (http://www.census.gov/population/www/cps/cpsdef.html).

———. 2007. "Marriage and Divorce: 2004 SIPP Report." Washington, DC: U.S. Census Bureau. Accessed April 13, 2010 (http://www.census.gov/population/www/socdemo/marr-div.html).

———. 2008b. "PPL Table 1B: Child Care Arrangements of Preschoolers Under 5 Years Old Living with Mother, by Employment Status of Mother and Selected Characteristics: Spring 2005 (Percentages)." *Who's Minding the Kids? Child Care Arrangements: Spring 2005.* Accessed May 6, 2009 (http://www.census.gov/population/www/socdemo/child/ppl-2005.html).

———. 2008c. *Statistical Abstract of the United States: 2009* (128th ed.). Washington, DC: Author.

———. 2008d. "Table PINC-03. Educational Attainment—People 25 Years Old and Over, by Total Money Earnings in 2007, Work Experience in 2007, Age, Race, Hispanic Origin, and Sex." Annual Social and Economic Supplement. Washington, DC: U.S. Census Bureau. Accessed May 29, 2009 (http://www.census.gov/hhes/www/macro/032008/perinc/new03_000.htm).

———. 2008e. "Historical Income Tables—Households." Accessed June 6, 2009 (www.census.gov/hhes/www/income/histinc/inchhtoc.html).

———. 2008g. "2008 National Population Projections: Tables and Charts." Accessed June 18, 2009 (www.census.gov/population/www/projections/tablesandcharts.html).

———. 2008h. "2007 American Community Survey 1-Year Estimates." American FactFinder. Accessed June 19, 2009 (http://factfinder.census.gov/home/saff/main.html).

———. 2009a. "Families and Living Arrangements." Washington, DC: U.S. Census Bureau. May 23, 2009 (http://www.census.gov/population/www/socdemo/hh-fam.html).

———. 2009b. "Educational Attainment." Washington, DC: U.S. Census Bureau. Accessed May 28, 2009 (http://www.census.gov/population/www/socdemo/educ-attn.html).

———. 2009c. "Tables of Alternative Poverty Estimates: 2007." Accessed June 8, 2009 (http://www.census.gov/hhes/www/povmeas/tables.html).

———. 2009d. "Person Income Table of Contents." Annual Social and Economic Supplement. Current Population Survey. Washington, DC: U.S. Census Bureau. Accessed March 28, 2010 (http://www.census.gov/hhes/www/cpstables/032009/perinc/toc.htm).

———. 2009f. *Statistical Abstract of the United States: 2010* (129th ed.). Washington, DC: U.S. Government Printing Office. Accessed April 5, 2010 (http://www.census.gov/compendia/statab/).

———. 2009i. "Historical Income Tables—Households." Accessed April 25, 2010 (http://www.census.gov/hhes/www/income/histinc/inchhtoc.html).

———. 2010a. "Families and Living Arrangements." Washington, DC: U.S. Census Bureau. Accessed April 11, 2010 (http://www.census.gov/population/www/socdemo/hh-fam.html).

———. 2010b. "Observations from the Interagency Technical Working Group on Developing a Supplemental Poverty Measure." Accessed April 25, 2010 (http://www.census.gov/hhes/www/poverty/SPM_TWGObservations.pdf).

———. 2010c. "The Questions on the Form." Accessed May 16, 2010 (http://2010.census.gov/2010census/pdf/2010_Questionnaire_Info.pdf).

———. 2010f. Statistical Abstract of the United States: 2011 (130th ed.). Washington, DC: U.S. Government Printing Office. Accessed May 23, 2011 (http://www.census.gov/compendia/statab/).

———. 2010g. "Table PINC-03. Educational Attainment—People 25 Years Old and Over, by Total Money Earnings in 2009, Work Experience in 2009, Age, Race, Hispanic Origin, and Sex." Annual Social and Economic Supplement. Washington, DC: U.S. Census Bureau. Accessed June 3, 2011 (http://www.census.gov/hhes/www/cpstables/032010/perinc/new03_000.htm).

References

————. 2010h. "Historical Income Tables–Households." Accessed June 9, 2011 (http://www.census.go=v/hhes/www/income/data/historical/household/index.html).

————. 2010i. "2009 Poverty Table of Contents." Accessed June 9, 2011 (http://www.census.gov/hhes/www/cpstables/032010/pov/toc.htm).

————. 2010k. "Fertility of American Women: 2010." Washington, DC: U.S. Census Bureau. Accessed May 8, 2012 (http://www.census.gov/hhes/fertility/data/cps/2010.html).

————. 2010m. "Voting and Registration in the Election of November 2010—Detailed Tables." Accessed May 24, 2012 (http://www.census.gov/hhes/www/socdemo/voting/publications/p20/2010/tables.html).

————. 2011a. "Families and Living Arrangements." Washington, DC: U.S. Census Bureau. Accessed May 31, 2011 (http://www.census.gov/population/www/socdemo/hh-fam.html).

————. 2011d. "Profile of General Population and Housing Characteristics: 2010." American Fact Finder, 2010 Demographic Profile Data, Table DP-1. Accessed June 20, 2011 (http://factfinder2.census.gov/faces/tableservices/jsf/pages/productview.xhtml?pid=DEC_10_DP_DPDP1&prodType=table).

————. 2011f. "Table PINC-03. Educational Attainment—People 25 Years Old and Over, by Total Money Earnings in 2010, Work Experience in 2010, Age, Race, Hispanic Origin, and Sex." Annual Social and Economic Supplement. Washington, DC: U.S. Census Bureau. Accessed March 14, 2012 (http://www.census.gov/hhes/www/cpstables/032011/perinc/new03_000.htm).

————. 2011g. "Who's Minding the Kids? Child Care Arrangements: Spring 2010—Detailed Tables." Accessed April 5, 2012 (http://www.census.gov/hhes/childcare/data/sipp/2010/tables.html).

————. 2011h. *Statistical Abstract of the United States: 2012 (131st Edition).* Washington, DC: U.S. Government Printing Office. Accessed April 5, 2012 (http://www.census.gov/compendia/statab/).

————. 2011i. "2010 Poverty Table of Contents." Current Population Survey 2011 Annual Social and Economic Supplement. Accessed April 6, 2012 (http://www.census.gov/hhes/www/cpstables/032011/pov/toc.htm).

————. 2011j. "Families and Living Arrangements: Households." Washington, DC: U.S. Census Bureau. Accessed May 3, 2012 (http://www.census.gov/hhes/families/data/households.html).

————. 2011k. "Families and Living Arrangements: Families." Washington, DC: U.S. Census Bureau. Accessed May 4, 2012 (http://www.census.gov/hhes/families/data/families.html).

————. 2011l. "Families and Living Arrangements: Marital Status." Washington, DC: U.S. Census Bureau. Accessed May 7, 2012 (http://www.census.gov/hhes/families/data/marital.html).

————. 2011m. "America's Families and Living Arrangements: 2011." Washington, DC: U.S. Census Bureau. Accessed May 8, 2012 (http://www.census.gov/population/www/socdemo/hh-fam/cps2011.html).

————. 2011n. "Families and Living Arrangements: Living Arrangements of Adults." Washington, DC: U.S. Census Bureau. Accessed May 8, 2012 (http://www.census.gov/hhes/families/data/adults.html).

————. 2011o. "Families and Living Arrangements: Living Arrangements of Children." Washington, DC: U.S. Census Bureau. Accessed May 8, 2012 (http://www.census.gov/hhes/families/data/children.html).

————. 2011p. "Historical Income Tables—Households." Accessed May 17, 2012 (http://www.census.gov/hhes/www/income/data/historical/household/).

————. 2011q. "Selected Population Profile in the United States—2010 American Community Survey 1-Year Estimates." American Fact-Finder. Accessed May 26, 2012 (http://factfinder2.census.gov/faces/nav/jsf/pages/searchresults.xhtml).

U.S. Census Bureau. 2012a. "Current Population Survey (CPS)—Definitions." Washington, DC: U.S. Census Bureau. Accessed May 2, 2012 (http://www.census.gov/cps/about/cpsdef.html).

————. 2012b. "Educational Attainment: CPS Historical Time Series Tables." Washington, DC: U.S. Census Bureau. Accessed May 15,

2012 (http://www.census.gov/hhes/socdemo/education/data/cps/historical/index.html).

————. 2012c. "Historical Poverty Tables—People." Accessed May 17, 2012 (http://www.census.gov/hhes/www/poverty/data/historical/people.html).

————. 2012d. "World Vital Events per Time Unit: 2012." World Vital Events, International Data Base. Accessed May 27, 2012 (http://www.census.gov/population/international/data/idb/worldvitalevents.php).

U.S. Commission on Civil Rights. 2009. "Racial Categorization in the 2010 Census: A Briefing Before the United States Commission on Civil Rights Held in Washington, DC, April 7, 2006." Briefing Report. Accessed May 16, 2010 (http://www.usccr.gov/pubs/RC2010Web_Version.pdf).

U.S. Customs and Border Protection. 2011. "U.S. Border Patrol Fiscal Year Apprehension Statistics: Nationwide by Sector and Border Area—FY 1999 through FY 2010." June 7. Department of Homeland Security, Washington, DC. Accessed June 12, 2011 (http://www.cbp.gov/xp/cgov/border_security/border_patrol/usbp_statistics/).

U.S. Department of Agriculture. 2007. "International Macroeconomic Data Set." Economic Research Service. Accessed August 6, 2009 (www.ers.usda.gov/data/macroeconomics).

U.S. Department of Health and Human Services. 2011. "The AFCARS Report." Administration for Children and Families, Administration on Children, Youth and Families, Children's Bureau. Accessed May 8, 2012 (http://www.acf.hhs.gov/programs/cb/stats_research/afcars/tar/report18.htm).

U.S. Department of Justice. 1999. "Ten-Year Program to Compensate Japanese Americans Interned During World War II Closes Its Doors." Press release No. 059, February 19. Accessed June 3, 2010 (http://www.justice.gov/opa/pr/1999/February/059cr.htm).

U.S. Department of Justice. 2011a. "Offenses Known to Law Enforcement." *Crime in the United States, 2010.* Washington, DC: United States Department of Justice, Federal Bureau of Investigation. April 23, 2012 (http://www.fbi.gov/about-us/cjis/ucr/crime-in-the-u.s/2010/crime-in-the-u.s.-2010).

————. 2011b. "2010 Crime Clock Statistics." *Crime in the United States, 2010.* Washington, DC: United States Department of Justice, Federal Bureau of Investigation. Accessed April 23, 2012 (http://www.fbi.gov/about-us/cjis/ucr/crime-in-the-u.s/2010/crime-in-the-u.s.-2010/offenses-known-to-law-enforcement/crime-clock).

————. 2011c. "Hate Crime Statistics 2010." *Crime in the United States, 2010.* Washington, DC: United States Department of Justice, Federal Bureau of Investigation. Accessed May 26, 2012 (http://www.fbi.gov/about-us/cjis/ucr/hate-crime/2010).

U.S. Department of State. 2009. *FY 2009 Annual Report on Intercountry Adoptions.* U.S. Department of State, Washington, DC, November. Accessed April 13, 2010 (http://www.adoption.state.gov/pdf/fy2009_annual_report.pdf).

U.S. Department of State. 2011. "FY 2011 Annual Report on Intercountry Adoptions." United States Department of State, Washington, DC, November. Accessed May 8, 2012 (http://adoption.state.gov/content/pdf/fy2011_annual_report.pdf).

U.S. Surgeon General. 1999. "Overview of Cultural Diversity and Mental Health Services." In Chap. 2, *Surgeon General's Report on Mental Health.* Washington, DC: U.S. Government Printing Office.

Utne, Leif. 2003. "We Are All Zapatistas." *Utne Reader,* November/December, pp. 36–37.

V

van den Bergh, Linda, Eddie Denessen, Lisette Hornstra, Marinus Voeten, and Rob W. Holland. 2010. "The Implicit Prejudiced Attitudes of Teachers: Relations to Teacher Expectations and the Ethnic Achievement Gap." *American Educational Research Journal,* January. doi: 10.3102/0002831209353594.

Van Dijk, Jan., John van Kesteren, and Paul Smit. 2007. *Criminal Victimisation in International Perspective, Key Findings from the 2004–2005 ICVS and EU ICS.* The Hague: Boom Legal Publishers. Accessed May 20, 2009 (http://rechten.uvt.nl/icvs/pdffiles /ICVS2004_05.pdf).

Vanderstraeten, Raf. 2007. "Professions in Organizations, Professional Work in Education." *British Journal of Sociology of Education* 28 (5): 621–635.

Vasagar, Jeeran. 2005. "'At Last Rwanda Is Known for Something Positive.'" *Guardian Weekly,* July 22, p. 18.

Veblen, Thorstein. [1899] 1964. *Theory of the Leisure Class.* New York: Macmillan.

———. 1919. *The Vested Interests and the State of the Industrial Arts.* New York: Huebsch.

Veenhoven, Ruut. 2012. Average Happiness in 149 Nations 2000–2009." World Database of Happiness, Rank Report Average Happiness. Accessed March 10, 2012 (http://worlddatabaseofhappiness.eur.nl /hap_nat/findingreports/RankReport_AverageHappiness.php).

Venkatesh, Sudhir. 2006. *Off the Books: The Underground Economy of the Urban Poor.* Cambridge, MA: Harvard University Press.

———. 2008. *Gang Leader for a Day: A Rogue Sociologist Takes to the Street.* New York: Penguin Books.

Venter, Craig. 2000. "Remarks at the Human Genome Announcement, at the Whitehouse." Accessed June 30, 2008 (http://www.celera .com/celera/pr_1056647999).

Villarreal, Andrés. 2004. "The Social Ecology of Rural Violence: Land Scarcity, the Organization of Agricultural Production, and the Presence of the State." *American Journal of Sociology* 110 (September): 313–348.

Virtcom. 2009. "Board Diversification Strategy: Realizing Competitive Advantage and Shareholder Value." A Whitepaper by Virtcom Consulting, prepared for CalPERS. Accessed June 22, 2009 (www.calpers-governance.org/docs-sof/marketinitiatives /initiatives/board-diversity-white-paper.pdf).

Vogt, W. Paul, Dianne C. Gardner, and Lynne M. Haeffele. 2012. *When to Use What Research Design.* New York: The Guilford Press.

Vowell, Paul R., and Jieming Chen. 2004. "Predicting Academic Misconduct: A Comparative Test of Four Sociological Explanations." *Sociological Inquiry* 74 (2): 226–249.

W

Wang, Wendy. 2012. "The Rise of Intermarriage: Rates, Characteristics Vary by Race and Gender." A Social & Demographic Trends Report, Pew Research Center, February 16. Accessed May 8, 2012 (http://www.pewsocialtrends.org/files/2012/02/SDT-Intermarriage-II.pdf).

Wais, Erin. 2005. "Trained Incapacity: Thorstein Veblen and Kenneth Burke." *KB Journal* 2 (1). Accessed May 13, 2009 (http://www .kbjournal.org/node/103).

Waites, Matthew. 2009. "Critique of 'Sexual Orientation' and 'Gender Identity' in Human Rights Discourse: Global Queer Politics Beyond the Yogyakarta Principles." *Contemporary Politics* 15 (1): 137–156.

Waldman, Amy. 2004a. "India Takes Economic Spotlight, and Critics Are Unkind." *New York Times,* March 7, p. 3.

———. 2004b. "Low-Tech or High, Jobs Are Scarce in India's Boon." *New York Times,* May 6, p. A3.

———. 2004c. "What India's Upset Vote Reveals: The High Tech Is Skin Deep." *New York Times,* May 15, p. A5.

Walker, Iain, and Heather J. Smith, eds. 2002. *Relative Deprivation: Specification, Development, and Integration.* New York: Cambridge University Press.

Walker, Rebecca. 1992. "Becoming the Third Wave." *Ms.,* January, pp. 39–41.

———. 1995. *To Be Real: Telling the Truth and Changing the Face of Feminism.* Berkeley: University of California Press.

Wallerstein, Immanuel. 1974. *The Modern World System.* New York: Academic Press.

———. 1979a. *Capitalist World Economy.* Cambridge, U.K.: Cambridge University Press.

———. 1979b. *The End of the World as We Know It: Social Science for the Twenty-first Century.* Minneapolis: University of Minnesota Press.

———. 2000. *The Essential Wallerstein.* New York: New Press.

———. 2004. *World-Systems Analysis: An Introduction.* Durham, NC: Duke University Press.

———. 2010. "Structural Crises." *New Left Review* 62 (March/April): 133–142.

Wallerstein, Judith S., Julia M. Lewis, and Sandra Blakeslee. 2000. *The Unexpected Legacy of Divorce: A 25-Year Landmark Study.* New York: Basic Books.

Wallis, Claudia. 2008. "How to Make Great Teachers." *Time,* February 25, pp. 28–34.

Walpole, Marybeth. 2007. "Economically and Educationally Challenged Students in Higher Education: Access to Outcomes." *ASHE Higher Education Report* 33 (3).

Warner, R. Stephen. 2005. *A Church of Our Own: Disestablishment and Diversity in American Religion.* New Brunswick, NJ: Rutgers University Press.

———. 2007. "The Role of Religion in the Process of Segmented Assimilation." *Annals of the American Academy of Political and Social Science* 612 (1): 100–115.

Warren, Patricia, Donald Tomaskovic-Devey, William Smith, Matthew Zingraff, and Marcinda Mason. 2006. "Driving While Black: Bias Processes and Racial Disparity in Police Stops." *Criminology* 44 (3): 709–738.

Wartella, Ellen, Aletha C. Huston, Victoria Rideout, and Michael Robb. 2009. "Studying Media Effects on Children: Improving Methods and Measures." *American Behavioral Scientist* 52 (8): 1,111–1,114.

Washington, Harriet A. 2006. *Medical Apartheid: The Dark History of Medical Experimentation on Black Americans from Colonial Times to the Present.* New York: Doubleday.

Waters, Mary C. 2009. "Social Science and Ethnic Options." *Ethnicities* 9 (1): 130–135.

Watts, Duncan J. 2004. "The 'New' Science of Networks." pp. 243–270 in *Annual Review of Sociology 2004,* ed. Karen S. Cook and John Hagan. Palo Alto, CA: Annual Reviews.

Weber, Max. [1913–1922] 1947. *The Theory of Social and Economic Organization,* trans. A. Henderson and T. Parsons. New York: Free Press.

———. [1904] 1949. *Methodology of the Social Sciences,* trans. Edward A. Shils and Henry A. Finch. Glencoe, IL: Free Press.

———. [1904] 2009. *The Protestant Ethic and the Spirit of Capitalism,* trans. Talcott Parsons. New York: Scribner.

———. [1916] 1958a. "Class, Status, Party." pp. 180–195 in *From Max Weber: Essays in Sociology,* ed. H. H. Gerth and C. Wright Mills. New York: Oxford University Press.

———. [1916] 1958b. *The Religion of India: The Sociology of Hinduism and Buddhism.* New York: Free Press.

———. [1921] 1958c. "Bureaucracy." pp. 196–244 in *From Max Weber: Essays in Sociology,* ed. H. H. Gerth and C. Wright Mills. New York: Oxford University Press.

Wechsler, Henry, J. E. Lee, M. Kuo, M. Seibring, T. F. Nelson, and H. Lee. 2002. "Trends in College Binge Drinking During a Period of Increased Prevention Efforts: Findings from Four Harvard School of Public Health College Alcohol Surveys: 1993–2001." *Journal of American College Health* 50 (5): 203–217.

———. 2007. "Earnings by Gender: Evidence from Census 2000." *Monthly Labor Review,* July/August, pp. 26–34.

Wechsler, Henry, and Toben F. Nelson. 2008. "What We Have Learned from the Harvard School of Public Health College Alcohol Study: Focusing Attention on College Student Alcohol Consumption and the Environmental Conditions that Promote It." *Journal of Studies on Alcohol and Drugs* 69 (4): 481–490.

Weinstein, Henry. 2002. "Airport Screener Curb Is Regretful." *Los Angeles Times,* November 16, pp. B1, B14.

References

Weiss, Michael J. 2000. *The Clustered World: How We Live, What We Buy, and What It All Means About Who We Are.* Boston: Little, Brown.

Wells-Barnett, Ida B. [1928] 1970. *Crusade for Justice: The Autobiography of Ida B. Wells,* ed. Alfreda M. Duster. Chicago: University of Chicago Press.

Werner, Carrie A. 2011. "The Older Population: 2010." 2010 Census Briefs C2010BR-09. Washington, DC: U.S. Government Printing Office. Accessed April 6, 2012 (http://www.census.gov/prod /cen2010/briefs/c2010br-09.pdf).

Wessel, David. 2011. "Big U.S. Firms Shift Hiring Abroad." *The Wall Street Journal,* April 19. Accessed August 4, 2011 (http://online .wsj.com/article/SB1000142405274870482170457627078361182 3972.html).

West, Candace, and Don H. Zimmerman. 1987. "Doing Gender." *Gender and Society* 1 (June): 125–151.

Wethington, Elaine. 2000. "Expecting Stress: Americans and the 'Midlife Crisis.'" *Motivation & Emotion* 24 (2): 85–103.

Whorton, James C. 2002. *Nature Cures: The History of Alternative Medicine in America.* New York: Oxford University Press.

Whyte, William Foote. [1943] 1981. *Street Corner Society: Social Structure of an Italian Slum,* 3rd ed. Chicago: University of Chicago Press.

Wickman, Peter M. 1991. "Deviance." pp. 85–87 in *Encyclopedic Dictionary of Sociology,* 4th ed., ed. Dushkin Publishing Group. Guilford, CT: Dushkin.

Wierzbicka, Anna. 2008. "Why There Are No 'Colour Universals' in Language and Thought." *Journal of the Royal Anthropological Institute* 14 (2): 407–425.

Wilford, John Noble. 1997. "New Clues Show Where People Made the Great Leap to Agriculture." *New York Times,* November 18, pp. B9, B12.

Williams, Alicia, John Fries, Jean Koppen, and Robert Prisuta. 2010. *Connecting and Giving: A Report on How Midlife and Older Americans Spend Their Time, Make Connections and Build Communities.* Washington, DC: AARP.

Williams, David R., and Chiquita Collins. 2004. "Reparations." *American Behavioral Scientist* 47 (March): 977–1,000.

Williams, Kristine N., and Carol A. B. Warren. 2009. "Communication in Assisted Living." *Journal of Aging Studies* 23 (1): 24–36.

Williams, Mike. 2008. "Rising Cost of Food Devastates Haiti." *Atlanta Journal Constitution,* June 17. Accessed August 12 (http://www .ajc.com/news/content/news/stories/2008/06/16/haiti_food_crisis .html).

Williams, Richard Allen. 2007. "Cultural Diversity, Health Care Disparities, and Cultural Competency in American Medicine." *Journal of the American Academy of Orthopaedic Surgeons* 15: S52–S58.

Williams Jr., Robin M. 1970. *American Society,* 3rd ed. New York: Knopf.

Wills, Jeremiah B., and Barbara J. Risman. 2006. "The Visibility of Feminist Thought in Family Studies." *Journal of Marriage and Family* 68 (August): 690–700.

Wilper, Andrew P., Steffie Woolhandler, Karen E. Lasser, Danny McCormick, David H. Bor, and David U. Himmelstein. 2009. "Health Insurance and Mortality in U.S. Adults." *American Journal of Public Health* 99 (12): 2,289–2,295.

Wilson, Carl. 2007. *Let's Talk About Love: A Journey to the End of Taste.* New York: Continuum.

Wilson, Robin. 2007. "The New Gender Divide." *Chronicle of Higher Education* 53 (January 26): A36–A39.

Wilson, William Julius. 1980. *The Declining Significance of Race: Blacks and Changing American Institutions,* 2nd ed. Chicago: University of Chicago Press.

———. 1987. *The Truly Disadvantaged: The Inner City, the Underclass and Public Policy.* Chicago: University of Chicago Press.

———. 1996. *When Work Disappears: The World of the New Urban Poor.* New York: Knopf.

———. 1999. *The Bridge over the Racial Divide: Rising Inequality and Coalition Politics.* Berkeley: University of California Press.

———. 2008. "The Political and Economic Forces Shaping Concentrated Poverty." *Political Science Quarterly* 123 (4): 555–571.

———. 2009. *More than Just Race: Being Black and Poor in the Inner City.* New York: Norton.

Wirth, Louis. 1931. "Clinical Sociology." *American Journal of Sociology* 37 (July): 49–60.

Withrow, Brian L. 2006. *Racial Profiling: From Rhetoric to Reason.* Upper Saddle River, NJ: Prentice Hall.

Witte, Griff. 2005. "The Vanishing Middle Class." *Washington Post National Weekly Edition,* September 27, pp. 6–9.

Wolf, Naomi. 1992. *The Beauty Myth: How Images of Beauty Are Used Against Women.* New York: Anchor.

Word, David L., Charles D. Coleman, Robert Nunziator, and Robert Kominski. 2007. "Demographic Aspects of Surnames from Census 2000." Accessed January 2, 2008 (www.census.gov/genealogy /www/surnames.pdf).

Worford, Justin C. 2011b. "Legacy Admit Rate at 30 Percent." *The Harvard Crimson,* May 11. Accessed June 4, 2011 (http://www.thecrimson. com/article/2011/5/11/admissions-fitzsimmons-legacy-legacies/).

World Bank. 2003. *World Development Report 2003: Sustainable Development in a Dynamic World.* Washington, DC: World Bank.

———. 2006. "India, Inclusive Growth and Service Delivery: Building on India's Success." Development Policy Review, Report No. 34580-IN. Accessed June 13, 2009 (http://siteresources.worldbank .org/SOUTHASIAEXT/Resources/DPR_FullReport.pdf).

———. 2009a. "Gross National Income per Capita 2007, Atlas Method and PPP." *World Development Indicators 2009.* Accessed June 11, 2009 (http://siteresources.worldbank.org/DATASTATISTICS /Resources/GNIPC.pdf).

———. 2009b. "Gross Domestic Product 2007." *World Development Indicators 2009.* Accessed June 12, 2009 (http://siteresources .worldbank.org/DATASTATISTICS/Resources/GDP.pdf).

———. 2010a. "Health Expenditure, Public (% of Total Health Expenditure): 2007." *World Development Indicators.* Accessed April 25, 2010 (http://data.worldbank.org/indicator/SH.XPD.PUBL).

———. 2010g. *The MDGs After the Crisis: Global Monitoring Report 2010.* Washington, DC: World Bank.

World Bank. 2012a. *World Development Report 2012: Gender Equality and Development.* Washington, DC: The World Bank. Accessed June May 17, 2012 (www.worldbank.org/wdr/).

———. 2012b. "GNI per Capita, Atlas Method (Current US$): 2010." *World Development Indicators.* Accessed May 17, 2012 (http://data .worldbank.org/indicator/NY.GNP.PCAP.CD).

———. 2012c. "GDP (current US$): 2010." *World Development Indicators.* Accessed May 18, 2012 (http://data.worldbank.org/indicator/ NY.GDP.MKTP.CD).

———. 2012d. "Income Share Held by Highest 20%." *World Development Indicators.* Accessed May 18, 2012 (http://data.worldbank .org/indicator/SI.DST.05TH.20).

———. 2012e. "Income Share Held by Lowest 20%." *World Development Indicators.* Accessed May 18, 2012 (http://data.worldbank .org/indicator/SI.DST.FRST.20).

———. 2012f. "Income share held by highest 10%." *World Development Indicators.* Accessed May 18, 2012 (http://data.worldbank .org/indicator/SI.DST.10TH.10).

———. 2012g. "Share of Women Employed in the Nonagricultural Sector (% of Total Nonagricultural Employment)." *World Development Indicators.* Accessed May 18, 2012 (http://data.worldbank .org/indicator/SL.EMP.INSV.FE.ZS).

———. 2012h. "Mortality rate, infant (per 1,000 live births)." *World Development Indicators.* Accessed May 18, 2012 (http://data .worldbank.org/indicator/SP.DYN.IMRT.IN).

———. 2012i. "Birth Rate, Crude (per 1,000 People)." *World Development Indicators,* Databank. May 27, 2012 (http://data.worldbank .org/indicator/SP.DYN.CBRT.IN).

———. 2012j. "Fertility Rate, Total (Births per Woman)." *World Development Indicators,* Databank. May 27, 2012 (http://data.worldbank .org/indicator/SP.DYN.TFRT.IN).

———. 2012k. "Death Rate, Crude (per 1,000 People)." *World Development Indicators,* Databank. May 27, 2012 (http://data.worldbank .org/indicator/SP.DYN.CDRT.IN).

————. 2012l. "Life Expectancy at Birth, Total (Years)." *World Development Indicators*, Databank. May 27, 2012 (http://data.worldbank.org/indicator/SP.DYN.LE00.IN).

World Health Organization. 1948. "Preamble to the Constitution of the World Health Organization." Adopted by the International Health Conference, New York, June 19–July 22, 1946; entered into force on April 7, 1948. Accessed June 30, 2011 (http://whqlibdoc.who.int/hist/official_records/constitution.pdf).

————. 2005. *WHO Global Atlas of Traditional, Complementary, and Alternative Medicine.* Geneva: WHO Press.

————. 2008a. "Traditional Medicine." Fact Sheet No. 134, December. Accessed May 21, 2010 (http://www.who.int/mediacentre/factsheets/fs134/en/print.html).

————. 2008b. "Air Quality and Health." Fact Sheet No. 313, August. Accessed May 21, 2010 (http://www.who.int/mediacentre/factsheets/fs313/en/print.html).

————. 2010. *World Health Statistics 2010.* Geneva: WHO Press. Accessed May 20, 2010 (http://www.who.int/whosis/whostat/en/).

World Health Organization. 2012 *World Health Statistics, 2012.* Geneva: WHO Press. Accessed May 28, 2012 (http://www.who.int/gho/publications/world_health_statistics/en/index.html).

World Values Survey. 2009. "Online Data Analysis." Accessed May 17, 2010 (http://www.wvsevsdb.com/wvs/WVSAnalize.jsp).

Wyatt, Edward. 2012. "Use of 'Conflict Minerals' Gets More Scrutiny From U.S." The New York Times March 19. Accessed May 18, 2012 (http://www.nytimes.com/2012/03/20/business/use-of-conflict-minerals-gets-more-scrutiny.html).

Y

Yinger, J. Milton. 1970. *The Scientific Study of Religion.* New York: Macmillan.

Yogyakartaprinciples.org. 2007. *The Yogyakarta Principles: Principles on the Application of International Human Rights Law in Relation to Sexual Orientation and Gender Identity.* Accessed May 11, 2010 (http://www.yogyakartaprinciples.org/principles_en.pdf).

Z

Zarembo, Alan. 2004. "A Theater of Inquiry and Evil." *Los Angeles Times,* July 15, pp. A1, A24, A25.

Zellner, William M., and Richard T. Schaefer. 2006. *Extraordinary Groups,* 8th ed. New York: Worth.

Zetter, Kim. 2009. "FBI Use of Patriot Act Authority Increased Dramatically in 2008." *Wired,* May 19. Accessed June 30, 2009 (www.wired.com/threatlevel/2009/05/fbi-use-of-patriot-act-authority-increased-dramatically-in-2008).

Zickuhr, Kathryn and Aaron Smith. 2012. "Digital Differences." Pew Research Center's Internet & American Life Project, April 13. Accessed May 17, 2012 (http://pewinternet.org/~/media//Files/Reports/2012/PIP_Digital_differences_041312.pdf).

Zimbardo, Philip G. 2007. *The Lucifer Effect: Understanding How Good People Turn Evil.* New York: Random House.

Zimmerman, Amber Lynn, M. Joan McDermott, and Christina M. Gould. 2009. "The Local Is Global: Third Wave Feminism, Peace, and Social Justice." *Contemporary Justice Review* 12 (1): 77–90.

Zola, Irving K. 1972. "Medicine as an Institution of Social Control." *Sociological Review* 20 (November): 487–504.

————. 1983. *Socio-Medical Inquiries.* Philadelphia: Temple University Press.

Zweigenhaft, Richard L., and G. William Domhoff. 2006. *Diversity in the Power Elite: How It Happened, Why It Matters,* 2nd ed. New York: Rowman & Littlefield.

Front Matter:

p. iv top: © AP Photo/Don Ryan; p. iv bottom: © Daniel Berehulak/Getty; p. vi top: © Jacob Wackerhauser/iStockphoto; p. vi bottom: © Pamela Moore/iStockphoto; p. vii top: © AP Photo/Elizabeth Dalziel; p. vii bottom: © David Lewis/iStockphoto; p. viii top left: © Nevada Wier/Getty; p. viii top right: © Thomas S. England/Photo Researchers; p. viii bottom: © Corbis RF; p. ix: © The McGraw-Hill Companies, Inc./John Flourney, photographer; p. x top: © Justin Sullivan/Getty; p. x bottom: © Ingram Publishing RF; p. xi top: © Pavel Filatov/Alamy RF; p. xi bottom: © Goodshoot/Alamy RF; p. xii top: © Dr. Parvinder Sethi; p. xii bottom: © Thomas Northcut/Digital Vision/Getty RF; p. xiii top: © The McGraw-Hill Companies, Inc./Barry Barker, photographer; p. xiii bottom: © Michael Steele/Getty; p. xiv: © David McNew/Getty; p. 1 © Brand X Pictures/Jupiter RF

Chapter 1

Opener : © Chip Somodevilla/Getty; p. 2 earth: © BLOOMimage/Getty RF; p. 4 (left): © Doug Pensinger/Getty; p. 4 (middle): © Ingram Publishing RF; p. 4 (right): © Mike Coppola/FilmMagic/Getty; p. 5 popcorn: © iStockphoto; p. 5 (bottom): © PhotoDisc/Getty RF; p. 7: © Doug Pensinger/Getty; p. 9: © Library of Congress Prints and Photographs Division [LC-DIG-fsa-8b29516]; p. 10: © Mark Downey/Masterfile; p. 12: © Ingram Publishing RF; p. 13: © Mike Coppola/FilmMagic/Getty; p. 14 Durkheim: © Bettmann/Corbis; p. 14 Durkheim frame: © iStockphoto; p. 14 Marx: © Library of Congress Prints and Photographs Division [LC-USZ62-16530]; p. 14 Marx frame: © iStockphoto; p. 14 Weber: © Hulton Archive/Getty; p. 14 Weber frame: © Lou Oates/iStockphoto; p. 15 (top): © Con Tanasiuk/Design Pics RF; p. 15 popcorn: © iStockphoto; p. 15 (bottom): © Mike Segar/Reuters/Corbis; p. 16 Adams: © Hulton Archive/Getty; p. 16 Adams frame: © Andrea Gingerich/iStockphoto; p. 18: © iStockphoto; p. 19: © Stockbyte/PunchStock RF; p. 20 (left): © Medioimages/PictureQuest/Jupiter Images RF; p. 20 (right): © Comstock Images/Alamy RF; p. 21: © Doug Menuez/Getty RF

Chapter 2

Opener: © Ocean/Corbis RF; p. 26 (left): © Georgina Palmer/iStockphoto; p. 26 (middle): © Sally and Richard Greenhill/Alamy; p. 26 (right): © Frank Trapper/Corbis; p. 26 (bottom): © PhotoDisc/Getty RF; p. 27: © Mike Kemp/Getty RF; p. 28 (top): © Jose Luis Pelaez Inc/Blend Images RF; p. 28 lightbulb: © iStockphoto; p. 29: © Stefano Maccari/123rf.com; p. 30 (top): © U.S. Census Bureau, Public Information Office; p. 31: © Jerry Koch/iStockphoto; p. 32: © Hill Street Studios/Getty RF; p. 33 earth: © BLOOMimage/Getty RF; p. 33 (bottom): © Bettmann/Corbis; p. 34: © Georgina Palmer/iStockphoto; p. 35: © Sally and Richard Greenhill/Alamy; p. 37 (top): © The McGraw-Hill Companies, Inc./Jill Braaten, photographer; p. 37 (bottom): Women in the Relay Assembly Test Room, ca. 1930. Western Electric Hawthorne Studies Collection. Baker Library Historical Collections, Harvard Business School; p. 38: © Penny Gentieu/Jupiter Images RF; p. 39 (top): © Scott Barbour/Getty; p. 39 (bottom): © Craig Blankenhorn/© AMC/Courtesy: Everett Collection; p. 40 (top): © Grafissimo/iStockphoto; p. 40 (bottom): © Frank Trapper/Corbis; p. 41 (top): © Columbia Pictures/Courtesy Everett Collection; p. 41 (bottom): © Siqui Sanchez/The Image Bank/Getty; p. 42 popcorn: © iStockphoto; p. 43: © Dennis Wise/PhotoDisc/Getty RF

Chapter 3

Opener: © Wu Kaixiang/Xinhua Press/Corbis; p. 48 (left): © Business Wire; p. 48 (middle): © Peter Menzel/menzelphoto.com; p. 48 (right): © Underwood & Underwood/Corbis; p. 48 (bottom): © The Granger Collection, New York; p. 49 (top): © The McGraw-Hill Companies, Inc./Jill Braaten, photographer; p. 49 (bottom): © Wicked Artwork and logo© *2011 Wicked LLC. All rights reserved; p. 50 (left, middle, right): © Peter Menzel/menzelphoto.com; p. 51 earth: © BLOOMimage/Getty RF; p. 52: © Business Wire; p. 53: © Jon Witt; p. 54 (top): © Warner Bros/Courtesy Everett Collection; p. 54 (bottom): © Little Blue Wolf Productions/Corbis RF; p. 56 (top): © TM & Copyright © 20th Century Fox. All rights reserved/Courtesy Everett Collection; p. 56 (bottom): © Jean-Christophe Verhaegen/AFP/Getty; p. 57: © Jupiter Images/BananaStock/Alamy RF; p. 58 (top left): © dbimages/Alamy; p. 58 (top right): © Mustafa Deliorkanli/iStockphoto; p. 58 (bottom): © Ballyscanion/PhotoDisc/Getty RF; p. 59 popcorn: © iStockphoto; p. 60 dress: © Igor Terekhov/iStockphoto; p. 60 jeans: © iStockphoto; p. 61 (top): © KarimSahib/AFP/Getty; p. 61 popcorn: © iStockphoto; p. 62: © Rob Crandall/The Image Works; p. 63: © Underwood & Underwood/Corbis; p. 64: © RubberBall Productions RF; p. 65 (top): © Marvy! Advertising Photography; p. 65 (bottom): © Frans Lemmens/The Image Bank/Getty; p. 66: © moodboard/Corbis RF; p. 67: © Digital Vision/Getty RF; p. 72 (top left): © Nevada Wier/Getty

Chapter 4

Opener: © Frances M. Roberts/Ambient Images, Inc./SuperStock; p. 72 (middle): © Thomas S. England/Photo Researchers; p. 72 (right): © Corbis RF; p. 72 (bottom): © Ariel Skelley/Blend RF; p. 73 (top): © PhotoDisc/Getty RF; p. 73 (bottom): © Mary Evans Picture Library/Image Works; p. 74 (top): © Nina Leen/Time & Life Pictures/Getty; p. 74 (bottom): © Glow Images RF; p. 75: © Ingram Publishing RF; p. 76: © Somos/Veer/Getty RF; p. 77: © AP Photo/Francois Mori; p. 78: © Corbis RF; p. 79: © Brand X Pictures/PunchStock RF; p. 80: © Mark Wilson/Getty; p. 81 (top): © Bill Pugliano/Getty; p. 81 (bottom): © blue jean images/Getty RF; p. 82: © Jose Luis Pelaez Inc./Blend Images RF; p. 83: © Michael Yarish/Fox Television/Courtesy Everett Collection; p. 84 (top): © Datacraft Co Ltd/Getty RF; p. 84 (bottom): © Creatas/PictureQuest RF; p. 85: © Purestock/SuperStock RF; p. 86 phone: © Tatiana Popova/iStockphoto; p. 86 (bottom): © Drew Myers/Corbis RF; p. 87 (top): © Glow Images RF; p. 87 (bottom): © Nevada Wier/Getty; p. 88 (top): © William Thomas Cain/Getty; p. 88 (bottom): © Thomas S. England/Photo Researchers; p. 90: © Justin Sullivan/Getty; p. 91 (top): © Paula Bronstein/Getty; p. 91 popcorn: © iStockphoto; p. 92 earth: © BLOOMimage/Getty RF; p. 92 (top): © iStockphoto; p. 92 (bottom): © Darren Greenwood/Design Pics RF; p. 93: © Kelly Redinger/Design Pics RF; p. 94 popcorn: © iStockphoto; p. 94 (bottom): © Harold Eisenberger/LOOK/Getty; p. 95 (top left): © Corbis RF; p. 95 (top right): © Lisa F. Young/iStockphoto; p. 95 (bottom): © Ronnie Kaufman/Blend Images RF; p. 97: © PhotoDisc/Getty RF

Chapter 5

Opener: © B2M Productions/Getty; p. 102 (left): © Jim Arbogast/Getty RF; p. 102 (middle): © Corbis RF; p. 102 (right): © Reza Estakhrian/Reportage/Getty; p. 103: © AP Photo/John Rooney; p. 104 (top): © Amos Morgan/PhotoDisc/Getty RF; p. 106 (bottom left): © Jim Arbogast/Getty RF; p. 104 (bottom right): © Jim West/The Image Works; p. 106: © ImageDJ/Alamy RF; p. 107: © Photo by Kevork Djansezian/Getty; p. 108 (top): © Courtesy of Central College, photographer Dan Vander Beek; p. 108 (bottom): © Keith Srakocic/AP Images; p. 109: © Corbis RF; p. 110: © Reza Estakhrian/Reportage/Getty; p. 111: © Stockbyte/Getty RF; p. 112 earth: © BLOOMimage/Getty RF; p. 113 (blue pattern): © iStockphoto; p. 113 (bottom): © Pixtal/AGE Fotostock RF; p. 114: © Bob Pearson/epa/Corbis; p. 115 (top): © Image Source/Getty RF; p. 115 (bottom): © Mark Evans/iStockphoto; p. 116 (top): © AP Photo/Yves Logghe; p. 116 wash line: © iStockphoto; p. 116 (bottom left): © Custom Medical Stock Photo; p. 116 (middle): © Adam Crowley/Getty RF; p. 116 (right): © Muntz/Taxi/Getty; p. 117: © Rtimages/Alamy RF; p. 119 popcorn: © iStockphoto; p. 121: © PhotoDisc/Getty RF; p. 122: © Frederick M. Brown/Getty; p. 123 earth: © BLOOMimage/Getty RF; p. 124: © Dennis Wise/Getty RF; p. 125: © Veer/Getty RF

Chapter 6

Opener: © Comstock/Jupiter Images RF; p. 130 (top left): © Leonard McLane/Digital Vision/Getty RF; p. 130 (top middle): © Ingram Publishing RF; p. 130 (top right): © Masterfile RF; p. 130 (bottom): © Scott Garfield/© American Movie Classics/ Courtesy Everett Collection; p. 131 (top): © Dave Robertson/Masterfile; p. 131 (bottom): © Moviestore Collection/Rex USA; p. 132: © From the film OBEDIANCE © 1968 by Alexandra Milgram, © renewed 1993 by Alexandra Milgram, distributed by Penn State Media Sales; p. 133 bottlecaps: © Luis Carlos/iStockphoto; p. 133 bottle: © Dimitry Bomshtein/iStockphoto; p. 134 (top): © MirkaMoshu/ iStockphoto; p. 134 (bottom): © Dave Moyer; p. 135 (top): © Leonard McLane/Digital Vision/Getty RF; p. 135 (bottom) © Jose Luis Roca/AFP/Getty; p. 136 (top): © AP Photo/Alberto Pellaschiar; p. 136 dice: © Comstock Images/Alamy RF; p. 136 (bottom): © Masterfile RF; p. 137: © Floortje/iStockphoto; p. 138 handprint: © Tamas-Dernovics/iStockphoto; p. 138 (bottom): © Ingram Publishing RF; p. 139 popcorn: © iStockphoto; p. 140: © HBO/ Courtesy Everett Collection; p. 141 earth: © BLOOMimage/Getty RF; p. 141 (bottom): © Trista Weibell/iStockphoto; p. 142 popcorn: © iStockphoto; p. 143: © Justin Lubin/NBC/Courtesy Everett Collection; p. 144: © 2009 Jupiter Images RF; p. 145: © Bear Dancer Studios/Mark Dierker; p. 146: © BananaStock/PunchStock RF; p. 148 popcorn: © iStockphoto; p. 148 (bottom): © Amos Morgan/ Getty RF; p. 149: © BananaStock/Jupiter Images RF

Chapter 7

Opener: © AFP/Getty; p. 154 (top left): © Brand X Pictures/Jupiter Images RF; p. 154 (middle): © TM and © Fox Searchlight. All rights reserved/ Courtesy Everett Collection; p. 154 (top right): © Justin Sullivan/ Getty; p. 154 (middle): © David Noble Photography/Alamy; p. 154 (bottom): © Jeremy Edwards/iStockphoto; p. 155: © ABC-TV/Eric McCandles/The Kobal Collection; p. 156: © 2009 Jupiter Images RF; p. 157: © S. Greg Panosian/iStockphoto; p. 158 (top): © TLC/Joe Pugliese/Courtesy Everett Collection; p. 158 (bottom): © Brand X Pictures/Jupiter Images; p. 159: © Comstock/PunchStock RF; p. 160: © Mistikas/iStockphoto; p. 161 (left): © Erica Simone Leeds; p. 161 (right): © Don Tremain/Getty RF; p. 161 earth: © BLOOMimage/Getty RF; p. 162: © Burke/Triolo Productions/Getty RF; p. 163 popcorn: © iStockphoto; p. 164: © TM and © Fox Searchlight. All rights reserved/ Courtesy Everett Collection; p. 165: © Splash News/Corbis; p. 166: © Corbis RF; p. 167: © Universal/Courtesy Everett Collection; p. 168: © Flying Colours LTD/Getty RF; p. 170: © Justin Sullivan/Getty; p. 171: © Angela Wyant/Stone/Getty; p. 172 wedding: © bitter/ iStockphoto; p. 172 frame: © sxasher/iStockphoto; p. 172 (left): © AP Photo/Evan Agostini; p. 172 (right): © Joe Stevens/Retna Ltd./ Getty RF; p. 173 (top): © Jennifer Trenchard/iStockphoto; p. 173 (bottom): © CMCD/Getty RF; p. 174: © Digital Vision/Getty

Chapter 8

Opener: © Gavriel Jecan/The Image Bank/Getty; p. 180 (left): © Challenge Roddie/Corbis Outline; p. 180 (middle): © Goodshoot/Alamy RF; p. 180 (right): © Pierre-Philippe Marcou/AFP/Getty; p. 180 (bottom): © Borut Trdina/iStockphoto; p. 181 earth: © BLOOMimage/Getty RF; p. 181: © Forest Woodward/iStockphoto; p. 182: © iStockphoto; p. 183: © Mandel Ngan/AFP/Getty; p. 185: © PhotoDisc/Getty RF; p. 186 (top): © Squared Studios/Getty RF; p. 186 (bottom): © PhotoDisc/Getty RF; p. 187 popcorn: © iStockphoto; p. 187 (bottom): © Mike Kemp/ Getty RF; p. 189: © Robert Hunt/iStockphoto; p. 190: © Challenge Roddie/Corbis Outline; p. 191: © Michael Ciranni/iStockphoto; p. 192: © Chris Ryan/OJO Images/Getty RF; p. 193: © PhotoDisc/Getty RF; p. 194: © Goodshoot/Alamy RF; p. 195 earth: © BLOOMimage/ Getty RF; p. 195 (bottom): © DAJ/Getty RF; p. 196: © Jeff Greenberg/ The Image Works; p. 198 (top): © Robert Davis; p. 198 (bottom): © Pierre-Philippe Marcou/AFP/Getty; p. 199 earth: © BLOOMimage/

Getty RF; p. 200: © George Doyle/Stockbyte/Getty RF; p. 201: © Pavel Filatov/Alamy RF; p. 203 popcorn: © iStockphoto; p. 204 (top): © M. Freeman/ PhotoLink/Stockbyte/Getty RF; p. 204 (bottom): © Syracuse Newspapers/The Image Works; p. 205: © Exactostock/ SuperStock RF

Chapter 9

Opener: © Brendan Smialowski/AFP/Getty; p. 210 (left): © Liu Jin/AFP/ Getty; p. 210 (middle): © Peter Macdiarmid/Getty; p. 210 (right): © Tony Savino/Corbis; p. 210 (bottom): © AP Photo/Don Ryan; p. 212: © Tony Savino/Corbis; p. 214 (top): © Rene Mansi/iStockphoto; p. 214 (bottom): © AP Photo/Paul Sakuma; p. 215: © Elliot & Fry/Hulton Archive/Getty; p. 216: © Comstock/Getty RF; p. 217 (top): © J.D. Poole/Getty; p. 217 (bottom): © Rob Wilkinson/Alamy; p. 218: © Liu Jin/AFP/Getty; p. 219: © Amanda Rhode/iStockphoto; p. 220: © Peter Macdiarmid/Getty; p. 221 (left): © Ashraf Shazly/AFP/Getty; p. 221 (right): © National Archives and Records Administration; p. 222 (left): © AP Photo/Chris O'Meara; p. 222 (right): © AP Photo/ Steven Senne; p. 223 earth: © BLOOMimage/Getty RF; p. 223 (top): © Ugur Evirgen/iStockphoto; p. 224 popcorn: © iStockphoto; p. 225: © Ben and Kristen Bryant/iStockphoto; p. 227 (top): © Brand X Pictures/Punchstock RF; p. 227 (bottom): © AP Photo/Nati Harnik; p. 228 (top): © Ryan McVay/Getty RF; p. 228 earth: © BLOOMimage/Getty RF; p. 228 (left): © Library of Congress, Prints and Photography Division [LC-USZ62-53202]; p. 229: © Blank Archives/Getty; p. 230: © Valerie Loiseleux/iStockphoto; p. 231 (top): © Capital Pictures/Courtesy Everett Collection; p. 231 (bottom): © Tariq Mahmood/AFP/Getty; p. 232 earth: © BLOOMimage/Getty RF; p. 233: © Amos Morgan/Getty RF

Chapter 10

Opener: © Janine Wiedel Photography/Photoshelter; p. 238 (left): © Dr. Parvinder Sethi; p. 238 (middle): © Dave Moyer; p. 238 (right): © Robyn Beck/AFP/Getty; p. 238 (bottom): © Bettmann/ Corbis; p. 239 (top): © Per-Anders Petterson/Getty; p. 239 (bottom): © Dr. Parvinder Sethi; p. 240 (top): © Jean Baptiste Lacroix/ WireImage/Getty; p. 240 (bottom): © Everett Collection/Rex USA; p. 241: © Sean Gallup/Getty Images; p. 242 popcorn: © iStockphoto; p. 243: © AP Photo/George Nikitin; p. 244: © Dave Moyer; p. 245: © 2010 CBS Photo Archive via Getty; p. 246: © AP Photo/Paul Sakuma; p. 247: © Lew Robertson/Corbis RF; p. 248 (top): © Michael Krinke/iStockphoto; p. 248 (bottom): © Mike Clarke/ iStockphoto; p. 249: © BananaStock/Punchstock RF; p. 250 (left): © Tana Lee Alves/WireImage/Getty; p. 250 (right): © Ivan Bajic/ iStockphoto; p. 251: © Brand X Pictures/PunchStock RF; p. 252 earth: © BLOOMimage/Getty RF; p. 252 (bottom): © Jason R. Warren/iStockphoto; p. 253: © Robyn Beck/AFP/Getty; p. 254: © Dr. Parvinder; p. 255 (top left): © James Pauls/iStockphoto; p. 255 (top right): © Edwardo Jose Bernardino/iStockphoto; p. 255 (bottom left): © Stockphoto4u/iStockphoto; p. 255 (bottom middle): © Ivar Teunissen/iStockphoto; p. 255 (bottom right): © David Buffington/Getty RF; p. 256: © Bfoto/Getty; p. 257: © Gary S. Chapman/Photographer's Choice/Getty RF; p. 258: © iStockphoto/ Alex Potemkin; p. 259: © FPG/Hulton Archive/Getty; p. 260 (top): © Digital Vision RF; p. 260 (bottom): © Dennis Wise/Getty RF

Chapter 11

Opener: © 2011 Gallo Images/Getty; p. 266 (top left): © Digital Vision/ Getty RF; p. 266 (middle): © The McGraw-Hill Companies, Inc./ Barry Barker, photographer; p. 266 (right): © Marco Di Lauro/Getty; p. 266 (bottom): © Dr. Parvinder Sethi; p. 267 (left): © Photofusion Picture Library/Alamy; p. 267 (right): © Caroline Schiff/Digital Vision/Getty RF; p. 268 earth: © BLOOMimage/Getty RF; p. 268 scales: © Rafael Laguillo/iStockphoto; p. 268 (bottom): © Digital Vision/Getty RF; p. 269: © Library of Congress; p. 270: © Warner

Brothers/Courtesy Everett Collection; p. 271: © Picturenet/Blend Images/Getty RF; p. 272 earth: © BLOOMimage/Getty RF; p. 273 (top): © Siqui Sanchez/The Image Bank/Getty; p. 273 (bottom): © Tom Stoddard Archive/Getty; p. 275 (top): © AP Photo/Suzanne Plunkett; p. 275 (bottom): © The McGraw-Hill Companies, Inc./ Barry Barker, photographer; p. 276 (top): Copyright © SASI Group (University of Sheffield) & Mark Newman (University of Michigan); p. 277 (quarters): © Image Club RF; p. 277 popcorn: © iStockphoto; p. 278: © Randolph Jay Braun/iStockphoto; p. 279 (top): © Glow Images RF; p. 279 (bottom): © Pixtal/age fotostock RF; p. 283: © Marco Di Lauro/Getty; p. 284: © Paula Bronstein/Getty RF; p. 286: © Amos Morgan/PhotoDisc/Getty RF

Chapter 12

Opener: © STR/Reuters/Corbis; p. 292 (left): © Art Montes De Oca/ Taxi/Getty; p. 292 (middle): © Thomas Northcut/Digital Vision/ Getty RF; p. 292 (right): © 20th Century Fox/Rex USA; p. 292 (bottom): © 1998 Image Ideas, Inc. RF; p.293 (top): © Michael Steele/ Getty; p. 293 (bottom): © Olivier Blondeau/iStockphoto; p. 294: © Art Montes De Oca/Taxi/Getty; p. 295 (top): © Dove/PA Wire URN:8069588 via AP Images; p. 295 earth: © BLOOMimage/ Getty RF; p. 295 (bottom): © Christine Balderas/iStockphoto; p. 296: © iStockphoto; p. 299 (top): Source: New York Times; p. 299 (bottom): © Brand X Pictures/PunchStock RF; p. 300 (top): © AP Photo/Gerald Herbert; p. 300 (bottom): © Scott J Ferrell/Getty; p. 301: © George Marks/Getty; p. 302 scales: © Comstock/Alamy RF; p. 302 groom & groom: © PhotoDisc/Getty RF; p. 302 bride & groom: © Image Club RF; p. 303 (top): © AP Photo/Hermann J. Knippertz; p. 303 (bottom): © 20th Century Fox/Rex USA; p. 305: © Hulton Archive/Getty; p. 306: © 2010 Jason LaVeris/FilmMagic/ Getty; p. 307: © NYC Department of Health and Mental Hygiene/ AP; p. 308 (top): © Thomas Northcut/Digital Vision/Getty RF; p. 308 (bottom): © Jason Lugo/iStockphoto; p. 309: © Corbis RF; p. 310 (top): © Comstock Images/Getty RF; p. 310 (bottom): © iStockphoto/Anton Seleznev; p. 311 popcorn: © iStockphoto; p. 311 (bottom): © Tetra Images/Getty RF; p. 312 (top): © Elisabetta Villa/Getty; p. 312 earth: © BLOOMimage/Getty RF; p. 312 (left): © Jack Jelly/iStockphoto; p. 312 (right): © Anna Bryukhanova/ iStockphoto; p. 313: © Exactostock/Superstock RF

Chapter 13

Opener: © John Moore/Getty; p. 318 (left): © AP Photo/Bob Child; p. 318 (middle): © William Campbell/Sygma/Corbis; p. 318 (right): © David McNew/Getty; p. 318 (bottom): © Image Source, all rights reserved RF; p. 319: © Jeff Greenberg/Alamy; p. 320: © Patrick Kelley/USGS; p. 321 (top): © Steve Granitz/WireImage/Getty; p. 321 (bottom): © Stephen Chernin/Getty; p. 322 (top): © Ryan McVay/Getty RF; p. 322 (bottom): © AP Photo/Bob Child; p. 323: © Bruce Roberts/Photo Researchers; p. 324 (top): © Duncan Walker/iStockphoto; p. 324 (bottom): © William Campbell/Sygma/ Corbis; p. 325 (top): © Skip Odonnell/iStockphoto; p. 325 (bottom): © Bettmann/Corbis; p. 326 (top): © Don Farrall/Getty RF; p. 326 (bottom): © Tom Carter/PhotoEdit; p. 328 (top): © Francis Miller/ Time Life Pictures/Getty; p. 328 (bottom): © Jim West/The Image Works; p. 330: © AP Photo/Gene Herrick; p. 331 popcorn: © iStockphoto; p. 331 (bottom): © Nicole Rivelli/© NBC/Courtesy Everett Collection; p. 332 (top): © Bill Rankin (Yale University), www.radicalcartography.net. Color version reprinted with permission of Eric Fisher; p. 332 (bottom): © Daniel Berehulak/Getty;

p. 333: © David McNew/Getty; p. 334 (bottom): © Ken Usami/Getty RF; p. 334 (top left & right): © Copyright 1997 IMS Communications Ltd/Capstone Design. All Rights Reserved.; p. 334 (bottom right): © liquidlibrary/PictureQuest RF; p. 335 (top): © Jaroslaw Wojcik/ iStockphoto; p. 335 (bottom): © Walt Disney Co./Courtesy Everett Collection; p. 340: © PhotoDisc/Getty RF; p. 341: © Ingram Publishing RF; p. 343 & 344 earth: © BLOOMimage/Getty RF; p. 344: © Steve Dibblee/iStockphoto; p. 345: © Comstock/PictureQuest RF

Chapter 14

Opener: © Paul Buck/epa/Corbis; p. 350 (left): © Anthony Saint James/ Getty RF; p. 350 (middle): © China Photos/Getty; p. 350 (right): © Brand X Pictures/Jupiter RF; p. 350 (bottom): © Digital Vision/ Getty RF; p. 356: © WireImage/Getty; p. 357 (top): © AP Photo/ Alberto Pellaschiar; p. 357 (bottom): © LWA/Dann Tardif/Blend Images RF; p. 359 (top): © Blend Images/Getty RF; p. 359 popcorn: © iStockphoto; p. 360 earth: © BLOOMimage/Getty RF; p. 360 (bottom): © The McGraw-Hill Companies, Inc./Christopher Kerrigan, photographer; p. 361 earth: © BLOOMimage/Getty RF; p. 362 (top): © Jean-Marc Giboux/Getty; p. 362 (bottom): © RubberBall Productions RF; p. 364 (top): © Fancy Photography/Veer RF; p. 364 (bottom): © Photo by Victor Keppler/George Eastman House/ Getty; p. 366 (top): © Comstock Images/Alamy RF; p. 366 (bottom): © Jules Frazier/Getty RF; p. 367: © Showtime Networks Inc./Courtesy Everett Collection; p. 368 (top left): © Chip Somodevilla/Getty; p. 368 (top right): © Grigory Bibikov/iStockphoto; p. 368 (bottom): © Anthony Saint James/Getty RF; p. 369 (top): © Duncan Walker/ iStockphoto; p. 369 (bottom): © Paul Miles/Axiom Photographic Agency/Getty; p. 370 (top): © Digital Vision Ltd/Getty RF; p. 370 (bottom): © Digital Vision/PunchStock RF; p. 372 (top): © Bruce Dale/National Geographic/Getty; p. 372 bottom: © iStockphoto; p. 373: © China Photos/Getty; p. 374 earth: © BLOOMimage/Getty RF; p. 374 panda, fish and frog: © Eric Isselée/iStockphoto; p. 375 (top): © Brand X Images/Jupiter RF; p. 375 (bottom): © Corbis RF; p. 376 (top): © Mark Trost/iStockphoto; p. 376 (middle & bottom): © Stockbyte/PunchStock RF

Chapter 15

Opener: © Mandel Ngan/AFP/Getty; p. 382 (middle): © Alex Wong/ Getty; p. 382 (right): © 20th Century Fox Film Corp. All rights reserved/Courtesy Everett Collection; p. 382 (bottom): © Daniel Berehulak/Getty; p. 383: © Lara Seregni/iStockphoto; p. 385 popcorn: © iStockphoto; p. 386 (left): © AP Photo/Alex Brandon; p. 386 (right): © AP Photo/Bristol Herald Courier, David Crigger; p. 387 (top): © Ryan McVay/Getty RF; p. 387 (bottom): © McGraw-Hill Companies, Inc.,/Lars Niki, photographer; p. 389: © Elmer Martinez/AFP/Getty; p. 390: © PhotoDisc/PunchStock RF; p. 391 calf & goat: © Eric Isselee/iStockphoto; p. 391 piglet: © Image Source/PunchStock RF; p. 391 kitten: © Blackbeck/iStockphoto; p. 391 rat: © Butinova Elena/iStockphoto; p. 391 (bottom): © Getty; p. 392: © Clint Hild/iStockphoto; p. 393: Library of Congress, Prints and Photographs Division [LC-USZ62-29808]; p. 395 (top): © Bettmann/Corbis; p. 395 (bottom): © Popperfoto/Getty; p. 396: © Mario Tama/Getty; p. 397 (top): © Alex Wong/Getty; p. 397 (bottom): © Digital Vision/PunchStock RF; p. 399: © AP Photo/Paul Schemm; p. 400 (top): © Bettmann/Corbis; p. 400 (top): © 20th Century Fox Film Corp. All rights reserved/Courtesy Everett Collection; p. 400 (bottom): © moodboard/PunchStock RF; p. 402: © Digital Vision/Getty RF